"IN SEARCH OF HISTORY is the most fascinating and most useful personal memoir of this generation."

—*William Safire*

Politics vs. Armies ~~Papers~~

"An important contribution to our history."

—*Henry Steele Commager*

Role of Gold 195 - 196 - 200 Forward

"Extraordinary . . . Teddy White's voyage of discovery over a remarkable half-century . . . compelling, provocative, entertaining."

—*Mike Wallace*

Reporting v. History

"A delightful and significant memoir that must be ranked with the best of our turbulent times."

—*John Toland*

Power of Press 233

"Nothing he has done comes up to *In Search of History*. It has all the pace and energy of the earlier work and more of many other things: more insight, more reflection, more candor, more intimacy, more humor, more humility, surer and sharper judgments of those he writes about, including himself."

—*New York Times Book Review*

American Vote 234

"White is the best, a great reporter and a great storyteller . . . a wonderful book about a wonderful man: a reporter, proud and questioning."

—*Washington Monthly*

Intellectuals / revolution £99

Stalinists / Communists ~ 44

Books by
THEODORE H. WHITE

*AMERICA IN SEARCH OF ITSELF	1982
*IN SEARCH OF HISTORY: A PERSONAL ADVENTURE	1978
BREACH OF FAITH: THE FALL OF RICHARD NIXON	1975
THE MAKING OF THE PRESIDENT—1972	1973
THE MAKING OF THE PRESIDENT—1968	1969
CAESAR AT THE RUBICON: *A Play About Politics*	1968
THE MAKING OF THE PRESIDENT—1964	1965
THE MAKING OF THE PRESIDENT—1960	1961
THE VIEW FROM THE FORTIETH FLOOR	1960
THE MOUNTAIN ROAD	1958
FIRE IN THE ASHES	1953
THE STILWELL PAPERS (EDITOR)	1948
THUNDER OUT OF CHINA (WITH ANNALEE JACOBY)	1946

*Published by
WARNER BOOKS

Theodore H. White

IN SEARCH OF HISTORY

A Personal Adventure

WARNER BOOKS

A Warner Communications Company

This Warner Books Edition is published by arrangement with
Harper & Row, Publishers, Inc., 10 East 53rd Street, New York,
N.Y. 10022

Cover art by Roy Anderson

Back cover photo by Carl Mydans. © Time/Life

Warner Books, Inc.
666 Fifth Avenue
New York, N.Y. 10103

 A Warner Communications Company

Printed in the United States of America

First Warner Books Printing: July, 1981

10 9 8 7 6

To Beatrice

CONTENTS

Prologue   The Storyteller   13

PART ONE—BOSTON: 1915–1938

1   Exercise in Recollection   27

PART TWO—ASIA: 1938–1945

THE SIGHTSEER   83

2   China: War and Resistance   93
3   Reporter in Asia: Episode and Personality   139
4   Stilwell: Jockey to a Dying Horse   177
5   Yenan: Takeoff for the Revolution   239
6   The Politics of Victory: Asia   283

PART THREE—EUROPE: 1948–1953

REPORTER IN TRANSITION   323

7   The Marshall Plan: Springtime in
a New World   347
8   The Politics of Victory: Europe   403

PART FOUR—AMERICA: 1954–1963

THE HOMECOMER   473

9   The Fifties: Incubating the Storm   499

THE OUTSIDER   567

10   John F. Kennedy: Opening the Gates   593

11 Camelot   641

Epilogue   Outward Bound   683

Acknowledgments   701

Index   702

IN SEARCH OF HISTORY.

A Personal Adventure

PROLOGUE

The Storyteller

Should he follow the sound of the drums?

He could hear it all beginning again: the nervous rattle of practicing drums, the shuffle that precedes the parade. The sound was almost irresistible, because in American politics it is when the parade is falling in that it is most exciting. He had followed those sounds for twenty years, across the country and back, again and again, and up with the crescendo to the conventions, on through the rallies with pretty girls in shakos and pompoms kicking in town squares and crowds yelling in big-city arenas until, suddenly on a November night, there would be a new President.

There is no excitement anywhere in the world, short of war, to match the excitement of an American Presidential campaign. He had loved that excitement and had made it his profession to be a storyteller of elections. Yet as summer faded in 1975 and the campaign for the Presidency reached speed, the more stories he gathered, the more confused he became.

Was there more to learn in one more story of the making of a President? There *was* something new in what Americans sought as they passed on their power —but how to define it? The excitement of the campaign was still there, but not the clarity that once gave the pattern to his stories.

Nor was there ever more than momentary escape from this confusion, behind any barricade. He would come back from his forays into the insane parade of the 1976 primaries with a sense of relief. For a few days, his office would be again, as it used to be, his cave. There were always chores at the office, and the mail to be answered—distractions he welcomed.

But now he found himself oddly irritated by the letters he used to enjoy most—those from students of history, young or old, inquiring about some corner of the past he had witnessed: the revolution in China, the victory in Asia, the renascence of Europe, the turning of the hinges of American politics. Usually, the questioners wanted to know if he had more to say than he had reported in his public writings. They were pursuing what scholars called an "argument," and wrote to him to mine his reporter's memories and notebooks for raw material that would support those "arguments." Good reporters organize facts in "stories," but good historians organize lives and episodes in "arguments." It was a very rare learned man who would change his "argument" because of a reporter's response to his question. Yet such letters from history students were innocently accusatory, and before plunging back on the campaign trail, the storyteller would wonder whether, in his appetite for anecdote and detail, he was missing the "argument," the connection between this campaign and what was really happening in this two hundredth year of the American experiment in self-government.

As a storyteller he had always liked the lines in Archibald MacLeish's poem "Conquistador," in which Bernál Díaz, MacLeish's storyteller, is made to say: ". . . but I . . . I saw Montezúma: I saw the armies of Mexico marching, the leaning Wind in their garments:

the painted faces: the plumes. . . . We were the lords of it all. . . ."

We Americans had, indeed, been lords of it all during this storyteller's time. But few serious students of history seemed to care about the sights, sounds and smells which now seemed to them irrelevancies on the trail by which America moved to its power, then disposed its power around the globe and at home. No one cared to listen about how it rained the weekend of the surrender and how drenched the Japanese must have been when the sun came out just in time for the thundering fly-by of American bombers; or how the same drought that had parched Europe in 1947 brought about not only the Marshall Plan but sugared the finest white Burgundy wines of the century; or exactly what the connection was between General Chennault's whorehouse in Kunming and the great debate between Chennault and Stilwell over the strategy of destroying Japan; or the wild and happy exultation in Boston's streets when John F. Kennedy came home in 1960, which seemed at the time like just another rally, but was not.

Strangers always ask reporters what it is "really all about." That question, now in mid campaign, began not only to irritate the storyteller, but to make him angry.

He was angry most of all with himself because for so many years he had neither paused nor dug deep enough to answer that question. Moreover, less and less frequently came those bursts of ecstasy when the hours of writing swept by like minutes, all the words flowing in paragraphs preshaped by unconscious thinking. This time his observations were outrunning his understanding. This America he was now reporting was swelling with strange, vague forms which his thinking could no longer shape into clean stories. No piling up of more reportorial facts, no teasing anecdote, no embracing concept, could hide from him what was wrong: his old ideas no longer stretched over the real world as he saw and sensed it to be.

Thus, as the campaign wore on, he found himself

more and more bewildered. How had America come to
this strange time in its history, and he with it? How had
the old pieties and the new technologies come to this
strange intermarriage in politics? He had seen most
of it; reported much of it; but, by the code of reporters,
had denied himself, in the name of "objectivity," the
meaning of it.

The thought crept in: it was probably more useful
to go back than to go on. It was just faintly possible
he might learn more from what he had left out of his
forty years of reporting than to go on and add more
observation. What more was to be added with one more
campaign swing, watching the wild mobs roar and
cheer, hearing the drums beat, seeing the arc lights
sweep the night sky—and reportorially wondering who
had "advanced" this crowd, putting together what voting groups, to win which votes in this particular place,
by what vision of how the American mosaic fits together?

To go back, however, meant that the storyteller
would have to identify himself to himself before he
could resume his old profession of spinning political
stories in public which, he hoped, the readers could
string together as history.

He had been, he now knew for certain, almost too
fashionable in his reporting for too many years. He
had been a mild Marxist at one time in his youth because that was the fashion of his generation. He had
become entranced by power and force during the war
years in Asia. Had become convinced of American virtue during the years of reconstruction in Europe. And
then had come home to American politics and begun to
see it as an adventure in which men sought their identity. If men made history, he would seek them out. This
thought had lasted for years, as popular fashion went
at the time—the thought that leadership is a quest of
men seeking to find themselves and that in so seeking,
they shape the lives of other people.

Though he could not give up that old thought entirely, he knew it was insufficient to explain politics. Identities in politics, he now realized, were connected far more to ideas than to ego, to id, or to glands. At the core of every great political identity lay an idea—an idea imposed on the leader from his past, which the leader absorbed, changed and then imposed on the others outside It was with some amazement that the storyteller realized that this simple thought was exactly where he had begun as Theodore H. White back in Boston many years ago, learning about ideas. He had discarded those boyhood teachings very early. He had later learned that money counted. That guns counted. That power counted. But the idea that *ideas* counted, that ideas were the beginning of all politics, was now, when he was sixty, pressing his thinking back to his adolescence. The men he had since reported in politics were all of them the vessels of ideas. The armies, the navies, the budgets, the campaign organizations they commanded flowed from the ideas that shaped them, or the ideas they could transmit and enforce. Whether it was Mao and Chou, or Nixon and Haldeman, or Kennedy and McNamara, or de Gaulle and Monnet, their identities came from the ideas that had been pumped into them, the ideas they chose in turn to pump out. Their cruelties and nobilities, their creations and tragedies, flowed far more certainly from what was in their minds than from what was in their glands.

You could separate people out into the large and the small, he thought, by whether their identities came from their own ideas or from the ideas of others. Most ordinary people lived their lives in boxes, as bees did in cells. It did not matter how the boxes were labeled: President, Vice President, Executive Vice President, Chairman of the Board, Chief Executive Officer, shop steward, union member, schoolteacher, policeman, "butcher, baker, beggarman, thief, doctor, lawyer, Indian chief," the box shaped their identity. But the box was an idea. Sir Robert Peel had put London policemen on patrol one hundred fifty years ago and the "bobbies" in London or the "cops" in New York now lived in the box invented by Sir Robert Peel. The Sterling Professor at Yale and all the great physicists at the Cavendish Laboratory in Cambridge, England, alike lived in a box, labeled by someone else's idea. When a pilot awoke in the morning, he could go to the air strip feeling that he was the hottest pilot in the whole air force——but he was only a creature of Billy Mitchell's idea. And even if he was the bravest astronaut in outer space, he was still a descendant in identity from Robert Hutchings Goddard's idea of rocketry.

All ordinary people below the eye level of public recognition were either captives or descendants of ideas. When they went out to work in the morning, they knew what they were supposed to do in the office, in the store, at the bench, on the line. They did their jobs either competently, or happily, or grimly. Sometimes they hated the man above or below them; more normally the attraction of the job, whether in a coal mine or in a newspaper city room, was not so much the money as the comradeship. Yet what a man did was what he was, and what you did, whether you knew it or not, fell to you from other men's ideas. Only a very, very rich man, or a farmer, could escape from this system of boxes. The very rich could escape because wealth itself shelters or buys identity. The very, very rich could become the greatest collectors of Picassos, Tang horses, rare books, stamps, stables, needlepoint, old coins or, simply, girls. They could exempt themselves from reality. And farmers, too, could escape from other men's ideas: A farmer made his own life in the fields; the weather, the market, the quality of his labor and devotion, connected him to another, primitive human condition which was not disturbed by ideas. Or——perhaps?——not even a farmer could escape. After all, at the time White was born, more than half of all Americans lived in villages or tilled the fields. And now only four percent worked the land. Some set of ideas——was it Justin Morrill's? or Mordecai Ezekiel's? or the Agricultural Adjustment Act?——must have had something to do with the dwindling of their numbers.

Thus, then, in the pauses between campaign rounds he began to ask himself: Whose idea was he? What was the label on the box that marked his trade?

The answer was not at all simple. The storyteller knew he was a trafficker in an undefinable trade, a popularizer of personalities, causes, revolutions, battles, campaigns; half public clerk, half private courtier. He told his stories, as troubadours had offered their songs, for attention, applause and a fee. But now, in the adventure of 1976 he no longer knew how to string the stories together in any way that connected them with history. He could read the notes as well as any—but the rhythm escaped him. For forty years, he had believed that any political problem could be solved with enough money, enough good will, enough common sense—and a dash of courage. But now, in the campaign of 1976 he could sense contradictions developing that completely upset such thinking. He could no longer fit his stories into the old patterns, nor himself into the old box labeled "reporter." Moreover, he was uncomfortable in the shelf box labeled "historian." There was this jangle between the ideas he wanted to believe and the contrary ideas his reporting forced on him.

To explain his confusion, it was necessary to go back to the beginning. There, even at the beginning, was the clash of ideas.

The beginning lay in Boston, and his awareness of the Depression, and the sense of terror and fright that politics had let into his house and family, and the nights he listened in the little bedroom off the kitchen when his parents talked and thought he was asleep.

The first memory was of the sound of his mother crying late one night, crying to his father because there was no money to buy shoes for the children, who had to go back to school. Then his father came to bed; his father slept with him in the same bed, the two little brothers on another narrow bed in the same room, his mother sleeping with his sister in the other bedroom.

That night his father did not sleep at all; he could feel his father twisting and turning and tossing in the bed, while he tried to make his father believe he was unaware.

The family was alone there in Boston. Except as a statistic, or to each other, they did not exist. He would always agree with the sociologues who said that the worst thing about a depression is not the hunger but the erasure of poor men's identities. The poor had no jobs; they were useless bodies; they fit nowhere; but worst of all, they were negatives in their own eyes, for they could not protect their own; as his father could not.

When his father died during the Depression, White was sixteen, and it was up to him, then, to protect his mother, sister and brothers. It was a sadness to him many years later, when his books won an audience, that his father, a compulsive reader, could not see them in bookstore windows. He had loved his father, and yet been resentful of him, for his father had thought of this son only as a "tough" kid, a child being swept into the rough culture of the streets, a culture that repelled the father. It was good, though, that he had been toughened, for his story began there on the streets. When a system breaks down, history always throws the breakage into the streets. It was there he found his first job.

It was a ten-hour-a-day job selling newspapers on the trolleys. Ten hours meant ten hours—from five in the morning until three in the afternoon, with no time off for lunch. He used to hop the streetcar, yell the headlines, squeeze through the crowded standees and then, if the motorman was friendly and slowed the car to reasonable jumping speed, he hopped out of the moving trolley and raced back to the corner to catch the next one—caught it, hopped out, ran back, caught another, and thus the treadmill all day long. It was good for the lungs and for learning.

The corner was "owned" by a rather friendly roughneck who "owned" many corners, and also "owned" the metal arm badges that the streetcar company gave out to newsboys or their bosses; the badge was the license that let its owner sell papers on streetcars. The boy had no right either to the corner or to the badge; that belonged to the boss. But at the time, he was grateful to the boss.

What he learned was important. He did not know then that he was in the news system, in the process. He was a newsboy, an old-fashioned newsboy. For each one hundred papers, sold at two cents each, two dollars came in—of which he could keep seventy cents for himself. When he took over the corner, it sold about three hundred newspapers a day; when he left, a year and a half later, the corner sold four hundred newspapers a day, and sometimes even five hundred, if he was smart enough to grab attention—or if history grabbed the headlines. That was the very beginning of learning—when to fake it with a yodeled subhead, and when to let history dictate the yell.

The yodel in Boston for newsboys on the streetcars always began: *"Globe, Post, Herald* and *Record* here! *Globe, Post, Herald* and *Record* here! Papers?"* After that chant followed the "sell." The "sell" was of the newsboy's imagination. It was very cold in Boston at five o'clock of a winter morning, and he would stand over the trolley motorman's electric heater reading the paper for a good "sell" headline. A perfect one would be something from the headlines of the lurid Boston *American,* one of the worst Hearst newspapers of the day. One afternoon the *American* did a story on abortion and the newsboy would yodel: "Oh, read all about it, read all about it! Twenty-seven babies' bodies found pickled in a barrel in East Boston! Twenty-seven babies pickled in one barrel!" That sold. But from the world outside, the "they" of history could do even better for the young newsboy. When in the bitter cold of 1933, the American economy collapsed, "they" intervened—or Roosevelt did. The yodel that morning ran: "Oh, read all about it, read all about it! Roosevelt closes the banks! All the banks are closed! Read all about it!"

The closing of the banks sold more papers than the pickled babies in the barrel. History, thus, was very important. The repeal of Prohibition brought an extra two dollars in newspapers sold that day, almost as much as the bank closing. What "they" were doing was obviously important, and he wanted to be "in on it"; and he got there by accident. He was granted a scholarship by a local college in Boston; and the boss who "owned" him and the corner agreed that he ought to take the scholarship, give up the corner and go on to college.

Now, in 1976, more than forty years later, he had been so long a part of the transmission system of news —of images, personalities, ideas—was so trained in packaging events as "stories," so convinced that if he caught the event right, he caught history right, that it was hard to go back to the boy who so suddenly and coarsely realized that Franklin Roosevelt and history sold newspapers.

He supposed his story should begin with that boy, who was given that scholarship to that local college. That local college happened to be Harvard, and Harvard was then at the apogee of its glory. It was there he would begin to rub the ideas of the street against the ideas of the academy. It was there he would begin to learn a trade, and his teachers would equip him to fit into an unfashionable box called "reporting." Reporters were supposed to *tell* what happened; scholars *explained* what had happened.

But, to be honest with himself, even Harvard was not the true beginning. The beginning of his search for history lay in his unabashed love of the American idea as it had been taught and passed on to him in his family. So that all the while he was trying to package the episodes of the campaign of 1976 into "events" that made a "story," the old idea of home, street and school kept intruding—the idea that America was the goal and the promise to which all mankind, including his immigrant grandfather and father, had been marching. He had followed this idea around the world. But now he knew that the old bundle of ideas made nonsense of the current story—or the ideas themselves had become nonsense.

Why this was so, what the connections were between the campaign of 1976 and the past—his past and America's past—slowly grew in his mind to be a more challenging assignment than one more book on one more campaign. It might take one, or two, or several volumes to tell such a story. How did America get this power? How had America used it? How had the various Presidents sucked up this power to kill or to heal from what was thought to be the American "people"?

What the end of such a story might be he could not, as he began to write it, imagine. He was certain only of the beginning—and that was Boston.

PART ONE

BOSTON:
1915-1938

CHAPTER 1

Exercise in Recollection

I was born in the ghetto of Boston on May 6, 1915.

No one ever told me it was a ghetto, because the Jews who settled there, like my father and my grandfather, had left the idea of a ghetto behind in the old country.

America was the open land. Though they carried with them the baggage of a past they could not shed, a past that bound all the exploring millions of Jewish immigrants together, they hoped America would be different, and yearned that it prove so.

We were of the Boston Jews.

Each of the Jewish communities then a-borning in America was to be different, as I came to realize later when I traveled the country as a political reporter. Each Jewish community was to take on the color and quality of its host city. Chicago Jews, whether in politics or in business, were tougher, harder, more muscular than, say, Cincinnati Jews. Baltimore Jews were entirely different from Detroit Jews. Hollywood Jews were different from

27

the Jews of university towns. Only New York had a community of Jews large enough to create a culture of its own, in which Yiddish newspapers could thrive, and Yiddish artists, poets, playwrights, actors, could develop an audience of their own; it was a culture in which Jewish employers sweated Jewish needleworkers, Jewish stonemasons built for Jewish contractors. Never, in all the history of the Jews since Titus plowed the Temple and sent them into exile, had so many Jews been gathered in one place at one time. New York's Jewry, before it dissolved into the suburbs and across the country, was unique in history—an implosion of hitherto suppressed and scattered energies and talents. The ferment of these New York Jews, as they came together from all over Europe in one city in a strange country, generated an uncontainable dynamic of its own which helped to reshape both New York's and the nation's culture. But all the other Jewish communities in America absorbed the ideas of their host cities, took standards and values which they could neither recognize nor word from the alien culture. Such standards and values reached from the outside in, magnetizing and orienting the ghetto particles, who did not know they were being reordered or being reshaped—and nowhere was this more true than in Boston.

In such a community I was born and by such Jewish parents I was brought up. How we must have appeared to old Boston on the Hill, or how Henry Adams might have seen us, I do not know. But about the time I was born, the scholars of Harvard and MIT collaborated on a series of studies examining the ways of the newcomers who were changing the interior of old Boston. After discussing the characteristics of the Canadians (then an important immigrant group), the Boston Irish (then the established menace), the newly arriving Italians (about to become the Italian community of Sacco and Vanzetti), they allotted a few pages to the Jews—who were characterized as a group with "an abnormal hunger to acquire real estate."

Among the Jews with that abnormal hunger for real estate was my grandfather Samuel Winkeller, a glazier by apprenticeship, a storekeeper out of need, but in his own eyes a musician, a part-time cantor with a copper-toned tenor voice. However much he may have seemed an acquisitive specimen to the antiseptic scholarship of sociology, he was a real man—a dandy when he could afford the clothes; slim, slight of build, proud of his Vandyke beard; possessor of a teasing sense of humor, yet ferociously Orthodox. He was also, all his life, stone poor; and his pride was the wooden-frame house on Erie Street, Dorchester, that he had bought in 1912 for $2,000. It was probably the first home, the first piece of land, owned by any one of his family, for in their centuries of East European life, most Jews were either forbidden to buy land or too frightened to do so. He loved that house. It had two floors and eight rooms. He, his wife and my unmarried uncle, Naman, lived on the top floor. On the ground floor lived his daughter (my mother), her husband (my father) and the children he expected them to bring forth.

There, in my mother's bedroom, in that house, I was born—home delivered by Dr. Knowlton, for a fee of twenty-five dollars. So my father's writing in the family Bible records. Jews had not yet become doctors in those days in Boston, and Dr. Knowlton, whom I remember from childhood illnesses, was a tart and twinkling no-nonsense Yankee who made visits to the houses of the poor in the ghetto.

That house rests at the beginning of memory.

The house on Erie Street is now a shanty deep in the troubled black ghetto of Boston. But it was, in my childhood, and in retrospect, beautiful: it still stood then as the fleeing Yankees had left it.

There is an ethnic ballet, slow yet certain, in every big American city that I have reported, which underlies its politics. The ballet is different in each city. In the larger cosmopolitan cities of the Eastern Seaboard, old-stock Protestants gave way to the Irish, who gave way in turn to Italians or Jews, who gave way in turn to blacks. Chicago's lower six wards also passed from Irish to Jew-

ish to black, the old Jewish synagogues, still engraved
with the commandments in Hebrew, converted to black
churches. So, too, did Harlem pass from Irish to Jewish
to black. In Los Angeles, Boyle Heights became Jewish,
then Mexican American. In the Midwest and along the
Great Lakes, the ethnic ballet involves other groups—
Poles, Slavs, Germans, Scandinavians. But in Boston,
specifically, the Jews leapfrogged the Irish, moving from
the West End of the core city to Dorchester, which the
old-stock Protestants were leaving for the southern suburbs.

The house on Erie Street thus connected me, unknowingly, directly to the New England past. It might
have been gardened by John Greenleaf Whittier, and its
yard was the most beautiful on the block. All the New
England flowers about which I read in school, in the
poems of Longfellow, and Whittier, and Emerson, and in
the stories of Thornton Burgess, grew in my own back
yard. Under the lilac bushes grew lily of the valley; we
continued to replant the tiger lilies and tulips until we
became too poor even to buy tulip bulbs. Out of the
parlor window we could see the peonies that Amy Lowell
wrote about, and across a little green space, the flowering
almond my mother loved so much. Honeysuckle and
daisies, petunias, phlox and pansy beds alternated; mari-
golds and hollyhocks grew in summer, dahlias in fall. To
the two original fruit trees—a pear and a cherry—my
grandmother added a peach tree and a grapevine.

The grapevine had a special significance. Prohibition
had been written into the law—but that was *their* law.
My grandmother and grandfather needed wine for the
Sabbath ceremonies and the Jewish holidays. So they
made their own, with their own grapes and cherries—
huge jugs of wine, stored in the cellar. And as a boy, I
would sneak with my friends into the cellar and sample
the fermenting wine before it was decanted for real drinking the next fall. Every family on the street had its cache
of wine, homemade or smuggled in, for the law of the
land was secondary to the command of custom. My
grandparents were very patriotic immigrants—but Prohi-

bition or its observance was not included in patriotism.

The house had one other connection to the old New England, beyond the flowers of its garden. Upstairs, in the attic, the original family had abandoned a treasure trove of left-behinds—brass bedsteads, stained-glass lamps, old *Scribner's* Magazines and *National Geographics,* and stocks of discarded books. Of these books, my favorite, which I preferred to the serious books in my father's library, was an old copy of *Blue Jackets of '63.* It was an account of the U.S. Navy's war against the Rebels in 1863, obviously part of a series, of which the other volumes were missing, but certainly published for the veteran audience shortly after the Civil War. I became a staunch Union man long before I was taught the Civil War in the sixth grade. "We" had freed the slaves. Upstairs, I met Admiral Farragut and General Grant. Downstairs, on the street, I was Jewish.

In that house and on that street, modern times came to us. When I was a child, milk was delivered in winter by horse-drawn sleigh, and you could hear the horses' bells in the morning before you woke. When there was a fire, huge fire horses pounded down the street pulling "Hook and Ladder," "Smokey," "Pipe and Hose." Erie Street was lit by gas; and a real lamplighter passed before our house each dusk just exactly as did Leerie the Lamplighter in the Robert Louis Stevenson poem my mother read to us. Life changed as I watched it, miracle following miracle. We began with one coal stove in the cellar, which I had to learn to stoke for house heating; there were also two kitchen stoves, on which my mother and my grandmother cooked over wood and nut coal—and then fuel oil arrived. The house was lit by gas, and I can remember both the delicate touch required to replace a fragile gas mantle in the ceiling light—and the year that electricity was strung into our house! With electricity, we were wired into a new world, for electricity brought the radio. One of our richer cousins gave us a radio—a crystal set—because he was buying one of those new radios with tubes. With enough ingenuity, one could tickle the crystal with a cat's whisker and pick up anything. In

that year, 1927, I could listen to the Yankees win the
World Series, hear the Sharkey-Dempsey fight from New
York and even the prayer for Lindbergh's flight to Paris.
As the telephone became general, the phone company
sent instructors to the schools to teach children of immigrant parents how to use the dial, so that the children
could, in turn, teach their parents. With radio, and telephone, and electric lights, the world changed and ideas
began to creep into boyhood.

The ideas descended in streams.

They flowed first from the family, but even within
the family they clashed.

My father, David White, called himself a Socialist.
He was proud that in 1911 he was one of the handful of
men who had marched on the Boston Common at the
head of a parade of suffragettes demanding the vote for
women. He kept us up in vigil all the summer night in
1927 when Sacco and Vanzetti were executed so that my
sister and I, the two older children, would never forget
what capitalism did to workingmen. He would walk with
us on weekends and explain the world. I recall one
particular Sunday afternoon when I was 12—I had been
leafing through the old *Literary Digest,* where I had seen
a cartoon of a squint-eyed giant bound to the ground by
ropes, slowly heaving himself erect, the ropes snapping. It
looked like a picture of Gulliver snapping the strings of
the Lilliputians in our children's copy of *Gulliver's Travels.* I asked my father to explain and he told me about
China; there was a revolution going on there and when it
succeeded, as he said it must, all of us would have to pay
attention to it. The only Chinese I had ever seen was the
Chinese laundryman on Erie Street, whom we taunted, as
all children did, with the call of "Chinkee, Chinkee
Chinaman." But my father said we should not do that; we
must respect Chinese: they were fighting imperialism.

However vigorous a radical my father may have
been in his youth, when I came to know him he was as
melancholy a man as I have ever met. Short, stout, bald,
with beautiful brown eyes and a deep, resonant bass
singing voice, he must once have been a man of enormous

physical vigor; he could bend nails with his fingers, had the chest and forearms of a steelworker, but thought of himself as a scholar; yet his spirit was already burned out when I was growing up. He had been born to a family of rabbis in a chain that claimed descent from the Baal Shem-Tov, founder of the Chasidim; his own father, Reb Todros, left Russia and ended his days in devotions, praying at the Western Wall in Jerusalem. We were told he had been heartbroken that his American son, David, having snapped the long chain of rabbis in our family, had gone on to become a godless Socialist.

But long before Reb Todros made his pilgrimage to the Holy Land my own father had left for his Promised Land—at sixteen a runaway from home, arriving in Boston from Pinsk in January 1891, one among the wave of Russian-Jewish migrants set in motion nine years earlier by the brutal anti-Semitic decrees of Czar Alexander III. Whether he was missed at home was questionable. Reb Todros had twelve daughters and five sons, my father being the youngest. His mother died in childbirth.

Whatever iridescence the American dream may have held for David White before he arrived soon faded. In Boston he had neither family nor home, peddling from a pushcart in summer, sleeping underneath it in the street, in winter finding what work he could and sleeping where he worked. Yet somehow he had the energy to learn English; to begin free law courses at night at the YMCA; then to save enough money to pay the fees for a true law school, at Northeastern University. In 1904 he passed the bar; eight years later he married, and before long he had a family of four children to support, though he cared little about money, except to buy books. His clients were poor, and he charged them no more than they could pay; in the end, in the Depression, they could pay nothing. So there was literally no money for food, no money to pay the rent to our grandparents upstairs, no money for clothes. He had always been a kind and gentle man, but now he was tattered and forlorn, with only his pride as a scholar left. He was reduced to collecting rents in the Boston slums for landlords almost as poor as their tenants, men close to or in bankruptcy, and then even his pride, too, was broken. In 1931, suddenly, his heart failed and he was dead.

My mother, Mary Winkeller White, was at once strong and fearful. She had been born in Boston in 1890; had been moved as a child to Cambridge, Massachusetts, where her family lived in a cellar apartment close to Harvard until the rocks thrown through the windows by the local Irish had driven the family back to storekeeping in the safe Jewish West End. Of Sam Winkeller, my maternal grandfather, I have spoken. But the dominant member of my mother's family and the dominant member of our household was our grandmother—a hard, shrill, vigorous woman of violent piety who, until she died, fifty years after her coming to this country, spoke no English. She spoke Yiddish—always in a rage, in a temper; a shrew who resented being wedded to a man who wanted to be a musician and singer, and saw her daughter married to a lawyer, a Socialist unbeliever, who spent his money on books and wrote poetry, and refused to speak Yiddish at all once he had mastered English. She was more man than any of the men around her, and she made life hell for them.

Her own background was interesting. Her village, her *shtetl,* had rested squat on a little river that marked the border between White Russia and East Prussia. Hers was one of the rare Jewish families that actually owned land and worked it; they were cattle dealers too; and on the side, they smuggled across the border. The most important part of their smuggling traffic was other Jews, young men escaping from the anti-Semitism of the Russian Army, into which they were being drafted, and attempting to sneak into Germany, whence they could make their way to a port like Danzig or Bremen and take off for America. So, too, her family had left, to become cattle dealers in Boston. But she was still a country woman and her garden was her joy; we American grandchildren would be ashamed as she dashed out into Erie Street after a horse's fresh droppings and swept up the steaming manure to fertilize her flowers. Nothing, she felt, must be wasted—especially money. Because there was so little of it, money was obsessive with her. Perhaps from her, more than anyone else, I inherited my obsession with money—and her phrases: "A poor man is a cripple, a rich man is free"; "Only a man with money can afford to have an opinion." She believed that unless you could bank it, touch it, hold it—all other rewards were vanity.

My grandmother despised my father; and this was the curse of my mother's life. My mother had met David White at the Workmen's Circle in Boston, a Socialist clubhouse in the West End; she was nineteen years old, a volunteer waitress who served tea at two cents a glass, coffee at three cents. There she had met this handsome young lawyer, a Socialist. Finally, after several years, she introduced him to her parents and they, so proud that their daughter had met a "learned" man, a lawyer at that, agreed to the marriage; and then all of them, after the purchase of the house, moved to Dorchester on what they thought was the way up.

There the conflict began.

Upstairs was Yiddish-speaking. Downstairs, we spoke English. Upstairs, Friday night, the eve of *Shabbas* was celebrated with candles, wine and challah, the twisted white bread. Downstairs, my father sat adamant—he, the unbeliever, had come to see religion as a superstition and would have no part of its ceremonies. I was a pawn between the two families, moved by my grandmother's tyrannical will and my mother's desire to please her mother and her husband at the same time. I rather enjoyed it all; my grandmother, after shaping her own white twistbread for the evening, would bake a special small challah, the size of a bun, for me. Then I would be called upstairs for the prayers of the *Kiddush*. I would make the traditional blessing in Hebrew, and would be given a goblet of red wine. When I did especially well, or lingered to eat dinner upstairs—usually chicken and chicken soup—my grandfather, a merry man, would be delighted, and would pour me a thimbleful of raw yellow Polish vodka. At which my grandmother would shriek that he was trying to make me a drunk, and after much shrieking and occasionally singing, I would go downstairs to my own family.

In this conflict of cultures, my mother was the pivot. Orthodox Jews in those days disdained their women; neither my mother nor my sister, a brilliant girl, was sent to Hebrew school. My mother had not even been allowed to finish public high school, but was put to work at sixteen. Near-sighted, she would never have been fitted with eyeglasses if the public-school teacher had not summoned my immigrant grandfather to school and indignantly insisted on it. Somehow, whether from this school experience or from her own children's experience, she belonged to the American system more than anyone else in the family. My father, as I say, was a Socialist; my grandparents were locked in their Jewishness; but she, American born, a favorite of her teachers, wanted to be "in"—if not "in" for herself, "in" for her children.

I did not realize for many, many years how very hungry my mother was for genteel respectability—and what she thought to be American. To the rigid underculture of Jewish Orthodoxy she added the Puritan customs of old Boston—down to the ever-handy bar of black tar soap with which she washed our mouths if we spoke a single dirty word. American holidays were to be celebrated as much as Jewish holidays, Thanksgiving with a feast and the Fourth of July with penny firecrackers. When, in 1919, the soldiers were coming home, she would stand, waving, by the railway siding that carried the doughboys from Boston's pier to the Fort Devens demobilization point. In that year, when I was four years old, she bought penny flags for my sister and myself so we, too, could wave to the "soldier boys," who waved back from the train windows and threw molasses kisses and hard candies to the children who cheered them home. She was as conservative politically as she was socially. In our home, only my father spoke of politics—and then only to underscore for us that Democrats and Republicans alike cheated the people. But my mother was a Republican. In all her life she has voted for only two Democrats—

Franklin Roosevelt and John F. Kennedy. She still recalls with pride her vote for Barry Goldwater, because he was a "much nicer man" than Lyndon Johnson.

What dreams may have passed through her mind, I cannot guess. In most marriages, there is usually a dominant partner and an indulgent one. In hers, there was no room either for dominance or for indulgence. My grandmother dominated the entire household, and life and poverty indulged no one. I am sure that my mother never dreamed of dances, or balls, or silken gowns. She told me once that the only thing she ever dreamed of having when she was a little girl was a doll—but no one ever bought her a doll. So she dreamed of dolls until well into her sixties, when her own grandchildren came along and she could buy dolls for them. What she wanted of life was security, and she dreamed for her children, dreaming always of a "good job," a "government job," perhaps even a schoolteacher's job, which was the farthest limit of her ambition. She wanted no factory jobs for them, nor did she want them in "business," for the small Jewish merchants of the neighborhood were even more insecure than their customers, the workers. Her children, she insisted, would be learned people, like their father, only "safe" because they would have jobs. Thus we were thrust out to learn, and there were several systems of learning—the Hebrew school, the street school, the public school.

The decision to send me to Hebrew school, to which I trudged off at the age of eight, was the common decision of my grandmother, grandfather and mother—with my father silently resisting, and myself hopelessly protesting. My father resisted, perhaps because he once had revolted at the narrowness of the rabbinical home in which he had grown up in Pinsk, and because of the memories of the Talmudic school which his own father had taught there. My revolt was purely animal—after getting up at eight in the morning and going to public school until three-thirty, I wanted to play in the streets. I did not want to race off to another school, where I must study for two more hours in a strange language, with intense, bitter teachers who slapped when you made a mistake, lacking the easygoing qualities of the Irish teachers in the public school.

But the Beth-El Hebrew School captured me. Most of our teachers were then newly arrived young immigrant scholars, who had come from post-World War I Europe to seek a secular education in Boston's universities; they taught Hebrew in the evenings to earn their living. They were rigorous in their teaching of the young, and violent of temper when the tired children failed to respond. They despised Yiddish, a language I knew from home, for to despise Yiddish was their form of snobbery; and as a matter of principle they would speak no English in class, for their cardinal political principle was Zionism. They were about to revive the Hebrew language and make it a living tongue; after a little pampering with English in the first and second year, as we learned the ancient alphabet and pronunciation, we were into the Bible in Hebrew—it was explained to us in Hebrew, pounded into us in Hebrew, and we were forced to explain it to one another in Hebrew.

It was a nightmare education, but I came to love it. By the time I was ten, when my father was still insisting that I should not be forced longer in this torment, and my mother was leaving it up to me to decide, and most of my friends, young street Americans like myself, were rebelling against the torture with tantrums and tears at home, I was moved up to the section that met from six to eight o'clock in the evening. I decided to go on, for the break between four and six let me do my public-school homework, and the hours of six to eight were not intolerable.

What I learned, then, from age ten to age fourteen, when I went on to evening courses at the Hebrew College of Boston, was the Bible. We learned the Bible from Genesis (Bereshith) to the Book of Chronicles, from the Book of Kings through all the Prophets, major and minor. We learned it, absorbed it, thought in it, until the ancient Hebrew became a working rhythm in the mind, until it became a second language. Its balanced cadences, its hard declarative sentences and its lacelike images structured the sentences we wrote in public-school classes.

Hebrew is a difficult language to learn, almost as difficult as Chinese; but the Old Testament in Hebrew draws one in, then clutches. Its themes and its stories are primitive—miracles; love; hate; killing; attack; sacrifice; wonder; above all, revenge! No child, however dull, can fail to be caught by the story of Joseph and the sweet revenge of Joseph when, as Pharaoh's first minister, he reveals himself to the evil brood of his brothers, holds them in his grasp, and at last relents. We were supposed to be able to hold in memory each line, each phrase, each episode. Examinations strung before us a list of quotations, asking: "Who said . . . to whom?" and we had to give book, line and episode, all in Hebrew. Some were easy, like: "I am Joseph your brother." Others were more obscure, like: "The arrow lies beyond you and farther," or "Today too many servants rise against their masters."

Memory was the foundation of learning at the Hebrew school, and the memory cut grooves on young minds that even decades cannot erase. Even now, when a Biblical phrase runs through my mind, I am trapped and annoyed unless I can convert it into Hebrew—whereupon the memory retrieves it from its proper place. The memory retrieves it from Boston, Massachusetts, where little Jewish-American boys, pulled and tugged by stickball, hit-the-ball, baseball and jackknife, and by the movies, were forced to learn of nomads and peasants of three thousand years ago, forced to learn how shepherds watched their flocks at night, to learn of spotted lambs, of the searing summer and the saving rains (*yohreh* and *malkosh*), without knowing that these rains were the monsoons of public-school geography. Long before the King James Bible was named supplementary reading for me in a course at Harvard, it belonged to me in my own translation; and though the Bible's English is sublime, I could, from memory, pick here and there a translation I had made my own and would not give up for theirs—as, for example, the phrase "vanity and vexation of spirit."

Memory had scored that into my mind as: "all is in vain and a shepherding of the winds." The ancient Hebrew can be translated either way, but "to be a shepherd of the winds" is the way nomads must have described futility, and the way little boys in Boston, forced to study Hebrew, did translate it to themselves.

The Bible drenched me in cadence and phrase, in imagery and folklore. But it did not occur to me then, as it occurs to me now, that I was being given my first intensive seminar in history. All religions—Christianity, Judaism, Islam, Buddhism—are, essentially, accounts of history. Religion is an effort to explain man's intrusion in time, how he got there, who put him there, for what purpose, and how that purpose worked out. All religions are embellished with stories of martyrs, teachers, sacrifices for the sacred cause. But they remain essentially stories, which explain to ordinary people their place in the now and the hereafter.

Jewish history, as I learned it in Hebrew school from the Bible and the tradition, was a very stark and perplexing history, with very unsatisfactory lessons to be learned. God had chosen the Jews; he had freed them from Egypt; when they grew stiff-necked and arrogant, again and again God would punish them. When they repented, they were saved. When they whored after false gods, they were destroyed. But it was all ancient history—fossil history. The last time God had done anything to help the Jews was two thousand years ago! And ever since then had come disaster after disaster, with the greatest of the disasters, the Holocaust, yet to come. Why? How long, O Lord?

Our stern young Zionist schoolmasters shared the same questions. Although their teaching contract with the local elders held that they must teach us tradition, prayers and the Bible, they had in their own hearts repudiated the simple historical theory of the Bible. They were Zionists all. For them, history lay in the future, when would come the redemption of the Jews by their own efforts, in their own land, without the help of God. Even more than they despised Yiddishists, our teachers despised rabbis. Their purpose was single-minded: to get an education in America and serve the cause of Zion.

Of what they taught of Zionism I remember very little—except for one phrase, again a phrase in Hebrew, which came from Theodor Herzl. *"Im tirtsu, ayn zeh hagadah"*—"If you will it to be so, this is no legend." It is a phrase I have heard in many languages since; and I have seen men and women, students and guerrillas, in hills and streets, lashed by the thought that if you wish, you can make the dream come true. I did not share the belief that the dream of Zion would make that dream reality; but among my most cherished memories is one of a summer night in Boston. We had gone picnicking in Franklin Park, which was then safe at night; the park was moonlit and the hills soft of shape. We had read in the papers that one of the great German Zeppelins would be coursing over Boston en route to its landing in Lakehurst, New Jersey. We hated the Zeppelin because it was Hitler's and Hitler was bad for the Jews. So we talked, and strolled, and sat, and boys and girls cuddled, until, exactly on time, the Zeppelin appeared overhead, its belly light sweeping the terrain below. When we saw it coming, we gathered in a circle and danced the hora in defiance, dancing and singing until it passed from view overhead. The dream of Zion and of Israel was then so ephemeral, so unreal, that the dance was a dance of hopeless, wishful intoxication. Yet thirty years later, the idea of Zion was an army, with an armored corps, with an air force, with guns; and as an American correspondent during the 1967 Six-Day War, I flew over the desert of Sinai and stopped off now and again on the morrow of the great victory, and saw the flag of Zion flying over the Suez Canal and at Sharm al-Sheikh—the flag with the white field and the blue Star of David snapping in the wind. The idea that had reached in to touch me as a youngster in Boston had also reached out to become an army, a power, a strike force that could defend and kill.

The recognition of the force of ideas was as far away from me, growing up in Boston's streets, as the thought of man reaching into outer space—but never was there a better demonstration of the force of ideas than in the streets of Boston's ghetto. There, the American idea was steadily, remorselessly, irresistibly eroding the walls of custom and tradition that had protected the ideas of the Jews of Europe for centuries. Even in the formidable person of my grandmother, the old ideas could survive only as bad temper. There were never more than 110,000 Jews in Greater Boston's population of one million when I was growing up, far too small a number to generate the cultural energy which, for decades, preserved so much of the European *shtetl* culture among New York's Jews. In Boston, as in every American city, immigrants might continue to practice their religion as their fathers had, and the wives would try—at home—to preserve all the old customs, from the blessing of the candles on Sabbath eve, to the Passover Seder, to the baking of *hamantaschen* for Purim, to the decoration of the *succah* in the fall. But the men had to learn the ways of American small business to survive, the mothers had to feed their children into the suction of American schools. So there perished first the old religious orthodoxy, then the old-country customs, until finally the essence of the tradition was stripped to its naked core. And there was nothing at that core but an idea, which was as much a genetic mind set as a theology!

The old religion was, as I have said, as much history as ritual. There are almost as many different sects of Jews, who quarrel with each other, in both the new and old forms of our religion, as there are among Protestants. But if a thread ties them all together, it is the thread of the *Shma*—the incantation "Hear, O Israel, the Lord our God, the Lord is One." The cantillation of this phrase was set long before the Crusades and the persecutions that scorched the Crusaders' trail; but its intonation shrieks with the agony of medieval Europe, where Jews were burned at the stake for their faith. We learned in Hebrew school that those Jews wailed the *Shma* even as the flames licked up at them; and we children argued, on our way home at night, whether it was sensible to give up your life rather than kiss a cross. Most of us admitted to cowardice; but we stood in awe of the countless forefathers who had chosen to burn rather than change their faith, and the *Shma* was the call of their courage.

The idea behind the *Shma* is the unity of all happenings; it was an idea of prehistoric shepherds who put out, in a world of idols, superstitions and numerous gods of random passions and contrary impulses, the new idea that there was but one God, who gave order to the entire universe. The mind set of all great Jewish thinkers since those shepherds has been to bind the variability of observed phenomena into one all-embracing theory. I do not believed in inherited *racial* characteristics beyond the obvious physical ones; but inherited *cultural* characteristics seem to me to be irrepressible. Thus, over the centuries, those Jewish thinkers who have moved out and been accepted in the larger world stage have been bearers of some one seductive all-embracing theory which is as unifying as the *Shma*. At its spectacular best, this mind set yields Einstein's unified-field theory, stretching from microcosm to macrocosm, binding energy to matter by irrefutable laws, substituting $E=mc^2$ for the *Shma*. At its most humanly compelling, the mind set produces a Christ, who replaces the tribal vengeance of the Old Testament with a theory of mercy and universal brotherhood that embraces every tongue, sex, skin color, and strange custom. Whether it is the all-embracing economic and dialectic theory of Marx, or the patterning of sex, ego and the repressions of modern man as in Freud's world, the passion of Jewish thinkers for a single, universal theory in every field of knowledge or behavior has been persistent, creative—and frequently subversive to settled establishments and order throughout Western history.

Boston's Jews have no place at all in the grand history of Western thought. But their community was a good specimen for thinkers to examine. History had delivered to them two equally compelling but hopelessly irreconcilable ideas. The community in Eastern Europe from which my grandparents had come believed that only

God could save. As they suffered in the ghettos, waiting
for redemption and the Messiah, all they could do was
pray to God to hasten the day of deliverance. God had
his own grand design for all. But as news of America
spread, the unsettling idea took hold that a man could
save himself by his own efforts. The confusion that resulted was overwhelming; and you could see the confusion in the street school of Boston, where I learned so
much. In Hebrew school, I learned about the God of the
Jews. In the street school, other Jews were learning the
American "hustle"; and I was part of both.

Erie Street was my street school. It was then a
bustling market street, ancillary to the main shopping
artery of Dorchester—Blue Hill Avenue. Storekeepers
had transformed Erie Street from the quiet residential
neighborhood my grandparents had sought as Jewish pioneers in the district into a semipermanent bazaar. Whatever you wanted you could buy on Erie Street. Or else
someone could get it for you. Herrings were stacked in
barrels outside the fish stores, and flies buzzed over the
herrings. Fresh-caught fish lay on slabs, and little boys
were allowed to keep the fishhooks for the trouble of
extracting them. All butcher shops were kosher, sawdust
on the floor, chopping blocks scrubbed clean every day,
unplucked chickens piled in flop heaps in the store window, from which housewives squeezed and prodded, then
picked and chose. There were four grocery stores, several
dry-goods stores, fruit and vegetable specialists, hardware
stores, mama-papa variety stores, penny candy stores.

But it was the peddlers who gave the street its sound
and motion. The banana man was Italian, but all other
peddlers were Jewish. Early in the morning, the peddlers
would go to their stables, hitch up their horses, and
proceed to Faneuil Hall or the Fish Pier to bring back the
day's glut in the city market. Then, leading their horse-
and-wagons through Erie Street, they would yodel and
chant their wares. For each peddler another chant: the
fish man would sing in a special voice, *"Lebediker fisch,*

weiber, lebediker fisch"; the secondhand-clothes merchant would chant otherwise; the Italian banana man would chorus only "Bananas, bananas, bananas," hawking a fruit previously unknown to Eastern Europeans.

Saturday night was the night of the fair. Friday was normally payday for the garment- and shoeworkers of the district, and Saturday was *Shabbas*. Thus Saturday night, when Sabbath was over, became shopping night—wives dragging their husbands after them, children skipping about the crowded corners, the women greeting each other, sharing gossip, the fathers stolidly enjoying themselves, the peddlers yelling their wares. Summer was best: the peddlers would bring in strange delights they had found in the Faneuil Hall produce market, and Jews could see for perhaps the first time wagons of watermelons (twenty-five cents each), pineapple wagons, grape wagons, as well as wagons full of rejected or factory-surplus socks, shirts, undergarments. I grew up with such weekly fairs, and later, reporting both China and France, I found their weekly fairs spoke of home.

I tried my hand at the peddling business. One summer I sold ice cream. For several winters, with my across-the-street friend Butsy Schneiderman, I peddled tin horns at New Year's Eve. Another entire summer Butsy and I sold stuffed dates from door to door in Quincy and Wollaston, of which venture I remember two things: the Quincy police drove us out, for they did not want adolescent Jewish peddlers in the neighborhood; and the best quick ice cream and hot dogs in the neighborhood came from a small counter stand run by a Swede named Howard Johnson. Howard Johnson's stores later expanded across the nation. But so did one of the local grocery stores on Erie Street, Rabinowitz's, which later grew into a chain of supermarkets now listed on the New York Stock Exchange. And Sammy Rosenzweig, my classmate who had a job as a soda fountain clerk in one of Erie Street's drugstores, later made his own drugstore chain the largest in New England.

But this out-migration into the larger community

was all to come later. Erie Street was the hub of a self-contained neighborhood, and it was a safe street. The mothers all watched each other's children. No one was ever struck or mugged or threatened, even late at night; and "late at night" meant ten o'clock on weekdays, eleven o'clock on Saturdays.

Within the boundaries of our community we were entirely safe and sheltered. But the boundaries were real. We were an enclave surrounded by Irish. To the south of us, across the railway tracks, lived very tough Irish—working-class Irish. The local library lay in such an Irish district, and my first fights happened en route to the library, to get books. Pure hellishness divided us, but after one last bloody-nose battle, I was given safe passage by the Irish boys whenever I went to the library. Across Franklin Park to the west lay the lands of the lace-curtain Irish, who lived in Jamaica Plain and Roslindale; they were, if not friendly, at least not pugnacious. South of Mattapan Square there were the original settlers, Protestants—and Protestants were not dangerous at all; they did not beat you. You could hitchhike all the way to Quincy or Milton or the great Blue Hill, and if you did not bother them, Protestants would not molest you. From my uncle, who worked in the produce market at Faneuil Square, I learned that "Taleners" (Italians) were easy to get along with, too, and would not bother you if you made friends with them. There was a tiny pocket of black people in the South End, but they were curiosities and one had to be kind to them. Beyond lay terra incognita—"Hic Sunt Leones" (Here Dwell Lions")—but I did not care.

Long before ethnicity became a fashionable political concept, we knew about ethnics, about each group living in its own community. But we were also all Americans, and even where the friction between the groups was greatest—in my neighborhood, along its borders with the tough Irish—it was not intolerable. Our house sat on that border; our yard backed against the yards of Irish families on the next street, a line of fence dividing them. In the house across the fence from ours lived a boy my age,

Johnny Powers, whom I had always considered my enemy.

But the day my father died I climbed over the fence to call Johnny to come out—and he came out, bristling. I explained that my father had died that morning, and asked him if he could keep the kids in his street quiet for the rest of the day. Johnny instantly agreed. Not to worry, he said; he'd make sure there wouldn't be a sound from his block. He'd take care of his gang. And he did.

Politically, we were an ethnic enclave in the Irish principalities of Boston politics. Our local district leader, a Mr. Goretsky, was a man who claimed to know Martin Lomasney; and everyone knew that Martin Lomasney was close to Mayor Curley. We voted, even my father, the Socialist, as did the Irish—a straight Democratic ticket. Only my mother, the Republican, voted otherwise, and she told no one. And the Jews of Ward Fourteen all voted! I read, much later, how my ward had voted in 1932 and 1936 when Roosevelt ran: Ward Fourteen's solid Jewish vote had gone 71 percent for FDR in 1932—but when they felt they knew him, by 1936, the Jews of Ward Fourteen ran up 85.2 percent for Roosevelt, the highest mark in the Democratic city! Roosevelt could reach out to ordinary people and stir them; even if the ward captains had wished or urged otherwise, Roosevelt's ideas would have caught the ward. His ideas were changing America.

For us in the ward, however, though Roosevelt was President, the Irish were Government. In the Boston of my youth, where the Irish clearly outnumbered all other groups, it was hard to perceive that their historic role in American politics was the teaching of government. They played this same role in the cities where they were only one of many minorities—in Chicago, in St. Paul, in New York and Philadelphia—just as they played it in my city, where they were the majority. Of all the immigrant groups, only the Irish spoke English at home, and more than that, understood the Anglo-American courts, law and officialdom—sheriff, alderman, bailiff, surrogate. They shared the anguish of other immigrants, but they were neither so voiceless nor so helpless. They knew how to deal with the boy in trouble, the peddler caught without a license, the street fights that brought in the police, the hunger for jobs; and with that understanding they acted as intermediaries between government and the bewildered immigrants. They could drop a word in a judge's ear, intercede with the school board to get, say, a girl into the city's teachers college. Their fee was gratefully and willingly paid, and might be as high as a dozen sure votes. Piling up votes, the Irish ran local government pretty much as they chose—in Boston under Big Jim Curley reaching a high, florid corruption that became a national farce. Farce, perhaps—but Big Jim Curley liked roses, and in our ward we knew that the rose garden in Franklin Park was there because Curley had put it there, and mothers could park their baby carriages in the rose garden and sun themselves and their children in fragrance because Curley liked roses.

So government for us was simple and direct, reaching only occasionally beyond our neighborhood. Far away, remote, there was FDR, who, thank God, believed in jobs for people. As I grew older, it also turned out that he was against Hitler, and we enshrined him in our hearts. Below the President was the state; Massachusetts, in those days, was run by Yankees. No one in our ward knew what a state was supposed to do, and as nearly as we knew, the State of Massachusetts did nothing. After that came the city, which was run by Curley and had little to do with us.

So that government, as it reached down into Ward Fourteen, was the police and the schoolteachers. The police were all Irish. They cuffed us, slapped us, kicked us when we gave them lip. The schools were just as Irish. Irish schoolteachers dried our tears, kissed and coddled us, and taught us what their Yankee overlords in the Boston public-school system directed them to teach.

In the descent of ideas, therefore, family came first, street next—and then public school.

Whatever the general theory of the Boston School Committee was, in the state in which Horace Mann had first broached the idea of free public education, its practice, when I was going to school, was excellent.

As the Boston public-school system absorbed me, it was simple. Each neighborhood had an elementary school within a child's walking distance—kindergarten through third grade. At the level of the William E. Endicott School, where I began, the Irish had replaced the Yankee schoolmarms and my teachers were Miss Phelan, Miss Brennan, Miss Murray, Miss Kelly. They were supposed to teach us to read, write (by the Palmer method) and add. They also made us memorize poetry, and the poetry was all New England—Henry Wadsworth Longfellow, James Russell Lowell, John Greenleaf Whittier. But memory was essential, as it was in Hebrew school, where one memorized the Bible.

Each neighborhood also had an intermediate school—in my case, the Christopher Gibson School. There segregation began, boys separated from girls for special periods. In the fourth grade, boys had special periods to learn carpentry, girls to learn sewing. In the fifth grade, it was electricity and wiring for boys, cooking for girls. Vocational and book learning were taught in the same building. I can still tell a ripsaw from a crosscut saw by what was taught me (by a lady carpentry teacher, Miss Sprague) in the fourth grade. I can still wire lamps in series or in parallel, insulate or install cutoff switches by what was taught me in the fifth grade. But—most importantly—I first became aware of the word "history" in the sixth grade at the Christopher Gibson School—and my teacher was Miss Fuller.

How can I say what a ten-year-old boy remembers of a schoolteacher lost in time? She was stout, gray-haired, dimpled, schoolmarmish, almost never angry. She was probably the first Protestant I ever met; she taught history vigorously; and she was special, the first person who made me think I might make something of myself. She was the kind of teacher who could set fire to the

imaginations of the ordinary children who sat in lumps
before her, and to do so was probably the chief reward
she sought.

Her course in American history began, of course, at
a much later date than the history we were taught at
Hebrew school. In Boston, history began in 1630—when
the Puritans came. It then worked back and forth, but
every date had to be impeccably remembered; Columbus
was 1492, Cabot was 1497. Cortés was 1519, as was
Magellan; and so on, moving through Jamestown, 1607;
New York, 1614; Plymouth Colony, 1620; then other
dates that led up to the settlement of Boston—1630!
1630! 1630! We also had to know the names in the tests:
William Penn, Sir George Carteret, King James (which
had to be written King James I, or else you were marked
wrong).

Miss Fuller did not stop with names and dates. First
you had to get them right, but then they became the pegs
on which connections between events were to be hung. In
this she was far ahead of most of the teachers of her day.
For example: Thanksgiving. How did it come about?
What would you have thought that first winter in Plymouth, if you had come from England, and survived?
How would you invite the Indians to your feast? She
decided we would have a play the day before Thanksgiving, a free-form play in the classroom, in which we would
all together explore the meeting of Puritans and Indians,
and the meaning of Thanksgiving. She divided the class,
entirely Jewish, into those children who were American-
born and spoke true English, and those who were recent
arrivals and spoke only broken English or Yiddish. I was
Elder William Bradford, because I spoke English well.
"Itchie" Rachlin, whose father was an unemployed trumpet player recently arrived from Russia, who spoke vivid
Yiddish, was Squanto, our Indian friend. Miss Fuller
hoped that those who could not speak English would
squawk strange Indian sounds while I, translating their
sounds to the rest of the Puritans, all of us in black
cardboard cone hats, would offer good will and brotherhood. "Itchie" and the other recently arrived immigrant

children played the game of being "Indian" for a few minutes, then fell into Yiddish, pretending it was Indian talk. Miss Fuller could not, of course, understand them, but I tried nevertheless to clean up their Yiddish vulgarities in my translation to the other little Puritans, who could not help but giggle. (*"Vos is dos vor traef?"* said Itchie, meaning: "You want us to eat pig food?" and I would translate in English: "What kind of strange food is this before us?") Miss Fuller became furious as we laughed our way through the play; and when I tried to explain, she was hurt and upset. Thanksgiving was sacred to her.

But she was a marvelous teacher. Once we had learned the names and dates from 1630 to the Civil War, she let us talk and speculate, driving home the point that history connected to "now," to "us." America for her was all about freedom, and all the famous phrases from "Give me liberty or give me death" to the Gettysburg Address had to be memorized by her classes—and understood.

She was also a very earnest, upward-striving teacher. I realize now that she must have been working for an advanced degree, for she went to night school at Boston University to take education courses. This, too, reached from outside to me. One day she told my mother about a project her night-school seminar was conducting in how much independent research a youngster of ten or eleven could do on his own—one of those projects now so commonplace in progressive schools. Would my mother mind, she asked, if I was given such an assignment, and then reported on it to her seminar? My mother said yes after Miss Fuller promised to bring me home herself afterwards.

My assignment was to study immigration, and then to speak to the seminar about whether immigrants were good or bad for America. Her seminar mates would question me to find out how well I had mastered the subject. The Immigration Act of 1924—the "Closing of the Gates"—had just been passed; there was much to read in both papers and magazines about the controversy, but my guide was my father. He put it both ways: the country had been built by immigrants, so immigrants were not bad. He had been an immigrant himself. On the other hand, as a strong labor man, he followed the A.F. of L. line of those days. The National Association of Manufacturers (the capitalists) wanted to continue unrestricted immigration so they could sweat cheap labor. But the American Federation of Labor wanted immigration restricted to keep the wages of American workingmen from being undercut by foreigners. This was a conundrum for my father: he was against the capitalists and for the A.F. of L.; but he was an immigrant himself, as were all our friends and neighbors. He helped me get all the facts, and I made a speech on the platform of a classroom at Boston University Teachers College at nine one night, explaining both sides of the story and taking no position. I enjoyed it all, especially when the teachers began asking me questions; I had all the dates and facts, and an attentive audience, but no answers then just as I have none now. I must have done well, for Miss Fuller kissed me and bought me candy to eat on the streetcar. It became clear to me, as we talked on the way home, that immigrants were history, too. History was happening now, all about us, and the gossip of Erie Street and the problem of whether someone's cousin could get a visa back in the old country and come here were really connected to the past, and to Abraham Lincoln, Henry Clay, Sam Adams, Patrick Henry and the elder William Bradford.

If I went on to the Boston Public Latin School, I think it was because of Miss Fuller and my mother; it was Miss Fuller who persuaded my mother that there was something more than a lump in the boy, and pointed me in the direction of the Latin School.

The Boston school system offered then what seems to me still a reasonable set of choices after intermediate school. You could go to a local high school—Charlestown High School, Roxbury Memorial High School, South Boston High School. Or, if your parents chose, you could go to a "downtown" high school. Today these central schools would be called "magnet schools," "enrichment schools," "elite schools." They served the entire Boston community—a Commerce High School to learn bookkeeping and trade, a Mechanic Arts High School to learn blueprints, welding, machining, and, at the summit, the Boston Public Latin School, the oldest public school in America, founded in 1635. It was free choice: you could walk to your local community high school, or you could go downtown to the central, quality schools. There were no school buses then, so if you did want to take the half-hour trolley ride to a downtown school, you bought student tickets, beige-brown tabs at five cents each, half the price of the dime fare for a regular rider on the Boston transit system. Ten cents a day, five days a week, for carfare was a considerable sum. You had to *want* to go.

My mother, my father, myself all agreeing, I chose the Latin School.

The Boston Public Latin School reeked of history. Harvard had been founded only in 1636, a year after the Latin School, because, so the school boasted, there had to be a college to take its first graduates. The school had sat originally on Beacon Hill, before being moved ultimately to the Fenway, where it was when I attended. The original school on the hill had given its name to the street which is still there: School Street in Boston. We learned that the legendary boys who had outfaced the British on the hill, and thrown snowballs at the Redcoats who put cinders on the icy streets where they sleighed, were Latin School boys. They were the first recorded student demonstrators in American history. In our Latin School assembly hall, the frieze bore proudly the names of boys who had graduated to mark American history. From Franklin, Adams and Hancock, on through Emerson, Motley, Eliot, Payne, Quincy, Sumner, Warren, Winthrop—the trailblazers pointed the way. The frieze might later have listed a Kennedy, a Bernstein, a Wharton. But all this history translated quite precisely to the immigrant parents of

Boston. The Latin School was the gateway to Harvard—
as much so in 1928, when I entered, as it had been for
hundreds of years before. No longer is it so.

In my day, the Latin School was a cruel school—but
it may have been the best public school in the country.
The old Boston version of "Open Admissions" held that
absolutely anyone was free to enter. And the school was
free to fail and expel absolutely anyone who did not meet
its standards. It accepted students without discrimination,
and it flunked them—Irish, Italians, Jewish, Protestant,
black—with equal lack of discrimination. Passing grade
was fifty, and to average eighty or better was phenomenal. Our monthly tests were excerpts from the College
Board examinations of previous years—and we learned
"testmanship" early, beginning at age fourteen. The entire
Latin School was an obstacle course in "testmanship," a
skill which, we learned, meant that one must grasp the
question quickly; answer hard, with minimum verbiage;
and do it all against a speeding clock. If you scored well
in Latin School classroom tests in arithmetic, the College
Boards held no peril—you would do better in those
exams; and at Harvard, almost certainly, you would qualify for the advanced section of Mathematics A.

The Latin School taught the mechanics of learning
with little pretense of culture, enrichment or enlargement
of horizons. Mr. Russo, who taught English in the first
year, had the face of a prizefighter—a bald head which
gleamed, a pug nose, a jut jaw, hard and sinister eyes
which smiled only when a pupil scored an absolute triumph in grammar. He was less interested in the rhymes
of *The Idylls of the King* or "Evangeline," or the story in
Quentin Durward, than in drubbing into us the structure
of paragraph and sentence. The paragraph began with the
"topic sentence"—that was the cornerstone of all teaching
in composition. And sentences came with "subjects,"
"predicates," "metaphors," "similes," "analogies." Verbs
were transitive, intransitive and sometimes subjunctive.
He taught the English language as if he were teaching us
to dismantle an automobile engine or a watch and then
assemble it again correctly. We learned clean English

from him. Mr. Graetsch taught German in the same way, mechanically, so that one remembered all the rest of one's life that six German prepositions take the dative case—*aus-bei-mit, nach-von-zu*, in alphabetical order. French was taught by Mr. Scully. Not only did we memorize passages (*D'un pas encore vaillant et ferme, un vieux prêtre marche sur la route poudreuse*), but we memorized them so well that long after one had forgotten the title of the work, one remembered its phrases; all irregular French verbs were mastered by the end of the second year.

What culture was pumped in came in ancient history, taught by Mr. Hayes; American history taught by Mr. Nemzoff, who enlarged on what Miss Fuller had taught in the sixth grade; and Latin itself, taught by "Farmer" Wilbur. "Farmer" Wilbur was a rustic who raised apples on his farm outside Boston, and would bring them in by the bushel to hand out to the boys who did well. Latin was drudgery; one learned Caesar, one groaned through Cicero, one went on to Virgil. I did badly in Latin, although ancient history fascinated me; and not until I came many years later to American politics did I realize how much of "Farmer" Wilbur's teaching of Caesar and Cicero had flaked off into the sediment of my thinking.

Yet, though the choice had been my own, my first three years at the Latin School were an unrelieved torment. I barely managed a sixty average, which put me somewhere in the lower third of my class. But then in June 1931 my father died, and I was plunged into an education that remains for all men and women of my generation their great shaping experience—the lessons taught by the Great Depression.

One reads now that the 1920s were boom years, that the Great Depression did not begin until the stock market crash of October 1929.

For those of us of the underclass, the Depression had begun long before then. I had started a schoolboy diary the same year I entered the Latin School, in 1928. On historic Black Friday, October 29, the day of the

great Wall Street crash of 1929, my diary makes no
mention of the event. It says: "No money all week, Pa
brought home $2.00 today, Mama is crying again."

The two years after that, the two years during which
my father's heart was broken, come back at me again and
again like a nightmare.

This was our country.

I was, by then, an American history buff. But even a
teen-ager could see that this country was not working for
us. There were no clothes—literally no new clothes for
over four years in the family; all of us wore hand-me-
downs. We traded at a delicatessen store where, occasionally, I had to ask Mr. Schiff if he could slice an *achtel*
(an eighth of a pound) of corned beef into six slices, one
for each of us in the family. Mr. Schiff could perform that
butcher's miracle, and a slice of a sixth of an eighth of a
pound of corned beef was so paper thin that you could
see the light through it if you held it up—but if you held
it up, it shredded in your fingers. For a passing delicacy, I
would walk a mile to the baking plant of Drake's Cakes,
and there, at the factory, could buy two pounds of day-
old stale cake for ten cents. A mile the other way was a
chocolate factory. For a dime, you could buy old and
moldy chocolates about to be thrown out; but such a
dime for chocolate was an extravagance. Movies vanished
entirely from the family budget—so the children read
books instead. I began to walk back and forth to the
Latin School, four miles away, whenever the weather was
fair, to save the nickel fare. And as one walked to school
by Roxbury Crossing and through the factory district, one
saw that the shoe plants were closed down, no workers
going in and out, no smoke from the cold smokestacks
that silhouetted my route. The year I entered Latin
School, in 1928, there were 948 shoe factories in Greater
Boston; a year later, only 817. By 1930, in the city of
Boston there were only eight thousand shoe workers; by
1940, only half that number.

What I saw and what I felt had no connection at all
with what I had learned of American history. The evidence before me said that Papa was right—capitalism

had ruined us. Capitalism did not care what happened to us. No one cared what happened to us. I worked on off-school days and during the school vacations for a house renovator, a small-time contractor who had me on the job from eight in the morning until the house was scraped of its old wallpaper, its crumbling plaster gouged out and respackled; for a twelve-hour day I was paid two dollars, and glad to have it. I was lucky—until the little contractor went broke, too, and that was the end of that job. People hungered. Lives ended.

The Depression was too immense an event to grasp. Our streets and my friends hived with young adolescents who were joining either the Young People's Socialist League (YPSL), or the Young Communist League (YCL) or the Young Worker Zionists, whose song ran: "Off we go to Palestine—the hell with the Depression." American politics seemed to offer nothing. When I was sixteen or seventeen, I visited the local Democratic Party storefront on Blue Hill Avenue, the first political headquarters I ever entered. I might get a job, I thought, by getting into politics—and a thug grabbed me by the shoulders, kicked me so hard that the base of my spine still tingles at the memory, and said that they didn't want any goddamn kids around this place. It must have been the year that Franklin D. Roosevelt was building his 1932 campaign for the Presidency; I now know he had Curley and the Boston machine with him; but from where I walked the streets, I could not see what Franklin Roosevelt would do, and I loathed the whole system. Revolution, only revolution, would save us—but how did you connect revolution with what Miss Fuller and Mr. Nemzoff taught of American history?

It was worse when my father died. I was sixteen then. My diary records a one-line sentence, June 16, 1931: "Pa died today." And the memory of the year after he died I cannot, despite every effort, bring back. I pushed it out of mind long ago. I know, technically, that my mother let me finish my last year of school before I went to work—I was to graduate in the class of 1932 at the Boston Latin School. But in dignity the price of my finishing the Latin School, instead of going out to hunt work, was crushing.

We were on home relief.

It was shameful—we, of a learned family, on home relief. With my father's death, we were five left. And for five people the city of Boston gave eleven dollars a week. We survived on eleven dollars a week, for my grandmother, upstairs, had ceased demanding that we pay rent. But to get home relief, in those days, my mother had to take a streetcar (ten cents each way) downtown to the relief office. And there, after standing in line for hours, she would receive a five-dollar greenback and six ones. Each week she made the trip, each trip brought her home desolate. It was intolerable. My marks at school rose spectacularly in the last year of misery. If there was no father left, I had to make it on my own. If I wanted to go to college, I would have to do it by scholarship, and scholarship meant getting good marks. Given this need, my marks jumped from a sixty to a ninety average. My final College Board examinations brought marks then called "highest honors." And immediately after graduation, there was an acceptance to Harvard. But the acceptance carried no scholarship money; no stipend, nothing but the right to enroll. And so the certificate became a trophy to put away in a drawer. The problem was how to get off relief—and yet survive.

The struggle to survive spared no one. My sister, Gladys, a woman of extraordinary gifts, had to leave college after her first year to find a job as a library assistant. My two younger brothers—Robert, then nine, and Alvin, twelve—were conscripted to sell newspapers at the corners before going to school. That meant they had to be roused from bed before six each morning, and thrust out into the winter cold. And I woke at five each morning, for I had won from the local news wholesaler the right to run the streetcars on the tough ride from Franklin Park to Egleston Square, peddling papers.

On the streetcars I met the Irish as workingmen. Except for Mr. Snow—I always called him Mr. Snow—

who was a motorman six days a week and taught a Congregational Sunday school on the seventh day, the motormen were all Irish. Most were Galway men. They were proud of being men of Galway, and they told me why men of Galway were different from men of Cork, or Tipperary, or Dublin. It sounded very much like Jewish talk—why Pinsk Jews were different from Warsaw Jews, or Odessa Jews, or Lvov Jews. They were hard men, but once they accepted you they offered the camaraderie that makes Irish radicals die for each other. Of these men, the meanest was Motorman Conley. He was hard-faced, surly and profane. Even though I wore the nickel-plated medallion which officially entitled me to sell newspapers on the streetcars, he wanted me to "stay the hell off" his car. I had to brace him, and hopped his car one day to sell the papers; I rode three stops trying to explain to him that I had to make a living, too, for my mother and the kids, and I had the right, and I didn't want to have a fight with him and on and on. Finally, he said, "O.K." And then, after that, he not only gave me the key to the booth of the Franklin Park station, where there was an electric heater to warm the fingers and toes of the motormen on the early-morning run; but he also began to help me get more money from the boss. I was doing well selling papers, making between two and three dollars a day. But I could also hand in returns and get credit for the unsold papers against my account with the boss. Conley figured out for me that we could screw my boss and I could make an extra half buck a day if he picked up for me the discarded newspapers at Egleston Square, the turnaround of his trolley run. He would bring me back a batch of newspaper throwaways at ten or eleven in the morning; and if they were neatly enough cast off, I could refold them and slip them into my returns, thus making 1.3 cents on each false return that I claimed from the boss. I am sorry now that I cheated the boss by half a dollar a day, but he probably cranked it into his calculations of the net he took from the newsboys he "owned." And since my cash return to him was high, I was not chal-

lenged; he sent them back to the newspapers anyway.
Conley and I became friends, in a surly way, as he helped
me screw the bosses; we were both against the system.

Newspapering lasted for over a year. I would scream
the headlines; and occasionally, when I saw an old Latin
School friend taking the trolley in town to Boston University or Massachusetts Institute of Technology, I would
scream the headlines in Latin. I could sell almost as many
papers, if I put emotion into the call, by shrieking, *"Quo
usque, O Catilina, tandem abutere patientia nostra, quem
ad finem nos eludet iste furor tuus . . ."* as I could by
shrieking anything else. But my old schoolmates of the
Latin School ignored me. I was a dropout, they were
college day students.

Newspapering led to cheating—all newsstand operations do, as I learned later when I tried to manage
magazines, or tried to find out how my more successful
books were selling on paperback newsstands. I converted
some of the regular streetcar customers to home delivery,
and within a year, I had a growing home-delivery route
which would bring in several dollars a week all by itself,
apart from what the boss knew I was selling in the open.

Far more importantly, I had won a steady job—
teaching Hebrew to children in the local Hebrew school at
fourteen dollars a week, subjecting them to the same
cruelty to which I had been subjected when a child.
Middle-aged men and women now approach me as I
travel and tell me they were my students and that I was a
stern but effective teacher of tradition to the young. But I
was then just eighteen myself, full of the juices of life.
Thus, rather than teaching children the Hebrew characters by reading in the standard books of the Bible, which
they were required to decipher but not understand, I had
them do their rote reading from the Song of Songs, which
is Solomon's. They could not understand that text either,
but to hear little boys and girls pipe the lines of love in
the ancient language soothed me in the dreary evening
sessions. Two books of the Bible are generally not taught
to youngsters in the modern Hebrew schools: the Song of
Songs and, for obvious reasons, Ecclesiastes. Ecclesiastes

I had won to myself by my own reading. But listening to the little children reading aloud the Song of Songs was, probably, the closest I came to erotic reading.

And then, in the fall of 1934, when I was two years out of Latin School, confused, angry and on my way to nowhere, two things happened. Harvard College gave me a scholarship of $220 and the Burroughs Newsboys Foundation gave me a college grant of $180 (I still ran a newspaper route). Two-twenty and one-eighty came to four hundred dollars—which was the exact fee for a year's tuition at Harvard, and so I could try that for a year. Harvard then required a bond that a freshman would do no property damage there, and luckily, our neighbor, Mrs. Goldman, who owned a house down the street, was willing to sign such a bond. So in September of 1934, cutting a corner here and amplifying a hope there, I took the subway into Harvard Square to enroll.

I have, in the years since, served as an overseer of that majestic institution Harvard University, a member of the Honorable and Reverend Board of the most ancient corporation in the Western world, the chosen thirty who tip their silk hats as they file, two by two, past the statue of John Harvard on Commencement Day in the Yard. But it was a better Harvard I entered in the 1930s than it was later, when I sat on its Board of Overseers, or than it is today.

One emerged, as one still does, from the subway exit in the Square and faced an old red-brick wall behind which stretched, to my fond eye, what remains still the most beautiful campus in America, the Harvard Yard. If there is any one place in all America that mirrors better all American history, I do not know of it.

The signature building of the Harvard Yard was the Widener Library, its gray façade and pillars dominating all the open inner space. Widener was the crownpiece of the largest university library in the world and its architecture made a flat statement: that books and learning were what a school was all about. But the rest of the Yard spoke history. Across the green was the chapel built to

commemorate Harvard men fallen in the First World
War, which would, in time, have carved on its tablets the
names of thirty-two of my classmates who were to fall in
World War II. Across the street from the Yard, on the
edge of Cambridge Common, stood the Washington Elm,
where, legend claims, George Washington took command
of the Continental Army in 1775. Beyond rose the gor-
geous Romanesque bulk of "Mem" Hall—the memorial
for the veterans of the Civil War. To the north were acres
and acres of a university no one person has ever fully
explored—law school, graduate schools, museums, laboratories. To the south the residential houses rose along
the Charles and there, beneath their turrets of red and
blue and yellow, one could lie on the grass beside the
slow-flowing Charles River with a friend and gaze at the
Harvard Business School across the river. The business
school, though few knew it, had its roots in history, too.
It had sprung out of the Spanish-American War, when a
few public-spirited alumni decided that America, for its
new empire, needed a colonial school of administration to
match Britain's imperial and colonial civil services. The
school they envisioned became, in the course of time, the
Harvard Graduate School of Business Administration,
eventually fulfilling the imperial dreams of its sponsors by
staffing the multinational corporations of the twentieth
century.

Revolutionary War, Civil War, Spanish-American
War, World War I, had all left marks behind at Harvard.
World War II was on its way; and Harvard was in change
under the leadership of James Bryant Conant, who was to
leave to head a secret project called the "uranium bomb."
Harvard had entered the modern world of learning in
1869, under the leadership of Charles William Eliot, who
presided until 1909; it had passed through twenty-four
years of the presidency of Abbott Lawrence Lowell, an
aristocrat of great personal wealth who had candied Harvard's overwhelmingly New England student body with a
top layer of the wealthiest adolescents of the Eastern
seaboard. And then came Conant, the greatest of them

all. Conant was of New England lineage as ancient as Lowell's or Eliot's, and was, like Eliot, a chemist of extraordinary creativity. Conant wanted to make Harvard something more than a New England school; he wanted its faculty to be more than a gentlemen's club of courtly learned men, wanted its student body to be national in origin. Excellence was his goal as he began shaking up both faculty and student body, and in the end, twenty years later, when he left in 1953, his insistence on excellence had made Harvard the most competitive school in American scholarship, a meritocracy in which students and professors vied for honors with little mercy or kindness.

But then, at the beginning of Conant's regime in the thirties, Harvard combined the best of the old warmth and the new strivings. Conant himself would address the freshman class. We all squatted on the floor of the Freshman Union, and he told us what a university was: a place for free minds. "If you call everyone to the right of you a Bourbon and everyone to the left of you a Communist, you'll get nothing out of Harvard," he said to us. And went on to explain that what we would get out of Harvard was what we could take from it ourselves; Harvard was open, so—go seek.

Students divide themselves by their own discriminations in every generation, and the group I ran with had a neat system of classification. Harvard, my own group held, was divided into three groups—white men, gray men and meatballs. I belonged to the meatballs, by selfclassification. White men were youngsters of great name; my own class held a Boston Saltonstall, a New York Straus, a Chicago Marshall Field, two Roosevelts (John and Kermit), a Joseph P. Kennedy, Jr. The upper classes had another Roosevelt (Franklin, Jr.), a Rockefeller (David, with whom I shared a tutor in my sophomore year), a Morgan, and New York and Boston names of a dozen different fashionable pedigrees. Students of such names had automobiles; they went to Boston deb parties, football games, the June crew race against Yale; they belonged to clubs. At Harvard today, they are called "preppies," the private-school boys of mythical "St. Grottlesex."

Between white men above and meatballs at the bottom came the gray men. The gray men were mostly public-high-school boys, sturdy sons of America's middle class. They went out for football and baseball, manned the *Crimson* and the *Lampoon,* ran for class committees and, later in life, for school committees and political office. They came neither of the aristocracy nor of the deserving poor, as did most meatballs and scholarship boys. Caspar Weinberger, of my class of 1938, for example, was president of the *Crimson* and graduated magna cum laude; he later became Secretary of Health, Education and Welfare, but as an undergraduate was a gray man from California. John King, of the same class of 1938, was another gray man; he became governor of New Hampshire. Wiley Mayne, an earnest student of history, who graduated with us, was a gray man from Iowa, later becoming congressman from Sioux City. He served on the House Judiciary Committee that voted to impeach Richard Nixon—with Wiley Mayne voting to support the President. The most brilliant member of the class was probably Arthur M. Schlesinger, Jr., who defied categorization. Definitely no meatball, Schlesinger lacked then either the wealth or the savoir-faire of the white men. Indeed, Schlesinger, who was to go on to a fame surpassing that of his scholar father, was one who could apparently mingle with both white men *and* meatballs. In his youth, Schlesinger was a boy of extraordinary sweetness and generosity, one of the few on campus who would be friendly to a Jewish meatball, not only a liberal by heredity, but a liberal in practice. Since Wiley Mayne, Arthur Schlesinger and I were all rivals, in an indistinct way, in the undergraduate rivalry of the History Department, I followed their careers with some interest. Mayne was a conservative, tart-tongued and stiff. I remember on the night of our Class Day dance, as we were all about to leave, he unburdened himself to me on "Eastern liberals who look down their long snob noses on people like me from the Midwest." Over the years Mayne grew into a milder, gentler, warmer person until in his agony over Nixon, wrestling with his conscience on whether to impeach or not, he seemed to be perhaps the most sensitive and human member of the Judiciary Committee. Schlesinger, by contrast, developed a certainty about affairs, a public tartness of manner associated with the general liberal rigidity of the late sixties that offended many—and yet, for all that, he remained as kind and gentle to old friends like myself, with whose politics he came profoundly to disagree, as he had been in boyhood. Both Schlesinger and Mayne, the liberal and the conservative, were always absolutely firm in their opinions. I, in the years starting at Harvard, and continuing in later life, wandered all through the political spectrum, and envied them both for their certainties.

I find some difficulty in describing what a "meatball" was. Meatballs were usually day students or scholarship students. We were at Harvard not to enjoy the games, the girls, the burlesque shows of the Old Howard, the companionship, the elms, the turning leaves of fall, the grassy banks of the Charles. We had come to get the Harvard badge, which says "Veritas," but really means a job somewhere in the future, in some bureaucracy, in some institution, in some school, laboratory, university or law firm.

Conant was the first president to recognize that meatballs were Harvard men, too, and so he set apart a ground floor room at Dudley Hall where we could bring our lunches in brown paper bags and eat at a table, or lounge in easy chairs between classes. The master of this strange enclave of commuting Irish, Jewish and Italian youngsters from Greater Boston was a young historian named Charles Duhig, whose argument was that the most revolutionary force in history was the middle class. Duhig had contempt for the working class ("slobs"), disdain for the upper class. His theory held that modern history is carried forward chiefly by the middle class, their children, and what moves them to the future. In us, his wards, he had a zoo of specimens of the mobile lower middle class and he enjoyed watching us resist Communist penetration.

Dudley Hall was plowed regularly by Harvard's intellectual upper-class Communists, who felt that we were of the oppressed. Occasionally such well-bred, rich or elite Communist youngsters from the resident houses would bring a neat brown-paper-bag lunch and join us at the round tables to persuade us, as companions, of the inevitable proletarian revolution. Duhig, our custodian, welcomed their visits because he knew his scholarship boys could take care of such Communists in debate as easily as they could take care of the Republican youngsters who staffed the *Crimson*. We were Duhig's own middle class in the flesh—hungry and ambitious. Most of us, largely Boston Latin School graduates, knew more about poverty than anyone from Beacon Hill or the fashionable East Side of New York. We hated poverty; and meant to have no share in it. We had come to Harvard not to help the working classes, but to get out of the working classes. We were on the make. And in my own case, the approach to Harvard and its riches was that of a looter. Harvard had the keys to the gates; what lay behind the gates I could not guess, but all that lay there was to be looted. Not only were there required courses to be attended, but there were courses given by famous men, lectures open to all, where no one guarded the entry. I could listen. There were museums to be seen, libraries and poetry rooms of all kinds to tarry in—and stacks and stacks and stacks of books. It was a place to grab at ideas and facts, and I grabbed at history.

One had a choice, in one's freshman year, of taking either one of two required courses—History I or Government I. Government I was a "gut" course, and the student underground passed the word that no one ever failed in Government I. History I had the reputation of being a nut-cracker; no one ever got an A in History I except by luck. But History I was the course most freshmen took because its professor, "Frisky" Merriman, was perhaps the most colorful character on Harvard's then vivid faculty of characters. He believed history was story—thus, entertainment.

In History I, Roger Bigelow Merriman stretched the story from the Age of the Antonines right down to the Treaty of Versailles—all 1800 years from the breakup of the Roman Empire to the breakup of Western Europe in 1914–1918. He is now considered a primitive by Harvard's present more elegant and austere masters of history—an academic histrionic who made his course in Western civilization a vaudeville sequence of thirty-six acts. Merriman could entertain a hall of six hundred students and hold them spellbound; he paced the platform from end to end, roaring, wheedling, stage-whispering, occasionally screeching in falsetto and earning fairly his nickname. We raced through the Antonines, enjoyed the Middle Ages, saluted Caliph Harun al-Rashid, thrilled with the struggle of Moors and Catholics in Spain, mourned for Boabdil, last sultan of the Moors. But the course was like an express train, pausing only at major stops on the track of history, and always, at every turning point, there would be "Frisky" Merriman, like a conductor calling the next stop and ultimate arrival, closing his lectures with "Unity, gentlemen, unity!"

Europe, he held, had sought the long-lost unity Rome had given it two thousand years ago as a man seeks to recapture a dream. Noted professors came from their own history courses to give a guest lecture or a week of lectures on their favorite subject, all falling into Merriman's mood as vaudevillians who try not to disappoint their producer. The last of these was the best, a young professor called James Phinney Baxter III, later to become president of Williams College and deputy director of the OSS. Baxter had observed World War I and thought that the machine gun was the instrument that ended the Age of Wars: he would crouch and go *hup-hup-hup* with an imaginary machine gun on the lecture platform explaining just what that machine gun had done to warfare and history between 1914 and 1918. I would have enjoyed hearing Baxter, twenty years later, on the nuclear bomb. But after Baxter, as after every other lecturer or turning point, Merriman would bring the course back on track: "Unity, gentlemen, unity!" he would roar. Charlemagne, Napoleon, Bismarck, the Hohenstaufen emperors, the Popes, the Hapsburgs, the Versailles Treaty—all had sought to give unity to Europe. It was a theme that would echo all the rest of my life; and resound again when I came to Europe to report the Marshall Plan, the Common Market and the dreams of Jean Monnet, who had never heard of "Frisky" Merriman but held exactly the same view of Europe.

History I led in two directions, both of them luring me from my past without my knowing it.

The first direction in which History I led, as I romanticize the beginning, came by mechanical accident. It led across a corridor in Boylston Hall—to China.

It happened this way: A reading room on the ground floor of Boylston Hall was set aside for the hundreds of students who took Merriman's course, and it would become crowded, sweaty and steamy on weekends as we crammed for the next week's sections. But across the corridor in the same building was the library of the Harvard-Yenching Institute—the library which would grow over the next forty years into the greatest collection of Oriental volumes outside Asia. It was easier to study in the empty library of the Harvard-Yenching Institute than in the History I reading room, so I would surreptitiously cross the corridor on Saturday afternoons. And if I was bleary with reading about medieval trade, or the Reformation, or the Age of Imperialism, I could get up and pick Chinese volumes off the shelves—volumes on fine rice paper, blue-bound, bamboo-hooked volumes with strange characters, volumes with their own particular odor, an Oriental mustiness different from the mustiness of Western books. As I became more and more accustomed to the Oriental atmosphere, and my eyes rested on the scrolls of calligraphy on the walls, I began to feel at home. The Boston Latin School had given me reading knowledge of Latin, German and French. Yiddish I understood from home. Hebrew was the language I knew I spoke best after my native English. Why not, then, take a giant step, and add Chinese to my languages—and find out what the blue-bound volumes said. And my father had told me to pay attention to China. The choice, then, at the end of my freshman year, as I had to choose a field of concentration for my sophomore year, became Chinese history and language.

And a more dangerous choice I never made.

Chinese is one of the simplest languages to speak, but the most difficult to read. The Chinese Department at Harvard, in those days, had the standards of the Emperor Ch'ien-lung laced with a dash of sadism. Their theory, entirely wrong, was that no youngster in his teens, no undergraduate, could possibly master the Chinese language. Conant had overruled such desiccated scholarship in his second year as president, and in my sophomore year the study of the Chinese language was thrown open to undergraduates for the first time. Chinese I, the introductory course, was conducted by one of the most brutal men I have ever met. The class had five students, three graduate students and two undergraduates; but our professor was determined to prove his point (that undergraduates could *not* learn Chinese) by trying to flunk both of us immediately. The other undergraduate collapsed quickly. I, however, was at Harvard on scholarship, and if I flunked, I would lose my scholarship and thus my dreams would end. The professor taught the language by main force—simple visual memorization. We were never taught that almost all Chinese characters have a phonetic element which gives the sound, and an idea element which gives the meaning. Chinese should be taught to children while young—while their minds are elastic enough to associate vision and meaning. Graduates of American high schools now learn Chinese with far greater ease than graduates of Harvard in the old days. In those days at Boylston Hall one pounded each character into the mind by sheer force of recall, as one pounds nails into a board. I was put on notice of dismissal within six weeks of joining the course; and since my survival depended on staying at Harvard, I must not flunk, I must study—until one and two and three in the morning, forc-

ing my memory to inscribe and retrieve Chinese characters. As the professor increased the burden in each session, the entire class, even graduate students, began to
wilt. He relented, finally, and I survived, to get an A.

What we learned in Chinese was almost entirely
useless. By the time I graduated from Harvard, I had
memorized and could recognize by sight three thousand
individual Chinese ideograms and as many more combi-
nations of ideograms; I still have the memory cards on
which each is written. But I can no longer recognize more
than a hundred of the characters I once mastered, and
can no longer read any kind of Chinese. All the characters and all the literature I was taught came from the
Chinese classics: we read and translated Confucius and
Mencius, histories and ancient odes. None of the spectacular Chinese novels of tradition (and the Chinese invented the novel form almost two thousand years ago),
none of the lyric poems of the Tang or the nostalgic
poems of the Sung were taught to us. We were taught the
classics as if we were training for examinations in the
Manchu civil service—and the classics were rules, regulations, moralities, history. And war. Those who think of
the Chinese as a sublimely philosophical and peaceful
people should be steeped in such Chinese classics. The
Chinese tradition seeks order, discipline, moral behavior
at all times; and when this order in the mind is affronted,
the Chinese system reaches, as their tradition records,
paroxysms of violence and ferocity.

Parallel to the path across Boylston Hall was the
second direction in which I was invited—to the History
Department. And history as it was taught in my four
years at Harvard is, in retrospect, a wonder. Quite simply,
history was not yet considered a science but was still
thought more noble than a craft. The professors were a
colony of storytellers, held together by the belief that in
their many stories they might find a truth. They still cared
about students and lingered after class for conversations.
No better preparation for what was to come to me in life
could have been planned than what came to me at Harvard, by accident and timing and osmosis of curiosity.

The best course in American history was given by Arthur Schlesinger, Sr., and Paul Buck. Schlesinger, a magnificent teacher, opened the course by telling us that American history was singularly poor in ideas, deficient in political theory, in philosophic system, in abstractions of all sorts. He insisted that American history swung in regular cycles of sixteen years, from hope to fear, from liberalism to conservatism. He concluded his masterly introductory lecture by saying: "The American people have not been governed by political theory, but purely by opportunism . . . because of this plasticity we have been spared violent and bloody convulsions. . . ."

At Harvard, thus, I made the third round in American history: Miss Fuller had guided me the first time around, the Latin School the second, and at Harvard a large covey of professors gave me the final tour. But Schlesinger and Buck had set the tone: proud and patriotic as Miss Fuller had been, they saw American history as a struggle from which the good usually emerged triumphant. I was thus early bent to this patriotic view, and confirmed in it by higher learning, before I went out to see the story myself.

Yet Harvard's History Department offered more than American history. It offered a banquet of invitations to the past, of famous courses, of byways and coves and special delights of learning. Professor Crane Brinton, an urbane and aloof man, offered a course in the French Revolution. Cynical, caustic, disdainful of all morals, Brinton claimed as his own particular hero Talleyrand; but he lectured on Marat, Danton, Robespierre with an insight into character that would now be called, by fashionable scholars, psychohistory. Forced by the syllabus to devote one lecture to the financial policies of the revolutionaries, the inflation and the *assignats,* he read his notes from cards, and halfway through that lecture, he paused, yawning, and said, "Gentlemen, I don't see how you can stay awake listening to this, I'm falling asleep myself, but money is always important"—and went on.

A magnificent teacher, whose importance in historiography was unknown to me, was a man named Abbott

Payson Usher. Usher taught economic history, but with
such infectious enthusiasm, with such a waggle of his jaw,
with such salivating eloquence, that he shook all my
adolescent Marxism. Here, ran the story of Usher's
course, was the way men made things and traded things;
and history rests on how they manage the manufacture
and exchange of goods. He took the Connecticut valley
and explained how the Yankee tinkerers there invented
mass production, interchangeable parts, and the American system of production. He traced on a map the coal
beds that undervein Europe from England's Midlands, to
France's North Country, to Germany's Ruhr and Silesia,
demonstrating how one could track the development of
political power in Europe by following the veins of energy
and the times when coaling was first developed in each
country. He taught about rivers, and how all the great
cities of the world grew up at the mouths or fording
places of rivers—London, New York, Paris, Rome. His
course was basic introductory material for any reporter
who would later write about the Marshall Plan. And in
Fire in the Ashes, a book I wrote on European recovery,
many years later, I plagiarized what I remembered of
Abbott Payson Usher's lectures shamelessly. His course
simply took all my previous ideas, shook them apart
gently, then taught me how facts and large affairs arrange
themselves in connections that made history seem like
intellectual detective work.

   Yet the teacher who, more than any other, spun me
off into history as a life calling was a young man who
arrived at Harvard only at the beginning of my junior
year: John King Fairbank, later to become the greatest
historian of America's relations with China. Fairbank was
then only twenty-nine—tall, burly, sandy-haired, a prairie
boy from South Dakota; soft-spoken, with an unsettling
conversational gift of delayed-action humor; and a pains-
taking drillmaster. He had himself graduated from Harvard in 1929, but on his way back to the Yard had made
a circuitous route via Oxford and Peking to become a
specialist in modern Chinese history. He had a freshly
minted Ph.D. and was on trial at Harvard both as a tutor

and Orientalist; since I was the only undergraduate majoring in Chinese history and studies, I was assigned to him as tutee. No two young people could have come of more different backgrounds. The tutorial system at Harvard was then in its early years, exploring the idea that each young mind needs an older mind to guide it. Tutors at Harvard now are usually embittered graduate students, rarely, if ever, emotionally committed to the undergraduates they guide. But Fairbank approached me as if he were an apprentice Pygmalion, assigned a raw piece of ghetto stone to carve, sculpt, shape and polish. He yearned that I do well.

It was not only that I was invited to my first tea party at his home, learning to balance a teacup properly; nor that, by observation, I learned proper table manners at a properly set breakfast table in the little yellow cottage where he lived with his beautiful young wife, Wilma. It was his absolute devotion to forcing my mind to think that speeded the change in me. We would talk about China and he would tell me tales of life in Peking as chatter—but only after our work was done. He was insistent that I read. I spent six weeks plowing through St. Thomas Aquinas, which, he agreed, was useless, yet necessary for a professional historian's understanding. He would make the hardest work a joy, and his monthly assignments were written with a skill and personal attention that no tutor at Harvard, or anywhere else, today gives to his students. One of his assignment memos, which I still treasure, shows how a great teacher goes about his calling.

WHEREAS [read his communication] it is not possible to live (long) without thinking, and not possible to live well without thinking well; and

It is not possible to think well without making *distinctions* between this and that, or heredity and environment, or cause and effect, or the group and the individual, or the law and the facts, or tactics and strategy, or rights and

duties, or man and woman, or nominalism and
realism, or communism and fascism, or collec-
tivism and individualism, to say nothing of up
and down, or backwards and forwards; and
whereas

It is not possible to go very far in making
distinctions without making use of *categories of
thought*, such as a category of laws and a
category of events, or a category of noumena
and a category of phenomena, or a category of
spirit and a category of matter; and whereas

It is not possible to think with critical
power without being *critical* of the categories
with which one is thinking; and

It is not possible to avoid receiving certain
categories at an early age from the contemporary intellectual environment;—

THEREFORE—

Philosophy is a most *necessary* and *admirable* subject, and

You are cordially invited to be present at
a meeting on Friday, January 8, 1937, at which
there will be a discussion of Whitehead's vol-
ume *Science and the Modern World* (entire)
conducted by none other than Mr. Theodore H.
White.

Thus I was introduced to Whitehead's philosophy as
to myriad other ideas by Fairbank's loving and disciplined tutelage.

Yet, though he molded me, he was pursuing his own
cause, too—which was understanding the revolution in
Asia in our time. The fossil Sinologists of Harvard's
Oriental Department felt that all Oriental history ended
with the end of the Ch'ien-lung dynasty, in 1799. Professor Elisaeff, the department chief, insisted that everything
after that date was journalism. Fairbank held otherwise—
that history was happening now. He was probably the
only man in all Cambridge who recognized that the Long
March of Mao Tse-tung, the year before he himself joined

Harvard's faculty, was epoch-making. Thus, then, in my senior year, young John Fairbank was allowed to teach a course—History 83b—on China from the death of Ch'ien-lung down to our times. It was a magnificent series of lectures, ground-breaking in intellectual patterns, and those few students who attended it caught the swell of what was happening in China and Asia from his wry, caustic, surgical stripping of myth from fact, noumena from phenomena, his separating Dr. Fu Manchu and *The Bitter Tea of General Yen* from what was really going on in China. His course reinforced what my father had told me of China and what I felt by instinct. It inflamed my itch to be off, away and out—to China, where the story lay.

We differed, Fairbank and I, in an affectionate quarrel, over my senior thesis. I was shooting for fellowships and highest honors and I wanted to write about the delicate interaction of force and order. I wanted to take as my thesis subject the war lords of modern China and their brutalities over the thirty-year span of collapse of China's civil order. Fairbank insisted it was too broad a matter for a college senior to write about. I had become obsessed with force as the engine of history: who gathers the guns together at what point to hammer at the state or the enemy. Fairbank wrote back to my remonstrance a long letter on the causes of human action in man, saying that "force forces them at times, fear of force more often—and ideals still more often." He insisted that I display my knowledge of Chinese historiography by writing about the Twenty-One Demands of Japan on China in 1915 from Chinese bibliographical sources. This kind of scholarly paper, he pointed out, might get me a fellowship in the Harvard-Yenching Institute as a candidate for a doctorate. I set out to pursue this thesis in my senior year; and did so. This study of Japanese imperialism may have been, in a tiny way, useful to scholarship. But already, in my senior year, after two years with Fairbank, I knew I was leaving home.

I had come to Harvard as an adolescent Socialist and Zionist. I had helped organize the student Zionist activists on the New England campuses in what was called the Avukah (Torch) Society. I had helped organize a boycott of German goods in Boston, and been driven off by the cops for picketing Woolworth's. But somewhere between my junior and senior years, I had been lured to other interests. Harvard and History had intervened. So many other things were happening: The Japanese had begun their war on China in the summer of 1937, and were shattering Chinese resistance everywhere. Hitler was persecuting Jews. The Spanish Civil War was in its second year, and campus liberals were all engaged. What upset me most, the proximate cause of changed orientation, as Fairbank would have called it, was the siege of Toledo. Loyalists there outnumbered the Fascists; they had more men, but they were badly commanded. The Fascists held on to the Alcázar; Toledo had been lost; and men of good will had been defeated because they did not know *how* to fight. If we were to face Fascism—and we could sense a war coming—all of us should know *how* to fight.

Thus, very consciously, I knew I was separating from my Socialist and Zionist friends on the Harvard campus when I went into the yellow frame building, which now houses the Harvard Alumni Association, to apply to Colonel Harris of the Reserve Officers' Training Corps and ask whether I could, as a senior, join the ROTC. Colonel Harris was stern. I was a minor campus radical. Such radicals had rolled toilet paper down the steps of Widener Library when the West Point cadets came to visit, had brandished signs calling for "Scholarships Not Battleships" to protest Roosevelt's naval rearmament program. But I explained to Harris how I had changed my mind and wanted to learn how to be an officer. The colonel said that it was impossible to join the ROTC in the senior year and qualify for a commission. But he would let me audit the course, without credit; and he also let me join the unit in exercises.

The Harvard unit was a field artillery unit, which drilled with its horses in the armory in Boston. I had never touched a horse in my life, except for peddlers' cart horses on Erie Street. At my first muster in the armory they presented me with a huge horse and played the Hoot Gibson comic Western trick on me. I stood at the right side of the horse, put my left foot in the stirrup, swung myself up to the saddle—and found myself facing the horse's tail. The ROTC students howled with laughter, and I was humiliated looking out at their laughing faces over a horse's behind. But then they did teach me how to mount correctly, and I attended the lectures on military strategy. What I most retained of my one year with the ROTC was this knowledge of how to mount, speed or slow a horse—which, when I was riding with Communist guerrilla units behind Japanese lines in China two years later, proved to be the most valuable practical skill I learned at Harvard. Some forty years later, as an Overseer at Harvard, I vehemently and fruitlessly protested the abolition of Harvard's ROTC unit as authority yielded to campus violence. Then, with only one other Overseer, I presented myself for the commissioning of the last of Harvard's contribution to the ROTC. All wars, by 1969, had become abhorrent to Harvard's undergraduates. We, in 1937, lived in a different time and knew we would have to learn to fight.

But that is to get ahead of the story. My senior year passed pleasantly enough. I was reading Chinese, steeping myself in history, writing about the Twenty-One Demands, slowly swinging in my politics from Socialist to hushed approval of Roosevelt's New Deal, concealing from friends that I was participating in ROTC exercises.

Graduation in 1938 was a pleasant June day. My mother and my sister came in by streetcar and subway to watch me graduate, and found nothing at all noteworthy in the program's statement that I had graduated summa cum laude under the rubric *"Qui adsecuti sunt summos honores."* That was what they had expected since I had entered the Boston Latin School. I left at noon, not staying to hear the commencement address by John Buchan, Baron Tweedsmuir. I was very hastily off that afternoon—by bus to Ann Arbor, Michigan, where they were giving a special summer course in reading Chinese newspapers, then back to Boston, then in a hurry to go to China.

Everything had come together in those last few months at Harvard.

In my own mind I was a revolutionary; but in reality I was the creature of other people, of another past, beneficiary of all the Establishment had packed into the Harvard processing system. My summa cum laude degree had won me a $1,200 fellowship from the Harvard-Yenching Institute. I could take that up, when I chose, and start on the long run of becoming a professor of Oriental history. But there was another surprise gift from the Establishment, which came in my last month at Harvard, something called the Frederick Sheldon Traveling Fellowship.

The Frederick Sheldon Traveling Fellowship was most important. Sheldon was a childless New England bibliophile who had graduated Harvard almost a hundred years before. When his widow died in 1908, she had bequeathed in his name half a million dollars for fellowships to let "students of promise" travel for a year as fancy took them. As it was explained to me, it was an invitation to spend a year traveling outside the United States, with no obligation either to study or work in the year of wandering.

The grant was $1,500—a fortune. For $600 (actually $595.27), I found, I could buy a series of tickets that would take me around the world: by U.S. President Lines to London, thence to Paris, thence to Marseilles; by Messageries Maritimes to Palestine, thence from Port Said to Hong Kong, then an economy passage from Hong Kong to San Francisco, and bus fare from San Francisco to Boston. This would leave $900 from the total. I could leave $600 of that behind for the family, as my contribution to the budget my mother and I had worked out—twenty dollars a week for eight months. There would still be $300 for me to eat, sleep and live on as I moved around the world to China. If I could not earn a living in China, if I could not earn enough to help my sister keep the family going back in Boston, I would have to come back and take up the route to my Oriental professorship.

A new thought had also crept in in my senior year—the thought that I could, conceivably, write of history as a newspaperman. Both Charlie Duhig and John Fairbank thought I was not really and truly of the stuff of scholarship. Without being specific, both implied that I had the manners, lust and ego of someone who might be a journalist. Fairbank had known Edgar Snow in China; and he thought I should try to do what Snow was doing.

So, then, with Establishment money in my pocket, and Harvard advice in my mind, I had begun to feel around the approaches to reporting. The Boston *Globe* was not then, as it is now, the best newspaper in Boston. But I was urged to try there before I went overseas. The name on the masthead that indicated "boss" was that of the managing editor, Laurence Winship, the father of its present editor, Thomas Winship. Larry Winship was a gruff man, but not frightening. In retrospect, he was the best of the old open-door newspaper editors. In his office on Boston's newspaper row, the Fleet Street of New England, he would, apparently, receive almost anyone—politicians, "cause" people, cranks, strangers, and Harvard seniors like myself. He gave me a brisk ten-minute hearing. I told him I was going to China, wanted to be a foreign correspondent and write for the Boston *Globe*. He listened, then said abruptly: All right. He could promise nothing except that he would read what I wrote if I mailed the copy to him personally; and if he liked what I wrote, he'd print it and pay for it. That was all, but he turned out to be as good as his word.

In the fall of 1938, then, I set out. I had a letter on stiff white Harvard stationery signed by James Bryant Conant, president of Harvard, recommending me to the good graces of the entire world as a Frederick Sheldon Traveling Fellow of the university. Charles Duhig, custodian of the meatballs at Dudley Hall, had always been upset by my vulgarity of manners and had given me a stern lecture about the graces of the world I was entering ("You've got to learn to clean your fingernails, White!"); then, as a gift, he also gave me his father-in-law's worn-out tuxedo. If I wanted to be a foreign correspondent, he said, I would have to go to diplomatic receptions and I would need a black-tie suit. John Fairbank's gift was more practical—a secondhand typewriter. My relatives gave me secondhand clothes. I bought a new suitcase and I had two hundred dollars in traveler's checks plus one hundred dollars in greenbacks in my wallet to get me to China.

I left Boston on the weekend of the great New England hurricane of September 1938, and my mother and sister cried seeing me off at the old South Station. All the way down to New York on the New Haven Railroad, the shoreline was littered with the wreckage of the hurricane; at New London, a huge ship's prow, blown on shore, hung within inches of the coach I was riding. It was a dramatic night. The next day I spent at the YMCA in New York and then boarded the SS *President Roosevelt* where, deep in the hold, above the throbbing engines, I shared a bunk with a young man whose name I still remember—Serafin Aliaga, a Spanish anarchist returning to fight Franco. Since the cause of the Republic was now hopeless, he said, he must therefore go back.

His sense of history was drawing him back to what must have been his death. My sense of history was drawing me outward, with no particular purpose of political passion. I hoped eventually to come back to Harvard. But first I must satisfy curiosity, my absolute lust to see what was happening in the China I had studied. How *did* history actually happen?

PART TWO

ASIA:
1938-1945

THE SIGHTSEER

Looking back now on the newly fledged college graduate leaving Boston, the storyteller could examine an almost comic figure. It was like squinting at something unrecognizable through the wrong end of a telescope. What the storyteller could see, looking back, was a bespectacled hustler, carrying one suitcase and a secondhand typewriter, about to round the world before coming home to be a professor of history—a prototypical juvenile sightseer.

That young sightseer had already been for years, and was to remain, a compulsive notetaker and diarist; and the diaries of his swift passage from Harvard to China are the only way to reconstruct the trajectory on which he was squirted out of one world into another completely different.

The sightseer came of two entirely different traditions: that of the Jews and that of the New England institutions that had set him on the road.

He was still reflexively Jewish as he set out from

Boston in 1938. He had not knowingly until then ever eaten lobster, clams, pork, ham or other conspicuously nonkosher food. At breakfasts with his tutor he had tried to push the bacon to the side of the eggs and hide it under the toast. He was also puritanically Jewish in the old social tradition. Neither he, nor any of his friends at Harvard—*not one*—had ever known a woman sexually before he graduated. In the old Jewish tradition, sex came only *after* marriage, no more than kissing was permitted until then; and then that was daring.

But he was also Bostonian. From the time Boston's Judge Baker Foundation, a vocational guidance center, had told his mother that her boy was very bright and tested in aptitudes best to be an electrical engineer, he had been pulled and tugged from the ancestral base by Boston good will. Boston good will had brought him the Burroughs Newsboys scholarship; had brought him other scholarships at Harvard; had finally graced him with this Sheldon Traveling Fellowship. If the founders and testators of such institutions and bequests had, with calculation, proposed to lure promising youngsters up into the Establishment, they could not have succeeded better than in first training this sightseer, then setting him on the road out of his origins.

The diaries of the swift journey started very personally, and changed swiftly, within weeks. The diary notes began almost totally concerned with three matters. With money first—records of bus fares, taxi tips, waiters' tips, arguments about hotel bills. With sex next —the sightseer entertained an athletic fantasy life about sex, and being on the road, meeting strange people, stimulated his sex fantasies. Lastly, politics—page after page of amateur attempts to stretch Harvard history courses over what he saw as he traveled. But what he was seeing then, in the fall–winter of 1938–1939, he would understand only later.

His passage through Europe was brief and did little to deepen understanding. Europe was there exactly as described in the newspapers and textbooks. The Munich crisis had just come and gone, but in October of 1938, gas masks were still being distributed in London, and the air raid trenches in Hyde Park were fresh-cut. Paris was as beautiful as Professor Brinton had described; and from Paris he was off to visit the land of his ancestors, Palestine.

There were, then, perhaps 450,000 Jews in what was later to become Israel, and already the Arabs and Jews were at each other's throats. A Harvard companion in the Avukah Society, Emmanuel Labes, a gifted young violinist in the Harvard orchestra, had preceded him to Palestine by a year. The sight of Labes, a year ahead of the new voyager, was startling. Labes had chosen commitment to a cause. He worked in a settlement growing oranges, drove the horse that collected the crates of harvest; his violinist's hands were horny with peasant work; he was bare-boned with exhaustion from his work in the fields. But Labes wanted to make an Israel and was learning to use a gun.

Everyone in Palestine seemed overworked, overstrained, hacking away at dry rock to make fields, eating groats and coarse bread, learning to grow vegetables and fruit, but all of them ready to fight for the idea that had gathered them. Pioneers manned mountaintops outside kibbutzim, learning by experience that they must hold the high ground, just as Colonel Harris had directed his ROTC cadets. When the young political sightseer took a four-mile walk in the countryside one day, he was greeted, on his return to a settlement, with genuine indignation; he had worried them and caused an alert. Arabs killed individual Jews walking unarmed on that road. Over this kettle of hatred the British watched with a garrison of sixteen thousand men, not basically anti-Semitic, but generally pro-Arab, disturbed because of the killings, and troubled because the Jews were unsettling this drowsy corner of their empire. "You Jews are simply a bloody nuisance," a young British officer told the Harvard sightseer.

The conflict of Arab and Jews, however, made a story, which, it seemed to the sightseer, would last for more than several weeks—it would last at least long

enough to send a "mailer" to Mr. Winship, who might
print it in the Boston *Globe.* Winship was to buy the
story, but Theodore H. White was not to know that he
had won his first by-line until he arrived in Hong Kong
months later, to find a clipping of his story from the
Boston *Globe* and a check for eight dollars. Eight
dollars was important, but the clipping was more so.
With the clipping he would be able to claim in Shanghai
that he was the Far Eastern correspondent of the Boston
Globe, stretching the single clipping as a credential
much farther than Winship ever knew.

From Palestine, off to Asia on a Norwegian
freighter, the M.V. *Tarn.* That leg of passage vividly
illustrated what he had been taught of Western imperialism. The freighter touched at every dot on the
map that marked the sweep of the British Empire, which
was then at the fading apogee of its orbit. Port Sudan.
Aden. Colombo. Singapore. Somewhere, perhaps in
the colonial office, there was a modular design for
colonial ports; each had its neat concrete piers, with
single-track rail lines running down to wharfside, from
which cranes ladled cargo in and out. There were native
variations of locality: Sudan unloaded its cargo with
Africans, Aden with Arabs, Ceylon with Tamils, whose
long black hair fell in tresses down their backs. Ceylon
was tea. A blue neon sign shone at night at the passenger terminal: "Ceylon for Good Tea." Singapore unloaded with Chinese. But everywhere the ship touched,
the British ruled. When the sightseer went to the post
office in Singapore, he stood in line to post a letter, not
noticing that Chinese, Malays, Indians, all stood in the
same line. He was pulled out of that line by a white
lady, who sternly said, "White people go to the head
of the line." It was as if he had been caught riding the
back of the bus in the old South. At each port of touch,
all around the rim of Asia, white people strode to the
head of the line, and the "natives" yielded.

Shanghai was the unrivaled Paris of imperialism,
exactly as the textbooks predicted it would be. For a
few months, the sightseer made Shanghai his base as

he alternately declared himself to be a Sheldon Fellow of Harvard and the correspondent of the Boston *Globe*. From Shanghai he traveled to Tientsin and Peking; and poked his way into Japanese Army press conferences to hear a military spokesman announce each afternoon that the war in China was over, the Imperial Army was now mopping up. The sightseer wormed his way shamelessly into the Japanese spokesman's good graces, persuaded him that the Boston *Globe*'s special correspondent should be given a pass to travel in Manchuria. But always, in those first few months, he wheeled out and back to Shanghai.

Shanghai was where the jobs were. Scores of American reporters in the thirties, tired of homeside jobs, were caught by word-of-mouth accounts of Paris or of Shanghai. In both cities, English-language newspapers hired unknown floaters like, say, Eric Sevareid or Edgar Snow. So there were too many experienced American reporters scratching coolie wages out of Shanghai's three English-language newspapers for them to take on yet another.

Some days the sightseer drifted; some days he spent pounding his typewriter in his room at the Shanghai YMCA; other days he shoved himself into unwelcoming offices looking for a job as reporter, writer, clerk, office boy. But he knew, after two months on the rim, that he wanted to stay in China and not go home to Boston to be a professor. For as he walked, or wandered, or rode the bus, or indulged in a rickshaw ride, he was seeing in this city of monsters and missionaries, of light and laughter, of gangsters and gardens, something unique. In this city of Chinese, ruled by white men, the despair at the bottom was as inconceivable to a poor boy from Boston as the delights of depravity at the top were inconceivable to Brahmins of Boston.

The British had set up their trading post in Shanghai in 1843. By 1939, Shanghai was the largest city in China, yet not really a city. Three million Chinese lived under the jurisdiction of the Shanghai Municipal Council, the expression of British-American-Japanese con-

sular authority. The French concession, adjacent, was
governed by Frenchmen in haughty independence. But
the Chinese of Shanghai were people who were not
people; their laws, courts, police, were all imposed by
foreigners from thousands of miles away. Shanghai was
an open city—cabarets, opium dens, bawdyhouses,
Blood Alley, the waterfront, gangsters. The sightseer
visited the bawdyhouses but did not touch the girls. He
drank at night with other jobless newsmen. The city
tingled; he tingled with it; and the city tingled thus in
the sightseer's memory as Sin City until 1972. Then,
visiting it with Richard Nixon, he recognized that it was
not the dirty gray buildings, the hulks and skyline of its
famous Bund which had given it enchantment, but the
long-vanished contrasts of sybarite pleasure and wordless sorrows. Under Communism, Shanghai had become a tenement city without pleasure or panic.

The sightseer's diary marked a day in Shanghai
when he was first tempted to stop sightseeing. It was
a day's tour of Shanghai's factories. No one then cared
about Chinese workingmen, least of all the Chinese
rich; but some reflex twitch of morality in the Anglo-
American overlordship of the city had caused the
Municipal Council to appoint a nominal factory-inspec-
tion system. One of the inspectors, a young Dane
named Chris Bojessen, hated his job because it was
more than his emotions could absorb. Bojessen wished
to shriek and took the young political sightseer with
him one day on his daily rounds, hoping White could
write a story.

Together they made the tour of the factories. There
was the glass vacuum bottle factory—the little boys at
work there were ten or eleven years old; they wore wood-
en clogs as they tramped over the splintered bottles,
which they dumped into the vats where the glass was
melted fresh. They made the next visit at a textile factory—Bojessen poked with his toe to show a cylinder
of bamboo mat in the dump of factory garbage by the
canal. In the mat was wrapped the body of a little girl,

a factory worker; two or three such mats were put out
each night to be collected with the garbage. Next stop
was a silk filature, an overheated, steaming loft—there
the little girls were six or seven years old, and their
duty was to stand all day long over the steaming tubs
of hot water in which the silk cocoons were dissolved;
they had to pick out the silk thread which unwound the
cocoon and fix it to a tiny hook. A job any child could
do—except that Bojessen led the sightseer down the
line and gently pulled the hands of the little girls out of
the tubs and showed how the joints of each hand, where
the fingers joined the palm, were rotting. The skin
blistered away, the flesh was open and festered with
eczema. Such children, Bojessen said, were bought
from peasant parents in the countryside; these little
girls would die, like the little girls in the textile factory;
and also be rolled in bamboo mats to be carried away
as refuse. The sightseer thought that made a story, but
when he wrote it no one bought that story, not even
the Boston *Globe*.

The sightseer was, at this point, being shaken in
his posture as roving observer, and the diaries record
him as deciding he must join the action, as a revolutionary, a partisan, an agitator, whatever. But the most
radical group he met in his few months in Shanghai was
a group of Trotskyites, all white men and drifters; they
threw him out of their group almost immediately; the one
he admired most told the sightseer, "White, you're
nothing but a goddamn Socialist and you ought to
know it."

So he sought other ways to join the action—and
the largest action going in Asia was, without doubt,
the war of the Japanese against the Chinese, with the
Nationalist government of Chiang K'ai-shek somewhere
way, way off to the west, landlocked beyond the mountains and gorges. That war, too, was part of the front
against the Fascists, as was the war of the Loyalists in
Spain. He made contact with the agents of Chiang K'ai-
shek, and offered them his help. But he could not stay

too long in Shanghai, for his money was running out. His plan called for him to be moving back to Boston, but first he wanted to see the inside of China.

The sightseer bought a ticket on a British passenger steamer from Shanghai to Hanoi. From Hanoi, he planned to travel up the French railway to Kunming; from Kunming he might find his way to Chungking, the mountain lair of Chiang K'ai-shek—then it would have to be back to Boston, quickly, before the Sheldon Fellowship money ran out.

A Butterfield & Swire ship carried him out of Shanghai in second class, with the wives of British noncommissioned officers being shipped from one outpost on the perimeter of empire to another. There was no third class: that was coolie class, deck class. But he enjoyed second class with the plain Englishwomen of thick girth and no style. He liked them because they hated Hitler. "A proper Bolshie, he is," said one of the soldiers' ladies, whose politics were confused, but whose loyalties were perfect. And they loved England. "We love our King and Queen and our royal family," explained another, as if affirming her religion and faith in God. Solid-bottomed ladies, with solid-bottomed loyalties, they added to the sightseer's ineradicable affection for the British, which persisted long after he recognized, years later, that the British had lost their greatness when they came to despise such simple ladies, whose men had made Britain great.

The sightseer arrived in Hong Kong in the afternoon, en route to Hanoi; he left the ship next morning to scout the job market at British newspapers in Hong Kong. It must have been eleven o'clock when he wandered into the office of the Chinese Republic's Information Service, with whose agents he had already been in contact in Shanghai.

They were waiting for him. The message they must have received could only have been extravagantly garbled. He was received as a "newspaperman" from

Boston, who had studied Chinese at Harvard, and was now a fellow of the University—and willing to serve the Chungking Government! In Chungking, the propaganda service was about to lose an Australian newspaperman who supervised a six-man staff of Chinese feature writers pumping out stories to feed the American and British press. Could the sightseer leave immediately for Chungking and inland China? They meant *immediately*—like the day after tomorrow, when there would be a night flight over the Japanese lines to the wartime capital in the interior. Could he?

He could. He was back at the boat in no time, packed his bags, argued with the purser for reimbursement of the unused portion of his ticket to Hanoi, was paid for it in cash, found a hotel room for that night and the next day. The sightseer's diary recorded the night's thoughts. Should he serve as a propagandist for a foreign government? Was this a way to help with the war against Fascism? Would the job forever disbar him from American journalism? Should he ask the American consulate for permission? Where would it take him?

But the night's self-searching was both irrelevant and hypocritical. He had already agreed to take the job. He would be part of a war as soon as the plane took off. He would see bombings, for Chungking was certain to be target number one for the Japanese Air Force. Whatever history was all about, he would be part of it, for he would be inside the Chinese "government."

It was the first plane flight he ever took; late on a Friday evening he stood in line to board a Chinese Junkers plane, which trundled down the runway of Kaitak Airport, seemed certain to hit the surrounding mountains, then rose in the air, leaving behind the blue and red and white lights that made bracelets about Hong Kong's peak, and was off into dark China, where no lights shone at night.

He was being flown into one of the greatest upheavals of the twentieth century, and quickly, more quickly than he could possibly guess, the last ties to home, Boston, family and Harvard were to be snapped. Even the eye of a fresh-minted college graduate would not fail to find startling what he was about to see.

CHAPTER 2

China: War and Resistance

I arrived in Chungking on April 10, 1939, landing in the Yangtze River.

I looked about. The runway was a sandbar paved with stone, and on both sides of the sandbar the river rushed by, yellow and muddy, carrying the silt of Inner Asia down to the ocean beyond the gorges below. The airstrip was usable only from winter through spring, when the river ran low; in summer and early fall, swollen with the melting snows of Tibet, the river flooded the airport. A footbridge now led across an eddy of the river to the foot of a gray cliff, and there, high above the cliff, ran the city wall of old Chungking.

The pilot hurried us out, reloaded the plane with waiting passengers, then roared away at once before any marauding Japanese overflight might discover his plane on the ground and destroy it.

I was at last in a country at war, in its capital fourteen hundred miles from the sea, up the Yangtze River, four hundred miles beyond the Japanese lines.

Sedan-chair bearers were called to carry me up the hundreds of steps carved into the cliff wall, and I was swung aboard a hammock of bamboo slats hung between two poles, a front bearer and rear bearer yoked to the poles. It was the first time I had seen men used this way, as beasts of burden, and I remember noticing the brown calluses, thicker than leather, on the bare shoulders of the lead carrier as he sweated his way up. *"A-ya-zillah, a-ya-zillah,"* he chanted in singsong at each step, and the rear bearer responded with the same *"a-ya-zillah, a-ya-zillah,"* as he lurched, heaving, up one step at a time. Up the cliff, up the road, into the city wall of Chungking, and I was in another world.

The city itself for the first weeks held my attention more than my job or my ambitions.

Marco Polo had written of cities like this when he visited the province of Szechwan almost seven hundred years earlier, and by rolling back the thin veneer of the twentieth century that overlay Chungking, I might have been again in his Cathay. Let me linger over what I could see, for it was the beginning of the story of China I was to learn:

The city sat on a wedge of cliffs, squeezed together by the Chialing and Yangtze rivers, which joined flow at the tip of the wedge. The city wall, with its nine gates, had been built in the Ming dynasty, over five hundred years earlier. Much of the wall had been torn down for building material a few years before I got there, but its nine gates still stood and one of them still functioned; its huge brass-knobbed beams swung shut at sunset, opened at dawn. The gate that had opened for the imperial cart road—the T'ung-yüan Men, the "Gate Connecting with Distant Places"—was now pierced for a motor road. This motor road, the "old" road, was twelve years old; until 1928 Chungking had boasted no wheeled vehicles, no autos, no rickshaws, not even wheelbarrows. The "new" motor road, circling the south rim of the wall, had been opened only the year I arrived. Sedan chairs, with their bearers, outnumbered rickshaws, with their pullers, three thousand to two thousand.

Neither road had yet significantly changed life in the city, and Chungking was still attached umbilically, as it had been forever, to the countryside. Rice paddy fields reached up to the city wall itself; down below on the fringes of the Yangtze's banks, peasants hopefully planted vegetables, gambling they could harvest before the summer floods overran their plots. As far as the eye could see, on both sides of the Yangtze, on both sides of the Chialing, the crescent paddy fields stretched to the hills, then in terraces over the hills, to the next ridge of hills, on and on to the great walled city of Ch'eng-tu, 275 miles away, and beyond that more paddy fields until the Tibetan escarpment forbade the peasants to try farther.

Inside the wall was a China I had never heard of. Flowers, for example. No one had ever told me how much the Chinese love flowers—but now, in springtime, there were more flower stalls than in my native Boston. In semitropical Szechwan, the flowers, it seemed, forgot to blossom by the season. Paper-white narcissi (*shui-hsien*) came in midwinter; plum blossoms spotted the hills and decorated the markets in March; azaleas bloomed all year round, and the stalls offered little pots of flowering shrubs, which lit the dingy, shadow-dark alleys around the calendar. Then, fruits: tiny orange cherries, sticky sweet, in baskets, as early as May; followed by peaches in June—huge yellow-skinned red-fleshed peaches, the best in all China except for those of Shantung; then the apricots and the lichee nuts of midsummer, followed by the watermelons of August and September; followed again by pears; by the red and rosy persimmons of late fall; to be overwhelmed finally by the magnificent citrus fruits of winter—pink pomelos, oranges and, at their glorious best, the tangerines of December. In a few years, I, like most Chinese in Chungking, learned to mark the rhythm of the seasons by the fruits.

Flowers and fruits gave the visual rhythm. But the real flow, the continuing beat of the city, connected it to the fields of rice where fifty million peasants in China's richest province, Szechwan, filled the granary of China at war. Rice came down from upriver in flat-bottomed

scows, was shoveled into sacks, was shipped off now in
wartime to the fronts instead of to the cities of the coast,
where it had gone before. The richest of the rich in
Chungking were the rich merchants and landlords of rice
fields. Meat came from the countryside, as it always had.
Pigs were carried in every morning to the city, four legs
trussed over a pole carried by two coolies, the eyelids of
the pig sewn shut, the pig squealing in agony until it
reached the slaughtering place. And then it reappeared as
fat slabs of red meat, oozing blood on butchers' counters;
or as fly-blown gobbets of gray pork; or as yards-long
black-and-brown dust-coated dry sausages hanging from
hooks in open stalls, from which the meat merchant
would sell from an inch to two feet to any customer. The
city repaid the countryside by returning all its bowel
movements; collectors emptied the thunder boxes of every
home each morning, and padded barefoot down the alley
stairs to the riverside, two buckets of liquid muck jiggling
from their bamboo staves, until they reached what foreigners delicately styled the "honey barges." There, they
emptied the excrement into the barges, where rivermen,
entirely naked, stirred the muck around at a collection
point famous for its stench. From that point, Chungking's
gift to the fields was carried upriver to be sold to peasants
as fertilizer. From the same river the water-bearers carried up buckets of muddy water, jiggling on the same
kind of staves as the honey buckets, to all the homes that
could not be reached by Chungking's new, but minimal,
piped water supply. The sloshings on the stone steps, up
and down the alleys, left them always slippery, and one
could never be sure what kind of slime one must avoid.

From the one main motor road in the city, on the
crest of the ridge, one descended, as if through centuries,
to the past. This main road had the façade of a coastal
city; its stores sold bolts of cloth, flashlights, auto parts
and canned foods, advertised in neon; its peddlers sold
needles, thread, vacuum bottles, imports from downriver.
But from the road, the alleys slipped down into darkness.
Chungking was always foggy, except for the clear, midsummer bombing months. The alleys were always shad-

owed, and some were so narrow that a passer could catch the drip from the eaves on both sides with his umbrella. They offered a symphony of smells, fragrant and stinking at the same time—fragrant with the smell of food and spice, the aroma of flowers, roasting chestnuts, incense, the sweetness of opium, yet stinking of uncollected garbage and the urine that ran in the gutters. The noises were a symphony of another kind—of yelling men, screaming women, bawling babies, and squawking hens, which lived with the families in the huts. To which was added the singsong chants of the coolies carrying their buckets or the peddlers carrying wares. Each activity had its own sound. The timbermen, swinging their logs, bellowed. The peddler of cottons announced his journey by clacking rhythmically on a wooden block. The notions dealer carried all his wares in one great black box and sang his wares with his own particular chant, as the banana man and the fish peddler had on Erie Street. The night-soil collectors gave out a warning chant peculiar to them. So, too, did the brassware man, who sold cat's bells, knives, toothpicks, ear cleaners, back scratchers, all dangling from a long pole, twirling as in a Calder mobile.

The people in these alleys lived as they always had, responding sluggishly to the changing times, wrinkling their habits as an animal wrinkles its hide and stirs at a prod. A few had learned to visit the three missionary clinics that had been established in the town. But most, when they were ill, visited the herb doctor or the acupuncture man, and sought medicines unheard of in the West—moldy bean curd for sore throats, potions of baby urine, powders ground from crystals of musk or rhinoceros horn. They bought their virility and fertility aids, their backache and headache cures, their beauty aids and lotions in their own tradition, seeking the same elusive magic of life, love and comfort that television advertises with the same futility each day in America. On the ridge of the motor road were strung the electricity lines that lit the neon of the storefronts and the offices in which government had found shelter, but down in the alleys, homes were still lit by oil lamps and candles. Paraders bearing green leaves asked the gods for rain in time of drought; traditional marriage processions followed behind the red-draped bridal chair, cymbals clanging; at funerals, the people trooped in white, as they had for millennia, behind the coffin—and sometimes on the body of the corpse mourners still tied a crowing cock to ward off evil spirits.

This Chungking, in the alleys and of the past, needed little of the kind of government of the coastal cities I had seen, where Westerners had planted outposts and seeded industry. Chungking's relation to the country-side was straightforward; its traditional government, though cruel, was simple. Local government policed an orderly place where merchants, moneychangers and shop-keepers could provide a market for the peasants of the valleys; government kept the peace. The merchants paid off to authority—to whomever had the spears, the sol-diers, the guns, the power to keep the trading place functioning. Such people had paid their taxes to a millen-nial succession of imperial civil servants, to mandarins and viceroys and, more recently, to warlords. They might have paid off forever, living undisturbed by any but local predators, except for the war. Not Chungking, but China, as a nation, needed a new kind of government. And I had come to Chungking to serve the government that had only recently taken refuge there.

The national "government" of the Republic of China had set up its command post in this old city because it controlled the entry to the largest and richest province of China—Szechwan. Landlocked by mountains and gorges to the east, backed against the roof of Asia to the west, cupping the most fertile fields of the entire land, Szech-wan was a semitropical inner empire of fifty million people, self-sufficient and all but impregnable. By spring of 1939, when I arrived, the Japanese Army had occu-pied all the cities of the coast—Shanghai, Canton, Tient-sin, Peking—apparently all of North China, and all the cities of the Yangtze valley up to Hankow. West of

Hankow, however, rose the impenetrable gorges; beyond the gorges, Chungking; and from this natural fortress the Nationalist resistance was to be directed for six full years.

Chungking had been a town of some 300,000 people before the war. A quarter of a million refugees, embodying the national government of the Republic, had arrived, fleeing from the Japanese, before I got to Chungking; another quarter million were to arrive before the war was over; and the strangers arriving to staff the government were as far from home as was this young man from Boston. They had grown up in the cities and universities of the China coast, accustomed to electric lights, flush toilets, sewage systems, buses, trolleys, newspapers, libraries; their wives were accustomed to kitchens, bathtubs, automobiles, movie houses, Western medicine. Chungking had few of these modernities. There was, for example, but one movie house, and in 1940 it was showing 1936 newsreels. So the refugees had been driven as far back into the past as into the interior, and the past exasperated them. It was as if the ablest and most devoted executives of New York, Boston and Washington had been driven from home to set up resistance to an enemy from the hills of Appalachia.

Chungking had been the capital of a self-regulating provincial society; now it had to be jolted into a new world. The forward echelon of the national government, as soon as it arrived, regarded the easygoing ways of the past it found there as wanting in discipline for the austere politics of wartime. Opium was banned at once, in late 1938. Four months before I arrived, the bathhouses were also banned—the famous bordellos where merchants might gather to dine and, between courses, dart in and out of the steaming tub rooms to be washed, scratched, oiled and serviced by the ladies of the establishment. Austerity was the theme of wartime reform— drinking of spirits was soon forbidden. The wastefulness of traditional marriage ceremonies was outlawed; later, an attempt was made to replace the lavish old funeral rites with the simpler ceremony of cremation. Rickshaws and sedan chairs were numbered and licensed. Even a campaign against spitting in the streets was undertaken. But none of the edicts, except that against opium, could be enforced in the old city, which gradually was smothered by the newcomers. The old city continued its old life, under the blanket of the new.

Heroic—that was my first impression of the people of this government in refuge. Any one of these thousands of civil servants might have remained behind on the occupied coast, as thousands of others did, servile to the conquering Japanese. But they would not. They would suffer the prickly heat of Chungking's torrid summer, the moist and chilling cold of winter in unheated rooms; they would see their children sicken and often die—but they would not submit.

Not only government officials chose the way of resistance. So did thousands of university students and their professors, taking refuge in makeshift college grounds for miles around Chungking. So did many small merchants of the coast, who came not to get rich but out of sheer pride of nationhood, the stubbornness of wanting to be Chinese. After them came the marvelous cooks who would not remain behind to serve the enemy. By the end of the war, Chungking offered better food than I have since eaten in any other city in the world, except occasionally Paris and New York. From Fukien, Canton, Shanghai, Peking, Hupeh, Hunan, arrived the fleeing chefs of great restaurants to display their mastery of table in every provincial variation.

I found all these people—government officials, scholars, soldiers, shopkeepers, restaurant men—historically romantic. And it is difficult to recall how easily they won admiration at that time when one looks back now. By the end of the war, when inflation had made their paper salaries worthless and thus made them corrupt, when American aid had separated the Nationalists from the countryside, when their private civil war with the Communists envenomed all their thinking, Chungking had become a city rotten to the core. But in the beginning, it was inspiring to visit officials whose children played on the steps of their government offices, whose wives hung the wet wash from the dormitory buildings to the office buildings, who ate in community messes, who drilled their children for the inevitable bombings that must come when the spring fogs lifted. Several sacks of rice and a bit of cooking oil was the official monthly ration. Entire families slept in one room in office dormitories, the room heated by a charcoal brazier in winter.

The newly arrived government had possessed itself of almost every hotel, semimodern office building, and school compound in Chungking and its neighborhood. Then it spread, as arrivals swelled, over the countryside—into shacks of bamboo wattles woven together, smeared with mud, then whitewashed.

Each morning, everywhere, opened with the mournful singing of the Nationalist anthem: *"San Min Chu I, wo tang so pao, i chien min kuo."* When I tried to translate the song that woke us every morning, Western visitors would laugh at the comic-seriousness of the words: "Three peoples principles our party will defend, to build people democracy." But the music was as stirring as it was melancholy, and I thrilled to the sound. I thrilled, too, at evening when bugles would blow everywhere in the city as the Nationalist banners with their twelve-pointed star were lowered from the staffs.

It was not only their cause that captured me, but also the fact that they were, apparently, so very American.

No government in Asia, or anywhere else for that matter, was ever so completely penetrated by "Americanists" as was the Republican government in Chungking. And no government, except perhaps that of the Republic of South Vietnam, was so completely ruined by American ideas, aid and advice. The men and women of this government were, as a group, not so much conscripted by Americans as they were seekers for American ideas, American ways. The missionaries had begun to disturb China's old ideas a half century before; mission colleges and schools had deepened American influence; and the upward mobile, the strivers, hungering for the modernization and westernization of China, sought American learning, technology, culture, as if America knew all the secrets of life.

The penetration started at the top, with Madam Chiang K'ai-shek, the Wellesley-educated wife of the Generalissimo, whom she had persuaded to become a Methodist. Chiang K'ai-shek's Minister of Finance was H. H. Kung, who had graduated from both Oberlin and Yale; his Minister of Foreign Affairs was Yale, 1904; his Minister of Education was a graduate of the University of Pittsburgh; the legislative Yuan was presided over by Dr. Sun Fo, with degrees from Columbia and the University of California. The Minister of Information was a graduate of the Missouri School of Journalism. The head of the Bank of China, T. V. Soong, later to be China's Prime Minister, was Harvard, class of 1915. The list of American-graduated Chinese in the government was endless— too long to count. It ran from the National Health Administrator to the Salt Administration to the Foreign Trade Commission. The ambassadorial list of China's foreign affairs was overwhelmingly Ivy League; in Washington, a Cornell-Columbia graduate; in London, a University of Pennsylvania man; in Paris, Wellington Koo, who had not only graduated from Columbia with three degrees but had edited its college newspaper and was now proud that his son had made the staff of the *Crimson* at Harvard. My Harvard degree carried me farther than it would have in Boston. Later, I organized a Harvard Club of China, which included a larger proportion of the high officials of Chiang K'ai-shek's government in Chungking than a Harvard Club would have in John F. Kennedy's Washington.

In retrospect, of course, all this was tragedy. It took me over a year to discover that any high Chinese official of the "national" government who spoke good English was so separated from his own people, and his understanding of his own people—his understanding, even, of the old city of Chungking—as to make him useless to me in trying to find out what was going on in China. Such people lived, dreamed, thought, spoke to each other in English—all except Chiang K'ai-shek.

Chiang was a Chinese Chinese of the real government. He was a man I learned first to respect and admire, then to pity, then to despise. Chiang spoke no English, read no English, had come of a peasant family poorer even than Mao Tse-tung's. The Americanists whom Chiang chose to man the façade of his government were, in retrospect, like the panel of a modern electronic system. When one pushed buttons, lights winked But the wires in back led nowhere, the switchboard did not connect to the operations system. And the parade of American advisers, aid masters and generals who were later to come to help all exploded in impotent fury when they finally realized the switchboard did not work. Only a few Americans were admitted to Chiang's presence. Most would be shown the rock wall of Chiang's compound; two sentries guarded the entrance, a curving road ran up the hill, then twisted away. Where it disappeared was where the other "government" of China began—the "government" that controlled the armies of the front, made the necessary alliances with warlords, reached down through the few modern highways to the villages, towns, the *pao-chia* system, which was where real government began.

Few Americans understood that other "government" of China, which began where the Americanized Chinese officials reached the limit of their authority. But few Chinese understood the American system which furnished them with advisers, either. Chiang invited such advisers to help his government because he thought Americans possessed some magic, some technology which could artificially be grafted onto his system without altering it.

The American advisory system in China was to be a thing of wonder years later. And in the thirty-five years since, I have seen American advisers and spies spread like a presence around the world, saving some nations, ruining others. But Chungking was the starting place for my tour of observation.

Briefly, that first summer, I was invited to join a dinner mess of American advisers, who gathered at the Methodist mission each evening for an American meal. Senior among them was a taciturn and courtly aviation adviser named Colonel Claire Chennault, U.S. Army Air Corps, retired. He was trying to reorganize the Chinese air force. Chennault would never take shelter in an air raid, but would study the Japanese formations as they came over, as a football coach studies films of a team he expects soon to meet in the field. He recognized the Japanese Zero for what it was—a highly maneuverable but underpowered plane, inaccurate in its fire. He figured that the new American P-40, with its platform-mounted gun, had the advantages of height, accuracy and speed. If it came to war, the American tactic should be to hold the height above the Japanese Zero, and then make one passing, striking swoop from above. Later, his tactic was proved correct. There was a civilian aviation adviser, William Langhorne Bond. He taught me how to recognize the shrill of a bomb from the air, and more importantly, how to sight on an enemy plane: if you stood behind a telephone pole and the plane seemed to climb directly up the pole in the sky beyond, head for the shelter; if it diverged from the pole sighting, the bomb wasn't going to hit you. There were financial advisers at the mess; they spoke very gravely about central banking and taxation and relayed such advice to Chiang K'ai-shek. My distrust of economists was probably born then: they taught the Chinese about modern central banking and how central banks could print money; which the Chinese government proceeded to do with great enthusiasm until paper money became entirely worthless. It was like teaching an adolescent how to shoot heroin.

By all odds, the most amusing of the American advisory corps was a man who called himself "Osborne," who purported to be a merchant of leather and hides. "Osborne" was a delightful man. His real name was

Herbert O. Yardley, and he was the creator and founder of the American cryptographic and code-cracking services in World War I, which have since developed into the National Intelligence Agency. Long before there was an OSS, even longer before there was a CIA, Osborne-Yardley was acting for us in Chungking, intercepting Japanese radio messages, cracking them for codes, serving Chiang K'ai-shek as a technician, getting the U.S. Navy ready for the code crackings of World War II.*

"Osborne" took a fancy to me. He was a man of broad humor and unrestrained enthusiasms, and among his enthusiasms were drink, gambling and women. He decided after we had become friends that he should teach me poker, which he did by letting me stand over his shoulder and watch him unfold his hands and sweep up the pots. He also felt I should be taught sex, and tried to persuade me to sample that experience by inviting some of the choicest ladies he knew to a banquet in his house. I would not learn; Boston was still strong in me. But he did teach me something more important than anything I have learned since from any official American adviser or wise man: how to behave in an air raid. Yardley's theory was that if a direct hit landed on you, nothing would save you. The chief danger of an air raid, he said, was splintered glass from windows. Thus, when one hears the siren, one should get a drink, lie down on a couch and put two

---

*Yardley was a professional code breaker. His most important book, *The American Black Chamber,* was a pioneer work in the long sequence of American secret agents who have since then gone public. *The American Black Chamber* told of American code cracking in World War I. Yardley told the story better in person than in print, but his reason for going public was impeccable. He had been fired when the noble Henry Stimson became Secretary of State. Stimson was dismayed to learn that Americans read and code-cracked the cables of foreign embassies with whom we negotiated. "Gentlemen don't read other people's mail," Stimson is reputed to have said in getting rid of Yardley's Black Chamber. Much more worthwhile of Yardley's literary output is his twilight book, *The Education of a Poker Player,* Simon & Schuster, 1957. This major contribution to the American folk culture is as important in the education of the young to poker playing as a sex manual is to a college freshman.

pillows over oneself—one pillow over the eyes and the other over the groin. Splintered glass could hurt those vital organs, and if the eyes or the groin were injured, life was not worth living. It was good advice for any groundling in the age before atom bombs; and I took it. Yardley was excessively kind to me, as were so many older men in Chiang K'ai-shek's Chungking.

I was thus, among American advisers to the Chinese government, the lowest man in the hierarchy, so low as to be almost imperceptible. Twenty-three years old, fresh from the Ivy League—which was accepted as fresh from the cathedral seminary by the Americanized Chinese government—totally inexperienced, I was titled Adviser to the Chinese Ministry of Information. In this job I was a thorough failure I did not understand the job. No one could explain it to me. I thought of myself in the stiff Socialist rhetoric of my youth as a "fighter against Fascism." But in reality, I was employed to manipulate American public opinion. The support of America against the Japanese was the government's one hope for survival; to sway the American press was critical. It was considered necessary to lie to it, to deceive it, to do anything to persuade America that the future of China and the United States ran together against Japan. That was the only war strategy of the Chinese government when I came to Chungking in 1939, and my job was to practice whatever deception was needed to implement the strategy.

Technically, I was supervisor of the news-feature stories of the "China Information Committee." I was paid four hundred Chinese dollars a month, worth at the then rate of exchange, sixty-five American dollars; but I was free to do my own free-lancing, for anything I could publish would serve the Chinese cause.

For the first few weeks I lived in a mission compound; then the expected bombings began and the mission was blasted out. After the bombings, I moved into a government dormitory on the downstairs floor of the information service office, where I slept with Chinese roommates and ate breakfast and lunch at their mess.

Later, when the bombings flattened more and more of Chungking, the Ministry of Information built, in the back yard adjacent to it, a press hostel for foreign correspondents, and I moved in with the press corps.

It took no more than a few weeks for everyone to discover that I was an amateur. The six Chinese news-feature writers whom I was supposed to supervise spoke English as well as I, they were all men between thirty and forty who had been reporters on the English-language newspapers of the coast, competent journeymen newspapermen who out of patriotism were serving their government for rice wages. And I, a boy of twenty-three, was supposed to direct and edit them. Moreover, I did not share their devotion to their government; their government was a mystery. I probed it critically; I tried to deliver to the American press corps what shreds of information I could gouge out of the government in which I worked. To me a good story was a good story, whether it was good propaganda or not, and my clients were the foreign newsmen, either resident in Chungking or passing through, who were starved for news.

These men were posted to cover a war, to file stories every day—but the war was hundreds of miles downriver; it took a week's journeying to get to the front, a week's journeying back. It was no simple tragedy that they were not allowed to cover the news; neither were the Chinese newspapermen, and no Chinese newspaper ever printed actualities. There was a quaint Chinese jargon one had to learn quickly in translating the war bulletins issued at midnight from the Ministry of War. The Japanese were never called Japanese, but were always referred to as the "dwarf bandits." In war bulletins, Japanese never "attacked," their armies "sneaked about" (the characters used in the phrase denoted the sneaking about of a robber at night). When the Japanese had seized Hankow, their climactic victory of 1938, the news was suppressed in Chungking for a week and then appeared as "traces of the enemy have appeared in Hankow." A Chinese retreat was always announced as an engagement of the army "in a major strategic outflanking movement." The loss of a

new town or city to the Japanese was always first reported as "our forces have successfully entrapped the
enemy" in whatever city had just fallen. And if a little
victory did occur at the front, it always ended with the
capture by Chinese forces of *"wu-ch'i pu suan"*—"war
weapons to an incalculable amount."

This kind of news dismayed the foreign press. Some
of the reporters could be controlled. The Associated Press
was represented by a young Dane with a Chinese wife;
Reuters by a Chinese bureau chief; others, too, had given
hostages of loyalty to the Chinese government. These
reported what the government put out. The two most
difficult reporters to control were a young United Press
correspondent, Robert Martin, who wrote excellent verse
when the mood took him; and F. Tillman Durdin of *The
New York Times*, one of the greatest foreign correspondents ever to report Asia, a man of such integrity that even
Chinese government officials flinched when they lied to
him. Easiest of all to manipulate, however, were the
famous names, the trained seals, the swooping stars of big
American and British newspapers who would fly in for a
four-day visit and then send out pontifical dispatches
about the war and the Chinese spirit of resistance. It was
with these I had my greatest luck in my brief career as a
propagandist; one correspondent arrived in Chungking,
was banqueted by the government the evening of his
arrival, stayed drunk for his entire four-day visit, lurching
from banquet to banquet, and let me, from my desk at
the Information Committee, write all his dispatches.

I was demoted gracefully within a few weeks from
editor; I was so good a writer, I was told, I should write
news features myself. Not only did this "save face" all
around, but it suited me better, and from my experience I
learned much about the self-propelling life of legends,
true and false.

The correspondents clamored at me, as an "insider"
of the government, for real copy to pad out the unpronounceable monosyllabic place names that marked the
military communiqués; the United Press bureau had to fill
a minimal five-hundred-word cable budget every day;

Reuters had to file two thousand words a day, whether there was news or not. I tried to meet their needs. A one-paragraph item in a Chinese newspaper caught my eye; somewhere in Chekiang province, then occupied by the Japanese, a Chinese woman named Tsai Huang-Hua had thrown a grenade into a theater attended by Japanese soldiers, killed several, and escaped alive. I translated the Chinese characters—"Huang-Hua"—of her name literally, and she became Miss "Golden Flowers" Tsai, the guerrilla chieftain, the Amazon leader of a band of Chinese resistants. I padded the story a bit, and it caught with the foreign reporters, all except Durdin. Their home offices demanded pictures to go with the story. My colleagues at the Information Service provided a photograph of a young Chinese woman in uniform, packing two pistols at her waist. She became the "Pistol-Packing Miss Golden Flowers." The reporters wanted more, and the Information Service provided more and more and more. For a few months, as I fed out the story, "Golden Flowers" Tsai became a heroine of the resistance, second only to Madame Chiang K'ai-shek herself. At the hands of rewrite men back in America, her exploits became legend. Three years later, long after I had left the service of the Chinese government, the now defunct *American Weekly* gave her a full front-page spread. By then I was temporarily Far Eastern editor of *Time* magazine in New York and when it was suggested that *Time* pick up the story, I had to demur and confess my role as father of a fraud.

More serious was my effort to describe the vastness of the dislocation and tragedy, for that effort concerns the writing of history, and its interlock with journalism. I wrote much about refugees and their suffering. The National Relief Commission claimed it had statistics. I examined them: the records showed that in the fourteen months between the beginning of the Japanese invasion in 1937 and the fall of Hankow in 1938, the Commission had served in and out of the refugee camps some twenty-five million meals—the count came from the refugees who trudged twice a day through the rice-gruel and chow line at the temporary shelter camps. Their figure was twenty-five million *meals*—not *people*. By some garble in my own story, the figure was transmuted to the statistic that twenty-five million people had fled the Japanese invaders in the first years of Chinese resistance. The figure was cabled abroad, remained fixed in morgues, appeared in magazine articles, constantly appears and reappears in learned accounts of the China war. The figure has become part of history. I know now that no one will ever know how deep and far-flung was the dislocation of the Japanese invasion. It may have been two million or five million Chinese who fled rather than submit. But the twenty-five million figure remains locked in most history books.

The Chinese were hypersensitive to American news reporting. Some dispatches were held up by the censors until Chiang K'ai-shek himself could read them in translation. Any minister of the government mentioned in a dispatch to America was informed by telephone and could hold up the dispatch until he approved it. I lived with the censors in our government dormitory; the two day censors, the one night censor and I were all friends; we ate, drank and partied together. The Deputy Minister of Information also lived in the dormitory in the same squalor we did, and if the night censor could not make up his mind whether a dispatch might clear or not, he would take it to the Deputy Minister. My room in the dormitory was next to the toilet, separated only by a wafer-thin bamboo wall, and sometimes at night I could overhear the inner dialogue of censorship. The sad Deputy Minister was chronically constipated, and would wait until late at night to move his bowels; it took him an hour of pain to perform this function, and he was decent enough not to hold up the rest of the staff by day for his personal needs. He would grunt, groan, sometimes almost sob, as he submitted to nature in the cubicle behind my thin wall. But there were those nights when the night censor would come trudging upstairs with a dispatch to America, position himself outside the door, and read the dispatch in English as Hsü-pei groaned over his seat. They would then discuss the dispatch in shouting Chinese, only a few

words of which I could understand. The poor Deputy
Minister would consider with the night censor the effect of
such a dispatch on American thinking; and jointly the two
would decide whether they had the authority to permit
such-or-so a phrase to go over the wires, or whether they
must tell the important correspondent that the phrase in
that dispatch could only be permitted transmission by
higher political authority. They were not attempting to
deceive America; they were serving their country. In
many instances they were themselves deceived and would
question not the correspondent's friendship to China but
his accuracy. "Do you think it's true, what he says?" one
would ask the other through the partition, wondering
about their own war. They did not know what was happening in China; no one did. They and I and all of us
served the command post of what we thought was the
resistance; but we were all, equally, ignorant.

The next step in learning was a violent one.

Chungking was bombed on May 3 and again on
May 4 of 1939. Those bombings are now forgotten mile-
stones in the history of aerial terror, but at the time they
marked the largest mass slaughter of defenseless human
beings from the air in the rising history of violence. And
the Japanese began it.

The Japanese hit once, in early afternoon of May 3,
but our office dugout was far from the trail of their
bombs. They came again the next evening; they outwitted
the Chinese air defenses by circling the city for almost an
hour until the Chinese pursuit planes had run out of gas
and landed for refueling. Then they came, and performed
massacre.

I was with my group of information ministry friends
that day and we had left our dugout, which had become
stuffy with the long wait inside, and descended to the
banks of the Chialing River to watch the sunset until the
all-clear would sound. Then, droning through the cloudless sky, came a formation of twenty-seven Japanese
bombers, a serene and unbroken line of dots in the sky.
The Chinese antiaircraft reached up through the gathering

dark, and the tracer bullets, like pink and orange puff-balls, made fireworks as they pointed to the Japanese formation. The shells burst in instant flashes—short, however, visibly short, impotently short of the line above. Then we heard the thudding from behind the ridge inside the old city, and the Japanese were gone, untouched.

I made my way back to the office, then began the four-mile walk to the Friends Mission, deep inside the walled city, where I was then lodging. By this time it was full dark, and what I was seeing was the reaction of a medieval city to the first savage touch of the modern world—which was total panic. Behind the slope, as I climbed up, was the red of spreading fire; and from the red bowl beyond the rim, people were fleeing. They were trudging on foot, fleeing in rickshaws, riding on sedan chairs, pushing wheelbarrows; and as they streamed out, an occasional limousine or army truck would honk or blast its way through the procession, which would part, then close, then continue its flight to the countryside. They carried mattresses, bedrolls, pots and pans, food, bits of furniture. They carried babies in their arms; grandmothers rode piggyback on men's shoulders; but they did not talk: in the silence one could even hear the padding shuffle of their feet.

At the crest, where one began the descent into the old city, I could get a larger view. The electric power lines had been bombed out; so, too, had the trunk of Chungking's water system, which ran down the main street. There was no light but that of the fires, no water to fight the fires, and the fires were spreading up and down the alleys of old Chungking. One could hear the bamboo joints popping as the fire ate the bamboo timbers; now there was noise, women keened, men yelled, babies cried. Some sat rocking back and forth on the ground, chanting. I could hear screaming in the back alleys; several times I saw people dart out of the slope alleyways into the main street, their clothes on fire, then roll over and over again to put out the fires.

I reached the room I had occupied in the Friends Mission those first few weeks, and knew at once I could stay there no longer. The mission had been shattered by a close hit, and in my room I saw a dead body. It had been thrown in by a bomb blast, and concussion had blasted off its face, crushed its rib cage; I could tell the body was a woman's only by the skin-stripped flesh of her breasts. I would not sleep there that night, or ever again, and continued walking, and finding by some chance the companionship of Martin of the UP, went on walking until four in the morning.

There was all through that night, as I walked with Martin, the bewildering contrast of the old and the new. Along the main street, with which I thought I had become familiar in a few weeks, the slopes had until now been hidden by bamboo-and-mud buildings. As I came to a blazing slope where all the buildings had already been burned off, I saw a Buddha. It was cut into the side of a cliff wall, and its temple had burned away so that the huge bronze cross-legged figure glowed with the reflection of the flames; and I could see its benign countenance softly smiling on a city that wept and wailed.

Chungking had reacted after the first day's bombing with what must have been the old community's normal response to danger. That first night between the two bombings, the town crier, clanging his bell, had paced the streets warning all who could hear his chant not to pick up cigarettes. The Japanese bombers, he called out, had dropped poisoned cigarettes over the city and to smoke them was to die. That same first night had been the night of an eclipse of the moon, and while the smoke was still rising from the afternoon's bombing, the priests had been exorcising the eclipse. Chinese folklore held that when the moon is eclipsed it is because the Dog of Heaven is trying to swallow it. That first night, the priests had beaten their bronze gongs, as was their duty, and sung the incantations to frighten off the Dog of Heaven. But now, the second night, after the terror bombing, there were no priests about, and nothing to defend the people of the old city from the killings of the new age.

Statistics often mislead. This time they did not. The official figures reported that between three and four thou-

sand people were burned to death that night by Japanese
incendiary bombs; how many more or less may have been
killed is almost irrelevant in retrospect. More people were
killed that night than ever before by bombardiers. But
what was important about the killings was their purpose
of terror. Nanking and Shanghai had already been
bombed; those, however, were military bombings. There
was no military target within the old walls of Chungking.
Yet the Japanese had chosen, deliberately, to burn it to
the ground, and all the people within it, to break some
spirit they could not understand, to break the resistance
of the government that had taken refuge somewhere in
Chungking's suburbs. I never thereafter felt any guilt
when we came to bomb the Japanese; when we bombed,
we bombed purposefully, to erase Japan's industry and
war-making power; no American planes swooped low to
machine-gun people in the streets, as had the Japanese.

I had not yet learned, as I was to learn later in
Vietnam, that senseless terror is worse than useless;
senseless terror denies even the craven, the submissive,
the potentially cooperative, the incentive or compulsion to
yield. The senseless terror bombings of Chungking had a
result that was immediate and primordial in my thinking
on politics.

What I learned was that people accept government
only if the government accepts its first duty—which is to
protect them. This is an iron rule, running from bombed-
out Chungking to the feudal communities of the Middle
Ages to the dark streets of New York or Rome where the
helpless are so often prey. Whether in a feudal, modern,
imperial or municipal society, people choose government
over nongovernment chiefly to protect themselves from
dangers they cannot cope with as individuals or families.

Thus, then, within days of the bombings of May,
with no political protest from anyone, the "guest" government, the "national" government, abolished the old
municipal government and proclaimed Chungking a
"Special" municipality, a ward of the central government.

They chose as the appointed mayor one of the Americanists—K. C. Wu, a one-time Princetonian, an aspiring novelist and short-story writer (in English). K. C. Wu did not depend on votes, as do mayors of American cities, so he performed arbitrarily and superbly. He cleared fire lanes, organized fire-fighting systems, repaired the water mains, and did all those things Americans do most efficiently. He was the very model of a modern American mayor, but he could not speak the dialect of old Chungking.

For the next two years, his town echoed to the muffled booming of excavations, as old-fashioned Chinese black powder was used to hollow dugouts. The government, which had brought the new world to Chungking and tempted the Japanese to pursue it by bombing, was responsible for protection. So, slowly, the people of Chungking and their government grew together, and the two years thereafter, as I observed both groups, were among the happiest of my life. There were no more panics; people old and new learned to live together.

I did not, however, serve this national government for long. The bombings were too exciting to write of as a propagandist; the tug of journalism, of writing my observations for myself, the ache for a by-line in print, were too strong. An opportunity to change my life was ushered in by happy accident.

The accident, as so often happens, was the random ricochet of a distant decision, and came about as follows: War was coming in 1939. In New York, Henry R. Luce was making ready his three magazines, *Time, Life* and *Fortune*, to cover that war. Luce was a China-born American; so, too, was his then favorite young man, John Hersey, fresh out of Yale and Cambridge, unknown to fame. And in the spring of 1939, Luce had sent young Hersey to the Orient to scout for "stringers" who might feed copy from Asia to his magazines.

John Hersey was only twenty-five when he arrived in Chungking at the end of May, and I had just passed my twenty-fourth birthday that month. Hersey stayed in

Chungking for little more than a week on his visit, inquiring what loose newsman might be available to "string" for *Time*. Blithe, handsome, tall, a Yale varsity football player, Hersey had every quality I then admired most in any contemporary, as well as self-possession and beauty. He was, at that age, an outgoing man. His singing, when he drank, was as rich in tone as my grandfather's; he could match any of us in any athletic feat, and once when Martin, a 180-pounder, got very drunk, Hersey carried him bodily all the way down a cliffside set of stairs, lest Martin fall. Hersey spoke easily and gently in those days, and wrote, as I and the world were later to learn, even better. Above all, he loved China, where he had been born, as much as I did or Luce did; and his fascination lay not so much with daily journalism as with history itself. This last quality was, of course, to make him one of the true progenitors of a new school of journalism when war came to America two years later.

Before the week was out, Hersey offered me the "stringer" job, which, as he explained it, was quite easy. Cable tolls from Chungking to New York were fifty cents a word. Expensive. Thus I should write backgrounders and "mailers." The magazines were not interested in overnight news, spot news from China; anything I wrote would have to be useful for a six-week or two-month span. In short, I should write the kind of copy I was sending the Boston *Globe* and other free-lance outlets, but not worry about the length; the New York office would edit what it found useful. I should try to tell not what had *happened,* but what was *happening.* This is the essence of the difference between daily and magazine journalism. For this I would be guaranteed a fifty-dollar monthly retainer, plus an extra fee for whatever was used.

I began immediately to churn out mailers for *Time* magazine and by the end of July there arrived in one of Chungking's sporadic mail deliveries a full harvest of checks. A seven-dollar check from the Boston *Globe,* and the same article I had sent to the *Globe* had been bought by the *Manchester Guardian* for four guineas! I had recycled the material for the Australian Broadcasting Commission and they had paid me five Australian pounds! On top of that came notice of a first check for fifty dollars from *Time,* and a supplementary fee of $125 for the first outgush of material I had sent them in June. All in all, more than I could earn in three months at the Ministry of Information. I could begin to think of myself as a journalist.

Poised thus, about to take off, yet still cautious, I needed only one more breakthrough to quit the Ministry of Information and secure my journalistic base. I needed a major story—a narrative, a scoop, not a feature—that would cement *Time* to me. The commerce of journalism and my education in history ran, fortunately, together; since all other newsmen in Chungking were bound by their jobs to the cablehead and daily deadlines, they could not take weeks to visit the war fronts, reachable only by long foot marches. But with a leave of absence from the Ministry of Information I could do so. Thus, in September of 1939, as the war in Europe broke out, I set off for the Yellow River in the north, and the province of Shansi, where a battle was going on. If I could catch up with actual combat, I could write of it for *Time* as something more vivid than the bombings of the capital, which had now become routine.

The Ministry of Information was happy to give me leave. I think my prying had begun to annoy them. They issued me a low-grade military pass to visit the war areas and arranged an airplane ticket to take me to Sian, whence I would be on my own to make my way to the war front two hundred and fifty miles beyond. I was lucky the pass was of such low quality. Had I been granted the VIP pass usually given to famous correspondents and important dignitaries, I would have been escorted to the war front and back in style and seen nothing—as happened to me in the Vietnam War, thirty years later, after I had become known and had to be cocooned from reality. My credentials recommended me to no one; they attested simply that I was authentic and not a Japanese spy—and let me move at worm's level through China at war.

The journey to China's north country was, on a larger scale, like the descent from Chungking's main road to its alleys—a backward progress through time, a journey down to the peasant culture of old China and thence back up again to the ferocity of the twentieth-century war which was burning away that old culture forever. I was seeing, from underneath, a civilization that had lasted for two thousand years just as it began to crumble, and on whose ruins, years later, the young Communists I met in the spreading chaos would build another civilization.

I was in Sian by plane within two hours. Then it was five days more to make the one-hundred-seventy-mile journey to the Yellow River crossing to the North China war front; another seven days by foot and horse to the front, eighty miles away; several weeks at the front; then an aimless roving through the rear areas as far as Lanchow, on the edge of the northern deserts.

I fell almost immediately into a mood I can only recall as part sightseer's, part anthropologist's. I could observe the people in their villages, but they were too strange to understand. No one spoke English; I had no interpreter; and my Harvard-taught Chinese was little more useful than classical Latin would have been in a Sicilian village. By the time I returned, two months later, I would be able to make my own way in rough street Chinese almost anywhere in China—but by then I had learned more than how to speak poor Chinese.

I learned first about villages. China was then and remains still, even under Communism, a nation of villages; and since one sees things for the first time only once, I shall stretch my notes of these villages over what I was to see again and again in the next six years, when all villages had become the same to my eyes, all of them too familiar.

The first village I saw was a nameless one. I had gone no more than twenty miles on the railway out of Sian when we came to a bomb-out. I flashed my pass at the local military headquarters; an officer grunted, and sent a soldier to take me to a hut a mile or two away. I slept there that night with the family—on a door spread flat, a mat underneath me, a cow next to me, the family sleeping on floor mats also, the chickens gurgling. I rose the next morning and saw the wife mill wheat: an ox tethered to a pole and turning it, pulling the upper grindstone over the lower one, the grain trickling out of the groove, the chickens pecking at it, the wife chasing them away. There was a pit outside the hut where we all defecated, teetering over two footstones to keep balance, using leaves for wiping.

If Chungking was noisy, as all Chinese towns were noisy, the village, as most villages, was silent—the somber, brooding silence of countryside which I later came to recognize as the sound of emotionless vacuum. Nothing happened in villages; people grew up, lived and died in their villages, lashed to the seasons, to the fields, to the crops, their lives empty of any information but gossip, any excitement except fear. A wall ran around this village, as about most villages in China, and inside the wall were five or six little lanes, enclosed by inner walls, within which were the huts. In a small village like this the lanes were beaten earth; in a larger village they were roughly cobbled. Sometimes there were trees on such lanes; more often not; the lanes were corrugated with ruts; cow droppings lathered them in spots; flies buzzed everywhere; the children wore rough cotton shirts with no bottoms and dumped where they chose; lean dogs slept in the sun. Electricity, newspapers, automobiles—these were faraway things, of no reality.

The villages I passed through for the next two months and for the next six years were all embroideries on the same stark pattern. The peasant and his family took from the soil, lived by the soil, returned their refuse to the soil, finally returned themselves to the soil. In the south, peasants lived by rice; in the north, they lived on wheat buns, millet and noodles; vegetables came as the main course; on feasts days, chicken. Only the rich ate meat.

As I wandered the war area a week later, I learned

how self-sufficient the villages were. They could live this
way forever, as they had always lived, except for the
intrusion of violence. One would come down by horseback from a hill to a village pocket which had not been
scourged by the Japanese or by modern roads. The young
women were healthy, their fine black hair glistening; some
mountain pockets were so backward that parents still
bound the feet of their young women although that had
been outlawed, along with the pigtail, when the Manchu
dynasty was overthrown thirty years earlier. In such villages, little children seemed happy; they played with
inflated pig bladders, bouncing them like balloons. Once, I
had a moment of sheer delight in recognition of kinship
when my horse stopped in the middle of a village street
and created a huge puddle of piss. Immediately, the little
children began playing "jump the pool," hurdling over the
puddle again and again, falling in, until an old lady came
up and began to shriek at them, scolding at the top of her
lungs as my own grandmother used to do in Erie Street.

But as one traveled, over the next ridge one found
the unhappy villages—where the war had come and passed, or the war had come and stayed. From one ridge to
the village in the hollow over the next ridge, the cycle of
life had been disrupted. Children with bloated bellies of
hunger, with scabs on their little shaven skulls, sulked in
the shadows of the stricken villages; in one village I saw
an entire community smitten by trachoma, men, women
and children alike with red crusted eyelids, some squeezing the pus from their eyelids so they could open them
and see. Then again, in most villages, anyone over forty,
man or woman, displayed rotting yellow teeth pitted with
black decay, the breath foul.

The villages lived by folklore, by word of mouth, in
the world of the past; all news was gossip, and the gossip
was inflammation of fear, hope, legend and fact. I learned
that villages literally kept no time. In any village, I could
ask the hour to check my watch, and if there were two or
three people with watches, all had different times. Each
village had its own time set by the county magistrate—the
hsien chang. It might be noon by the *hsien chang*'s time in

one village; but twenty miles away on either side, the time might be eleven-thirty or twelve-thirty, or even an hour ahead or behind. No time was official, all times were inaccurate; all recent dates were reckoned by the moon festival or the fall festival, and more important dates by the warlord who had commanded in such-and-such a year, or by whether someone was born before the revolution (1911) or after. There was only one operational time measure in a village—that of sunrise and sunset. At sunrise, men went to work in the field. They knew when it was time to come back by the way the sun slanted; the wife cooked the meal; and then, perhaps, an oil lamp flickered for a few minutes in the dark. One could watch the wisps of smoke, each one a tiny gray plume in the darkening sky as the evening meal was prepared or finished and then, quickly, it was dark, and the oil lamps went out, and all over China, except in the cities, it was night. No other marking of time had any reality to it, except the seasons which framed the days.

Through and about some of these villages ran the new roads. We take roads for granted. Chinese peasants did not, because roads were fresh. They knew the dates (by famine, warlord or season) when the roads had been put through and the roads had connected them to big outside government. The roads were useful: peddlers came off them to sell wares to village markets. But roads were also dangerous. It slowly came to me what the phrase "king's highway" must have meant in Europe years and years ago—how much opportunity the king's highway must have promised, yet how perilous it was. I can do no better in describing the perils of a road for peasants than in transferring to this page some jottings I made on that trip of 1939.

I had been hitchhiking my way on army trucks or "yellow fish" buses shortly after I left the front, and the following occurred, according to my notes that evening.

> On the way, our truck overtook a donkey loaded with lumber. The donkey swerved and broke the headlight with the projecting log on

its back. Then out hopped the driver, the mechanic and several soldiers, and they seized the peasant and began to beat him. They beat him mercilessly and he cried horribly, he fell on the ground, twirled into a ball and began to kowtow with a wailing servility that was disgusting. Every time he brought his head up from the ground as he pleaded for mercy, the mechanic kicked him in the face. The little boy who was with him began to cry and plead; the soldiers seized him bodily and flung him up to the top of the baggage. They kept on pounding and beating the peasant until the *t'ui chang* [lieutenant] came up, and the *t'ui chang* made them let the peasant go. The peasant got up, staggered away, his face a puffy mass of welts and wounds, and thanked the *t'ui chang*. The *t'ui chang* told the soldiers, *"Pu-yao ta t'a, mei yu yung"* ["Don't hit him, it's no use"]. Then the *t'ui chang* explained to me that the bus driver and mechanic were angry because they would have to pay the twenty dollars the headlight cost.

Modernizing China required roads, roads meant training drivers and mechanics not to steal auto parts or gasoline—and punishing them for mistakes or damage, whether their fault or not. So the drivers and mechanics saw the peasants who used their roads as, at best, an inconvenience and, at worst, a threat to their jobs. I, as a Westerner with an official pass, was safest on the king's highway; but a peasant was at his most vulnerable.

Dangerous as this new world of his own government was to the village peasant, the Japanese who now followed such roads introduced him to an even more dangerous world.

I had not come to write a study of village sociology. I had come to cover the war, and I had chosen Shansi because it was the only active front in China. Had the

Japanese broken all the way through in the summer and fall of 1939, they would have held the dominant heights of the Yellow River, could have closed easily on Sian and, quite possibly, have cut China in two, cutting Nationalists from Communists for good. The Japanese victory would have been styled an epic one and achieved a grandeur in the retelling. The fact that the Chinese held, however, wiped out the narrative value of the Southeast Shansi campaign for any history of war. Tens of thousands of men died to hold the lines exactly where they had been before the summer of 1939 and where they would remain until 1944. In the eyes of history they died uselessly, unworthy of record. For myself, it was the first real battlefront I had seen, and a giant step in education.

The scene of action was the Chungtiao mountain range of Southeast Shansi province, the province that snuggles into the elbow of the Yellow River. In the summer the Japanese Army had mounted a three-divisional offensive to clear the mountain range and reach, then cross, the river. But the fall rains had come early, mired their trucks and artillery, and given the Chinese foot soldiers time to gather and to cut off the Japanese in garrison pockets. Isolated thus in villages and towns, trying to extricate themselves, the Japanese went absolutely berserk before they were driven out.

The action I saw in the fall of 1939 was in the Ch'in River valley, where imperial road markers dating back to the Manchu dynasty still flagged the stone-paved carters' trace. I was following the Chinese soldiers forward, and they moved on foot, fifteen to twenty miles a day, crawling up and over and through mountain gaps, their officers ahead on horseback. Whatever they needed they carried—each soldier toting his bedding, his sausage roll of rice, his ammunition and grenades, some doubling up to carry telephone wire, machine gun parts, cartridge boxes, medical supplies. Mules brayed under dismantled pieces of artillery. Sick soldiers straggled back from the front, hobbling with staves, on the five- or ten-day hike to the nearest aid station; beggars clustered pleading as the columns trudged through villages; sometimes one could

see peasants impressed to carry those too sick or
wounded to walk; flies buzzed over the stretchers where
men in coma, or groaning, were carried on with undressed
wounds. And then I caught up with the path of Japanese
retreat through the villages they had savaged. I have since
so often exaggerated in retelling what the Japanese did
that perhaps it is best to restrain memory to the text of
my original dispatch.

> . . . village after village completely de-
> stroyed. Houses shattered and burned, walls
> fouled, bridges torn up. Houses were burned by
> the [Japanese] soldiery both out of boredom
> and deviltry and because they were cold and
> needed fire and warmth.
>
> The Japanese looted indiscriminately and
> efficiently. Everything of value was stripped and
> taken away. Telephones, wires, clocks, soap,
> bedding, collected for transfer to their own sup-
> ply department. On their own, the soldiers went
> in for simpler forms of looting. Clothes and
> food were what they wanted, and they were not
> very discriminate in their tastes; women's silk
> garments, peasant cotton trousers, shoes, un-
> derwear, were all stripped off the backs of their
> possessors whenever Chinese were unfortunate
> enough to fall into the hands of Japanese de-
> tachments.
>
> The Japanese soldiers were caked in mud,
> chest high; their beards were bristling with two
> weeks' growth; and they were ravenously hun-
> gry. The peasants, in fleeing before the ap-
> proach of the Japanese, had taken their pigs,
> cows, grain and other food with them into the
> hills where the Japanese could not follow. All
> through the valley, tiny Japanese garrisons were
> mired in mud, unable to communicate with one
> another and slowly starving. . . . The names of
> the villages (Liushe, Wangchiachuang, etc.)
> are meaningless 100 miles away, but in some,

every single woman without exception was raped by the soldiers in occupation. In villages whose occupants had not fled quickly enough, the first action of the Japanese was to rout out the women and have at them: women who fled to grain fields for hiding were forced out by cavalry who rode their horses through the fields to trample them and frighten them into appearance.

Male villagers were stripped naked, lashed to carts and driven forward by the Imperial Army as beasts of burden. Japanese horses and mules were beaten to death in the mud; and on any road and all the hills of the valley, one can see the carcasses of their animals rotting and the bones of their horses whitening in the sun. The Chinese peasants who were impressed to take their places were driven forward with the same pitiless fury until they collapsed, died, or were driven mad.

The action I saw in the Ch'in valley was all I expected, and made a fine story for a fledgling combat reporter.

But what I left completely out of my reporting and what I find buried now in my notes was far more important—the story of how revolutions begin.

I wish I could describe better what was spread before me in that combat area; in particular what I saw in one five-day period, which was to change all my understanding of politics.

In those five days, I was being passed from unit to unit, over and behind Japanese lines, into guerrilla areas and penetrated areas—but I was with Chinese officers, recent college students of my own age, men who were leading guerrilla bands, and I could not accurately tell a Communist unit from a popular-front unit from a Nationalist unit, in the spectrum of their loyalties, alliances and suspicions.

The only metaphor that occurs to me is from local folklore. Those valleys in the Chungtiao Mountains, through which I rode, are noted for their local fogs and mists, exactly the kind of "fogs in mountain" one sees in great Chinese paintings. Chinese travel writers would remark, as a curiosity of these mountains, how one could look across a bed of low-lying fog in the valley and see on the next ridge horsemen riding a trail as if floating in the distance. I was now seeing this myself. All the way across the valley, on a far ridge, were distant horsemen climbing over a pass slit in the crest, as if rising from a bowl of mist—horsemen in the sky. Now and again the far horsemen would disappear in the clouds as they descended, then rise again above the clouds as they followed the trail, and turn around a bend, and disappear.

I could see carts, or files of soldiers, appearing and disappearing in such mists beyond, and their officers on horseback at the head of the column. But in those five days I did not know who was who on the far ridges, so I cannot put this story together correctly, for I was lost in mist myself—political, linguistic, fear-ridden mist.* Yet the episode of those five days was important.

The politics that moved this local theater of revolu-

---

*The serious reader must regard this adventure in and behind the Japanese lines, as related by me now, with extreme caution. I had just been dismissed from the large politics of Chungking and went to North China with a smattering of Boston-taught Chinese language. It had taken me weeks to adjust my classical Chinese to spoken Chinese: when I set out I did not know, with all my education, how to ask to go to a toilet, until I was caught in a Chinese troop train, in distress, and was taught by common soldiers the proper word. My Chinese improved quickly and I soon learned the words for guns, rifles, machine guns, companies, regiments, bombs, shells, division headquarters, airplanes, distances, etc. Military dialogue is the simplest interchange in any language. But I never did learn, even after six years in China, the vocabulary of motivation, personal history, political purpose, or how and why things come to be. My blurred memory of the politics of the combat in Southeast Shansi is highly defective. But my notes, on which I base these recollections, are real—usually written by candlelight at night, as I tried to puzzle meaning out of conversations and stories I only half understood.

tion rise now in memory from a preposterously small stage; but the politics were far more important than the fighting. The stage was the Ch'in River valley, no larger than thirty by seventy miles. If gridded with a modern American highway, it could have been traversed in half an hour one way, an hour the other way. But it then had neither a working highway, nor radio, nor communications; only people held in villages which had not changed for centuries, yet which now *had* to change. It took days of walking and horseback riding to get through the valley. And in that valley the most efficient people, the most indomitable defenders of the helpless, the best killers, the most persuasive couriers of the ideas that move people into politics, were young Communists of my own age.

Three counties, of about 200,000 to 300,000 peasants each, spread over the valley, each county with its walled-about, crenelated county seat—Yangcheng, Chincheng, Kaoping. In two of these, Yangcheng and Chincheng, the new magistrates were twenty-six years old, and in one county, Kaoping, the magistrate was only twenty-four years old! Two had graduated the National University in Peking, China's Harvard. And these two had majored in ancient Chinese history! The other was a graduate of the Shansi Provincial University, and he had majored in government. When the Japanese war had broken out, two years earlier, these students had fled from the occupied towns to the hills and the resistance rather than stay under the Japanese. They knew history; they were young, with the energy and muscles of young men— and so they were useful. Whereas, as both provincial and national governments had so quickly discovered, the traditional appointed county magistrates of Southeast Shansi were totally useless in war.

For example: in the county seat of Yangcheng, when the Japanese had first come raiding a year earlier, in the summer of 1938, the old magistrate and the elders had walked down the road in their long black silk gowns to greet the marauders, and offer them obeisance, civility and local bearers. This they did for all banditti and warlords. The Japanese column had passed through; and then the Japanese planes had followed, swooped and machine-gunned the peasants who stood in Yangcheng's streets; the peasants had never seen planes before, so they stood in the streets to look, and they were murdered. Then, returning, the Japanese raiders massacred all the peasants who had not already fled. The Japanese had raided like this again in the fall of 1938, and by then, whatever the motley commands of the Chinese armies were, their commanders were calling for more effective local civilian support. Thus, by the time I got there in the fall of 1939, with the war entering its third year, the old long-gowned, black-silk elders had been replaced by new young men in all thirty counties of bloody Southeast Shansi. And although all these new men may not have been as effective, or of the same background, as the three young men I met, they were the nerve controls, the leadership elements of local resistance. The army needed them for support, for contact with the peasants; and the peasants, sickened and terrified by Japanese butchery, were willing to turn anywhere for guidance to survival.

The Yangcheng county magistrate, twenty-six years old, was the one who had majored in government at Shansi Provincial University. The night I slept in his courtyard, I woke the next morning to find him lecturing village elders on what "government" is. They must not beat peasants, and they must not collect the taxes themselves; the grain taxes were to go to his deputy magistrates directly, so that the food could be given to the army.

The Chincheng county magistrate, also twenty-six years old, was from Peking University; he was an attractive poseur, and dangled a cigarette in a holder from his lips. Since there was much coal and iron about Chincheng, he was organizing little forges in the hills which could make grenades, to be filled with black powder and used against the Japanese vehicles; one workshop was making pistols for soldiers and officers of scrap steel from abandoned Japanese equipment.

The Kaoping magistrate was exactly my own age, twenty-four. He wore a captured Japanese overcoat that hung loosely over his plump frame down to his ankles, and his conversation, as well as his round face with its wire-rimmed spectacles, made him resemble a graduate student back home. We talked about history over the barrier of my halting Chinese, and he would shift from history to the problem of organizing village self-defense corps. The county of the Kaoping magistrate, Ts'ao, marked the hazy junction where Japanese occupation troops, Communist guerrillas, government troops and Nationalist guerrillas all intersected. Ts'ao was loyal to Chiang K'ai-shek; but he was also very friendly with the Communist guerrillas. He was also loyal to Yen Hsi-shan, the warlord provincial governor; to the Nationalist units when they marched through; and to anyone else fighting Japanese. Since he was a student of Chinese history and hated only Japanese, his only purpose was to organize resistance.

All three young men had, by the time of my arrival, thoroughly learned the business of war. The enemy must get no cooperation in their areas as they had from Chinese elsewhere. Anywhere from a third to half of the Japanese forces that occupied the province of Shansi were "puppet troops"—Chinese turncoats, Manchurian Chinese, Formosan Chinese, North China peasants with no sense of nationhood, who served the enemy for warmth, for pay, for food, or out of fear of reprisal against their families. My trio of student officials in Shansi was reinstalling a sense of nationality.

Everyone must fight, was their message. Women must fight against the Japanese—thus a Women's National Salvation Movement, which spun, made blankets for the troops, wove sandals. Students must fight—thus a Students' National Salvation Movement. Every village must have a self-defense corps—thirty men for each large village, five grenades to a man, two guns or more to a unit. Children must be scouts. Old people who could not flee must become spies as Japanese passed through. It was better to waste the countryside, burn their own homes, desolate the land, than to serve the Japanese. Every village had signs painted on the walls, instructing: "Burn the Crops, Empty the Rooms, and Flee."

The three young men knew they were consciously modeling their efforts on what they had learned from Communist organizing efforts; they were making the countryside an environment of hate for all invaders; they were writing on blank minds, teaching people how to defend themselves and kill. They, themselves, all three, were simple Nationalists, but they were in no way hostile to the Communists, who were their allies; and the closer I got to the front, the warmer became the relationship.

The enthusiastic Kaoping magistrate was the most friendly to the Communists. His county was occupied, incomprehensibly but clearly, in three halves, or over-lapping layers—one half by the Japanese, one half by Nationalist armies, one half by Communists. The three layers overlapped three-dimensionally, permitting the three halves. Since I wanted to see Communists, and he dealt with them every day, it was he who passed me on to the Communist guerrillas.

The Communist leader—my notes record his name only as Captain Wu—was older; he must have been all of twenty-eight or twenty-nine, a tall, unsmiling young man who, to my puzzlement, hated the government of Chiang K'ai-shek as much as he hated the Japanese invaders. We talked all through the night at his encampment behind Japanese lines. I knew why he hated the Japanese; they were killers. But he was angry at Chiang K'ai-shek, too, because Chiang was supposed to be a national leader—and Wu's Communist volunteers were paid only one dol-lar a month (fifteen cents in American money), while the government soldiers were paid eight dollars a month ($1.20 in American money). Government troops had their food sent to them over the passes in sacks, whereas his troops had to get their food by "persuading" the peasants to give it. Government troops had their rifles and ammunition *given* to them, but his soldiers had to capture the rifles and machine guns with which they fought. In this unit there were eight different kinds of guns, and how could you get ammunition to fit eight different kinds of guns?

Captain Wu was a stern, energetic, thoroughly capable young man. But I recall how, with a sudden shift in mood, he went off into an inexplicable rage against the *T'ê P'ai*. I finally began to understand from his tirade that the *T'ê P'ai* were the Trotskyites! Here in the hills, the war had nourished his politics with a green and native Communism; he had never met a Trotskyite. But his anger at this invisible faction of Trotskyites was as fierce as his anger against Japan or against Chiang. Trotskyites, he said, were *I-chi-fan* people. Such people, said Captain Wu, opposed everything (*fan* being the Chinese character for opposition). Trotskyites opposed Japanese (*fan Jih*), opposed Chiang K'ai-shek (*fan Kuo*) and opposed Communists (*fan Kung*); thus, opposing everything, they were called *I-chi-fan*. His unit had executed a Trotskyite recently. How did he know the person was a Trotskyite, I asked. Because he was helping the Japanese, replied young Captain Wu in fury. His rage against the Trotsky goblins was as unmistakable as his ability; but as incomprehensible to me as the factional battles over sibylline doctrine under Mao in the name of Communist against Communist thirty years later.

In the morning it was my turn to show anger. I had, by that time, become so exasperated by the different measures of time in these old Chinese villages that I was explosive. I wanted to be up at six, and astride the horse at seven. Seven came, eight came, nine came, and finally the Communist platoon came to fetch me. So, I thought, the Chinese Communists have no more sense of time or timing than Nationalists or warlords—they simply do not understand time. But when I rode out of Captain Wu's village I could see why he had detained me. The children were lined up in the street, waving banners. The banners said in Chinese that America and China were friends. America and China would fight to the end against the Japanese bandits and imperialism. And one magnificent sign said in English: "Welcome Theodore H. White, Famous American Journalist, Friend of the Resistance." I could not be angry. The children sang songs and I was escorted out of town as a hero. Captain Wu gave me a captured Japanese overcoat and hat, and we went on.

Captain Wu explained Communist tactics to me. They were textbook simple. Guerrillas never attacked in late fall or winter, because there was no cover after the fields were harvested; summer and early fall, when the grain was high enough to hide them, was their time for assault. And always when they had superiority in number. They never, never offered positional resistance to a Japanese foray; they ran to the hills, to the villages, and disappeared, or dissolved, to regather at another point later. To have the peasants with them was essential—for intelligence, for shelter, for food, for care of wounded. Mao's phrase "The people are the sea, we are the fish in it" was supreme doctrine.

Mao's sea seemed, however, more like a moving stream as we rode along. As we rode, or paused, or forded a river, I slowly became aware of the clutter of little boys who trooped or clustered where we stopped; they had been sucked into the stream by the romance of guerrilla life and had become part of it. Called *hsiao kuei* ("little devils"), they were anywhere from ten to fifteen years old and had left home as the war dissolved the countryside. They trotted after their older brothers, helping in any way they could. They sat in camp at night and listened to the older soldiers tell stories; they must have grown up on hand-me-down, word-of-mouth legends of the Long March of 1934–1935. They cooked, fetched, carried; the army was their home. When their unit came to a stream too deep for them to ford, the older soldiers carried the little ones across on their shoulders. Such little boys, if they survived, probably now command the Chinese Red Army. The world they came from is obliterated; the army became their parent, shelter and home.

The panorama of the old world that was being wiped out was made quite clear to me when Captain Wu took me to a ridge overlooking a Japanese outpost in a large walled town in the valley below. We could see scores of lesser villages dotted in the valley, and as we lay peering, Wu identified which ones were "ours" (meaning Communist), which were "friendly" (meaning Nationalist in loyalty), which villages were held by Japanese.

It was like seeing a huge photographic enlargement of a microcellular structure. China was then a nation of five hundred million people, and there were, perhaps, three million such little villages, each one a single cell, in a society hitherto the most changeless in the world. Somehow, in China's time-frozen history, these cells had coagulated under the glistening patina of successive imperial governments in a culture of breathtaking beauties and cruelties. Underneath the patina, however, a deliquescence had set in, a melting away of the jellies of life. The forms remained but the forms were brittle—brittle to the touch of Western commerce, to the touch of warlords; now, finally, brittle and incapable of survival as the Japanese carried war across the country into villages. In each village, leadership had to change, new ideas creeping in with the need of survival, with the need that government must offer protection. From the ridge where I lay watching with Captain Wu, the pragmatic young guerrilla leader could point out villages which I can now, symbolically, translate into the political deliquescence of my imagination. Those villages below that were Communist-dominated could be identified by the fact that their walls had been torn down! Guerrillas, said Wu, could flee or enter such villages before or after Japanese thrusts without fear of being trapped by the walls.

This Chinese Communist hatred of walls, this hunter-hunted reflex, was later, in victory, translated, alas, to the destruction of the most beautiful of all city walls in the world, the magnificent ramparts of old Peking. But then, as the Communists fought the Japanese, and knew the world required changing, the tearing down of the walls was the visible signature of their presence—and the deliquescence of old China.

About me, in the five days of hard riding at the front, I saw all this but could not fit it into any pattern of reporting that would make a good story. As the old system melted or crumbled under the Japanese penetration, the Communists melted themselves into what was left. The Japanese shattered structure after structure in their offensives, raids, forays, bombings of China. What was left was not a society, but a spongelike mass, a honeycomb of mashed cells in most of which some sting was left. Some villages supported the Nationalists, others the provincial government, and yet others supported the Communists—but they supported whoever could serve their need of protection best, who could save their women from rape by the Japanese, their men from impressment as coolies. The Japanese had come to kill; the Communists were the most efficient counterkillers.

A single episode will give the flavor of this honeycomb of resistance. On one particular evening, I was riding with a lieutenant, a Nationalist guerrilla leader, and his horsemen. The Japanese flushed us and we rode hard to get away, and came to a village on a hill as the sun was falling. I was riding, as I recall, a white horse with wooden saddle frame, and I was horrified to discover during the chase that between the saddle frame and the horse's back there was only one thin woolen blanket. The blanket had been worn thin and the horse's skin rubbed raw; its back was bleeding, as we jounced over brooks and I flogged him to keep up with the others. We had to get water and food for the horses, and I wanted padding for my bleeding horse. The lieutenant stopped our little group in a village and asked the few peasants there for food and water for the horses. Then he said (and I could understand that much colloquial Chinese by then), *"Wo-men shih pa-lu-chun"* ("We are of the Eighth Route Army"), which meant that we were Communists guerrillas. I asked him why he said that; we were a Nationalist group. And he snapped at me, "Shut up! If we tell them we're Nationalist guerrillas, they won't feed our horses or water them."

The episode, which I thought then to be unimportant, keeps coming back to haunt me. The message that the Communists bore, true or false, had penetrated into the hills; they held the "hearts and minds" of these people who could neither read nor write. The people were certainly not unfriendly to Nationalist troops, who, like them, hated Japanese; but their political leadership, in the most primitive way, had been won over to the Communists, who were beginning to introduce ideas.

But the crazy patchwork of interlocked or conflicting loyalties was not limited to the valley Captain Wu had shown to me from his hill. It was larger. I had, for example, been passed up the way to the active Kaoping front by the 40th Army. Inquiring as I did about the 40th Army, I learned that its soldiers were Manchurian Chinese, who had been driven out of their homeland in 1931 by the Japanese seizure of Manchuria. Yet they still fought. They had been part of the group of divisions that had encircled, then kidnapped, Chiang K'ai-shek in Sian in 1936. They were now a dwindling band of men who had been fighting for ten years and wanted to go home. The 40th Army was very friendly with the Communists, although it stood officially on the muster as a Nationalist Chiang K'ai-shek army. From the Kaoping sector of the 40th Army command, I had been passed to the Communist units, then passed from them on the way back with some stiffness to the 27th Army. The 27th Army was commanded, absolutely, by Nationalist central government officers, and I was received there, after coming from a guerrilla area, with intense suspicion. The 27th Army was the only army I saw on that front which had telephone communications with the rear. Being suspicious of me, its forward regimental commander let me linger, hungry and tired, in his anteroom as he telephoned back up the chain of command to find out who this person was—a Japanese spy, a Communist spy, a wanderer, or whatever. Someone on the line must have had the number of my pass, and when he learned I was truly an American journalist I was well received: my feet were washed in hot water by his soldiers, I was offered hot perfumed towels to bathe my face and fed an extraordinary dinner.

On my way back from the front, I could see things more clearly. The 27th Army, for example, was made up of provincial draftees from Yunnan and Szechwan, far to the south. But they were adequately supplied because all their officers, from captain up, were graduates of Chiang

K'ai-shek's military academy. It was different from the
40th Army, which had once been the property of the
Manchurian bandit-warlord Chang Tso-lin, then became
the property of the "Christian general" Feng Yu-hsiang.*
That army in turn was different from the old syphilitic

*Feng Yu-hsiang was called the Christian general not only be-
cause he baptized his troops en masse with a hose, but because he
had a rudimentary social conscience. He forbade rape and punished
his troops for rape, for one thing, and occasionally, on inspection
days, after checking their rifles, he would order all soldiers to hold
out their hands to be examined for clean fingernails. My preoccupation with the warlord era of Chinese life, as an exercise in
political anthropology, came to an end shortly after this trip. The
warlords were fascinating as individuals, more fascinating yet as
an episode of government degenerating to brutality—but they were
of the past, not of the present. I was still collecting warlord folklore at this time, but I remember best my last impression of Feng
Yu-hsiang after the war in New York, when we exchanged visits.
His apartment, on Riverside Drive, had a spectacular view of the
Hudson River; but it was barricaded by cases and cartons of
groceries, coffee, soup, canned meats. He was prepared to live in
New York under siege, with the supplies of his personal staff entirely under his control. He was persuaded to leave America for
Russia in 1948. He was probably considered useless to the Russians, for he died in a fire on a steamboat in the Black Sea—
burned to death. Other warlords were equally colorful. Wu P'ei-fu,
for example, was not only the warlord of Honan, but a lover of
flowers and trees. He had tried to plant his province with many
flowering trees, but only succeeded in accomplishing this along the
rail lines he controlled. Having had a victorious clash with the warlord of Manchuria, Chang Tso-lin, Wu pursued—and Chang Tso-
lin, in retreat, would halt his command train wherever he could
find a pause, to send his troops out to chop down the young trees
Wu P'ei-fu had planted. The troops who had done this were probably the troops of what I called, on this trip, the 40th Army. There
were many other remnant warlord groups involved in the fight
against the Japanese; particularly the troops of the province of
Shantung, who, ultimately, went over to the Communists. The
great warlord of Shantung for a period of ten years in the twenties
was Chang Tsung-chang, who was remembered as "Old Eighty-six
Dollars." The nickname came from the rumor that Chang Tsung-
chang's penis, even in repose, was as long as a stack of eighty-six
silver dollars, one coin placed on top of the other—which would
make it nine inches long.

army of Yang Hu-cheng, just south of them. Yang-Hu-cheng had been a bandit, pure and simple, and when I left the 27th Army to return, I was given a military escort to protect me not from the enemy but from the bandit soldiers of Yang Hu-cheng, who might be on the loose.

Of all the memories of my visit to the front—of the villages, the mountains, the killings, the poverty, the hardships—the three young county magistrates I met and liked remain outlined most firmly in my recollection, they and Captain Wu. Old men with ideas stir up young men; but only young men know how to choose other young men. Generally, students are the best vehicles for passing on ideas, for their thoughts are plastic and can be molded, and they can adjust the ideas of the old men to the shape of reality as they find it in villages and hills of China—or in ghettos and suburbs of America.

Old men grow rigid, and keep their shop of ideas at the same storefront; they know what goes wrong when it goes wrong, but are too brittle to know how to fix what goes wrong. Young men grow old, too, and move from passion to politics to power soon enough.

A year after I had left Southeast Shansi, trying to keep track of my friends there, I learned that the young *hsien chang* of Yangcheng, the one who had majored in government, had been purged—but by whom, or which group, or for what cause, I never found out. What happened to all the others is equally unknowable. Young men following a successful cause sometimes succeed with it. The lucky among them harden into bureaucrats and abandon their old companions of the field when another logic, that of government, seizes them. Most die or have their spirit broken on the way to success—and I am sure that is what happened to my young men when the revolution hardened about them years later.

I came back by bus from the war areas, and remember of the long journey south only how wonderful it was to cross the range of the Ch'in-ling Mountains, which separates North China from Szechwan. One crosses through the pass, and in half an hour, one has left behind

the eroded hills that face the arid country of the north to
find oneself in the warm moist air of Szechwan, where
bamboo begins to grow on the south face of the range.

Szechwan was the peaceful interior, the war far
away again, and my first night back behind the range I
spent in a Buddhist temple fragrant with incense. It was
surrounded by bamboo thickets; a pool in its courtyard
reflected the full moon and in the moonlight paddled
several ducks. The priests chanted and it was exactly like
the China I had read of in Boylston Hall's books. All
dynasties running back for centuries had preserved such
ancient places of grace. But after what I had seen in
North China, I questioned how long such graces would
stay the course of history.

I had learned the first real lesson of politics, government and history: governments are instituted among
men in the first instance, and accepted by men gratefully,
to protect them from random violence and killing. I had
begun to observe that when the central government replaced the local government of Chungking after the
bombings. But I had now seen what government meant in
the hills of Shansi, where the Communists, not yet calling
themselves government, were becoming government. They
offered protection.

Many other lessons in politics and government were
to follow over the years, but none more important than
that.

Thus, wending my way back to Chungking, I could
no longer see Chiang K'ai-shek or his Americanized administration as a real government. They had no control of
events, and I had an immense desire to separate from
them.

CHAPTER 3

Reporter in Asia:
Episode and Personality

I did not know that I had become a recognized reporter until two weeks after my return to Chungking.

Time had cabled its pleasure with my reporting from the front—but then the magazine itself arrived. I had received a full page and a half for my dispatch, with a by-line!—the first by-line *Time* had ever given anyone it called its own "special correspondent." It illustrated the story with a map that showed in a red line the meanderings of that correspondent through the hills of Southeast Shansi. John Hersey had edited my prose to a high polish. A telegram arrived from a New York publisher, Random House, inviting me to write a book about the war in China. There could be no doubt that I had made a score.

It was December of 1939; I was only a year and a half out of Harvard, but *Time* was willing to raise my monthly guarantee, and the Chinese Ministry of Information willing to accept my resignation. With as much friendship as relief at my departure, my comrades in the ministry gave me a banquet to celebrate the fact that I would now be a recognized foreign correspondent, on the receiving not the disbursing end of their attentions.

For those men who, sooner or later, are lucky enough to break away from the pack, the most intoxicating moment comes when they cease being bodies at other men's command and find that they control their own time, when they learn their own voice and authority. For most, this moment of breakthrough comes in the wonderful years of the thirties, when life floods men with peak vigor, and vigor is tempered by experience. For some it comes later, in their forties. But for those of us who came of age in the war years, the war, terrifying as it was, gave us the opportunity to break out of the management chains and the lockup of training programs at a very early age. If one was lucky enough to be where the action was, and if one could find a way to insert himself in the action, the breakout might come in one's twenties. Luck had brought me to China. Luck had carried me to a war action exciting enough to be published. War incubated opportunity: the number of American foreign or war correspondents was to go from perhaps two hundred when I left Harvard in 1938 to a guesstimated three thousand by 1945. War was a growth industry; I rode with that wave and was swept up by it.

It was clear to me that I was never going back to Boston to be a professor of history; that dream had vanished sometime between the bombings of Chungking in May and the action in Shansi. I was no longer a student sightseer. And yet, since no one had ever told me what a reporter does, or how he does it, or what a foreign correspondent is supposed to do, I remained, as I can see now, still a sightseer but of a different kind—a collector of impressions of whatever could be typed or pasted into a dispatch. I collected sights, sounds, personalities, famous names, episodes. *Time* was then a far less responsible magazine than it is today, and delighted in quips, curiosities, anecdotes and quotes, whether true or not. If there was a history that framed it all, then the editors back in New York decided what the history meant, and reporters simply supplied raw material. As a purveyor of such raw material, their collector of anecdotes, personalities, episodes, names, in the Far East, I thrived—and left the history to New York.

Many good things followed on my new status.

Invitations came to *Time*'s China correspondent, particularly from the diplomatic colony, where the exiled envoys to this half-forgotten Asian war spent their evenings entertaining each other and picking each other's brains for shreds of information. With the diplomatic invitations came, by chance, my introduction to sex. I was invited to the Belgian legation for a formal dinner one evening, but the Japanese air force arrived to raid. We scuttled for the legation's dugout, and in the dark I began conversation with the lady accepted as the "mistress" of one of the Belgian attachés. She was Chinese; he spoke very little Chinese; snuggled in the dugout, waiting for the bombs to thud, she and I began to talk in Chinese, which none of the other foreigners could understand. And so, two days later, I met her in a Chinese hotel, took a suite, and she introduced me to what had so long fascinated me. The meal we ate was good; but the experience was disappointing. The windows of the bomb-racked hotel had been replaced by greased paper; Chinese waiters poked their fingers through the paper to peek in; we went to bed; I fumbled at her; my inexperience was obvious; and she wailed, in Chinese, "You're nothing but a little boy." What I needed of sex during the early years of the war thereafter usually came casually; love came much later. Yet I had been initiated, and a good deal of fantasizing could be discarded.

Far more important than my dugout encounter on the diplomatic circuit, however, was my acquaintance with my first man of importance—or "representative character," as he would appear in a history book. This was a particularly wise man who, by good fortune, had been made British Ambassador to China—Sir Archibald Clark-Kerr, later Lord Inverchapel and Ambassador to Washington. Old men take pleasure, I now know, in talking to bright young men, thinking aloud to them, instructing them. Clark-Kerr, after our first few meetings, let me call him "Sir Archie"; and then he would ramble on to me, at lazy times, about history, the British Empire, and diplomacy as it had been and should be practiced. It was good education, for it ran from the last century into the new. He had been recruited, as had all young British diplomats at the turn of the century, by the permanent Under Secretary of the Foreign Office, a pederast who scrutinized all young candidates for posting to their unpaid secretaryships around the world. Archie had, at one time, as a very junior diplomat been apprenticed to the great Lord Bryce in Washington, and to hear someone talk of Lord Bryce, who had written the classic *The American Commonwealth,* was like hearing of Plato when he was writing *The Republic*. Archie had left the diplomatic service to fight with his Scots regiment in the trench warfare of 1914–1918, then returned to the service, and his assignments had given him a world view that no other Western diplomat in Chungking could rival.

For me, most importantly, Sir Archie was a teacher of politics. I was pasting interviews into my notes like stamps in a postage album. Clark-Kerr would rescue names from my conversation and pin them into politics and history. I would come back from the field or the war fronts and report raw observations. He would listen; then sort out for me what I had seen. And always he would come back to the Communists; he was convinced that the Communists would ultimately win in China, but did not grieve about it; that was the way history went, he said. Clark-Kerr was probably the best senior diplomatic reporter out of Chungking in the war years.

"Names" are to young reporters the same as money in the bank; they are credit references; they lead to other contacts, other sources; their invitations translate into circles of acquaintances, thus stories. For years, until 1963, my search for stories would be a search for names and personalities. Starting with Archibald Clark-Kerr, in the spring and summer of 1940, my circle of names widened, my stories cast a wider net, and Time Incorporated came up with the irresistible idea that I tour Southeast Asia for their morgue—meaning I would fill their background files with features, personalities and the kind of tourist observation I was good at. The war in Europe had flamed, the Netherlands, Belgium and France had fallen, combat was sure to spread to Asia, and *Time* wanted enough background material in their files to color up events when they happened. They would pay all my expenses for three or four months of travel, which meant that I might live for the first time as I had always believed I should live—at the best hotels, eating at the best restaurants, without hassling over bills, rickshaw fares or add-ons.

Of the three or four months I spent on my tour of Southeast Asia, only two impressions are worth reproducing. I was chiefly seeking names, quotations and color—but what I was observing was one of the great thrusts of the twentieth century. Without recognizing it, I was also stumbling into the first chapter of the Vietnamese story, and into a major personality, Douglas MacArthur, whom all then disdained.

The thrust, of course, was the thrust of the Japanese. All through the 1930s, the Japanese thrust in Asia, like that of the Nazis in Europe, magnetized all politics and all events on the continent about them. The Japanese were on the threshold of their industrial expansion and their appetite for industry and modernization was translated into the most naked lust for overseas sources of oil, rubber, tin, coal, rice; they meant to have it all. France had fallen, Holland was occupied, the British were beleaguered—and the bits and pieces of those old empires seemed open for the looting. I was to pass along the rim of this Japanese thrust in the South Seas—France's Indo-China, Britain's Malaya, Holland's Indonesia, America's Philippines—trying to document the nature and range of Japanese pressures.

I bristle still at the Japanese. I recognize this as prejudice. But I was first introduced to violence by Japanese action in Chungking and in North China; and confirmed in my antipathies by this long voyage of examination of Japanese purpose in Southeast Asia in 1940. I found them repulsive in the openness of their ambition and the coarseness of their manners. They brandished their planes and their armies with none of the normal niceties of diplomacy. They might wear Western business suits and be coldly technical, as they were in Indonesia, delivering ultimata to the Dutch colonials for delivery of oil. Or they might sit around the rococo old Hotel Metropole in Hanoi in brown undershirts, and grunt and spit on the floor, courteous to no one, as they demanded of the French colonials that three air bases in northern Indo-China be given to their air force for bombing South China. Wherever one met the Japanese on the thrust, they were brutal.

My first stop was in Hanoi, where the Japanese were coercing the French colonial administration to submission. I envied the correspondents who were filing daily bulletins; both the French colonials and the Japanese bullies were so obviously contemptible that they made good copy. But I had to content myself with mailers, and so I concentrated on politics, and on what I called, in my dispatches, the "Annamites" or "natives." I watched them crouching in the streets and reported that they would "sit on their haunches, chew betel nuts, and do nothing," whether the French remained or the Japanese marched in. They had, I reported, a certain "native" exotic flavor; I was particularly taken with the beauty of their women, who walked so marvelously erect, and I attributed that, in my anthropological mood, to the training of Vietnamese girls to carry baskets on their heads, balancing them as they walked. Further, anthropologically, I ascribed their beauty to the mingling of the Malaysian and Chinese strains of their heredity, giving them the robust body, hips and bosoms of the Malays, and the delicate facial features of the Chinese. About their men, whom I accepted as "natives" and of whom I learned only from Frenchmen, I was more harsh. Trying to estimate for an American magazine what local resistance might be offered to the Japanese if it came to a showdown at arms, I offered the observation that the "natives" would support neither the French nor the Japanese. And speaking of what later would become the nation of Vietnam, which humiliated our own country in battle, I finished one dispatch by dismissing Vietnamese as "a whining, cringing, gutless mass of coolies, part mule, part goat, part rabbit."

It was, perhaps, inevitable that traveling and dining with white men in French Indo-China, I should come to such a conclusion. But nothing could obscure the prime political fact that all politics in this white man's colony revolved around hate. The French Army was an army of oppression—seven thousand Frenchmen, three thousand Foreign Legionnaires and scores of thousands of black African colonial troops, Moroccans with their fezzes, Algerians in distinctive uniforms. The French made money out of Indo-China, and they despised the people who lived there. In Hanoi, for the first time, I saw a white man slap a native—a Frenchman slapping a rickshaw driver who had protested the fare paid. Sometimes there was provincial Ku Klux Klan mischief in provocation of natives—as, for example, the "tableau." A group of Frenchmen would get into rickshaws to go to a bordello, exhort their pullers to high speed in a race; then they would pick out the sweating, exhausted winner, take him upstairs and urge him to make love to one of the prostitutes as they watched. They enjoyed observing his desire as he was pulled exhausted from servitude between the rickshaw shafts and even more when he showed inability to achieve erection with the girl they had paid to please him. I could relate such sights easily to the politics of race hate, but had no idea that those politics would reach across some thirty years to wreck American politics, too. I contented myself with observing that none of the Vietnamese would die for white man's rule; they distrusted Chinese; the Japanese were simply a new set of conquerors; they seemed to be enjoying the humiliation of the French and would wait for years to make their country their own.

In Hanoi learned French scholars, from the École Française de l'Extrême Orient, provided most of the learning the West still has on the arts, the culture, the tradi-

tions of Cambodia, Laos, Vietnam. French colonials provided wine, good food, good manners, good coastal roads
to the natives—but also opium. The colonial government
imported opium, licensed opium dens, poisoned people
with the drug on which the government revenues
thrived—and in a sublime act of hypocrisy erected in
Hanoi a tiny replica of New York harbor's great Statue of
Liberty. There was no contact, however, between Frenchmen and the people they ruled, no contact except hate.
And there is no greater irony today than that the French,
who debased, defiled and degraded the Vietnamese people, should act on the world stage as public friends of
Vietnam, and we, Americans, should be accused as the
ravagers of a civilization we tried to save. The exercise
cost Americans fifty thousand lives, and the Vietnamese
more than a million.

But all that was in the future. As I passed through in
1940, I found only that the Vietnamese women were
beautiful, the men sullen, the French colonials stupid or
cruel, and I felt that Americans should not engage themselves in this matter. On Vietnam I was then an isolation-
ist, and I should have remained so forever.

I went from Vietnam to Thailand, to Malaya. Then,
on through the East Indies to see the Japanese squeeze
that Dutch colony for oil, and from there to the Philippines, where I met Douglas MacArthur.

Douglas MacArthur is, probably, historically far
more relevant to the history of Asia than to American
politics. He remade Japan. But I should like to pause
over him as an American, nonetheless. Outcast as he was
in 1940 from power or influence, he was a genuinely
"representative man," who stood for something. In the
fluctuating market of historic values, MacArthur stands
presently at low discount. He was outrageous in his rhetoric; and any sophisticated scholar can make him look like
a fool simply by quoting him in his moments of transport,
when, indeed, he was a fool. But underneath it all, he was
an extraordinarily able man, a good general, sparing of

his men's lives in combat, a technician who won larger victories with less bloodshed than any other American general of record. It was only in politics that MacArthur was slightly mad, and then he was daft only in the politics of America, not in the politics of the Orient.

When I met him, on this trip, I was very young, and still more sightseer than reporter. He was then, by my youthful judgment, a very old man—over sixty! I went to see him in the Philippines only because in my military survey of Southeast Asia I had been so disappointed by the U.S. Army in the Philippines—commanded by dull men, with an even duller spokesman in Manila, who had contempt for the "aging" and retired one-time Chief of Staff of their army, Douglas MacArthur. They called him "the Napoleon of Luzon," and the press spokesman, a stout U.S. Army major, told me in 1940 that he "cut no more ice in this U.S. Army than a corporal." MacArthur was just an adviser to the Philippine Army, he said, not worth seeing. So I went to see this relic of history, this great soldier, now a field marshal in the Philippine Army.

MacArthur at sixty, on the eve of his great war command, was, I found, still a spectacle. His hands trembled; his voice sometimes squeaked; but he could not talk sitting down. He paced, and roared, and pointed, and pounded, and stabbed with his cigar, and spoke with an intelligence and a magniloquence and a force that overwhelmed. He was holding himself, he said, in readiness to command the American expeditionary force in Asia when the war broke out. This was a year before Pearl Harbor, but he insisted war was coming. He spoke of the Japanese Navy—and he thought it was first class. Beware of the Japanese Navy, he said, and continuing, he said that Japanese carrier-based aviation was superb. He believed, however, that the Japanese Army was not even second class, that it was shot through with venality. He, himself, was building the new Philippine Army for Manuel Quezon, and if he had enough time, he could make it into a fighting force. MacArthur had a real respect for Asians as fighters and, generally, liked the Asians, much as William

McKinley had liked the "little brown brother." From this, on to tonnages, distances, mileages, fire powers, and he was altogether impressive as he lectured to me.

I wrote my dispatch on the defenses of Asia for *Time* and then, provocatively, sent it upstairs from my room at the Manila Hotel to his penthouse suite to see if I had violated his confidence. I had written that after three months of seeing all the generals—American, French, Dutch, English—in Southeast Asia, by far the best in every respect was General Douglas MacArthur, U.S. Army, retired. With this judgment MacArthur totally agreed, and I was immediately summoned up to his penthouse to be told what a grand dispatch I had written.

It was late in the afternoon, and he was dressed in an old West Point bathrobe of blue and gray wool which displayed the Army "A" on its back; his skinny shanks protruded as he paced, and occasionally he puffed on a corncob pipe. We rejoiced together that we alone understood the Japanese peril to America, the Japanese thrust; in this sympathetic mood, he began to reminisce. He had been a young first lieutenant when he came here with his commission after graduation from West Point in 1903; he had fought the little Philippine brown brothers in the Aguinaldo insurrection. He had commanded a U.S. division in combat in World War I and in the occupation of the Rhine that followed; had been Chief of Staff of the U.S. Army under Hoover, had retired. But he felt that our fate and Asia's were intertwined. His father, Arthur MacArthur, had been a Civil War general. Arthur MacArthur had done his duty; he, Douglas MacArthur, would do his duty. It was a memorable conversation, and at one point, as the sun was setting over Manila Bay, he turned to me from the balcony and said, "It was destiny that brought us here, White, destiny! By God, it is destiny that brings me here now."

MacArthur was to be in Asia from 1935 to 1951 without ever coming home, conquering the Pacific islands, occupying and restoring the Japanese islands, commanding Korea until Harry Truman fired him. Harry Truman fired him for good cause, of course, but there was in their clash a quintessence of the century-old clash in American history between military and civilians, a clash I was to report more closely in the Stilwell episode: How much of war is politics? And if so, whose politics? MacArthur understood the politics of Asia, and not only in his legacy to Japan but in his parting admonition to his successors ("Anybody who commits the land power of the United States on the continent of Asia ought to have his head examined") demonstrated this understanding. What he could not understand were the politics of America, and above all, the politics of the Presidency. He was convinced that the military and the political executives were co-proprietors of American history, equal partners in the great adventures of war.

I was to see MacArthur several more times over the next six years, but it did not occur to me that he was flawed politically until two years later. By that time, we, too, were at war with the Japanese. He had just escaped from Corregidor, was again an American general, not a Philippine field marshal, had been named commander of all U.S. forces in the Southwest Pacific—but with no visible support in troops, ships or supplies from the homeland. He was indignant. I visited him, as a war correspondent, in his headquarters at Melbourne, Australia. In our conversation he managed to denounce all at once, and with equal gusto and abandon, Franklin D. Roosevelt, the President; George Catlett Marshall, the regnant chief of staff; Harry Luce, the publisher of my magazine; and the U.S. Navy. He felt that the U.S. Navy was a poor navy. ("White," he said, "the best navy in the world is the Japanese Navy. A first-class navy. Then comes the British Navy. The U.S. Navy is a fourth-class navy, not even as good as the Italian Navy.") He was completely wrong in this in the spring of 1942, for the U.S. Navy was about to prove it was the finest navy that ever cut water; and Franklin D. Roosevelt and George C. Marshall were men greater than he.

In December of 1940, however, I had nothing but admiration for Douglas MacArthur, and an affection that still remains, however much I later separated from his politics. MacArthur had helped me on the way; he was the most vivid of the paste-up characters I was trying to file to the *Time* morgue, and *Time* liked what I wrote. While I was in Manila, *Time* decided to hire me as a staff correspondent, on full salary. Not only that; I was cabled a bonus of one thousand dollars, and all expenses for my Asian tour. When I reached Hong Kong, en route back to China, there was also an invitation to join the staff in New York, whenever I wanted. My instructions were only to return to Chungking, to stay at least through the spring of 1941, until Harry Luce, the distant owner of *Time,* could come to visit China, his birthplace—and I, as *Time*'s correspondent, might serve as his escort.

I did not know what was happening in China that first week of my return in January 1941. I doubt that anyone ever will. It was an episode called the New Fourth Army Incident, and since I was collecting episodes as well as personalities in those days, I thought I could interest *Time* in it. I have still a mound of documents—government papers, secret instructions, and unpublished notes and interviews—which testify more to my diligence than to my understanding. *Time* was profoundly uninterested in the episode of the New Fourth Army. Perhaps I might have won the editors' attention if I had been able to connect the episode to the flow of history, but I could not, for I had not yet learned how. Though I pursued the story of the massacre of the New Fourth Army as diligently as any in all my life, no more than a paragraph or two appeared in print. But now that that massacre takes its place in the tragedy of modern Chinese history as one of the four or five great turning points at which the choice was made for blood rather than conciliation, I would like, briefly, to tell it as I came across it.

The story begins with a point on the map—a village named Mouling on the south bank of the Yangtze valley, in which on January 13–14, 1941, some ten thousand Chinese Communist partisans were wiped out by Chinese Nationalists. The precise point on the map is inconsequential, for the larger movements, snagged at that point on the map, reached all the way from Manchuria in the north to the tropics of South China. On this map, ever since 1927, three great forces had been contending—the Japanese, the Chinese Nationalists and the Chinese Communists.

For ten years, starting in Manchuria in 1931, the Japanese had been pressing down from the north on split and quarreling China south of the Great Wall. And when, in 1937, the Japanese had made a formal war of it, all the Chinese factions—Communists, warlords and provincials—had joined to support the recognized Nationalist government against the invader. Despite this union, by the end of 1938 the Japanese had seized the three great river valleys of China, occupied all the coastal cities, controlled ninety percent of its railroad net and confronted Chinese armies of all kinds dug into hills and mountains, as I had found them in Shansi.

But as the Japanese had spread, and the map had become splotched with swelling patches marked "Occupied," the Communists had followed. Wherever the Japanese staked out garrisons in the countryside, the Communists felt entitled to organize the countryside against them. At the war's beginning, the central government of Chiang K'ai-shek had seen this Communist response as one of a dozen regional or warlord responses, all bracketed together in war zones commanded by loyal Nationalist generals, all more or less irregularly supplied by the central government. But the Communists lived by the doctrine of the offensive—and their guerrilla forces spread behind the Japanese lines of "occupation" with a zest, a speed, a wild imagination and a strategic brilliance that defied all rules of conventional warfare. They spread eastward first, across the Yellow River from Yenan through Shansi province, crowding the provincial government of Yen Hsi-shan until, in the summer of 1940, despite the common war against the Japanese, Yen Hsi-shan turned to fight them. The Communists spread north to the deserts, crowding the Muslim generals. They spread farther east, crowding out or absorbing all other

Chinese resistance until, by the summer of 1940, they shared the "occupation" with the Japanese right down to the hills of Peking and beyond to the Pacific shores of the province of Shantung, Confucius's birthplace. Then they turned south.

When they turned south, control of their armies by a single army command became too much for their rudimentary communications and primitive logistics. Thus they spun off a new army—the New Fourth Army, vaguely recognized by the central government as an anti-Japanese force under Communist leaders. Down from the province of Shantung this new army had moved, in symbiosis with the Japanese armies of occupation—down, down, down south into the province of Kiangsu, which includes Shanghai, down into the province of Anhui, down across the Yangtze valley, down toward the province of Chekiang, Chiang K'ai-shek's birthplace, which was over one thousand miles from their headquarters in Yenan.

It was a stupendous feat of arms—bewildering to the Japanese, but terrifying to Chiang's central government armies.

The Communists on the move proclaimed themselves to be a patriot Chinese army, so they demanded arms, bullets, money, rice, supplies from the national government. But the numbers of the New Fourth Army, in their growth, had passed 100,000 men, totally unauthorized by the national government. True, the Communists were resisting Japanese—but in a new way. If they could get no support from Chiang K'ai-shek, they must get rice, clothing, help, hospital service, from the peasants. The Communists needed to create an entire new civilian base—in short, a form of government. They also needed guns. So they took guns in battle as they could grab them—from the Japanese, or from Chinese mercenaries of the Japanese; from warlord units in the grand alliance if they had to; occasionally from central government units, too.

Over and over again, Communist units as they spread clashed with other Chinese divisions and units in sputtering, sniping, bloody little actions. Society had dissolved in occupied areas; loosely disciplined troops might be warlord troops one month and free-booting banditti the next. The savagery of the Japanese, the feral resistance of Chinese of all kinds, had divorced the war from all civilized custom. Only the Communists had the doctrine, the ideas, the political techniques, to make people jell again into groups with a cause; they were different from other regional and warlord groups because, though they could be as violent as any other, they could mesh the violence to a purpose and strategy.

By October of 1940, clashes of Chinese Nationalists, warlords and Communists had become so commonplace that Chungking ordered the entire New Fourth Army back north of the Yangtze River immediately, within a month. Then matters grew worse. In November, the commanding general of the Nationalist 53rd Army, Li Shou-wei, was killed in an obscure clash with the New Fourth Army in Kiangsu. Since the logic of war demanded some intelligent Chinese response to the Japanese, both Chinese parties despite their mutual hates sat down in Chungking to work out a more reasonable timetable for separation of war zones. On paper they agreed there would be an expansion of the recognized area of Communist activity: the entire sweep of Japanese occupation in North China from the Yellow River to the coast would become a Communist theater of operation, a vast extension of their "legitimate" authority. In tough reality, however, the agreement meant the Communists must withdraw the New Fourth Army from south of the Yangtze, from the provinces of Anhui, Hupeh, Chekiang and Kiangsu, by January 1 of 1941, then withdraw even farther north to the Yellow River.

This would have to be an intricate operation. Japanese garrisons pocked the route of Communist withdrawal. Where Japanese garrisons did not bar the way, vengeful Nationalist government troops and generals manned other positions. Negotiations of zones, timetables, routes of withdrawal, continued through December of 1940, the Communist army in the field responding reluctantly to the agreement made between their high command and Chiang's high command. For the Communists in the field to withdraw meant that scores of thousands of local peasant recruits must say good-bye to wives and families, leaving villages behind defenseless against the Japanese, dependent for protection on Nationalist troops with no love for Communists. Communist headquarters in Chungking clung to the agreement, but their messages, transmitted by makeshift radio, couriers and bamboo signals, lacked the crisp edge of command. In the field, central government armies were pressing on the withdrawing Communists, urgent to move into the zones the Communists were leaving—and eager to revenge the November killing of Li Shou-wei.

In Chungking, negotiations dawdled on between Chiang K'ai-shek and the chief of the Communist emissaries, Chou En-lai. Both were passionate men; both had tempers; but they had been friends and enemies for so long by then—some fifteen years—that they felt they might work out some agreement to avoid the bloody and profitless clash that impended. On Christmas Day of 1940, Chiang K'ai-shek, Methodist, had invited Chou En-lai, Communist, to have dinner with him. They had finally settled on the terms and details of the withdrawal of the New Fourth Army from south of the Yangtze and then pushed on, according to Chou's account (which is the only account I heard), to talk about the long-range relations between Communists and Nationalists in China. Chou described the Communist complaint to Chiang K'ai-shek: that Chiang treated them like a warlord army, not like a political force; he said there must be a recognition of the politics as well as the logistics of war; and he told Chiang to his face that his Nationalist government was undemocratic. Then, recounting the tale, Chou said, in that chuckling way of his: "Do you know what he answered? He said, 'You mean you call me undemocratic?' " Neither one understood what a democracy is, but both recognized that the test of ideas is their ability to move men to use, or accept, force. And in that situation, Chiang had the force.

I arrived back in Chungking the week that the Chinese were moving to kill each other eight hundred miles downriver. I could sniff the trouble, I could sense it as I tried to make contact again. But it was like being once more in the mists and mountains of Shansi, with fragments of detail surfacing above clouds. I could catch echoes of the killings, but only muffled echoes. Nothing appeared in print in the controlled press of Chungking, the capital. I had to reconstruct the episode from men who lied not only to me but to each other; and by the time I had put together a reasonable outline of what had happened day by day, the news story had disappeared, and I had nothing to tell except for history.

What happened, as best I can reconstruct it now, is that most of the New Fourth Army had moved across the Yangtze to the north by the end of December. South of the river there remained in that first week of January only the New Fourth Army headquarters—which meant their command staff, their hospitals and their political school, which was as essential to a functioning Communist army at that time as the thyroid gland is to the human body. But the regional Nationalist command (Third War Area) had directed the withdrawal of this critical Communist command echelon northward over a route that would carry them across the Yangtze directly into the guns of a Japanese river garrison posted to cut them down. The Communist commander of the New Fourth Army, Yeh T'ing, in the second week of January thus decided to repudiate the designated route. He would take his headquarters command—in all, ten thousand troops, officers and cadres—and move east downriver, to cross the Yangtze at a point where he felt the Japanese would be less on guard. He distinctly diverged from the agreement made by his principals in distant Chungking; to have accepted the route set by the local Nationalists would have been suicide. As he moved thus, the Nationalist generals caught and encircled him, and in three days' fighting, while the Japanese stood by, presumably enjoying it all, the Communists were massacred. Their chief, Yeh T'ing, was thrown into prison. Other Communist leaders were shot outright. Some five thousand or six thousand of the ordinary troops were killed or massacred. Those who lived were disbanded, and assigned to patriotic service in other government armies against the Japanese.

We, in Chungking, did not know of the massacre of January 14, 1941, until days later, and then by word of mouth or underground leaflet.

From distant Yenan, Mao Tse-tung cabled his office in Chungking to issue a Communist statement of defiance. The prose is blunt enough to be his own.

> ... those who play with fire ought to be careful. We formally warn them. Fire is not a very good game. Be careful about your skull. ... Our retreat has come to an end. We have been struck with a hatchet and our first wound is a serious one. If you care for the future, you ought to come to offer medical treatment. It is not too late. We have to give this warning for the last time. If things continue to develop this way, the whole people of the whole country will throw you into the gutter. And then if you feel sorry, it will be too late.

A week after Mao's statement and two weeks after the episode, Chiang, on January 27, 1941, spoke secretly to his National Military Council. The council was the decorative proscenium of his grand coalition, which included restive central government generals, regional army commanders, and aging warlords who had turned over their troops to the alliance. The massacre had probably most disturbed the old warlords; Chiang might someday treat them similarly. Chiang tried to calm them, in the magisterial language of the mandarins. Said he, in a cold, straightforward speech whose text I managed to abstract: "The affair was unambiguous; the issue was uninvolved; the incident not abnormal. Disobedience and insubordination among army men naturally bring down punishment upon them. Acts of revolt, attacks on comrades in arms ... demand the disembodiment of the troops. ..."

Chiang went on, recalling other generals who had disobeyed his orders. His remarks illuminate the command of China at war: "Han Fu-chu, Li Fu-ying and Shih Yu-san ... disobeyed orders. ... The first of them was executed because he failed to obey the government's order to hold his ground in eastern Shantung and instead wanted to withdraw westward. ... Li Fu-ying was shot for his persisting in retreat when retreat had been forbidden him. Shih Yu-san ..." etc. Finally, Chiang said: "I am resolved to demonstrate to the nation the essential qualities of sound discipline. ... I have often compared the army to a family wherein I look upon the soldiers under me as a father regards his children. If his children behave well, the father feels they reflect honor upon him; if badly, they disgrace him. ... My solicitude failed, however, to move them [the New Fourth Army]; they interpreted it as weakness and even timidity. ... Now the New Fourth Army has been abolished; the question has been settled and no other question remains. ..."

Yet there *were* other questions, which I pursued for months because it occurred to me that these killings were more significant than the larger combat killings I had reported in Shansi. Why did the Chinese have to kill each other? I asked that as I jounced on rice bags going to the central front, or dozing in the sun with young Nationalist officers, or drinking tea with generals at their headquarters. They were disturbed, all of them. But I caught their sense of satisfaction, or retribution exacted for the killing of General Li Shou-wei of the 53rd Army. Revenge was sweet to them. I tried to put together chronologies and causes at military headquarters in Chungking; but each Chungking general started the chronology of reactions with a different date; none was sure how it all came about. In June of 1941 I finally managed to see the Generalissimo himself in a stiff interview. His view of the war had changed since 1937; now he summarized the episode with an epigram: "The Japanese are a disease of the skin, the Communists are a disease of the heart."

I got the story best, I think, from Chou-En-lai, with whom, by then, I had become friends. Two weeks after the massacre, on February 1, when his rage had cooled, he spent several hours with me, and he was in his best analytical mood. Chou En-lai had an amazing mind, for detail as well as for synthesis, a memory that could with ease recollect dates, quotations, episodes, incidents. He went through the story of the breakup of the alliance of all Chinese against the Japanese, date by date, from 1937 to 1940, then moved, with amazing facility, to the dates and hours of the climactic ten days in early January of 1941. He explained, as he went, the nature of the Chinese government, the Chinese Army, the telephone communication system, the dangle of forces that Chiang must balance and manipulate. He was cool enough by then to separate his rage at the massacre from his clinical measurement of Chiang K'ai-shek. He said he was sure that Chiang did not command and specifically order the massacre—but Chiang must have led the field commanders at the front to believe he would not mind if they liquidated Communists in their own fashion. Chiang had personally promised him, Chou, at Christmas in Chungking, safe passage for the New Fourth Army. Chiang had not known of the killings until they were well under way, when Chou himself, who had been reached in his Chungking headquarters by Communist radio from Yenan (which in turn had been contacted by sputtering radio from the killing ground), had reported to the Generalissimo what was happening. The Generalissimo had replied it was impossible, it could *not* be happening. But it was.

Was Chiang lying to you? I asked. "No," said Chou. "Someone was lying to the Generalissimo. But the Generalissimo lies to a certain extent, too. The Generalissimo lies because he wants to strengthen his position among the factions. His success is in utilizing all the contradictions in the country to his own ends. The greater the contradictions in the country, the greater his power. If this tendency continues, he will be a failure."

As for the future, Chou was again clinical, and even more cold. All agreements with the central government he now considered over. The remaining ninety thousand men of the New Fourth Army would withdraw no farther; they would stay on the coast, around Nanking, around Shanghai. They would fight their own war against the Japanese. "It will be difficult to exist without supplies from the government," said Chou, "but we will do it. We will turn to the people for support." As he went on, I began to absorb the departure in his thinking, Communist thinking: There were now, in 1941, two independent governments in China fighting Japan—one the coalition government of Chiang, the other the Communist government. After the war, they would settle their differences. The gears were engaged. Matters would move to their own appointed climax.

By this time, I had long since come to know Chou En-lai. He had become a full man to me, not one of the personality cutouts with which I filled my journalistic album of famous names made live.

Now, older and wiser, and having been tugged too often by friendship and affection for men I have reported, I am as wary of friendship with the great as a reformed drunkard of the taste of alcohol. But Chou En-lai was, along with Joseph Stilwell and John F. Kennedy, one of the three great men I met and knew in whose presence I had near total suspension of disbelief or questioning judgment. In all three cases I would now behave otherwise, but most of all in the case of Chou En-lai. I can see Chou En-lai now for what he was: a man as brilliant and ruthless as any the Communist movement has thrown up in this century. He could act with absolute daring, with the delicacy of a cat pouncing on a mouse, with the decision of a man who has thought his way through to his only course of action—and yet he was capable of warm kindness, irrepressible humanity and silken courtesy. The Chinese revolution is singularly tongue-tied when it comes to words of tenderness; but even the jargon of Peking refers to Chou En-lai, and Chou En-lai alone, as "our beloved leader." He had a way of entrancing people, of offering affection, of inviting and seeming to share confidences. And I cannot deny that he won my affection completely.

Perhaps the best way of getting at the twinkling character of the man and his charm is to describe the ripening of our relationship into friendship and laughter in 1940, which climaxes at what I remember as the dinner of the pig.

I had begun to cultivate Chou even before I became *Time*'s correspondent, when I was still attached to the Chinese Ministry of Information, trying to free-lance my reporting. As a young reporter, I asked the questions that provoke the quick quotable answers we now see in television interviewing, as, for example: Q: "What did you feel at the moment?" A: "Uh . . . very upset." In the case of Chou, I began by asking: "Sir, you are a Chinese Communist. Are you more Chinese or more Communist?" Chou: "I am more Chinese than Communist." White: "Sir, Russian Communism has abolished religion; if the Chinese Communists come to power, will they abolish religion, too?" Chou: "Chinese Communists respect all religions; all forms of worship will be permitted."

But Chou had the knack that few public men have when confronted by such canned questioning—he would throw a decoy into his answer, an odd teaser of new fact. And if the questioner pursued the decoy, Chou might lead him on and on in conversation in the direction he wanted the conversation to go, to deliver his point.

In my case, Chou was amused by my preoccupation with the folklore of Chinese warlord politics; and he enjoyed himself, sometimes for hours, by his tale-telling and his instruction of this novice. Chou had much time then, for the six- or seven-man staff of the Chinese Communist headquarters in Chungking was a lonesome group; and the visit of a malleable young American reporter gave them an opportunity, as they saw it, of influencing *Time* magazine.

However it was, after a year of growing friendship, Chou En-lai invited me to a banquet in my honor. His headquarters had, presumably, a budget for reaching

American opinion; and they would use *Time*'s correspondent as a pretext to eat a meal grander than the noodles, rice, vegetables, occasional chunky meat stews they normally ate at their own mess. So we went to the finest restaurant in Chungking, the Kuan Sun Yuan, to dine—Chou, the Communist headquarters staff and myself, the only Westerner.

The reader must remember now how far I had come from home. I had learned to drink. I had had my first experience in bed with a woman and that was behind me. I knew I had been for months eating nonkosher food, but always tried to delude myself that the meats I ate were lamb, beef or chicken. This habit was my last link to family practice. I was still so pinned to Jewish tradition that to eat pig outright seemed a profanation. Chou En-lai's banquet, however, was extraordinary—first the Chinese hors d'oeuvres, both hot and cold; then the bamboo shoots and chicken; then the duck livers. And then the main course—unmistakably pig, a golden-brown, crackle-skinned roast suckling pig.

"Ch'ing, ch'ing," said Chou En-lai, the host— "Please, please," gesturing with his chopsticks at the pig, inviting the guest to break the crackle first. I flinched, not knowing what to do, but for a moment I held on to my past. I put my chopsticks down and explained as best I could in Chinese that I was Jewish and that Jews were not allowed to eat any kind of pig meat. The group, all friends of mine by then, sat downcast and silent, for I was their guest, and they had done wrong.

Then Chou himself took over. He lifted his chopsticks once more, repeated, *"Ch'ing, ch'ing,"* pointed the chopsticks at the suckling pig and, grinning, explained: "Teddy," he said (as I recall it now, for I made no notes that evening), "this is China. Look again. See. Look. It looks to you like pig. But in China, this is not a pig—this is a duck." I burst out laughing, for I could not help it; he laughed, the table laughed, I plunged my chopsticks in, broke the crackle, ate my first mouthful of certified pig, and have eaten of pig ever since, for which I hope my ancestors will forgive me.

But Chou was that kind of man—he could make one believe that pig was duck, because one wanted to believe him, and because he understood the customs of other men and societies and respected them.

At that time, Chou En-lai was only forty-three years old, and though he was isolated in Chungking, whether he knew it or not, he was at mid passage in his career. His job, as scout in the tower for Mao Tse-tung, was to keep contact with the outside world, at all costs. Later, that assignment would make him Foreign Minister, then Prime Minister of the People's Republic of China, its liaison with the entire globe. But at the moment, in Chungking, the assignment was to buffer the Communist Party and its armies from the wrath of Chiang K'ai-shek, and wheedle what aid he could from the central government for the Communist war against Japan.

He conducted this mission from a ramshackle old compound called simply No. 50, Tseng Chia Ai—the fiftieth house on the alley of the Tseng family. It was a shabby place; when it rained, the alley was ankle deep in mud, which was tracked inside all over the reception room. In the reception room were several armchairs and one sofa, spring-broken, lumpy, uncomfortable, all covered with the same coarse blue cloth worn by Chinese peasants and workers. I was to meet in the next five years in that reception room a revolving cast of characters, many of them already famous, others to become even more famous. There I met Tung Pi-wu, a pink-eyed old man, one of the legendary twelve founding fathers of Chinese Communism, who, along with Mao Tse-tung, had gathered for the party's first meeting in Shanghai in July of 1921; no one could have seemed milder, frailer, kindlier than Tung Pi-wu. There I met Yeh Chien-ying, a gay, frolicking man, already a hero for his leadership of the Canton insurrection of 1927, who was to go on to become Chief of Staff of the Red Army and then Minister of Defense; and Lin Piao, a dour man, strategist of the Red Armies that destroyed Chiang K'ai-shek in the civil wars of 1946–1949, Mao's choice for succession until 1971, when Lin struck for the mantle prematurely and was erased. The Communists did not seem to want to confide their Chungking liaison post with the government to just one man. There were always two. And always, the senior character in the Communist mission in Chungking was Chou En-lai.

The young Communists of Chou's personal staff also went on to fame. His personal favorite, and mine by far, was the most beautiful Chinese woman I ever encountered, Kung P'eng, the Christian-educated daughter of an opium-smoking warlord. She spoke not just flawless but eloquent English, and before being assigned to Chungking had been a fighting guerrilla against the Japanese in North China, a true pistol-packing heroine. Her first husband died in the guerrilla mountains of the north; in Chungking she met and fell in love with a fiery revolutionary journalist named Ch'iao Kuan-hua, who became Foreign Minister of China. I casually employed for a while, as a stringer on Communist affairs, another youngster at Chou's headquarters, called Ch'en Chia-k'ang. He, after the revolution succeeded, went on to become Ambassador to Cairo, Peking's first diplomatic mission in the Middle East, and helped forge the Third World alliance against Israel. There were several others; and those who belonged to Chou, like those who later belonged to Kennedy, were almost a family of politics—a family that came to dominate, and still tenuously monopolizes, China's relations with the outside world.

Chou had credentials rare for a Communist Chinese leader. He was, of course, to begin with, a genuine warrior, like all the other Communist leaders. He had been the insurrectionary leader of the Shanghai uprising of 1927, and barely escaped execution; then been a field commander in the civil wars from 1928 to 1934, and been wounded in battle; then marched the Long March, and skirmished in all its frays in 1934–1935—and had been carried from his horse, sick almost to death, when the Communists at the end of that march had found refuge in the hills of the northwest. There was no question of his physical courage, or his command ability, or his wounds. He did not show his hurts while I knew him, but later, as he aged, he carried his wounded left arm cocked ever more rigidly and stiffly until the day he died. But many other Communist braves could boast similar heroism and bodily punishment.

What set him apart from the others was that he was, by education, a larger man; and by temperament, an elastic man. He had come of a well-to-do mandarin family; been educated not only in an American missionary school in Tientsin, but also in Japan and in Europe; had joined the Communist Party in Europe; had come home and joined the revolution and, at the age of twenty-seven, had, though an avowed Communist, become an ally of Chiang K'ai-shek and acting political director of the Nationalists' revolutionary Whampoa Military Academy. The two had broken in the civil wars of the thirties—but it was Chou, supple enough to forget Chiang's massacres, who had arranged the release of Chiang K'ai-shek by his warlord kidnappers in the Sian incident of 1936. He could fight ruthlessly—but when the time came, Chou could give up hatred, which made him unique among Communists. He had, for example, in 1945, pleaded with friends at the American Embassy to be allowed to fly to the United States to visit Franklin Roosevelt and explain the revolution to him; he had been turned down. He had sought to have Communists included with Nationalists in the Chinese delegation to the United Nations in 1945—and been turned down by the Americans again. He had helped design the Geneva conference of 1954, which temporarily halted the Vietnam War. But at Geneva, when he extended his hand in friendship to shake that of American Secretary of State John Foster Dulles, Dulles humiliated him in public, refusing to shake the proffered hand. It was probably the most expensive display of rudeness of any diplomat anywhere, ever. Chou became a dedicated enemy of American diplomacy for many years; yet still, at the end, he broke with his Long March comrade Lin Piao, who wished to cement China's alliance with Russia. It was Chou who swung Mao's mind to accepting once more the bridge to America that he and Nixon built together. If that bridge endures in peace, it will be Chou's greatest contribution to both peoples.

This world eminence was far in the future when I first knew him. Early in our acquaintance, he would insist on speaking to me only in his choppy English. Later, he grew more relaxed; instead of appearing in his customary neatness, he would wander out to greet me, late for appointments, in baggy rumpled clothes, unshaven. He had a dark, almost Mediterranean face and coloring, and when he unwound, the face became animated with a thousand expressions as he acted out all the parts of a remembered conversation. As my Chinese continued to improve, he began to talk to me in Chinese, with Kung P'eng occasionally attending to translate the more subtle passages in my continuing course in Chinese politics.

Chou had a novelist's art of characterization, and would have made a superlative dramatist. He liked to tell stories. It is very rare that a young reporter meets a great man who has nothing at all to do except play watchman at a political outpost, and who has the human need to gossip about what he learns. Chou, if triggered properly, or if caught on the proper rainy afternoon, could spin a tale of questions and answers almost Arabic in its dialogue and casual acceptance of cruelties. Example: Several years after the New Fourth Army incident, I was trying to find out what had happened in the court murders in faraway Chinese Turkestan. The local warlord, Sheng Shih-tsai, had murdered Mao Tse-tung's younger brother (in retaliation, so Sheng Shih-tsai said, for the Communists' murder of *his* younger brother). The web of intrigue in faraway Turkestan had proved too much for me to understand even after a two-month trip to that Inner Asia desert of oases, melons, flowers and dancers, so I came to talk to Chou, as a friend. Chou relished a good political problem, and as I remember, his final analysis (with gestures) ran like this: "Why do they tell you that we [the Communists] killed his [Sheng's] brother first? We liked his brother better than we liked him. We could have killed either one, and if we had done the killing we would have killed him, not his brother. They know this and they slander us when they say we killed his brother."

The Communists' information net reached all through Chiang's government and occasionally Chou would tell me of stupidities he found particularly amusing. As, for example, Chiang's projected national mobilization bill of 1943. Chou relished that story: Ho Ying-chin, the Nationalist Minister of War, and H. H. Kung, the Nationalist Minister of Finance, had tried to collaborate in drafting a new mobilization bill that would solve the problems of each. Inflation was raging, the army was short of troops. They agreed, so said Chou, that conscription must now apply to all classes, upper, lower, middle alike. Every young man must go to war—except those who could afford 5,500 dollars in Chinese money (then worth only 250 American dollars) to buy a year's exemption. Since there were no less than *forty million* Chinese of draft age, the two cabinet ministers figured that at least thirty million would buy exemption, thus giving the finance minister billions and billions of dollars a year for his budget; and the war minister would have left a pool of ten million men to draw on. Chou acted all the parts of the dialogue, then burst out: "This is stupid, utterly stupid—but not only stupid, considering they have been in the cabinet for ten years; it shows lack of experience."

There were many such conversations. I do not know whether he was trying to persuade me, as an American correspondent, and through me, *Time* magazine, that Chiang's government was a useless one and the Communists were the wave of the future; or whether he was simply enjoying educating me. I learned much from him and finally he actually accepted his role of teacher. One day he was explaining a particularly intricate point of Chinese subterranean politics and I interrupted to finish his sentence with the answer, which was rude. But he laughed and said that now I was no longer a freshman in China, I was a sophomore and on the threshold of beginning to understand the country. I was flattered by the accolade; I do not know how many times Chou said this to foreigners, but I am told that his ultimate flattery of Secretary of State Kissinger was to tell him that he, too, was finally beginning to understand China.

I retain an irrepressible affection for Chou En-lai still, even though I know he, as any Chinese Communist, would have sacrificed me for his cause, or for the greater glory of Mao Tse-tung and the Chinese people, at any moment when persuasion failed to bring me over. Our personal relationship ended when he returned in 1943 to Communist headquarters in Yenan, the seat of the power he sought to make.

I saw him, of course, again and again in the years 1944 and 1945, but those were severe occasions which I forget, except journalistically. I would rather remember Chou the last two times I saw him, on the occasion of Richard Nixon's visit to China, many years later, in 1972.

The first glimpse of Chou on that visit was in Peking's Great Hall of the People, at a banquet of fine food and elaborate ornamentation, while the orchestra was grinding out such American favorites as "Home on the Range" to honor the American President. The main table, where sat Chou En-lai and Richard Nixon, was surrounded by a ring of lesser tables, where sat other dignitaries; and the rows of tables descended in importance the farther removed they were from the Chou-Nixon table, until they came to the tables where the American journalists, whom Nixon had invited, sat, at the far rear of the hall, which reputedly seats ten thousand. When President Nixon rose to circle the innermost ring of tables of the mighty, I thought I might sneak through the ring of American and Chinese security men at the big table where Chou En-lai sat next to Mrs. Nixon. Nixon's seat was momentarily unoccupied.

I wove my way through the tables and was abruptly stopped by agents of our American Secret Service as well as by Chinese security. I was too determined, in 1972, to accept such a rebuff cheerfully; but as it happened, Chou En-lai and Mrs. Nixon, next to him, saw my predicament simultaneously. Perhaps they were bored with their con-

versation, for I do not think that Patricia Nixon and
Chou En-lai had much in common to discuss. Simultaneously both waved to their agents to let me through, and
each, as I came forward, tried to explain to the other why
they had beckoned to me. Chou En-lai, his English by
now rusted away, could only say that I was "old friend,
old friend," pointing at me. And she, believing that I had
approached to talk with her, was saying the same thing. I
was amazed that Chou recognized me after twenty-five
years, but then I fell into my role as interpreter, trying to
interpret Mrs. Nixon to Chou En-lai, and Chou En-lai to
the President's wife. I must have hung there awkwardly
for two or three minutes, hovering over the President's
empty seat, but when Nixon returned, I fled. The conversation between Chou En-lai and Mrs. Nixon is not noteworthy.

I saw Chou for the last time seven days later, after
he flew with Nixon down to Hangchow, one of the beauty
spots of China, as San Francisco was in America, or
Carcassonne still is in France. It was a grisly afternoon,
all organized for television crews and cameras, for sym-
bolism and manipulation, with posts and positions roped
off, stakeouts set, each journalist assigned his two square
feet of observation space. My position was at the end of
one of the several moon bridges over the lake, with the
CBS and the NBC crews. Nixon and Chou strolled over
the bridge, with affected nonchalance, as if it were a
chance meeting of old friends who go walking together in
the countryside. Nixon, who noticed me first, pointed me
out to Chou, and I could not catch what he said. But
Chou tried out his English at that point, and said, "But
that is Teddy White. He has not come back to China
since the liberation." I was angry with the entire manipulative voyage; I had tried without success for twenty years
to reach Chou En-lai and ask him if I might have a visa to
revisit China, so I shot back: "It's not my fault I haven't
been able to come back." At which Chou En-lai, who
understood but no longer could speak English easily, shot
back a jest in Chinese. My command of Chinese had by
then also rusted away, so I relied on the official interpret-

er, who said that Chou En-lai had responded, "Maybe it's both our faults."

I would like to think the interpreter's translation of his riposte was authentic; it sounded like the Chou En-lai I had once known, who was amused by Westerners' efforts to understand China, yet appreciated the effort. He was willing to admit error in the old days, privately. And his public doctrine—that we Westerners could not understand China and therefore must not meddle in her affairs—was sound. He might have accepted the Kipling paraphrase of that thought: "East is East and West is West, and never the twain shall meet." But I like the way he said it better: "Maybe it's both our faults."

I was never to see Chou En-lai again after 1972, but more than thirty years before he had overlapped in my education—in timespan, influence, friendship and bitterness—with another man, who was to make that early year, 1941, memorable not only for its historic dramas but as a turning in my life.

That man was the exact contemporary in age of Chou En-lai. But just as passionately as Chou En-lai believed that the Chinese revolution was irrevocable and irrefutable, and insisted that the Chinese "government" had failed because it could not protect its people, the other passionately believed that it was the duty of the American government not only to protect its own but to reach out and protect the whole civilized world. For the next five years I would walk hand in hand with that second man in the belief that the reach of American power was limitless and the American Century upon us—for that man was my maximum boss, founder and editor of Time-Life-and-Fortune, Henry R. Luce of Chefoo, Shantung and New York, New York. I had, at that point, never met Henry Luce, but he owned my immediate future.

When Harrry Luce arrived in Chungking, in May of 1941, he was only forty-three years old, but an authentic press lord, and he knew it. Not only that. He was, in the eyes of the Chinese government, a natural resource—

almost as much a resource as the Yangtze gorges from which the government hoped to draw hydropower once they were dammed after the war. Luce was China's single most powerful friend in America, a man who had already spoken out boldly and forcefully for America's entry into the war. Luce believed, and meant to persuade America, that England's fate and China's were her own; that Fascism menaced our civilization as well as theirs. No restraint bound him in using his magazines to spread the message of his conscience.

No visitor I had seen previously in China, no eminent journalist, no diplomat, no Asian eminence, not even Jawaharlal Nehru, was received with the deference given to Luce and his wife, Clare Boothe Luce. Whisked from the airport immediately by a limousine, guest in the mansion of H. H. Kung, banqueted endlessly, sensing his own importance, Luce enjoyed all of it. He was in Chungking for the bombing that followed the day of his arrival—and delighted in it. He wanted to see more, and asked the Generalissimo for permission to visit the war fronts. He was given access almost immediately; a special plane was laid on to take him to Sian, a special train set up, with spotless seats and dinnerware, to take him to the Yellow River bend that had taken me, two years earlier, five days to reach; and he was treated to a Chinese shelling of the other side of the Japanese-held river.

Yet he was no captive of the government. His curiosity gobbled up fact after fact, and wanted more, more. Conversation with Luce, someone remarked, was like conversation with a vacuum cleaner: He could strip almost everyone clean of all they knew in a first conversation, leaving them exhausted; and the next morning he would have more questions; and more questions at the end of the day.

Luce delighted in his return to China. Only now can I imagine what it must have meant to him: a missionary lad shipped off from China to boarding school in cold New England; returning now as the most powerful opinion-maker and publisher in America, with this beauty as his wife; courted by the Christian government his father had hoped might come about in China.

One morning he commanded my presence and ordered me to get him away from the smothering government escort—and as we mounted rickshaws and sneaked off, it turned out he wanted only to practice his Chinese. He had not spoken Chinese since he was a boy growing up in a Shantung mission compound, but the tongue came back to him, and with glee at rediscovery, he commanded the rickshaw man this way and that, poked in and out of shops, examined prices and stocks, bargained in Chinese with ever-growing gusto. Another evening he canceled a banquet of state and ordered me to assemble whatever graduates of Yenching University I could find, for he wanted to dine with them. His father, Henry Winters Luce, one of the great missionary figures of the century, had helped found that university in Peking as a Christian enterprise and Luce wanted to find out what had happened to Yenching and its graduates since the Japanese occupation. He questioned the Yenching refugees about the Christian condition in China, lectured them on the joint mission of China and America in the modern world, and the evening closed with the note of chapel.

In Luce's mind, the purpose of Christ and the purpose of America joined in a most simple, uncomplicated fashion, and the purpose of both embraced the Chinese people. This emotional skew to his thinking colored all his politics and later, in the fifties and sixties, would make him one of the most vocal, and certainly the most eloquent, of the cold warriors of his time. His Americanism, his patriotism, his unquestioning loyalties, were twenty years later to become unfashionable; but along with Douglas MacArthur, he was the most vehement and instantaneous flag-waver I have ever known. He and MacArthur, though they disagreed, spoke for the dominant thought mood of their time. Luce's Christianity was simple; he reminded me of the famous Bishop Odo of Bayeux, who insisted on going forth to do battle with the Duke of Normandy's enemies and bounded across the

battlefield, wielding a mace (because his scruples forbade
him to use a sword), bashing in the skulls of the duke's
enemies with a right good will, for the greater glory of
Christ. Luce was never in doubt about right or wrong; yet
he could occasionally be persuaded of the truth of new
ideas when the facts were mobilized. But what ideas he
held, his staff was supposed to hold. I, of course, was one
of those whose skull was later bashed by Harry Luce, but
on first meeting him I was as captivated as by Chou
En-lai.

He conquered all Chungking in that ten-day visit. At
the height of his powers, burly, magnificently muscled,
bursting with energy, his overset brows frowning from
under a Panama hat, he struck Chungking like a storm.
And in that storm I was swept up. Two days before his
departure he turned to me and, in that peremptory half-
stammering speech of his, asked me if I could be packed
and ready to leave in forty-eight hours. I asked why and
he coughed out that I was going home with him to New
York. He did not ask me whether it was convenient to
leave China at that time or what my plans were. He had
decided that I was to be Far Eastern editor of *Time*. Now.
So thus, three years after graduating Harvard, I would be
returning home to my family in triumph.

We paused in Hong Kong, then stopped for two days
in Manila, where I was finally released from the fortnight
of endless questioning and interrogation as his China
expert. Then came five days of lazy flight across the
Pacific by the old Pan American Clipper, stopping each
night on the old stepping stones: Guam, Wake, Midway,
Hawaii. Each evening, at dusk when the plane landed, he
would send me out in a car to examine the island's
defenses and find out how well prepared it might be for
the war which he, and I, were sure was coming. Then, in
the morning, the interrogation again.

Of the trip home, I remember several conversations;
one was a short history of *Time* magazine, climaxing with
Luce's philosophy that *people* are important, names make
news. *Time* had been founded with a picture of a man,
"Uncle Joe" Cannon, on the cover. Even the tired busi-

nessman who reads *Fortune,* said Luce, wanted to read
about people.

The last conversation instructed me in office deport-
ment. We had by the end of the voyage home become
friends; I had been instructed to call him "Harry," as he
called me "Teddy." Then, as we were coming in to San
Francisco, he harrumphed me over, stammered again,
and said, "Teddy, you've read all this stuff in business
magazines about how the boss's door is always open to
everyone?" I said I had, and he continued, "Well, that's
not the way I run my magazines. Everybody's door is
open to me. But my door is open to people only when I
want to see them."

I remember coming in over San Francisco, after
almost three years in Asia, and marveling at the sight.
There were the automobiles on the Golden Gate Bridge
as we slipped low for the landing—shiny little things seen
from the air, yellow, red, black, and endless in procession.
What a strange, rich country it was, and so far from Asia,
and still thinking itself at peace.

I was off from San Francisco directly for Boston to
see my family again, arriving in tropical sharkskins and a
pith helmet. My family laughed at my costume; and I was
annoyed. But I loved them and told them of my promotion and they rejoiced.

But Boston was no longer home, the old ghetto no
longer my place. My place was Asia, if anywhere; or New
York, if I could not be in Asia; and so I went on to New
York, to begin work, within five days of my return to
America, in the magic circle of mid Manhattan. There the
news system of America is commanded, though the ideas
that move it are brought by strangers and wanderers like
myself from all across the world. Years later, New York
would become my home, and I would live there in another ghetto, the ghetto of men who merchandise news,
names, stories and the history of the day, and love it.

It was in the brief summer and fall of 1941 that I
first began to learn the main ways and alleys of this
new ghetto—in the chambers of *Time* magazine, in the
machinery that had grown up around Harry Luce's ideas.

There was, on that twenty-ninth editorial floor of *Time,*
more of the personality of the editor than in conversation
with him. All great editors are men able to see how
stories, episodes and personalities flow and merge one
into the other to reproduce the pattern of a world that
only their own inner eye perceives. Luce insisted that the
world, his reporters and his magazine all conform to the
pattern his perception traced over random events. What
he chose to display of his reporters' reporting was his own
personal art. He made instant history of the mosaic
fragments of his choice; and his choice in turn influenced
events in that oscillation between fact and report that
was later to fascinate me so much.

Luce was never less than warm personally—except
when he chose to be absolute autocrat and executioner.
His wife Clare would invite me to weekends with the
famous at their country home in Greenwich, where I
might meet the head of British Intelligence in the United
States, famous writers like John Gunther and Walter
Duranty, Broadway personalities, various Rockefellers.
Luce would drily instruct me as to who was whom and
who did what, enjoying both my goggle-eyed wonder and
his wife's pleasure in her great parties. But he was,
fundamentally, a very serious man. The day after Pearl
Harbor I was writing one of *Time* magazine's stories on
the episode when he stalked into my cubicle. His father,
the missionary, had just died. I was sad for him. He was
dry-eyed. He said to me, "He lived long enough to know
that now China and America are both on the same
side."

It was that particular episode, Pearl Harbor, which
released me from the lockup of the desk and the organization and the formal processing of news into story.

That Sunday afternoon I was writing a rehash of the
tensions in Asia, shaped by my conviction that, no matter
what the Japanese were saying in Washington, we would
have to fight them, when the telephone rang. One of my
office mates, James Aldridge, who later quit journalism to
write novels, lifted the phone, let it drop, and yelled,

"Jeezus Christ! The Japs are bombing Pearl Harbor; it's on the radio." We rushed to the news ticker, and it was hammering out a bulletin: *Flash ... White House Says Japs Attack Pearl Harbor.*

We went back to our office and we looked out the windows from our tower in Rockefeller Center. Down below was the jostle of a Sunday afternoon in mid Manhattan, the streets crowded with automobiles of parents showing their children the Christmas trees and holiday sights of the great city. We made paper airplanes and sent messages sailing through the air to the streets below, saying: "We are at war," or "We are at war with Japan," or "The Japanese are bombing America."

We were gleeful; I most of all. In that first hour none of us knew how badly the American fleet had been damaged at Pearl Harbor. But it was the right war, a good war, and it had to be fought and won. This is the only conviction of mine that has lasted unchanged for thirty-five years: it was better for America to have fought that war and won, than to have let the world be taken by those who killed and had no shame in killing. Or even worse, to have fought that war and lost.

For myself, I knew it meant release from the desk. I would be back in Asia, where I belonged. But now I would no longer be a sightseer. We, ourselves, were involved. That would change my view.

CHAPTER 4

Stilwell: Jockey to a Dying Horse

I was a full year away from Asia—from the summer of 1941 to the summer of 1942—and returned not as a sightseer but as a war correspondent in uniform.

Somewhere along the way the uniform itself would drag me to a commitment. But I associate the tug with the man who wore the most important uniform in Asia— Lieutenant General Joseph Warren Stilwell, Commanding General of the U.S. Forces in the China-Burma-India theater. Stilwell could not be reported as I had reported other men. He was a military craftsman and patriot, thrust unprepared into an arena of politics where no one had defined the problems and all decisions rested on unpredictables. His anguish, his tragedy were too large for my young experience then to grasp. But, as I slowly came to learn from this good man, I could see that he stood at the very junction of politics and war. That lesson took more than two years to sink in.

I had left New York after Pearl Harbor, assigned to Singapore; but Singapore and the Indies had fallen so

swiftly that my ship was diverted to Australia. From
Australia, after revisiting MacArthur, I was directed to
India, the apparent crisis point in Asia. Rommel was
closing with his Afrika Korps on Alexandria in the Middle East; the Japanese had just occupied Burma in the
Far East—and the Indians, seeing the Empire caught
between these two geopolitical pincers, recognized this
as the moment to overthrow the British Raj.

I was in India in the summer of 1942 for two
months of violence and uprisings, watching almost all
men, even the largest, borne along by events they could
do little to control. I visited Jawaharlal Nehru—eloquent,
melancholy, fatalistic—moving along to lead the uprising
he did not want, yet knew he could not halt. I visited with
Field Marshal Sir Archibald Percival Wavell, his adversary, a man already exhausted at fifty-nine, in command
of India, listlessly mouthing clichés about colonials and
empire, and moving to crush a revolt he could not understand.

The most poignant of my personal memories of
events overbearing purpose or desire came on a sweltering
August day—the morning after the Indian Congress Party
had voted revolt. I found myself riding in a column of
British Bren gun carriers through Chāndni-Chawk, the
crowded main way of Old Delhi. Our column was manned by Scotsmen, tough young soldiers from the Glasgow
slums, Labor Party all, foul-mouthed good fellows at any
level of brotherhood. They hated their effing English
officers and the effing Wogs alike, but this morning they
had no choice. The street was full of rioters, and bloody,
beaten students were waving the green-and-gold Indian
Congress banners and screaming, *"Inquulab Zindabad"*
("Freedom Forever"); from the rooftops they were heaving rocks down on us. My heart was with the rioters, but
I knew, and the young Scottish soldiers knew, that if, at
this moment, British rule was smashed and the Japanese
seized India, the war might go on forever—and, moreover, if the protesters overwhelmed us that morning, they
would tear us apart with their fingernails. But the Indian
students had no guns; and the young Scottish Socialists of

the Bren gun carriers began methodically to shoot Indians down from the rooftops, their bodies plopping into the street. In a few minutes the column had "pacified" Chāndni-Chawk, and though it was a bad day's work well done, I approved of it. For me, China was what mattered; my assignment was to get back there and report it; if India fell to revolutionaries, mutineers or the Japanese, there would be no way for America to get aid to China; and so whatever had to be done to keep the link with China had to be done.

Inevitably, thus, on my way back to China I would meet "Vinegar Joe" Stilwell, charged with the defense of the Chinese Republic.

Until this time, I had approached the famous men I reported as sightseer, trying to wheedle out of them the choice phrase, anecdote, insight or fact that would illuminate the scenery they dominated. But Stilwell was to be different. He was to be the first American shaper of events I was to observe closely—the leader as the man who must make things happen in the lives of other men. Stilwell was to be trapped in a drama he loathed; he performed superbly in this drama—but as a soldier. No one explained to him that this was a drama of politics and revolution, nor did anyone realize until too late that he had been miscast. He was the first to recognize this, and as I watched him over the next two years, the excitement lay in that recognition—that it was up to him, by his own leadership, to set policy in which command of troops was the lesser part of his responsibility.

I called to see him first in Delhi. He had flown down to India from China to see whether the August uprising would wipe out his strategic CBI rear base. When, in a few days, it was evident that the British Army could quench the mutiny, he found time to see me.

I was ushered into his office, an enormous suite at the Imperial Hotel; he was smoking a cigarette, and he scowled at me. Stilwell was then fifty-nine—wiry, ugly in the most attractive fashion, his face wrinkled and gnarled, yet full of vitality; to a stranger, a forbidding personality. I flustered my questions: I was en route back to China;

he was theater commander; I needed to write about the war. Could he give me a quick overview of the situation I would be writing about or what he planned to do? He assessed me quickly as I wriggled, put down his cigarette, decided he *would* speak to me and said:

"The trouble in China is simple: We are allied to an ignorant, illiterate, superstitious, peasant son of a bitch."

I gulped. I had never heard Chiang K'ai-shek described that way before, not even by Chou En-lai. And then Stilwell went on, bitterness exploding from him.

I did not know him then, or his honor, kindness and candor, as I came to know them later, but his bitterness, as I now reflect on it, was far more than the bitterness of just that month; it was the bitterness of his life. History had cursed him with China. Stilwell was an outstanding command soldier, an infantry tactician, a star in the U.S. Army's exercises of 1940 and 1941, George Marshall's favorite officer. But in the drowsy years before the second war, when the U.S. Army offered little challenge to a restless mind, Stilwell had become the Army's China specialist—had studied its language until he could speak and read it, traveled with warlord armies, become American military attaché in Peking during the first years of China's war with Japan.

That intellectual curiosity had now earned him this present cursed command. Two weeks after Pearl Harbor, Stilwell had been chosen to command America's first blow against Germany: he would head up Operation Gymnast, the planned landings in North Africa, preliminary to the ultimate strike at Europe. Had Stilwell held on to that assignment, his name would have been inscribed at West Point along with those of Eisenhower, MacArthur, Bradley and Patton as one of the great American soldiers of World War II. But Chiang K'ai-shek in China was, at that moment, petulant, querulous, demanding American aid, indignant as the early weeks of war revealed to him how low his China ranked in America's strategic priorities. Thus, in one of those casual Washington political decisions that so fatally shape other men's lives, it had been decided to placate Chiang K'ai-shek. A distinguished American soldier was promised to assist him—and who else but Stilwell, the Army's China expert? The North African landings were still almost a year away, while Burma was under attack and China desperate; thus Stilwell was trapped by his own past, by the expertise he had made his specialty in time of peace.

He had arrived in Asia just as Burma was falling, British and Chinese troops retreating before the Japanese assault. With no American troops of his own, Stilwell was placed in command of the Chinese divisions, whose morale was already gone. He, an American, would have authority over Chinese troops—authority even to execute officers up to the rank of major. Stilwell discovered quite soon how limited that authority was. The Chinese chief of supply on the Burma front was a General Yu Fei-p'eng, who, in the disaster, tried to use the few trucks of the Chinese Army not to evacuate retreating troops, but to evacuate all the merchandise he could grab for sale in blockaded China. Stilwell wanted Yu Fei-p'eng shot immediately but was told that was impossible; he was the Generalissimo's cousin. When, finally, the front broke totally, Stilwell had walked out on foot, a thirteen-day, 140-mile trek through jungle and mountain, and when he arrived at civilization in India, he had told his first press conference: "I claim we got a hell of a beating. We got run out of Burma and it is humiliating as hell. I think we ought to find out what caused it, go back, and retake it."

He had been finding out why ever since, and when I first met Stilwell in August of 1942, he was just beginning to understand his horrid fate. His overall responsibility had been to modernize and retrain China's armies into a real fighting force; then, specifically, his strategic duty would be to use this modernized army to break the blockade of China by cutting his way back through the Japanese occupying army of Burma; and, ultimately, to create within China a much larger force that would join the Pacific Allies in the grand assault on Japan. It was a soldier's job. But it is better to see Stilwell as the last in the long parade of missionaries, advisers, teachers, West-

erners, all of whom, for a century, had been trying to
remold the Middle Kingdom and succeeded only in disturbing it. What Stilwell was beginning to learn then,
when I first met him, was that all war at its supreme level
is dominated by politics and that no fighting army could
be created in China without changing the politics of
China.

The root of Stilwell's trouble lay in the accepted
political concept of his command: that China was a great
power, like England, Russia and America; and that
China's "government" was entitled to the same dignities,
respect and support as that of the other major Allies. This
concept of the Grand Alliance soothed and misled Chinese and American public opinion alike. But Franklin
Roosevelt was the President, responsible for realities. Sick
and ailing as he was, Roosevelt knew that a President
must set priorities, and with all the pressures of a clamor-
ous world on him, as well as war strategies, domestic
politics, Congress, Churchill, de Gaulle, Stalin and Tito,
Roosevelt set China at a very low priority in his thinking.
It was a military matter, to be handed over to military
men—with no one reaching beyond combat considerations to the problems of politics and policy. Thirty years
later, a succession of generals would all leave for Vietnam, again with no political or policy briefings on the
Asia war they must fight—and thus became blind, unlucky
failures all. Stilwell, however, was the first of American
military theater commanders to be handed an assignment
of policy and politics disguised as a combat assignment. It
was impossible to make war without politics, as Stilwell
soon learned.

The formal definition of Stilwell's assignment was
meaningless, because the two principals in the agreement
read it differently. Stilwell, the American, was to be
"chief of staff" to Chiang K'ai-shek, the Chinese "commander in chief" of this theater of Allied war. What that
meant, in Chiang's mind, was that he would tell Stilwell
what he needed; and Stilwell would order it up. Stilwell
would be like a cashier at a bank. Chiang wanted guns,
planes, gasoline, arms, supplies. His American chief of

staff would indent for these supplies in Washington, and presto, they would materialize. Over and over again in the past thirty years I have reported on frustrated allies of America, convinced of both American generosity and their own virtue, all of them feeling they knew far better than Americans how America's resources should be disposed of. But there were to be none as demanding as Chiang K'ai-shek—nor as convinced that the American "no-sayer" whom he faced directly, in this case Stilwell, was, individually and maliciously, denying him what the American people, the American press, the American government, rightfully sought to provide.

For Stilwell personally, the clash was exacerbated by Madame Chiang K'ai-shek—a beautiful, tart and brittle woman, more American than Chinese, and mistress of every level of the American language from the verses of the hymnal to the most sophisticated bitchery. Madame Chiang, always stunning in her silk gowns, could be as coy and kittenish as a college coed, or as commanding and petty as a dormitory house mother. She swished briskly into any room like a queen, and could bustle even sitting down. She was interpreter on many occasions for her husband and Stilwell, and when matters snarled, would take them into her own hands. A typical conference on supplies, which Stilwell recorded in his diary, had taken place just before he came to Delhi, when I first met him. Madame Chiang had dressed Stilwell down over the telephone that afternoon for "sabotaging" a Chinese demand for four-engine bombers and hundreds of transports; then briskly, on her own authority, she called a conference of the two top generals of the Chinese air force, Generals Chou Chih-jou and Mao Pang-chu, and two of Stilwell's own subordinate American generals, Chennault and Bissell. Then, in Stilwell's presence, she went through her shopping list. In Stilwell's words in his diary:

"How many planes do you want, Mao?" she asked. "Two hundred, with twenty percent monthly replacements." "How many do you want, Chennault?" "Three hundred, with twenty percent ditto." "All right," said

Madame Chiang, "now we'll tell Washington, and T.V.
[Soong] will put on pressure, and General Stilwell can get
busy and tell them, too." When Stilwell brought up the
limit on stocks of bombs, ammunition and gas, her reply
was, "We won't talk about that. That's your job to get it
in." Then, when the others had left, like the house mother
promising a prize to a good boy if he really was a good
boy, she added, "And we're going to see that you are
made a *full general!*" To which comment Stilwell added
in his diary: "The hell they are."

Stilwell's concept of his mission was, in the beginning, entirely different and rigidly military. His concept
was framed by George Marshall, not Franklin Roosevelt.
The superlative mind of Marshall saw the grand war in
steps. Europe and the relief of England and Russia was
first priority. Then came the Pacific, where the Navy and
MacArthur's troops would slowly close on Japan and
isolate her. Then, third, when the Navy had cleared the
ocean, the Americans would land in China and, in combination with a reorganized and retrained Chinese Army,
close on Japan, both on the mainland and at home. China
was the greatest potential pool of Allied manpower, but
that manpower had first to be trained, then re-equipped,
then committed to grand action. Stilwell's job was to
shape the Chinese armies for combat—to shape them as
the continental anvil on which the American Army, as the
hammer, could smash Japan to pieces.

It was a simple mission, although enormously intricate, and was, apparently, devoid of politics. But devoid
of politics it was not—and the story of how Stilwell was
led into those politics was the story of his disaster. If
Chinese soldiers could not fight, he would ask why.
"Why" was simple: generals stole soldiers' pay; soldiers
were not fed; they were sick; they were undernourished.
To make them combat ready again meant finding out:
Who stole their pay? Why could not incompetent generals
be relieved? Or shot? Why could the Chinese government
not use Communist troops in a crisis? After all, both were
fighting Japanese. Why did Chiang K'ai-shek deploy
200,000 of his best fighting troops not against the Jap-

anese but in blockade of the Chinese Communists? Why? Wherever Stilwell turned for two and a half years there was the same why, the same mystery. And in the end, it always came down to a question of government. An army is an expression of a society and its beliefs; each army reflects the government that sends it out to do battle. Slowly, over the years, it became apparent to Stilwell that China had a government, recognized by America, which did not govern; and as an American, Stilwell came to the awful conclusion that the government of China had to be changed if it was to be made useful to America—even if its chief of state must be shoved aside.

But that is for later.

When I flew back to China, following Stilwell, in the fall of 1942, I found that Stilwell was embroiled in yet another feud. This feud was with my old friend and messmate, the one-time Colonel Chennault of the Methodist dinner mess, now Brigadier General Claire Chennault of the Flying Tigers, commander of the U.S. China Air Task Force.

This was a thoroughly American feud, one whose shadows would reach longer and longer over the years and fashion American military doctrine—for it was a feud over instruments and purposes in war.

Brigadier General Claire Chennault was a man as rich in texture as Stilwell and probably more complicated. Stilwell was pure Yankee; strait-laced; crisp in diction. His sense of duty bound him; whatever George Marshall and the United States needed of him, he would do. Chennault was a Southerner, Texas born and bred, of French descent, as his name indicated; he was dark, almost swarthy, his face seamed with straight-up-and-down lines. Chennault talked with the normal Southern accent, but when he relaxed, as at the poker games to which I was occasionally invited, he fell back into a thick delta dialect which, to my Boston-trained ear, was almost incomprehensible.

Perhaps the only thing Chennault and Stilwell had in common, beyond their uniform, was their bitterness. Where Stilwell snarled, Chennault smoldered, and both men had been embittered by what befell able and ambitious men in the peacetime U.S. Army. That army, which counted no more than 174,000 men as late as 1939, had been regarded strategically as an American self-defense corps. But that lean and muscular United States Army of the 1920s and 1930s bred military geniuses by the dozen. Their famous names were later to run almost as long as Napoleon's roll call of marshals. In the pinchpenny military of those days, all officers, army or air corps, had to be skilled craftsmen, sparing of manpower and matériel. For some—Eisenhower, Bradley, Stilwell, Clay, Gavin—service of flag and country was primary. Others—like Patton and Chennault—served chiefly for love of the craft, possessed by their fascination with instruments. Chennault's craft was airpower, and his bitterness, like that of Billy Mitchell, his superior, rose from his long and losing struggle to break through budget and bureaucracy to prove what air power could deliver in war. Retired in 1936, he took his skills to China as a mercenary to build Chiang's air force. His master stroke was to organize the American Volunteer Group, the snouts of whose P-40s were painted with the Flying Tiger insignia and who dazzled the world with their performance in the Burma campaign. When Stilwell took command in the early spring of 1942, Chennault was already a figure of world fame.

Stilwell and Chennault despised each other, but their feud was not merely personal. They fought over a conceptual difference about war, a conceptual difference which to this day splits all American defense and war plans. It was the concept of ground war as against the concept of air war.

I backed into the feud inadvertently. *Time* magazine had directed me in early 1943 to write a field study of Chennault, out of which they would carve the story that would run with his portrait on the cover as an authentic hero of America's war. By then the Stilwell-Chennault feud could not be ignored.

I began by asking Chennault, off the record, as an

old friend from Chungking days, where and how his great feud with Stilwell had begun. "That whorehouse of mine," he said obliquely, "that's worrying me" (so my notes recorded him as saying). "The boys have got to get it, and they might as well get it clean as get it dirty." From that to the story of his first breach with Stilwell —over a whorehouse! Chennault's early strategy in 1942—how puny and minuscule it now seems in after-look!—rested on a strike force of less than eighty planes. But sometimes as many as half his planes might be grounded by accidents of casual copulation—ground and air crews both being hospitalized for infections acquired in Kunming's famous Slit Alley. Venereal disease reduced Chennault's combat effectiveness as if his planes had been bombed on the ground. Intolerable. Thus, since he could not pen up his young Americans in stockades, he must recognize their appetites, yet protect their health to keep his planes flying. Therefore Chennault had sent a U.S. Air Corps plane, with a medical crew aboard, over the "Hump" (the spurs of the Himalayas) to India, where twelve nondiseased Indian prostitutes had been inspected, medically cleared and recruited for the service of the China Air Task Force; and had flown them back in an American plane to our forward strike base, where the air and ground crews might dally with them and not be infected. I had never heard of the episode. What was more important, Stilwell had not authorized it, and ex-ploded when he heard of it. Stilwell was the theater commander; he was a puritan. Stilwell knew that the Japanese had whorehouses for their troops; the Prussians had whorehouses for their troops; the French had whore-houses for their troops. But not the U.S. Army, goddamn it; the U.S. Army would not fly whores across the Hump in Air Corps planes; it established no brothels for its men. Chennault wanted only to keep his planes flying and would do anything necessary to keep them in the air, to deliver his message with bombs. Stilwell had the morality of Oliver Cromwell—he was pure, absolutely pure, of graft, adultery, lying, thieving, or any transgression of the Ten Commandments. Such men served the United States Army in those days. Both were necessary—but Chennault had to close down his whorehouse.

The episode was both amusing and trivial; but it served to set off the difference in the two characters, both of them American absolutists. And the two characters colored a far greater and infinitely more important difference: a difference in the concept of war and power, a difference that has run through American geopolitical strategy for all the years since.

Chennault was an absolutist of air power. He believed, and in this he was proven correct, that air power could destroy Japan. Though he was never to participate in the great holocaust over Japan's burning cities, he knew Japan was uniquely vulnerable from the air. And he knew that he, with his few planes, was uniquely situated on the plateau of Southwest China to hit Japan's naked and exposed rear. In 1942 and 1943 he was the only American commander—except the U.S. submarine commanders—who could reach Japan's interior sea lanes. For Chennault, China was simply a platform, speckled with the bases from which his planes could take off to rowel Japan. His was a surgical concept of war, China a table for his instruments.

No one could have been more pleased by Chennault's concept of war than Chiang K'ai-shek. Chennault's message to the Chinese was simple: Get Washington to give me enough planes, and I will destroy Japan as you rest from your exertions. Chennault and the Chinese in Washington thus became palace allies at the White House, to overturn the strategy of Chennault's nominal superior, theater commander Stilwell.

Where Stilwell broke with Chennault, intellectually, was in his practical assessment of where Chennault's air strategy might lead. Stilwell was convinced that if Chennault's air strikes punished the Japanese as severely as promised, the Japanese would have to react. If Chennault ripped out Japan's interior sea lanes, the Japanese would have to protect their entrails by striking at the American air bases in East China—and the Chinese armies defending those bases simply could not hold. Stilwell was as absolute as Chennault in his insistence on the need for battleworthy, motivated Chinese ground forces. Thus, then, it appeared imperative to Stilwell that he first build such Chinese armies, equipping and training them to fight Japanese. To Chennault this strategy appeared not only of insufficient daring, but also stupid: he, Chennault, had the opportunity no other Allied general then possessed to gut-punch the Japanese where they were most vulnerable; the opportunity must be used.

The argument between the two generals, like the argument between the British (Montgomery) and the Americans (Bradley, Patton) in the fall of 1944, hinged on supplies. The quarrels of warriors usually begin with the accounting of supplies, and only later escalate to matters of spirit and politics, but the accounting of supplies in China was particularly grotesque.

From the spring of 1942 on to the spring of 1945, all the supplies for beleaguered China, and all its forces, both American and Chinese, came in over the Hump. When one flew the Hump, it was high romance—sorties of blockade runners, little C-47s and later C-46s, ducking Japanese planes by darting into mountain-stuffed clouds, a handful of American boys, itching, scratching, sick, malarial, sometimes cracking under the strain they said made men "hump-happy." ("Yonder lies Tibet," they would say, pointing out snow-topped landmarks.)

But on the ledgers of war they were simply cargo carriers of the Air Transport Command, and their cargo was the substance of a bookkeeper's quarrel. Hump flights had started in April of 1942, after the Japanese seized Burma and blocked the land route. From eighty tons a month the lift figure rose to three hundred tons a month by fall; then jumped with increasing manpower and planes to three thousand tons a month by early 1943. Two or three thousand tons a month, however, at the time of the great Chennault-Stilwell quarrel, was nothing. China had 500 million people; an army of at least four million and possibly twice that number, for no one knew; a war industry with endless needs; and an inflation which alone demanded an airlift of hundreds of tons of paper currency, printed in America. Thus Chiang K'ai-shek needed all the tonnage for himself. But Chennault also needed all the tonnage or more just to keep his strike command flying. And Stilwell, too, needed all of it or more to retrain and re-equip the Chinese armies for George Marshall's strategy. "Trying to manure a ten-acre field with sparrow shit" is what Stilwell called his nominal responsibility for dividing the cargo among all claimants. When, in February of 1943, the old cargo carriers had threaded the Himalayan corridors with 3500 tons of supplies, Chennault had been promised 850 tons for his air force; he had received only 330 tons. "I lie awake at night, dreaming gasoline," he said to me. "My stomach is getting nervous. I used 40,000 gallons this past ten days, and I got only 17,000 gallons in." There was no way of satisfying Chennault's appetite; nor Chiang's; nor Stilwell's.

By May of 1943, Franklin D. Roosevelt had to intervene in the three-way dispute. Both Stilwell and Chennault were summoned to Washington, where the supreme American warlord made the grand decision. The quarrel between Stilwell and Chennault, with Chiang K'ai-shek backing Chennault, seemed simple—a matter of tonnages. A technical solution to a political problem is always seductive, and the British, the Chinese and the palace strategists of Roosevelt all agreed that Chennault's way was easiest. Roosevelt thus decided that 10,000 tons a month must immediately be shipped over the Hump; told that it was impossible, he decreed 7,000 tons a month must be airlifted in July, rising to 10,000 by year end. Chennault promised that with enough tonnage he could sink 500,000 tons of Japanese merchant shipping by Christmas, ten percent of all Japan possessed; and in return was promised 4,500 tons of Hump supplies for his air force alone, with Chiang and Stilwell left to squabble over the remainder. At the game of palace politics Stilwell was hopelessly outsmarted. "My point [to Roosevelt]," wrote Stilwell in his diary after the May conference, "was that China was on the verge of collapse economically. . . . That the first essential step was to get a ground force capable of seizing and holding air bases, and opening communications to China from the outside world. . . . They [Chennault's planes] will do the Japs some damage, but at the same time will so weaken the ground effort that it may fail. Then what the hell use is it to knock down a few Jap planes?"

But Chennault had his way, and, by the end of the war, claimed to have sent to the bottom two million tons of Japanese shipping. His was, without doubt, one of the spectacular feats of the Pacific war, yet there remains in my mind, still, the thought that if Stilwell had had his way, the Communists might not have won China—or if they had, would have won as our allies or at least not regarded us as enemies.

Looking back now, I can see in the Chennault strategy—as in the strategy of Curtis LeMay and H. H. ("Hap") Arnold—one of the roots of America's formidable, yet musclebound, strength. Airpower was so tempting a concept: swoop and strike; let economists set the strike targets. To fight from the air is so clean and so logical—as neat a form of combat as football, where the goal posts and markers are clearly defined on the gridiron. The concept of American air power as the most American form of superiority continued for decades, until the final disaster in Vietnam.

I was among those early seduced by airpower in World War II, and not simply out of my friendship with Claire Chennault. True, he had befriended me years earlier, when I was lonely in Chungking and he self-exiled. True, he favored me and let me fly on any mission liable to make a good story whenever I asked to join the bombers. But he was an extraordinarily persuasive man in his mumbling way. If total victory was sought, total annihilation of the enemy's cities and production lanes was necessary. The plane was the instrument, in Japan as in Germany. What other purpose was there in a war, Chennault would ask, except to get the enemy? Chennault loved the instruments.

I would not say that it was Stilwell who persuaded me otherwise—nor can I say when it was that I went over to Stilwell's side of their argument. Perhaps my shift began with the questions that grew in my mind. What if the purpose of war is not just to "get the enemy," but to defend what one sets out to defend as well? What if the preservation of a plateau of resistance depends as much on politics as on armies? What if those politics are more important than immediate combat opportunities? What if you lose what you began to defend by the manner of winning?

These were quite unshaped questions in my mind in the spring of 1943, although they had begun to nag. I was no longer a sightseer nor yet a Harvard historian. I was in uniform, my own brothers (one in the Pacific, one in Europe) were actually in the fight, pawns in the game I wrote about. Even as a correspondent, I was being forced to take a position, as most correspondents knowingly or unknowingly do. Without any pressure at all from Stilwell, I now know I was coming down on his side against Chennault. I was beginning to believe that the Chinese government was totally incapable of governing. China was not just a platform, from which we exercised our instruments; China was There. In and of itself it was enormous, mystifying, cruel—and it was as much our purpose to befriend what was decent in these changing people as to use their territory as a platform to destroy Japan. In the long shaft of afterlight, I now see what Stilwell was trying to do. He was trying to find a responsible government to deal with—a task that should not be forced on generals in uniform.

It was the Honan famine that transferred me from agreement with Chennault to commitment to Stilwell. It should have taught me, even then, how hopeless Stilwell's task was, and how he would come to his end. Yet what the famine taught me immediately was more than that: it taught me of anarchy and order, of life and death. Of all marks on my thinking, the Honan famine remains most indelible.

It happened in the winter of 1943.

The scene, Honan, was a province about the size of Missouri, but inhabited by thirty-two million peasants, who grew wheat, corn, millet, soybeans and cotton. Honan was not a backward province like mountainous Shansi or a Westernized province like coastal Kiangsu. It was a fine, flat plain, resembling Iowa in its rolling sweep, except that the soil was not the rich black loam of the Iowa prairie, but powdered yellow loess which, when wet with rain, oozed with fertility. And which, when the rains did not come, grew nothing; then the peasants died. The rains had not come in 1942, and by 1943, Honan peasants, we heard in Chungking, were dying.

Famines come and go in China's history. They are like earthquakes or hurricanes or the changes of dynasty. Men dated family histories by famines. But what a famine was, I did not know—nor did I know that the Honan famine of 1943 was one of the worst in modern history. But it sounded as if it would make a story.

So, then, at the end of February 1943, I flew to North China again (with my friend Harrison Forman of the London *Times*), and won permission to travel the Lunghai railway from Paochi through Sian to the gap. The gap was the pass through which the Yellow River flowed and the railway ran. Here, the Japanese artillery on the north bank of the Yellow River would sporadically shell the rail line on the southern bank and deny exit through the pass, which was the main entry to Honan.

The station at the gap, where we spent the evening, stank of urine, stank of shit, stank of bodies—and all around us were acres of huddled peasants. The peasants were bundles of flesh lying in the cold on the ground, waiting for the next train to take them east, to the rear area and food. Some were swathed in blankets, some in padding. Many wrapped their heads in towels against the cold or, occasionally, wore a fur hat, earmuffs down. They had fled in their best clothes, and the old bridal

costumes of middle-aged women, red and green, smeared
with filth, flecked the huddle with color. They had fled
carrying of their best only what they could—black kettles,
bedrolls, now and then a grandfather clock. What they
could sell, they were exchanging for paper money, or
bargaining away at the food stalls, which cooked rice or
meat over charcoal fires, spitting blue flame when the box
bellows were pumped. Babies cried; but no one paid any
attention, even if a baby was crying in the arms of a
lifeless woman lying on the ground. Soldiers patrolled the
mob as if they were cattle—else they would have stam-
peded for the food or to board the trains which rolled at
night.

In the morning a handlebar car was ready for us.
The Japanese shelled only real trains; three refugee trains
a night made it across the gap, but a pumpcar, with two
soldiers at each handle, was too small a target for the
Japanese to shoot at by daylight. And thus, bundled in a
soldier's padded robe, seated in the cold wind on an open
pumpcar, I traveled thirty miles that day as if I were in a
box at the opera, or a general reviewing his troops. But I
was reviewing a famine.

There was, of course, much blood. But blood is not
what marks a famine. The blood was from the debris of
the refugee trains, the people who had fallen off the
flatcars, or fallen from the rooftops of boxcars because
their fingers froze on the night run and the numbed
fingers could not hold their grip. First a man, lying by the
rail line, still alive, crying, with his leg severed at the shin
and the shinbone sticking out like a white cornstalk. He
must have fallen under the wheels of the train. Then
another man, still alive, his hip mangled and bloody. I
forced the pumping soldiers to stop the car this time; but
I did not know what to do, and so gave the man sulfa-
nilamide, water, money, and promised to find a doctor to
send to him.

The blood, as I say, was not my chief distress; it was
my inability to make any sense of what I was seeing. In a
famine, where no one kills but nature, there are no marks
on the body when people die; nature itself is the enemy—

and <u>only government can save from nature.</u> I could not understand this at the beginning.

All day, along the railway tracks, as far as I could see, trailed an endless procession—solitaries, beads of families, or groups. They walked in the cold, and where they dropped of hunger or cold or exhaustion, there they lay. There were the wheelbarrows, piled high with family goods, father pushing, mother pulling, children walking. Sometimes between the shafts of the wheelbarrow hung a babypouch, with the baby peering black-eyed up into the cold; sometimes fathers hung their babies from pouches around their necks, papoose fashion; old ladies hobbled with bound feet; sometimes young men carried their mothers piggyback on their shoulders. No one stopped in the trudging procession on either side of the tracks. If children cried over the body of a father or a mother, they were passed, soundlessly. Some young men rode bicycles, other carried all their possessions slung over their shoulders on sticks like Huck Finn. I was seeing people in full flight where no armed man pursued.

I was glazed with the sight when I arrived in Loyang, the provincial capital of Honan; and there at the station, in the dark, they were packing refugees into boxcars like lumber, stacking them together so they could not move, cursing them aboard the car roofs, with fathers hauling children up by the hand, dangling like packages, as they swung aloft for the night run over the gap. And again, the stink of urine and bodies; then through the deserted streets to the Catholic mission.

Its master was Bishop Thomas Megan, of Eldora, Iowa, a stocky, cheerful, healthy man, devoutly Catholic and American. I learned in the next two weeks that he was not only a good man but an effective one, for he was my thread to the Christian missionaries, and the Christian missions were the only connection to reason as I understood it. The Christian missionaries had come to spread the gospel—in rivalry. But buried in the gospel is a message of kindness. Now, in this theater of death, the missionaries were partners in charity, Americans joining with Europeans, Catholics with Protestants. Megan was

Irish-American Catholic; two Italian Catholics, Father
Fraternelli and Dr. Danielli were his liaison in Chengchow; and though Americans and Italians were killing
each other in Europe, here in Honan they were united in
charity. In Chengchow, the Italian Catholics were joined
by Mr. Ashforth, an American fundamentalist, in their
hopeless struggle against desolation. What outside relief
came in, came through the missionaries; and where we
located them on our travels they were beleaguered, with
crowds around mission compounds, children and women
sitting at their gates, babies dumped each morning at their
threshold to be gathered into makeshift orphanages. Missionaries left their compounds only when necessary, for a
white man walking in the street was the only agent of
hope, and was assailed by wasted men, frail women,
children, people head-knocking on the ground, groveling,
kneeling, begging for food, wailing, *"K'o lien, k'o lien"*
("Mercy, mercy"), but pleading really only for food. The
handful of missionaries who staked out the Christian
underground in the area of famine were the only thread of
sense—the sense that life is precious.

Of their nobility there was no doubt; also of their
futility. Ever since Caesar and Christ delivered their messages to Western civilization, government has rested on
order and mercy. The Christians wished to deliver mercy;
but what they tried to do was futile because government
provided no order.

With Megan, we set out on horseback through the
winds of February and March, because he felt we should
see the people dying. As he rode ahead, he chanted—and
he taught me to say the Pater Noster in Latin each
morning. In one abandoned Catholic chapel in a deserted
village, overborne by tragedy, I kneeled for mass and felt
no profanation of my own heritage. On the road, to keep
my spirits up, Megan taught me to sing the Requiem for
the dead: *"Requiem aeternam,"* he would sing out, and
when I got it right, he would teach the next phrase:
"Dona eis, Domine"; and so on. Then we would sing
together, in responsive verses, he from his leading horse, I
from the following horse, mourning over what we saw.

What we saw, I now no longer believe—except that my scribbled notes insist I saw what I saw. There were the bodies: the first, no more than an hour out of Loyang, lying in the snow, a day or two dead, her face shriveled about her skull; she must have been young; and the snow fell on her eyes; and she would lie unburied until the birds or the dogs cleaned her bones. The dogs were also there along the road, slipping back to their wolf kinship, and they were sleek, well fed. We stopped to take a picture of dogs digging bodies from sand piles; some were half-eaten, but the dogs had already picked clean one visible skull. Half the villages were deserted; some simply abandoned, others already looted; spring compost rested in heaps, untended. To hear a sound or see a person in such a village was startling: an old man tottering through the street all by himself; or, in another village, two women shrieking at each other with no one else in sight, where normally there would be a crowd to watch them scold— and what were they arguing about in death? One saw, as one traveled, people chipping bark from trees, with knives, scythes and meat cleavers. They were stripping bark from all the elms that warlord Wu P'ei-fu, the tree-lover, had planted, because you could grind the bark and eat it.* The trees would then die and be chopped down for firewood; perhaps all China had been deforested that way.

The orphanage of central government General Tang En-po stains memory with its smell. Tang En-po was an

---

*In a famine, almost anything becomes edible and can be ground, consumed and converted to energy by the human body. But it requires the terror of death to provoke the imagination to eat what, hitherto, is unedible. Ground elm bark, apparently, was edible, as were ground straw and chaff, roots and scum algae, if dried. What the peasants did was to dry out anything that seemed to be alive, then grind it, and bake it in hotcakes. The doctor of the Italian Catholic mission in Chengchow gave me a nauseating clinical description of the obstructions, illnesses and absorption processes of the human body as he saw inoperable peasants carried to his clinic. Cottonseed cake, of all the inedibles, was, apparently, the most nutritious food; but it created intestinal obstructions and reactions difficult to comprehend.

able general; he had fought well in his first two years of
war, 1937–1939, hated Japanese, was loyal to the cause.
The perimeter of the war area to which he had now been
promoted ran along the line between the belt of famine
and the belt of Japanese occupation. Tang was, I think, a
good person. He forced all his officers to accept one
famine orphan each in their quarters; all his soldiers'
rations were cut one pound a month to give the extra
pound to the starving. Also, he had ordained this orphanage, which I was invited to visit. It stank worse than
anything else I have ever smelled. Even the escorting
officer could not stand the odor and, holding his handkerchief to his nose, asked to be excused. These were
abandoned babies. They were inserted four to a crib.
Those who could not fit in cribs were simply laid on the
straw. I forget what they were fed. But they smelled of
baby vomit and baby shit, and when they were dead, they
were cleared out.

So I saw these things, but the worst was what I
heard, which was about cannibalism. I never saw any
man kill another person for meat, and never tasted human flesh. But it seemed irrefutably true that people were
eating people meat. The usual defense was that the people
meat was taken from the dead. Case after case which we
tried to report presented this defense. In one village a
mother was discovered boiling her two-year-old to eat its
meat. In another case a father was charged with stran-
gling his two boys to eat them; his defense was that they
were already dead. A serious case in one village: the
army had insisted that the peasants take in destitute
children and an eight-year-old boy had been imposed on a
peasant family. Then he disappeared. And on investigation, his bones were discovered by the peasant's shack, in
a big crock. The question was only whether the boy had
been eaten after he died or had been killed to be eaten
later. In two hours in the village, we could not determine
the justice of the matter; anyone might have been lying;
so we rode on.

What appalls me most, as I read back into my past
and the notes of my trip, written each evening, is my

increasing callousness. At first I was frightened; and of course, the matter was too large for grief. But then I became increasingly hard. Riding a horse through a cluster of beggars lying in wait for you in a village street was a serious matter, dangerous. If you stopped, they might tear the horse down and eat it, and then you yourself would be left on foot with the starving. So I learned to flog my horse to a gallop through any cluster of people, sometimes whipping hands off, sometimes throwing out handfuls of peanuts or dried persimmons to make a safe getaway, and sometimes casting Chinese dollars into the wind to decoy them with paper. My notes became less colorful, more analytical, more statistical, as I tried to find out what happened.

Chengchow was the epicenter of the famine and also the seat of the Italian Catholic mission. The snow was falling as we came into Chengchow, a powder snow, and it was falling on the hunger-stricken who slept in the courtyard of the mission. The snow continued next day as we continued our inspection on a walk through the city. There had been 120,000 people in Chengchow before the war; now its population was down to something over 30,000. Each day, the count of the dead ran between 150 and 180 corpses. And those who remained fluttered through the streets in rags, like scarecrows, whining and crying, or stumbling in silence. Nor was it always easy to tell the quick from the dead. One saw a wheelbarrow trundled through the snow, and the body on it was jiggling as it bumped; but then one realized that the flopping of the hands and legs was mechanical, and it was a dead body being carried off for dumping. We found a man in the gutter and Father Fraternelli shook him to see whether he was alive; the man stirred under the snow and murmured. We pressed paper dollars into his hands; his fingers curled on the bills, and then uncurled. We got him to his feet, and he staggered, so we were stuck with him. A woman with a crying baby came by and we conscripted her with money to help us—to help the man to the mission compound, where he could lie in the courtyard and might be fed. She tried to help him, but her baby fell;

then she lifted the baby again, and supported the leaning man, and they wandered off to the mission station, while we went on to the relief station, where the missionaries had organized food. Food was sacks of flaked bran, and with the proper tickets the supplicants would get enough bran to give them six ounces a day till the next handout. But since it was obvious that there was not enough bran for all those in line, we left before the expected riot broke out.

From then on, I tried to work my mind, rather than my emotions, to understand what had happened.

What had happened became slowly clear; and anywhere on the chain of linking causes one could become morally indignant. The war was the first cause. If the Japanese had not made war, then the Chinese would not have had to cut the dikes of the Yellow River to stop them by switching the river's course. Then, perhaps, the ecology of North China would not have changed. Or, perhaps, food might have been packed in from food-surplus areas. But in addition to the war had been the drought. That was nature's guilt. Rains had not come in 1942, and so the fields had not produced their normal wheat and millet. At this point, men had become guilty—either for what they did or for what they failed to do. And here, then, I found my indignation point—at what purported to be the government of China; or at the anarchy that masqueraded as government. For though the famine had come from the heavens, in the worst drought since the reign of Emperor Kuang-hsu in 1893, death might have been avoided had government acted. But this death was man-made.

Night after night, I wrote up my notes after talking to local officials, as a political pollster writes up his notes in America today. And the only verdict was that the Chinese "government" had let these people die, or ignorantly starved them to death. The government was fighting a war against Japan; it was relentless in collecting taxes for the war. But since it did not trust its own paper money, its armies in the field were instructed to collect taxes in grain and kind for their own support. ("If the people die," said an officer to me, "the land will still be Chinese. But if the soldiers starve, the Japanese will take the land.") What the army had done in Honan was to collect more in grain taxes than the land had raised in grain. They had emptied the countryside of food; they had shipped in no grain from grain-surplus areas; they had ignored the need of the people to eat.

Technically, I began to compile statistics *in minimo,* noting the yield of wheat per *mu* wherever I could find a peasant willing to talk. A *mu* is one sixth of an acre and I would ask how many pounds per *mu* the peasant had raised. Eight pounds? Twelve pounds? Twenty pounds? The army's tax, I found, was usually equivalent to the full crop, but in some cases it was higher—and where the grain tax was higher than the yield, peasants were sometimes forced to sell animals, tools, furniture, for cash to make up the difference. Moreover, the peasants were required to feed the army's animals when they marched; and though I was told that peasants generally cheated and lied to officials, nonetheless, said one civilian official of his peasants, "It's very hard to make them give grain to army horses when I know they're eating straw themselves." And then came the tax for the civilian government officials. Each civilian official was allotted four and a half pounds of grain a day to feed his family, however large; and in army units soldiers were supposed to get two pounds a day. Where units were under strength, army storehouses bulged with surplus grain—which officers sold for their own profit, and which missionaries and good officials bought from the black market to feed the starving.

One night, I sat at an army headquarters, the safest place to be, and several peasant officials asked entrance to see the foreigners. The room was heated by charcoal pans and lit by candles. The local officials held papers in their hands which they asked us to deliver to Chiang K'ai-shek in Chungking—an accounting of what their district had grown and what it had paid in taxes. Of their county of 150,000 people, 110,000 had absolutely nothing to eat; about 700 a day, they guessed, were dying. We asked one of them whether he owned land. Yes. How much? Twenty *mu*. His harvest last fall? Fifteen pounds per *mu*. His tax? Thirteen pounds per *mu*. The commander became furious and yelled at the local official, who then handed him a copy of the plea he had written for us. The officer pocketed it. Then he demanded that we yield him our copy. I said no. He said yes. It was very ugly for a minute; then I gave him the papers, because we had nowhere else to go if he threw us out into the night; and if we refused, his anger would be vented on the peasants when we passed on.

Statistically, putting it together, county after county, village after village, it appeared to us that in the forty worst-hit counties still lived eight million people. And then there were fringe counties, where others were dying. Extrapolating from sights we had seen and the figures of death that local officials had given us, we could guess two or three million people had fled on the refugee trail; and another two million had died. We calculated that since we stood there in March, and the new crops. if they came through normally, would not come through until May and June, another two or three million would die. I concentrated my last week in the famine area on estimating figures. My best estimate was five million dead or dying— which may have been twenty percent off the mark, one way or the other. But figures that large become statistics, thus forgettable. My sharpest memory is not of the figures I assembled, nor even of our own callousness in the probing of the disaster, but a glimpse, at evening as we were riding, of two people lying in a field sobbing. They were a man and his woman, and they were holding each other in the field where they lay, intertwined to give warmth to each other. I knew they would die and I could not stop; but it seemed to me that it was a loving if tragic way to end a hopeless life, curled with one's wife against the cold and the indifferent world, on hard soil, in snow, still committed to each other.

What I saw was anarchy. Anarchy is a condition where no order prevails. The government in faraway Chungking had decided in October that it would remit the

Honan grain tax. This was either ignorance or hypocrisy, for the locals had already collected the grain tax of the fall harvest of 1942 and, thus, the central government was remitting the tax on next year's crop, not yet even in sight. The government in Chungking had appropriated two hundred million paper Chinese "dollars" for famine relief in Honan but had shipped in only some eighty million, and that in hundred-dollar bills, to the famine area. The government banks, however, would discount their own currency; for a one-hundred-dollar bill, they would give back only eighty-three dollars in small bills—singles, fives and tens.

Some army commanders sold the surplus food of their troops to refugees, and made fortunes. But some unit commanders put their troops on half rations or, like Tang En-po, set up army orphanages for young children. Some civilian officials deducted taxes due before giving peasants their handout. Other officials wept with shame. There was no administrative control to enforce what the nominal government said should be done to help the peasants.

Fundamentally, there was no idea that could embrace what was happening—no idea, even a Chinese idea, that could hold human beings together. Compassion, kinship, customs, morals, were swept away. Families sold their children; nine-year-old boys brought four hundred Chinese dollars, four-year-old boys two hundred dollars. Adolescents husky enough fled from home to join the army, where they could be fed; brothelkeepers came from the outside to buy girls.

Food was the only idea, hunger the only command. Food was currency, and the greedy used it like a club. Speculators now came in early spring with their own sacks of food and paper money to buy up land. Land that yielded up to twenty or thirty pounds of wheat per *mu* could be bought, and was being bought, for the equivalent of sixteen to eighteen pounds of wheat in outright spot payment.

One could hold on to reason only by identifying, here or there, the individual officers or officials or leaders who were senselessly trying to do good. In Chengchow an official gave refugee families a red-ink chop on a patch of cloth, which entitled them to free passage on the railway to the east—if they could get to the railhead. But he had no food to give them with the passage patch. Even at their best, people were cruel. On the fringe of the famine area was a military academy for young officer trainees, and several were so carried away by the general barbarism that they had looted an abandoned village. This infuriated their commander, Hu Tsung-nan, and he ordered that three of the young looters be buried alive in sand. Which was done.

It is easy to recreate from my notes an animal theater. But these were not animals. These were people descended from one of the great cultures of the world; even the most illiterate had grown up celebrating the festivals and rituals of a culture that set order above all else. If they could not find order from their own kind, they would accept order from whoever offered it. Had I been a Honan peasant I would have acted as they did when, a year later, they went over to the Japanese and helped the Japanese defeat their own Chinese troops. And I would have, as they did in 1948, gone over to the conquering Communists. I know how cruel Chinese Communists can be; but no cruelty was greater than the Honan famine, and if the Communist idea promised government of any kind, then the ideas of mercy and liberty with which I had grown up were irrelevant.

I chose to return from the north by an old green postal bus, tracing again my 1939 route over the mountains—and there again was the spectacle of the peaceful interior in springtime, the white of apple blossoms, the pink of the cherry trees, the deep rose of the peaches. In Szechwan, the barley was already ripe for harvesting, the wheat dark green and coming to head, the lowland paddies pooled with water just before the rice planting. Honan and the dead were beyond the range, only a few hundred miles away; but here men were insulated from the horror and no one knew.

In Chungking, literally no one had any sense of dimension about what was happening in Honan. By the time layer upon layer of officials in Honan had covered their tracks, and layer upon layer of reports had been softened on their way up to Chungking, not even Chiang K'ai-shek knew there was anything more than a food shortage for which he had appropriated two hundred million dollars in paper money.

I was uncontrollably indignant as I tried to reach Chiang K'ai-shek with the story: I ran about screaming, in almost insane fashion, "People are dying, people are dying." And I probably would have screamed bootlessly had not the general anarchy up there in Honan let the American press be accidentally mobilized. So impatient had I been to get the story out from the famine area that I had filed it raw from Honan, from the first telegraph station en route home—Loyang. By regulation, like any press dispatch, it should have been sent back via Chungking to be censored by my old companions in the ministry, who would certainly have stopped it. This telegram, however, was flashed from Loyang to New York, via the commercial radio system in Chengtu. Either the system had broken down, or some unknown telegraph key-tapper at the Loyang telegraph office had been pushed by conscience to scoff at regulations and route the dispatch to New York, direct and uncensored. Thus, when the story broke, it broke in *Time* magazine, of all places—the magazine most committed to the Chinese cause in all America. Madame Chiang K'ai-shek was then in the United States, and the story infuriated her; she asked my publisher, Harry Luce, to fire me; but he refused, for which I honor him. Our own quarrel would come later.

In Chungking I became controversial overnight; I was denounced by some officials for avoiding censorship, and accused by others of having plotted with Communists in the telegraph administration to slip my story out. I reported to Stilwell through army intelligence. I reported to the American Embassy. I reported to the Chinese defense minister (who told me, baldly, that either I was

lying or others had lied to me). I besought help from the
head of China's powerless legislature, who said that only
Chiang K'ai-shek could act; I was told the same by the
governor of Szechwan, a kindly man. It took five days to
get through to Chiang K'ai-shek, and then only with the
help of his sister-in-law, the sainted widow of Dr. Sun
Yat-sen. She had family rank, being one of Madame
Chiang K'ai-shek's older sisters, and it was she who
insisted the dictator receive me. Madame Sun Yat-sen
was physically a dainty woman, but her spirit was hardened by the revolutions she had lived through. She stiffened me for the meeting with a last note, in which she set
up the appointment. " . . . I was told," see wrote me,
"that he [Chiang] was very weary after his long tedious
inspection tour and needed a few days rest. But I insisted
that the matter involved the lives of many millions. . . .
May I suggest that you report conditions as frankly and
fearlessly as you did to me. If heads must come off, don't
be squeamish about it . . . otherwise there would be no
change in the situation."

Chiang received me in his dark office, standing erect
and slim, taut, holding out a stiff hand of greeting, then
he sat in his high-backed chair, listening to me with
visible distaste because his meddling sister-in-law insisted
he had to. I talked of the dying; then of the taxes; then of
the extortions. He denied that the peasants were being
taxed: he had ordered that taxes be remitted in distress
areas. I quoted peasants, and he said to one of his aides,
"K'an wai-kuo jen, shuo le" ("They see a foreigner and
tell him anything"). It was obvious he did not know what
was going on. I tried to break through by telling him
about the cannibalism. He said that cannibalism in China
was impossible. I said that I had seen dogs eating people
on the roads. He said that was impossible. But there I
had him. I had sensed I would need corroborative evidence and so I had asked Harrison Forman to accompany
me, for he had photographs of famine conditions. Forman
fumed in the anteroom as I spoke to the Generalissimo,
but when the Generalissimo denied that I had seen dogs
eating people, Forman was summoned. His pictures

clearly showed dogs standing over dug-out corpses. The Generalissimo's knee began to jiggle slightly, in a nervous tic, as he asked where this picture had been taken. We told him. He took out his little pad and brush pen and began to make notes. He asked for names of officials; he wanted more names; he wanted us to make a full report to him, leaving out no names. In a flat manner, as if restating a fact to himself, he said that he had *told* the army to share its grain with the people. Then he thanked us; told me that I was a better investigator than "any of the investigators I have sent on my own." And I was ushered out twenty minutes after entering.

Heads, I know, did roll, starting, I assume, with those at the hapless telegraph office of Loyang, which had let slip to America the embarrassment of death in Honan. But lives were saved—and saved by the power of the American press. Months later, by slow post, I received a letter from Father Megan. I excerpt it here to show that power:

> After you got back and started the wires buzzing [wrote Father Megan], the grain came rushing in from Shensi by trainloads. They just could not unload it fast enough here at Loyang. That was score No. 1, a four-bagger to say the least. The provincial government got busy and opened up soup kitchens all over the country. They really went to work and got something done. The military shelled out SOME of their MUCH surplus grain and that helped a lot. The whole country really got busy putting cash together for the famine-stricken and money poured into Honan.
>
> All four of the above points were bullseyes as I see and confirmed my former opinion that the famine was entirely man-made and was at all times within the power of the authorities to control had they had the inclination and desire to do so. Your visit and your jacking them up did the trick, jerked them out of their stupor,

and put them on the job, and then things did
GET DONE. In a word, more power to Time &
Life, and to Fortune Long Life. Peace! It's
wonderful! . . . You will be long remembered in
Honan. Some remember you in a very pleasant
way, but there are others who grit their teeth
and they've got reason to do so.

I was not to see Chiang K'ai-shek again, except at
receptions, until after the war; but I left convinced he was
not only useless to us—as Stilwell had said—but useless
to his own people, which was more important.

History has now cast Chiang K'ai-shek off. But for
twenty years, from 1927 to 1947, we Americans made
him a crossroads character in the history of Asia—and I
should like to pause over him for a few pages as a
specimen in the politics of an Asia we never understood.
For some Americans he was a Methodist deacon in arms,
an Oriental Miles Standish, a selfless national hero; for
others he was a merciless Fascist, leading a gang of
looting warlords. He was none of these things, of course;
simply a man ripped out of the old world too soon,
plunged into a new world he could not understand.

During all the years I wrote about Chiang K'ai-shek,
and all the times I met and spoke with him, I never once
thought I even approached understanding him. He was
Chinese, true Chinese, and in the days I was reporting
China, the ethic of the time forbade one from reporting
the world in terms of race. Today we still speak of world
brotherhood, but we recognize that the difference of culture, behavior and perception between the West and the
Orient is real. To ignore this difference is perilous; and to
ignore the perception of China by the Chinese themselves
is to walk blind into their world. Despite the erasure of
surface dignity by pestilence, famine, invasion and brutalities; despite the smothering of the ancient culture by
revolutionary new ideas, there still lies underneath Chinese manners an extravagant pride in descent and race
which nothing can wipe out.

Chiang embodied this stiff-necked Chinese pride.

This was the first quality that came to mind when one reflected on Chiang—his pride. A slim man, rigid in posture whether erect or seated, always immaculate whether in black cloak or khaki uniform, thin-lipped for a Chinese, his skull clean-shaven, he behaved with ice-stiff self-discipline—except for the moments when he flew into a tantrum, yelled, threw teacups or plates about, tore up papers and raged out of control.

Chiang's pride was more than a nationalist pride. It was racial (not racist), and in his teachings (for he, like Mao Tse-tung, considered himself as much a national teacher as a national leader), he habitually used the phrase *min tsu* ("race") to iden.ify his Chinese people, not the word *min kuo,* which means "nation."

With his people he shared, and shared personally, a century of humiliation that had cut him so sharply it edged every facet of his personality. "My father died when I was nine years old," he once wrote, " . . . the miserable condition of my family at that time is beyond description. My family, solitary and without influence, became at once the target of much insult and maltreatment." He had been born in 1887, to a farmer's family in Chekiang province, and had thus seen in his adolescence the dissolution of the old Manchu imperial regime; must have heard of the Boxer Rebellion in 1900 and its bloody suppression by foreign troops; then seen all order come apart. He had become a soldier; an officer cadet; studied military tactics in Japan, a nation he learned to hate; had later been sent by the Nationalist revolutionaries to study Soviet institutions, especially the army, in Lenin's Russia, which he hated even more. He suspected and mistrusted all foreigners. The independence and unity of Chinese were his only politics; and his political base was his personal will—inflexible, unswerving, dedicated.

Yet he knew that foreigners knew things that Chinese did not. Chiang saw the outer world as Chinese tradition taught it—as a world of barbarians. Yet the barbarians had tricks, and he wanted to learn those tricks. Thus he had about him constantly a court of foreign advisers, starting with Mikhail Borodin, his Russian adviser in 1926; through the Prussians who, under Generals von Falkenhausen and von Seeckt, reorganized his army; through the Australian, W. H. Donald, who instructed him in diplomacy; to the sequence of American advisers that came to instruct his government in agrarian reform, potato raising, artificial insemination of cows, infant care, truck maintenance, artillery and combat aviation. Of all his American advisers, Claire Chennault was his favorite—master of all the tricks of the air. If he bore affection for any other foreigners, it was for American missionaries—for he had become, under the influence of his second wife, Mei-ling, the youngest of the famed Soong sisters, an American Methodist; perhaps the Methodists knew best the way to God.

What Chiang probably wanted most in his own confused mind was to refurbish Chinese tradition with Western manners and Western precision. One of his younger ministers of cabinet came to him one day dressed in the traditional long gown of the Chinese bureaucrat. Chiang was infuriated and tongue-lashed him: the minister was too young a man, said Chiang, to be wearing a long gown; he must wear pants, necktie, jacket and shirt, as modern China must. He insisted, in the old tradition, on punctilious ceremony; only in modern dress. I once went to visit a graduation ceremony at a Chinese staff college at which he would speak. The graduates were dressed in uniform, with orange silk sashes around their waists; they were piped up, inspected physically; the middle-aged officers would tremble, click heels à la Prussian, salute, retreat, pace, be dismissed. Then Chiang held them all at attention while a half-hour essay was read from the works of Sun Yat-sen, which the dictator explained textually, as teacher, paragraph by paragraph. He was leading them, through war, to China's new glory and the modern world.

Stilwell caught the flavor of one such ceremony far better than I ever could. In Stilwell's diary I later found a notation that should be reproduced in full. "Graduation exercises at [Chinese] Military Academy," Stilwell wrote.

"As Peanut [Stilwell's diary code for Chiang] mounted rostrum band leader counted 1-2-3, but unfortunately band sounded off at 2. Peanut was furious, stopped band, bawled out leader: 'Either start playing on 1 or start on 3. Don't start on 2.' Then a speaker pulled his notes out of his pants pocket. This infuriated Peanut. He bawled him out and told him that *tsai wai kuo* [in foreign countries] you could put a handkerchief in your pants pockets but not papers. Papers go in lower coat pockets, and, if secret, in upper coat pockets. Then someone stumbled on procedure and Peanut went wild, screaming that he ought to be shot . . . '*Ch'iang pi*' [Shoot him], and repeating it at the top of his voice." Stilwell could barely conceal his exasperation and amusement with Chiang; but he called him "Peanut" only in private.

Chiang was fascinated by everything Western. Once, being flown in an American plane over the Hump, he became interested in the parachute and survival kit provided for each passenger on VIP planes. An American officer watched, horrified, as Chiang, out of curiosity, undid the parachute pack, unfolded its flaps, untied the survival kit and examined its contents. He was trying to understand; but if the plane had gone down, it would have been one parachute short, and some GI of the flight crew would have to go down with the plane, for Chiang was too precious to lose.

But he was sincere, sincere in his love of China, truly dedicated to his country—and to Methodist morality. In the summer of 1944, when all East China was falling to the last great Japanese offensive, Chiang summoned to his garden for an off-the-record conference and tea party a number of foreign correspondents as well as a group of his high inner circle. I still have the *official* transcript of his remarks, which we correspondents were forbidden by censorship to send out " . . . Of late," said Chiang, "rumors about my private life have been in circulation in Chungking . . . you have heard of these serious calumnies . . . without telling me. . . . What are the rumors? One says that I had secretly kept a woman last year. Another says that there has been an illicit relationship between myself and a nurse and the latter had given birth to a child. . . ." He went on. He denied the rumors. He went through his daily calendar; he declared "the future of our revolution is jeopardized" by such rumors, for he considered it his moral duty to set an example to others. And then Madame Chiang K'ai-shek, who was also present, rose to say daintily that "I wish to state that never for a moment did I stoop or demean myself to entertain doubts of his uprightness."

I have no doubt that he was telling the truth. But this rigid morality was locked in one compartment of Chiang's mind; while other compartments concealed animal treachery, warlord cruelty and an ineffable ignorance of what a modern state requires.

Of his personal treachery there could be no doubt. I had come to China believing him a national hero. Then, incident by incident, as I accumulated notes, the hero became to me first an unlovely character, then an evil one. He had been kidnapped, I knew, in late 1936 by the Manchurian Chinese of young Marshal Chang Hsueh-liang's army; Chou En-lai had extricated him; Chiang had promised forgiveness to the young Marshal. But later, bringing the trusting Chang Hsueh-liang back to Nanking, the dictator had thrown him into prison for a life term. And carried him, besotted with opium and weakened by concubines, in captivity to ultimate exile in Formosa. Explainable. Chiang had, I learned later, executed scores of officers for dereliction of duty. Excusable. But then there was the Kwangsi general, Li Chi-sen, who had come to see Chiang before the Japanese invasion to offer national cooperation against the enemy. When they disagreed, Chiang had thrown him in jail after dinner. He had entertained another general—Chang Fa-kuei—and granted the general's request that a derelict subordinate not be executed. But when Chang Fa-kuei returned from Chungking to his headquarters, he discovered that the subordinate had been executed as soon as he left Chungking. I talked with a Yale-educated professor of economics, Ma Yin-ch'u. Before the war, Ma had been invited by Chiang to his residence to give the dictator private instruction in economics—much as he invited missionaries to instruct him in theology or Prussians to instruct him in infantry tactics. Ma thought he was close to Chiang. But during the war, lecturing to his university classes, Ma began to denounce the government's inflationary policies. Chiang then invited Ma once more to dinner to talk economics. After dinner, as Ma was being driven home in the dictator's limousine, the two gunmen in the front seat told him he was under arrest—and he was not to see his home again for two years.

Chiang's anger came in spasms, and went from casual beatings to killing. He knew there was something wrong with the conscription system that his government imposed; one day, walking the road on his afternoon stroll, he saw a file of peasants roped together, being led off to the army, a sight familiar to all of us in China. He was angered by the stories the conscripts told him when he halted them. So, with his walking stick, he began to beat the recruiting officer over the head and shoulders mercilessly for such cruelty.

Chiang tried to do good. He tried to do good in Honan when that story was brought to his attention; he tried to do good about the conscription system when Americans protested its cruelty. As late as the spring of 1945, he was still astonished at excesses in the system he commanded, and ordained the summary execution of the chief of the national draft system because it was so corrupt. He was probably the last of the long chain of tyrants who believed a problem could be solved by shrieking: "Off with his head!" or *"Ch'iang pi!"*

I can see Chiang now as a pathetic man. He loved his two sons, his wife and his country—his country most. But he did not know how to be a good ruler or a good father: the pathos came in his trying to do good and failing. At times, in his fumbling and fury, he reminded me of the stories and legends of Charlemagne—of the nights that old king would spend in bed, holding a scroll in the candlelight, turning it this way and that, up and down, trying to decipher the words which the priests were teaching him to read. And not succeeding at the

clerical tricks, and growing furious! Chiang fumbled and
fumbled at his tasks; he had achieved his greatness in the
1920s by clearing the Yangtze basin of old warlords and
setting up the Nationalist government there; he had
reached heroic stature in the first two years of the war
against Japan, organizing the coalition of resistance,
drenching his cities in blood rather than yield them to the
Japanese; after that, the fronts stabilized and the war
froze him. Then, sometime after America entered the war,
or possibly because America entered the war, his Mandate of Heaven ran out. By Chinese tradition, dynasties
rule only so long as they keep the Mandate of Heaven;
when, mysteriously, the Mandate is withdrawn, the dynasty crumbles. It came as a personal mystery to Chiang
when slowly he began to realize his Mandate of Heaven
had vanished, and that he was powerless outside his
palace. Thus the spasms of fury. And as his inner bitterness grew, so did his bitterness at America, which he held
duty bound to save him from the Japanese and Communism—which it would not.

It must have been sometime in early 1944 when the
crumbling of the Mandate became visible. In a pocket
anthology of verse I carried with me through the war, I
had read T. S. Eliot's "Rhapsody on a Windy Night."
Three lines in it began to haunt me as a precise description of what I was seeing, "A broken spring in a factory
yard,/Rust that clings to the form that the strength has
left/Hard and curled and ready to snap."

Wherever one reported, wherever one poked in
Chungking or outside—at government bureaus, offices,
hospitals, army headquarters, universities, provincial ad-
ministrations—structures proved hollow at a probe; or
snapped.

The snapping was soundless, but you could touch
and feel it simply by pulling out of your pocket the paper
money of China and looking at the inflation. The Chinese
had, of course, invented paper—as they had invented
gunpowder, the compass, block printing. But when emperors were persuaded to combine paper with printing to

yield money, they produced the world's first currency. The Chinese had experimented with every form of money before they came to paper: copper, stones, shells, leather wads, silk sheets. When finally, however, the Sung dynasty (960–1126) issued paper notes that passed as money, they were off on a course no one could control. The Sung dynasty collapsed in inflationary implosion; the Mongol dynasty which succeeded it also toyed with paper currency; and Marco Polo marveled at least as much at this wonder as at any of the other wonders of Kublai Khan's Cathay; but that dynasty, too, died in a blizzard of useless paper money. Since then, almost always, whenever a government has perished it has done so in a paroxysm of inflation. From the Sung dynasty to the French Revolution, from the Confederacy of the United States to the Weimar Republic, inflation has accompanied the death rattle. This is because paper currency is nothing; its value comes only from the faith and the strength of the government that issues it, and the price index in Chiang's China traced the collapse of his government.

I cannot recall when I first began to sense inflation as a threat. At the beginning it was all so amusing to watch. It was amusing to see an American soldier pulling out a Chinese dollar bill, lighting his cigar with it and saying, "I always dreamed of doing this"; amusing to see a little Chinese girl cutting up blue twenty-cent notes into paper dolls. It was also convenient at first to carry paper change and not a pocketful of heavy copper coins, as I had in 1939 when I first arrived.

But then one realized that there was no more copper in anyone's pockets. Then came the time when Chungking's writers split off from Chungking's playwrights. Playwriters were paid percentages of the theater's weekly take, as they are here; so their income rose with the price of tickets, and playwrights rode with the inflation. Writers, however, might wait months to be paid for publication; so they insisted on being paid in rice: seventeen pounds of rice per thousand words was their demand. Finally, inflation was publicly accepted. Our black-market moneychanger no longer sneaked into the Press Hostel. By

1944 he marched in openly, his bearer behind him carrying a basket, and in the basket—bundles and bundles of wadded Chinese banknotes to trade for American greenbacks.

One could trace a quickening collapse statistically. The war had begun in 1937 with the Chinese currency stable at three Chinese dollars to the American dollar. The exchange rose, officially, to six to one, by 1939; prices stayed in line, doubling. By the spring of 1940, however, prices had doubled again; and again by late fall of that year. By June of 1941, when Luce took me home from China, prices were sixteen times higher than prices at the war's outbreak; when I returned in the fall of 1942, they were thirty-two times higher; and then, by winter 1942, they doubled to sixty-four times the prewar mark.

The trouble with China, said one American adviser at this point, is not that the Generalissimo doesn't understand economics, but that his Minister of Finance doesn't either. Chiang's finance minister was a flabby, pudgy man, claiming lineal descent from Confucius. But H. H. Kung was not only seventy-fifth in lineal descent from Confucius; he was also married to Ai-ling Soong, sister of Mei-ling Soong, who had become Madame Chiang K'ai-shek. Kung's understanding of economics remained, however, at the level of the silver-and-copper moneychangers on the Bund of Shanghai. I interviewed him several times and remember one memorable statement about inflation. "Inflation," exclaimed Dr. Kung, "inflation! You American reporters talk about our inflation all the time. There is no inflation in China! If people want to pay twenty thousand dollars for a fountain pen [a favorite item of hoarding at the time], that's their business, it's not inflation. They're crazy, that's all. They shouldn't pay it." His advice to his government was similarly perceptive. I remember an American-trained Chinese engineer in China's War Production Ministry who reported to me, boggle-eyed, of a conference with the finance minister. The arsenals had now found it impossible to buy either raw copper or raw iron on the domestic Chinese market; steel production in the country had dwindled to ten thousand tons a year—and that steel was priced beyond reason. Kung had offered the sage thought that if the arsenals began to make cigarette-rolling machinery, they could sell them at a spectacular price because cigarettes were in such demand—and then, with the profit from making cigarette machinery, they could afford to buy raw material for the arsenals!

Americans who dealt with Chinese slowly developed a mean and surly suspicion of every Chinese official. The official rate of exchange had been raised to 20 Chinese dollars to 1 U.S. dollar by the time America entered the war. But as the Chinese currency shriveled in value, the true rate of exchange became 100 to 1; then 200 to 1 by early 1944; prices outstripped even those true rates, and the gouging of American needs by the fictitious official rate became intolerable. To pay 200,000 Chinese dollars at 20 to 1 for a latrine at an air base cost Americans officially $10,000 in American dollars, while at home such an outhouse could still be built for $500. By 1944, the friction between Americans and Chinese over the dollar rate of exchange, or, fundamentally, over how the American Army could pay to operate in the inflationary climate of a decaying government, was critical to the breach between Americans and Chinese that was approaching.

Nor could one be reasonable about it. One was told by responsible Chinese that one must understand that in China at war there were two budgets: the paper-money budget and the grain budget. Entirely separate. The paper-money budget projected on graphs like an abnormal case of hysterical finance; but at least it was understandable. Then there was the grain budget, which I had seen at work in Honan; the army collected the grain tax for army needs in each war area.

But beyond the two recognized budgets was the third budget—the Generalissimo's personal budget, uncountable and huge. The Generalissimo could write a personal check on any government bank: $100 million for a favorite general whose troops were in short supply, $60 million for a provincial governor faced with a local crisis, a score of millions here and a hundred million there. No one, even the Ministry of Finance or the cabinet, where several score bewildered but sensible Chinese officials labored to keep matters under control, knew how large an injection of paper currency would be needed to honor the General-issimo's personal government checks. They knew, finally, only that paper currency was as much an ingredient of war as bullets and fought for their share of tonnage over the Hump to ship in bales of paper currency.

Inflation is the haunting pestilence of the middle classes; it is the hidden threat that disorganized government always holds over those who try to plan, to save, to be prudent. To be honest in one's day-to-day dealings in a runaway inflation does not make sense. To pay a debt on time is folly. To borrow and spend as fast as possible is prudence. Every man suspects everyone else. I remember trying to supply my Chinese friends with whatever medicines I could cadge from U.S. Army supplies—sulfa drugs, quinine, paragoric, Atabrine—and then discovering that some of those who pleaded illness were not truly ill but were selling the drugs for the wild paper prices they brought on the open market. So I distrusted everyone who asked for an American medicine, an American tool, an American artifact.

In 1943, I took notice of prices in the large provincial capital of Chengtu. The local price index had risen by 174 times since the outbreak of the war, workingmen's wages had risen by 104 times—but the salaries of professors at its distinguished university had risen by only 19 times! Inflation meant such scholars must starve or beg. For government officials of the same social background, there was a third alternative—to steal or solicit bribes. No official could remain honest for long unless his rice, cloth and oil ration were fattened by his superior's favor, and supplemented with handouts. It was easier to steal. Chiang's response was, as usual, shoot the profiteers, shoot corrupt officials, stop the prices. In 1944, the *Ta Kung Pao*, the most courageous newspaper in the capital, reported such executions with satisfaction: "Recently there has been a joyful aspect of politics," its editorial began; but then it went on, mournfully, to warn that "government should pay attention to one prerequisite—salaries of officials should be sufficient to keep them honest . . . if suffering of government employees is unbearable and if salaries are so low they cannot sustain life, occurrence of cases of corruption is worthy of sympathy."

What the West calls *le trahison des clercs,* the desertion of the intellectuals, is considered by most historians to be a forerunner of revolution. Unless a regime can find learned men to serve it, it cannot serve the people. In China, inflation made it impossible for learned men, honest men, decent men, to serve their national government except at unbearable personal cost—or self-corruption that revolted them. They sought any alternative—and the only alternative was the Communists. Inflation made life unreasonable.

I remember fragments of breakdown more vivid than statistics or price indexes.

For example: the first tax revolt in 1943, in isolated Kansu province. There the farmers took pitchforks and guns to oppose collectors of the grain tax; then they were strafed by government planes. Another revolt followed in the province of Ningsia; yet another was reported in Yunnan.

For example again: arsenals were closing down. The Minister of Economics told me that only twenty percent of Chinese steel-making capacity was being used because the government arsenals' budget could not meet the prices set by government-controlled steel mills! On the other hand, the large coal mine fifty miles upriver from Chungking was also closing down—because it could not operate within the government-fixed price for coal!

For example yet again: the familiar two-hundred-dollar Chinese bill, which I had thought of for a year as being equal to an American dollar bill, was replaced by a fresh green five-hundred-dollar bill at the beginning of 1944; and the inflationary fever swept everyone, myself included. I began to hoard incense pots, silks, satins, embroideries. By 1945 I became accustomed to carrying my money on shopping trips in a knapsack; I would hold the knapsack between my knees on the rickshaw. When I got to a shop, I would hand over wads of money, bundled in rectangles as big as a man's fist—and shopkeepers would not unbundle the wads to count bills individually, but would count the wads as money. Though I was paid in American dollars back in New York, insulated by the distance of my bank account from China, I caught the sense of panic. I learned to fear inflation as much as the cruelty of joblessness and depression in which I had grown up. What the famine had done to the peasants of Honan, the inflation was doing to the middle class of the cities and universities: wiping out all loyalties, denying all effort except to survive.

The irreversible crumbling could be concealed from none of the outside parties of interest in the Chungking government—fom the Communists, the Japanese, or the American Army.

The Communists broke off any serious attempt to negotiate with Chiang's crumbling government in the summer of 1943. Chou En-lai had been joined in Chungking by General Lin Piao, who was later to become the Generalissimo of Communism; perhaps Mao thought Lin Piao would be tougher than Chou in putting pressure on Chiang K'ai-shek. But there was little left to be tough against. And so, in the summer of 1943, having wheedled several trucks from Chiang to return to Yenan for consultation, Chou and Lin heaped their personal files, baggage, bedrolls and belongings on top of the trucks and jounced out of the old house on Tseng Chia Ai. They had a safe-conduct from Chiang; but their headquarters could not relax until word was relayed that they had passed Sian safely en route back to Yenan. The next time I saw either of them was a year later, in Yenan, where they were earnestly preparing to erase the government for which they had such contempt.

The crumbling tempted Japanese action as much as

it earned Communist contempt. In early spring 1944, the Japanese launched their convulsive ICHIGO offensive. The Japanese knew the war was lost by then. But they might, by this final action, put themselves in a negotiating position—or, like Oriental Samsons, bring down the pillars of China with them in their defeat. They struck across the Yellow River into Honan, knowing what the famine had done to loyalties; and as I have said, the peasants came to their side. Then they moved south through East China against the American air bases which Chennault had installed there. As Stilwell predicted, Chennault had punished the Japanese too much; and Chiang could not provide ground cover for Chennault's bases.

The crumbling, it seemed to me, could no longer be concealed from the American government, either. All that summer I had followed the disaster in East China from the combat zone, both from our own air bases and on foot with Chinese infantry. I had come over to Stilwell's view completely by early fall of 1944: American policy must act to refashion the Chinese government and its army if it was to fight; or must abandon them completely. Since we could not afford to abandon China, we should act. What I did not know, there in the field, was that Stilwell had already persuaded the American government that his position was correct; and now, too late, American policy had changed.

American policy in Asia used to combine missionary purpose and merchant's greed. In China, however, missionary purpose had come to outweigh, by far, mercantile greed, and in defense of China's nationhood we had invited Japanese attack.

When that attack came, in 1941, Washington policymakers looked on Chiang K'ai-shek as a precious ally, master of a great Asian reservoir of manpower, lord over an endless airstrip from which the ultimate air war against Japan would be launched and sustained. The defense of China's government had been, for us, as the defense of Poland's sovereignty had been for the British in 1939—the immediate cause of a war which may or may not have been inevitable.

Three years later, in 1944, the official American attitude to China had totally changed.

The map of war told one part of the story:

By the summer of 1944 that map was a joy for American leadership to examine: there were the blue slashes of American armored divisions racing across France toward Germany, MacArthur moving on the Philippines, the U.S. Navy raiding in Japan's coastal waters, B-29 bombers beginning to strike Japan's wood-and-paper cities. Only in China did the map dismay: there, the Japanese had crossed the Yellow River, plunged south from the Yangtze, seized Hengyang, were moving relentlessly to wipe out the American air bases in East China, which had cost hundreds of millions and so much effort to build. The airlift that Chiang had demanded for the Hump and for Chennault had absorbed so much American air-freight capacity that now there was not enough in Europe to settle the dispute between Patton and Montgomery; had there been enough air-supply capacity to supply both, then either might have finished off the war against Germany in the fall of 1944. The American exertion in support of Chiang had been enormous; yet incessantly Chiang insisted he was being cheated, that the fall of East China was due not to his incompetence but to America's niggardliness and Stilwell's machinations.

The other part of the story was told in the classified dispatches of American military personnel, reporting regiment by regiment, position by position, Chinese incompetence, decay and graft. It was not simply Stilwell, all alone, reporting such matters; the story came from every level of the growing American combat and advisory corps, all of whose reports could be summarized as Germany's Ludendorff had summarized his visit to the Austrian Army in World War I: "We are allied to a corpse." Early in the war Stilwell had been admonished by Marshall, at Roosevelt's specific request, to stop treating Chiang K'ai-shek "like a tribal chieftain." Now

Roosevelt's good will, too, was strained. By summer of 1944 he knew he must act.

If Chiang could not mobilize China effectively for the war against Japan, then someone else must. Roosevelt could not, of course, order Chiang to step down as chief of state of China. But he would ask him to step aside—and on July 6, 1944, by cable, Roosevelt urged Chiang to turn over command of all Chinese armies to the American Chiang most loathed—Joseph Stilwell. It was a ticklish matter; Chiang stalled; a month later Roosevelt cabled Chiang that he was sending two eminent Americans, Donald Nelson, former chairman of the War Production Board, and Patrick J. Hurley, former Secretary of War, to speed negotiations on the proposition that would reduce Chiang to an impotent figurehead.

Historically, the documents show events quickening in pace. As the Japanese tore through East China, panic gripped Chungking. By September 12, 1944, Chiang had agreed in principle to the appointment of Stilwell as Commander in Chief of all Chinese ground forces. On September 13, Stilwell received two Communist emissaries at his headquarters in Chungking. On September 14, Stilwell flew down to the threatened American air bases in East China, to confer with General Chennault and Chinese General Chang Fa-kuei.

Stilwell returned from the front to Chungking on September 15. He had the previous day given orders to blow up the great American air base at Kweilin lest it fall into Japanese hands. So much for the Chennault-Chiang strategy of a year earlier. He now reported to Chiang K'ai-shek on the confusion in the Chinese East China command, and on another Japanese offensive in North Burma. Chiang and Stilwell differed in weighing the strategic threats. Chiang insisted that Stilwell halt the combined American-British-Chinese offensive hacking its way through Burma, and fly those troops to the threatened East China front. Stilwell wanted Chiang to use his personal anti-Communist reserve of 200,000 troops in the north to save the threatened front. They clashed. Stilwell radioed Chief of Staff George Marshall in the Pentagon

that the East China situation was "hopeless," that
Kweilin was about to become a "rat-trap," that the Generalissimo would not "listen to reason, merely repeating a
lot of cock-eyed conceptions of his own invention."

General Marshall was not, however, in Washington
to receive Stilwell's message. He was in Quebec, with
Franklin Roosevelt and Winston Churchill at the
OCTAGON conference on the prosecution of the war.
There Stilwell's combat report and his vignette of
Chiang's reaction reached Marshall, thus Roosevelt.

Poor Franklin Roosevelt—directing a global war in
the middle of a Presidential campaign; trying to solve all
the problems of Asia six weeks before voting day! The
British, with their contempt for the Chinese, had, all
through the war, considered Chiang K'ai-shek a tribal
chieftain. So, too, had Stilwell; so, too, did the soldier
Roosevelt most relied on, George Marshall, who supported Stilwell. And Chiang and China's friends in Washington had both overpromised and nagged away at the
White House enough to try any President's patience.

So Franklin Roosevelt, on September 18, 1944, responded: directly to Chiang K'ai-shek, with the full approval of Churchill, the British, the Americans and the
Combined Chiefs of Staff.

Roosevelt must have been tired. His message to
Chiang was probably as blunt as any that an American
chief of state has sent to a friendly or allied chief of
state—laced with a touch of that marvelous Hudson
River valley snobbery, the tone of the squirearchy to
stablemen, housemaids and errant children. It was a six-
hundred-word telegram ordering Chiang to put Stilwell in
charge forthwith, but its rhythm ran thus:

> After reading the last reports on the situa-
> tion in China, my Chiefs of Staff and I are
> convinced that you are faced in the near future
> with the disaster I have feared . . . if you do not
> provide manpower for your divisions in north
> Burma and, if you fail to send reinforcements
> to the Salween forces and withdraw these ar-

mies, we will lose all chance of opening land
communications with China.... For this you
must yourself be prepared to accept the consequences and assume the personal responsibility.
I have urged time and again in recent months
that you take drastic action to resist the disaster
which has been moving closer to China and to
you. Now, when you have not yet placed General Stilwell in command of all forces in China,
we are faced with the loss of a critical area in
east China with possible catastrophic consequences.... In this message I have expressed
my thoughts with complete frankness because it
appears plainly evident to all of us here that all
your and our efforts to save China are to be
lost by further delays. [Signed] Roosevelt.

It was now Roosevelt himself who was treating
Chiang K'ai-shek as a tribal chieftain. Moreover, he in-
structed that this message be sent to Chiang *not* via the
State Department, which dealt with the Chinese Foreign
Office, which, in turn, habitually softened the words of
the American President to their own maximum dictator.
It was to be delivered, ordered Roosevelt, via Stilwell—
with instructions to deliver the message personally.

No more enthusiastic messenger could have been
chosen than the four-star American general who had
suffered so long from the duplicity and false courtesies of
Chiang K'ai-shek. By five-thirty on September 19, Stilwell
had arrived at the Generalissimo's country residence,
Huang Shan, where the Generalissimo was meeting with
his chief military counselors and American emissary
Patrick J. Hurley, charged with negotiating the details of
transfer of command to Stilwell.

Stilwell paused on the veranda to tell Hurley what
was in the Presidential message. Hurley was appalled; he
believed that that afternoon, in a few minutes more, he
might have the Generalissimo's chop, or great seal, on the
transfer of command. But Stilwell had the President's
orders to deliver this message personally. The group

drank tea together for a few minutes. Then Stilwell announced that there was a personal message for the Generalissimo from the President. Until now Chiang's control of American support and recognition had been his greatest strength with his courtiers and subordinate warlords. Now, in the presence of his staff, he was to be humiliated. He read through the Chinese translation quickly; then said, "I understand"; and closed the meeting.

Stilwell's diary notes that evening went: "I handed this bundle of paprika to the Peanut and then sank back with a sigh. The harpoon hit the little bugger right in the solar plexus, and went right through him. It was a clean hit, but beyond turning green and losing the power of speech, he did not bat an eye. He just said to me 'I understand.' And sat in silence, jiggling one foot. We are now a long way from the 'tribal chieftain' bawling out. . . . I came home. Pretty sight crossing the river: lights all on in Chungking."

Stilwell was a master of punctilio and courtesies as taught to West Point cadets and American generals. In all public ceremonies with Chinese, he honored the rituals. But there was a private boyish streak, a Mark Twain Connecticut Yankee bubble in him, which he shared only with his wife. Three days later he wrote a letter to Mrs. Stilwell, with a bit of doggerel that expressed his sense of triumph:

> I've waited long for vengeance—
> At last I've had my chance.
> I've looked the Peanut in the eye
> And kicked him in the pants.
> The old harpoon was ready
> With aim and timing true,
> I sank it to the handle
> And stung him through and through.
> The little bastard shivered,
> And lost the power of speech.
> His face turned green and quivered
> As he struggled not to screech.

The poem went on for several more verses, but it is not worth anthologizing.

Stilwell was, apparently, totally unaware of the turbulence he had set up in the court of the Generalissimo, though he should have anticipated it. He had for so long seen Chiang ignore the dignity of other men, known how casually this dictator could kill, that he, too, had become emotionally callous—and forgotten how important the personal dignity of Chiang K'ai-shek was, as it is to any leader in an unstable society, where the most precious attribute of success is dignity.

Thus, unaware of the mood he had left behind, Stilwell was astounded when he learned a week later of the message Roosevelt had received from Chiang on September 25, in which, finally, the Chinese Generalissimo took the stand he could not help but take: either he or Stilwell could direct affairs in China, said Chiang to Roosevelt, but not both. And since he, Chiang, was chief of China, it was Stilwell, the American, who must go. ". . . it was made manifest to me," wrote Chiang to Roosevelt, "that General Stilwell had no intention of cooperating with me, but believed that he was in fact being appointed to command me. If you will place yourself in my position, I believe you will understand how in the future I can never direct General Stilwell, or in all seriousness depend on General Stilwell to conform to my direction. If ignoring reason and experience, I were to appoint General Stilwell as Field Commander, I would knowingly court inevitable disaster."

Indeed, Chiang would have. This personal disaster for Chiang K'ai-shek might have been good for China— but one cannot expect any political leader to accept castration, however necessary for the good of his country. Chiang did not feel it necessary, and resisted. For almost a month—from September 24 to October 18 of 1944— this deadlock between Chiang and Roosevelt persisted, and then, finally, politics dictated the inevitable outcome.

Almost all the story of the previous few pages, as I tell it, was unknown to me at the time. I have written it from the documents, archives, letters and memoirs that professional historians have uncovered in the thirty-five years since. And few sequences illustrate better the usefulness of history than the understanding it has brought to the chain of events I reported episodically in the summer of 1944. The connection between events and decisions is the domain of the historian. But the true connection becomes clear only years after the events tumble over the participants. Thus I am grateful to the historians who have come since and clarified what to me was a summer of absolute bewilderment.

I was following the reporter's trade in 1944, and a young reporter in a war is best advised to get as close to the sound of guns as possible; the closer he gets to combat and the in-tight view of battle conditions, the more useful his dispatches. If he stays at headquarters and writes of grand strategy, then he must accept the prospect that historians in years to come will write it better than he.

My view in the summer of 1944 was an in-tight view of events. I marched up to the front, walking through July heat to the hills above Hengyang, to watch the Chinese 62nd Army make its counterattack. For the "grand counterattack" it marshaled its batteries of old 75-mm guns; each gun had 20 shells; I watched them fire; when they had fired their 20 shells to no purpose, the counterattack was over. Only later did I discover that down the rail line, the only remaining East China rail line in Chiang's hands, was Chiang's stockpile of 40,000 tons of munitions at Tushan; but Chiang was saving that stockpile for an "emergency"; and Americans later blew up the dump lest it fall into the hands of Japanese.

The U.S. Air Force provided air cover for the East China rail line. Thus I watched appalled when under our air cover a troop train stopped in broad daylight and the engineer dismounted to smoke his opium pipe. The American officers on the train insisted that since I spoke Chinese, I do something about it. I did; I strode forward, berated the engineer, kicked him up into his booth, and the train went on. But I did not know then that we

Americans were not supposed to be helping this particular front with ground supplies; and that when we did help this collapsing front of warlord Hsueh Yueh, Chiang protested our aid! I *did* know that Chiang favored American air support, à la Chennault, over ground support, à la Stilwell. But I did *not* know that summer that Chiang sought air aid with such extravagant unreality that he demanded operations control over our B-29 force, the strategic air force that later burned Japan to the ground! This demand, I later learned, Roosevelt had flatly refused, though he countered with the offer to raise Chiang's title from Allied Commander of the China Theater of War, to Allied Supreme Commander of the China Theater of War. I knew there was no coordination between ground and air in the defense of East China. But I knew so only because I lay paralyzed, sweating, screaming, in a drainage ditch with a battalion of Chinese troops one hot afternoon when American P-40s swept down on us, shooting, strafing, swinging back and forth—and I knew the pilots in the squadron were not *trying* to kill me, but were ignorant of where the front was and who held what. I knew that Chiang was suffering a bout of execution fever; he had executed the general in command of the artillery at Changsha, then executed the commander of the Chinese 93rd Army; but I did not know then how deeply he suspected Stilwell of conspiring against him; I thought simply that Chiang had come unbuttoned again.

Nothing made sense in the field. I sat outside the room when Chennault and Stilwell conferred at Kweilin with General Chang Fa-kuei; and had no idea until years later that Chang Fa-kuei had offered right then to break with Chiang K'ai-shek, and accept his orders only from the American, Stilwell. I knew only that Stilwell had given orders which Chennault obeyed, to blow up the airfields at Kweilin. What followed that night was a wild and wonderful thunder-popping, flame-streaked, explosion-rocked orgy of destruction that is the most scarlet-and-brilliant night of my memory.

Then I was out of the story, and was hospitalized in Kunming. The story of the East China retreat could not

compete for space in *Time* magazine with the great victo-
ries in Europe, the liberation of Paris, the advance on the
Rhine. So I lingered in the hospital awaiting the arrival in
China of a war correspondent who would join me in the
Chungking bureau of *Time*—Annalee Jacoby, widow of
my old friend Melville Jacoby, with whom I had fallen in
love within days of meeting her. With her, I flew from
Kunming to Chungking, where I felt I might use the time
I had earned at the front for a bit of rest and pursuit of
romance.

But that was not at all the way it was to be. Annalee
and I, flying to Chungking, were flying into the eye of a
hurricane. I was *Time*'s bureau chief, their senior war
correspondent on the mainland of Asia. She was to report
politics in Chungking and China. But it was impossible,
by then, in the last week in September, the first weeks in
October, to separate politics from war—or Chiang's ambition from the Communist counterthrust, or Hurley's
diplomacy from Stilwell's purpose. We were in the midst
of the Stilwell crisis in Chungking, and however wisely
and clearly historians see it now, none of us, not even
Stilwell, knew what it meant while it was happening.

I checked into the secret story in Chungking the last
weekend of September, at the height of the deadlock
between Roosevelt, Chiang and Stilwell.

It took me days to realize that the obscure story here
rose above gossip into history. Returning to Chungking
from the front was always to return to rumors, for
Chungking rippled with them. The rumors these first few
days in October were choice. The rumor that Chiang
K'ai-shek was sleeping with a nurse had been spiked by
his manly denial. But: Had Chiang really beaten his chief
of conscription, Chin Tso-jen, over the head with a stick
and then locked him up in a recruit-training camp because conditions in such camps were so bad? That, I was
ruefully told by a cabinet minister, *was* true, "but," he
added, "it's the first time in twenty years the Generalissimo has actually beaten a *high* official." Was it true that
China was now down to its last ten thousand rolling and

usable trucks? No, said the Minister of Communications to me: China had six thousand trucks operable—three thousand in the army, three thousand for all the rest of the nation. Was General Hsueh Yueh conspiring with the Japanese, as some said? Was the Generalissimo himself dealing with the Japanese occupying command to counter American pressure, as others said? Bubonic plague had broken out in Fukien: Was it spreading inland? Could it be stopped? Yen Hsi-shan and the Communists were fighting each other in Shansi again: could anything be done to stop the fighting, short of giving American aid to both sides?

It was a hot and sultry autumn in Chungking, itchy and wet; rumors flourished, begat and multiplied as they can do only in a community with no open communications system, where anxieties and heat incubate rumor to fever. Yet after ten days back in Chungking, out of all the blur of rumors, I could begin to range in on some very large shapes that were indisputably real: We Americans were being forced to a choice. The choice was being forced on us by the Japanese. They meant to wipe out our continental base on the mainland, and we were apparently compelled to choose between Chinese Communists and Chinese Nationalists to hold that continental base.

The first rumor I heard, the first week back in Chungking, was that Stilwell himself was in Yenan visiting the Communists! Not true at all, I learned instantly. The facts were: Henry Wallace, the U.S. Vice President, had passed through Chungking, and had backed Stilwell in the demand that the U.S. Army be allowed to maintain an observer's mission in the Communist capital of Yenan, in North China. That mission of contact, called Dixie Mission, was already in operation by the end of September. (Only later did I learn from the historians that Wallace, while supporting Stilwell against Chiang to make contact with the Communists, was also supporting Chiang against Stilwell, and urging Roosevelt to replace Stilwell in China.) But Stilwell himself had indeed made contact with the Communists in Chungking.

U.S. Army headquarters was not entirely forthcom-

ing about what was going on. But gradually, there
emerged from friends at headquarters the outline of the
Allied command that Stilwell believed was already his.
Stilwell planned to carve out of the mass of plodding,
road-bound Chinese foot soldiery a thirty-division American-directed army, which he would modernize, equip and
deploy personally. Then, only then, would he distribute
the rest of American aid to Chiang K'ai-shek—and to all
other Chinese armies fighting Japanese. In short, Stilwell
planned to cancel Chiang's exclusive franchise of American aid—and meant also, with no effort at all at conceal-
ment, to share some of that aid with the detested Communists. Moreover, Stilwell proposed to fly directly to
Yenan to bring the Communists under his personal command. For Stilwell, anyone who fought Japanese was a
friend of the American cause.

Chiang's intelligence service must have told him of
Stilwell's contact with the Chinese Communists; it must
also have reported to him the efforts of independents, like
Chang Fa-kuei, to make direct alliances with the Americans. For Chiang, the perspectives were clear. Japan was
already being destroyed by the Americans. The future of
China, therefore, was being decided now in the struggle
between himself and Mao. No Americans must interfere
in that struggle except to help him—so Stilwell must
go.

I had been at the front, in the kind of combat
isolation now unimaginable to American soldiers, reporters or officers, who read of their national politics as a
matter of course wherever they are posted. Coming back
to Chungking, I was in a political world and nothing was
more startling than to tap in again on the negotiations
between Communists and Nationalists that had resumed
under American pressure. The Communists were now as
intransigent as the Nationalists; they wanted recognition
not only of their entire political independence, but also of
their area control, which was now widening behind the
spreading conquest of the Japanese. Most pathetic was
the statement of the chief Nationalist negotiator, Wang
Shih-chieh. Wang asserted there could be no compromise

for the reason that the national government was too *weak* to compromise. It would take a year to overhaul the national government enough to give the people efficient government, which was the only way to compete with the Communists, and so—shrug of shoulders!

Where the truth lay in all this sputter of word-of-mouth news, I did not know for two weeks after I returned to Chungking. Was Stilwell in command? Was Chiang in command? Where did Roosevelt stand? Were the Americans planning to accept a Communist alliance? Was Chiang threatening to go over to the Japanese?

Then on Monday morning, October 16, I was summoned with Brooks Atkinson of *The New York Times* to visit Stilwell.

How great a breach this invitation was with Stilwell's tradition of discipline I can only now understand. He sat there behind his desk in his austere headquarters, a flat-topped villa with a sweeping view of the Chialing River, and suddenly he seemed frail. Brooding, vituperative, bitter, he spoke. I remember him scratching at his arms, infected with the jungle itch he had contracted in Burma, glaring, not in anger at us but to make sure we understood his points. Someone, he said, must know the truth; for the time being we were not to print a word of what he said; but for the next few days, we could come and go at his headquarters, read the "eyes alone" cables the commander of the theater received from Washington. When all was over, one or the other of us must tell the story to the American people so they should understand. It was my first sense of the American press as the supreme court of political appeals—that this man should violate his military oath of secrecy, his personal loyalty to George Marshall, to carry his story to the court of future opinion. He wanted us to know, in the historian's phrase, "the way it really was."

He was going to be relieved of command in the next few days, Stilwell began. And suddenly I could see him as an old soldier stripped of authority, shriveled overnight. He wore the four stars of a full general, which was a rare honor in those days, and his mandate still ran from the

Yellow River, across China, through the jungle of Burma, over the sprawl of American troops in India as far as Karachi, a continental expanse larger than the United States itself. For a few more days he might, if he wished, command sorties, retreat, killing. But now, already, the personality was broken.

He wanted us to know that from the day of Pearl Harbor on, "this ignorant son of a bitch has never wanted to fight Japan." He went on supporting the large facts with combat details. "Every major blunder of this war is directly traceable to Chiang K'ai-shek." Orders given by Stilwell, countermanded by Chiang; telephonic orders from Chiang to frontal troops decreeing assault or withdrawal over distances and terrain Chiang K'ai-shek simply did not know. Lying. Thieving. Hoarding. Hoarding of all supplies for the few politically reliable troops needed to fight the future civil war against the Communists. And with that, Stilwell's paradoxical love of China and Chinese: how wonderful these troops and these people were when fed, trained, and led by honest people. All he had wanted was to help these people. Then, in stunning simplicity, he told us what he had demanded: the authority to move, shift, deploy, command any unit in China; the right "to reward and punish, to promote and demote." Then the push of his duty: We had hoped the war in Europe would be over by this fall, 1944. But the Germans had held, not broken. It might be six months, another year, before we could get at Japan; meanwhile, we could not let the Japanese transfer their main base of resistance to China, from their homeland to the continent, as the resistance front in East China collapsed. Chinese had to learn to resist, to organize and command armies, to push Japanese back—for the common purpose of China and America. Stilwell could not wait. "We can't expect to be *told* about the future," he had once written in his diary. "If we want to find out, we must march toward it." As an actor in history, he had undertaken that march too late; and then marched too fast.

It was the end of the long missionary road. The man, whom I then adored, I can now see as a political innocent: a man with the old West Point code of honor, seeking to get things done, as the purpose of America wished them to be done, in a world that does things otherwise; a man too proud and too old-fashioned to dissemble. Stilwell had found it necessary to change things, but then found that to change China he must act far beyond the historic experience of any American. What he had come to seek, step by step, was the replacement of an Asian leader useless to our war purpose, and the installation of a leadership that would be effective in the American way. Yet politics did not permit that, even then, at the height of American power. America would have to deal with what Asia chose as leadership—or stay away from such leaders.

I was there at Stilwell's headquarters again, usually with Brooks Atkinson, on Thursday, Friday and Saturday of that same week—installed in the basement, reading cables we should not have read, watching the distant Roosevelt, another of my political gods, slowly accepting the superior reality of politics over Stilwell's reality of combat. On Thursday, officially, without public announcement, Roosevelt relieved Stilwell of command and ordered his departure for home immediately. On Friday, a minor Chinese functionary arrived at the headquarters where Stilwell was packing, to offer him, in the name of the Generalissimo, China's highest decoration for a foreigner, the Special Grand Cordon of the Blue Sky and White Sun. Stilwell told his aide to tell the Generalissimo's aide to shove it. Later that afternoon, he had tea with the Generalissimo. And the next day he was off.

He left early on Saturday afternoon. Only a few of his inner staff knew what was happening. They packed his bags and his briefcase; and Stilwell carried his own trophy, a Japanese Samurai sword, much too long for his short stature. At the airfield, he was given farewell by T. V. Soong, about to become China's Prime Minister; Soong would be the chief temporary beneficiary of Stilwell's insistence that the government of China be reorganized. A touring car splashed through the mud of the overcast and drizzling day to disgorge China's Minister of

War, Ho Ying-chin, who, with exquisite relish and equal courtesy, had come to see the departure of the American who had demanded his dismissal from office. Stilwell took their greetings, turned to his personal aide and said, "What the hell are we waiting for?" then climbed aboard. Atkinson climbed in with him, determined, as all *New York Times* men traditionally are, to tell the story first where it counted most. I gave Atkinson my dispatch to sneak through censorship to *Time* magazine. And I was the only one left to wave Stilwell off as his plane rose from the runway and he left China.

It was years before I could see Stilwell correctly. He came of a tradition which has now all but vanished—the tradition of Americans who felt so strongly we were the good people that wherever they went they were convinced they, as Americans, brought virtue. Nor could Stilwell conceive that what was good for America could possibly be bad, or wrong, for other peoples. In the years since, American ambassadors, generals and agents, like the emissaries of other, much crueler people, have continued to try to change governments, replace governments, have helped to sustain or tried to eliminate foreign chiefs of state. It was a diplomatic technique to which we came late and at which we are not very adept. But Stilwell was the first American to insist that our interests required political elimination of a major foreign chief of state. This policy perplexes me with its arrogance. But paradoxically I know, in Stilwell's case, that he was absolutely right. It would have been better for China, for America and for the world had Chiang been removed from China's leadership in time. There might then have been some hope of a Chinese leadership more humane, less hostile, just as effective yet more tolerant than the one that succeeded Chiang.

Several years later, in 1946, visiting my home in New York, Stilwell summed up what lay ahead on the day of his departure. "Chiang," he said, "was a man trying to fight an idea with force. He didn't understand the idea, and he didn't know how to use force."

He could not have said it that well on that Saturday

afternoon in the drizzle at the Chungking airfield. Nor could I have formulated it, either. What was at issue in the Stilwell crisis was what kind of China there was going to be after the war was won. What had most alarmed Chiang K'ai-shek, I knew even at that time, was not the Japanese victories of 1944, nor even Stilwell's command temper. What had most alarmed Chiang was Stilwell's effort to establish contact with the Chinese revolutionaries of the north—the men of Yenan, Mao's Communists.

And so, before Chiang could cut the tendrils of contact between Americans and the Chinese revolution, I felt I ought to go north. I knew, as did all field correspondents, that the men in Yenan were not the simple agrarian reformers described by distant American liberals. They were, instead, a swelling, pressing force, banging at the American command for a decision, one way or another. They could cause men to die, could set back the Japanese, could govern. They had much to offer and much to teach.

CHAPTER 5

Yenan: Takeoff for
the Revolution

I had waved Stilwell off the mud-slick runway of Chungking late Saturday afternoon, October 21, 1944.

And now I knew I must hurry.

With Stilwell gone, it would be only a week or ten days before a new American commander in China would be arriving. The American Embassy was in disarray, with no authority. The Chinese, shocked by their own temerity in forcing Stilwell out, would not move overnight to penalize me, or halt my movements—but soon they certainly would. Stilwell's staff, however, still controlled American military headquarters that night. An American courier plane, I knew, would be leaving the next day for the Communist capital in Yenan; my friends could still airlift me there if they cut my orders that evening. Which they would; and did; and the next afternoon, the rain still drizzling, I was Yenan bound.

We were over the loess uplands and in the sun in two hours—first the Szechwan hills fleeting away below to the south, then the walled rectangle of Sian passing be-

neath our wings; then the tawny hills, the mesas with their
tops sliced off, and the brown and yellow fields in their
sere fall colors draped over the hills; then a solitary
yellow pagoda pricking into the blue sky, the crenelated
sentinel which was the landmark of Yenan. Three arroyos
below slashed the sandy hills, then ran together in a gully
which broadened into a riverbed, and our plane as it
twisted its way on wing end through the gullies displayed
to us the slope sides—cut with hundreds of oval cave
entrances, a panoramic honeycomb that might have been
a bandit's lair. Then we were bouncing over the airstrip
in the valley, flanked by green vegetable patches, and I
was in Yenan.

Time, by its miracle, gives a clarity to all great
events the further they fade into the past, burning off
detail to reveal the track of history and decision. I had
come to Yenan as a war correspondent, to write a story
of politics and pressures. But what was happening in
those three weeks I lingered in Yenan was far more
important: a revolution was groping for its shape; the
People's Republic of China was preparing to declare its
sovereignty as Communist leaders filtered through from
the vast all-China underground to Yenan to prepare for
the first national congress of their party since 1928. Not
only that; in those weeks, in the immediate aftermath of
Chiang K'ai-shek's repudiation of Stilwell and Roosevelt's
repudiation of Chiang, the Chinese Communists were
preparing to offer a full, perhaps permanent, alliance to
the United States—military, economic, political—which
they hoped, and some of us also hoped, would endure
into the future. Had that mood in Yenan continued, there
might have been no Korean War, no Vietnam War.

Those were the honeymoon weeks between America's war purpose and the Chinese revolution, and the
agent of the honeymoon, the matchmaker, was a young
American diplomat, John Paton Davies, Jr., then thirty-
six years old, China-born to missionary parents, fluent in
Chinese; a lithe, handsome, witty rising star of the Foreign Service, who had taken it on himself to explore

history on his own. I hope I do my old and dear friend John Davies no disservice in saying that brilliant as he was, he was as innocent of American politics as I was at that moment; and he was to suffer humiliation and degradation far greater than mine for those lyric fall days in Yenan.

Davies and I had flown to Yenan together that Sunday afternoon, in the same plane. I was journeying to get a story. What his purpose was, he did not say; close as we were in friendship, diplomats like Davies in those years kept their secrets from friends in the press like me; and I would not intrude. We parted at the Yenan airport, he to lodge with the American military observers' section, Dixie Mission, and I to lodge at the civilian guesthouse of the Communists, a mile away. We saw each other again and again in the two weeks of his stay, with affection and frolic, as we pursued our differing ways in that hill city which is now legend; but not until years later, when all documents were published and he wrote his own superb memoirs, *Dragon by the Tail,* did I know what he was doing, or fully understand what was happening.

The Chinese have a saying for such moments: "The heavens are high, and the Emperor is far away." That week the heavens were, indeed, high; and there was no emperor. There was no superior to John Davies, for no one either in Washington or in Chungking presided over American relations with the Chinese revolution. Technically, Davies was a State Department political officer, detached to give political advice to the military commander, Stilwell. But that weekend, there was no Stilwell, no American military command. So Davies pursued an exploration of his own: Could the Chinese Communists be useful to America's war against Japan? What was their value to us?

Davies had begun on the evening of his arrival with a late-night session with Mao Tse-tung, Chou En-lai and Chu Teh, Commander in Chief of the Red Army. If our forces were to land on the China coast, would the Communists be able to develop support, cut rails, mobilize peasants? It was a legitimate inquiry. But it came at a moment of confusion. The Communists were fully informed of Chiang's break with America over Stilwell; even better informed of the decay and collapse of the Nationalist armies; and preparing for the shaping of an independent government. All their great military leaders were back, or were trickling back on foot, from the underground and guerrilla resistance areas, for the Seventh Party Congress—the first in more than sixteen years! Chu Teh, Chou En-lai, Mao Tse-tung, Liu Shao-ch'i, were all in residence, but Lin Piao, P'eng Te-huai, Ch'en I, Nieh Jung-chen, had also just arrived—the name marshals of the future conquest of China, the men who would seize control of a civilization. And here was Davies, exploring the possibility of military cooperation, an alliance! Davies could not have been there at a better time. Nor could I.

We were seeing a revolution hardening from embryo to form; I was the only newsman there, and since I was sheltered by old friendship with Chou En-lai and acquaintance with Yeh Chien-ying, and clothed with spurious importance by the accident of my arrival with John Davies, I was accepted as part of the great purpose of exploring the alliance between America and the Chinese Communists.

Those weeks in Yenan were a time of laughter and gaiety. Those of us who have been so criticized for romanticizing the Chinese Communists can claim forgiveness for those weeks in October and November; Chinese Communists were different then; we were not duped. The wine of friendship flowed; Chu Teh and Chou En-lai would wander around on foot unannounced to visit the outpost of Americans as friends, chatting and whiling away the hours. Their own comrades, the men of the underground, the battle-scarred veterans of combat, the commanders of sprawling, invisible, yet violently successful guerrilla armies, were arriving for the great congress. It was a time of good will—with men open, warm, trusting. Later, twenty years later, they would purge each other, kill each other. Later they would command armies to kill Americans. But their trust in each other and their yearning to make friends with us was real. What it must have been like at the Smolny in St. Petersburg when the Russian Communists struck for power, I cannot imagine. Certainly Americans, with rare exceptions like John Reed, were not welcome. But Yenan, at the transition moment, embraced us as allies and friends.

In my cave quarters each morning at the guesthouse, I would be awakened by the sound of bugles, silver-bell tones shivering off the hills. Breakfast was brown wheat buns—sliced, toasted and served with eggs. I would go out to the ledge looking down over the valley and see tufted camels coming in from the northern desert, bells tinkling from their throats. And mules, and horsemen, and teamsters cracking their whips, and people gathering at the marketplace. The people were healthy, dressed in shaggy tan woolens or thick blue cotton paddings. The Communists, in those days, believed that soldiers, officials, students, should all be fed—fed enough so they could work and stride with the vigorous step that differentiated them from the sluggish officials and feeble soldiers of the Nationalists.

All were healthy; but I noted that complete equality fell short in luxuries: milk, for example, went to the sick or wounded in the hospitals. But after that, the milk went to the families and children of the high officials. I pressed that question: Whose children got the milk?

It embarrassed them. So I did not press further, for they were my hosts.

I could wander anywhere unescorted: to the leather market, which stank as tanneries do; to the fruit and vegetable stalls; up and down roads. And thus, as I wandered about, the encampment slowly clarified for me into two rough visible centers of power. I could see these centers, and visit them at will because I was considered a friend. Party headquarters and army headquarters were nuclei of unseen, yet interacting, systems. Party headquarters was three miles from my quarters—two gray brick

buildings, one for the offices of functionaries, one housing
an auditorium for meetings. There I did most of my
political interviewing. Army headquarters was another
gray brick building, surrounded by lesser buildings of
yellow adobe and enclosed in a garden called the Pear
Orchard by the Americans of Dixie Mission though, to
me, it seemed to hold more fig trees than pear trees. I
understood the military talks better than the political
talks because my Chinese could absorb the plain, technical language of war, while the nuances of their politics
were so new and revolutionary that Western languages
had not yet invented terms to translate them. Yet the
language of this hill town would someday become the
clichés of revolutionaries all around the world and stir
even American changemakers in the streets of the 1960s.

All seemed to chuckle with a joviality that, even
now, I cannot conceive as feigned. There was Chu Teh,
for example, a pug-nosed, burly man of fifty-eight, Commander in Chief and father of the Red armies, dropping
in to visit Americans, sample their Western food, drink
tea, chatting away as if time did not exist. One day after a
two-hour talk at his headquarters, he insisted I stay for
lunch. As we sat down, we were joined by his Chief of
Staff, Yeh Chien-ying, who had just finished a talk with
John Davies; and then, as casually as if we were at a
house party, we went out into the sunny garden and joked
in a word game. We tried to see which of us could use the
phrase *"so-wei"* (which means "so-called") most often in
a sentence—as, for example, "The so-called government
in Chungking under its so-called President Chiang is
trying to extricate the so-called Nationalist armies from
the so-called front." We laughed and laughed and ate
ice-cold pears and drank tea unhurriedly.

These two Chinese commanded armies that ran from
bases on the tropical island of Hainan to the deserts of
the Gobi in the cold north. But nowhere in all my travels
have I met men who seemed more at ease in authority or
enjoyed it more than in Yenan those weeks. I look now at
the somber faces of present Chinese leadership, photo-

graphed as they stand on the rostrum at Tien-An Men, stiff and stern, and I wonder if they themselves can recall the days when they were young and made puns and danced. Perhaps power changed them before they knew they were changing, when they learned that power meant they could afford the harsh luxury of purging and killing each other.

In those days, however, they were comrades—with a natural, easy quality of friendship and equality that the power of state has since erased. After lunch, Chou En-lai might invite his young interpreter, Ch'en Chia-k'ang, to play Ping-Pong with him in the big mess hall, which they would sometimes do even in the presence of foreign guests. Chu Teh, P'eng Te-huai, Lin Piao, would roar with laughter at each other's jokes. They had been together for so long, hungered and suffered and trod the Long March together, that they were brothers. It was only ten years from that epic; they had dismissed Chiang, and outfought the Japanese. Back now from the various fields of command against the invader, they were enjoying this wartime reunion, and a bubble of mirth, the swagger of confidence, attended their rendezvous. They were the first team of command; they had transformed their guerrilla ragamuffins into an organized army of 600,000, with a militia support of over a million. Lin Piao would go on to conquer Manchuria and North China; P'eng Te-huai would go on to command Chinese forces against Mac-Arthur in Korea. Then both would be purged and Lin Piao would be killed.

The best moment to savor this comradeship was at the Saturday-night dances in the party headquarters auditorium. A few Chinese string instruments would saw away, drums would beat, harmonicas and paper-covered combs would carry a melody, and the high command of party and army would sashay around the floor. The dance I attended while I was there seemed to me reminiscent of the old-fashioned Jewish weddings I had known as a boy, while to John Davies it seemed more like the church sociables he had known when he was young. Chu Teh did

not dance, but sat at a table drinking tea and cracking
melon seeds; but Madame Chu Teh was like the grandmother who wants to dance with the youngsters. Yeh
Chien-ying brought his three-year-old daughter, Niu Niu,
who darted in and out among the chairs with other
children, while Yeh, himself the Chief of Staff, danced
with abandon. Yeh, a man of almost Mexican cast of
countenance, sporting a pencil-thin mustache, swung his
partner about the floor, no matter what the music, in a
combination of free-flowing tango and waltz. Lin Piao
preferred the fox trot. American enlisted men, forlorn at
their observers' outpost in the hills, were also invited. But
these were dances of innocence; one American once made
a pass at a Chinese lass and the incident was followed by
a formal visit of protest from Chou En-lai himself to the
commander of the American outpost, Colonel David D.
Barrett. Chou explained that the matter was inadmissible,
unless the American enlisted man did, indeed, love the
Chinese girl with his whole heart.

I recall the music now because today it seems like a
melodic midpassage in a minor cultural stream. Five
years before, in the hills of Shansi, I had heard Communist soldiers marching as they sang Chinese words to
"Onward, Christian Soldiers." Now, in Yenan, in 1944,
their leaders danced to strains from "Yankee Doodle
Dandy" and "Marching Through Georgia." And twenty-
eight years later, in 1972, when I attended the reception
for Richard Nixon in the Great Hall of the People in
Peking, the accomplished first orchestra of the triumphant
revolution played in his honor "America the Beautiful."
But the folk music of America sounded most authentic in
China in 1944 as the drums went thump, thump, thump
at the Saturday-night dance, while men and women in
thick padded woolens wore their caps as they danced on
the beaten mud floor—and all of us swung in a rhythm of
brotherhood into the night.

Historic documents present events in mannered
prose. For example: in the bible of Chinese Communism,
The Collected Works of Mao Tse-tung, is embedded the
"great" speech he made on October 30, 1944, in Yenan,

entitled, forbiddingly, "The United Front in Cultural Work." As it reads now, manicured into a state document, it gives no feel of the man Mao Tse-tung who spoke that day. The Chairman entered the hall that afternoon, walked about among the local officials and invitees like an American politician meeting the medical and public health workers in Kenosha, Wisconsin. He shook hands as he walked; he was dressed in a drab brown woolen suit, buttoned at the neck, and shortly mounted the platform to begin his speech. He rambled a bit before he found his theme, then fished out a few notes from his pockets, began by interpellation, the questioning of the listeners, the seeking of answers to set questions, involving the audience of local health officials in his discourse, before he began the serious part of his lecture. He was the teacher, his theme the necessity of using witch doctors, herb doctors, acupuncture specialists, all the resources of native Chinese medicine, to help the people and the army since the people and the army were deprived of Western medical science.

I remember two things of the lecture. The first was the marvelous folksy, histrionic quality of his platform presence; only Hubert Humphrey among the American stump speakers I have since heard was as good as Mao. Mao would mimic, gesture, pace back and forth, hold on to his haunches to make a point, squeak, screech, drop to sotto voce. I could not understand half of what he said— but as a performer, in his prime, he was gripping. And I remember also Chou En-lai sitting in the front row with the other leaders at this medical exhortation. Chou had a pad and a pencil with him; perhaps he was showing his loyalty to Mao, perhaps he was setting a good example to others to pay attention. But he held his little pad very high in the air, sitting there in the front row before Mao, and with a tiny extra bit of flourish, conspiciously wrote notes on the great lecture for the Chairman and all others to see his respect of the Master Teacher.

The time frame as well as the catalytic presence of John Davies set the mood.

The time frame was the Communist perception of

the events of 1944. They knew, better than any others, the extent of the battle disasters of Chiang K'ai-shek in East China. Nationalist armies were dissolving; Japanese were gobbling up entire provinces; the Communists were following the Japanese advances and organizing counter-resistance. Whatever fell to the Japanese, the Communists felt was theirs to undermine and organize—and organization was moving even faster than the Communists had hoped. Chiang had lost a quarter of a million Nationalist troops in six months; but their own Communist recruits were multiplying each week. They had now organized no less than sixteen political-military regional bases in the rear of the Japanese, each called a "liberated area." In some of these areas, they now controlled patches of one hundred by two hundred miles in which neither Japanese nor Nationalists dared enter, patches where the only government was their government. The prime political matter under their consideration was how to knit all these "liberated areas" into one "people's government," a real government that controlled the ninety million people they protected. So far as they were concerned, the so-called government of Chiang K'ai-shek had evaporated with its troops in East China; it now existed in West China only as the proprietor of the American franchise. And lo, at this point, here were the Americans, Davies and Barrett, exploring Communist willingness to share this American franchise. Thus, as the leaders of these local governments gathered, and more importantly, the military commanders gathered with them, to consider the calling of their first national congress in sixteen years, and the possibility of making a Communist government, the accident of Stilwell's removal teased them to consider also whether this new government a-borning would cast its lot with America or not.

A reporter could not have found himself in a happier situation. There were apparently thirteen members of the Communist Politburo in Yenan, each a vivid character, each anxious to accept the American embrace, each open and forthcoming. I interviewed no less than eleven of the thirteen, and, perhaps, should have tried for the full house. But interviews with Communist leaders in those days ran two, or three, sometimes four hours, in unhurried, leisurely sessions. I did a rough survey, which may prove inaccurate in the light of later research, on who and what these founding Communist fathers were and where they came from. The names, in Western transliteration, are a roll call of monosyllables. But the persons were, overwhelmingly, intellectuals. Eight had gone directly from college or school into the revolution twenty years earlier. That included Mao and Chou and Liu Shao-ch'i (the party boss, later purged). Only four had come from the peasant or working class—Chu Teh himself, P'eng Te-huai, Ch'en Yun and Teng Fa. Po Ku had been both a college student and a worker, a man of humor who could speak in both idioms. After the new congress, this Politburo would change to include more military commanders—but these new marshals were also, overwhelmingly, men of intellectual background who had begun as scholars.

This was one of the things I learned firsthand in Yenan as I searched for history: revolutions are made by intellectuals. Not all intellectuals are revolutionaries. But if intellectuals can weave their ideas about what bothers ordinary people, they can ensnare and mesh them together. If they are shrewd enough to describe conditions to workers and families so that simple people recognize what is cramping them or destroying them—then they can mobilize these people to change things, to kill, to hunt, to die, to be cruel, with the moral absolution that intellectuals can always give simple killers and terrorists.

All of the high command in the Politburo were willing to talk with me. And all—except Chou En-lai and Mao Tse-tung—were convinced, apparently, that I was a semi-official and friendly reportorial arm of the American government.

The generals in the Politburo admitted they knew nothing of the use of modern artillery; that they knew nothing of aviation; that their own staff work was primitive; that their communications net was rudimentary, dependent on wires snipped from Japanese lines or radios they put together from parts smuggled out of the Japanese-occupied cities. But their intelligence service was spectacular: they knew precisely the order of battle of Japanese divisions; enemy lines of communication; the spectrum of occupation zones. Their intelligence reached into studies of personalities of various Japanese field commanders and classified Chiang's generals by ability, background, meanness, cooperation. The net message in each military conversation was: We can help you. Chiang K'ai-shek cannot.

The conversations ran with remarkable similarity, with no contradictions, no matter which general one spoke with; and their frankness, in wartime, on their dispositions, plans, movements, was to me astounding. One conversation must do to cover all military conversations—with P'eng Te-huai. He was a small man, balding, of crumpled face, his eyes set in a perpetual squint. He had been fighting since 1926 and had now risen to Deputy Commander in Chief of the 18th Group Army; with no reluctance at all, he lectured me for three hours on war. He began as if I were a man from Mars, explaining first the doctrine of partisan warfare; from that to the military tactics that partisan warfare implied—total cooperation with the people so that the army could fade and disperse into the countryside, melt away into the people, then regather; then a description of his own forces and their levels of competence—from the evanescent and diaphanous guerrilla command outside Canton; to the semi-organized, more sophisticated base in Japanese-occupied Hainan island; to the full-force regulars of the New Fourth Army in central China; to the established governments of the "liberated areas" in the north, where he could collect and maneuver units up to twelve thousand men in strength. Twelve thousand was his limit as a force of maneuver simply because, as he explained, they could not feed more than twelve thousand men in one concentration for any length of time. From that to staff structure, training commands, the function of the combined chiefs of staff here in Yenan.

P'eng went back twenty years in his history of the Red Army; knew the caches of buried rifles and weapons left behind in Nationalist-occupied areas; spoke matter-of-factly of different tactics of battle used against Japan and Nationalist armies. He mentioned casually how "we destroyed two regiments of the 61st Army [a Chiang K'ai-shek army] this summer with few casualties." Then he brought the conversation up to the contemporary history of October 1944. The Eighth Route Army alone, he said, had 400,000 regular troops within operational distance of the North China coast; these could call on a further 1,000,000 armed militia bound by family to their villages and towns. "With these forces," said P'eng, "we can aid any American landing in North China." Thus to his techniques of disruption; he could tear apart any railway north of the Yellow River, for as long as we wanted. In 1940, said he, in the Hundred Regiments offensive, Communist troops had ripped up all Japanese rail communication in North China so thoroughly that it was from three to six months before the Japanese could rebuild. Now, in 1944, they could do even better. If we, the Americans, landed anywhere between Shanghai and the Shantung peninsula, with enough advance notice, said P'eng, "we can guarantee you one million regular troops on the spot plus our people's militia." Every Communist commander was making the same guarantee, and to Davies and Barrett in even more specific terms. I for my part, as an American reporter, was willing to accept the alliance.

These military conversations were happening in late October 1944 and, to me, seemed critical. But I was parochially bound to a China vision of war. In the Pacific, war was taking on a happier coloration. October 20 was "Assault Day," as the battle of Leyte Gulf began; in the next four days followed the greatest sea battles of all time, with Americans spectacularly victorious; by November 1, MacArthur had 101,365 men ashore in the Philippines—and the Japanese grand battle fleet had been wiped out, erased from history. As seen from Washington, clearly, by mid-November there was no need of Chinese support to destroy Japan; China could safely be demoted to a tertiary theater of war; no American in Washington need be faced with the messy problem of deciding that month whether to support Communists or Nationalists in China or ignore both. On that unrecognized political decision hung the future of Asia, and America's relations with Asia—which was tragedy.

In Yenan, however, politics were supreme. Yenan was, above all other things, an idea factory. Perhaps never before in history, except perhaps for the Christian revolution in Rome or the French and American revolutions of the eighteenth century, have ideas been so important—or been so consciously perceived as forces in themselves, as the manipulators of action.

Again, I must cast away notes of hours and hours of conversation, skip from interview to interview, bowdlerize and distort in order to make the idea of ideas manifest.

I should start at the bottom with the two minor functionaries, Kao and Nan, who directed the local government of the Yenan base area. "Base area" meant to me a logistical base—a secure area from which arms, supplies, food and support were shipped to a war front. I thought of a base area in terms of what Americans called in those days the "ZI," or Zone of Interior, meaning Detroit, Pittsburgh, New York, the manufactories and training camps of our power. In Yenan, not so. Kao Tzu-li and Nan Han-ch'en told me flatly that the Yenan base area shipped *nothing* to the front. All war areas were self-supporting. What Yenan shipped out was people—"cadres" who could spread ideas. Yenan, of course, had problems, but basically they were experimental problems—as, for example, finance and currency. The breach with Chiang K'ai-shek in 1941 over the New Fourth Army incident had forced the Communists to enter finance; the week after Mao's statement that January (see page 156) denouncing Chiang, Yenan had decided to print its own paper money. Currency control is an essential attribute of sovereignty. Without knowing it, the Communists had thus accepted one of the prime problems of states: finance, currency, reserves. Now, in 1944, they were training cadres to ship out to the liberated zones to manage finance and the economy.

Yenan was a continuing experiment in "do-it-yourself" government, with people learning, as they do not learn in Poli-Sci I in any American university, how you go about choosing the proper men to govern other men—or improvising all the multitude of technologies needed to govern. How does one make paper to print books, leaflets or money in a hill country? They were learning by themselves. What do you do after you dip buckets of oil from traditional oil pits and try to make kerosene out of it for lamps, and the badly refined oil sputters in the homemade lamps? How do you refine oil? How do you melt iron and make guns? How do you care for sick and wounded? How, after all, do you make a revolution and a new government without ideas? That was Yenan's main function; to cycle and recycle individuals through the base area and teach them to think in new ways. Forty thousand people lived in the Yenan area. Twelve thousand of them were locals, peasants, merchants. The rest were party people—functionaries, leaders, officials and, overwhelmingly, students. Students ranged from eighteen to forty-five, from adolescents just arrived after fleeing their schools in the occupied cities or Nationalist areas, to grizzled middle-aged guerrilla commanders undergoing courses in remedial reading, learning how to put staff orders in writing.

Yenan was a community of schools—for doctors, for nurses, for commanders, for political commissars, for party functionaries. The Politburo members were charged, each one, with some area of idea training.

There was Liu Shao-ch'i, chief of what the Russians would have called the Orgburo. He controlled party training and organization. Later, in 1959, he would become the Chairman of the People's Republic of China, under Mao's superior party chairmanship, and would be ruthlessly purged in 1966. I could understand the later purging, for in talking to Liu Shao-ch'i one found that he had the mind of a great administrator—or a mechanic. The world of his life was the interior of the party and, dryly, he lectured me on party cell organization from village branch, to railway branch, to county branch, to all-area branch; and how the hierarchy operated. Liu Shao-ch'i had a neat mind, but there was no poetry in it.

Teng Fa was not an intellectual, but certainly a memorable interviewee. He was one of the few authentic proletarians in the Politburo, a waterfront organizer in his youth, a riverboat cook on a British vessel, a dedicated revolutionary. Like most untutored people, particularly seamen who read in solitude, he had come upon ideas as a virgin illiterate. Ideas had struck him as virulently as venereal disease had struck the Hawaiian Islanders after Captain Cook had passed through. Teng Fa was in charge of mass organizations and his specialty was slogans. He loved slogans, explained why one slogan worked and another did not, how critical they were. For the masses an idea had to be clear, simple, easy to understand—and correct. *"Yu chien kei chien, yu li kei li"* was, he thought, a good example of clarity and simplicity; it meant: "Have money, give money; have strength, give strength." That was a great resistance slogan; translated, it meant that poor peasants had to give their strength, their lives, their guts to the revolutionary resistance; and the rich landlords, who had money, had to deliver money, or face the consequences. Communists were cruel in extorting money from landlords and the rich, moving to excesses of brutality. But I note with wry amusement that their feeling then was that the maximum income tax on a rich man should not be more than 35 percent. When Teng Fa spoke, with professional enthusiasm, of how you get ideas to women, to peasants, to workers, to masses, through slogans, I felt he might have made a great Madison Avenue ad man. But he wanted to overturn two thousand years of history with his slogans; words were weapons.

Then there was P'eng Chen. P'eng Chen was an intellectual; he had gone directly from school into the Communist underground; been imprisoned by his local warlord for six years, until released in 1935; thus may have been the only Politburo member who had not made the Long March; but had seen combat action against the Japanese for four years, from 1937 to 1941 He had returned from the field to K'ang-Ta ("Fight Japan") University at Yenan in 1942 and now headed that most elite of Communist academies—a combination of West Point, MIT, Leavenworth Staff College and Harvard. P'eng Chen fascinated me.

P'eng Chen believed quite simply that history was an ingredient of the revolution—not something handed down by tradition, but something you mixed, compounded, rearranged and packaged just as you packaged gunpowder by formulas for land mines. He had a reverence for history. Each of the succeeding dynasties of China had edited the official history of its predecessor and thus the twenty-four dynastic histories, where they were not simple chronologies, were probably entirely misleading. P'eng Chen felt the party also needed its own new Chinese history; unless you had theory, you could not trace social roots. But no one knew any Chinese history. he said; there were no Chinese histories. No one knew anything about Chinese economics. either. When Karl Marx wrote *Das Kapital.* P'eng Chen said, he had used the reading room of the British Museum; but in China there was no such thing. The party, he continued, did not even have a history of its own revolution—only a handful of documents for students to study, plus *The Party History of the Soviet Union.*

P'eng Chen made no effort to conceal his contempt for such classics of Marxist hagiography, as well as Lenin's *Two Tactics* and *Left-Wing Communism, an Infantile Disorder,* Engels's *Socialism. Utopian and Scientific,* and others. He dismissed *Das Kapital* as being too hard to understand. The result was that his students— tested party and army functionaries being groomed for higher-level responsibility—were writing their own textbooks in history and economics. They met in groups as large as fifty, sometimes as small as twelve. They studied from documents, news reports, articles, but mostly they exchanged their experiences in the field. From what they knew and had observed, they devised their own theories of economics and development and when they came to questions they could not solve, classes appealed to the Central Committee, or even to Mao himself, for the applicable theory or instruction.

P'eng Chen grieved that the three thousand students of his new university could be spared to study for only two years before being recycled to higher duties. He explained his fundamental problem in a phrase: "brain remolding." The men who came in from the field, he said, whether semiliterate battalion commanders or college-trained intellectuals, had to have their minds washed out, had to be remolded in ideology. At first he thought this could be done in only three months; he had now learned that a full year was necessary to "remold the brain," before they could go on to study military matters, or economics, or health, or administration. His interpreter and I searched for a word better than "brain remolding" and finally the interpreter came up with the phrase "raising their level of consciousness." This was the first time I heard that phrase, which, over the years, moved out of China and into the streets and fashions of America in the 1960s.

P'eng Chen took his history very seriously—theoretically as a scholar, militarily as a man of action, politically as a party man. He left leadership of the university in 1945 to join Lin Piao for the campaign and victories in Manchuria; became the mayor of Peking after victory in 1951; and then was purged in the Great Cultural Revolution of 1966. At last account, he had been sent back to his native Shansi and been spared indignity because he, like all others in Yenan, early acknowledged the godhood of Mao Tse-tung. If he were writing his memoirs on his own search for history, they might best explain the revolution to which he consecrated his life yet finally could not explain to Mao's satisfaction.

The godhood of Mao Tse-tung was already recognized in Yenan, though it was not called that. He was simply "The Chairman," but like Jesus, he preached, and others listened as he taught. The reverence given him had been earned over the years: earned in battle, where he had swum rivers, crossed mountains, led riflemen; earned by his sorrows, which had embittered him—his first wife and his sister executed by the Nationalists, both brothers killed, the younger one strangled to death in 1943, the year before I met him, by the governor of Sinkiang; earned by his example—he hoed his own tobacco patch, for he was a chain smoker. But above all, the reverence rose from his authority as the teacher. He was the man who had been right when all others had been wrong; he had first split with the Russian Communists in 1927, then welcomed back and forgiven people like Chou En-lai, who had briefly flirted with the ideas of Stalin on proletarian urban insurrections. It was as if Mao held before him the book of history, written in cabalistic symbols only he could decipher, and from this book he lectured the comrades and their leaders, telling them where China was going, how he would take them there, what they must do when they arrived. No one disagreed with Mao Tse-tung; his power of mind was theological. He had been a librarian once and his reading was immense though disorganized; but his will, his personal will, his insistence on seeing that will executed, was probably, with the exception of Lenin's, the most formidable personal will of the twentieth century.

I was awakened one morning at seven and told that if I wanted to see the Chairman, I should prepare to breakfast with him at once. He received me not in an office, but in his personal cave—an immaculate cave, the mud floors swept clean, the table dust-free. He had been a sloven in his youth, his dormitory room at the Hunan First Normal School thirty years before filthy, cluttered and appalling to classmates, who later told stories of him. But he had arrived at a fetishistic neatness of habit that, later, would be imposed as dogma on all the spick-and-span lanes and streets of the China he created.

What struck me about the man was not his appearance but the command of his presence. Husky, with a receding hairline, the faintest trace of mustache hair on his upper lip, a tiny mole on his chin, he was in no way handsome. When he spoke, it was in a flat, soft voice, unlike his platform manner, and with no intent of persuading. He was telling me exactly how it was. What he said was perceived reality. He was the sage, instructing. When he walked, it was with a shuffling, rolling amble, a bearlike gait. But mostly he sat still, his mind speaking out of the slouching body.

I began with the standard set questions of an interview with a chief of state. Since American purpose was to unify the factions of China so that all could fight together with us against the Japanese, I asked whether there was any hope of reform in the Kuomintang, of "untying the knot." The answer came flat: "There is no way of untying the knot." Would negotiations do any good? There was only the faintest hope, he said. Negotiations were a means the Nationalists were using to deceive the Americans: ". . . the Nationalists hope that the United States will defeat Japan, and they can turn their own forces to wipe out the Communist Party of China." And on and on. He would not attack the government of Chiang K'ai-shek now, but if attacked, he would resist. Chiang, said Mao, accused Communists of being "running dogs of Red Russia," of seeking communization of land, communization of women. There had been three great campaigns by Chiang against his party in the last four years. The party had survived them all. And so long as Chiang kept his part of the front against the Japanese, "We will not raise the slogan of overthrowing his government." Yes, they were now considering linking all the guerrilla base areas and liberated areas in a new "People's Political Council"; the pressure came from his leaders in the field, but "no decision has yet been made." And as for America, he did not object to America's limited supply to Chiang's armies, but if we equipped ten or twenty divisions of Chiang's armies with modern arms, Chiang would turn them

against him. It would be better for the United States to
supply neither side; or if they were to do so, then his
demand was that the United States distribute supplies to
both sides proportionate to their effectiveness in fighting
against Japanese.

So much for the formal interview, which lasted
about an hour. I promised to submit it to him for clearance, since he was making a pronouncement of state. But
when it was returned to me, it was so edited as to be
useless for publication.

Then he went on, as we chatted informally. What
scored on my mind most was his composure; there was no
knee-jiggling as with Chiang K'ai-shek, when Chiang betrayed the tension of a question not in his mind but in his
body movement. No one entered with telephone messages, or interrupted with notes as he talked, as in
Chiang's chambers, or in the Oval Office of the White
House. This was the thinking place of Communist China.
He, Mao, was obviously neither executive nor administrator, but the sage, and he must not be interrupted as he
thought. And he was thinking aloud to me as he rambled.
There was no dialogue; I was a student; he was instructing me. The personality was majestic, permitting of no
contradiction or dispute. And frightening. I asked, after
the formal questions were over, about policy in the big
cities once they had won. Big cities were so different from
the villages he had organized into resistance; in big cities
there were newspapers and magazines. Would he let rival
newspapers publish what they would, even if hostile?
Certainly, Mao replied. In the new Communist China
there would be freedom of speech, freedom of rights,
freedom of press. In his China of tomorrow, anyone
would be able to publish in any newspaper whatever he
wanted—except "enemies of the people." I did not think
then to ask him who would define what an enemy of the
people was.

His knowledge, too, seemed askew. His conversation
was that of an autodidact, who had read as whim and
taste took him. He could discuss, with the precision of a

Marxist, landholding and feudalism in Western Europe
and the bourgeois leap in France when the Revolution
gave peasants their own land. But then, instructing me, he
went on to a comparison between his China as seen from
Yenan and the American Revolution as a foreign reporter
might have seen George Washington at Valley Forge.
Foreigners might now see the primitive conditions in
Yenan, he said, as they might have seen Washington's
headquarters, without realizing that Washington's ideas
would make him the winner. Did George Washington
have machinery? he asked. Did George Washington have
electricity? No. The British had all those things and
Washington did not, but Washington won because he had
the people with him. I realized that in his reading of
Marxian texts he had not placed the era of industry and
the era of electrification in their proper centuries. But it
made no difference: this man knew his country. This man
knew that ideas made people bear guns; power was what
came out of the muzzle of the gun. He had invented the
modern doctrine of partisan warfare, war in which uniforms are meaningless, where there are no neutrals, where
men, women, children, must all, willing or not, be involved in struggle and revolt. His was the doctrine of the
ceaseless revolution—and he knew his people better than
any leader I have talked with.

In the simplest historic terms, he was not campaigning against Chiang K'ai-shek; he was campaigning
against Confucius and two thousand years of ideas he
meant to root out and replace with his own.

I had come for breakfast and thought the interview
would soon be over. But he seemed to enjoy the off-the-
record conversation of instruction and I had been well
recommended to him, so he went on. I was startled when
he said it was time for lunch and asked whether I could
stay. I could. His wife Chiang Ch'ing (his third) came
into the room to serve us. She had been a movie actress in
Shanghai before she joined the revolution, and her figure,
even smothered by the thick brown wool pants she wore
that day, was stunning. She served and joined us for the

simple lunch and was charming. She was then thirty-two, almost twenty years younger than Mao, and I relished the sight of her as he must have. Later, much later, as she aged, she became herself a member of the Politburo and one of the architects of the bloody Cultural Revolution; an actor or actress in politics is very dangerous because politics exaggerate the native dramatic instinct with the intoxication of substantive command. Chiang Ch'ing became, and probably remains, a dangerous woman. But she seemed quite harmless there in the cave serving the great thinker—smiling, pleasant, compliant, not at all the Dragon Lady of later Western reporting.

I saw Mao several times in those weeks, and a year later in Chungking. Those were formal meetings. The indelible impression was the first—a man of the mind who could use guns, whose mind could compel history to move to his ideas.

All too often the dialogue of great historic forces is skewed by the spin of the initial conversation—and the dialogue of the American Democracy and Chinese Communism was thus skewed by their first official contact. The spokesman of China was Mao Tse-tung; the spokesman of America was Major General Patrick Hurley. Mao was a genius, Hurley was an ignoramus, and Hurley's arrival in Yenan during that first week in November 1944, to begin American negotiations with Chinese Communists, is a classic instance of the derailment of history by accident.

I can see Hurley now in split image—both as he appeared on the airstrip in Yenan, and as he must have appeared in the corridors of American politics I later reported. Both are relevant. He was, I know now, a hustler in domestic politics, of the type I later came to recognize in Washington. He had made his mark as a politician in the Republican convention of 1928 in Kansas City, where he was one of the floor managers corralling delegates for Herbert Hoover. When Hoover won the nomination, Pat Hurley, an Oklahoma corporation law-

yer, got his piece of the traditional share-out of office after
a Presidential victory, being named Secretary of War in
1928. That post brings the eminence so many American
cabinet members seek, which leads to the world of big
deals and big captaincies in private industry. Hurley, returning to his law practice in 1932, had negotiated an
agreement between the Mexican government and five
American oil companies; the Mexicans had expropriated
American oil holdings, but Hurley came away with a
multimillion-dollar, happy settlement. Thus his reputation
as a man good at the negotiation of foreign affairs. War
came, and Franklin Roosevelt, making the war a bi-
partisan effort, not only adorned his cabinet with such
stately and patrician Republicans as Stimson, Knox,
Lovett and Forrestal, but also sandwiched in other decorative Republicans of lesser quality for minor, symbolically
ceremonial tasks. Since China was low on Roosevelt's
priorities, he had sent Patrick J. Hurley, now accoutered
as a major general of the United States, to negotiate with
Chiang K'ai-shek for both the creation of a coalition government between Communists and Nationalists, and the
supersession of Chiang K'ai-shek by Stilwell as Commander in Chief of the Chinese land forces.

Hurley had already failed to make peace between
Stilwell and Chiang when he decided to take off for
Yenan in November of 1944. But the making of peace
between Communists and Nationalists seemed to him to
be less difficult. What he knew of revolutionaries he must
have learned in his Mexican adventures, for he regarded
the Chinese Communists as kindred to Pancho Villa.
Hurley was talkative, with the Southwestern garrulousness
that marked Lyndon Johnson—his concept being that, if
he held a conversation together by his own chatter long
enough, he might find out what he himself was talking
about while creating a mood of good will which might
trigger other conferees to compromise. Hurley always
talked a lot and his style was caught best by a young
congressman, a one-time college instructor in Far Eastern
history, sent by Roosevelt to China in November of 1944.
The freshman congressman was Mike Mansfield, later to

be the Majority Leader of the United States Senate, and Mansfield reported pithily to Roosevelt: "I saw Major General Pat Hurley and we had a very long talk. He talked for two hours and forty-seven minutes, and I talked for thirteen minutes, which was about right."

To say that Hurley was colorful is an understatement, and the flourish of his arrival in Yenan on November 7, 1944, creased the minds of all who by chance were at the airfield the day of his unannounced visit.*

Hurley loved dramatics—and what could be more dramatic than the personal representative of the President of the United States dropping in, from the air, for the first summit conference of the American state and the Chinese revolution, unannounced, unheralded, accompanied only by a sergeant stenographer who would write up the notes of one of the great rendezvous of history.

Because it was a dull afternoon, Davies, Barrett and I had gone to the airstrip to see one of our rare weather-service planes arrive, we hoped with mail for us. But there was a second plane in the air, which we recognized as the one used until a few weeks before as Stilwell's personal command plane. A little knot of curious Chinese had gathered, as they always did, to see a plane land— but out of this plane descended a six-foot-three-inch character in American uniform and overcoat, the pants pressed knife-sharp, a silver-haired, bushy-mustached major general, whose chest was covered with ribbons from shoulder to rib cage. It was Hurley, whom we all recognized. Barrett, as senior American military officer, approached, and dressed as he was in a Chinese cotton-padded blue overcoat, he must have seemed to the martinet emissary as distinctly out of uniform. Barrett, an

---

*There were three of us at the airfield to see Hurley arrive, and the mark of that visit appears in all our writings. Both John Davies, in *Dragon by the Tail* (New York, W.W. Norton & Company, 1972), and Colonel David Barrett, in his magnificent memoir *Dixie Mission* (Berkeley, Center for Chinese Studies, University of California, 1970), tell of that day. Although our accounts vary, probably all are correct. My memory of the day is written from notes made at the airfield and retyped that evening.

irrepressible wit, compounded the error instantly by looking the general up and down, from head to toe, and
offering the observation, "General, it looks as if you have
a medal there for every campaign except Shays' Rebellion." This caused the general to frown, for he had no
sense of humor. Barrett was to suffer for this, as were I
and Davies, and all who tried to instruct Hurley on
China.

The reaction time of the Communists in action always amazed me. There must have been an instantaneous
telephone call from the airstrip to headquarters. No more
than five minutes could have elapsed before a ragged
group of soldiers raced down from the hill to line up in an
honor guard. And almost instantly thereafter, apprised of
the arrival of Franklin D. Roosevelt's personal representative, appeared the Communist high command: Mao Tse-
tung himself, in a baggy unpressed cotton-padded blue
cloak; Chu Teh, the Commander in Chief, in the orange-
tan thick woolen uniform of a common soldier; Yeh
Chien-ying, the Chief of Staff, in the smart khaki-colored
wool uniform of an officer; and Chou En-lai, in a dingy
brown leather coat. There were only four automobiles in
Yenan then, and when Mao required one, his vehicle was
a converted ambulance. Out of this ambulance they now
rushed, trotting pell-mell to greet Franklin Roosevelt's
emissary. Hurley, all six foot three of him, immaculate
and glistening, towered above the stocky Chinese like
Captain John Smith surrounded by Powhatan's tribal
braves.

Hurley advanced on the honor guard of disheveled
soldiers, stood for a moment, and then let out a loud
screech—"Yahoo!"—giving the Choctaw yell of his native Oklahoma. We gaped; but this was President Roosevelt's choice. We got into the ambulance—the four leaders of the Chinese high command, Hurley, Davies, Barrett
and I. We jounced over the ruts toward Dixie Mission; a
mule on the road swerved; the mule driver, paralyzed by
the sight of an automobile, clubbed the mule. Hurley
bellowed, "Hit him again; hit him on the other side." He
then offered the observation to Mao Tse-tung that he had

been a cowboy in his youth and knew about animals. Mao responded that he had been a shepherd in his youth. Barrett was translating and his command of Chinese was exquisite, in tone, nuance, slang and decorum. As the ambulance jounced through the ford of the dry Yen River bed, Mao explained how this gully rose and fell with the rains, now a torrent, now again a parched gulch. Hurley recalled Oklahoma and its dry creeks. In summer, he said, you could tell when a school of fish was swimming upriver by the cloud of dust they raised. Barrett translated and the Communist leaders laughed; here was a real man of the people. We went on to Dixie Mission, and all of us sat down to tea and happy conversation. It is a reporter's dream to insert himself unobserved into the presence of great men as they talk history; my notes, alas, ran out at that point because I was enjoying myself too much in the company of the great. And that evening, since the Communists had already prepared a banquet in honor of the November 7 anniversary of the great Russian Revolution, we were all invited. Of that banquet I remember little, except that when Hurley was called on to speak, he rose, paused, and then yelled again at the top of his lungs, "Yahoo!"

Of more consequence to me was my conversation with Hurley between our tea and the banquet. I had spoken to Mao Tse-tung, formally, only a few days before. I told Hurley what Mao had said, briefing him as I thought an American reporter must brief any major American in high place when asked. I told him that Mao had said there was no way of "untying the knot," no way of negotiating a peaceful end of the embryonic civil war, unless America recognized the existence of a de facto Communist government, and saw it as an independent ally in the great war against Japan.

For this briefing I was to suffer in two ways, because then, in my naïveté, I did not realize how potent, yet how vulnerable, was the calling of journalism. I did not know, when I told Hurley that his unannounced and unbriefed mission was probably futile, how much it would enrage him. But twenty years later, when the documents were

published, I read that the next morning, November 8,
Hurley had sent a dispatch to the State Department
concerning my disruptive presence: "Theodore White,"
wrote Hurley in his classified message, "... told me that
he had just talked to Chairman Mao and Mao had told
him that there was not any possible chance of an agreement between him and Chiang K'ai-shek. White told me
many reasons why Mao should not agree with the National Government. White's whole conversation was definitely against the mission with which I am charged."

That report would remain filed in the dossiers of
American intelligence for years, and would return to
plague my life many years later, when I was accused of
being one of those who "lost China to the Reds."

More importantly, and immediately, Hurley quoted
me directly to Mao Tse-tung in a gambit of their conversations; and Mao's wrath was roused.

In the only open yelling argument I ever had with a
Chinese Communist, I was accosted by Mao's interpreter,
a young Chinese named Huang Hua, now Foreign Minister of China. Furiously, he denounced me for repeating to
Hurley what Mao had said to me. "But we trusted you,"
said Huang Hua in anger. "Mao trusted you; we thought
you were a friend."

It was an impossible situation, but highly educational. Neither Hurley of the American government, nor
Mao, the Chinese sage, understood the code of American
journalism. Hurley expected an American reporter abroad
to be an arm of American purpose; and thus I had
betrayed him. (Our relationship ended six moths later,
when, in a blaring face-to-face argument, he denounced
me as "un-American" and called me "you goddamn sedi-
tious little son of a bitch," and we parted forever.) If
Hurley distrusted me, so now did the Communist high
command, for revealing their thoughts to the American
government; and the three days of Hurley's conversations
in Yenan, from which I was excluded at the threshold,
were of transcendent importance.

Once all the documents were published, years later,

the story of Hurley's three days made the dimensions of tragedy clear. Hurley had come for a simple American purpose: to work out some truce or agreement between Chinese Nationalists and Chinese Communists so that, in alliance, they might multiply rather than divide their strength against the Japanese, our common enemy.

Hurley began the morning after his arrival (his sergeant stenographer attending to make the report), in a conference with Mao and his leaders, by presenting the terms Hurley and Chiang K'ai-shek had previously worked out together: a five-point program. By this program, both parties would pledge themselves to unity, the Communist party would be recognized as legal, all would work to establish at some future date a government pledged to progress—and in return, the Chinese Communists would disband their armies, give up their "liberated area" governments (which already governed ninety million people); and their troops would be "reorganized" in obedience to the National Military Council.

In the afternoon, Mao responded—explosively. He denounced the Nationalist regime from top to bottom, pointed out that one seat for the Communist armies on the National Military Council, which met rarely and only as a cosmetic convocation of castrated warlords and provincial generals, was not enough for him to give up the most effective army in China and its largest effective government. The agreement will give you a foot in the door, said Hurley. It does no good to enter a door if you have your hands tied behind your back, said Mao. They suspended that afternoon on Hurley's wise negotiating suggestion that he would be glad to entertain a description of what the Communists thought would be adequate terms for a settlement.*

*The full history of these vital and watershed conversations can be reconstructed from two State Department volumes (*Foreign Relations of the United States, China 1944, 1945*). But the best account, the most vivid and the truest in spirit, is that of David D. Barrett in *Dixie Mission,* an authentic contribution to scholarship, published, alas, too late, in 1970.

They met again the next day, Thursday, November 9, in the afternoon; the Communists had worded their proposals in language smooth enough to conceal from Hurley their stubborn meaning. Expansively, Hurley declared that the Communist proposals were indeed fair, but that they did not go far enough. He wanted another day to reword them.

So that evening and into the next morning, Hurley reworked and reworded the Communist proposals. I linger over his rewording of the proposals because it concerns meanings, idioms and the sorrow-burdened attempt of men of different cultures to understand each other's ideas in translation.

Our most hallowed word is "liberty." But translated into Chinese, the concept requires the words *tsu-yu-chu-i,* whose written characters mean "the idea of self-will" and connote "selfishness," or every man for himself. "Democracy" in Chinese translation goes back to the original Greek, coming out in ideographs as *min-tsu-chi-i,* "the idea of the people" as governing imperative. In American idiom, democracy is a process; translated into Chinese, it becomes theology. Of these linguistic difficulties Hurley had no perception whatsoever. He was no intellectual; he was a cartoon character out of American folklore. But in the cave quarters of Dixie Mission that night, he rewrote the Communist proposals in the finest American tradition—and to the Communists, the rewording of their proposals must have been dazzling when they met on the morning of the tenth.

First, in the Hurley draft, came unity: the "Government of China," the "Kuomintang of China," the "Communist Party of China," would all agree, as three equals, to fight together against Japan. Then came an almost inadvertent phrase—startling in concept—which indicated that the National Government of China (Chiang's dictatorship) would be reorganized into a "Coalition National Government" in which all parties were equal. There would be a new "United National Military Council" under this Coalition Government, representing all armies fighting against Japan, and *"supplies acquired from foreign powers will be equitably distributed,"* meaning that America would arm both Chinese armies simultaneously. But coloring the entire document as it came from Hurley's American retouching was a glowing, untranslatable synoptic echo of the American Constitution and political faith. This new Coalition National Government, wrote Hurley, would "establish justice, freedom of conscience, freedom of the press, freedom of speech, freedom of assembly and association, the right to petition to the government for the redress of grievances, the right of writ of *habeas corpus,* and the right of residence." Hurley was committing the United States to underwrite a new China, an Oriental society which would accept the American Bill of Rights, the binding faith by which James Madison and George Mason had sealed the original American revolution to its people. For good measure, Hurley threw in Franklin D. Roosevelt's revolution, too: "The Coalition National Government will also pursue policies intended to make effective those two rights defined as freedom from fear and freedom from want."

It must have appeared to these Oriental gun-slinging revolutionaries as too good to be true, because it *was* too good to be true. Yet if Franklin Roosevelt's personal emissary would guarantee it as a basis of negotiations, how could they say no? They were about to be recognized; the Americans were promising to abolish Chiang's government and replace it with a coalition government in which their armies, their government, would qualify for the guns they wanted. The Bill of Rights, on which Hurley insisted, must have seemed to them in translation as both incomprehensible and irrelevant, as it would certainly seem to Chiang. But if the Americans could compel Chiang to sign this curious document, certainly the Communists would sign it.

Nor did they have to wait for this important ceremony. It was Hurley who insisted they sign. On a flat rock, in the crisp sunshine of a perfect fall day, the document was laid down. Hurley signed. Then Mao, rather than placing his chop on the document, which was a formality, signed his personal name, his signature—far more important. And a blank space was left for Chiang K'ai-shek's signature, which Hurley undertook to try and get. Marvelous; transporting; history being made. Mao did not want to fly down to Chungking on Hurley's plane leaving that afternoon; he was still cautious. But Chou En-lai would fly with Hurley to conclude the negotiations in Chungking.

Chou En-lai kissed his wife at the airport—one of the rare moments when I have seen a proud Chinese display private emotion in public. But he was probably disturbed; Chiang, as I have said, had been indulging his execution frenzy that fall, and though Hurley would try to protect Chou as a negotiator, who knew whether Chou would return alive?

I joined the plane trip back with Hurley and Barrett, Chou En-lai and his secretary, Ch'en Chia-k'ang. I remember it as a bumpy ride, with turbulence in the air, and Chou En-lai being cold to me. He was either angry because I had told Hurley of what Mao had said to me; or he was worried, disturbed, knowing himself on a hopeless mission. We landed in Chungking; and I raced to type my dispatch, a rhapsodic dispatch, an emotional dispatch, about how peace had come to China at last and how we stood on the threshold of heavenly harmony.

Time magazine did not publish my dispatch, the filter of distance removing the desk editors from my emotional writing, which was in truth winged with a hope and passion that were entirely unreal.

Negotiations proved purposeless. Both sides were unmalleable. They had killed each other for too long. They would go on killing; and the only instantly meaningful question was who could best persuade the Americans to give them guns with which to kill each other. In less than a month, Chou En-lai, claiming his safe-conduct under the American flag, requested a plane to fly back to Yenan. Hurley, with honor, granted it. Barrett flew back with Chou and spoke with Mao Tse-tung once more, on which occasion Mao broke into temper. He had been betrayed by Hurley, he said. Mao had been betrayed so often by white men—both Russians and Americans—that this episode must have been demonstration of his doctrine that revolutions in Asia can only be conducted by Asians. All whites were untrustworthy. Mao twitted Barrett, whom he liked, and indicated that he might make public this American betrayal by exposing to the world both his signature *and* Hurley's signature on the secret document of coalition peace. When Barrett reported this astute political reaction back to Hurley, Hurley roared. According to Barrett, "I was afraid for a moment he [Hurley] might burst a blood vessel. 'The mother f——,' he yelled, 'he tricked me.' "

This was in December of 1944, and I had seen it all: I had seen famine and rout; I had been there with Stilwell as he was relieved; been there as Davies tried to explore the revolution; been there to see Hurley arrive, been there with Hurley and Chou and left with them for Chungking. I knew at least as much as any other journalist about the nature of the struggle in China, and knew I knew so. The Communists, I knew, no longer trusted me. The American government no longer trusted me—or at least Pat Hurley, the President's man in Chungking, considered me an enemy. The Kuomintang distrusted me, and had since my talk with Chiang on the Honan famine. But I was confident, even arrogant, knowing that I wrote for *Time,* for *Life,* and was Harry Luce's man in Chungking.

And then Luce, too, repudiated me. I was no sooner back from Yenan than Chungking intelligence services intercepted a dispatch of the Japanese news agency, Domei, which reported *Time* magazine's story on Stilwell's relief from command, with Stilwell on the cover. I read the Japanese summary, stunned. I could not believe it. I had smuggled back to Luce on the plane carrying Stilwell from Chungking a thirteen-page personal letter giving a blow-by-blow, fact-by-fact account of the events that led up to Stilwell's relief, which I knew to be a genuine scoop. *Time* must have received it, discarded it,

and then apparently turned it upside down in a story so
fanciful, so violently pro-Chiang K'ai-shek that it could
only mislead American opinion—which it was Luce's
duty, and mine, to guard against.

My quarrel with Harry Luce in the winter and spring
of 1945, as the war pushed to its close, was, I think,
somewhat more important than the usual reporters' quarrels with their editors.

First, the subject was China. An event was swelling
there that was more than a military defeat, more than a
conspiracy. A revolution was changing the landscape of
politics forever, but America was bound to a decaying
system and regime on which rested all its hopes for
postwar Asia. To try to halt or threaten this revolution
was impossible, and would cost America incalculable lives
in the future. That was clear even then. But between this
revolution in Asia and its perception in America was a
screen.

Second, the most inflexible guardians of this screen,
the most distorting of the lenses through which Americans saw China, were the publications I worked for—and
their editor-proprietor was my friend Harry Luce, one of
the grandest of the great press barons of American history.

To try to break through the screen meant that I had
to accept Henry R. Luce as an adversary.

Luce was a formidable man. Even were he not so
important to the China story, he would rank in his own
right as one of the giants in the history of American
journalism. And it is useful to pause over the personality
and thinking of Harry Luce if only as a study in power—
the power of the press to shape public policy, and the
autocratic power of the proprietor in those days to shape
policy unchallenged within the portion of the press he
controlled. The power of the press has since grown; but
within that press the power of the proprietor over what he
publishes has dwindled. Luce is a crossroads figure in
both developments.

Luce was conscious of his power as few press lords are today. He was responsible to his balance sheet and conscience alone, thumbing his nose at advertisers, politicians, correspondents, critics, anyone who stood between him and the view of reality he expected his magazines to deliver. He knew instinctively what has since become a public cliché: the power of the press to set the agenda of public discussion. Luce introduced the personality of the week. the man of the year. *"Life* Goes to the Movies," and half a dozen other agenda-setting dockets which are now taken as commonplace. In his time. in his great period, Luce made and unmade men, elevating nonentities to national leadership. destroying careers with the snap of his whip. And Luce brooked no nonsense about who controlled his magazines and what they said: he did. His reporters assembled facts from all around the world. The facts were important; provocative, quotable, salable, they were the raw stuff of the magazines. Luce knew, as few editors know, how much depends on the quality of raw reporting. And he paid generously for reporting. But in New York. those facts were assembled by his editors to his design. Freedom of the press. he held. ran two ways: His reporters were free to report what they wished; but he was free to reject what they reported, or have it rewritten as he wished.

It was his attitude to China that had first brought us close. He loved America; he loved China; with his power and his influence he meant to cement the two together forevermore. Luce was a surprisingly learned man, a true intellectual as well as a great business executive; but he was, above all, a Christian, and Christianity was the cement by which he meant to bind China and America together.

In these days of watered-down religion, of mouthed pieties and social fashions that masquerade as new faith, Luce's Christianity would seem anachronistic. But faith was his motive force, a muscular, thoughtful Christianity, infused as much by gospel folklore as by theology. When he summoned a cowering editor and remarked that he had thought all night about that boy who came home, the editor scoured his mind, wondering what story he had missed in the papers—but it would turn out that Luce was thinking of the prodigal son in the Gospel according to Luke. Luce, along with DeWitt Wallace of the *Reader's Digest*, who came of an equally clerical background, was probably among the last of the great editors who was moved by the generative dynamic force of believing Christianity. Luce might stray from the Christian past and teachings in personal dalliance and romance, or in cruel executive decisions as a great publisher must. But Christianity guided the best of his editing, leading him to his bold championing of black liberties in America, and to his denunciation of Senator Joseph McCarthy. At the moment of our breach, however, Luce's Christianity had impaled itself on the figure of Chiang K'ai-shek. Luce's missionary forebears had helped to plant Christianity in China. Chiang was their creation, and bore their message. With the Stilwell crisis, Luce felt, rightly or wrongly, by his morality, that he must take his stand: support Chiang, or else godless Communism would take over. The lesser facts of events must be suppressed for what he considered the greater truth; and his magazines were his instruments.

With this view I violently disagreed.

Our quarrel had not been overnight in developing. I had been one of his favorites for several years because both he and I thought it was evil of the Japanese to reduce China from a great nation to a territory owned by Japan. We had begun to differ when China became our ally, and in the spring of 1944 I had flown back to New York to persuade him that we must now, finally, tell the truth about China, for Chiang K'ai-shek was doomed unless he could be shocked into reform by America. From our colloquy emerged a major article, *"Life* Looks at China," in which I pushed Luce as far as he would go (publishing that Chiang's Kuomintang combined "the worse features of Tammany Hall and the Spanish Inquisition"), and he restrained my angers, still heated by the Honan famine, as far as I could let myself be restrained.

What we were arguing about was the soul and purpose of Chiang K'ai-shek, whether redemption was possible for the sinner or whether America (meaning Time-Life-Fortune) must cast him out. He published my piece much as I wrote it—after a remarkable intellectual volleying between us.*

*The quality of Henry Luce's mind and learning is so often distorted by the more colorful and bumptious qualities of his conduct that it is perhaps appropriate to quote from our colloquy to show why so many of us served him so loyally for so long. Luce and I exchanged multipage memos frequently. As we argued that spring about whether to do a skin-flaying exposé of Chiang's government, or a sorrowful, hopeful story, he responded in a two-thousand-word memo to this reporter, from which I quote him, at his best, thus:

> Different policies and different leadership might have led to different results under the same physical conditions—that is at the core of any belief in God and man. . . .
> But there is something here that needs to be sympathetically understood—and that is the effort of Chinese to discover the moral basis of their Reconstruction not in the morality of the West, but in their own, as they think, indigenous morality. (Perhaps the hardest thing for men to understand . . . is that true morality springs not from here or there, but is, as Emerson said, at the "center of the universe," over which citadel flies the flag neither of Britain nor of Jerusalem nor of Mecca nor of Confucius.)
> Now I find it very strange to be defending the cause of Confucius. But I do. . . . It is necessary to see this matter steadily and see it whole. . . . What happened [in China], to oversimplify, was . . . a great spill-over of evangelical zeal from a nineteenth century West which profoundly believed in a paradox: Christianity and Progress. . . . The people of the West, misled by their shoddy intellectuals and bewitched by a spawn of technological toys, have done precisely what Chen Li-fu does. For the people of the West, as the nineteenth century marched on to Verdun and Dunkirk, they too, voted Christianity irrelevant and Progress the thing. This schizophrenia of the West hit China. Christianity in its various guises (including Science as Reason) overthrew the idols of superstition . . . and reinvoked the moral law. . . . [But] Progress . . . in its various guises (including Science as Materialism) exploited China . . . challenged China and shamed China.

But then, on returning to China in the summer of
1944, I found that decay had moved faster than even I
had anticipated, that the Japanese were destroying what
remained of the East China front, and that Stilwell was to
be sacrificed. Luce had my full report of the Stilwell crisis
in hand when he let the story of the crisis be edited into a
lie, an entirely dishonorable story.

And, thereafter, the breach between us widened to
anger. Luce's court favorite at that moment in New York
was Whittaker Chambers, a former Communist *appa-
ratchik* of remarkable literary gifts who had become foreign editor of *Time*. Chambers edited the Stilwell story of
the chaos, decay, misery, sadness and dissolution in
China simply. Admitting that Chiang K'ai-shek was governing "high-handedly," *Time* declared that Chiang was
doing so

> in order to safeguard the last vestiges of
> democratic principles in China . . . engaged in
> an undeclared civil war with Yenan, a dictator-

. China's reaction was slow, painful and confused. But it
was clear that China must some day take her reformation in
her own hands—a development devoutly wished for by the
representatives of Christianity. . . .

The memo ran on page after page; few editors today would
take the time to expose a whole philosophy to a correspondent at
such length. I responded in a memorandum of equal length, in-
voking Alfred North Whitehead and Science and Reason, against
Christ and Confucius. It was exhilarating to be working for a man
who could discuss, all at the same time, the Bible, Confucius and
the itchy gossip and color which sells readers on a magazine. But
Luce's quotient was the same as my quotient at that time—that
though Chiang's government was wicked, it was less wicked than
the Japanese or than Stalin's Communism; and that in Chiang lay
our hope. Thus, jointly, Luce and I excoriated Chiang's government and praised Chiang. Only when I returned to China, after the
colloquy, was I persuaded by facts, murder, execution and incompetence that Chiang was no longer a useful vessel either of American or of Christian purpose. I was more pragmatic than Luce. I
could not ignore what I saw; and he would not print it, for it destroyed his philosophy of the world.

ship whose purpose was the spread of totalitarian Communism in China . . . If Chiang K'aishek were compelled to collaborate with Yenan on Yenan's terms, or if he were forced to lift his military blockade of the Chinese Communist area, a Communist China might soon replace Chungking. And unlike Chungking, a Communist China (with its 450 million people) would turn to Russia (with its 200 million people) rather than to the U.S. (with its 130 million) as an international collaborator.

America must choose, was the message of the story—to support Chiang or yield China to Russia. The story had the tone of apocalypse and, as usual with apocalyptical stories, had the forces and the future all wrong.

When I had first read the Domei summary of the story, I had exploded and cabled Luce: "If what Domei said is true, I shall probably have to resign as have no other way of preserving my integrity. . . ." Luce had cabled back: "Keep your shirt on until you have full text of Stilwell cover story. . . . Your views have always been respected here but I do not think it becomes you to get angry if for once your editor does not instantly follow your instructions. . . ."

The published story, when it arrived in Chungking, proved worse than the Domei summary. I drafted a forty-five-page letter to Luce, arguing my case that neither Nationalists nor Communists were democratic in the American sense and that our immediate interest was to support the ones who could help us most against the Japanese. But to aid Chiang against Mao, I said, was to commit us to a disastrous "meddling" in a civil war in which we could only lose. Luce cabled back that his support of Chiang was no more a "meddling" in other people's politics than American support of Churchill in England.

Our argument rose in intensity. I threatened by cable to resign three times more in the next few months. Luce

raised my salary, but would not change *Time*'s policy. I
was sad. This man, Luce, had plucked me out of nothing
and given me eminence; he and his wife, Clare, had
fostered me, sheltered me in their home, introduced me to
the famous. Now he was repudiating me, and it was as if
my father had denied me in public.

I would have done anything I could to keep or
regain his affection. But he had trained me in the importance of the news, and the by-line he had given me bore a
responsibility with it—to the by-line, not to *Time*. I was in
China, seeing this great revolution scream for simple
reporting. But he was in New York and felt it must be
crushed. I *could* not yield from what I saw. He *would* not
yield from how he saw it. I still insist, and know, that I
was right and he was wrong in the telling of the story of
China. But we could never be friends again so long as I
worked in his house—and so I used him for the next two
years and he used me, warily, suspiciously, until we
broke; and we would not become friends again for another twelve years, when our affection surmounted the
anger of old disputes.

The beginning of our final breach came in February
of 1945. The Communists had consented to another
round of negotiations with the Nationalists in Chungking,
and these had broken down. I wired a cable warning of
what would follow, which began thus: "This was New
Year's week in China, the time for the giving of presents.
And the leaders of China took the occasion to send their
people a cruel and bitter gift . . . future civil war to be-
queath to their children." The tone of the dispatch, chast-
ened as I now was, was scrupulously neutral, predicting
only tragedy.

Not a word of my dispatch was used, as Chambers
edited my story thus:

> In Chungking another parley between the
> central government and the Communists ended
> in deadlock. Encouraged by jovial U.S. Ambas-
> sador Patrick J. Hurley, the Communists' ace

negotiator, smart, suave General Chou En-lai, had flown down from Yenan for one more try. . . . For two weeks he had talked long and earnestly with Chungking's ace negotiator, scholarly, liberal . . . Wang Shih-chieh. . . . Chungking was ready to give the Communists legal status and minority posts in the national defense council. . . . but when Chungking asked Yenan to put the Communist army under Generalissimo Chiang's control, General Chou balked. . . . When would Chou En-lai return to Chungking? Darkly he answered: "Not so soon."

The cables between myself and my editors sputtered for weeks thereafter and then in April came one like this: "After consultation with Luce here's what he (and most emphatically he) would like you to do: stay in and near Chungking for at least four or five weeks to report not political China . . . [but] mainly small indigenous colorful yarns." There followed then a sample of the kind of reporting he expected of me, an excerpt from a London bureau cable on England's two thousandth day of the war, ". . . yellow crocuses bloomed, daffodils sold for dollar and half per bunch, Commons passing bill making rear lights compulsory on bicycles." The cable went on to tell me: "in other words, good-fashioned Time news. . . . This assignment interesting but not taxing . . . so you've good chance getting stories in magazine. . . . Maybe you should consider coming here for brief refresher. What say?"

I said no to the "refresher" and put myself to reporting what "good-fashioned" news I could find. But though the azaleas and plum blossoms of Chungking made spring as colorful as did daffodils in London, in England victory was at hand—and in China, the Communists had launched an all-out offensive behind Japanese lines which was giving them control of the Yangtze valley. I could not report that, and did not want to report daffodils. Yet I wanted to stay in China and the price had to be the filing of light, sun-filled copy in an arena of despair and absurdity.

At this light, sun-filled reportage my partner in the China bureau, my then beloved Annalee Jacoby, was a masterly craftswoman. Though she hated Luce, Chambers and their policy more than I did, her touch at the typewriter preserved both our jobs. She discovered that in the spring season, Chinese could, traditionally, make eggs stand on end. Indeed, in spring a properly chilled egg can be made to stand on its oval bottom anywhere in the world, for reasons I still cannot understand. At her dispatch, feature editors of the war-drugged Western press came alert. Someone interviewed Albert Einstein, who declared the feat to be impossible. Annalee arranged for photographs for *Life* magazine to show that Einstein was wrong, Chinese were right, eggs did stand on end. It was microcosmically sensational, and Annalee was congratulated for her "eggstraordinary story." I tried to emulate her but I was, in that season, unable to write "happy" copy.

I could score, when I tried, with a story, say of Dr. Chiang Chien-tsai, the most famous herb doctor in China, whose clientele included most of the Westernized cabinet of Chiang as well as the Generalissimo himself. Dr. Chiang diagnosed all diseases on the basis of the four "winds" that might invade the body, and blended his prescriptions of gallstones taken from horses, powdered snakes, ground goat horns, ripened child's urine, musk from the navels of Tibetan musk deer, and dried testicles of little animals; he was also a master at acupuncture. That story was published.

But for the politics of China and their hidden convulsion I could find no outlet, and remembering Chicken Little squawking, "The sky is falling, the sky is falling," I wondered whether it was I or my proprietor who was mad. It seemed to me that this was the history I had come to seek out—a revolution, with myself at the observation post, and a story so immense that no overdramatization could exaggerate it.

Since I had to see it through for myself, whether *Time* wanted to tell the story or not, I had to keep my job with *Time* to hold on to my credentials as war correspondent. Thus, from the beginning of 1945 on, I realized that my only insurance against dismissal would be combat reporting. We were a patriotic magazine, and our American men in action were splendid. So, as often as I could, I left political surveillance of the capital to Annalee, and for weeks and months on end I followed the American forces in the field.

Combat reporting was an escape from politics and I took it lightly. I gave myself over to reporting soldiers, charges, tanks, artillery, the sound of guns.

I did not realize then that this story was equal in importance to that of Yenan—and just as political. For the story of the American forces as the war drew to a close was a story of valor victorious. And the courage and spirit of American men at war flowed from a fostering politics as compelling as the politics of Mao's guerrillas. The American forces in 1945 were magnificent—as magnificent in Asia and the Pacific as they were in Europe— and no book on modern politics or history would be complete without recalling how truly impressive and effective were America's fighting men who brought the Pacific war to a close.

CHAPTER 6

The Politics of Victory: Asia

It was easy to make clear the politics of the Chinese Communists and their peasant boys, who so willingly died and so skillfully killed for their cause. It was and is equally easy to make clear the grand strategy of the United States at war, as historians reconstruct day by date the landings and armored breakthroughs, the bombardments and air strategy, the convoys menaced and victories at sea, technology mastered and triumphs in laboratories.

But to make clear the underlying politics of the American men who fought the war, and died, is more difficult. Those unspoken politics were too simple. They were so taken for granted that only now do I realize how critically important those politics were: the millions of nameless Americans who fought the war loved their country with a mute and unquestioning loyalty and died when they had to, if not willingly, with full heart and devotion.

The mood and temper of those times is now so far

away, in the afterlight of America's disaster in Vietnam, that the valor of the Americans at arms seems vaguely and disturbingly anachronistic. Perhaps it was F. Scott Fitzgerald who, after the earlier world war, caught best the spirit that was to move an innocent America. In *Tender Is the Night,* Fitzgerald's hero, Dick Diver, and a group of Americans visit the British battlefield of the Somme, seven years after that war ended, and gape at the hills, the relics of slaughter, the stupidities of generalship. Diver insists that the thrust came from the past. "See that little stream," he says, "we could walk it in two minutes. It took the British a month to walk it—a whole empire walking very slowly, dying in front and pushing forward behind. . . . leaving the dead like a million bloody rugs." Someone disagrees, and Diver continues: "You had to have a whole-souled sentimental equipment going back further than you could remember. You had to remember Christmas, and postcards of the Crown Prince and his fiancée, and little cafés in Valence and beer gardens in Unter den Linden and weddings at the *mairie,* and going to the Derby, and your grandfather's whiskers." Fitzgerald wrote in 1934 of a scene revisited in 1925. But the spirit that moved the men to fight in 1918 was the same as still propelled Americans to action in 1941, and was as potent a political force as any other I then observed and reported. All my combat reporting from 1942 to 1945 was a reporting only of the vivid outer expression of that spirit.

I had begun reporting Americans in action only in 1942, but in the next three years one could sense the rising pulse of American power better in Asia, at the tail end of the effort, than in Europe. In Asia it flickered first faintly, then rose, then throbbed, then, in its last exertion, surpassed anything war had ever known before. But the dynamics of the pulse came, I am sure, in Europe and in the Pacific, as it came in China, from that spirit of valor which rests on faith—and which is the essence of politics in war.

The spirit is difficult to describe, for no American soldier would admit aloud that he loved his country; that was for politicians. No one admits his devotion to the general or the President when he is at war. Except that, as it turned out, in World War II that love was there. The men I lived and flew with groused constantly—at the food, at the "Slopies" (our Chinese allies), at the mud, at the sergeant, at the general (whether Chennault or Stilwell), at Franklin Roosevelt. Yet I saw several cry like children when Roosevelt died. They had no songs except pop melodies: "You Are My Sunshine, My Only Sunshine" was our favorite in 1942; and in 1943, "Pistol Packin' Mama"; then "Blues in the Night." Some of us tried to sing, one drunken night, "John Brown's body lies a-mouldering in the grave," but that stopped when a Southern lieutenant tightened his lips and said, "We ain't going to sing that song anymore, and I'll bust the next son of a bitch who sings it in the mouth." He had a century of other memories and songs worked into his spirit. So we sang that no more. But we sang "Lili Marlene," taken from the Germans; and "There's a Troopship Just Leaving Bombay," taken from the British; and "Waltzing Matilda," taken from the Australians. There was no great American war song; Americans needed none; nor did "Mom and Apple Pie" stir them—the spirit came from the sentimental equipment of a century past, wordless but powerful.

The thread by which to lead into the valor of the Americans is, perhaps, the Eleventh Bombardment Squadron, which I unashamedly wish to celebrate. The squadron counted sixteen B-25s and until 1943 was the only striking instrument of American power on the mainland of Asia. It had been put together as a unit before the war, and was thus largely volunteer in its manpower. The squadron specialized in hit-and-run strikes, for it was, in function, an airborne guerrilla unit. It struck Hong Kong for the first time, Hanoi for the first time, Haiphong for the first time, on all of which strikes it permitted me to go along. But after playing red dog, or poker, or after a good raid in which no one was killed, or after getting drunk in the wildest drunken bashes I have ever enjoyed, the men would grouse about the command. They would grouse aggressively—about what we should be doing that we were not doing.

Combat morale actually outran command.

On Christmas Eve of 1942, I recall, the squadron disagreed with General Chennault, who had ordered a stand-down for the holiday, because most American generals hate to order troops to attack on Christmas Eve. But any number of the flying men in the squadron felt that Christmas Eve was just the proper time to jump the Jap, because they would not be expecting us. Thus, after the party in the barracks, they recruited themselves into scratch crews, found enough men to get four B-25s off the ground, and unauthorized, all of them volunteers, took off in the night to bomb the Japanese across the Salween River. Most of us were slightly alcoholized when we took off, but the raid was performed splendidly. We coursed up and down the gorge of the Salween, locked in tight formation, the moon lighting the walled Chinese villages below like fossil rectangles. We located our target, Tengyueh, and as we strung our bombs down the main street, where the Japanese depots were located, Japanese answered back, their pink and yellow tracers scratching for us; then we turned, locked on the flight leader as he turned, as if this raggle-taggle band had practiced such a formation maneuver for years, and heeling over, our planes delivered a broadside of our own, our red, blue and white tracers flaring until we had extinguished those of the Japanese. Then, as we lifted and gained height, we adjusted our earphones and the pilot tuned in the armed forces shortwave broadcast out of San Francisco; they were playing Christmas carols for the men overseas, and we joined the broadcast, caroling "Oh Come, All Ye Faithful" as we homed on Kunming. We expected to be court-martialed for violating orders, but Chennault only chuckled at the idea of his men exceeding command.

Upon this spirit, this absolutely reckless desire of the young Americans to get the war over, rested, first, on our tactics and then our strategy, for bravado gave lift to daring planning and one could see the American reach spreading.

A year later, again on a holiday, Thanksgiving Day, 1943, the reach had spread to Formosa, and again it was the Eleventh Bomb Squadron that led. Formosa lay twelve hundred miles from our main base at Kunming. But Chennault had packed in to a secret coastal field, Lingling, by coolie carrier and truck, enough gasoline to refuel the squadron sufficiently to get from that field to Formosa and return. We hedge-hopped down on the afternoon before Thanksgiving, refueling once at Kweilin; then touched at dusk at Lingling, where we were gathered under the wings of one of the planes and were told that the target for tomorrow was Formosa.

Not only was it Formosa, but it was the Shinchiku air base there; and Shinchiku was the great staging base of the Japanese air force as it flew its bombers and fighters down the island chain from the homeland to the Southwest Pacific, where they were deployed to fight MacArthur. Air intelligence had reported a Japanese force of forty bombers and twenty fighters paused at Shinchiku for relay south.

The men shifted uneasily as they learned that there was just enough gas to reach the Japanese base and get back to refuel at Kweilin. Success, said the briefing officer, depended on three things: surprise above all, for if the Japanese had even five minutes' warning they could rise from their fields to overwhelm us; next, weather—a cold front and clouds were coming down from the north; and last, pinpoint navigation—Shinchiku lay by the shore, and we must make landfall directly on target, for an error of navigation of even one degree would let the Japanese get their fighters aloft. After that, we were told that since the next day was Thanksgiving, Chennault had ordered a special dinner sent down with the squadron, complete with canned turkey and cranberries, which would be waiting for us when we came home from the raid. At which came the only rebellion of the squadron, and it came instantly. Since it was very likely that quite a few would not be returning safely from the raid to eat that dinner, they wanted their Thanksgiving dinner now, before they took off. Our forward commander was Colonel Clinton ("Casey") Vincent, all of twenty-nine years old; and the actual strike commander in combat would be Colonel David ("Tex") Hill, also twenty-nine. They were both young enough and sufficiently combat-blooded to understand the insurrection. They yielded. So we had Thanksgiving dinner the night before, and on Thanksgiving Day, before dawn, as the rising sun was pinking the hills, we took off.

The Formosa raid was one, I am sure, of hundreds and hundreds the U.S. Air Force executed with perfection all around the world. But this was the first time I had seen a strike go so well. We cleared the coastal mountain range with a few feet to spare, dropped to the ocean so low that our propellers sucked salt spray into the cabin, prayed that our navigator, an earnest Polish-American lad named Ray Mazanowski, would find Shinchiku exactly where he pointed us—and there it was. The Japanese planes were all there, wing tip to wing tip on the ground, the red balls painted on their jungle-green camouflage coloring, waiting for us. Our pursuits, up above, were impatient; one P-38 overflew us by seconds to get at a slow Japanese transport plane in the sky ahead, and as we came in, the transport was already twisting down in smoke and flame. We lifted to fifteen hundred feet so as to clear the fragments of our own bombs, and then we were over them, our frags opening up the parked planes, unfolding in flame, with the characteristic orange-and-black smoke coronas of burning fuel flowing from the tanks. Then our pursuits were strafing what was left, and strafing barracks, and Japanese were running, and the whole operation, by my stopwatch, had taken no more than three minutes, from the sea approach, over the airfield, to the turn, and back out to sea—and only eight minutes from first sight of landfall to the smoke vanishing over the horizon. Then Mazanowski was up in the top turret, counting, counting, and screaming that every single plane was safe, we had not lost a plane, nor a man, and we were on our way home. We destroyed, by the records, some fifty enemy bombers and fighters on the ground and in the air on that strike—and it meant, for the Japanese, that the interior lanes of their empire were now no longer safe, since Formosa was only 750 miles from their homeland. And for the American command it meant that Americans could go anywhere; Japan itself was the next prey.

On such spirit rode the victories; and on this spirit and the vast American investment in education and technology married to the spirit came the power lift; and after that, even if I could not distinguish it then, the "stretch"—the beginning of the obsession with air war that was to delude American strategy thirty years later in Vietnam.

I would mark my first awareness of the stretch that evening in August 1944 when the B-29s took off from China to reach for the homeland of Japan in the first daylight strike at the enemy. The B-29s belonged to the Twentieth Bomber Command; they were the most advanced airplanes of their time, with a range of well over five thousand miles, and were at the disposal only of General "Hap" Arnold and President Roosevelt in Washington. They had been built specifically to destroy Japan, and the closest safe bases the United States could locate for their design and distance capacity in 1943 had been China. Thus they arrived in Chengtu from over the Hump in the spring of 1944, divorced from all local command and control, either Stilwell's, Chennault's or Chiang's. They were a "pure" strategic instrument, the best the air force could put into the sky—and watching them prepare to hit stretched my horizon along with that of our generals.

The Twentieth Bomber Command briefed its crews the night before the August 19 strike scientifically, not at all in the romantic, football-jargon, happy-go-lucky style of our local China strikes. First on weather and meteorology, with huge charts; then on rescue procedures if they were downed in any given area; then on the topology and layout of the steel mills in Yawata in Japan's homeland,

which we were going to hit in broad daylight; then, a
matter-of-fact pep talk by Brigadier General Laverne G.
("Blondie") Saunders, who was going to lead the strike.
He spoke in the slurred, blurred syllables of common
American talk, but his instructions were precise. "Gentlemen, we've got to do better work, we've got to get at our
aiming points. . . . You pilots have got to get in there at
the altitude set and you've got to keep your speed steady.
How do you expect your bombardier to do his work if
you're flubbing around back there? This raid is going to
be rough, but goddamnit, it's a rough war and you're
flying in a good ship, better than anything they ever
dreamed of having. You'll have to fight your way through
to target, but you're better than they are, you know it,
that dirty bunch of yellow-bellies. . . ."

The technology of the first daylight raid on Japan
was impressive. So was the long briefing. But most impressive, in retrospect, was the reach and the spirit. In the
briefing, they spoke of errors and successes in the early
raids the B-29s had already made from the China base:
they had hit at Anshan in Manchuria, thirteen hundred
miles north; at Palembang, on Sumatra in the Dutch East
Indies, over two thousand miles to the south; their arc of
destruction was so impressive that my notes recorded for
the first time that the spread of American power was now
global. A Catholic chaplain, named Adler, closed the
briefing by reciting the Lord's Prayer, which all the crews
in the briefing room repeated. Then all of them, Catholics, Protestants, Jews alike, listened as he blessed them
"In nomine Patrius et Filii et Spiritus Sancti," and the
room mumbled the words after him. It would be very
dangerous.

The next morning in the dark the planes took off.
They were overloaded, carrying enough gasoline in their
fuel tanks to go all the way to Japan and back; the
runway at Chengtu was the longest in China, but still
perilously short for comfort. I went to the end of the
runway to see if the planes could clear with their heavy
lift, and found Chaplain Adler there. As the planes one
by one rumbled by and the pilots squeezed aloft, he

would chant aloud from his prayer book as if trying to give the wings just an extra bit of lift in Christ's name, amen.

All the planes on that raid took off safely. They bloodied the Japanese homeland. But it was far more dangerous than planned and we paid too heavily for American logistics to bear. Fourteen planes, or twenty percent, did not come back—an intolerable loss, which we were forbidden, rightly, to report. Simple geography had compelled the B-29s to return to the Chengtu base across occupied China; on the way back, Japanese fighters rose to hit the laggards as they limped home. China was apparently not a good place to base long-range aircraft in those days; and shortly thereafter, when the Marines moved across the Pacific, the entire B-29 operation was tranferred to the Pacific islands, from which the "Superforts" devastated Japan and then dropped the atomic bomb. But the instrumentation was already there; and the power that comes with long-range devastation, which seemed so thrilling that evening, grew later into the blind intoxication in which instruments influenced American decisions more than politics.

The grass-roots politics in those days, however, were very sound. Wherever one touched the dispersion of American force, one found the same kind of men— bitching and drudging, but willing to die, giving that critical extra effort which transforms soldiers into warriors, persuades leadership to boldness, and lights imagination with newly perceived realities.

The Hump, for example. No one knows when the first flight across the Hump was made, not even Don Old, who made that first flight on what he thought might have been the ninth or even the tenth of April, 1942. The men who flew the Hump (including a young lieutenant named Barry Goldwater) did, simply, what they thought they must do. They flew in the beginning against clouds, against the Japanese, who dominated the air in 1942, and against the Himalayas. They flew in old DC-3s, whose service ceiling was so low they must fly the passes in sunlight, which exposed them to the Japanese; or fly

through clouds, where the Himalayas might poke up
crags to bring them down. Casualties were so high that
the DC-3 was replaced by the C-87; but those four-engine
planes could not be maintained. The Hump command
then accepted the whale-bellied C-46s, fresh from the
factories, not yet test-flown and tried, and they test-flew
and tried them in the Asian mountains. They made their
own maps of uncharted peaks, bases and landing fields.
The charts at the end of the war carried the designation
of a landing field called Dumbastapur. All the other bases
of the Air Transport Command were named for the
points on the British Indian Survey maps, but Dumbastapur was named for an episode during a Japanese raid
on an airstrip laid out on a British tea plantation. An
American colonel named Gerry Mason saw his men in the
open, gazing at the planes overhead, realized they were
enemy planes and yelled, "Take cover, you dumb bastards!" After which this airstrip was officially charted on
the maps as Dumbastapur, India, and may remain so still,
for all I know.

Out of the flights of the Hump, as they rose from
eighty tons a month in May 1942 to eighty thousand tons
a month by the end of the war, came the entire art of
modern air logistics, replayed once more in the Berlin
airlift of 1948–1949, and then transmuted to the air-cargo
transport practice that is now common in the modern
world.

For myself, admiring as I did the valor and technology which took the men over the Himalayas day and
night, came a rather long-lasting lesson and understanding
in the measurement of human spirit, couched in the first
and one of the rarest reasonable explanations of psychiatry to me. By good planning, someone in Washington had
been wise enough to send to the Hump command as
"Wing Surgeon" a lieutenant colonel named Donald D.
Flickinger. Flickinger was an easygoing man, a psychia-
trist, and seemed to spend much of his time simply going
from base to base and chewing the fat aimlessly with
young pilots. I queried him and he explained, as I recall,

thus: His was the difficult job of deciding whether a man was a coward, too chicken to fly; or whether the man had been stressed so far he was too sick to fly. Every man, said Flickinger, pulling a teacup over to him, is like a cup. But men come in different sizes, big cups and little cups, each with a different capacity to hold strain. With too much strain, every cup spills over and anything can happen. Then men can crack up their planes, go berserk, make errors in judgment, become reckless in the air. Some men, he said, could take only ten trips across the Hump; some could do thirty; some even sixty—but eventually, sooner or later, a man would reach his limit of strain and he, Flickinger, had to recognize that point of strain, ground the man, or ship him home, before he harmed himself or his crew. Flickinger was more concerned about men who tried too hard, and pushed themselves too far, than by the occasional coward. His measure of the outreaching spirit was the best index of valor, as well as the best use of psychiatry, that I have come across, before or since. And thus, two years later, I would use what I learned from Flickinger of stress and strain to measure myself.

By then, in early 1945, I had given up on my effort to report esoteric Chinese politics, or the crescent civil war, in the columns of *Time* magazine. I was still under political strain; so I found actual combat a relief from thinking, or trying to force thinking on my editors. And it seemed to me that I could get through to the end of the war only by joining the men in the field in that happy-go-lucky comradeship that comes in the company of men when all goes well.

From January of 1945 until the end of the war, I did my best to stay with the action—but the action always, and ultimately, brought me back to politics and history.

After January 1945, the war went well in the field. Stilwell's training effort was now paying off; the thousands of Americans posted as liaison and training officers with Chinese troops, sleeping in hammocks in the jungle, in mud huts, in old Chinese temples, were now proud of the force they had created.

From the beginning, the object of the American effort had been to cut through the Japanese blockade of China and reopen the Burma Road. The end came in a ten-day period in mid January of 1945, starting with an assault on the last stronghold of the Japanese, atop Mount Huilungshan; and there again came another of those vignettes that mark a turning point. Huilungshan was 7,500 feet high; the American-Chinese command of three Chinese divisions was to stage out of a ridge 6,000 feet high to clear Huilungshan—and once more, perfection of execution. It was a long, hot day of mountain climbing, and it began with American planes circling the peak: a tattoo of three smoke shells from the artillery to mark the Japanese positions on the crest, then American pursuits and bombers peeling off one by one, dropping their napalm, dropping frag bombs, dropping heavy bombs. Then the artillery: three eight-minute salvos every hour, then after each salvo a rush of Chinese infantrymen to the next height through the shell-shredded trees; then another salvo, and one could see the Chinese in their blue-gray uniforms tumbling into trenches or circling Japanese blockhouses and dropping on them from the top. Then, finally, at four o'clock, in the brilliant sun, the final fusillade from the American-directed artillery and an old-fashioned bayonet charge as the Chinese infantry reached the crest. In a few minutes, from our observation post, we could see them strolling outlined against the sky on the height that commanded the junction of the historic road where Burma meets China. From that height, any Japanese pocket remaining on lesser heights could be pounded under with ease. The blockade, we knew, would be over in days.

What remains most vivid in memory now are two things: the vultures flying over the slopes of the mountain picking away at the Japanese corpses which had been lying in the sun, rotting, for days. And the spirit of the Japanese. None surrendered. They died far from home.

My only trophy of the ending of the blockade, which I still have, is the Japanese battle flag that flew over Hui-lungshan, signed in the dried-out, rusty blood of the Japanese soldiers who chose to die rather than surrender, who must have signed it from their own wounds that last day of battle. They, too, had spirit—and the leaders of their empire had wasted it.

Thus, then, in the closing months of the war, I was almost schizophrenic. What was happening in the field was, simply, so exciting that I could not help but thrill with American pride. But whether or not we wasted the spirit, skills and valor of our men in the field, as the Japanese Empire had wasted its men, would remain for the coming years to decide. My heart was with the men I knew in the field making victory, but my mind told me we were already deep in blunder in the politics of China. The warping of my emotions to a patriotism which is my worst weakness as a professional journalist had begun in Boston, when Miss Fuller taught us of Miles Standish and Elder William Bradford. It had continued through Harvard; but now this sense of the American purpose as Triumph over Evil became unshakable in me, almost maniacal as I began to flick around the map of Asia which was opening to our conquests.

My movements in the last few weeks of the war were frenzied. I forgot about politics, forgot about my quarrels with Luce, and intoxicated with the victory that intoxicated everyone, moved anywhere I wanted. I was into Nanning in June, as soon as the Chinese pierced the cordon in East China and began to unravel the Japanese victories of 1944. I was off by plane to visit MacArthur's command in the Philippines in July, when news reached us that the air force could now make direct flights between the China and Pacific commands. I flew on to Okinawa for the last days of the mop-up and saw bulldozers pushing the sun-dried bodies of dead Japanese off newly built roadways as if they were garbage. I flew back to Manila and woke to hear that we had dropped an atomic bomb on Japan. The news came on the armed forces radio while I was shaving, on a day of terminal madness and joy. My instinct was to

hurry to my post in Chungking, but first I wanted to talk
to MacArthur himself. He received me two days after the
bomb dropped, the day after he himself had been briefed
for the first time on the bomb and its nature by Karl
Compton of MIT. After some pleasantries of reacquain-
tance, he got at once to the bomb, no longer roaring as he
used to roar. "White," he said, "White, do you know
what this means?" "What, sir?" I asked. It meant, he
said, that all wars were over; wars were no longer matters
of valor or judgment, but lay in the hands of scholars and
scientists. "Men like me are obsolete," he said, pacing
back and forth. "There will be no more wars, White, no
more wars." With that assurance, I was off again, back to
the mainland, up to Chungking to find out how the
surrender was being taken, lingered in Chungking for a
few days, then decided the story was elsewhere. I flew
back to Manila to hedge-hop to Okinawa, whence I
hoped our plane could make it to Tokyo Bay, where,
apparently, the Japanese were about to surrender.

Reading again the dispatches I kept cabling back
from my wild circuit about the rim of the shrinking
Japanese Empire, I can see once more the contradiction
between events and decision. The world was fluid and
about to be remade. An empire had vanished; a half-
dozen victors raced for the spoils. Boundaries were to be
drawn fresh, armies disarmed, entire states abolished.
And once more, as always, as news of events flowed into
the seat of command, Washington, the events must have
been sorted out there not by their own nature but by the
shapes and categories ready in men's minds to receive
them. I was following only the crash and sound of events
on the rim, waiting for decision at the center in Washington to give them coherence and meaning.

The decision in Washington was to give all priority
to the orderly opening and occupation of Japan. The Japanese had formalized their surrender on August 14; had
sent their first personal emissaries to Manila on August
19 and 20; and agreed to accept MacArthur's General
Order No. 1, outlining the terms of surrender. But was
this surrender real? Or a trap? We had designated Atsugi

airfield outside Yokohama as our first touchdown point of occupation. The Japanese argued: Atsugi was a training base for Kamikaze pilots, it was too dangerous; the suicide pilots had mutinied on first news of the surrender, invaded the Emperor's palace to protest, killing the general of the Imperial Guard Division. Another 300,000 soldiers of veteran divisions had been assembled in the Tokyo plain before the surrender to fight off American invasion; the Japanese were unsure of the control of their command structure in the vicinity.

But MacArthur insisted: we would penetrate Japan at Atsugi.

Thus, then, I found myself on a hot night in Okinawa waiting to fly to Japan and Tokyo Bay—where the Japanese were supposed to surrender, and the war was supposed to come to an end.

Ceremonies are little more than punctuation marks in history, to be ignored except by schoolchildren, who must learn their dates. But the ceremony of the last great American victory was of an order so important and colorful that I shall tell it here, before I touch on the real history of the disaster in Asia which happened, almost instantly thereafter, unnoticed.

It was the night of August 31, 1945, that we moved on Japan.

The negotiation of surrender had taken a little more than two weeks, and we had been gathering planes, from the Hump run, from the North Atlantic run, from the mid-Pacific and mid-Africa runs—and they were jammed together here in the night on the airfields of Okinawa. Ten beacon ships were strung north over the sea from Okinawa to Sagami-Wan, to blink the air train on its way.

The planes went off into the night, spitting back blue flames from their nacelles, tightly timetabled. I was scheduled out of Kadena airfield, on a plane of the Eleventh Airborne Division, combat-packed and combat-ready, departing in sections at two-minute intervals. The plane I rode took off about an hour after the first echelon, before anyone had yet landed at Atsugi airfield, which would be the first pinpoint of occupation. This would give us enough time to turn back if trouble developed at Atsugi—but enough honor to say that we were in on the first landing, at least two hours before MacArthur himself.

It was a short flight from Okinawa to Japan, three hours on bucket seats. The sentiment of the men was simple: "Don't trust the sons of bitches"; and no one slept, the men fingering and plucking at their guns, opening them, cleaning them again and again as combat troops always do before action. We were flying under an overcast and dawn seeped in at six. Below we could pick out the tips of the volcanic islands that lead to Tokyo Bay. Our plane rocked in a rain squall, bobbed about, then slipped into a patch of sun. And there in the morning sun, stretching as far as we could see in the inner arms of Tokyo Bay, was Halsey's Third Fleet—flattops and battleships, cruisers and destroyers, more ships than anyone had ever seen before in one place, or is ever likely to see again. Then to the left, in the distance, a gray, unmistakably perfect mountain cone, Fujiyama, so lovely one's eyes had to caress its slopes and flanks. Then the surf breaking on sand shores below, the green rice fields, nothing moving on any road, and down to the landing at Atsugi, which is twenty-two miles southwest of the Imperial Palace in Tokyo and perhaps twelve miles from Yokohama.

The first touchdown could have preceded us by little more than an hour, but it had softened the sharp edge of confrontation. Off at one end of the field, crowded together, wings crazy-cocked to the sky, were the camouflaged green planes of the Japanese air force, their propellers stripped. What I had feared for so long was now stacked as junk. The Stars and Stripes were flying from the control tower. Our planes were coming down in unbroken sequence. The troops unloaded, their guns cradled ready; and then they slung up the guns when American jeeps rolled up to lead the Japanese trucks that would take them to the perimeter points. As we watched, the perimeter of American presence swelled, men hammering up their assigned rendezvous signs: FEAF. THIRD BATTALION. SEVENTH AACS. ATC. And more signs, and more, as the web grew, and Americans clustered in their units about the expanding perimeter of the field, the power of one civilization pressing on, and about to squeeze out another.

It was ten in the morning before we felt the field secure, and our own strength large enough to test beyond. I joined the point, the Third Battalion of the Eleventh Airborne, as it pushed off in a column of Japanese trucks, led by the jeep of Brigadier General Frank Dorn. Dorn was an old friend of China days, an artist of watercolors, a creative gourmet, a skilled troop commander—a man competent either to fight the Japanese or to perform the tea ceremony if required.

Yellow and red tapes marked off our route. Japanese gendarmes and troops lined the roads, their backs to us, rifles slung across shoulders, scanning the countryside for possible troublemakers. The fields were empty, no farmers in sight, straw flats of grain drying in the sun, wash hanging on the line near the shuttered wooden bungalows; but almost everyone indoors—except for the few curious teenage girls, who would peek around corners to watch the invaders pass, and then dart away when they saw they were observed by the American soldiers. Their men had raped their way through China; we would not, but they did not know it. It was silent all the way into Yokohama, paddies rising in crescents beyond the shrublike trees, but no one there. We came into Yokohama by the Sakuragicho station; and our battalion, the spearhead of the occupation, made for the Grand Hotel on the Bund.

It might have been make-believe, it went so fast. Two American infantrymen, grenades at the belt, guns ready, took over the door. A few minutes later, an American sergeant and a captain, assisted by a Japanese girl with thick-lensed eyeglasses, were ready to billet arrivals. Then the assistant manager, in frock coat and striped trousers, made his appearance in the lounge—a huge room, wood-paneled, with overstuffed pink furniture—

and, wringing his hands, he tried to find out from us what General MacArthur would like to eat for dinner.

We went out shortly to look around. Perhaps a quarter of a mile of the Bund was still intact, and from the Bund we could see Yokohama's harbor—empty. On the waterfront: burned-out fishing boats, abandoned lighters, decaying launches rising and falling with the lapping of the waves; a single Japanese warship, one turret blown half overside, its guns poking askew like broken pipestems. Beyond in the distance one clean American battleship and two escorts, guns leveled at the city.

There was no need to level any guns at Yokohama. It was cinder. We had told each other for years that the wood-and-paper houses of the Japanese would burn at the first touch of fire-bombing. So they had. The city was flat—acre after acre of rubble, above which three features repeated themselves over and over again, signatures of desolation against the sky: the speckling of big iron safes, iron cubes intact on plots where shops, offices, factories had been burned out; the stubble of brick smokestacks rising high across the horizon; and a crust of corrugated-iron shacks, all rusting, where people still tried to live. Dreary, beshawled figures trudged about in these ruins.

The city was dead. So apparently was Japan. It had needed no atom bomb to crush Japan; the B-29s had already done it with their fire bombs, killing more, by far, than both atom bombs did. The atom bombs had been essential only as a pretext for the Japanese to give up an idea—of their eternal invincibility. But the fire bombs had already wiped out the vitality of the nation. I felt no shame at that moment over the slaughter of Japanese, either by fire bomb or by nuclear fission: I had cowered under their bombs, under their machine guns, seen the victims they had savaged with knife, bayonet and club. And they had bombed my country first. Revenge is a dry form of satisfaction; but the dryness was clean to my taste, even though I could not bring myself to hate the stooped and forlorn people of the street.

Friday night and all day Saturday, as we waited for

the ceremony, I probed about in a jeep, in the rain and mist; and the fog made all outlines in the beaten country soft and blurred, as in Oriental paintings. Then on Sunday, the day of ceremony, all came sharp.

A destroyer picked our group of China-based reporters off the Bund in Yokohama in early morning, and we climbed aboard the U.S.S. *Missouri* in the bay. The U.S.S. *Iowa* lay to one side, the *South Dakota* to the other. An old flag with thirty-one stars hung from one of the *Missouri* turrets, the same flag that Commodore Perry had brought to Tokyo Bay when he opened Japan to the West ninety-two years earlier. At the very top of the mainmast was the same flag, we were told, that flew over the Capitol on December 7, 1941.

This was to be no cloistered surrender, as had been the surrender of the Germans at Reims, three months earlier. MacArthur wanted everyone there, and the world to watch. The *Missouri*'s veranda deck bristled with high command: five full four-star generals (Stilwell, Krueger, Spaatz, Kenney, Hodges); eleven three-star generals backing up the four-stars, followed by twenty two-star generals and fifteen one-stars. The Navy had equivalents in admirals; the Marines had their delegation of Leatherneck generals. Then were grouped, in their various splendid and many-hued uniforms, clusters of Russians, Chinese, Britons, Australians, French, Dutch. A space was taped off for eleven Japanese, sternly limited by our orders to "3 Army, 3 Navy, 3 Government, 2 Representatives of the Press." Then came the American press pack. The Marines, the Navy, the various Army commands had all insisted on having *their* war correspondents present to report the war as *their* victory. The crush held everyone erect, each of us allotted two square feet of tiptoe space from which we could watch. The enlisted men who had fought the war, the sailors and the marines, found what space they could, and very few of the *Missouri*'s crew could have remained below. Sailors in dress whites sat with their feet dangling over the long gray barrels of the sixteen-inch guns on which they perched; they hung from every line and rope. This would be a sight to remember, to tell their children, to tell their grandchildren. None of us knew then that this was the last war America would cleanly, conclusively win. We thought it was the last war ever.

A shrill piping announced the arrival of the Japanese. The first aboard was Mamoru Shigemitsu, the new Japanese Foreign Minister, in silk hat, morning coat and striped trousers. Limping on his wooden leg and a cane, he pulled himself up the catwalk, clutching for a grip. He had lost his leg in an assassination attempt before the war; the young radicals of prewar Japan, believing he was soft on Japan's destiny, had tried to kill him because he wanted peace with America. But that had been long ago; none of us knew it, so none of us offered a hand to the crippled old man as he dragged himself to the veranda deck where he would seal the surrender in the war he had once sought to avoid.

Then came Japan's Chief of Staff, Yoshijiro Umezu. He was a sturdy man, with a face easy to hate, stolid, stiff, blank of expression. I could imagine him giving orders to loot, rape, burn, devastate. His uniform was crisp; ribbons on his chest, gold braid over his shoulder. I recall brown pocks on his cheeks, and his teeth must have been tight-clenched, for as his face muscles flexed, the brown pocks went in and out. He seemed a mean man— but he had the honor to commit suicide, I was told, shortly thereafter.

The other Japanese followed. When they were all there, at eight minutes past nine on September 2, 1945, Douglas MacArthur emerged from a cabin and took the curse off the savage moment. MacArthur could always savor a moment and this one was worth savoring. If television had been available then, he would have delighted in displaying himself to it. He was master of the Pacific. He had spent some time composing his remarks, and what emerged was a mixture of Abraham Lincoln's Gettysburg Address with phrases plucked from the William McKinley school of American rhetoric. Out of respect, I shall quote the Lincolnian phrases, not the McKinley purple.

His hands quivered as he read his text and we listened. "We are gathered here . . . to conclude a solemn agreement whereby Peace may be restored. . . . Nor is it for us here to meet . . . in a spirit of distrust, malice or hatred. But rather it is for us, both victors and vanquished, to rise to that higher dignity which alone befits the sacred purposes we are about to serve. . . . It is my earnest hope . . . that from this solemn occasion a better world shall emerge out of the blood and carnage of the past—a world founded upon faith and understanding—a world dedicated to the dignity of man and the fulfillment of his most cherished wish—for freedom, tolerance and justice. . . . As Supreme Commander for the Allied Powers, I announce it my firm purpose . . . to proceed in the discharge of my responsibilities with justice and tolerance, while taking all necessary dispositions to insure that the terms of surrender are fully, promptly and faithfully complied with."

Here MacArthur looked directly at the Japanese and intoned: "I now invite the representatives of the Emperor of Japan and the Japanese Government, and the Japanese Imperial General Headquarters to sign the instrument of surrender at the places indicated."

Shigemitsu took off his silk hat and limped forward to sign the document. Someone finally took pity and gave him a chair to sit on. He signed, withdrew. Umezu followed. Umezu took off his white gloves, and refused the chair. He bent from the hips, like a folding rule. His stocky frame was rigid for a moment, then he took the pen and signed.

It was as Umezu straightened again that the last thing happened—and happened to the split second in the perfect timing of the victorious forces we then commanded. The rain of Saturday had ended, the skies were lightening, and now the clouds above the ship were breaking with sun patches when a drone sounded. It began as a light buzzing in the distance, then a roar, then the deafening tone of countless planes converging. Four hundred B-29s, the fire bombers that had leveled Japan, had taken off from Guam and Saipan hours before; the fleet carriers

had coordinated their planes. They were to appear over
the *Missouri* all at once. And they did. The four hundred
B-29s came low, low over the *Missouri,* and fifteen hundred fleet planes rose above and around their wings.
There they were, speckling the sky in flecks of scudding
gray; it was American power at zenith. They dipped over
the *Missouri,* passed on over Yokohama, inland over
Tokyo to brandish the threat, then back out to sea again.

They had laid waste this country, its empire, its sea
lanes; they had blasted open not only its cities but its
mind. Ours had been Victory Through Air Power, and
the planes paraded their triumph over Tokyo Bay as
Caesar's legionnaires had paraded theirs in Rome when
the short sword was queen of the battlefield. It was the
supreme moment of Air Power.

And so, after gaping, as we all did, at the planes,
and shivering slightly, I was overside on a destroyer
taking correspondents to shore to file their dispatches;
and I remember debasing the moment to beat my rival,
the *Newsweek* correspondent, with the quickest story on
how the Japanese had surrendered. And then, after filing,
I strolled at dusk the Bund of Yokohama with my old
friend "Pepper" Martin, and we sat down on the wharfside looking out over the Pacific. The surrender was then
no more than eight hours old. We knew the First Cavalry
Division was coming ashore somewhere in the vicinity,
and Martin pointed to the dirty water lapping the pier.
There, bobbing in the water, was a freshly opened, but
empty, wax package which clearly said "Cracker Jack."
He, from Seattle, and I, from Boston, had both grown up
eating candy-coated Cracker Jacks. Now the Americanization of Japan would begin.

Frenzy seized me again the next morning. *Time* and
Life had an entire platoon of writers and photographers
and reporters already ashore; but I was the China correspondent, and must get back to base.

But why Chungking? I asked myself. I had control
of a plane that would go where I wanted. General Wedemeyer, commander of the China theater, had put at the

disposal of the correspondents who covered his command a C-54, loaded with mountain rations and staffed by two full crews. I was by then senior among the correspondents and responsible for the flight. MacArthur could not give Wedemeyer's press corps orders; we could fly as we wished; and the plane's crew, all younger than I, were ready to frolic through the open skies that belonged to the white-winged stars of the American air force. So, too, were the other correspondents of the China command—if we could agree on the story. The story, all of us knew, was probably in Shanghai. So we plotted our route in skip-hops, as tourists through a victory, to move in leisurely return to Chungking: Shanghai, Nanking, then Chungking.

Our C-54 left early from Atsugi. We had already decided that we would make our trip, in this new plane, the first nonstop flight between Tokyo and Shanghai. But on the way we circled over Hiroshima because all of us wanted to see where that bomb had hit four weeks earlier. Hiroshima was not at all impressive from the air. There was nothing to describe, not even the smokestacks that I had seen poking up from the barrens of Yokohama. Hiroshima was bare, only the rivers running through brown flats below. The center was so neatly clean it could not be reported—as if the bomb had swept out the heart of the town in a single stroke.

Thus at dusk into an airdrome near Shanghai. It was a tight moment. We landed unannounced on the field, and when we pulled our door open, there stood Japanese soldiers, bayoneted guns pointed directly at us. They did not seem about to shoot, yet there was none of the obsequious bowing to Americans I had just seen for three days in Japan. A young Japanese officer came up the stairs, very angry. He could speak no English, I no Japanese, so we tried to make ourselves understood in the Chinese we both spoke. I did my best to explain to him that Japan had surrendered, that I, personally, had just seen it in Tokyo. He said he had heard this on the radio, but that he had no orders from his chain of command to let American planes land here at this field. But the heart had gone out of him; he did not want to shoot or seize us, only wanted us to fly on our way elsewhere. I insisted he give us trucks to take us into the city and place his guards around our plane. Finally, he gave in, but only because he had to: he was of the defeated, I of the victors, and his sullen confusion at the disorder was the story of the grand tragedy written in minuscule.

The tragedy of the victory revolved around one great question: To whom the fruits of victory? The answer was blurred by ignorance and events jostling decision. To whom, in occupied China, should the Japanese yield? Mao, in one of his flaring metaphors, described the political dilemma in peasant terms: Who collects the fallen pears? If the landlord has run away from the bandits and abandoned the orchard, asked Mao, and the tenants have remained to tend the pear trees, fertilize them and guard them—who, then, at harvest time has the right to collect the falling pears? The runaway landlord or the peasants who tended the orchard? He, Mao and his Communists, had occupied the coastal zones of China which Chiang had yielded to the Japanese. Who now should harvest the pears of victory in the areas that Mao's troops controlled?

From the neatness of the surrender ceremony in Japan, which our arms and logistics alone controlled, I was thrust into the confusion that determined Asia's fate.

I can best put a frame about this confusion by citing from three sets of now yellowing documents which I collected in those last six weeks of ecstasy and tumult, documents which I read, stripped for news and filed to *Time* magazine (which did not print them). I was filing convulsively, as all correspondents do when speed and action seem more important than reflection.

The first set were Communist documents—orders to the Communist armies which I had snatched from Communist headquarters in Chungking in early August. These Communist orders were signed by General Chu Teh, Commander in Chief of all Chinese Red Army regulars, partisans and guerrillas. Their dating is striking testimony of historic decision-making. Chu Teh, and his Communists, were quickest off the mark.

The Japanese had first sued for peace to the Allies on August 10—an open- message crackling over the wireless of the world, intercepted by the Communist listening posts in Yenan. The Communists must have gathered instantly at that old gray, sprawling, adobe-and-brick headquarters which I remembered so fondly from my visit a year earlier. And they must have reacted at once, for General Chu Teh's General Order No. 1, over his signature, is dated the same day: August 10.

"Japan has surrendered unconditionally," read General Chu Teh's Order No. 1. "... I hereby issue the following orders to all the armed force in the liberated areas: (1) Any anti-Japanese armed force in the liberated areas should, on the basis of the Potsdam Proclamation, deliver an ultimatum to the enemy troops ... ordering them to hand over their arms within a certain limit of time. ... (2) If they do not surrender over a certain limit of time, they will be disarmed. ... (3) If the enemy or puppet forces refuse to surrender or to be disarmed, the anti-Japanese armed force in the liberated areas should determinedly annihilate them. ..."

Then, the next morning, came a tattoo of further orders from Chu Teh, radioed area by area. At eight o'clock on the morning of August 11, by Order No. 2, Communist armies in Shansi and Suiyuan were to move on Chahar and Jehol, the troops in Hopei to move toward Liaoning in Manchuria; the details outlined a northern thrust whose ultimate objective was still obscure. At 8:00 A.M. also came Order No. 3, simultaneous with No. 2, an order coordinating the main Chinese Red Army forces with the Mongolian Communist army. At 10:30, Order No. 4: all forces in Shansi to move to take over the railway from the Japanese, and seize the provincial capital of Taiyuan. At 11:00 A.M.: orders to all commands down through Central China to South China, to seize all railways from the Japanese instantly, and again: "If resistance is encountered we should determinedly annihilate

our enemies." At noon, Order No. 6: to move to cooper-
ate with the Soviet Red Army coming into Manchuria. At
six in the evening—obviously after consultation with
Mao—Order No. 7: a sweeping full-scale order of insurrection to "control all ... depots, factories, schools, barracks and forts. ... Control all ships, trains, military
trucks, wharfs and piers, post offices, telephone and telegraph companies and radio stations. ..."

The reaction of the Nationalist government followed
the next day. It came in a personal telegram from Chiang
K'ai-shek to Chu Teh: "... The government of China has
made all necessary preparations to deal with Japanese
collapse and re-establishment of order and administration. Let Communists be warned: to maintain dignity of
government mandates and to abide faithfully by decisions
of Allies. ..." More specifically, I was told by the Generalissimo's headquarters: "In the past when military
orders have been disobeyed, military action has been
taken. The Generalissimo's orders *must* be obeyed. Those
who disobey them are to be considered as a common
enemy."

It was clear, then—the Communists were moving in
the field, relying on muscle and gun. The Generalissimo
was relying on the decisions of the "Allies," which meant
the United States. Chiang still held the American franchise. The United States recognized only the Republic of
China, Chiang's republic. The United States had the
power, the planes, and command over Japan if it wanted
to exercise it. Which meant that MacArthur was in total
command.

A week later I was again in Manila, and on August
20 had come Douglas MacArthur's General Order No. 1.
That order was backed with the world's mightiest army,
navy and air force—and the threat of nuclear devastation.
It was directed sternly to the conquered Japanese and
their Emperor, and it was a prescription of what the
Japanese Emperor must say to his scattered and hopeless
troops, of whom two million still stood in arms on Chinese soil, encircled by both Communists and Nationalists.

"The Imperial General Headquarters," read Douglas

MacArthur's draft of what the Emperor must say, "by direction of the Emperor, and pursuant to the surrender to the Supreme Commander for the Allied Powers... hereby orders all of its Commanders in Japan and abroad to cease hostilities at once ... to remain in their present locations and to surrender unconditionally to Commanders ... as indicated hereafter or as may be further directed by the Supreme Commander. ..." Then General Order No. 1 ran on for four and a half pages of detail.

We Americans would decide, so ran the burden of the message, who would harvest the fruits of victory on the mainland of China. We had driven the Japanese from the orchard; thus we would decide who should harvest the fallen pears that Mao disputed with Chiang.

The surly confusion of the young Japanese officer who now met me at the airport in Shanghai was thus only a reflection of the larger confusion of the beaten Japanese in those weeks. They still occupied China's cities. But to whom should they yield? To Mao or to Chiang? They knew they were defeated; they wanted only to go home again. And in those three weeks, while they still held the great cities of China, they did not care to which Chinese they yielded, so long as MacArthur would spare their homeland. Among the many messages coming into our signal centers from the Japanese several now stand out stiffest in the sheaf of our harvest of their melancholy. "The situation in China," began one of their humble messages to MacArthur, "following the cessation of hostilities is as follows: (1) Various military authorities of Chungking and Yenan and troops under their command are rushing unwarrantedly and without discipline into the area under Japanese control and separately demanding the Japanese to disarm. (2) Meanwhile the Japanese troops are executing their best effort for the protection of the people as well as their own nationals, scarcely succeeding in preventing further aggravation of the confused situation. ..."

Each day the Japanese messages to MacArthur reflected the growing confusion of their defeated garrisons caught between American power at the top and the conflict between Chinese Communists and Nationalists in the field. As, for example, on August 23: "In Manchuria, Inner Mongolia and North Korea, the disarming of our forces is making progress. However, in certain localities, disarmed Japanese forces and civilians are being made victims of illegitimate firing, looting, acts of violence, rape and other outrages. . . . The situation is certain to get out of control in the very near future. . . ." On August 24: "The Communist troops and the Chungking troops around Psinian are plotting activities and likely to cause local engagements. . . ." August 25: "Japanese first front troops on the continent find themselves under complicated circumstances, and the situation is so peculiar that the delivery of their arms may occasionally be made to the Allied Commander [i.e. Communists] in direct contact, who may not be designated in your General Order No. 1. Your agreement is requested."

It was up to the United States, therefore, to decide to whom Japan must surrender China. I was writing all this in the brief half hours a newsman takes to file a dispatch, but I had lost the frame of the story. Journalism is a profession whose imperative is "now," and I was intent on the "now" story, the "today" story, as I bobbed and weaved about the collapse and the insurrection to come. I knew I could make copy for *Time* by writing about the "today" story, and as I flew back from the Tokyo surrender to Shanghai, the "today" story of liberation was too enticing and vivid not to file.

Shanghai cried for visual, anecdotal, color reporting. In the sky were American planes; the air rescue missions of the air force had preceded us by a few days; and they were guiding the planes above dropping parachute packs of food and medicine into the prisoner compounds where wasted American prisoners of war and internees were still held. The Chinese in the street clapped and cheered when American planes came low. And if a parachute pack opened and fell into a zone outside the prisoner compounds, the Chinese raced to open and loot it, and instant carnivals burst out. It was carnival all over town. As our truck from the airport came down Bubbling Well Road, Chinese clogged our path, cheering, waving little American and Nationalist flags. I noticed at the waterfront, where peddlers normally sold dried fish, that they were already selling silk-screen portraits of Chiang K'ai-shek, the Liberator.

The international settlement in Shanghai had had an exemption from war. Its polyglot population had survived under Japanese occupation, and the black-market underground was now furnishing luxuries to us that we had not seen in China for years. Good Scotch was being poured, steaks were an inch thick, champagne and French wines were on sale. Four currencies circulated simultaneously—the Japanese yen, the American military dollar, the Nationalist currency, puppet-government banknotes. One could have made a fortune by trading in currencies whose values fluctuated almost hourly. Leicas, Rolleiflexes, all German cameras, could be bought for twenty dollars in American money if one caught the exchange rates right. Silks and artworks were equally cheap; and few Chinese merchants haggled with the victorious Americans. Even the whoremasters and cabaret owners welcomed the first Americans. On our first evening in the liberated city our group went out through cheering crowds to a cabaret. The White Russian owner was so delighted to see Americans in uniform that drinks and meals were free—and to cap it, he offered us our choice of any woman in the house, any race, any color, any size—and he had them all.

I tried to make contact the next morning with politics; and because I had learned how the Communist underground worked, and could drop the names of Chou and Mao, I was in touch with the Communists within twenty-four hours. But I found their underground paralyzed. They had moved immediately on General Chu Teh's orders No. 1 and 7. The "Red Workers" had seized ten factories, and were holding out against the "Yellow

Workers," who supported Chiang K'ai-shek. Their New
Fourth Army had closed in on Shanghai and now ringed
the city within ten miles round. The students wanted to go
out on full strike; so did the General Union of Red
Workers. They explained how they still controlled any
number of districts in Shanghai city, and named which
districts. But ten days earlier, on August 25, Yenan had
suspended its call for an insurrection. Now, said their
orders, everyone must hold still. It was, they said, because even at this moment Mao Tse-tung himself was in
Chungking negotiating with Chiang K'ai-shek, and discipline held them firm while Mao tried to work out a
peaceful solution.

    In Shanghai, the Communists might have moved
irresistibly to take power from the Japanese in the first
two weeks after their surrender—but American power lay
off the coast, and they would, almost certainly, have been
forced to disgorge. The Americans in Chungking and
Washington would decide how and to whom to hand over
power. And since Mao and Chou were both in Chungking
talking with Chiang K'ai-shek and Hurley, the harvest of
victory would be decided there. So I must be off back to
Chungking at once, without pausing to enjoy the revels of
Shanghai.

    Mao and Chou, I found when I reached Chungking,
had arrived on August 28, while we were preparing for
the ceremony in Tokyo Bay. General Hurley had flown to
Yenan to offer them safe-conduct to come and negotiate
with Chiang. It was the first airplane trip ever for Mao
Tse-tung, a landbound man. He had hugged his little girl
and said good-bye to his wife openly at the airport, as
throngs in Yenan cheered him off: "like a man going to
his execution," said one of the Americans who was there.
Mao had boarded nervously, but when he alighted in
Chungking, dressed in his baggy blues and wearing an
incongruous Indian sun helmet, he had been cheered
again. Then he had been whisked away to the Generalissimo's compound in the hills above the city and installed
in a mansion of his own, with a flush toilet in a modern

bathroom. Mao refused all guards, even American military guards. For several days, before serious negotiations began, he and the Generalissimo, murderers of each other's men and families for so long, had paid each other visits, and strolled through the gardens together—the Generalissimo wearing his neat Sun Yat-sen suit or, occasionally, a black silk mandarin gown, Mao Tse-tung invariably dressed in the baggy blue cotton paddings of Yenan.

Then, the very day of the surrender in Tokyo Bay, serious negotiations had begun—Chou En-lai negotiating with Chiang's government at the practical level, while Mao and Chiang talked of the future of China in terms of history.

The conversations had already broken down when I came back to Chungking late in the first week of September. What lay at issue beyond all the large words of China's unity and purpose and independence was the territorial imperative of power: Who would control what provinces of China? Whose armies, whose guns, whose police, would control what the Japanese were surrendering? Chiang's promise and premise were the same as ever—that China was a unity, that Mao and his Communists would have a place in the government if they put their troops under his discipline as the warlords had done. But Mao and Chou were adamant. They would yield all the Yangtze valley and South China to Chiang. But they would not yield nor accept orders from Chiang in the provinces of the Yellow River basin in the north. And as for Manchuria—there, Chu Teh's troops under Lin Piao's command were already reaching for contact with the Russian Red Army, racing for occupation, on foot; there they would not yield either. In effect, they declared themselves willing to accept two Chinas; Chiang would settle for only one China—his.

There come moments in history when all is confusion. To be caught in such a moment is bewilderment. One hopes that somewhere, at some distant center of command, someone can make sense of all the contrary

fragments which the daily reporter collects at random.
Where, or who, or at what level Washington was collecting the fragments, we in the field could not tell.

But some of the fragments in my notebooks give the
feel of the chaos.

Item: Our own intelligence reports in Chunking,
relayed from Moscow, indicated that Stalin distrusted
Mao, considered him too much a nationalist to be a loyal
Communist, and would probably purge him if the Russians took over North China and disciplined the Communist Party there, as they had disciplined the Communist
parties in Eastern Europe. Washington must have had the
same information. Would Mao choose to throw in with
the Americans or with Stalin?

Item: Reports were received of the first contact between the Russian Red Army and the Chinese Red Army
near Kalgan, the gateway to Mongolia. The Chinese Reds
had been rebuffed by the Russian Reds; some had even
been disarmed; in Manchuria, the Russians were looting
and holding cities to hand over to Chiang's troops, not to
the Communists.

Item: The Sino-Soviet treaty had just been signed. It
shocked the Chinese Communists. Did it mean that Stalin, as the words indicated, was recognizing Chiang K'aishek, not themselves, in return for Chiang's concession of
special rights in Manchuria to the Soviets? Was there a
fissure there we should explore for friendship with Mao?

Contrariwise:

Item: A young American captain in air force intelligence had just been killed by the Communists. He was
John Birch, a blue-eyed, red-haired, peppery, hot-tempered young Georgian ex-missionary who spoke excellent
Chinese. I had known and liked him and regretted his
killing. But the story of his death was obscure even then.
Birch had become military adviser to a Nationalist unit
behind the lines; they had clashed with a rival Communist
force. Whether Birch was killed by the Communists in
cold blood as a prisoner, or in the heat of combat, we did
not then know. But his memory would be the seed of the
John Birch Society, which I was to meet in American

politics twenty years later. More importantly, however, he was the first American killed by Communists in a civil war we did not understand.

Item again, and overwhelmingly important: The Republic of China was our recognized ally, and Chiang K'ai-shek was its president. We had entered this war, invited the Jap attack on Pearl Harbor, to save Chiang K'ai-shek's "Free China." He was the talisman of the accident that had brought us into this war. The British has been brought into the war to save Poland, only to see it seized by the Communists seven years later. Were we to see "Free China," for whose sake we were drawn to war, also taken over by the Communists?

All things were fluid, the world map to be redrawn, Asia to be reshaped. But how? By standing with Chiang? By recognizing Mao? By standing apart totally and letting the Chinese armies settle the issue?

One last fragment of my last few days in Chungking seems particularly pertinent. The talks of Mao and Chiang were deadlocked. We had already begun to fly Chiang's troops, in our planes, to the cities of the coast and north. General Wedemeyer had flown to Washington for command consultation on the takeover, but the lesser generals on his staff were already having second thoughts about the giant troop airlift just getting under way. Thus I was called in to a staff session during the absence of Wedemeyer. I was only a war correspondent, but I had enough acquaintance with Chinese politics and Chinese battlegrounds to cause one or two of the staff to think my opinion might be worthwhile. I was invited by then Brigadier General George Olmsted, a West Point graduate, but a civilian in peacetime life and a politician to his fingertips, who later ran for governor of Iowa. Olmsted knew the politics of the American move were more important than the logistics of airlift capacity. He wanted me to come, I am sure, to make his point that the airlift of Chiang's troops to the big cities in Communist-controlled regions was political folly, a participation in a civil war which was neither our obligation nor our commitment.

Olmsted had asked me to speak to the generals. I

pointed out that airlifting Chiang's men into Manchuria
and North China, where the Communists held the countryside about the cities, was terribly risky. We would be
airlifting these men into garrisons and pockets that could
be resupplied only by American airlift capacity—and if
the Americans withdrew, as I felt we would, we would
have deflowered Chiang's army of its best troops, to
replant them where they could not be nourished. The
other generals were exasperated at my presence; my statements were only political judgments, not measurable military certainties. My sole participation in American policy-
making thus ended. As the conference broke up, one
brigadier general yelled at me, in a fore-echo of all the
denunciations of the press I would hear later: "They
aren't there, those Communist guerrillas you say are
there. They're a fiction of the American press." He went
on: "They haven't got the guns and manpower to keep
those railways closed. Their only strength is what American newspapermen tell Americans about them. Guys like
you and Edgar Snow, who talk about the Communist
guerrillas and their areas—you guys are what makes their
strength. They aren't there, I tell you; they exist only on
paper."

Unfortunately, the Communist guerrillas *were* there.
Just as our planes and airlift capacity were there. And the
planes, the capacity, the surplus crews, all now unneeded
for our own purposes, were too tempting to ignore. Lo-
gistically, that huge, now unneeded, capacity could be
used at the snap of command to help China if we wanted
to—and Chiang's influence in Washington was overwhelming. There, in Washington, the airlift of Chiang's
troops into Communist-controlled areas seemed mechanical, a geographical and logistical decision on a map of the
world which we dominated. And it would be politically
palatable at home, too—an errand of mercy, an act of
generosity, helping the Free Chinese back to their home-
lands.

No one explained, nor could I publish, that at the
moment when Mao had to choose between the Russians
and the Americans, we forced his choice back on the

Russians, where he would rest uneasily for the next twenty years.

Nor was it understood that we were involving America in an Asian civil war for the first time.

So the airlift began, our thinking trapped by our airpower, moving us and China toward inevitable disaster.

And I had reached the end of the war at odds with my government's policy and at sword's point with my boss at *Time*. Luce decided that for its first two postwar issues, *Time*'s cover would show two great heroes, Douglas MacArthur one week and Chiang K'ai-shek the next. The Chiang story was assigned to me. I felt it would be most unwise for *Time*, with its customary panegyrics, thus to legitimize China's somber tyrant yet once again. I cabled a rude refusal of the assignment directly to Harry Luce. He answered immediately, accusing me of political partisanship. I cabled back: "This office is working flat out under enormous conditions of strain. . . . I resent being called an avowed partisan . . . only a compromise this week can avert civil strife and the resultant total triumph of one side or another . . . here in the field I am in touch with the facts. . . . Every major treatment of the China problem [in *Time*] in the past year has displayed our divergence of views." This time I offered to come home and explain; and this time there was no temporizing. He ordered me home forthwith.

A few days before I left Chungking, I felt I must say good-bye and that night climbed my favorite hill. High on this topmost point in Chungking was a patch of grassy land from which one could look down on the valley of the Chialing River as it flows to join the Yangtze. From the summit, I could see both the winding course of the river and the spiraling chains of light that now twisted, in full illumination and without fear, about the ridges of Chungking. A full moon shone. I thought I would be alone. But the grassy patch was huddled with little groups of people—Chinese, who were looking down on what had been a city of hope, Chinese who had fled seven years earlier from the Japanese occupation, who had grown older and bred children in this city of exile. They had believed in Chiang K'ai-shek and in China, and now, I assumed, they would be going home again to rebuild, in Shanghai, or Tientsin, or whatever city they had fled, the China they had dreamed of. They were silent, utterly silent, under the moon, looking down on the river, and looking forward to going home. But the past to which they hoped to return could never be recaptured.

I, too, was going home. And like them, I would find there was no way to go back. I had first come here as a boy who hoped to be a professor of history; but I had seen too much to want a professorship in history ever again. I would now, and for the rest of my life, be a journalist; and if I could get home fast enough to be first with the story of China, I might stretch journalism into a book.

Contacts are the only bankable capital on which a journalist can ever draw. I had contacts in headquarters, and could wangle a No. 2 priority—an air-flight category that could get me out of China to New York in a week. So on Tuesday, September 18, two weeks after the end of the great war, at the beginning of another war, I was off to New York. The great airlift of Chiang's troops to the disaster which would engulf them in the east had already begun. The airlift loaded Chiang's troops in planes going east. I boarded a plane going west. Across the Hump for the last time; across India; across Africa; a delay in Casablanca; then across the Atlantic and in to Floyd Bennett Field, just outside New York. Miraculously, there I could hire and pay for a taxi into Manhattan without army travel orders. I was still in uniform, but I was once more a civilian, free and uncommitted.

New York was a city I would come to love more than any other in the world. I drove into the city and checked in at the old New Weston Hotel; the very next morning, I was off to buy a suit. I had left America with cast-off clothes and one new suit, which my mother had picked out for me. Now, seven years later, almost to the week, I was buying an American suit myself. Not a uniform, but a real suit. Because I was still in uniform, the salesman gave me a cut rate, or so he claimed, on the brown pin stripe that made me a civilian again. I could no longer go home to Boston; nor would China be home again either, though I did not know it then.

My immediate task was clear: to write a book that explained what was happening in China. The book must say it not only first and best, but quickly. "Quickly" was of the essence, for, if information is to guide public understanding, it must be delivered in time to press its way through the people up to government, where decisions are made in response to such pressures. My information was important. It was news, not history. Over the years, I was to learn how much more dangerous news is than history—both for the reporter and those he reports. At that moment, returning from war, I was determined to be first with the story of the inevitable collapse of Chiang K'ai-shek—even if it meant full clash with *Time* and Harry Luce. Annalee would be following home from China within weeks to join me in the enterprise. All of us in those days entertained the illusion that we could make events march in the direction we pointed, if we pointed clearly enough.

PART THREE

EUROPE
1948-1953

REPORTER IN TRANSITION

The storyteller was locked in his purpose when, six days after leaving China, his plane touched down in New York.

China filled his mind, as it had for ten full years. The China war had taught him his trade, and in the past year, as that war rolled on to victory and revolution, China had opened his eyes to the way daily events fall together in clusters that make natural stories. He had learned further that each story is a step in a zigzag march that takes on a discoverable direction only later, when men look back and see it as history. But he thought he already knew how stories in China fit together; and he wanted to tell them instantly, as he saw them, not processed through the editorial mastications of a news-magazine. He would tell the story in a book, and then be off to China again to witness the climax of the revolution.

But he was not to return to China for almost thirty years, for New York was to ensnare him, then remold him. Not, of course, all at once. *Time* had granted him a six-month postwar leave of absence, and until his book was finished, he cloistered himself with his notes. Within two weeks of homecoming, he settled into a sunless apartment on East Twenty-ninth Street, where, working with Annalee Jacoby, he began to pound away furiously at the typewriter. They were joined in passionate purpose—not just to be first with the true, hitherto censored story of China at war, but to spread the message: America should get out of China, *now,* should let China find its own way into the future, by itself.

New York, however, could not be completely shut out of awareness. The city glowed with its postwar phosphorescence. When at night, that first fall, the lights came on in the skyscrapers and stood out in shafts against the dark, streaked and holed with golden-yellow light, it was indeed the imperial city. Washington might rival New York in the claim to be capital of the Western world, but New York was more exciting. Ballet was there, theater was there, music was there. The culture of New York, high and low, was part of what the war had been fought to preserve, and it now stood on the threshold of its postwar exuberance. The city was still mostly law-abiding, the girls mostly pretty, the streets and parks safe and inviting. A subway ride cost only a nickel, the best seats on Broadway four dollars and eighty cents, the food was cheap and excellent.

New York has always been that city of the Western world which gives wayfarers and wanderers the quickest chance to better themselves. But never more so than in the winter of 1945–1946.

He felt lucky. He had a place, a job, a niche into which he could fit when his leave was up. About him swirled the story of the great homecoming, which he could not see as a story because he himself was a digit in the numbers. In those postwar months thirteen million young Americans released from the military were returning to seek the place into which they could best fit back. All across the country, young men were asking the same questions: Where to come to rest? Where to seek one's fortune? Where to find one's friends and place? For millions of men, now, if ever, was the time to change jobs, styles of life, homes, ambitions.

For the China reporter, locked into his book, the question of where *he* himself fit in did not pose itself immediately. He was a born organization man, most comfortable when he had a place in a collective body that would pay him regularly and fairly and offer a dash of honor and dignity as well. Ten thousand dollars was a large salary in those years, the cutoff point between the men and the clerks, between the potato-sack bodies and the executives who pushed the sacks around. Already, overseas, *Time* had raised his salary to ten thousand dollars, and as soon as the book was finished, he knew he would go back to work for more money.

For he knew he was going back to work for *Time*. True, he had threatened to resign again and again during the last year of anger in China. But because he liked Harry Luce so much, he believed that the justice of his rebellion would be recognized once the book was published, and he would return to some new and glamorous post on the field-correspondent staff. He believed, in naïveté, he could have it both ways—that he could say what he wanted to say, and yet enjoy the comfort and benefits of the parent organization that disagreed. With boy scout simplicity he believed that organizations are as loyal to their employees as they expect those employees to be to them. He did not yet know that organizations and corporations have an internal loyalty only to the thrust that drives them forward and that individuals are sacrificed to that momentum. Of his own loyalty to *Time* he had no doubt. He disagreed with it, denounced it, made speeches about its journalistic distortions; but he belonged to *Time*. Years after he had left, when a telephone ringing by his bed would awaken him from sound sleep, he would, by reflex, snap into the mouthpiece: "Teddy White here, Teddy White of *Time* magazine."

The China book rolled off the partners' typewriters almost by itself, and when it was finished he sent the manuscript to Harry Luce—not for censorship, but for courtesy's sake—and without breaking stride reported for reassignment as foreign correspondent at the *Time* magazine offices.

Luce took some weeks to respond. The maximum editor and his one-time China favorite had seen each other socially several times over that first winter; and the reporter had needled the editor severely, believing the editor was smothered by sycophants. But now there came a terminal session in their relations. It took place in Luce's sunlit thirty-third-floor offices in New York's Rockefeller Center, a room with an intoxicating view of the lesser piles and summits of Manhattan's executive range.

The session was highly emotional, a cross-conflict of paternal and professional relations, more personal than political. Luce, the master and proprietor of the house in which the reporter worked, was terribly angry. He felt that all too many of his bright young men had used *Time* as a personal mount, had galloped to fame on the magazine's back. Young John Hersey, for one. He was breaking with Hersey; it was unclear from Luce's words whether he had fired Hersey or Hersey had quit. But Hersey had told Luce to his face that there was as much truthful reporting in *Pravda* as in *Time* magazine. White later learned there was an even more substantial reason for Luce's anger. Luce had sent Hersey back to postwar China for *Life* magazine at *Life*'s expense and Hersey had written several superlative reports for *Life*. But on his way back from China, Hersey had paused at Hiroshima, and then, on his own time, written that masterpiece of modern reporting, *Hiroshima,* which he had then submitted to *The New Yorker,* not *Life.* Luce summarized, his eyes glowering under the dark brows: White and Hersey were ingrates!

Therefore, said Luce, he now had a yes-or-no question for White. He himself was going off on vacation; White could reflect on his answer, but Luce wanted the answer as soon as he came back. Now his voice lacked any affection; it was the voice of the organization, examining an eccentric cog which no longer fit into the machinery. Luce asked: Would the reporter accept, or would he not, any assignment Luce chose to give him in the future—even if it meant drudgery in the ranks, even if it meant serving on the rewrite desk in New York for a year or two? In short: Did White *belong* to *Time* magazine, or was he using *Time* only to advance his personal interests? The reporter quailed, but demurred. He pointed out that he was now trained as a foreign correspondent; he was an outdoor reporter; he could not possibly be useful to *Time* except as a man in the field. The reporter flailed wildly, insisted that he had proved his loyalty to *Time* by risking his life in action for *Time* to get the stories that made him useful. Luce froze at this point. He refused to tell the reporter what his next assignment would be. The reporter wanted to go to Moscow; but that could be discussed, said Luce, only after the reporter first answered the publisher's question: whether he would prove his loyalty by accepting any assignment offered for the good of the magazine. The voice was inflexible.

The reporter was given a week to reply and pondered whether he must be an organization man, at Harry Luce's command, in Harry Luce's generous court —or dared venture out to find his own place. He wanted desperately to remain a foreign correspondent; such an assignment combines the best of adventure with the base of security, and he would have been content to go along all his life as a foreign correspondent. But on the other hand, dignity had invaded his personality, for now his by-line, he felt, must be a certificate of some honor. And he could not write with honor for *Time* magazine at its desk.

Thus, on Friday, July 12, 1946, with Luce himself away on vacation, he gave his answer precisely at noon to one of Luce's deputies. No. He could not continue on Luce's terms, he would not accept just any assignment unless it was agreed on in advance. Luce's deputy listened and replied that Harry had expected that answer and left word that if the answer was as expected, the reply must be that Luce felt White had no place in the organization—as of now, and for as long as White persisted in his obstinacy. Although, so ran the reply, at some future time, when they saw the world alike again, Luce would be glad to consider White's return.

Thus, not knowing whether he had quit or been fired, he went to lunch with a war companion, *Life* photographer Carl Mydans, one of his dearest friends; and together the two gloomily considered his future and where he could find another job, and whether freelancing was possible; or whether he had made a mistake.

Carl, having seen so many departures from *Time,* had advised making a clean break: when one is fired, get out as fast as possible, don't let them be sorry for you, don't linger, don't mourn. So White went back to his office to clean out files, memos, papers, and decided he would write his letters of farewell to office companions from home. He had to do what he had done; but it was still difficult explaining why.

Then the world somersaulted.

The judges of the Book-of-the-Month Club had just risen from their lunch; and his publisher reported that the book on China was to be a Book-of-the-Month Club selection! White was too astonished to ask more than what that meant—and the answer was that it meant at least $80,000 for the two authors. He had been desperate before lunch, abandoned and cast off; now he was free and, in his own terms, rich, rich, rich! So instead of sneaking out quietly with his packages of papers and notes, he made the rounds of the floors where he had earlier hoped to spend his life, and rather than announcing that he had just been fired, he reported modestly that he was leaving that afternoon—and that by the way, the Book-of-the-Month Club had just chosen the book as a fall selection. It was better to leave with a posture of pride—but he was now on his own again, belonging to no one; and he was acutely, inescapably faced with the problem of finding out where he fit in.

His first purchase with the anticipated book club money was an automobile, the first he owned. His next purchase was a complete indulgence: he would spend the time that now belonged to him, between this July weekend and the October publication of his book, simply driving across the country, coast to coast, to see America. There must be stories out there.

He had been living in a cocoon in New York—physically in his cave apartment, emotionally in the small world of China friends and returning war correspondents. The exercise of writing the book about China had kept him sealed up, wrapped him in a war that was now over. What better way of finding out about America than crisscrossing the country visiting his old comrades of the Eleventh Bomb Squadron and finding out how *they* were fitting in?

So he was off in his secondhand car to see the country whose politics someday would absorb him even more than China's. He plotted his journey: down through the Shenandoah valley, across Tennessee and Georgia, on to Florida, across to Mississippi, up the valley to Iowa, across the plains and mountains through Colorado; then to Utah and Idaho and Washington; then down the coast all the way to San Diego; and east again through Arizona and Texas and Arkansas and Chicago and Ohio and back to Boston.

He filled long notebooks with America as it looked to him on the ten-thousand-mile journey, but it was all written in the war mood of reporting—episode without frame.

The episode that gripped him first and introduced him to American politics was a last whiplash curl of the violence Americans had learned in the war. It happened in Athens, Tennessee, in McMinn County; it was not only unique, but even more perplexing in retrospect for the fact that it *was* the only episode of its kind. It was too small an episode to make history, yet it was the first exposure of the journeyman reporter to American politics at the dirty level.

McMinn County, Tennessee, was a tiny fiefdom on the fringe of the Memphis duchy of Boss Crump. The local county boss governed Athens, the county seat, with thugs; its courts, its police, its structure, all, except for its little daily newspaper, were corrupt. And now in 1946 Athens was holding an election for sheriff and other county officials. But the Tennessee mountain boys who had made such good infantrymen and sharp-shooters in the war were just recently home, full of the simple ideas that army indoctrination and motivation sessions had pumped into them. For example: the idea that Germany and Japan were dictatorships, but America was a democracy where men voted freely for their leaders. The mountain boys took that idea seriously, and formed what they called the GI Party, whose single platform promised: "Your vote will be counted as cast." This was a principle not then generally accepted in pockets of the American hinterland, but in Athens, Tennessee, the time had come for the idea to ripen.

The GI's—most of them combat veterans and non-coms—ran their ticket against the Crump machine's ticket, and the afternoon of the election, key ballot boxes were gathered as by prewar custom into the county jail-house, where the machine would count the ballots without observers. This enraged the GI's. They knew how to shoot; some had been combat engineers who knew about demolition; the local armory, not too far distant, held rifles and machine guns; a local farmer had a cache of dynamite. And so, as if they were storming Omaha Beach or Aachen, they first raided the arsenal, and then shot and blasted their way into the courthouse, where the potbellied civilian deputies could offer no resistance to the men who had helped to destroy the Wehrmacht. Then the GI ticket counted the votes in the open, to fulfill their promise, and of course, when the ballots were counted as cast they had won—cleanly, fairly, definitely.

The episode made a fine story, a natural, and when

the China reporter sent it to New York and learned that
Harper's Magazine had accepted it for publication, he
became excited. It occurred to him, trying to find his
place to fit in, that the writing of American politics might
become his place; American politics, he mistakenly
believed from this first exposure, were so much simpler
than Chinese politics!

But it was a false start—the beginning of a chapter
that would take shape only much later in his reporting.
Looking back, however, from that later American chapter to its beginning in Athens, Tennessee, he would
realize how lucky he had been. Simply by wandering the
country looking for old buddies in Tennessee, he had
seen an era of American politics just beginning to close,
an underview of old Southern politics before enlightenment and prosperity changed them forever. Those politics—cruel, corrupt, vicious—were also sometimes
murderous. This he learned in the Florida panhandle
from an old companion of the Eleventh Bomb Squadron,
who had seen his brother-in-law knifed to death on a
dance floor—and then, appalled, seen the local sheriff
refuse either to arrest or to prosecute the killer because
of his connection with the courthouse crowd. The Northern political machines of Chicago, Boston. Philadelphia,
New York, were corrupt; but not murderous. In the
South, they condoned murder: the killing of blacks
casually. the killing of whites only if they were extremely troublesome. All the better Southern politicians who
have made their way to center-stage national politics
have translated this folklore of Southern corruption and
bossism to a call for revolt against the bosses everywhere. From Estes Kefauver of Tennessee. standing in
the snows of Bemidji, Minnesota, at seventeen degrees
below zero in the primary of 1956. denouncing Boss
Crump. to Jimmy Carter of Georgia, denouncing the
bosses of labor and the big cities in the campaign of
1976 all progressive Southerners have for a generation
campaigned against the hangover of the courthouse
gangs and machines.

But the reporter was seeking a larger story than

this in his solitary but not unpleasant journey across America in the first postwar year, before four-lane highways, suburbs and supermarkets changed the face of the land. He wanted to find out what his comrades in China, the men of valor and devastation, were doing to find their way back into America: that would tell whether dreams could become real. He found the fresh veterans puzzling, yet pleasing. These men, who had been accomplished warriors only a year before, were now as ordinary, as peaceful, as comfortable to be with, as if no thought of killing had ever crossed their minds.

By the time White had reached the West Coast, pressing his car up through Idaho and the Camas valley, and over into the Yakima valley of Washington and down through Oregon and the redwoods and the escarpment of the Pacific to California and San Francisco—by that time White knew he had had a good time but knew also he could not weave a story out of the return of the Eleventh Bomb Squadron to civilian life. They were too diverse. The war had unified them in an adventure; peace dispersed them. They had gone back to being teachers, farmers, liquor store dealers, gasoline station operators.

The most talkative, among the men of the Eleventh Bomb Squadron, had been an enlisted man, Ed Sullivan. Sullivan had been politically excitable and the two had enjoyed many an argument during the war. But their reunion in San Francisco was flat. Sullivan was hustling a living in advertising, with no politics at all. Several weeks after their meeting, Sullivan sent a letter to White's New York address, which read: "I know I disappointed you. But really, I have to make a living now, and until I have it made, there's no point in talking anymore about the issues we talked about in the war."

Nothing of this lonesome driving around America for three months seemed to make a story except for the battle of Athens, Tennessee. Thus, as so often happens, what seems to the reporter too ordinary or too obvious to report is what causes him to miss the real stuff of history. In those summer and fall months when the story-seeking reporter had been driving through the country, history was venting in the campaign of 1946. But the war reporter was then uninterested in the mechanics of an election campaign in America; its importance was far above his perception.

The election of 1946 was the election that attempted to erase the war. The Republicans won both houses of Congress overwhelmingly, that fall. But somehow, they accepted their election as a mandate that America stand still, a plea that time stop its clock and reverse the pointers and bring America back to some unreal memory of how it had been before the war, a retreat through time to, say, 1925, or 1928, or 1936. The men of the Eleventh Bomb Squad probably voted overwhelmingly for the Republicans. They wanted simply to be home and undisturbed, with mothers, new wives, families; they wanted houses, cars, jobs; they had had their bellyfull of excitement, and their families too much of concern. America beckoned with what would become the greatest unbroken stretch of prosperity in its history.

Many veterans ran for office that fall, and historically their entry into politics was the undiscerned story of the elections of 1946. The returning veterans, having altered the outline of the world abroad, were preparing to alter the outline of politics in America for the next thirty years. John F. Kennedy and Richard Nixon, both back from navy service in the Pacific, made their first runs in 1946. So, too, did "Tail-Gunner Joe" McCarthy of Wisconsin. So, too, did Jacob Javits, the enduring liberal, and Otto Passman, the enduring reactionary. So, too, did Peter Rodino of Newark, New Jersey, and scores of lesser men, running down from the two future Presidents to ground level with George Smathers and Thruston Morton. Few, if any, young black veterans ran for office that year; blacks had two congressmen, Powell from New York, Dawson from Chicago, and, so it appeared, they must rest content with only two as far into the future as one could see.

The reporter, who was pursuing a war that was

fading and friendships that were withering, entirely overlooked this veterans' surge into politics as the young-
ster-politicians sought their place in the public arena.
So he came back to New York without the major story
he might have had, had he been able to see it—and
came back to find himself something of a public figure.
The book, now published, had made its author eminent-
ly controversial, praised or denounced on editorial
pages across the nation as the papers' varying politics
required.

White enjoyed the public attention enormously.

His luck, it seemed, had continued, and the book
crested it. He had been lucky in the publisher. William
Sloane, whom he had first met in the war years in
Chungking. Sloane had wanted then to found his own
publishing house, its first book to be the story of China
at war. Sloane put all his effort behind this book and
was as thrilled by the success of his first publication as
were its two writers, White and Jacoby. The book was
further lucky in that a fatherly gentleman named Harry
Scherman, president of the Book-of-the-Month Club,
liked it; and though Scherman rarely interfered in the
club's editorial policy, he gently suggested as a friend
that the book would sell better if its title was changed
from the original ("A Point in Time") to something that
explained what the book was about, say, "Thunder Out
of China." Scherman's suggestion was so obviously
appropriate that *Thunder Out of China* it became, and
under that title became a best seller.

Bestsellerdom is one of the most ephemeral invitations to public notice that any art holds out. Few
Americans buy books; even fewer remember them. But
while the author's name is there on the lists, while the
book is in the window of the bookshops, the author
can entertain delusions of grandeur. This author flew
his mother and sister in from Boston to walk them down
Fifth Avenue and point to his book in the window of
every bookstore. The sight impressed his mother beyond

words; his sister, who had become an accomplished librarian over the years, was just as enthusiastic but more realistic. She knew how quickly books rise and then vanish—to be remaindered by publishers, or cut-rated as overstock, or cleaned out of libraries, which try always to catch the swing of public taste.

Thunder Out of China had a wild, quick-blooming, quick-fading existence. It sold, when one included book-club purchases, over 450,000 copies, more than any other book on China until then except for two famous novels, Pearl Buck's *The Good Earth* and Alice Tisdale Hobart's *Oil for the Lamps of China*.

But *Thunder Out of China* was about politics; about revolution—and it was published in 1946, as the country moved in the cycle of its ideas to its most violent anti-Communist stance, toward the internal suppression that climaxed later in the McCarthy era.

White found himself, as an author, discovering the world of the book-reviewing mechanisms, and the literary politics that dominate it. Best sellers were made in two ways: They were made, most easily, by the fashionable critics of New York, from which they spread to the "little old lady in Dubuque," who wished to be up to date with the most advanced thinking. Or else they were made by word of mouth, creeping in from the hinterlands of simple book readers to affront fashionable opinions with their success. The two worlds of American taste used to clash, and this writer, in his time, has had it both ways, denounced or praised by fashionable New York, with the readers beyond the Alleghenies almost always reacting contrariwise.

On this, his first exposure to the politics of the book world, White found himself denounced by most major newspapers of the Midwest; and praised, on the other hand, by the chorus of liberal journals that take their cue from New York. White now found himself in Manhattan rather enjoyably a figure of dispute; savored the brief notoriety without realizing that its longest-lasting effect would be to list him as a leader among those "who lost China to the Reds"; and was completely unaware that with the publication of his book, the FBI was instantly on his trail, noting his speeches, his actions, the meetings he attended, scrutinizing his private life for detail running back to the war years. That realization would come later. For the moment he was only "controversial," not yet "subversive"—meaning that he spoke, appeared on radio programs, enjoyed his spurious importance.

For more years than a historian can make sense of, China had been an emotional symbol in American thinking: businessmen thought of it in terms of four hundred million customers; missionaries thought of it as a land to be saved for God. By 1946, Chiang K'ai-shek had become a symbol, too, replacing Doctor Fu Manchu in the mythology of China, which intrigues both right and left. As the outside world polarized issues in American politics, one had to be either *for* Chiang and *against* the Communists, or *for* Mao and against the "fascism" of Chiang. White was uncomfortable with either category of thinking, but caught between factions and flattered by invitations to speak out, he unhesitatingly chose the liberal left. If America was to get out of Asia, as White felt necessary, the liberal left was right, the other side wrong.

As sales of *Thunder Out of China* increased for a few months at the end of 1946 and before the new Congress took over, all things seemed possible. He was offered a choice between joining the *Saturday Evening Post* as a correspondent or joining the *New Republic* as an editor. He felt he no longer needed money. The *New Republic* offered little, the *Saturday Evening Post* more than twice as much. But the *New Republic* now had a new editor, Henry Wallace, a hero of his then politics, and White decided to express himself by joining the *New Republic*.

His experience there was brief. White was still groping to find his place to fit in and thought the *New Republic* would become that place—where a new journalism, a liberal journalism, could paint the nation's postwar portrait free of prejudice. But that was not to be. The *New Republic* was dominated by the grave and heavy presence of ex-Vice President Henry Agard Wallace. Wallace could be fascinating, thoughtful, kindly on occasion. He was at his best when he talked of what he knew: the mysteries of the earth, the farm, the garden. At plant genetics, Wallace was a genius, and was at that time producing giant strawberries at his New York farm. Henry Wallace's giant strawberries and corn hybrids may be his most lasting contribution to the pleasures and vitality of American civilization. But in politics Wallace was a bitter man; eccentric, ambitious, self-righteous; an inspired mystic as his friends saw him, a "bubblehead" as his enemies called him, a guru type as later generations might have described him. He was the first of the evangelical Presidency-seekers White was to meet, in a line that later ran through George Romney and George McGovern to Jimmy Carter. Of all these, however, Wallace was the most devout seeker for the Truth and Peace of God.

Like everyone on the *New Republic* staff, White recognized that the magazine was to be Wallace's campaign organ for his presidential race of 1948. But he was dismayed, when he came to know the man, to discover that Wallace literally loathed Franklin Roosevelt. But for Roosevelt, Wallace, not Harry Truman, would have been renamed the Vice Presidential nominee of 1944 and thus would have been President now in 1947. Moreover, White was to discover, and was to learn again and again in the next twenty years, that "liberalism" in politics does not always extend to personal courtesy or intellectual tolerance. There was less freedom to deviate from the line of the *New Republic* than from the line of *Time* magazine. White, in a few months, was numb with shock; what he wrote at the *New Republic* had to fit that line which supported Henry Wallace's views, just as what he wrote at *Time* magazine had to fit the line of Harry Luce.

Nor was that all. It was inescapable to any observant staff member of the *New Republic* that Wallace not only was running for the Presidency, but was aided by, counseled by, and in his innocence acquiescent to, Communists. These men were quite different from the Communists White had known in China, openly willing to die for their cause. These were American Communists, then, as now, an unpleasant breed of neurotics trying to use the complaisant Wallace as their front to found the Progressive Party of 1948. Wallace was susceptible to flattery; the Communists flattered him, burned incense in his nostrils, inflated his opinion of himself, wasted his name and honors, and left him beached years later in history as an eccentric, a hissing word in American politics. Had he passed his life in the furrows and never left for politics, he might have ranked with Luther Burbank, Joseph Henry and Eli Whitney as a native American genius.

White had discovered another truth: that a magazine committed to, or dominated by, a single man, as most sectarian magazines are, is as rigidly restricted in opinion as those magazines which depend on the marketplace and profit. Henry Wallace was a handsome man, his light-brown hair just turning silver, his clean, open face and muscled form instantly attractive to men and women alike, his personal kindliness well known. But underneath it all, he was a self-intoxicated man with but two subjects of conversation—botanical genetics and himself, the latter subject complicated by an abnormal suspicion of others. When White told Wallace, as a friend, that he was going to marry a young lady who worked for Harry Luce's *Life,* Wallace said gravely, "Ah . . . conjugal infiltration."

White soon left the *New Republic,* in the summer of 1947, because in that spring and summer the *New Republic* was as tolerant of the foreign policy of the Soviet Union as *Time* had been tolerant of Chiang K'ai-shek. Henry Wallace's bitterness at Harry Truman was unappeasable; and so White had no place there.

White left the *New Republic* as he had left *Time*— because of a breach in politics that no amount of good will could bridge. He told himself he was going back to the politics of Asia, his own history turf—but two large events led him to postpone his departure.

The first event was a political, personal and historical temptation.

Mrs. Stilwell needed his help. Stilwell himself had died in the fall of 1946. She had been left with his diaries, papers, memoranda, and wanted her husband vindicated in history. White had been as close to "Uncle Joe" as any reporter had been; so he offered to give six months of his time to the chore of editing and ordering the papers. *The Stilwell Papers* were glorious in their frankness and revelations; Stilwell's neat, legible handwriting each day, which White tried to pin against the larger background of the events he had seen, made the Chinese-American entanglement a carnival of personalities. *The Stilwell Papers* were published to acclaim from those he respected most; sold well; but only reduced further White's chances of joining the Establishment of the time. He was denounced by editors for having distorted, violated, clipped and cut the private thoughts of a great American war hero, to make a leftwinger's political point in the debate about China. Thus evaporated all the offerings and jobs he had rejected a year earlier to join the *New Republic*—all the major magazine assignments, all the staff posts, all the opportunities. The McCarthy years were about to close in, and there was nothing but the money from *Thunder Out of China* to fall back on; and money gives no one a function or a purpose in life. Very few people have, or ever get, enough money to be absolutely free and spend their lives in self-contemplation. It was clear, by early 1948, that White would have to find a place and a purpose all over again—and would have to do so propelled by the second event.

The second event rose from the nature of youth and the mood of the time—and climaxed, after considerable anguish, in his marriage.

The anguish came in parting with the past, and

with Annalee. He had begun *Thunder Out of China* in love with his China partner, but a collaboration of two such strong-willed persons in a book of such complexity had, rather than drawing them closer, widened differences of temperament. Moreover, he felt it was time for marriage, as did so many war veterans; but she, still deep in widowhood, did not. By the end of 1946, though their book was a success, their partnership had come to an end.

In that swirling turbulence of postwar New York, however, he had already come to know and then fall in love with one of the beautiful researchers at *Life* magazine. She was young, gay and loving, and became more and more necessary to him. He proposed to Nancy Bean; she accepted; and the date was set.

So substantially had the war erased old social differences that it never occurred to him how far behind he was leaving Jewish tradition when he made his choice. To marry out of his faith did not weigh against his conscience at all.

It was natural that his bride, Nancy, did not want to be married in a synagogue, as he would have liked; he understood that. She similarly understood his refusal to be married in a church, as her parents would have liked. They both felt simply American, and decided a civil service would be most appropriate performed by some New York judge. That turned out to be difficult to arrange. There was only one New York white Protestant judge left on the magisterial bench at the time; and as a white Protestant in a community of ethnics, that judge was exhausted by his appearances at brotherhood dinners. Seeking another judge to marry them, the pledged couple found that no Jewish judge would marry a young Jewish man to a Gentile; that was political suicide in those days. Finally, they found a tolerant Catholic, Justice James B. McNally. When told that the bride was a Protestant, the groom a Jew, that neither one was Catholic—for it would be political suicide for a Catholic judge to marry a Catholic to a Jew—he observed that both were pagans in the eyes of God; therefore he as a civil magistrate could marry them without exposing himself vulnerably in politics. Which he did, recessing his court in a murder trial to come upstairs, read the civil ceremony and pronounce them man and wife.

It was a strange marriage ceremony. Nancy Bean's parents stood on one side of the chamber, glowering. White's mother had come with his younger brother, Robert. White's sister, who loved him, refused to come for such a ceremony. One or two old war-correspondent friends and the court reporters filtered in to the chamber. And so they were married.

It did not seem to White then that he had abandoned any beliefs, or any tiny part of heritage, in marrying this young woman. They hoped for children, but the children would belong to the America that was coming, when all Americans would be free of categories, classifications, and any discrimination or privilege that descended from heritage or origins.

These were, of course, not at all dominant considerations in White's mind as he stood for marriage, upstairs over the Scottorigio trial. What was serious though unrecognized was not difference of religion, tradition or faith. What was serious was the sense of class. She would always assume that as a daughter of the local squirearchy in Connecticut, she would have her place at the head of the table, there to upbraid governor, senator, or chief of staff as she chose. And White would always fear that he would be expelled from the table unless he proved his right to sit there.

So they went off to married life. White was never to meet any man in politics or in letters who was not thoroughly influenced by his wife, if he loved her. Nancy Bean, for the twenty-odd years they were married, influenced all he wrote. They argued more and more violently—but he listened.

She was beautiful—fair-haired, hazel-eyed, round of face. She was full of gaieties; her presence made

any gathering a party, and parties became a way of life
for them until, too late, he realized he hated parties almost as much as she loved them. Nancy Bean was,
moreover, absolutely fearless. She, too, had been overseas in the war and had come back a flaming liberal.
Furthermore, she knew corporate life and despised it:
her father was President of his local chamber of commerce; a superlative engineer and executive, author of
a textbook on malleable iron, a man of quality. But he
had been crucified by his corporation in an executive-
suite struggle for the top; at the time she wanted no
part of the corporate life, though, ultimately, she would
go home to it.

All these qualities in his new bride influenced the
reporter in his choices. But the choices were narrowed
by larger realities. He had now, in effect, been black-
listed by the mass publications that had only months
before sought his copy and his by-line. He could publish, if he wanted to appear in print, only in small left-
wing magazines. He could, if he permitted, let himself
be made a martyr by those who would see him as a man
penalized for writing two books of unpopular political
bravado; or be caught in the schismatic groups of
literary intellectuals whose lives were, at the time, raddled by their sectarian approach to revolution and the
American upheaval. But the sectarians and their quarrels bored him.

Old friendships were dissolving, too; the bonds of
war-made comradeship were fraying. His best friends
were old China hands, but they enjoyed, and mourned
simultaneously, the continuing collapse of Chiang K'ai-
shek and the continuing advances of the Chinese Communists as fuzzily reported in the news pages. Endlessly, old China friends chewed the cud of their wisdom
and recalled their warnings against American intervention in the China struggle. They lived in the past. His
other companions were former war correspondents, but
they, too, were dividing as if by some internal law of
nature. Some could not give up the war, such as Jack

Belden, perhaps the ablest of all war correspondents, who went on forever listening to the echo of the combat sounds that had stirred his heart. Others drifted into the talk world of New York, greeting each other at fashionable drinking places like the Stork Club or "21," which White found exquisitely uncomfortable; or disappeared. And there were yet others, ex-war correspondents, the men White admired, who had found their place and were on their way into the future—Edward R. Murrow and Charles Collingwood, Eric Sevareid and Cornelius Ryan—all of them packing their war laurels away in memory trunks and going on to new endeavors.

White himself was very late in sorting out his choices. His new wife giggled at his attempt to find a way into publishing or corporate life. She was brave enough, always, to face life on her own. She had become part of White's circle of friends among war and foreign correspondents; their stories enthralled her; she wanted to be moving with the people who were moving, dispersing to Paris, or Tokyo, or Hong Kong, or Vietnam. And that was his own bent, too. Being a foreign correspondent had been the finest part of his life until then. He loved it and his wife loved the promised romance of the trade. So he began in the spring of 1948 to seek a post overseas again.

It was difficult. No large or distinguished magazine or newspaper would hire a known "left-wing" writer. After seeking, telephoning, groveling for openings, he could finally tell his wife in May of 1948 that he had found a place—not a distinguished job, to be sure—with a marginal news-feature service called the Overseas News Agency, a service which was still unafraid of the growing paranoia against liberal journalists. They would name him correspondent in Paris for a year. The salary was not large, but he still had money in the bank from *Thunder Out of China*. Moreover, the story that was offered him was large: the Marshall Plan had been announced, America was to save Europe from Communism. He would report that. White doubted that Americans could do better at saving "Free Europe" than they had at saving "Free China." But the adventure would certainly be exciting—and Paris, where he would be based, was, above all, Paris! That was enticement enough. He could no longer fit in at home; he knew that. He had already been summoned to appear before one Congressional committee; he was devoting too much time to fighting off investigations, charges, allegations. So he would drop China until the controversy died down, then after a year in Europe he and his bride would be off to Asia again. It seemed like the best solution: if he could not fit in in New York and America at that moment, he could still fit somewhere in Paris, plying his trade as a reporter.

Thus they left New York in June of 1948 for Europe, en route, they thought, to China.

But they were to remain in Europe for five and a half years, discovering not only each other but the idea of Europe.

He had no idea of what Europe meant. He would discover that Europe is the parent land of all civilizations. He would discover its wonders, its brilliance, the beauties of the countries that lie on the fertile peninsula which falls steeply, then gently, away from the crown of the Alps. He would discover how Europeans tormented each other and continued to torment each other, all the while creating the values by which civilized men lived. He would discover that this was a civilization at the point of death, hollowed out by the epicentric blasts which Europeans had unleashed in two great wars; and also discover that if it could be saved for civilization, only the Americans, with their Marshall Plan, of which he was so suspicious, could save it.

At that moment, Europe was the best place for him to fit in—professionally, as a reporter; historically, in an arena where America would do as much good as it had done harm in Asia. He accepted himself now as a journeyman reporter. He had no map to follow, but was seeking in the stream of history stories to tell. Best of all, history spun on a turntable that year in Paris.

Paris! Nancy would love Paris, with its grays and copper greens, its florets of chestnut blooming and fragrance of chestnuts roasting. As a journeyman he would have stories to carpenter, and they would have Paris.

CHAPTER 7

The Marshall Plan:
Springtime in a New World

I came to Europe in the spring of 1948 to see the Marshall Plan unfold. Surly and suspicious, I set out to watch—and for the next five years I was to watch Europe being remade by American power at its most intelligent and benevolent best.

I came by air, still something of an adventure. The nineteen-hour flight from New York to Paris, as well as the six-day sea passage chosen by most visitors, choked down the number of casual sightseers from overseas, while the aftermath of war choked off the bus-borne tourists of Europe. Thus the Paris I prospected in June of 1948 was still, in its green and leafy heart, blessedly French. The old lavender and pewter buildings rose in the familiar *fin de siècle* shades and shapes of gray, the mansard skyline of the Impressionists still unspiked and unspoiled by new skyscrapers, all seemingly unchanged from the city I had passed through ten years before, en route to war.

The Paris I came to was, as always, in transition; yet

that spring was something more than a season of the
year: it was the beginning of a spring that lasted several
years, a romance of politics between France and America,
whose common purpose bloomed in Paris. Frenchmen
were beginning to feel French again, but with a returning
pride that still embraced Americans.

I had come because history momentarily had given
America and Western Europe a common purpose: the
cold war was under way, Stalin was at his most malicious
and the Communist parties of the West at their most
aggressive. Paris was not only field headquarters of the
cold war, but also one of its chief battlegrounds. The
years since the Liberation of 1944 had not soothed
France, but snarled it. The occupation, followed by the
cold and hunger of 1945 and 1946, and the drought and
crop failure of 1947, were capped in the winter of 1947–
1948 by the nightmare challenge of Communist uprising—and with it, the end of the alliance of French
patriots who had fought the Germans as brothers in the
underground. When the break came, as it had to, riots
had bloodied a dozen different French towns. In Paris,
only the quick dispatch of several hundred navy electricians from coastal bases had frustrated a Communist
attempt to put the capital's electric generating plants out
of commission in a protest strike. In Lyons, Marseilles,
Brest, police and security forces battled Communist-led
demonstrators for control of the streets. In the coal mines,
Communist-led strikes had escalated quickly to critical
sabotage, and police and workers had battled in the
pits.

By the spring of 1948, when we arrived, the Fourth
Republic of France had shakily but miraculously survived. Though we reporters made its politics a subject of
comic journalism because of the flutter of arrival and
departure of its coalition governments, one had to recognize in the French leaders an earthy political heroism.
Preserving all republican and democratic traditions of
decency and freedom, they not only had established
themselves as *the* government, but obviously meant to
govern. They held forth no dramatic goals; they promised

neither glory, nor adventure, nor revolution, nor upheaval—only a healing process, and the slow restoration of the soft *douceurs* that Frenchmen fondly remembered from prewar days. Even for these modest goals, however, they needed vast help to restore the still war-shattered country; and for this kind of help there was only one source—the United States, which had promised a "Marshall Plan." Thus, then, as the winter of 1947 gave way to the transient stability of 1948, and the Americans prepared to unload the goodies of the Marshall Plan in Europe, the atmosphere of Paris and the attitude of the French government to Americans were those of a wedding party.

Americans were welcome, American reporters particularly so. The embossed press card, the tricolored *coup fils* of the accredited correspondent, was a *laissez-passer* anywhere; the French Ministry of Information made tickets to state concerts, festivals, municipal opera and theater available at all times and instantly; cabinet offices were open to all American reporters, down to the lowest crawling order of our species. We enjoyed semidiplomatic privileges—such as participation in the American National Interests Commissary, where we could buy American luxuries which the still-strangled French economy could not provide, as if we were war correspondents at an army outpost in Bavaria. An American reporter did not have to wait for a year to buy an automobile, as did most Frenchmen, who had to put their names on waiting lists; his passport and his dollars let him buy an automobile in days, fresh off the Citröen factory line in suburban Paris. Gasoline was tightly rationed for Frenchmen; but an American reporter was entitled to 120 liters a month. Down the empty boulevards, down the Champs Élysées, one could sweep at forty miles an hour, parking anywhere, free of traffic regulations, while the police smiled. And the highways beyond Paris, still deserted, beckoned with privilege.

Not only was the government indulgent of Americans; so were the people. I recall going to visit the D-day beaches in Normandy during these spring years of friendship. Coming off Omaha Beach, I pulled out into the main road, speeded up, swerved out from behind a truck, and forced a motorcyclist into a ditch, where he tumbled to the ground. I was horrified, and ran to pick him up. He rose, glaring, brushing himself off, and turned on me, then recognized my accent. Was I an American? he asked. I said yes and began to bumble apologies and offer help. But he smiled, said it was unimportant: all Americans were friends. He remembered when Americans had come ashore five years before on those beaches and so he would make no argument of this accident. He shook my hand, would have no help, told me only to be careful next time.

In this happy Paris we settled down, Nancy and I, in the springtime of our marriage, young, and untroubled by money. We were silly, to be sure, in the way we lived, for within weeks of taking up the post of the Overseas News Agency in Paris, I learned that my new employers were on the verge of bankruptcy, and that part of my job was to finance the operation of the Paris bureau with what I earned by selling the agency's reportage to European newspapers. Within two years the agency had fallen behind by six months in payment of my salary and so I quit; but by then springtime was over in politics, too.

In the beginning, however, there were no worries. We still had the savings of *Thunder Out of China* to live on; and a draft on dollars in New York could be cashed for French francs that summer at the rate of 500 to 1 on the black market. Our particular black marketeer was a jolly old lady full of gossip and good will who became a friend of the family, and Aunt Klavdia to our children. She would bustle in with a large parcel of paper francs, slip us the penciled name of a Swiss bank account to which our New York check must be sent—and disappear. We kept the paper francs in a satchel under our bed; and into this satchel Nancy and I dipped at will, with no sense of budget or restraint. A fine meal in Paris cost only 1,000 francs, or two dollars at our rate, and we could gorge endlessly and cultivate gourmet appetites; we could buy a second car; we could hire a servant, then a nurse for the first child. Very quickly we moved to a fashionable apartment on the Rue du Boccador, a block from the Champs Élysées; at the black market rate the rent was only one hundred dollars a month. There on the Rue du Boccador we made our base, watching the chestnuts put out their first green fuzz each spring, then their blossoms; then we would wait for the tulips to unfold around them. There we could watch the seasons pass, and French governments come and go, and we could delight, as did the French about us, in the quickening pulse of spring and revival.

We arrived as food rationing was coming off, and each morning there were hot loaves of long bread which Frenchmen could again waste as they wanted. Gasoline came unrationed. The railway and electricity systems began to work. With the resumption of traffic, market life returned, and all the little pleasures of normal being returned one by one, so that the fruits came back in season, and oysters appeared on corner stalls, as well as flowers and berries and citrus and chocolates and aromatic cheeses. We fitted not only happily but shamelessly into this returning rhythm of life, knowing it to be ineffably bourgeois, inexpungeably Right Bank in quality, obnoxiously self-indulgent and sneered at by our unmarried friends who were artists and musicians of the Left Bank. But what could be more pleasant, for example, than the invitation to indulgence of our Sunday routine? The maid began by picking up for us the British Sunday newspapers about ten in the morning to read with coffee; then I went to the magic cheese store of Courtois, just beyond the Étoile, where Camembert cheeses, selected for perfect ripeness each week, were displayed to greet the churchgoers coming home from Sunday mass; then to the baker on the Rue de Berri for the butter-drenched croissants; then to the Russian stalls in the sixteenth arrondissement to pick up fresh eggs, cold meats and, above all, fresh green pickles. Then home for the long leisurely lunch with friends; then out to the flea market to browse in winter, or to the parks to sun the children in spring and summer.

And at night, if one wanted, in those early days one could go to a cellar café on the Left Bank to sing with young French people.

Paris was experimental at every level in those spring years, but even so, our apartment house on Rue du Boccador was unusual in the neighbors it offered us. On our third floor, directly across the hall, lived a dark-haired young Frenchman, a raconteur of mimic gifts, named Raoul Levy. He was a film producer, hyperbolic in his schemes and fancies, forever entertained by and entertaining others with the shrewdness of his film coups, like tricking the Paris police force to turn out for riot call as extras in one of his movies. Raoul Levy went on experimenting with cinema until he discovered a full-bosomed, pouty beauty called Brigitte Bardot, whom he made into a sex symbol and star, and who in turn made for Raoul a fortune, which he lost.

Upstairs, in the garret, dwelt a forlorn American reporter trying to earn a living by contributing to the Paris *Herald Tribune* an experimental food and nightclub column. This youngster was a sweet and melancholy ex-marine of twenty-four. But his sweetness rubbed into his reporting an apparent child's naïveté, which made his humor all the more biting and wise. The *Herald Tribune* finally let him write a column, "Paris After Dark," with his own by-line, Art Buchwald, under which name he was later recognized as a social critic and, still unspoiled, earned fame. We all lived together in the apartment house, and took one another not at all seriously, and became friends; as we did with the mistress of the most important jeweler of Paris; and with the British arms salesman who sold outworn American combat aircraft to shadowy regimes; and with the Spanish Republican veteran, Germain, who was our concierge, and presided over entry and exit to this unusual house; and with the last of the arrivals, Irwin Shaw and his wife, Marian, he having given up the short story form he had mastered to come to Paris to write novels and movies.

By all odds, however, the most memorable tenant was a handsome, flamboyant, dramatic character named

Theo Bennahum. By chance, I rode up with him one evening in the apartment's elevator and recognized him as the same Palestinian traveler Bennahum I had met in Singapore in 1940 one night at the Raffles Hotel. He had been utterly destitute that night but so outrageously charming that even the staff command of the Royal Malay Rifles and the Seaforth Highlanders had smiled at him. Bennahum now lived, eight years later, on the floor below us in Paris and was, with his wife, to become closer than kin—and his charm was at its peak.

Bennahum was extravagantly and eloquently Jewish, and had fled as an adolescent from Bolshevik Russia to Palestine. That experience had taught him to sneer at rules and regulations, or at most to regard them as puzzles that could always be solved. He had grown up in Israel; and became an American only because his beautiful wife, Midge, was a Massachusetts girl. He later came to love America and New York more than anyone I knew, with an exaggeration that was at times painful. He was, at the moment in Paris, a maker of ballpoint pens in six European countries and his description of European trade and the exchange of finmarks, German marks, French francs, Swiss francs, Belgian francs, was not only high comedy but shrewd analysis. He knew so much of the absurdity of postwar European trade regulations and restrictions that he soon graduated to adviser and counselor to larger and larger American corporations. We watched Theo and his enterprises grow. He was there at the birth of the multinationals—negotiating for General Electric to buy all of France's computer industry, for El Paso to move into Algerian natural gas, for others to exploit Mauretanian nitrates, manganese and oil, Libyan petroleum.

Bennahum loved money in the best way—not out of avarice, or any sense of investment, but the way some men love horses. With money he could prance, he could race. Money incubated both his tastes and his generosity, and he loved to give it away. He enlarged our life with his enthusiasm for arts and antiques, but he collected actors, violinists, singers and scientists as enthusiastically as their creations. Theo was even more grandiose in his aspirations than Raoul Levy, who lived just above him. Where Levy, at Levy's end, was reaching even beyond the Brigitte Bardot period of his life to make a deal with the Chinese Communists to coproduce a film on Marco Polo, Theo was reaching even further. Theo, just before he died, was circling between Paris, Tokyo, Teheran and New York on a year-round globe-girdling safari. He had foreseen the energy shortage and was trying to break up the international oil cartel by negotiating a direct barter exchange between the Shah of Iran and a consortium of Japanese utilities—Iranian oil for Japanese capital equipment. It would have been a spectacular triumph had Theo lived, but it was the grandeur of the dream, even more than money, that moved Theo.

Home remained for me all the years I was in Paris at 24 Rue du Boccador, where Nancy made a salon of graces. There young musicians like Isaac Stern and mature ones like Sasha Schneider or Burl Ives might come to fiddle or to sing; young diplomats lounged there on Sunday afternoons; summers, when the Casals festival in Prades was either gathering or disbanding, violinists slept on our floors en route. Home was where my heart was; but the excitement of my life was five minutes away, in my office at the Herald Tribune Building at 21 Rue de Berri. There almost all American foreign correspondents congregated except those of *The New York Times,* who, in those days, did not choose to run with the pack. It was there, so many mornings, before my rounds of reporting, that I would sit peering either up over my office balcony toward Sacre Coeur, or darkly down into the blind keys of my American typewriter, wondering how I could convert this particular passage of history into the tellable stories, the feature snippets, that were the market wares of our news agency. For the story, the real story, the history story, was too large to report day by day.

I was late in learning the great story that underlay the news stories, but that was because Paris seduced me in so many ways.

The first of the distractions was, I suppose, environmental—the panorama of history prickling imagination as I strolled. The second was intellectual—the French press and its beguiling French belief that facts plus logic always lead to truth.

The panorama of Paris caresses, and thus seduces, the mood of every reporter who has ever worked there. A reporter who is not waylaid by Paris's beauty probably lacks the sensitivity to be assigned there—but I found that to live and report out of Paris was like trying to do business in a museum. The museum had been erected by the public builders of the city over the centuries, centuries going back beyond Notre Dame. Public buildings reflect the imagination of princes and taste-makers, and tell as much about princes as do their laws and their wars. And so, as I walked or drove from round to round, I found I could not hurry. Here were the ruins of the baths built by the Romans, there was the cloister of St. Germain-des-Prés, there across the river, dominating all, was Notre Dame; then came the Louvre, the Madeleine, other numberless pockets of memories in stone, anthems in gray, celebrating past stories I had known only in books. All these stories connected somehow, but the buildings would not speak, and I had to string episode and panorama together, to make past connect to present.

The United Nations, for example, met that first fall of 1948 at the Place du Trocadéro. The Trocadéro session of the General Assembly was a major event, for the target of United States morality at that session was Holland: we were getting the Dutch out of the East Indies at the time, as, in those days, we were busily urging all white empires out of everywhere. The debates, however, were dull, and when I shirked the indoor rhetoric I could sit on the broad stairs that creep down from the Trocadéro to the banks of the Seine; and at dusk, watch the people going home from work. There, on the other side, rose the Eiffel Tower; on this side Marshall Foch sat on his horse in an equestrian tableau, staring east over the fields of his victory beyond the Marne. Museums rose all about the Trocadéro, starting with the Musée de l'Homme, the best

museum of anthropology anywhere in those days, and
going on through all the other lesser museums in the
neighborhood.

Museums tempted me from duty at every step of
reporting in Paris. The Ministry of Finance, which drew
me often, was housed in the northeastern wing of the long
gray Renaissance palace built by Francis I. But the
southern wing of the same palace, along the Seine, was
the Louvre, sheltering the Venus de Milo, the Winged
Victory of Samothrace, the Mona Lisa, as well as the
scarlet pietàs of David.

That particular plaza of Paris was an entrapment.
From the Ministry of Finance I could walk across the
Gardens of the Tuileries, bearing in mind that this park,
full of flowers and beauties, once fronted Marie Antoinette's favorite palace, which the great revolution had
burned to the ground. On the north side of the park ran
the Rue de Rivoli, where the Marshall Plan came to have
its headquarters a few months after my arrival. But on
the way to the Marshall Plan, I could pause to visit the
Jeu de Paume, a cameo museum which held the most
vivid of the Impressionists in historical sequence. And the
offices of the Marshall Plan were even better than a
museum, for the Marshall Plan occupied the Talleyrand
mansion. There Talleyrand, the old master diplomat, had
once bounced his lovelies in bed upstairs, and downstairs
had entertained princes and generals, weaving what Victor Hugo called "the spider's web of Europe." There, too,
old Talleyrand had passed away, a paradigm of successful
flirtation with power, having lived skillfully through
France's most turbulent generation without ever once
having been in danger, even when Napoleon told him to
his face that he was nothing but "a silk stocking full of
shit."

A visit to the Talleyrand mansion was usually productive of some kind of story, but whether it was or not, I
would always rendezvous at the Crillon Hotel nearby,
where the British reporters gathered at dusk to drink and
gossip.

British journalism is most impressive only at long

remove, as is the BBC when its great productions are filtered from its dross. Close up, I found my British colleagues divided into three groups—scholars, pomposities and "jollies." The scholar journalists usually lived in walk-ups on Île St. Louis or the Left Bank and wrote with enormous erudition, seemingly with a goose quill pen, of what the facts meant. The pomposities were unaware that the Empire had perished, and their haughtiness of manner was that of British inspectors examining American and French colonials for shortfalls. The "jollies" were workaday reporters who could invent, inflate or embroider any scrap of fact or gossip into overnight excitement beyond the talent of any American. The scholars sought history, the pomposities sought nothing, the jollies sought circulation for their masters on Fleet Street—and at the Crillon, such British reporters would meet American reporters. On a large occasion, like a foreign ministers' conference, the bar of the Crillon was the only place to be at the end of a day, and we all drank together, trying to decipher the day's story or agree on what we should report it as being. None of us, of course, usually knew anything beyond the agency facts, the daily rumor, the press-conference statement, or the calculated leaks of our governments, which we traced; but we could put together a reasonable facsimile of what was happening, and were content. I would then make my way home through the greatest outdoor museum of them all, the Place de la Concorde.

I would have time on the twenty-minute walk home to think how I must put that day's particular fragments of story together so they would read usefully ten days from now, and occasionally, how this episode compared to other episodes the great space had witnessed: There, across the Seine, to the south, rose the hulk of the Palais Bourbon, where the Assembly sat. There, to the west, up the rise, loomed Napoleon's Arc de Triomphe; there, across the street, the American Embassy was housed in a Rothschild mansion, just as the Marshall Plan was housed in the Talleyrand mansion. And thus across the cobblestones, picking one's way around the Place de la Concorde—where not only Louis XVI and Marie Antoinette had been beheaded, but also Danton, Robespierre, Lavoisier and so many others, all victims of the Terror. When I learned that the figure for the entire harvest of terror came to only some fourteen hundred killed, I was astounded. But the great square still brooded over the past and it was difficult to get the dimension of this past into daily reporting. I could sit, for example, with one of my favorite young Gaullist vitalists, Diomede Catroux, and he would sneer at me openly for my democratic weaknesses. "Look," I recall him saying one dusk, "look around you. Everything you see that is beautiful, everything that makes you love Paris, was built by a tyrant or a dictator. There will be nothing beautiful here again until Paris has a strong government to build."

So I would saunter home to play with the children and wish I had worked harder, and had not been seduced by the distractions of the great museum of Paris.

The second distraction was even more difficult to ignore in reportorial life than the balm of Paris's beauty: this was the passionate absorption of the French press with the factual detail of politics. Political detail has always been a weakness of mine and in Paris I was drugged by a press environment which believed that out of multiplication of detail emerges truth. Nowhere else did I so quickly yield to the misleading belief that to know more is to understand more. The Paris press of 1948 was so beautifully written, engraved with such incision of phrase, enameled with such subtlety of sarcasm and subjunctive, that I did not realize for months after my arrival that its literary talents were devoted chiefly to the embroidery of trivia.

What was wrong with the Paris press flowed from its history—for its history was that of authentic heroes, the reporters and writers who had outbraved the German Gestapo. Never had there been a freer, more gallant press than the French under the German occupation. Those who had written for the underground sheets had gambled their lives in order to write the truth as they saw it; if caught, they knew the Germans would be merciless; thus they wrote freely without fear of any lesser penalty than death; and were fearless of death, too, for to tell the truth justified life.

As their reward, these journalistic heroes had been given by the Liberation government of France what every reporter hopes for but knows can never come to pass—ownership and control of the press itself! The guerrilla-Maquisard-journalistic groups entering Paris with the Deuxième Blindé seized and held as their property not only the buildings of *Le Figaro, Paris-Soir* and other publications, but the distribution net. Printing presses were nationalized, their time shared by journalist-publishers of the Resistance. The newsstand distribution monopoly, Hachette, was similarly nationalized and put at their disposal. Paper was rationed by the government; and each journalist group that had earned its honors underground was entitled to a share.

Twenty-eight such daily newspapers, all written by heroes, still saw light in 1946 in Paris. Within four years their number had fallen to sixteen and would later fall to nine. When I arrived, however, the Paris press was still controlled by the graduates of the underground and Resistance, but all were confronting the realities of profit-and-loss publishing, the needs of circulation, promotion, advertising. The discipline of the balance sheet was a more inflexible menace than the German armies of occupation, and ultimately enslaved them; but all of them then still believed, as had Harry Luce, that in the name of the great truth, fact could be subordinated to passion and polemic.

Each morning, when I went to my office, a stretch of ten or fifteen French dailies was waiting for me. It was my duty to scan them all for stories, and at first I tried. But then I realized I must not be lured; such graceful writing brought a novelist's art only to record commonplaces. Each set of facts was always presented, then refracted somewhere in the opinion spectrum by its own prism of truth. In the wartime Resistance all underground groups—Catholics, Communists, Socialists, Gaullists, patriots, romantics—had used the same prism: *La Patrie!*

Liberté, Liberté Chérie—Conduis, Soutiens Nos Bras Vengeurs! Now they screeched at each other in violent discord, arranged their facts and endless details of politics to suit their sectarian truths, and agreed only in their general undertone of suspicion of the American enterprise called the Marshall Plan.

Most Frenchmen, most politicians, most of the French press, agreed that America should, by right and moral obligation, help France. Some considered the Plan, however, to be a capitalist plot against French workers; others a finance plot against French industry itself; others a plot against Russia; yet others a plot against French culture, a step in what the Communists called the Coca-Colanization of France. But what the Plan was, and what it was doing, was scarcely ever reported factually in the Paris press.

Reporting from Paris, I found after a few months, was entirely different from reporting out of China—and more difficult. In China, the local press had always been useless. Whether Communist or Nationalist, the press came of the tradition of the court gazette. No important *political* fact was ever clearly printed publicly; it had to be deduced from omissions or two-line paragraphs. In France, however, *everything* was always reported *somewhere* in the press—which meant that the searching citizen as well as the baffled foreign correspondent was smothered, digging himself out from the overburden of daily facts. And each editor of the journals born of the Resistance felt entitled to drive his own particular logic through the facts, fearlessly presenting his arrangement as the real truth.

The Marshall Plan was the largest political event in French politics; I was there to report it; but it took me months to shape the story out of the events I was reporting daily. There was, I knew, a mother lode of history under the stories I was sending to New York. But not until I threw off the spell of Paris's beauty, and rid myself of dependence on the British and the French press, did I begin to see what I was writing about.

I was writing at the start, apparently, about trade;

and by using trade figures, aid figures, import-export figures, sterile as I found them, I had to lure editors and readers to understand that our kind of civilization was significantly mirrored in such figures. It was much more difficult than writing out of China, or describing a plane twisting down to its death in a spiral of its own smoke. But the story, once I found my way to it, was the most intellectually exciting I was to report for the next ten years.

The story of the Marshall Plan, it turned out, began with the Meaning of Money. It was also about Money and Europe, and Money and the Peace—but above all, Money and Power and America.

We bestrode the world like a Colossus, challenged only by the Russians. I knew that the Marshall Plan was an adventure in the exercise of American Power. I knew the Russians had the ground troops and we had the atom bomb—but the language of our push for loyalties in Western Europe was money. I had first to master the grammar of money: discount rates, equalization rates, exchange rates, interest rates. But if I wrote in that grammar, my copy would be consigned to the purdah of the financial pages. And my news agency depended on me as a "color-feature" writer to write stories people would read: Were the Europeans grateful for our foreign aid? Could the Marshall Plan stop Communism? Was there any graft? Was the money wasted or well used?

The concept hometown newspaper editors and even sophisticated commentators had of "foreign aid" in 1948 was descended from the concept of "subsidies." One wrote of the Marshall Plan from abroad to fit this concept because people can hear only what they are prepared to absorb. One wrote as if the Marshall Plan descended from England's subsidies to its continental allies against Napoleon—bulging sacks of golden sovereigns, the coins clanking as straining men unloaded them from brigantines in the dark across the Channel. But Marshall Plan money was not coinage. Marshall Plan money was a field of force, as invisible yet as energizing as electricity.

Although I could not write it so, I had to start with the Idea of Money. In Western culture, this idea conceals the idea of command. The idea of money grants command to any man who holds a tiny coin of silver or copper, or a heavy coin of gold; or to any man who holds paper which commands silver, copper or gold; or to anyone who controls credit, which is better than coin because it can control tons of coinage—the idea of money shares dreams of power unequally between poor and rich and men of state. Money can command a cigarette in a blockade, or heroin at the corner; or a turnip, or a pot, or silk for your wife, or a new plow; or the services of a killer. Whatever else money is, it is a medium that can translate one kind of command into another kind of command, up to the command of armies. Kings and states once came to Rothschilds and Morgans to gather moneys so they could pay and command their soldiers, officers and generals to go out and kill.

What was novel about the Marshall Plan was that the command quality of money, used on such a scale between nations, was being used for the first time not to kill but to heal; money provided the energy for a field of magnetic force, like electricity, in which things happened. And since the Marshall Plan has become one of the schoolboy parables of American political history, it is worth some effort to go into the condition that brought it about, the mechanics of its application, the abstractions that made it, and then into the tough-minded characters who forced the dollars to do good.

The condition that brought about the Marshall Plan could be described metaphorically as that of a beached whale that has somehow been stranded high beyond the normal tides and which, if not rescued, will die, stink and pollute everything around it. Europe was the whale, and its carcass could not be left by Americans to rot.

Less dramatically, the condition could be described as a bankruptcy—not the bankruptcy of a corporation or a city but of an entire civilization. The civilization of Western Europe had wasted its men, its wealth, its credit in two great wars and could no longer meet its bills. Like a profligate, it had spent its strength around the world, and now the world was repudiating it.

More specifically, the situation read like this: In the previous two centuries, the half-dozen West European states that share the rockfall of the Alps and the shoreline of the Atlantic had not only conquered the world by arms and technology, but unified the outer states as communities of tribute-bearers. Now, internally gutted by wars and faced with revolutions across the oceans, the Europeans could neither command nor pay for what they needed to live decently. Whether it was the hot red tea in the morning in London, the tobacco in the cigarette in Paris, the coffee with *schlag* in Vienna—Europe lacked it and could not pay for it. That was bad. But what was critical was the necessaries: it had no wheat for bread, no cotton for clothing, no petroleum to fuel the automobile. People were hungry; some starved; others stole; most hoarded; everyone cheated.

For the first two years after the war, only American gift and grant had financed the minimum needs of this European civilization, America's parentland. But in 1947, American leadership had undertaken to persuade the American Congress that they must make one new massive effort to help old Europe, to save it from starvation and Communism—one last try. Thus, then, in early spring of 1948, the United States Congress had passed the European Recovery Program (ERP) to help preserve freedom and put down Communism in Western Europe, and had swallowed its many and justified exasperations with its old allies.

Americans had good reason to be exasperated with Europe in the spring of 1948. They had already contributed all that their domestic politics would permit. America's Congress had pumped over a billion dollars into the United Nations Relief and Rehabilitation Administration —and Tito of Yugoslavia, who had received the largest proportionate share of this money, had reciprocated by shooting down American planes. Congress had endowed the new French government of liberation with a billion and a quarter of direct dollar aid; and it had disappeared. Americans still hated the Germans; but the U.S. Army, occupying Germany, could not let Germans starve in the streets—and the Army thus had claimed and received over half a billion dollars to feed Nazis, ex-Nazis and German innocents alike. To America's gallant senior allies, the British, the United States had given in a single grant in 1946 no less than three and three quarter billion dollars! These were in the good, heavy dollars of the postwar years, each worth three of the diluted dollars of our time—and all had disappeared, tracelessly. In one single six-day period of August 1947, the British Treasury had seen $237 million slip from its reserves as its bankers yielded to international traders what the traders had right to claim. Then, to prevent monetary catastrophe, the British had broken their promise to the Americans, suspended convertibility, and waited to see what the Marshall Plan might offer in relief.

Thus, in the spring of 1948, Europe trembled on American decision, victors and vanquished alike. For me, reporting this anticipation was most difficult because the drama was, above all, invisible. I had, in the service of Time Incorporated, learned how to "hype" a dispatch with color; but no amount of "hype" got at this kind of narrative. I could tell a true story: say, a Solomonic parable of the quarrel of the French and the Italians in the fall of 1947. Four ships, each bearing thousands of tons of American wheat, were on the high seas crossing the Atlantic; each country pleaded with the American dispensers of foreign aid that it needed all four of these American aid ships to maintain its meager bread or pasta ration of half a pound a day. Or else. Or else Communism would take over. That could be built into a vivid story. But in the larger, true story this was a minor bureaucratic quarrel. And one could scarcely write a realistic story about Germany. The days of gloating over their defeat were gone; but it was still too early to write a sympathetic story about the hated Germans, reduced in 1947 to a ration of 1,040 calories a day, with men and women fainting at their desks, or dropping in the streets with hunger. If the downspiral went further, of course, there would be riots in all the streets of the Continent, bloodshed, cracked skulls on the old cobblestones. But the Marshall Plan had been passed by Congress precisely to prevent such bloodshed, for only the Communists would gain from civil violence.

If the mythology as taught to schoolchildren insists that American good will fostered the Marshall Plan, it is right. But so also are the realists who insist that fear of the Communists and Joseph Stalin was equally important. George Marshall had come back from the Foreign Ministers' Conference at Moscow in the spring of 1947 convinced that the Russians meant to have all Western Europe. The Russians, he felt, would never cease pushing Western European democracies on the downspiral of 1946–1947 unless we, the Americans, did something to reverse that downspiral. In this sense, the Marshall Plan was the most successful anti-Communist concept in the past fifty years.

The American political memory which holds that the Plan was an act of national unity is thus true. It won the support of the hard and the soft, the fearful and the hopeful. The Marshall Plan was more than a foot-dragging, nibbled-away compromise of lobbying and conciliation grudgingly passed by Congress. It was a whole-hearted resolve of the United States Congress, like a genuine declaration of war, or the Civil Rights Act of 1964. Such authentic Congressional resolves are markers in American history, and they call forth from American life its very best.

The mythology of the Plan is far more true than its debunking by revisionists. Where the mythology breaks down and misleads is in holding that success rested chiefly on American good will, lavishing money like rainwater on the ruins and deserts of Europe. This mythology has led since to the entirely erroneous belief that money and good will can solve anything. Which is untrue, for brains and leadership are also required. And the men who directed the Marshall Plan were not only very attractive and humane custodians of power, but also very hard-

minded men who had come out of a war in which they
learned that mechanics were as vital as purpose to the
success of a good cause.

Thus I had to explore the mechanics of the Marshall
Plan in Paris—which led, inevitably, to the Château de la
Muette, where high purpose had to be brought down into
trade ledgers and the nastiness of national greeds. Most
liberal high purpose collapses in fraudulent accounting;
the Marshall Plan did not; at the Château de la Muette,
tough Americans held Europeans to tough figuring.

At the Château de la Muette—a lovely old yellow-
and-beige mansion with high scalloped windows, and
floors that creaked properly—gathered the sixteen nations
who had accepted America's invitation to be helped, plus
Trieste and West Germany, states under Allied military
occupation. Each had a voice in the Organization for
European Economic Cooperation, the OEEC. The OEEC
was empowered to negotiate with the Marshall Plan administrators how America's money should be parceled
out, but their voices were babble. To listen to each
European nation's plea for aid could carry one back in
conversation to Charlemagne; the Duke of Alba; traditional fishing rights; the three sons of Louis I, the Pious;
the Peace of Westphalia; as well as the consequences of
the treaties of Versailles, Rapallo and San Remo. Europe
carried too much history; Europe was split by too many
boundaries, too many fossil ridges. It was impossible for
American aid managers to listen to arguments over the
traditional markets of Greek against Turkish tobaccos; or
the complaint about the blockage of Dutch artichokes
from their traditional Ruhr market in Germany; or why
the Belgians, who had excess rolling-stock manufacturing
capacity, were blocked by currency regulations from making rolling stock for German railways, which desperately
needed it only forty miles away. All wanted their aid
portion, directly and immediately, from the U.S.A.—just
as Chiang had. The Europeans, talking to either American reporters or American officials, were like starving
tribesmen jostling each other for a share of the meat.

At the Château de la Muette, the Americans took a

simple tack. Let the Europeans first diagram their own problems, deciding who could physically supply whom on the Continent with what they needed of each other, ignoring the payment difficulties in European currencies. Then, finally, all should bring to the Americans, as Dispensers and Overlords of the Great Purse, what the net margin of their needs was in dollars and supplies from the outside world, which the Marshall Plan would cover. It was a practical, common-sense solution. In just such a practical way, Henry of Anjou, King of England, had let the jury system begin, when he despaired of understanding or getting at the facts of dispute among his quarreling English underlings and permitted them to decide the facts of a case while his appointees decided which laws must apply. So the Americans, without trying to force Europe to a common market, nonetheless pressed an idea on Europeans which became the Common Market, for Americans would yield dollars only to the common consensus of all claimants.

With this as their first tough decision in June 1948, the Marshall Planners went on to the even more intricate mechanics of getting the dollars threaded through the beggar governments into the hands of the people who could use them fastest, most productively, most accountably. Only learned economists and professional financial experts could follow all the detail, but when simplified, the mechanics of flow worked this way: Congress appropriated the dollars and placed them at the disposal of the Marshall Plan. After the most esoteric of bargaining processes, the Planners put at the disposal of each European government its share of the annual total of dollars recommended by the OEEC. At that point, matters became even more complicated, for the European governments did not, in turn, *give* the dollars away. Their central banks made such dollars available to importers of national necessities like food, oil, machines, cotton and sulfur. The importers *paid* for such dollars in local currencies, which accumulated in huge digital columns called "counterpart funds." Such "counterpart funds" could not be used by the receiving country without the consent of

American authorities, which generated much bickering and ill will between the American donors and the recipient cabinets. Moreover, the ultimate recipients of Marshall Plan aid (except for the starving) did not feel particularly grateful, either, or sense they were getting anything for free. They had to pay in francs, pounds, marks, lire, to buy the Marshall Plan dollars from their own government. They could not be accused of being "bought" by the Yankee dollar, for what they were getting in effect were the tickets to enter and buy on the world market—tickets purchased at the standard, not the scalper's, rate. They were getting the dollars that commanded wheat, coffee, tobacco, dried milk, as well as airplanes, rolling mills, computers and raw materials. The United States was handing out tickets of admission to the circling globe of world trade which Europe itself had once dominated. For the next generation, the Europeans were to move in that world trade only with American dollars and by American permission and policing—after which they were to turn on America, repudiate her dollar and denounce her leadership.

The immediate solution of 1948, the share-out of the first five-billion-dollar appropriation of the American Congress by a group of Europeans forced to look at their continent as a whole, was reached in July, little more than a year after George Marshall had proposed his plan at Harvard's commencement—which is lightning speed in terms of diplomatic proposal and effect.

It was pleasant to see how efficiently the dollars were put to use. For the Americans, the experience was exhilarating. They were not only doing good; they were doing good efficiently and smartly. It was as if they were faced with an enormous puzzle; they embraced the puzzle with the enthusiasm of game-players.

High purpose had assembled to guide the Marshall Plan, the finest group of American civilians in government since Roosevelt had gathered together his war cabinet of 1940–1942. It is an axiom first enunciated by Eugene Meyer, when he was head of the Reconstruction Finance

Corporation, that in the first two years of any national emergency the American government can freely call on its citizen best. But not for more than two years; the best then drift back to private life, and are replaced by the job-seekers.

In its first two years, then, the purpose of the Marshall Plan recruited America's best. And the nature of the talent is essential to explain the plan's success.

The high command of the Marshall Plan was two men: Paul Gray Hoffman of Chicago and Pasadena, and W. Averell Harriman of New York. Both would now be certified as Establishment types, but two more dissimilar characters would be difficult to find; the former folksy, the latter imperious; the former warm and persuasive, the latter haughty and peremptory; the former a Republican, the latter a Democrat. But both were men of extraordinary ability, devoted to their country.

As chief of the Economic Cooperation Administration (ECA), Hoffman was also chief of the Marshall Plan (or ERP) in Washington. He is difficult to describe, as is his genius. Paul Hoffman came closer to being a saint, in the secular sense, than any man I have ever met in politics except for Jean Monnet (with whom Hoffman became friends during the Marshall Plan years). Hoffman was a stocky, ebullient, inexhaustible man; people smiled almost reflexively when they met him, as they did at Hubert Humphrey, for Hoffman spread joy around him. He was a businessman, and sounded naïve when he talked politics, until I learned he had a knack of twisting politicians to his every whim when his salesman's blood raced, his eyes twinkled and his enthusiasms swept a room. The spell he cast around him was quite simple: he was obviously a *good* man; and obviously a *wise* one. People trusted him; he sought nothing for himself; he managed first to accumulate a large private fortune, then to get rid of it, and ended his days in modest circumstances, having toyed with millions and billions of dollars in absolute honor.

As chief of the Marshall Plan, Hoffman kept the U.S. Congress in line. He never promised Europeans

more than Congress authorized, or Congress more than
he expected Europeans to deliver in response. Hoffman
never sounded profound; indeed, sometimes his exhorta-
tions rang like those of a sales manager at the annual
sales weekend. But his simple manner was deceptive: he
believed it was America's duty to help the weak and
suffering; he also believed in the work ethic; he also
believed in making the terms of the contract clear at the
end of the sales exhortation. Thus everyone on either the
giving or the receiving end of Marshall Plan aid knew
Paul Hoffman required that good will and performance
must balance. Hoffman had entered the Establishment
through the business-executive stream, as president of
Studebaker; he had organized the Committee on Economic Development, and was one of the first great business
executives who insisted that business must have a social
conscience. As a millionaire, an industrialist, a phrase-
maker, he had been called into the war effort and risen to
command the postwar Marshall Plan because he was so
obviously competent, trustworthy and "plain folks" that
Congress would accept as truth anything he said.

Averell Harriman, his unlikely overseas partner in
command, was field director of the Marshall Plan, head-
quartered in Paris; he kept the Europeans in line. Harriman was an American aristocrat who had well earned his
post; if his accomplishments during the war had been
rewarded with diplomatic hash marks, they would have
run up his sleeve from wrist to shoulder. One of his minor
problems was that people generally, and newsmen particularly, thought he was stupid. This was an impression one
might easily gather from his mumbled diction, his apparent inattention to conversation, his groping for the proper
figures when making a point. But Harriman was not at all
stupid—only single-minded. He loved the United States
(as did Hoffman), and he loved it with passion, devotion,
and total contempt for personalities who might stand in its
way. Once Harriman was wound up and pointed in the
direction his government told him he must go, he was like
a tank crushing all opposition. From America he expected

nothing in return except recognition, for he was as vain for honor as he was wise in experience.

The jovial Hoffman and the lordly Harriman made one of the oddest partnerships of all time—incomprehensible to outsiders, but too rich in contrasts not to amuse friends of both. Hoffman was still a Midwesterner at heart, of the breed of Chicagoland industrialists and makers of things who baffle Eastern financial men. Hoffman's family still owned their manufactory of plumbing equipment in Indiana, though Hoffman, like so many Midwesterners, now thought of himself as a Southern Californian. His modest villa overlooked the slopes of Pasadena. Harriman was a polo player, a Yale man (Skull and Bones), of the elite; and his mansion in New York was just across the street from the Metropolitan Museum of Art. Harriman had enjoyed an imperial domain larger in acreage than the Rockefellers' on the Hudson, but had given most of it to New York State. He also owned a small dacha of several hundred acres on Long Island; and a winter sunning place in Hobe Sound, Florida. Harriman collected Klees, Mondrians, Picassos and great sculpture wherever he went, whether in Paris, London or New York; as in his youth he had collected polo ponies and ladies. Hoffman was still Midwestern in his tastes; he preferred collecting awards, silver cups, bronze plaques, and teaching his parrot, in Pasadena, to squawk odd kitchen phrases. At that time, the second Mrs. Harriman was Marie Whitney, a delightful lady of Edwardian style and candor, a patroness of arts and music, an authentic *grande dame*. The first Mrs. Hoffman, by contrast, was a sturdy Midwestern lady, very much down to earth, with strange religious views and a great devotion to her husband, a lady who collected and adopted orphans, not fine arts. Averell Harriman was a genuine gourmet and set one of the great tables of our times. Hoffman, by contrast, ate heartily of anything; one night, having promised us a treat, he arrived at my home carrying a basket of warm, dripping take-out Chinese food.

Between these two, Hoffman and Harriman, American leadership spanned a large range. Both were good men; but when they had to, both could be rough as a rasp, Hoffman with regret and Harriman with relish. Hoffman knew how the American system worked from the foundry, through the combustion chamber, through the assembly line, through the sales system. And still he believed in human kindness. Harriman knew how the affairs of nations worked; from his youthful negotiations with the Soviets on a fur deal, he had accumulated more knowledge of the simplicities and deviltries of foreign leaders than almost any other American of his time. On any list of the top ten diplomatic heroes of World War II, Averell Harriman could claim a place. They made a fine pair. Hoffman trusted people, Harriman distrusted them.

Beneath these two came a second range of leadership, of equally impressive quality. The names are too many to list, and I choose only two as prototypes of what the American system could then offer—David Bruce and Milton Katz. Both were to become ambassadors in service to the Marshall Plan. Each had a specific contribution to make.

David Bruce, then fifty-one, needed no lens of imagination to transform him into a novelist's hero; by all odds he was the most romantic of the leaders of the Marshall Plan. Though an amateur of all professions, he was the model for all professional diplomats. In his youth he had served for several years in the Foreign Service; when he came back many years later to diplomacy, he served at one time or another as Ambassador to France, to Germany, to Great Britain, to NATO, to the People's Republic of China. His father had been a United States senator from Maryland and a Pulitzer Prize winner; he himself was a man of letters, a biographer of presidents, a contemporary at Princeton of F. Scott Fitzgerald and Edmund Wilson. Bruce's honors and bizarre achievements pin-pointed his record like sparks. In his youth he had, as a lark, run for the Maryland legislature from a tenement district populated largely by poor Jews—on a promise to legalize fox hunting, which so amused his Jewish voters that they elected him forthwith. He had been a businessman, dabbling in ventures from denicotinizing cigarettes, to race tracks (Suffolk Downs in Boston), to French vineyards. He had been Colonel Bruce of the OSS during the war, spymaster of the French underground and Resistance; had been an Assistant Secretary of Commerce, and then, as Ambassador to France during the Marshall Plan, he made his great achievement: mobilizing American diplomatic support for Jean Monnet's dream of a United Europe, and then seeing that dream through to reality. He was both a diplomat and an ambassador: as a diplomat he was graceful and elegant, but as an ambassador he knew the clout and compulsion his country could exercise and used that clout to make "a Europe" come into being. Bruce loved beautiful things: old French veneers; good furniture and paintings; his exquisite wife, Evangeline; and what Europe, at its best, stood for.

If Bruce was the very model of what was best in the old American Establishment, in Paris his counterpart of the new Establishment was Milton Katz. Milton Katz was a professor. I had heard about professors during the war who made bombs, perfected radar, served the OSS. But Katz, a professor on leave from Harvard Law School, was an entirely new type in my political experience—the academic as operator. He was general counsel to the Marshall Plan in Paris, then successor to Averell Harriman. Harriman had the most imposing office in the old Talleyrand establishment—huge windows opening on the Tuileries, green carpet, gilt chairs with wine-colored silk cushions, the whole scene surveyed by its marble bust of Benjamin Franklin. Katz sat in a rather dingy office, little better than an office at the Harvard Law School, though more spacious—but Katz could explain the purpose and mechanics of the Plan better than anyone else. Katz was brains; his specialty was to translate ideas to action. He brought brains to bear on decision, and recruited brains for action.

Dark-eyed and handsome, then only forty-two, a spellbinding conversationalist, Katz was one of those priests of academe then just emerging from their studies to become American Cardinal Richelieus—or at least, policy-makers.

And through Katz I met others. Katz's scholarly counterpart in Washington was Professor Richard Bissell of Yale, an economist. Just as Katz was personal wise man to Harriman in Paris, Bissell was personal wise man to Hoffman back home. Katz went on to the Ford Foundation, then back to Harvard. Bissell went on to the CIA, where he, alas, was one of the masterminds of the Bay of Pigs invasion. They were the senior academics in the Marshall Plan, as Oppenheimer, Conant, Bush, Langer, had been senior scholars in the war. And beneath them were countless other professors and scholars interwoven with businessmen, soldiers and diplomats in the Plan's operations. The Chief of Trade and Payments for the entire Plan, a man required to understand all the esoterica of trade balances, was Joseph McDaniel, formerly Professor of Economics at Dartmouth. A young Milwaukee law school instructor, Henry Reuss, arrived to pursue the European cartels as deputy general counsel of ERP—and later continued as congressman, still distrustful of big business and banks, to become head of the House Banking and Finance Committee. Scholars and academics buzzed about the missions and the committees, from my old classmate Arthur Schlesinger, who was briefly a summer consultant, to a contemporary of ours from Yale, Kingman Brewster. Brewster was then a bright young Harvard Law School graduate, a favorite of Professor Katz, who brought him to Paris as an assistant. Brewster served for a year, returned to Harvard to become a professor of law, and then on up the ladder of academe to the presidency of Yale, and out to the big world again as Ambassador to the Court of St. James's in London.

The best of American talent was attracted to Marshall Plan headquarters as if by a political law of centripetal attraction; but what made them so remarkable historically as a group was the change they made visible in the character of America's political elite. The traditional Establishment still commanded at the top, to be sure; but the foreshadow of a new governing class was plainly to be seen below. The roster of white male Protestants, born to the kinds of families that had been governing America since the Civil War, began with George Marshall himself, who had first been tapped for leadership by John J. Pershing in World War I, and then in World War II had been given command of the nation's army by Henry L. Stimson, Secretary of War, and Franklin Roosevelt, themselves classic establishmentarians. Paul Hoffman's grandfather had been a wealthy man with a social conscience far in advance of his time; a century before he had been chairman of the Chicago School Board, and had commandeered the land along that city's lakefront for one of the nation's most imposing public green spaces. Harriman's father could hardly be called a man of conscience, yet the railroads of E. H. Harriman had undeniably served the public interest, particularly the Union Pacific, which spanned the West and created the national market that had made America rich. So, too, were Dean Acheson and Bruce men of the Establishment, and each of these men of the old Establishment had earned his way to public dignity and responsibility.

Yet the Marshal Plan needed more than generalized ability and devotion to the national interest; it needed expert knowledge. And so its older leaders chose as associates men of the academy, men of knowledge and expertise. Professors Milton Katz and Richard Bissell came of a new growth in public service; they were among the first of a fast-growing corps that would, in a generation, dominate the political landscape. In that new landscape, such men would eventually spurn their old advisory role in policy and insist on actually setting policy themselves.

That was, however, still far away. The command of the Marshall Plan was an accidental mixture of the new America a-borning—of businessmen and professors, of generals and diplomats, of men of heritage and men of ambition. Together their energy, talent and dollars soon infused a despairing Europe. Less than a year after George Marshall's speech in June 1947, first proposing the Marshall Plan, the first vessel of Marshall Plan cargo

arrived in Europe, in Bordeaux, France—bearing nine
thousand tons of wheat out of Galveston to make bread.
Two years later, by June of 1949, the tough mechanical,
distribution and payments problems within Europe had
been solved; at which point the planners, new and old
alike, intellectual and executive, historians and bankers,
ran into the insoluble problem—which was England.

Of the first eighteen months of the Marshall Plan it
can be written that the United States saved Western
Europe and discarded England. The problem was that
England did not fit into the world the Americans were
remaking. The English had acquired a whole new set of
ideas; and we were fashioning a world on the old English
model of ideas which the English themselves had rejected.
The breaking of England's trading strength was inadvertent and inevitable at once; it was performed without
malice because between the hopes of the new British
Labour government and the demand of the postwar
American Congress, no bridge was possible. To understand what was happening required a close examination
of the connection between trade figures, culture and history, which, of course, neither the American nor the British
man in the street cared to read.

It had proved easy in 1948–1949 to patch up the
trade balances that European nations owed each other.
American dollars could start the Dutch artichokes moving
to the Ruhr, the Greek tobacco moving to England, the
German coking coal moving to French steel mills, simply
by picking up a four- or five-billion dollar deficit a year.
But to connect Western Europe, as an industrial community, to the greater cycle of world trade—that was far
more difficult. World trade was infinitely more complicated; and grew continually more so as overseas luxuries,
like bananas and oranges, became as familiar as tea,
while overseas requirements, like oil and food, became
indispensable. Americans wanted to revive fair, open
world trade, a system which had been invented by the
British. But by 1949, as the Marshall Plan pushed into its

second year, it was becoming quite obvious that the British, under their Labour government, could not survive as a great power in the old open trading world England had invented.

Trying to understand the face-off between the British and American policy-makers of the Marshall Plan in 1949 exposed me to the effect of legend on politics—or how myths control action. In my dispatches, I described the dilemma as that of the memory of the Century of England, or the myth of the Golden Yesterday.

The Golden Yesterday was a period of history which, as I saw it, stretched from the last minuet of the Congress of Vienna in 1814, when the autocrats buried the memory of Napoleon, to the last waltz in London in 1914, when no one noticed that international civility was being buried for all time. In that explorers' century, the entire globe was made one. Europe made it one—and England led Europe. At the beginning of that century London was about to become the capital of the world. Chicago was a fur traders' post; Los Angeles was a mission station; South America and Africa were wilderness; Shanghai did not exist. By the end of that time the price of bread in Europe was not only what bread actually cost at the bakery, but also a statistical intersection of prices in London, reflecting the wheat yield in Kansas and the Ukraine. In that period, the plantation millionaires of the Amazon had flourished and then passed away as international trade stole the rubber culture from them, and transplanted rubber to Malaya and Sumatra. Cables and telegraph wires linked prices and markets together so that men in London or Liverpool could make fortunes on futures in copper, pepper, cotton, bristles, zinc or cocoa, and be sure of delivery and payment in recognized standards of quality and money. From the ports of Europe, all oceans, sea lanes, cargo carrying, insurance rates, were interlinked as one. Gold measured all values; London set the price of gold; the phrase "payable by draft on London" meant anyone, anywhere, could buy or sell, secure in London's guarantee to deliver gold.

The stability of the pound, and the globe-girdling authority of the British Navy as it brought the heathen to accounting, set up a rhythm of economic progress never before matched. It was this echoing rhythm of an open and fair world trade that the Americans of the Marshall Plan wanted to recapture.

This rhythm, or memory, or image, was the closest thing to doctrine in the Marshall Plan. The Marshall Planners had been sent out by Washington with nothing like a blueprint, least of all a *plan*. What guided them was this image of a world that educated Americans had learned about from teachers, from historians, from grandparents. They meant to restore it—though shorn of the grossness, the abuse, the extortions and inhumanities of the nineteenth century. Although, initially, the American technical experts described their purpose in such dreadful jargon as "the automatic, multilateral, international integration of trade balances," they meant far more than that. They meant the restoration of a culture. In the century of the Golden Yesterday, not only did goods pass freely for gold, but men and women traveled freely from country to country without passports; no nation toyed with export-import controls except in time of war. At the beginning of that century, science was considered above war, and scientists could cross borders into enemy country even in time of war; and art was universal, provocative, humane and fashionable, all at once. Indeed, it was this open world that was most threatened by Nazi Germany in the 1930s and by Stalin's Russia in the late 1940s. A civilization was involved, whose foundations the Marshall Plan was trying to restore—and it had to do so with dollars.

Only the British understood this American dream of restoration. The British had centralized the nineteenth-century world that America was now trying to recreate. Except that now, in the aftermath of the war, British politics had been ripped by other political dreams. Britain, the motherland of capitalism, had gone Socialist. And the British diplomats and civil servants in Paris who presented themselves at once as our partners and supplicants were thus schizophrenic.

To begin with, the British spokesmen in Paris were well-educated, upper-class men, steeped in their own history. They knew their nation had created world trade, but they understood better than anyone else what was involved in "automatic" integration of trade balances. They knew that the surest thing about the automatic world market of the nineteenth century had been the way the gold standard "automatically" squeezed out the weak. As a banker automatically stops cashing checks from an overdrawn depositor, so the great "automatic" trade world of the Golden Yesterday cut off credit to a pauper nation. If a nation could not pay in gold or pump out enough goods or services to pay for its needed imports, it was squeezed down to what it could pay for. The currency mechanism took care of that: if England (or more likely, France, Spain, or Italy, or one of the lesser breed of countries) could not buy what it needed, the nation went without. Only not everybody in the nation went without; some went more without than others. If the price of imported cotton, coffee, tea, wool, shot up, the poor went without; and their wages dropped and dropped until they were paid so little that their products could be exported at a profit; and so the cycle went from giddy prosperity ("a penny for the old man, a farthing for the boy") to apocalypse.

The British emissaries in Paris understood far better than the Americans both the glories and the cruelties of the Golden Yesterday. Now they were speaking for the new Labour government of the United Kingdom. And the men of the Labour government knew, not only in their minds but in their bellies, what the old "automatic" mechanisms had done to them and their families. They had seen coal miners coughing to death in Yorkshire; dwarflike, pigeon-breasted longshoremen hauling cargo off wharves in London; little beshawled ladies in Lancashire whose sons went off to fight England's wars and, if they lived, came home to work for bread and jam, to marry girls like themselves who worked in the mills. The new leaders of the Labour Party had been elected to abolish such injustices. They believed in their own good

will. Half a century of protest had given the movement
heroes, bards, martyrs; now it had given the movement
power. With this power they meant to conduct a bloodless
revolution that would bring brotherhood not only to victorious England's green and smiling land but to lesser
people also. Yet somehow, the same power insisted, of its
own, that England hold on to its imperial past and its
share of the great victory over Fascism.

Except Labour's leaders could not.

The contradictions of British Socialist purpose were
too large. If they wished England to remain the world-
girdling trading power it had been before the war, they
would have to use harshly their share of victory over
Germany and Japan, two potential rivals, and restrain
them as victors can. But if they were to act in brotherhood, as Socialists, and forgive and forget, they would
have to make their own workers compete against Germans and Japanese, who lived on sausages or rice balls.
There was the further conundrum of empire. The British
Labour Party could not hold on to the old Empire and
exploit it; that was forbidden by Socialist morality. Doctrine suggested they free the Empire as fast as possible—
which would have been commonsensical if they had simply called quits to the Century of Empire. What they did,
however, was not only to free such dominions as India
and Egypt, but to free them with such staggering dowries
of conscience money as to make a reasonable economy
impossible in the home country. In India, Burma and the
dependencies of the Middle East (including Egypt), the
bookkeeping of Empire and war had notched some 1,929
million pounds sterling as debts of the mother country for
protecting her subjects from Nazis and Japanese! This
was the equivalent of 8 billion postwar American dollars
(the old hard dollars), which England owed as a debt of
honor to the newly independent Commonwealth. To India
alone, the most demanding and difficult of the newly freed
dominions, the English acknowledged a paper debt of 750
million pounds. The British Labour Party was the first of
the great political enterprises I witnessed to sacrifice common sense to morality. They had no idea how much good

will costs, and even less idea how to use their share of victory and world power.

This contradiction of good will and common sense led Britain's Labour leaders inevitably to the court to which all moralists seeking refuge from reality eventually turn—the government of the United States, which was then held capable of solving anything. The best way of holding on to power while simultaneously advancing Socialist brotherhood around the world was for the English to persuade the Americans that the Marshall Plan was a joint enterprise—i.e., the Americans would put up all the money, but the British would share the direction. It seemed to Labour's leadership like a continuation of the wartime comradeship embodied in the Combined Chiefs of Staff.

But by the summer of 1949, when the British trading crisis became acute once more, the wartime comradeship had faded. Americans were in no mood to change their program—the establishment of a free and fair world trade—to protect their old companions in arms, the British. Moreover, had the Americans accepted the implied premise of governing the world in partnership with British victors, no chorus of voices would have been quicker in denunciation of American imperialism than the intellectuals of the British Labour Party, already discontent with their leaders' dependence on American power. There was also American opinion to consider. Most Americans had been conditioned to adore Churchill, salute the Royal Air Force, revere the defiance of 1940. But now it was time to face the new world; we were going one way in our politics, the British another. We were not about to break the British openly as a great power until the Suez crisis of 1956, when we broke their will and pride. But by 1949 we were content to cut them adrift to sink or swim in the new world we were making.

The new British Labour cabinet had not yet mastered the rhetoric of international economics—not even the governing trio. The most colorful member, Ernest Bevin, a tough union leader, had now mastered, as Foreign Secretary, the coarseness of dialogue necessary to negotiate with the Russians. But the Prime Minister, Clement Attlee, a social worker by profession, a bandage dispenser, was one of the great nonentities of British history; and the Chancellor of the Exchequer, Sir Stafford Cripps, a brilliant man, was an intellectual who combined the cutting mind and tongue of a barrister with the icy manners of a doctrinaire Socialist. Both Attlee and Cripps were, moreover, sincere religious Christians. None of these three could adequately present the selfish, primary, nationalist case for Britain, or invoke, with the hearty rumble of comradeship, shared memories and good brandy, the brotherhood of war, as might a Churchill, an Eden, a Beaverbrook, if then in power. Thus it was left for the nonpolitical British civil servants, not the guiding politicians, to make the case for England and reality.

I recall a conversation at my home with Sir Edmund Hall-Patch in August of 1949. That night I had gathered six of my fellow correspondents who met regularly and privately and who, collectively, for almost five years, hoodwinked famous European statesmen into the belief that we held the keys to American public opinion. We all respected Hall-Patch as the best professional diplomat of the old school in Paris at the time. A meticulously groomed man, a clipped and precise speaker, he was Britain's senior spokesman at, and also chairman of, the Executive Committee of the Organization for European Economic Cooperation, where in the contest among the eighteen rival nation claimants for the American dollar he performed best of all. But his task humiliated him. Begging for the American buck was not his style. So now, privately, as soon as dinner was over and we gathered in the easy chairs of our apartment, Hall-Patch shed his diplomatic manners and spoke bluntly, as Englishmen and Americans had spoken to each other during the war.

The whole trouble, declared Sir Edmund, was our American "surplus"; the world's problem was how to deal with this "surplus production of America," which it so desperately needed, but for which it could no longer pay. He compared America's dominance of the mid twentieth century with Britain's dominance of the nineteenth century; declared that our power far exceeded Britain's power at its peak; and then waxed eloquent about the difference between Britain's world and America's.

In the old world of the nineteenth century, said he, Britain not only dominated but also depended on the outer world. And that outer world reciprocally depended on Britain, as well as resented Britain. Now Britain was left with this still-dependent backward world making economic claims on it. And the Americans, in the Marshall Plan, were insisting in the name of free trade that Britain meet such economic claims. Did we realize, he asked us, that even then, in 1949, more people around the globe settled their bills with each other in pounds sterling than in dollars? Twice as much trade went on in the old pound as in the Yankee dollar! The Malays with their rubber and tin, the Australians with their wool and wheat, the Argentinians with their beef, the Africans with their cocoa and coconuts—all traded and banked in pounds sterling. Sir Edmund made trade figures dance and jiggle around the globe: If we Americans cut down on buying Malay rubber (as we were just then doing), Malaya earned fewer dollars; then England had to supply Malayan needs in dollars. What happened to Africa when the cocoa market cracked totally, as it did in New York in the spring of 1949? England had to supply Africa's dollar needs!

Hall-Patch then went beyond trade balances and came to the nub of it. What would happen to our Marshall Plan if all the people who dealt in pounds sterling suddenly demanded American dollars in exchange? If all of them tried to claim their share of the great American surplus by squeezing dollars out of the old pound sterling? India and Egypt, now free but owning sterling, were steadily drawing down dollars from England's shrinking reserves. But what if there were a famine in India next year and England had to spend half a billion of her dollars to buy wheat for India? What then? Was America willing to see Britain cut off India? Play rough with her? Remember, he warned, what happened when Britain had its last pound crisis in 1931, remember "what happened all over the world." And Britain was approaching such a pound crisis now, right now.

For the European participants in the Marshall Plan Hall-Patch had contempt. Sit with them in a meeting with Americans, he continued, and they grovel. If a junior American economist told a pleading minor nation that it might be wise to increase its production of triplets next year, the European pleader would probably say, We'll go into that right away and report back. As for the French— the French entered a meeting with American aid-givers with their legs spread so wide apart they seemed to be saying *"Baisez-moi"* ("Slip it to me").

A concerted *Putsch* against the pound was impending said Hall-Patch; the lesser European nations were ganging up. Only one response was possible: refashioning the great English-speaking alliance that had won the war! We needed a merger, a total merger of the resources of America and Britain, so that the dollar and the pound would become the obverse and reverse of the same coin of value, an economic union run by a single board in Washington ("on which, by God, Britain has a say"). Together we could create a globe of free movement, of free circulation of goods, of free men. But it must begin with the union of English-speaking people, for "our word is our bond, we know what good faith is," while our Latin friends—well, Sir Edmund thought that Latins were flatly untrustworthy. "Not since the time of Delcassé has a French diplomat's word been reliable."

So on and on with ever-increasing eloquence went Hall-Patch, until we realized that the senior British diplomat in Paris, emotionally under strain, was talking from the heart. America must move to save and take over the British economy that very fall, or Britain would fade from world power. He had little faith, either short range or long range, in the Labour government he spoke for publicly. He doubted whether England had the stomach to go the rough road it must go if it went alone—to cut the Empire adrift, to repudiate its distant and inner obligations, to hold on only to military command of the oil resources of the Middle East, which he thought someday must become the trump card of international diplomacy (!). He left us, as correspondents, perplexed both professionally and historically. We could not, in honor, quote or report what he had said, because he was appealing privately, off the record, over the head of his own government, to the court of American opinion. But we could not escape the lesson he had meant to teach: the U.S. must, that fall, decide whether we were going to govern the new postwar trading world in partnership with the British, or support it all by ourselves as long as we could. And there were very few weeks left for this decision.

I have never mastered the reporting of international financial crises, for their details are usually kept almost as secret as the internal debates in the United States Supreme Court. From outside, in the summer of 1949, one could sense that the shove was on—but whether the United States shoved the British to a devaluation of their money, or simply urged the Italians to do the shoving, I do not know. I enjoyed the leak furnished me for publication by the American authorities to help speed the crisis. Italy was then one of the most docile and obedient partners in the Marshall Plan, and, for a year, American authorities had frowned on Italy's desire to cash in her pounds in London for dollars. In its recovery, Italy had been selling so much of its wines, fruits and traditional luxuries to countries which could pay her only in British pounds that Italy had a surplus of pounds in her reserve, when what she really wanted was dollars. Now, finally, American authorities had winked at this Italian desire to convert pounds into dollars and slipped the leash. Along with all the other drainage on London's reserve came the Italian drain—and the British Treasury cracked.

On the weekend of September 17–18, the British dropped the value of the pound from $4.03 to $2.80. And England headed on that long downward slope to which good will had led her; from which America refused to rescue her; and from which only North Sea oil might, eventually, give a temporary respite.

It was a moment in history worth recording and I

meant to see it. I knew that if the United States had not
pressed the event, it had at least invited it. The Marshall
Plan sought to create a twentieth-century trading world
even more efficient than the old nineteenth-century world
—but a world in which we would be the chief guarantor,
the senior armorer, the central banker and permanent
umbrella holder. Under our umbrella there would be no
favorites; not even our great allies the British could expect special privileges.

It scarcely occurred to me then, and certainly not to
the Americans of hope who directed the Marshall Plan,
that in this new trading world the vanquished would
become the victors, that the Japanese and the Germans
would become the greatest beneficiaries of our exertion.
And that, ultimately, we would drive the British from the
Middle East, too, and leave all of America's economy and
civilization in debt to, and uncertainly dependent on, the
oil of Middle East sheikhs and strong men, whom the
British had previously policed for us.

The timing of my visit to London could not have
been better, for I had booked my arrival for the Monday
afternoon after what turned out to be the weekend of
devaluation. But if my timing was correct, my anticipation could not have been more delusive, which was better
for my education. I had expected the British crack-up to
come, if not with a bang or a whimper, at least with a
snarl of anger that would be reportable. But in London I
found that the British had set out on the long road
leading off and away from the mainstream of world affairs with complete, affable and cheerful indifference. Perhaps all financial crises are similarly unreportable except
for panic inflationary bursts.

I had boarded the *Golden Arrow* out of Paris very
early Monday morning bound for London, with a lapful
of newspapers, both British and French, describing the
drama of devaluation. But from the moment I passed
through the turnstile of passport inspection on the British
side of the Channel, the intensity of what I thought was a
historic crisis withered. The passport inspector ticked off

the questions: Occupation? Purpose of trip? Et cetera. And when I answered, "Journalist . . . to report devaluation crisis," he looked at me, said, "Really? But nobody's at all excited," and waved me on to the train. The British trains in those days seemed quicker than the French, perhaps because they were bumpier; and the napery in the dining car was certainly thicker and stiffer. The English villages of Kent, through which the train rolled, seemed neater and cleaner than the grim rock-walled villages of France; no crisis there. I went looking for crisis immediately in London, but was taken by my friend Denis Plimmer that evening to the pubs in the council housing at Wapping, a waterfront district. They were tranquil—men playing darts in one pub and their youngsters watching them; in another pub, a man with an accordion played while people sang, chanted, stomped. Walking away, I noticed the big bulletin board of the London County Council's offering of evening school courses; and then the houses, all of them postwar, were pointed out to me, clean, neatly gardened, well lit. Whatever glories Labour had sacrificed abroad, the new government had been generous to its own. If there was a crisis at this level, it required a detective to get through to it. The world was distant; whether Labour had managed or mismanaged the pound meant nothing here. Labour had been good for Wapping.

I scoured offices, factories and the port of London. The port was quite busy and I spent a full day there. It was picturesque and made good vignettes; I might have strung the thread of a story through my observations had I been writing of the old Empire. The wharves made good feature copy: the Canary Wharf, with its fresh fruits, tomatoes and bananas from the Canary Islands; the meat piers with lamb coming in from Australia and New Zealand; the Blue Star and Royal Mail Lines slinging beef from South America overside. There was the tobacco pier, with huge, yellow-pine hogsheads of tobacco swinging down to the warehouses; there were the ships loading and unloading cargo, whose ladings in my notes read like the manifests the Marshall Plan monitored in Paris: in-

coming sugar stacked in piles under Quonset huts; logs of
timber from Rumania and West Africa. And going out,
simultaneously, on one ship to Durban, a load of British
Fords, of Ferguson tractors, cases of whiskey, green ce-
ment-mixing machines, cement in paper sacks.

One ship, however, made the story come to point—a
gray ship called the *Triberg*, out of Vancouver. The
Triberg carried ten thousand tons of wheat and it would
take days to unload her. A huge vacuum pipe endlessly
sucked a stream of grain to the top of a huge elevator
while, from the bottom of the elevator, a dusty workingman presided over three chutes, milking away at the
bottom as if at the teats of a cow, directing the chutes to
pour the golden-red grains into railway wagons that
waited to carry North American wheat to the millers. In
order to eat bread, England needed five such ships every
single week!

The story I was writing had, somehow, to do with
keeping this flow of grain for bread coming in to England;
and how the English might pay not only for the wheat but
for the timber, the tobacco, the Canary Islands luxuries
and, above all, the oil and cotton that were unloaded at
Merseyside or Bristol. But, between the contentment in
the council flats, where the new Labour government cared
for the workingmen, and wharfside, where the goods went
in and out but did not balance, the story became confused. The new Labour government meant to protect its
workers from the ups and downs of the old world and its
new competitors in trade. Benevolence oozed from the
Labour leaders, but they could not say how they proposed to do what they proposed to do.

In search of the story, I interviewed not quite as
many English Labour leaders as I had Communist Politburo members in Yenan. I was in no hurry and had more
time; but the English Labour leaders, whom I then cherished as men of my own philosophy, made far less sense.
They offered a limited, shopworn store of ideas, all resting on the unspoken premise that whatever went wrong
was America's fault. And their querulous debate, now
that I reread my notes, had as its central theme the

familiar question that amuses British intellectuals still: Were the Americans kindly but stupid people? Or were they outright cold warriors, breaking England to the yoke of their anti-Communist crusade?

Two previous acquaintances spanned the debate.

Sir Stafford Cripps was on the American side of the debate. He was a man I had come to admire when I had first met him, out of power, in China years before, as a Christian Socialist. Now, when I looked him up again, as Chancellor of the Exchequer, he stated his feeling that America (by which he meant both the United States and Canada) did not understand its true importance to Europe. Historically, felt Sir Stafford, America's role had been to offer homes to European immigrants, thus draining off the excess population of Europe to work the mines and fields of America; and having been given this second chance in life, these exiled Europeans furnished in return to the old continent wheat, cotton, bread and raw materials. But a generation ago America had closed its gates; Europe was now stuck with a bloated population in a ravaged world; Europe was now forbidden to ship its poor to America, while America would not ship food and raw materials for the poor of Europe without dollars. Cripps's bitterness that day was most intensely focused on the Canadians. Canada was a member of the Commonwealth, yet insisted on charging for its wheat exports in dollars, not pounds—four hundred million dollars a year for the nourishing wheat brought over in convoys of *Tribergs!* And England already had so crushing a dollar burden to bear, furnishing the dollar needs for foods of such dependencies as India, Malaya, Africa, as well as its zone of occupied Germany!

Sir Stafford could make me feel guilty for both Canadians and Americans; we did not understand Britain's global trading burden, and thus had just broken the value of its pound.

Cripps was intelligently instructive. But a much more emotional British Socialist could not make me feel guilty at all. He was Harold Laski, a sparkling personality, the idealogue—if there was one—of the British La-

bour Party. British Labour boasted many fine minds, but
no theoretician: no Lenin, no Trotsky, certainly no Mao:
Laski was the closest thing to a theoretician in chief that
the Labour Party had developed. For this reason, he was
distrusted by the men who had to form a Labour government for England after the war, and was left out of both
government and honors. In some way, his personal bitterness focused on American policy and the government of
Harry Truman, with whom, perforce, his governing comrades were now associated. Laski was one of those European intellectuals who were personally fond of most
Americans they met, but always ready with a word or
essay of criticism on American life.

Laski invited me to his home one evening, not as a
journalist, but as a fellow writer whom he had met in
Paris—where, the previous year, he had assured me that
insurrection was coming ("I smell gunpowder in the air,"
he had said). He was a talker, convinced of his own
brilliance, and that evening was doing several things at
once: he was penciling an article for some publication or
other; he was occasionally pawing through a litter basket
at his feet from which now and then he would extract one
apple-green piece of White House stationery after another
and say, "Oh, yes, Franklin Roosevelt wrote me this."
And all the while he talked in a tirade against American
imperialism. Laski's view—to summarize the evening—
was that the Americans had outwitted and outmaneu-
vered Ernest Bevin, the British Foreign Secretary; they
and Churchill had lured England into the cold war; they
had made Attlee a pawn; our American policy was forcing Labour's new England to disaster. The politics and
the economics of the cold war did not make sense to
Laski. He felt Britain's first priority was to make friends
with Russia; that England's technology and Russia's resources together made for a natural alliance whether in
trade or in atomic secrets; that a greater community of
interests for the future lay between the Socialist countries
of Europe than the freedom countries of the Atlantic.

Laski was one of the great minds of England in his

time; he had been a reference point in the thinking of my generation at college, a humanitarian Socialist theoretician in the time of gathering of Fascism and war. Now, in London, this thin little man, with a brush mustache and wire-rimmed spectacles, sitting by his fireplace, was convinced that the Marshall Plan was a device of corporate American imperialism. I was sad that he had not been knighted by the Labour government; but he was chirpily above such honors as he gossiped away about his onetime comrades, now ministers of state in the cabinet.

I can see Laski now as a symbolic figure, in a parade of symbolic figures who mark the various time junctions when a primitive emotional movement gains strength and the movement becomes a party, then gains power and is transformed into government. The Labour Party was now in power, and honored Laski, but it could not employ him; he was left behind to talk.

Yet Laski and other advocates of Labour swayed me. They had come to power by persuasion, and I was vulnerable to their persuasion because their good will was so complete. They were translating the Christian Socialism of Labour's past into fair shares today—into orange juice for everyone's children; into a national health service; into council flats; into social services of new and imaginative quality. American economists of the Marshall Plan cautiously pointed out that the British were thus making their major national investment in social benefits, not in production. But if the British wanted fair shares from the encircling world as well as at home, they would have to invest in production to compete; we would not protect them. It seemed to me that this American position was much too rough; that we were depriving the British of their war-won share of victory simply because they would not sacrifice their priorities of social benefits to the priorities of production we set for the rest of the trading world.

And so I wrote a screeching series of articles, defending the British effort for fair shares, denouncing Marshall Plan imperialism—only to see that conviction of mine dissolve in the next nine months, the last nine months of the Marshall Plan before the invasion of Korea ended the era of American good will.

I was persuaded of how effective an enterprise the Marshall Plan was, not by the forceful men who directed it, nor by the attractive young men who staffed it, but by the evidence I had to report.

My change of heart came gradually. My memory marks a winter trip through the fields of the Beauce, France's wheat basin, the speckling of the stubbled fields with tractors—and my discovery that the Plan was now shipping tractors to France at such a rhythm that now, by 1950, France had four times as many as before the war! Wheat was about to be plentiful; France not only ate of her own, she could *export* food. I stopped off at one of the farms; the burly young farmer, in French hip boots, and his full-bosomed wife were proud of these tractors, for which they had paid in French francs; they were convinced that they had done it all on their own. American aid was something so remotely upstream in the financing of their new tractors as to be incomprehensible. They, like everyone else helped by the Marshall Plan in Europe, were convinced that they had struggled the road back all by themselves. But they extended their *politesse* to me because they were courteous people.

The road back began to open everywhere in Europe, and by the spring of 1950 it had become politically fashionable for Congressional junkets to tour the Plan's triumphs, as in war they had visited the battlefields. The Zuyder Zee was a showplace; the great postwar poldering projects which added so vastly to the Netherlands' placid and arable acres were financed by Marshall Plan funds. Sardinia was also a showplace; its malarial marshes were being drained, and not only would its people thrive but tourists would rediscover its beauty. In the cleft of the Rhone, the French were building with Marshall Plan funds and equipment the dams and channels of the Donzerre-Mondragon project, which would add 10 percent, by itself, to the generating capacity of prewar France.

By the spring of 1950 the evidence was overwhelming. One day in the winter of 1950, I dug into the dreary cargo manifests of the Marshall Plan in Paris, hoping, like a good investigative reporter, to discover sin. All I could find out was that on that day an estimated 150 ships, all bearing American aid, were on the Atlantic en route to Europe. On that particular day, the cargo train to France alone included five cotton-carrying vessels (for the record: S.S. *Geirulo,* S.S. *Delmundo,* S.S. *Lapland,* S.S. *Cotton States,* S.S. *Velma Lykes*) to supply the mills and lofts where 170,000 French textile and clothing workers depended on American cotton, but voted Communist or Socialist; such workers were more likely to vote Socialist (with us) than Communist (against us) if they had jobs. In addition, *Godrun Maersk,* out of Baltimore, was arriving that day with more tractors, resin and cellulose acetate; the *Gibbes Lykes* was pulling into Marseilles with American Gulf sulfur; the S.S. *Rhondda* was arriving with more farm machines, chemicals, oils; and so on and on, in detail and statistics, to the conclusion that we had well and fairly done what we set out to do. By the end of 1950, industrial production in Western Europe was not only 45 percent higher than in 1947, the year the Marshall Plan was proposed. It was also, despite all war devastation, 25 percent higher than in 1938, the last prewar year! By the time I left, three years later, Europeans were putting out almost three times what they had made in 1938—and were shooting even higher.

What happened between 1950 and 1953 is another story, which requires a separate telling. But historically, the Marshall Plan lasted for only two years, 1948–1950, and it was in those two years that the old civilization regained a sense of its own workability. In those two years, as Europe began to earn its oil and produce the steel for its automobiles, the new traffic jams that infuriated those who loved Rome, or Paris, or London, also began. But the traffic jams, as they clogged the rhythm of the streets, also clogged the rhythm of politics—and somehow, just as planned, the rising rhythm of Communist appeal to the discontented either faded or froze.

Those who loved the old civilization, as I had come to love it, who loved its graceful tolerances, its layer upon layer of memory, its vices as well as its vitality, knew that Europe would now change. I objected, as did all my French friends, to the American-style supermarkets that were spreading through the provinces, and even more to the hot-dog-and-hamburger emporia and the airline offices on the Champs Élysées, the sudden rash of American comic strips in French papers. But it was quite obvious that the down-spiral which George Marshall had feared would give Europe to the Communist idea was over. Europe was no longer an object of our sympathy. By 1950 it was about to be put to harness again, because American policy, and freedom's policy, required that it be done.

Halfway around the world on June 25, 1950, the Communist bureaucracies of Russia, China and North Korea misread their signals and invaded Korea. At which point, all Europe was mustered, half-finished in purpose by the Marshall Plan, to support the war of American purpose against Communist purpose halfway around the globe.

There was much more to be learned in the next three years—of armies, countries, government, diplomacy. But by fall of 1950 it was clear to me how very far I had come in my thinking.

The innocent first two years of the Marshall Plan could be described, as I tried to do, in terms of people and trade balances. But to leave the Marshall Plan memorialized only with figures and names is misleading, for its inner dynamic was as important as its outer frame of action.

The frame had been the cold war, the clash of Communists with the free systems of the West; and in this clash the Marshall Plan had been the master move. When George Marshall had come back from Moscow in the spring of 1947, he had been in no doubt that Stalin meant to occupy that ancient seat of culture, Western Europe. Had Marshall not mounted an American program to buttress that old culture, the Stalinists might well have succeeded. Americans described the confrontation as one of freedom versus Communism, which no doubt it was. But in the many fronts and facings of that war in European politics, we were enlisting once again the dynamics of the trading world against the statics of the Pharaonic world. Most liberals do not like to think of themselves as being linked historically with the traders because the drive force of trade is profit, a dirty word to moralists everywhere. But it came to me slowly, as I reported affairs from 1947 to 1950, that the values that liberals cherish flourish better in the trader's world than in the Pharaonic world. Art and music can flourish in both worlds. But learning and religion, letters, poetry and science, thrive better in the trader's world than in Pharaoh's world. There are no other ways of governing men; one either lures them forward by hope of gain and selfish betterment, or one drives them forward by bayonet, club and fear of the knuckle-breakers.

This I had learned in my first two years in Europe; and with it an inescapable corollary: The Marshall Plan had won because it had linked gain with freedom, had assumed that the movement of minds and the movement of peoples must go with the movement of goods and of merchants. In the noblest terms, it had enlisted the good will of free peoples against the discipline of orderly peoples. In the crudest terms, it had enlisted greed against terror. In any case, we had won. Somehow, I had left behind not only the thinking of my English friends across the Channel and my Yenan friends in China, but also the unquestioning thought processes of the American liberals, of whom I still thought myself one.

Since the Marshall Plan is one of those rare happenings in American history which, like the Boston Tea Party, has passed into the political mythology of both American liberals and American conservatives, I feel I should close this chapter by stating what I later recognized I had learned that made the Plan more than a myth.

I learned that speed and simplicity in large affairs are most essential; that severity in preserving an idea is vital; that in a democracy, the public must be informed; and that good will without competence, or competence without good will, are both equivalent formulas for political disaster. As follows:

• The masters of the Marshall Plan insisted on simplicity; they had too much responsibility and too little time to absorb detail, either from their own staffs or from the European claimants. Each country that begged our aid and help was invited to state its goals; the directors of the Marshall Plan then shook off details as a dog shakes off water; and then after analysis and approval by our experts, the American government delivered its aid, its dollars, its procurement of supplies, on time and on target. The Plan could move swiftly, for it enlisted minimum personnel and that only of the best. At its peak, the Paris headquarters of the Marshall Plan held only 587 people on payroll, and another 839 all across Europe. These people dispensed $13,350,000,000— efficiently.

• If speed and simplicity were the first of the qualities of the Marshall Plan, the next quality could only be called a benevolent ruthlessness.

The administrators of the Plan, being sure of their own good will but not of the unstable good will of the U.S. Congress, were ruthless in requiring performance as promised to Congress. The Marshall Plan put every recipient government and its politicians to enormous temptations—for the dollars the Americans gave to central banks and governments generated billions upon billions of so-called counterpart funds. And every single European government, except perhaps the Belgian, was tempted to use these local currencies politically for social services or social benefits. The Marshall Plan insisted that such use would be inflationary, and coldly forbade it, insisting that the counterpart of our aid funds be used for solid productive investment or else be held sterile. This was a violent intrusion on sovereignty by the American gift-givers, and thus the program was most successful where our armies and air force had wiped out sovereignty and least successful where in Europe our allies had maintained real governments.

    • Yet another major observation concerned the management of the press. Never had I seen the press more skillfully enlisted for American purposes, in a pattern of government only too rarely emulated in the years that followed.

The press policy of the Marshall Plan derived, I am sure, from Averell Harriman, whose relations with American reporters during the war had been dismal. Harriman loved power. Harriman's wartime power stemmed from the affections of Franklin Roosevelt and Winston Churchill. He did not need newsmen then and his manner with the press was ducal, distant and disdainful. But in the Marshall Plan, Harriman's sense of power dictated a change of manner. The plan needed Congressional support. Congressmen did not read documents in those days; they read the hometown papers; and the way to move congressmen was to move the press corps in Paris that reported home.

Thus the magisterial Harriman press briefings, twice a year, for a closed circle of correspondents in Paris were the best exercise in public diplomacy that I know of. Under the beautiful paintings that Marie Harriman hung in their apartment, the Harrimans would offer superb cheeses, the finest French wines—and solid information. Harriman would mumble briefly about our major current problems in France, England, Germany and Italy, the personalities involved, and the view from the top of the hill. Harriman, the multimillionaire, handled money figures as casually as Nelson Rockefeller: "Oh, I don't know how much it will cost, but we figured it cost a billion dollars to install a million tons of new steel capacity during the war, so take that as a bench mark," would be a typical Harriman phrase. Then he would usually turn the instruction over to Milton Katz. And Katz would transform the press briefing into a seminar, his professorial mind enjoying the provocation and the answering of questions. Our text would be the semiannual report of the Marshall Plan to Congress or to the Executive. We would get the text three or four days before its official release. This would give us time to read and study the entire thick-woven document if we wishd, and then listen to Katz's tutorial summary before the public report we made in the press.

What resulted from such briefings was the thorough education of the reporters in immensely intricate subject matter. Timed deadlines gave us days to master our subject before writing. We were made to understand what was going on; we could thus make the editors understand; they, in turn, made the people understand; which forced the hand of Congress. And when Congress, press and Executive all move together, they can reshape events.

• A further observation I should add was the Marshall Plan's subdued but precise emphasis on competence. One of the most vile cartels in Europe for half a century had been the steel trust, now renamed in France as the Comptoir des Produits Sidérurgiques. Thus I could not have been angrier in my early months of reporting than to discover that millions of ERP dollars were being given to finance two American-style strip-steel mills for France— both of them to be owned by members of the wicked old cartel, the Comité des Forges. But it was pointed out to me that first things came first: France had to have modern steel production to compete. And the rolling mills must be given to people who knew how to use them, just as American tractors had to pass through the hands of efficient tractor distributors to efficient farmers, not novices. We were conducting a restoration, not a revolution. When Katz succeeded Harriman as chief, and before the Korean War closed out social perspectives, he almost wistfully suggested that the next phase of the Plan should be to get at the working class; we had taken care of the middle class and the next problem was to work down. But he, too, had supported the philosophy of first things first, to put Europe to work again.

In retrospect, Harriman, Katz and the others were right: competence must play bodyguard to good will, for without competence American good will can become political plague. Knowing how disastrous American aid was to the incompetent government of Chiang Kai-shek, and how iatrogenic it became to the even more incompetent Saigon regime in Vietnam, I now look on American aid as an addictive political drug, as dangerous to its recipients as would be our outright political hostility. The money that Americans gave away in the years 1948 through 1950 worked best when it found its way through governments to groups, or industries, who knew how to use what they could buy with the money, and turn investments into results. Generally, those who benefited first from our money were the poorest, the neediest, the most hungry; but those who benefited longest and most were some of the most unlovely and greedy men of Europe. Yet the latter went with the former, and to get Europe working again, those invited to America's table were not at all those whom one would invite into the home.

Which brings me finally to the last and most unsettling lesson the Marshall Plan taught: a demonstration of what learned historians call the Law of Unintended Consequences.

• The Law of Unintended Consequences is what twists the simple chronology of history into drama. The operation of this law, as instrumented by Americans in the early postwar years in the areas of their dominance and conquest, is classic. Both in Asia and Europe we were bound politically and realistically by gratitude to old allies—England and China. On both continents our enemies, the Germans and Japanese, were to be treated with the utmost severity—and our proconsuls, with no affection for Germans or Japanese, meant to impose discipline and subservience.

I watched the Law of Unintended Consequences operate only in Europe, where the logic of the Marshall Plan was the governing writ. I could not believe then that what I was watching and reporting was really happening, for it did not appear in daily dispatches. But what we were doing was dismissing the British from greatness and elevating the Germans, our killer-enemies, to the status of Europe's senior power.

This historic reversal was not at all intended. Twice

in one generation Germany had been our most violent enemy. The fact that we had no policy for governing Germany meant that it was too complicated for simple solution. Its military governor, General Lucius Clay, took up his duties while the guns were still firing. Slowly, when peace came, he learned that his duty was to hold things still until Americans *could* come to a decision on what to do with Germany—a matter complicated by the suspicious brutality of the Russian Red Army he faced, and the cost of feeding the servile Germans we had just conquered. Neither Clay nor anyone else in the United States Army enjoyed asking the Congress for "Army" appropriations to feed or help Germans. Thus it was essential to get the cost of saving Germans from starvation off the Army budget onto some civilian budget like the Marshall Plan.

The result, thirty years later, is amusing to consider. I first stumbled on its roots in a conversation with one of Lucius Clay's economic experts in the Villa Hügel, the quintessential private Teutonic mansion of the Krupp family in Essen, all smelling of walnut oil and echoing of Wagner. The Villa Hügel was the command point and surveillance center for Allied occupation of the Ruhr. Clay's expert was quite simple. "Our policy," he said, "is to make these bastards work their way back." The American Army still hated Germans; he saw no reason why the Army's budget should carry the cost of feeding German children. The Marshall Plan should carry the humanitarian costs of the Occupation, he felt; but since the U.S. Army dominated West Germany, he thought the Germans should be forced to work, and work hard, to pay for the food, fiber and raw material that American humanitarians believed we must ship in.

Other West European governments were democratic governments; as all modern elected governments must, they promised more—more good houses, more schools, more health insurance, more equality. The most democratic and responsible government in Europe was the British government; it promised its people most. The most autocratic government in Europe was West Germany—and its autocrat was the United States Army. England, France, Belgium, had governments that could vote on how many hours went into a working week, and what maternity benefits should be, and how many days or weeks of vacation people should have. But in Germany, no legislature or parliament had, initially, to be consulted. Lucius Clay and his advisers decided that Germans must work a forty-eight-hour week, and work they did. The U.S. Army, advised by its experts, said the Germans must rebuild their factories, roads and bridges first; meanwhile, let them shiver in cellars, ruins and rags; no housing or clothing until they earned their way back.

It was years before I could fully measure the results of the Law of Unintended Consequences. When I first reported Europe, shortly after the war, the British standard of living was roughly three times that in refugee-crammed West Germany. Britain, though pocked by the bombings, still functioned, while Germany was a moonscape of desolation from the Ruhr to Silesia. Since then, somehow, England has gone its jovial way across its pleasant plateau of civility, but Germany has boomed. The average per capita income in victorious England had risen to $3,871 thirty years later—while in defeated Germany it had reached $7,336, and the gap was widening. Somehow, the severity with which the Americans policed Germany and directed the flow of aid proved more fruitful than the affection and support we gave the free government of the English people to do as they wished with our billions.

Neither Clay nor MacArthur nor Hoffman nor Harriman nor George Marshall nor Dean Acheson nor Milton Katz could have envisioned that what they tried to do in the reconstruction of Europe and Asia would result in the rise of Germany and Japan—and that thirty years later, our two former enemies would threaten, like giant pincer claws, America's industrial supremacy in the new trading world we had tried to open to all.

This was an entirely Unintended Consequence of the

Marshall Plan—but for a generation, which is long enough. an uneasy balance of politics between the East and West was created; and with that balance came the longest unbroken stretch of peace Europe has known in this century, which is no small thing.

CHAPTER 8

The Politics of Victory: Europe

In the beginning, I had hoped my stay in Europe would be only a year's stopover on the way back to China and the revolution. But by the summer of 1950, when the Korean War broke out, events both personal and historic had outrun all my planning.

Nancy had already become pregnant in the fall of 1948, at a time when the news dispatches reported that Lin Piao and his Communist troops had cut the railroads of Manchuria, and were picking off Nationalist garrisons there one by one. One could not travel to a revolution with a pregnant wife, so regretfully I stayed in Paris. By the time our daughter Heyden was born in July of 1949, not only Manchuria but Peking and Tientsin, then Shanghai, Nanking and the lower Yangtze valley, had all fallen to Mao. And when the Korean War broke out, in June of 1950, Nancy was again pregnant. Our son David was born in January 1951—but I no longer regretted being kept away from war and revolution in Asia. That story was now part of my past, too far away to seek again.

Europe had now completely caught my imagination, teasing me with a story I felt must be there but could not capture. That story was larger than the Marshall Plan. I had mastered the grammar of the Plan, enough at least to know that the political story was larger than Europe's need for grain and gold, more complicated than America's solution of free trade in a free world. There was something even more vital—and I picked away at it, still trying to chip news stories off history, but also hoping to find a core.

I had carried with me to Europe a vague expectation that at the end would come a ceremonial story such as the signing of a peace treaty, whose terms would outline the future, just as the Peace of Westphalia had shaped the seventeenth century, or the Treaty of Versailles the Europe of the 1920s and 1930s. Peace treaties were historical markers, and made great news stories. So it had always been before, and I had myself seen such a marker as it was being made, at the cloud-gray ceremonies aboard the *Missouri*, where the Japanese, surrendering to MacArthur, formally gave up their imperial ambitions.

Europe in these years now bustled with minor ceremonies and conferences, steps in the diplomatic minuet, and I thoroughly enjoyed witnessing every one I could. But these were not what I had come for—the great Settlement, the great Treaty, the great formal understanding among all the states that had blown Europe apart and now would agree how to put it together again. I was looking for that visible climax to events, that landmark from which, as the wave recedes, one can see how the shoreline has changed.

Looking for that crest, reading the present as if it had to repeat the past, was a mistake—and for the first two years in Europe had confused my reporting. I could report only what I could see, but what a reporter like me could see was only what a man in a small boat can see of the ocean—ripples or whitecaps or great breakers, the surface as the wind moves it, not the powerful tides nor, underneath them, the irresistible sea currents.

History is all those things—waves, tides and currents

—and like the sea, no matter how tranquil the surface, it is never still. A sequence of events is like a series of waves, one crest following upon another; and the trick, for statesman and reporter alike, is to tell which crest is a surge of the tide and which a mere accident of the wind.

I had come to Europe assuming that as soon as we, the Russians and the English settled the disposition of Germany, peace-making would take shape. By 1950, however, even before the outbreak of the Korean War, I had learned that there was no settlement possible with the Russians; that the British were powerless to affect any settlement we meant to impose on our allies; and that somehow, through the Marshall Plan, we had set in motion a wave effect that had vaguely but discernibly begun to move men toward something called "a Europe." My ultimate story would have to describe this new "Europe." But if it did, then at the center of the story I would have to focus tightly on those eternal antagonists Germany and France, about whom the history of the continent had revolved for so long.

The reader must go back with me, thus, through the waves prior to 1950, to see what had been set in motion in France and in Germany and how, now, in 1950, European politics would change because America was so involved. A jolt to the United States in the Pacific moved like a seismic vibration to the Atlantic, where the American presence carried it all through Europe. My journalistic beat had originally carried me through Western Europe from Belgium to Calabria, from Spain to Poland. After 1950, however, I visited and reported no other countries but France and Germany, with an occasional trip to London for affection and friendships. As a newspaperman of the war-correspondent generation, I cherished the British, was delighted by the French, feared and hated the Germans.

Living in Paris, I would go to Germany twice a year for spring and autumn trips: spring for reporting politics, and autumn to report military exercises. My first trip

came in February of 1949. And I arrived carrying in my
American baggage all the ancestral nightmares of the
Jews, nightmares I thought I had discarded years before.

As soon as I crossed the border of the Saar, at dusk,
and heard people speaking German, I bristled with the
memory of Poland, where I had just finished a reporting
survey. In Poland I had visited both the rubble of Warsaw's ghetto and the ruins of Auschwitz. I had cried in
the ghetto. But at Auschwitz I had had neither tears nor
words. The moldering concentration camp was then three
years out of service, but its museum of atrocities preserved its terror fresh: The Nazis' cache of gold-rimmed
spectacles was piled in a giant mound, each pair of
spectacles some traceless Jew's lens on life. There were
mounds of shoes—slippers, boots, women's high-heeled
shoes, babies' booties. The curators had found and
stacked the hanks of women's hair—black, blond, red,
but overwhelmingly gray tresses—which the Nazis had
thriftily gathered from the victims whose skulls they
shaved before incineration. The neat logic of Auschwitz's
assembly line was clearly visible, from railway siding to
"shower stations" (where the prisoners were told that
they would be getting a sanitary douche but in which the
overhead ventilators whirled gas into the air), to the
furnaces. At that time, the furnaces of incineration had
not yet been cleaned; ashes and a few fine bone fragments
were still scattered around. I had also visited the pits and
pools in the forests just beyond the camp limits where, I
was told, they dumped bodies at the end; and the dank
pools would emit a bubble now and then, a big, popping
bubble that stank. I had hated Nazis from my Asian
distance during the war, out of atavism, ideology and
patriotism. Now, after seeing Auschwitz, I hated all Germans with animal ferocity.

All this was on my mind when I lost my way after
crossing over from the Saar into Germany. I was American. My car was French, with French license plates. I had
nothing to fear—but I shook with fear. And I found I
had strayed from the main road into the villages between

the Saar and the Rhine. In most of these villages electricity had not yet been restored, and where it had been, it furnished only a string of dim yellow lights along the main streets. Elsewhere there was no light. I hated and feared these villagers. I did not want to be caught among them. Now my car developed a bearing knock; it had to be fixed. But there were no road signs, no garages, and the night grew darker. Wherever a light appeared, I stopped and stalked into the place to demand that a mechanic be found, as gruffly as an *Übermensch*. I must have been insufferably overbearing. At last a mechanic was found who could, actually, fix a French Citroën bearing, and when he was finished I drove on into the night as if I had just won a battle. I was headed first for Frankfurt, headquarters of the American occupation force, en route to Bonn, where we Americans had just assembled some Germans to write a new constitution which would allow Germany a limited self-government. But I trusted no German, and my drive through that night convinced me that the American occupiers were taking far too little care to patrol these desolate yet menacing villages. It was another hour before I could find anyone who could direct me to the ferry across the Rhine. When I reached it, I yelled at the captain, demanding instant passage. Then, as I reached the other side, my eye caught a sign in English and I swerved, following it. Suddenly I was up on the autobahn.

Dazzled by autobahn lights and autobahn traffic, I found myself in another world, the American world of superhighways. What I had left behind there in the darkness of the villages, without electricity and probably without enlightenment, was the nightmare Germany. And I realized I was wet with sweat.

The autobahn world belonged unmistakably to the U.S. Army. An American convoy rumbled ahead, its train of lights marking a conqueror's parade. An army jeep, headlights blazing, roared past me. I passed two American sedans in five minutes, their white occupation plates gleaming. The lights and American signs and American presence grew steadily until I reached the Rhein-Main air base outside Frankfurt. That was the winter of the Berlin airlift and the red and green wing lights of our planes rose in never-ending procession from the yellow runway lamps. I now relaxed, because we Americans held the high ground, Germany was our conquest, and when I woke in the morning the nightmares would surely be gone.

In the morning, when I drove out of the Park Hotel, a German policeman, directing traffic, tried to halt me; and I lost my temper. I knew that the Germans had organized their army, much as we had organized ours, with civilian reserve clusters to be mobilized in emergency for specific military assignments. But whereas, for example, the University of Pennsylvania Medical School had organized the great base hospitals of the CBI theater, where I had been hospitalized, German municipal police force reserves had helped organize and staff the concentration camps. The Frankfurt police force had not patrolled the worst of the camps of the Holocaust, like Auschwitz or Belsen; but it had provided cadres for the murder camps in Belgrade and Yugoslavia; or so at least I had been told. So when the policeman tried to stop me, I went into a temper tantrum, of which I am now ashamed, and having impressed myself on him as an accredited American correspondent, I was finally waved through. I bristled thus at most of the Germans I met, for this was the first of my trips to Germany. I saw crypto-Nazis everywhere.

My hatred of all Germans lasted a full ten days or two weeks—until I came to Bonn. Bonn was to be the centerpiece of my story; there we had gathered a handful of "good" Germans to write a new constitution for the ruined land Hitler had left behind. So I was visiting Bonn, suspicious as I was, to see whether the American supervisors of this experiment were monitoring it with proper severity for resurgent Nazism, Nationalism, Conspiracy and Plot.

What I was to see instead was a classic episode in the behavior of the defeated in the presence of their conquerors. Any conquered people will choose to ingratiate themselves with either the strongest or the kindest of their conquerors, seeking by instinct if not by conspiracy to divide their overlords. It is best to be defeated and occupied by Americans, for they restore and nourish what they conquer; second best is to be conquered by a coalition which includes Americans, to whom appeal can be made. The victorious coalition that had conquered and occupied Germany had included the Russians, with whom we had just irrevocably broken. It also included our partners the British, led by Labour visionaries who wanted a Socialist Germany; and the honorary conquerors, the French, who wanted no Germany at all.

In all this, the central character was our engineer general, the military governor of Germany, General Lucius Clay—and the Germans chose Clay as their judge of appeal.

Clay was an extraordinary character; he combined the utmost intelligence with the utmost self-assurance, and was loyal only to the United States Army, the United States Government, and his sense of order. He had, before taking up his post, sought instructions of the State Department on American policy for Germany. Told that we had none, he proceeded unabashed to govern Germany on his own, deciding the most important thing was simply to make Germany work. He was the only American general always accessible to the press: his door in Berlin was not only figuratively but literally open, and a reporter could walk in at almost any time and ask him questions.

Clay's problems were not minor problems—to uproot Nazism; to get Germany working; to revive its economy; to implant democracy; all the while trying to outface the bullheaded Russian commander, Sokolovsky, who was tempting war in the Berlin blockade; and simultaneously resisting the nibbling of our caviling allies, the British and the French.

It was Clay's decision that the situation demanded a German government, and his memoirs are amusing in tracing the roots of power. In April of 1948 Clay had entertained one of the more civilized French diplomats, the dapper and urbane Couve de Murville, and found a weakening in de Murville's spirit, a faint dilution of the hate all Frenchmen bore for the Germans, who had invaded them so often. Said Clay in his memoirs: "With this thought in mind, on the last day of his visit I rushed to the office and dictated a simple memorandum. . . ." Clay's memorandum outlined an eight-point program of getting the Germans from where they were to democracy. Point One of this private memo gives his tone of conquest and command: "The several states will be advised that a constituent assembly will be held not later than 1 September 1948 to prepare a constitution for ratification by the several states." The memo then proceeds to outline hastily the constitutional structure of the German Republic as it still exists today.

The French say that *"rien ne dure que le provisoire"* ("nothing lasts as long as the provisional"); Clay's memo was an army engineer's quick answer to the quick question of how to get the Germans back to work: You let them run their own country, but under strict controls. The Germans, in response, requested that the meeting be called not a constituent assembly but a "parliamentary council." This council they hoped would be writing a "Basic Law," not a "constitution"; no final structure of Germany, they pleaded, should be settled until West and East Germany were reunited. In any event, they had obeyed and taken what was offered: elections of delegates by the parliaments of the eleven states concerned in August, to convene in Bonn by September of 1948, to write a provisional document to govern Germany, subject to the approval of the three military governments of West Germany, American, British, French.

Thus, when I arrived in Bonn in February of 1949, I knew a new German government was forming; and if I could expose any taint of sin or Nazism in these new constitution-framers, it would make an exciting story. I had seen a moment of political conception at Yenan five years earlier. I had seen power move from an embryo of purpose into a state, and remembered Yenan by then with a romantic coating. Perhaps Bonn would be a counterpart.

I found, however, nothing romantic about Bonn. Bonn was a drowsy town on the banks of the Rhine, hitherto famous only for its university and as the birthplace of Beethoven. (The university was less visually exciting than Beethoven's birthplace, where, if you persisted, you found, in an upper garret under sloping eaves you must stoop beneath to enter, the four-foot-high servant's hutch in which the genius was born.) The town, relatively untouched by bombing, was now full of refugees from the East. And within this town of plodding and shuffling refugees and students were two centers of politics.

For the sake of my story, I had hoped to find the two centers as polar opposites, the German center, or "parliamentary council," opposed to the American center, in charge of surveillance. But rather than the tension I had anticipated, the two centers were swaying smoothly together, both dancing to the same political waltz. The Americans and Germans here were happy partners. Or, in another analogy, the Americans had let these Germans out of reformatory and now as guardians were choosing new clothes to garb them for normal life. A German newspaper cartoon summed it up very well. A puzzled man is looking for a new suit. There is Model Lohengrin, with horns and helmet and Wagnerian regalia; there is Model Weimar, with striped trousers, cutaway and high hat; there is Model Adolf, with swastika armband, brown baggy-pants uniform, the hair-slick over the forehead. And the salesman is saying, "This time, *etwas anders* [something different]?" In Bonn, we as salesmen were suggesting to the Germans *"etwas anders,"* and they were eager to comply.

I found it impossible to keep sharp the edge of hatred in Bonn. These German delegates had been screened, rescreened, de-Nazified and purified by every intelligence agency of the occupation before being allowed to come here. But not only that. It was as if the Anglo-American presence of the occupation, particularly the

American presence, had magnetized and drawn out from the wreckage of German politics a collection of waifs, strays, victims, outcasts and resistants to Hitler's politics more devoted to liberty, republicanism and democracy even than ourselves. They had suffered from freedom's loss. The chief American concern in Bonn was whether these forlorn and seedy constitution-makers would know how to use power if we turned it over to them, whether they would be tough enough on their own to crush any revival of Nazism, yet crafty and businesslike enough to get their country working again. Though the Russians in Berlin saw these middle-aged and docile Germans as American puppet leaders for a revanchist, anti-Communist Reich, we saw them as an experiment in self-government. And they, the Germans at their center in Bonn, saw us not as dictators and enemies, but as partners.

The American center of control was amusing, both for its setting and for its ambivalence. Bonn was a university town not unlike Cambridge, Massachusetts, fifty years ago; and on its outskirts, at 12 Joachim Strasse, was, as I recall it, a yellow stucco three-story building not dissimilar to a boardinghouse for graduate students at Radcliffe. In beleaguered Berlin, Clay negotiated with Sokolovsky at the edge of war; he directed the American airlift that flouted the Russian blockade; he was told by Sokolovsky that the blockade would go on until the American plans for a separate West German government were abandoned. But here, on quiet Joachim Strasse, where the American mission was supervising the architecture of this dreaded West German government, children played on the street, and the blockade crisis seemed as far away as it might at a college seminar on European politics.

No conquering legates could have been more ambivalent than the amiable group whose duty it was to sternly control the German menace yet nurse the makers of its new Republic. As in Paris at the Marshall Plan, the academics had already established a vigorous beachhead. Two professors, Edward H. Litchfield of the University of Michigan and Hans Simons of the New School for Social

Research, were cranking in political science and learning, but seemed usually to be traveling elsewhere. Several State Department diplomats occasionally dropped in, either to sample progress or to offer advice. But the permanent and most engaging member of this group, described as so sinister by Russian propaganda, was a New York trucking man—Anton F. Pabsch, of Syracuse, New York, the proud boss of the Onondaga Freight Company in civilian life. Pabsch had been a good army officer in the war, was kept on later in military government to supervise the Länderrat of Stuttgart; and had now moved up, as a civilian again, to this control group in Bonn.

One could make much of Tony Pabsch's politics. He had learned what he knew of government not from Plato but from upstate New York politics, then steaming and redolent with practices now prohibited, but as superior to the practices of Hitler's Germany as those of Pericles' Athens to the practices of Susa. Pabsch, as well as the others of the supervisory group, had as his overriding directive the American injunction to create a central German government strong enough to govern, but not so strong as to crush provincial or individual rights. That was the thrust and the sum of American political thinking on Germany, and men like Clay, Pabsch, Litchfield, Simons and other experts were given complete freedom to supervise, guide or yield to the "good" Germans of the parliamentary council in all detail within this major frame. Pabsch applied his pressure not with bayonets but as the truckers' or teachers' lobby applies pressure in Albany. "We observe them," said Pabsch, no political scientist, "then we cocktail them, dine them and lunch with them." Then the Germans, within this shell of American pressure and protection, wrote their own rules.

The "good" Germans who were writing the "Basic Law" met in what had been a young ladies' normal school before the war. The tranquil mood of Joachim Strasse reached all the way across the small town to the normal school, which sat on the banks of the Rhine, and whose lawns, in the old-fashioned German way, were kept cropped by dirty yellow sheep which passed and repassed

outside the windows where the councillors wrote the Basic Law. These "good" Germans were old people, seventy
percent of them over fifty. The English and American
occupations had scoured Germany for decent pre-Hitler
leadership, so the delegates were all, in one degree or
another, anti-Nazi. They were far more intellectual or
academic than their supervisors. No less than thirty-seven
of the seventy were Ph.D.s. Another eighteen were aging
pre-Hitler civil servants. Several clergymen, a small handful of women and two Communists sat among them. They
gathered together in the school auditorium overlooking
the riverbank at blond-wood desks and tables which had
been designed for lithe German maidens, not stiff old
German men. They caucused almost constantly in former
classrooms, then gathered in the stuffy auditorium to
debate with intensity the power vacuum that the Americans were inviting them to fill. One could almost see the
rifts and divisions of future German politics take shape as
these powerless people debated such abstractions as
taxes, union rights, school control, emergency powers,
cabinet structures and the nine different subject areas into
which their deliberations were channeled by committees.
They seemed harmless enough as one watched them, and
one hoped that under the scar tissue of Nazism lay the
other Germany, the country of Beethoven, Goethe and
Schiller, which, with luck, we might call back into being.

Several key characters had already appeared in this
council of emerging Germany, and I, being in haste,
asked Pabsch to suggest the most important. The most
important, said Pabsch, was "old Konrad Adenauer," and
with conqueror's authority, he picked up the telephone and
made a call which resulted in almost immediate consent
to my visit. Adenauer's bio file reported that he had been
mayor of Cologne before Hitler; had refused all cooperation and been twice imprisoned by the Nazis; been released under surveillance later in the war years, and had
spent his time since cultivating roses. He was now seventy-three years old, but was our American favorite to run
Germany, while Kurt Schumacher, the Socialist, was the
favorite of Britain's Labour Party. The British were

particularly opposed to Adenauer. British Intelligence reported him to be "politically incompetent"; Dean Acheson reported that the British opposed Adenauer's accession because he was "conservative and strongly Catholic [in] orientation." But we thought he was our man, the Americans' man as against "their" man, the British choice, Kurt Schumacher; immeasurably more palatable than the Russians' "man," Walter Ulbricht; and more reliable than the most charming of them all, Carlo Schmid, the man the French wanted to run Germany. As it turned out, Adenauer was *Germany's* man—and whether by guile or sincerity, used us all to restore Germany to power. The Germans later came to call him *Der Alte Fuchs*—the Old Fox.

When I called on Adenauer at the schoolhouse, it was as if I were visiting a painted bishop. He sat woodenly erect in his chair, his semi-Oriental eyes rarely blinking, listened intently, answered questions with precision. My first notes read: "very gray, clean, immaculate, aging, starched, detachable collar." Then I began to listen. It was difficult to talk conversationally with Adenauer, for intelligent as he was, any time he spent with newsmen become a Q and A quiz, with no suggestion of jest or zest. With me, he went through the pros and cons of each of the main questions still under constitutional debate: of centralization of government (which, he felt, depended on who controlled the purse—the central or the state governments), of the powers of the two houses (he felt Germany's lower house, like ours, should be the superior power in the new German union), and the controversy over schools. Only on this third issue did any juice come into his dry voice. Parents, he insisted, must have the right to send children to schools of their choice—Protestants to Protestant schools, Catholics to Catholic schools—the state must aid both, and state schools must provide religious instruction to all children.

There are a thousand reasons for hating Hitler; each good man and tradition claims his own. Adenauer hated Hitler as a Catholic for separating the souls of children from the guidance of their parents; he loathed the Hitler

Jugend, the bonfires, the pagan mystique, and as he spoke, passion quivered in his voice.

He was impressive when he spoke thus, but he seemed to me a wrinkled mummy breaking into voice. He was then, as I say, seventy-three years old and I gave him, hopefully, a year or two at most at the helm if we succeeded in setting up this new German Republic. I could not, of course, have been more wrong. By September 7, 1949, Konrad Adenauer was Chancellor of West Germany and he was to remain Chancellor for fourteen years, until he was eighty-eight years old! Though he had been separated from active life by Hitler in 1933, it was as if all his inner circuitry had remained intact, ready to function once the switch was turned on and the power began to flow. Power is an adrenaline which no doctor can provide, and the same power that circulated, by design, through Adenauer and the old men of Bonn flowed through the entire defeated country and caused it to flourish.

Transfer of power comes, in the Marxist and revolutionary catechism, by upheaval and cataclysm, by the *Putsch* at midnight or the swoop on the palace at dawn. But transfer of power in Germany came gradually and peacefully, by America's will with British acquiescence, to the men and women meeting in the old school for girls. Within our constitutional design the Germans had packed as much as they could of the old Weimar constitution, and in the detail, it was largely their handiwork. The most important and venturesome departure in constitutional theory came about almost by itself, a happy marriage of Anglo-American politics and Continental parliamentary tradition. The Continental tradition, on which the Weimar Republic had foundered, held that power is to be shared by coalitions, or partnerships of parties, which depend on flickering, shifting or unstable parliamentary voting majorities. The Anglo-American tradition is much simpler: you either wield power or you do not, you are "in" or you are "out"; politics are the way of getting the people directly involved in choice of leaders. The Bonn compromise, nearly Platonic in its simplicity, combined the best of the two traditions. The new German parliament, or *Bundestag,* would be able to eject an unpopular chancellor by a vote of no confidence, but only if, by the same vote, it named and gave its majority to another man as chancellor. The accidental compromise of Bonn has given Germany the strongest government in Europe since.

Nothing has intrigued me in political reporting, anywhere at any time, as much as this process of transfer of power. Power at transfer is attended sometimes by ceremonies of peace, by blessings of church, by murder, by riot, by brutalities, by the invisible rites of elections and public splendor of inaugurals. In retrospect, however, the process of transfer at Bonn was the most intriguing of all—a handful of Americans, having derived authority from armies now three years disbanded and shipped home, delivering authority to another handful of timorous and tentative old Germans, as if urging them to stand up, stride forth on stage, and play the roles history assigned. Whereupon, in the next few years, this fragile group found itself able to sink roots, rewire to its nervous control old bureaucracies, and make police, tax collectors, schoolteachers, respond to its direction so naturally that what began as a group of role-players became a state.

Were I to become the scholar I once hoped to be, I would choose such moments of political embryology as my field of study, and concentrate first on Germany. I would choose Germany because in 1933 a handful of men had seized a modern state and made its people into the most hated nation in the world. In 1949 and 1950, I saw another handful of men take over in Germany—dull, dreary, plodding men—and saw them convert Germany in the next twenty years into a decent society. What frightened me then, and frightens me still, is how very few men it takes at the head of any state to give it its character of good or evil, of freedom, tyranny, torture, butchery or benevolence.

I would return to Bonn again and again over the years to watch German politics, but the nightmare I had brought with me began to fade on the very first visit until finally it vanished. I could not stay in Bonn, on that first

visit of 1949, to see the new Basic Law approved by the
Americans. The action in Europe then was elsewhere—in
Berlin, where Clay was facing the Russians, or in Paris,
where Acheson was outfacing and outwitting Vishinsky.
When, finally, negotiations ended the Berlin blockade,
and the Russians accepted our decision to let the West
Germans administer their own affairs, the war on Germany by the Allies was over. The military occupation
would come to an end in all three Western zones as soon
as the German states ratified their new constitution or
Basic Law; and the three commanding generals of the
occupying forces would be replaced by high commissioners (who would, in a few years, be replaced by ordinary
ambassadors).

The Merlin of the transformation, the man who
waved his wand over the ruined enemy and prepared it to
be an ally, was, of course, Lucius Clay. Clay, who had
outlined the new constitution in his quick memo of 1948,
flew down to Frankfurt to exercise his conqueror's authority in a brisk review of its terms on April 25, 1949;
insisted on a trifle more tinkering; but was, on the
whole, pleased with the handiwork carved to his desires.
On May 8, the parliamentary council adopted the new
Basic Law. It awaited only the conqueror's approval. On
May 12, Clay, in Berlin, harvested the diplomacy of Dean
Acheson as the blockade came to an end; and flew to
Frankfurt to put his signature on the Basic Law. On May
15 he flew back to the United States, to become a Wall
Street banker, leaving behind a Germany on her way to
independence, equality and bursting prosperity.

The story changed after the blockade.

I would travel, as I say, twice a year to Germany,
sampling political tissue for traces of Nazism as a doctor
tests a patient for traces of returning malignancy. Fear
had been the original motive in my reporting of Germany;
the blockade, and the making of a new German constitution later, had been a first-class, straightforward challenge
to the storytelling of any journeyman reporter. Now I had
to write of Germany as a feature writer, and this too was

not difficult. Though the men who governed Germany under the new Republic were, perhaps, the dullest group of politicians I had ever encountered, they governed a people so rich in remembered excitement that whenever one delved beneath government level, a journeyman storyteller could not miss. The dullness of their government was a genuine merit in the eyes of a people who had known too much excitement and experienced too much history. It was a phenomenon no American could then understand—a shrinking away of a people from its past.

As, for example, among other people of the next four years of visits:

• Heta Fischer; a blond, straight-haired Viking lady whom I had tracked down in the catacombs of Hanover —as handsome and proud a woman as I have ever met, and a heroine. She had been a member of the Communist Party's underground in Hitler's Germany, and had emerged with her *Lebenskamerad*, Kurt Mueller, into leadership of the Communist Party in West Germany after the war. Then the Communist leadership *apparat* had come to distrust her man, Mueller, kidnapped him, spirited him off to East Berlin and Russia, and eliminated him tracelessly. No one cared but her. Bewildered, she had now lost both her man and her faith in Communism. Sensing a good scavenger's story in all this, I traced her to her home and we were moving through our conversation on Soviet wickedness very agreeably until, somehow, I inadvertently ran up my American flag with too much emphasis. At which she exploded. She had been in Hanover during the war when American planes bombed it, she said. She had *seen* those planes with white stars dropping bombs on people's homes. Killers, killers, killers, she shrieked, her voice rising in horror, a political Sadie Thompson playing *Rain* and proclaiming that all men were pigs and killers. The Russians were killers, the Nazis were killers, the Americans were killers. She was so brave, blond and handsome, I squirmed when she broke out like this.

But out of such people the stodgy leaders of Bonn had to fashion their dull Republic.

• And out of people like Willi Schlieker. Willi became the closest I knew to a friend in Germany, which is a great deal to say, for he had been, at the age of twenty-eight, the boy genius of the Speer *Ministerium* that produced the arms for Hitler's Wehrmacht: Of Willi's boyhood and career I have written elsewhere,* but what I found captivating about him was his love of steel and steel-making. He was totally apolitical, in the sense that he would work for anyone of any regime that let him make steel. He had been jailed, freed, liberated, jailed again so often by so many occupiers in the first few years of the occupation that he reacted like a jack-in-the-box when the British, who then controlled him, first took me to his cabbage-smelling and squalid apartment on Breitestrasse in Düsseldorf, and ordered him to tell me about the steel-making facilities of the Ruhr. He stopped jumping to command rather quickly thereafter as the occupation ended; and as I continued to visit him, he in his growing steelmaster's wealth would patronize me as a peripatetic American free-lancer. But I did not mind the transposition of our roles. Willi taught me about steel and industry; Willi exposed to me the affection of Germans for the forge and the rolling mill, as certain Frenchmen exposed to me their mysterious affection for wine. I learned also, after Willi grew very rich, that he loved flowers, loved Meissen ware, loved medieval art.

But most of all he loved steel and loved work, which is a particular German virtue, out of which the shrewd leaders of Bonn had to fashion their dull Republic. And that leadership had to deal with other large and small characters I came across:

• A twenty-seven-year-old student leader at Heidelberg University. The student leader, his friends and I drank in a beer hall as we talked. Anyone can seduce a student of any age by asking seriously for his opinion; and Heinz offered the ideal of a United Europe as the animating spirit of his group. Germans devoted to a

---

*For a fuller account of Willi Schlieker and his times, see Chaper VIII of *Fire in the Ashes*.

peaceful United Europe were what I was seeking, and so I pressed him. He held forth about how only the Germans had seen Europe whole, how only the Germans had managed a Europe united from the Pyrenees almost to the Urals, and how wonderful it was for there to come about, finally, this Europe. He himself had seen Europe as a tank commander from Paris to the outskirts of Stalingrad. This conversation led backward to the war and he began to talk about ground forces and tanks. He told how his tank platoon had been there outside Stalingrad, while I told about the American air force and how we had outreached in Asia. There we were, two men of roughly the same generation, engrossed in comparing war stories. I was probably as offensive as he, doing my *hup-hup-hup* of machine guns going down on the bridge north of Sian, while he was doing his *hup-hup-hup* of the machine guns of his tank platoon in Russia. But he grew more excited than I; he was recreating that tank advance over the snows of Russia which almost gave Hitler victory, and as he swiveled in his seat, moving his imaginary guns this way and that, I realized that the son of a bitch was one of the people I ought to hate and fear. And it was good that he was a destitute student at old Heidelberg while I was—by self-assumption—one of the American conquering team. Yet he taught me a lesson: There was little in shriveled Germany that excited his imagination for the future; and since he no longer wanted Hitler's mad dream, he wanted to dream of a European Europe in which he could lead a larger life than Germany offered him. Politics need dreams to lean on.

• Or the labor leader. He was one of those men who, without trying, could supply in conversation the enzymes of common sense to make nourishing the raw sights one has been ingesting. He was a middle-aged man, grizzled, a steelworker, a Socialist, an anti-Nazi. We met in a bar in 1950 in Essen; he headed the union at the Krupp works, which I had once hoped to see torn to the ground; Krupp was the heart of Essen; Essen was at the heart of the Ruhr; and the Ruhr was the most thoroughly destroyed place I had seen except for Hiroshima—worse than

Tokyo, worse than anything in China. For miles around, the ground had been churned by the Allied bombings and even now, more than four years later, it was like a panorama of waters, hurricane-lashed; except that the waves and troughs were made of earth, frozen to immobility by peace. The only place I have seen ground so torn, so irrevocably frozen in convulsion, is in what is preserved of the battlefield of Verdun.

I was, at that point in learning, passing out of my total hate of all Germans; and I had, after several visits, come to like the Ruhr, and its capital, Düsseldorf. I had originally questioned in my own mind whether we should raze it flat, which morality and revenge required, or help rebuild it, which reason and compassion told me the Marshall Plan required. And could we? It was the historian's version of Ezekiel's old question: Can these bones live again? Can these dead stems of a civilization destroyed be made to thrive again? I was asking the labor leader specifically about reparations.

The labor leader was a man much older than I and, like most labor leaders, stubborn in conversation. He was pleading with me to stop dismantling, because he was pleading for jobs. But he left me with another thought, paradoxically contrary, yet overriding, which I called the Law of Invisible Social Capital.

Like this: Even if we Allies finished dismantling all of Krupp's plants and all the other steel mills we could see on the skyline, what would we accomplish? he asked. His union members would be unemployed and hungry for a year, or two, or three. But then the Communists would tell his workers that the Allied capitalists of the West were only trying to crush German competition; his steelworkers would accept Communist leadership to get jobs as readily as they had welcomed Nazi leadership. And in the end, we would gain nothing because it was *impossible* to dismantle the Ruhr. Yes, we could ship out dismantled machinery—which would be junk and scrap iron when it finally got to Russia. The strength of the Ruhr, he insisted, lay not in the rolling mills but in the fingers, the hands, the skills, the minds and memories and crafts of men whose fathers and guildmasters had taught them to dig coal, bake coke, distill tar, machine gears, roll steel. Unless we physically wiped out the people who embodied the Ruhr's skills, we could not wipe out the Ruhr at all. The worst would be to let the men of the Ruhr stand idle, as they had in 1932 and 1933, their skills unused and unemployment growing. Unemployment had brought Hitler; more unemployment would bring evil again. So *"Schluss mit* dismantling"; let Germans work.

This Invisible Social Capital of experience, skill and know-how, this atavistic yearning to trudge to a job in the morning to exercise the skill, then trudge home unbothered by politics in the evening, underlay the *Bundesrepublik* Germany that was being born—a politically inert Germany. Of all the clichés of world politics, the cliché that Germans like to work seems to hold most true. In Germany, I learned that on holidays miners wore their own special uniforms with special buttons, to show their pride in their craft. Other craftsmen, from steelworkers to brass founders, also had special garb or insignia, which came down, perhaps, from the Middle Ages. The fact that these Germans had been, since the time of Tacitus and Caesar, the world's most savage and sometimes most stupid warriors, I also knew. But now they were spiritually burned out; and out of these people with a lust to work and a desire to forget their past, Adenauer netted the working majority, which stretched the thin film of civilized government authorized by the "provisional" constitution of Bonn.

My returning trips to Germany, at spring and autumn intervals, were like cinematic speed-up frames—as if I were seeing villages growing again on the sides of a volcano that had erupted and spewed out destruction over an entire continent. I did not enjoy seeing the Germans thrive, but being caught up in the American purpose, I could agree with the logic of it. We had not set out to make a powerful Germany again; we were letting Germany thrive just as we were letting the British wither, not out of policy but because in the field of American force these things had to happen. To have exercised control of

British or German affairs more aggressively would have made us, truly, into imperialists.

I could mark the wave of German resurgence creeping higher and higher at each visit to Germany, but 1950 marked a forward surge that was also a turning. The Korean War, which so widened the split between the Americans, on the one hand, and the British and French, on the other, had made us, suddenly, eye West Germans as allies. In the old days, whenever Lucius Clay had summoned, the aging Adenauer had docilely journeyed from Bonn to American headquarters in Frankfurt to bow his head and nod acquiescence. When I had passed through in 1949, a single telephone call from the American mission had delivered Adenauer to me for an immediate interview. By 1950, with the new "Constitution" in effect, there was no longer an American occupying general, and Clay had been replaced by an American high commissioner, who, like the French and British high commissioners, must journey to Bonn to see Chancellor Adenauer. Adenauer would see them one by one, when he chose, at his eighteenth-century baroque Palais Schaumberg in Bonn. But the West needed Germany by 1950—it needed German soldiers, German armies, German steel. The Korean War had made rearmament necessary; the Germans were there to be recruited; and Adenauer made the most of the leverage the Communist war in Asia provided.

By 1951 the war in Asia had so reshaped history in Europe that the following charade regularly took place in Bonn: The three uniformed members of the Allied Military Security Board would meet informally in the morning at the Petersberger Hof, across the Rhine from Bonn, with two former German generals, now civilians—Hans Speidel and Adolf Heusinger. The five would discuss the creation of a new German army to help the one-time Western enemies of Germany defend it against its present Eastern or Communist enemies. Then, quite conscious of the irony involved, the same three Allied generals would cross the Rhine to meet in the afternoon as the Military

Security Board, without Germans, to discuss the demilitarization of Germany, as required of them by their postwar compact to keep Germany forever disarmed.

Adenauer presided over this charade, and the historic shift. But it was very difficult to work up emotion about Adenauer or make American editors interested in stories about him. Except for Jean Monnet, he was certainly the shrewdest of postwar European statesmen—but more inscrutable than any Oriental. Adenauer was uninterested in fine art, books, culture or women. Questions of economics he left to his pudgy economics minister, Dr. Ludwig Erhard. Erhard could explain the German "miracle"—which was the spectacle of the defeated Germans overtaking their conquerors' standards of living month by month, year by year. Adenauer was interested only in politics, and Adenauer's miracle was greater and more difficult to describe than any other. Erhard had only to persuade Adenauer to do what was right for the German economy. But Adenauer had the task of persuading Germany's conquerors to do what was right for Germany.

Adenauer was a curious man to have been so great, and I puzzled at him each time I came to Germany. Hitler had been a fanatic, a killer. Adenauer was at heart an *Oberbürgermeister*. Adenauer would send police to pursue and punish pornographers, but no honest or decent person would be hurt by Konrad Adenauer. Bismarck, the Iron Chancellor, would have looked down on Adenauer. Bismarck actually enjoyed using armies; Adenauer did not, for he was not a Prussian of the goose-stepping tradition. He was a Rhinelander, which meant he did not cheer for German generals though he liked the bands, the lively music and the splashy colors of standards on parades. Adenauer's miracle, I finally decided, was a miracle of gravity and guile that rested on his sense of time, place, strength and the relationship of forces. With these qualities he achieved more than all German warriors had achieved in a century—persuading Germany's enemies of yesterday, American, British and French, not only to set Germany free to compete with their economies, but also to provide troops, planes and guns to defend Germany against Russia, and to pay for all this to boot.

Adenauer could not have achieved all this, of course, without the relentless public malice of Joseph Stalin, who frightened the world. Nor could he have achieved what he did without the cleaving stroke of Communist armies in Korea, which made America seek allies anywhere, of any kind. But he knew how to use his opportunities. There was this contradictory quality of open stealth about his leadership of a renascent Germany —as if he knew it was wisest not to rub awareness of Germany's resurgence into its erstwhile enemies' minds.

Adenauer had led Germany out from under military occupation, in September 1949, by agreeing to something called an occupation statute, which converted the military governors into Allied high commissioners. Within three years, he had wriggled loose from the high commissioners, also. One day in May of 1952 in Bonn he signed a mound of papers which celebrated the "Contractual Arrangements"; the next day in Paris, at the Salon de l'Horloge, he signed a fatter mound, outlining the so-called European Defense Community. These papers effectively deprived me of the great Settlement of Peace which I had so long hoped to report. What the Contractual Arrangements were has long since been forgotten; they reduced the Allied high commissioners in Germany to ordinary ambassadors. The story of the European Defense Community, which was never to come about, follows later.

But I recall the scene in the Salon de l'Horloge, with its lovely gilt-and cream décor, the great men all assembled before the fireplace under the clock, the Seine flowing by outside the Quai d'Orsay. Photographers, of course, swarmed over the ceremony to record its importance permanently. But it was sparsely attended. The price of Germany's full and free equality in the Western world had been to sign away command of its proposed new army to the proposed new European Defense Community. Adenauer, the old fox, was perfectly willing to sign this document which would never come to govern or embrace anything—and Germany would have an army to bargain with. When the cameras turned away from him to the dazzling Dean Acheson, to Anthony Eden and the French and other foreign ministers, I watched the old man as he slowly, surreptitiously, turned over one by one the sheets of the treaty he was about to sign. He was peeking like a schoolboy, yet he was smiling, one of Adenauer's rare smiles, smiling to himself. It was the closest any German statesman in a hundred years had come to a lasting peace, and ended the most terrible of all its modern wars.

To see Adenauer in Paris was, of course, an occasion. Adenauer was a man whom I observed on my rounds in Germany. But Paris was where I lived, and I loved France.

Yet Germany always made a good story and France did not. It was so much harder to report France and French politics than Germany—not because nothing was happening but because so much was. In Germany, for years, there was only one story: Would the beast, Kurt Schumacher's *"innerer Schweinhund,"* rise again? In France there were so many stories. But what was happening was going on under the surface, a series of contrary stresses which only now and then cracked open with strain to produce fragmentary news stories.

Central to this strain was our American Presence. And from 1950 on, with the Asian war aflare again, as events urged our diplomacy ever closer to the Germans, the same events embittered and exacerbated our relations with the French, who only two years earlier had been our favorite allies.

One could not blame the editors back home for the way they assigned space to French affairs. Only in France were so many things happening at once, so many waves overlapping, cross-ripping, chopping in the tide that one could not tell where the current was truly moving. At least five massive historic movements cut through Paris at the same time. Simple French recovery, first. But then, also: the final abandonment of any Western hope of a general settlement with the Russians; the search for a settlement with the Germans; the genesis of a European union under French inspiration and leadership; and the slow decay of France's war in Vietnam, coupled with the French effort to get Americans involved in that war.

By the laws of their being, journalists hunt where space on the front page invites them, trying to flush out of the tumbling of affairs an understandable, disposable event which may persuade a competitive editor or TV producer to yield daily space or time. In the early days, the Vietnam story, ultimately the most important to Americans, was smothered in unpronounceable place names and unrecognizable personalities. The story of European union seemed too visionary and hopeful to warrant more attention than the United World Federalists. Thus, then, a reporter was left with the superficial stories of stress, when strains surfaced in the French cabinets and French "governments" rose and then "fell." The "fall" of a French government could be made to sound like Jefferson Davis fleeing Richmond, or Napoleon fleeing Paris as Marshal Blücher closed in. The two words "collapse" and "government," when combined, can make journalism sound like history and push its way onto the front pages. By 1950, I had learned how to do that, was not very proud of the trick, but had learned a great deal about the nature of government in general, of what was flowing in Paris specifically—and of the stress and support we Americans by our very presence were contributing, whether we wished or not, to the rustling passage of French governments.

My experience was illustrative. When I came to France in June 1948, a government "crisis" impended— the fall of the first government of Robert Schuman (later called Schuman I, as in de Gaulle II and Ramadier III). Schuman's successors, the Marie government, would be the tenth government of France since liberation! And before snow fell that year, there would be two more changes of government, one government lasting only a week. After that, I lost count, and by the time I left

France in the fall of 1953, I could almost automatically type the story beginning: "The twenty-second government of France since liberation fell last night as the National Assembly balked at . . ." and then continue as I filled out the routine paragraphs giving the reasons and the Assembly vote count as if I were filling in a multiple-choice question-and-answer test.

I discovered that reporting the fall of a French "government" was a minor art of political journalism— much like covering an American Presidential primary in later days. It was work for journalistic needlepoint men and folklorists; few important correspondents stooped to the drudgery of such detail work as engaged me and which I so thoroughly enjoyed.

One could almost smell a "crisis" brewing in the Palais Bourbon, where the French Assembly met. Journalists and deputies normally mingled and buttonholed each other in the imposing marble-paved lobby of the Salle des Pas Perdus; but forty-eight hours before a government fell, old contacts would become sullen or elusive. Those reporters who specialized in "crises" recognized early that several long nights would be coming, and we usually so informed our wives, for a crisis was the occupational hazard of a Paris journalist's social life; for me, in the beginning, each crisis held out the false hope of a really great story. Only after a great many did I realize their connection to futility.

A "crisis" was usually formally signaled by a National Assembly vote of no confidence. The vote would clack in over the tickers if one was at the office; but if one had sweated it all out at the Palais Bourbon, one could have heard the *huissier* with the shiny chains on his breastplate announce the result of the critical vote that tumbled a government from the rostrum. By the time the vote was announced, the outgoing Prime Minister would already be on his way home to the lovely Left Bank beige-colored mansion of Matignon, the living and working quarters of French Prime Ministers. Journalists in taxis would chase after him. The doomed Prime Minister would closet himself with the loyalists of his just-smitten cabinet, and we would wait in the walled courtyard for the ritual statement: did the fallen Prime Minister intend to rise and fight again, or would he accept fate? Usually, he accepted fate in a few hours; emerged; made his gloomy statement from the fan-tiered steps of the threshold, and took off for the Élysée mansion, across the Seine on the Right Bank. Again we would chase him in taxis. There, at the Élysée, he must hand his resignation, as chief of government, to the President, as chief of state. Then we would all sit on the same kind of fan-tiered stairs, badgering with questions incoming and outgoing candidates for the next premiership, then gossiping among ourselves, as we skipped pebbles across the courtyard while the moon rose, the moon fell, dawn came and the night passed.

Some of those long nights, particularly that first balmy summer and fall of 1948, are among the most professionally pleasant and nostalgia-evoking of my memories; they are part of that indefinably important attendance on large events which reporters call "hanging around." Most of the French correspondents assigned to such lowly duty were veteran political reporters, but they accepted the three or four American/British reporters who joined them on such vigils as comrades. In the morning, their papers and editors would all thunder and denounce each other as well as the fallen government; but the controversies did not affect the reporters, who had become friends on many such long nights. It was a good camaraderie, but since men assigned to such duty lacked polemic or political passion, none ever advanced to the star level of French reporting.

Over the years I learned how futile it was to cover each French cabinet "crisis" in person—as "futile" as I later learned it was to cover every American Presidential primary. But from the "hanging around" at French cabinet crises I learned to distinguish between "state" and "system," as later, in American primaries, I learned to distinguish between "party" and "people."

For example: France was a republic, as in the phrase *"Vive la République!"* To defend that republic millions of Frenchmen had died. But when "republic" was modified by a phrase, as in "the Fourth Republic," which I was reporting, it became simply another form of state with which the French system of republican freedom had been experimenting for two centuries. Underlying freedoms were never in danger all the while I was in France because the Fourth Republic was a state designed to preserve the system Frenchmen loved. But the Fourth Republic could not move this system in any historic direction because that would have hurt or cost some group or another more than it thought it should yield. Thus what all would proclaim as a government "crisis" was simply a falling out of several parties in a cabinet which, temporarily, had squabbled over the share-out the state must give their clients.

A French cabinet was thus a housekeeping group. When it fell out, the governing executive majority temporarily dissolved, and its members changed seats and responsibilities Those of us who watched from the Salle des Pas Perdus, or from the courtyards, cynically regarded all the figures of the Fourth Republic as political comics. The characters who huffed, puffed, trotted, sauntered, stalked, marched, smiled, scowled, at their entries to and exits from the governing mansions in crisis wore always the same familiar faces. But as I watched them come and go, it slowly became clear that all these faces were members of the same company: a Schuman, a Pleven, a Mayer, a Moch, a Bidault, a Pinay, a Queuille, and other such forgotten names, would usually turn up in the next cabinet as either foreign minister, finance minister, defense minister or prime minister. They were a permanently revolving coalition that could govern, but could not move or lead.

I laughed at the processions in the pebbled courtyards—and now regret that they will not come again. For I knew, and took for granted, that these very ordinary Frenchmen would, in any major crisis, close ranks against Communists to the left or Fascists to the right; that they believed in making consumers happy; in raising old-age pensions; in peace in the streets; and in a security force which defended the liberty of all. Though they lied, cheated, wiretapped, they did not stoop to the torment or malediction of other Frenchmen; and finally, they supported the American alliance long after it went out of fashion, which was both loyal and brave but not politically smart.

France flourished under the Fourth Republic; but the exaggerated democracy of its politics was too sensitive to stress. All its crises were variations on the same theme: What burdens must the state now accept—and who will pay for them? When the coalition parties could not agree on an answer, then a cabinet fell; and so the answer became, in practice, to give something to everyone, which translated into another shot of inflation. Anything at all might bring a French cabinet down. In the crab bucket of French problems—the future of Germany or the price of meat, the war in Vietnam or the cost of electricity, the Communist menace or the wages of civil servants—all clawed and pinched and tore at each other. We, as Americans, held the lid on the crab bucket from on top; domestic politics heated the bucket from below. Inside the bucket, French premiers did their best to govern. But the scratchings and clawings did not lend themselves to front-page stories.

There was another way of reporting French politics, which was to try and get to know its leading personalities —by the time-honored device of the "inner few." The press device of the "inner few" was not necessarily more effective than the press practice of "hanging around," for "hanging around" at a public crisis transmitted best the sense of directional paralysis which afflicted the Fourth Republic. But the device of the "inner few" could provoke great statesmen and public figures to try and formulate themselves to the American public. In every capital I have ever worked, from Chungking to London to Washington to Paris, there has always been a select group of American newsmen who presented themselves as surrogates of the entire American people, and demanded that men of state explain themselves—off the record. Press conferences are for the record and for everybody. But the "inner few" device is for trying to draw perspectives which the principals may deny, but which may guide the reporters' writings. The best "inner few" gathering of reporters I can remember was ours in Paris. It had its *New York Times* man, Harold Callender; its CBS man, David Schoenbrun; its Time Incorporated man, Frank White; its *U.S. News & World Report* man, Robert Kleiman; and several lesser personalities, all presided over by the dean of the Paris press corps, Preston Grover of the Associated Press. *Newsweek,* NBC and the Washington *Post* were, in those years, still outsiders.

Through this group, which for five years made a practice of inviting Europe's key statesmen to dinner, filtered much of the politics of Europe as our guests wished them to be reported to the American public. Our first evening guest was Paul Reynaud, the ex-premier of France. Reynaud wanted us to come to a showdown with Russia immediately; *"Pistolets sur la table, messieurs!"* was the message Reynaud felt we must pass to our people to pass to the American government to pass on to the Russians. He appalled us. A much larger guest was Sir Edmund Hall-Patch, whose plea for an Anglo-American union stirred our emotions, as I have said, all the way to the threshold of agreement. But chiefly, our guests were French premiers or foreign ministers, and by their procession through our closed dinners one could gauge what was pushing French governments in what directions, and how large a factor the American presence was in their thinking.

The finest evening for metaphor was early in 1952, when René Pleven, then premier of France, came to dinner in the home of CBS correspondent David Schoenbrun. On this occasion what lay on Pleven's political platter as Prime Minister of France were, first, the price of meat, which was rising, and, second, the proposed treaty of European defense, which required France to merge and marry its troops with a reborn German Army. Either matter could tear the coalition apart once more. Pleven had not only to hold his Assembly majority stable on meat prices (should the farmers be subsidized?) but also to deliver it intact to support this treaty proposal (which ultimately never passed) because it was part of the American grand design and Americans insisted on it. Caught between American pressure and the popular lust for cheap beef, Pleven gave us the metaphor of the chase as the metaphor of leadership in the Fourth Republic. He, the Prime Minister, played the fox. "Ah," said Pleven, assuring us, Americans, that the treaty would pass, "if I let the treaty come to vote now, I would lose. The deputies this week are interested only in the meat price. But they will not catch me. No, they will not! For I am like the fox. They may chase me in the hill, and they may chase me in the brush, but they will never catch me in the open. They will not catch me with a vote on Germany until the meat price goes down, and then I choose the time to vote. Then, after the meat vote, will come the vote on Germany . . . no vote on Germany until after the meat, and I will choose the time to vote. . . ."

Pleven's problems were the kind that crabbed and clustered toward the end of the Fourth Republic. Pleven's was a good stewardship, but the stress was by then growing, and the French state could not sustain the contrary stresses at home and abroad. One of the last of our memorable visitors was the then relatively unknown Pierre Mendès-France, whose political star rose in measure as the war in Vietnam worsened. Mendès-France provided the epitaph for the Fourth Republic in the title of his book *Gouverner, C'est Choisir*—"To Govern Is to Choose." Mendès-France had not yet been premier in any of the governing coalitions when he came to visit with us in 1953, so he was unsoiled by compromise. He meant flatly, and said so without mincing, to abandon Vietnam, even if it meant breaking with the United States. To ourselves he pleaded simply, and I recall his phrase, *"Aidez-nous à décrocher,"* which means "Get us off the hook." To me that sounded preposterous at the time, but a year later Mendès-France *was* premier; he *had* abandoned Vietnam; and at Geneva in 1954 he somehow persuaded John Foster Dulles not only to help France off the hook but to substitute the United States.

But I get ahead of the story. History is always full of the overlapping of events and ideas, and 1950 was a vintage year. If the Korean War seems now the largest event of that year, that is because it was hot war; it brought America back to the mainland of Asia; it saw the first American arms and advisers arrive in Saigon; it reversed American policy in Europe; it urged Japan to revive her industries. Yet it may be that history will record that another, greater departure overlapped war in 1950—the first revival of an old vision, the vision of a United Europe, an idea placed on the agenda of world politics six weeks before the invasion of Korea.

Who conceived that Communist attack in Asia remains a mystery. But there is no mystery at all about who conceived the idea of a Europe united; that was Jean Monnet. Monnet was one of only two major Frenchmen who refused to talk with our "inner few," the other being Charles de Gaulle. Monnet was a personality as large and as seductive of my thinking as had been Chou En-lai. He had been a businessman, like Paul Hoffman, and was now a dreamer. Monnet's dream was in the next two or three years to change the politics of Europe.

I would like to pause at the personality of Jean Monnet not because of the magnitude of the personality, nor because he, ultimately, was the man who provided, in his dream of Europe, the grand settlement for which I was looking—the substitute for the peace treaty—but simply because he introduced me to a craft which I have since come to consider the most important in the world.

This peculiar craft can be called the brokerage of ideas. Monnet was a businessman by origin, cool, calculating, caustic; but he did love ideas, and he could sell ideas to almost anyone except Charles de Gaulle, his great historic rival, and the succession of British Prime Ministers who followed Winston Churchill. Ideas were his private form of sport—threading an idea into the slipstream of politics, then into government, then into history. When he talked of how and where you plant ideas, he talked not like an intellectual but like a good gardener inserting slip cuttings into old stock. He coaxed people in government to think, and enjoyed the coaxing process almost as much as the coopering of the ideas themselves. There were at that time few counterparts to Monnet in other countries; I had to invent the phrase "idea broker" about Monnet in 1950. Later, I used that phrase about certain Americans; I changed it subsequently to "delegate broker"; and then finally to "power broker," a phrase which passed into some general usage.

The Monnet whom I met first in 1948 already had a prodigious reputation as a planner. There were so many Monnet Plans that he sounded like a fraud—or a huge American management consultant company. But he was one man alone. He had devised a Monnet Plan for pooling French and British war purchases in Canada and America as far back as World War I. He had devised a scheme for reorganizing the Rumanian currency in the early twenties. He had devised a scheme for reorganizing all Chinese railways and their financial system in the early thirties. He had managed to break through the Washington bureaucracy just before we entered World War II to sell Franklin Roosevelt on the idea of an effective War Planning Board.

All this was of record, and I expected a perfunctory meeting when in the summer of 1948 I first met this little man, known for his abrupt manners, tart tongue, sharp mind. The French plan for postwar reconstruction was also called the Monnet Plan, and all I sought was a quick interview, which would give me a handful of quotes to feather my reporting. The man who met me at his office at Rue Martignac was a full-chested, round-faced, acid Frenchman with a needle-pointed nose. He had the reputation of either cutting reporters off with one stroke, or else enthralling them with anecdotes and ideas to make a point. I was admitted as an unknown; within ten minutes he suggested we sit by the fireplace in his office; and within another hour he had captured me as completely as had Chou En-lai.

I came to know him much better over the five years that followed. His reminiscences were at once homely and historic: of his old mother, Madame Monnet of Monnet Cognac, bustling around cooking for the entire family until she could no longer walk; of being sent as a youngster to Hudson's Bay in the cold Canadian winter in an ankle-length raccoon coat to sell Monnet cognac to the fur trappers; of his courtship of his beautiful wife, Sylvia, whom he had persuaded to leave her first, Italian, husband and marry him—in Moscow. He could sprinkle any conversation with the stardust of names, from Lloyd George to Clemenceau, from T. V. Soong to Dwight Eisenhower. But he would reminisce only when totally relaxed. Otherwise he was tart and to the point, peremptory and questioning.

I learned much from Monnet's questionings. After each major trip I made out of Paris I would visit him, and he would suck me dry of observations. He had an irritating habit of abruptly presenting a critically important question; you would open your mouth to answer; he would snap, "Don't explain. Just answer yes or no. We both know your reasoning either way. I just want to see how you add things up." He loved maps, and was at his most eloquent talking in front of a map. He was both warm-hearted and cold-blooded. I remember once talking with him about several problems of European unity, and the need of a particular decision. "Right," said Monnet. "*Exacte!* But *dites-moi,* on whose table should I pound to get the decision?" Monnet was convinced that ideas marched into politics only by reaching key people; his job was to find those people and use them, to pass the proper proposals through the proper offices over the proper tables to get the effects he wanted.

The Monnet Plan for postwar French reconstruction was a marvelous demonstration of Monnet's mind at work. His operation was understaffed, with less than fifty people tucked away in a quiet corner of Rue Martignac. As much detail as possible was exported to other French ministries, bureaucracies or industries. Monnet himself hated to read long, detailed explanatory papers. He would have his young men stay up nights absorbing details from papers, then summon them to brief him.

He wanted only the essence of what they accumulated. But the governing idea of the national Plan was his and could be compressed simply: that if a freely elected government makes a simple plan clear, free people can imaginatively adjust to it. Businessmen could plan investments, working people could plan savings, shopkeepers plan inventories and farmers plan their fields. The Russian kind of state planning was an abomination to Monnet —dictated, policed, compelled down to every crevice and crack, even the shoe-repair shop. A democratic plan, Monnet held, set out the large goals—and then freed anyone under its roof to do his own, or his corporation's, or his school's, or his family's future planning, projected against the plan targets set out by the state. By 1949, Monnet's planning was so obviously superior to the thin-lipped planning of British Socialists, to whom planning and regulation was a religion, that even the most dedicated free-enterprisers in Washington recognized that this businessman turned dreamer, turned planner, was the most imposing, though officeless, leader in his country.

Monnet's prestige in French politics was akin to that of George Marshall in American politics. He was not only thought to be virtuous, he *was* virtuous; he was not only thought to be wise, he *was* wise; he belonged to no political party, yet enjoyed the confidence of all except the Communists. Thus only he had the temerity and prestige to present to both American and French governments the plan that would give flesh to an idea which, ultimately, both would have to accept as the substitute for a grand settlement of peace.

The idea was the idea of Europe—an old idea, but this time clothed with a plan. Visionaries had dreamed of a United Europe since Caesar and Charlemagne. Napoleon and Hitler had more recently tried to unite Europe by killing. But Monnet was the man who saw the opportunity in modern times, and found a word for it: community. He had lived through two wars of the French and the Germans, seen them kill off his own friends and companions. Then came the spring of 1950, with Europe still struggling, the French still starved for coking coal, with-

out which steel cannot be made, the Germans rich in
coking coal, short of iron ore, and pinned down by the
rigid controls imposed by the victors on their steel production. It would be good for both Germans and French
if someone could "pool" their joint resources and needs,
and Monnet's idea was simple. The French would propose that the victors release their clamp on Germany's
steel production if Germany freely share its coal resources
with France, that a new Coal and Steel Community be
created in which not only Frenchmen and Germans, but
Italians, Belgians, Netherlanders, Englishmen, would
share resources, facilities and markets. It was the beginning of the Common Market and a grand idea, the greatest French contribution to world peace and progress since
Napoleon fled Waterloo.

Watching Monnet thread his suggestion through the
bureaucrats and foreign ministries of Europe was to take
delight in his political art. The idea was called the
Shuman Plan, because he had first sold it to Robert
Schuman, then French Foreign Minister. Schuman had
had a rendezvous with Secretary of State Acheson in May
of 1950; he was shopping for ideas to present to the
Americans; Monnet packaged the idea of a coal and steel
pool for Schuman as one which would please the Americans—both as an immediate solution for the vexations of
Ruhr control in occupied Germany, and as a long step
down the road to true peace. Schuman, an old bilingual
man of Lorraine, embraced the idea. More importantly,
both U.S. Ambassador Bruce in Paris and Secretary of
State Acheson in London proved enthusiastic about the
idea. The idea, indeed, found full American backing before either the French cabinet or the American cabinet
had been informed that a new Europe was to be born and
this was the route. Each was persuaded by the enthusiasm
of the other; it was a Monnet trick.

Ideas frequently capture control of events and then
outrun them, as American politics were to prove in the
1960s and 1970s. But the first demonstration I witnessed
of an idea outrunning reality came in that critical year of
1950. Monnet's original idea of a Coal and Steel Com-

munity of Western Europe, presented in May 1950, was
thoroughly creative and practical at once. Then came the
Communist attack in Korea. Then came the stretching of
Monnet's concept of an ultimate United Europe to the
creation, overnight, of a European army called into being
and governed by a European Defense Community
(EDC). The idea would not stretch that far; it became an
almost insane scheme to have Frenchmen, Germans, Italians, Walloons, fighting in one army with trilingual command systems, and contraptions of supply and recruiting
which met no idea of common sense. Only on paper did it
make sense; but not to common voters or men who had
fought as soldiers. Everyone knew that the Communists
were a menace to all; but no one quite knew how to bind
the new Europe together. A large idea was needed.

I remember that shortly before the politics of the
EDC began to reach the voting stage in European parliaments, I went out to visit Monnet at his cottage in the
village of Houjarray. I had seen him previously only in
his Paris apartment or his offices. In the cottage, under its
thatched roof, lived a hoot owl, whose sound Monnet
mimicked. The cottage had one large living room, full of
career marks: Steuben crystalware from America, Chinese porcelains, Japanese screens, old leather-bound volumes running from *L'Histoire de la Civilisation Arabe* to
La Sainte Bible. By Monnet's bedside was a book about
Franklin Roosevelt; and on the wall of the bedroom hung
a black-rimmed portrait of Roosevelt.

By the fireplace, as he scratched his kitten, Pool
(named for the coal and steel pool), Monnet spoke of
"us" and "them," and the difficulty of organizing the
West against the East, and the prospects for this new
Defense Community which he was trying to persuade to
reality. Though he was still optimistic, I remember best
his last balancing thought: "The central thing about the
Russians is this mystery. We have let ourselves be hypnotized by this mystery. . . . We should have a central idea
on our side. The old armies can't be made good by
adding on increments of conventional arms . . . they have
to be reorganized and reshuffled totally. . . . People will

only fight for what is inside them and what they believe, and we must give them something to believe."

Monnet could see farther than I could. He knew what was lacking in his own plan for a European Defense Community; and, I believe, grieved little when it was rejected. But I was not yet ready to explore the ideas acting on politics, and so for the next three years I went on writing in conventional terms of the Communist menace, of the new Europe being born that must be defended, and of the American presence, which, at that time, was overpowering.

I had come to Europe believing that a peace was possible. First a historic climax, then a general peace that would shelter a century or half century ahead. I was to leave Europe knowing that no formal peace would come about in our time—but neither would we have war, if we were strong enough and smart enough. We would hover between peace and war all the rest of my time.

It was in 1950 that I was pushed across that divide —and it was the Communists, I know, who pushed me, along with most of the civilized governments of the West.

It is easiest to recapture that general change in political mood by recalling the pinpoint moment when I came to that first recognition.

It came at the moment of the Korean War. There could be no doubt that the Communists had deliberately, clumsily, but with calculation, launched a violent war of conquest. But however stupid their command decision, there should have been somewhere in the world community of Communist opinion a loyal opposition—the counterpart of the intellectual opposition that, while loyal to democracy, questions constantly any action by the world's democracies.

But there was no opposition. I could find none—not even in Paris, where, theoretically, Communists were free to say what they thought, and feared not their state but their party. In exploring the French Communists in 1950 I passed my own divide.

I had come to Europe with a vivid suspicion of the

Russians but a substantial suspicion of the State Department as well. I had seen American diplomacy rebuff the Chinese Communists, and make them into enemies; I had seen, or so I thought, America discard the British simply because we disagreed with British Labour's social priorities. I had no particular respect for the Russians or the Communists—their coup in Czechoslovakia had outraged me, their blockade of Berlin alarmed me—but I had no particular hostility to Communists either, until Korea.

Among European Communist specimens, I found the men and women of the "Partisans of Peace" particularly interesting. The World Peace Movement was a classic mélange of party-liners, fellow travelers, headline names; but it also included some of the most graceful and sparkling French intellectuals, and for them Picasso had designed his famous white Dove of Peace. I enjoyed visiting their world headquarters in Paris, testing them, occasionally squeezing out a story. But just two days after the Communist push into Korea I remember losing my temper for the first and only time in an interview—at their headquarters. I was insisting on a statement from the Peace Movement about the North Korean invasion of South Korea. The conversation heated up. They said this was a different kind of war, the war of the peace forces against the imperialist forces; therefore, it was not war, but peace-making. At which point I remember yelling, pounding with my fist on the table, declaring they were neither fools nor liars but madmen, for they did not believe what they were saying, they did not expect me to believe it, and only madmen would say such things.

Then I walked home, feeling very much better for the catharsis of my tantrum, and I realized that for too long the image and friendships of Yenan had hung over me; that these European Communists were not only different, but repulsively different; and that in the old-fashioned journalistic code of "fairness" I had been unfair in not reporting them as they were. I had done my best to explore the hierarchy of European Communists and their thinking; but what the Communists did showed what they thought; talk was useless. Someone had led the Communists to believe that I was an agent of the CIA. When the Communists accused me of this strange identity, I did not deny the charge; it then became easier to see them—but their conversation was so arid, so unreal, so sterile, so factually misleading, that even had I been a CIA agent (which I was not), I would have found the assignment a bore. At that time they were a branch office of Russian policy as much as the IBM office in Paris was a branch of the policy set in New York.

Moreover, as I began to notice, European Communists differed in style from country to country; and French Communists in particular had a style that made me bristle. They believed in the "tough" style; *dur* was a word of praise. The Chinese Communists, whom I had known so well, had never playacted "tough." They were, when it came to chill killing, as tough as the toughest ever. But their manners could be charming and their conversation most civilized. Italian Communists were also civilized. But French and Iron Curtain Communists were repulsive at almost every level and in all their recognizable sects. There were, in every country I visited, the Communist intellectuals who repaid the valet service of Communist publicity with unqualified party loyalty; then the bureaucrats of the apparatus, draymen, diligent, as persistent and dependent on the *apparat* for a living as a career clerk at Sears, Roebuck; and at the base, working-class people, mostly union men and women, who struggled for a living and believed in the dream of brotherhood and equality that the Communists peddled. The Communists had inherited the dream franchise.

Most of these types I had met, in less developed form, in America at one time or another. But in Europe, where Communism had matured, I met a new type: the Communist as thug. These last bothered me most. I, who had known only Chinese Communists, was appalled by how easily young European Communists could be persuaded to slug for truth.

The quality of thuggery varied at the point where

one met it; unlike street thugs, who cripple out of random psychopathia, Communist thugs are always directed and, thus, coldly reflect policy.

There was, for example, the simple animal thuggery of young Red Army troops whom I saw briefly in 1949 on their weekly visit in Berlin to the monument to the Red Army dead, which lay about a quarter of a mile west of the Brandenburg Gate. On their treaty-permitted visits to lay wreaths on the monument to their fallen comrades, the young Red Army men simply kicked, shoved and slugged people in their way, including American correspondents. There was also the purposeful thuggery of Communist union leaders. For example, when I went out to cover a strike at the Renault works and managed to cajole a few auto workers into having a drink with me, I was suddenly threatened with a beating by union stewards (Communist) unless I got the hell out of there. That was directed thuggery, as in the American Teamsters Union or the old ILA. But there was also senseless thuggery. One afternoon, much later, in 1952, when the cold war was truly hot, I was reporting a Communist demonstration on the Champs Élysées. The Communists had threatened to tie up all Paris as a protest against General Matthew Ridgway's arrival to assume command of NATO. A traffic jam, at rush hour, on the Champs Élysées would be a useful artifice of demonstration, so the Communists did tie up traffic. I watched as several young men ran down the line of stalled cars. Most of the drivers had their windows down. And the young Communist toughs would reach into the open windows and slug or slap the faces of the trapped drivers. But by that time, in 1952, I had become so reflexively anti-Communist that nothing could ever push me back to neutrality.

I regretted what was happening to me, but could not escape it. In Korea, there was no doubt that the Communists had attacked. In Europe, there was no doubt that we were no longer protected by the bomb; since the Russians also had a bomb, we were at the wrong end of a military balance. The direction of my reporting changed. Like so many who had hoped for so much from the Marshall Plan, I had been full of anticipations in 1950—anticipation for what Monnet's European Coal and Steel Community might become, anticipation for what Milton Katz, who had just replaced Harriman as field chief of the Plan, might do; for what sense David Bruce, who had recently become Ambassador to France, might bring to the Vietnam War; and then the hopes were over, killed by a single Communist stroke in June.

So I was off for the next three years, watching the story of the Marshall Plan sliding somehow into another story, called NATO.

NATO—the North Atlantic Treaty Organization— was the military alliance of the same free European civilization the Marshall Plan was trying to make thrive by aid and trade. But the American NATO effort I would henceforth report would be an effort to add standby armies for a war that only this effort could forestall. The great peace settlement would never become the story at the end of the road because it was being worked out wordlessly, bit by bit, by American and Russian soldiers who dug ditches at night and tank traps by day, and strung barbed wire along both sides of the Thuringian ridges. There they faced each other in central Germany, immobile because on neither side surged the suicidal impulse of overt military conquest and push.

I approved of NATO, supported it wholeheartedly, and applauded what we were doing. But being a military or defense correspondent was in no way as exciting as being a war correspondent. A war correspondent reports combat, and practices a form of journalism that most closely resembles sportswriting, full of personalities, dash and heroism. A military correspondent, however, must be a technical expert, able to recognize instantly what tactical changes the enemy may adopt from a glimpse of his new 135-mm gun, able to spot a new type of fighter plane in a ceremonial fly-by. A war correspondent can watch actual tanks moving across the fields through banana groves or hedgerows; a military correspondent must take his story out of flip charts turned too swiftly in the briefing

room for him to absorb. I had been a good war correspondent in China because I was of the right age to move
with troops; but I was now in my mid thirties, when I
could make friends with generals, who are less interesting
as stories. Thus, for the next three years, enjoying Europe
more every year but finding the story more technical, I
followed the story of NATO defense.

The story of NATO's efforts is dramatic only if
drastically shortened. When, in 1948, the Russians threatened Western Europe with the Berlin blockade, only the
atomic bomb held them off and only the American airlift
balanced their ground encirclement. The United States
had, by 1948, dismantled the American armies around the
world. At the time of the Berlin blockade, the United
States Army mustered on the line in Europe just one
division, the First Infantry or the Big Red One; plus other
scattered units of the American constabulary, not remotely of divisional strength, engaged in hunting down Nazis
and imagined German insurrectionaries. Robert Lovett,
later Secretary of Defense, said that all the Russians
needed to march to the English Channel was shoes.

When, in 1949, the United States, as the leader of
the West, called upon the European allies for a first
estimate of what they would need in response to a Russian threat, the various national and regional staffs added
up their fears area by area, region by region, as if the
Russians could hit everywhere in full strength at the same
time, and estimated that the United States must equip and
field a full 406 Allied divisions to offset the Russians in
combat! The real crisis, when it came in 1950, blew such
hysteria away almost overnight and replaced it in Paris
with a planning command headed by Dwight D. Eisenhower that set as target a ninety-six-division Allied force
to be ready in Western Europe and the Mediterranean by
1954; and by spring of 1952, so well had NATO functioned that not even the ninety-six were necessary. By
1952, twenty-one to twenty-three divisions of Allied
troops manned the line of the Thuringian ridges, and
these far outweighed the Russians of the Red Army in

numbers, skills and metals. By then, too, NATO was functional: it had some seventy operational or alternative air bases that could menace the Russians from Norway to Turkey; it had signals, lines of communication and naval coordination; it had backup, timetabled reserves. The story of this superb force of 1952, now totally obsolete, was a story I might have written better, but wrote as well as I could; and from that story I learned much about the relations between civil and military in a democracy.

I learned, for example, that all public military numbers must always be suspect, whether body-count figures or divisional figures. I learned in Europe that to count "divisions," either enemy or friendly, was to count beer cans without knowing whether they were full or empty. If indeed we had, as we did in 1952, twenty-one to twenty-three "divisions" ready to fight on the line in Western Europe, one could not include in that figure, say, the backup French Sixth Division, stationed in Paris; that division was of a quality that could be wiped out in a day, even by the New York National Guard. On the other hand, the British Army of the Rhine was probably the equivalent in impact power to all the other Allies combined, except for the Americans. And then, among the Americans, the Big Red One, commanded by General C. T. Lanham, was listed as a single division but possessed what was probably the firepower of a full corps in World War II. I learned, too, the historic necessity of waste—for the most effective military expenditure a nation can make is to equip a force that is never used. The B-47 strike force, all the planes, the early atomic warheads, the artillery and the tanks of the spectacular force created in the emergency of 1950–1954, are now rusted away or entirely obsolete, a phantom army that never went to war. The billions spent on these arms were, in balance-sheet accounting, entirely wasted; yet in a political sense, never was money better spent. The armies of NATO, purchased by the United States and manned by the United States and its allies, bought Europe the longest-lasting internal peace since the Franco-Prussian War of 1870. The peace these armies bought lasted from 1950 to 1978, twenty-eight years stretching on until today—and may yet continue from one generation to a second.

But the settlement, the Grand Settlement I had been unconsciously seeking, was never to be more than the old military line on the map which the Allies and the Russians had provisionally agreed on in the first weeks of the long truce in 1945. Where the Red Army had come it meant to stay; and the lines to which the U.S. Army had been withdrawn that spring it meant to hold. If there was to be any change in this settlement, it would come not from any initiative here in Europe, not even from that of Jean Monnet, but from what was going on somewhere else. Europe had ceased to control history; it was a "reaction" story and would remain so for thirty years. What the French, British or German governments were to do would be because of what someone else did: Chinese, Russians—above all, Americans.

I do not know precisely when it came to me during 1952, or why, that I would be going home to America—any more than I can say when it came to me in 1949 that I was never going on again to China, where I had longed to be.

There must have been the same mixture of the personal and the professional in the decision to return home as when I had decided that Europe was a more seductive story than China and I would stay there. The professional part of the decision to move homeward must certainly have come from watching the parade of famous Americans pass through Paris and Germany. Here in Europe they bestrode the stage of their assignments like giants, larger than men. Here in Europe they were the American power presence in the flesh; yet always, if one came to know them well, one found them hesitant, uncertain, unsure—not of this outer world, but of that base back home from which their power came. And of the long parade of movers and shakers that began with Harriman, Clay, Hoffman and Bruce, there were two who, pre-eminently, symbolized for me the American of power abroad—and who gradually made me realize that the drama to be worked out in the next twenty years lay on the home side rather than the far side of the Atlantic.

These were Dean Acheson and Dwight D. Eisenhower.

I knew their power descended from politics, just as did that of Europeans. But powerful Europeans, except for Jean Monnet, were part of the political process, involved in it. These two Americans were, however, derivative of politics. The power they exercised was so real as to make all Europe tremble, but they personally were so vulnerable that the power they exercised could be taken from them as easily as it had been given. American politics apparently were different, and somehow these two could stand for what was leading me home to explore American politics professionally.

There was Acheson first.

If any man offered himself as personal silhouette of American supremacy in the postwar world, it was Dean Acheson, Secretary of State. He stood very tall, physically, over the short and stocky European statesmen he dealt with; with his bushy mustache and British guardsman bearing, he looked altogether as a British viceroy of India might have looked preparing for a durbar. But not only did he dominate physically; he dominated intellectually, in eloquence, in humor and in leadership quality. I watched him at his first major testing in 1949, the Pink Palace negotiations in Paris following the Berlin blockade. Acheson conducted the negotiations almost with a swagger, dragging along the timorous French under Robert Schuman, rousing the admiration of Britain's table-thumping Ernest Bevin, frightening with his brinkmanship the then mild-mannered John Foster Dulles of the American delegation—and backing the surly Vishinsky into a no-exit corner by relentless obduracy and mockery.

I remember Acheson best at this first crisis not only for the quality of his triumph—the Russians had yielded on the blockade with no counterpart concession from our side—but for his sense of humor. Most Secretaries of State are more candid and forthcoming overseas than in

Washington, and the morning after his triumph Acheson decided he would brief a small group of American newsmen on what had happened. His purpose, I rather think now, was not to crow over the victory he had just won, as he had every right to do, but to play it down so as not to humiliate the Russians. As we gathered around him in a parlor in the embassy, he told us first the details and then a Sambo story. Acheson was a man as devoid of prejudice as Martin Luther King, Jr., himself, and the story was innocent, but it is the last time I can recall an important man of public affairs telling such a story. We asked him how he would summarize the weekend deal with Vishinsky on lifting the blockade, and he said it reminded him of the story of Sam and the plantation manager. The plantation manager came riding round the day before Christmas and tossed Sam a bottle of whiskey; then came back a few days later and asked Sam how he'd liked that whiskey. To which Sam replied, "Well, jes' about right, boss, jes' about right." What did Sam mean by "jes' about right," asked the boss. To which Sam said, "Well, boss, I figure if that whiskey was any better you wouldn't have given it to me; and if it was any worse it would have killed me." That described his deal with the Russians, said Acheson—any deal with the Russians. You couldn't get any better from them, and any worse terms would have killed us, either in Europe or in Congress.

At the height of his prestige and power abroad, Acheson had no counterpart. He was like the sun god or a Benjamin Franklin with thunderbolts. He came through for a moment of celebration at the end of May 1952 to witness and seal the treaties that were supposed to bind Germany and France in one army, the capstone of the "grand design" some outsiders attributed to American policy. Few foreign ministers have the right to summon any other nation's cabinet to a hearing. But Acheson one morning that week entertained what was, in effect, an executive committee of the French cabinet, and asked Anthony Eden, the British Foreign Secretary, to come along to be instructed also. And then that day came to lunch with our group of correspondents in his finest storytelling mood, and presented us with a vignette of the American diplomat among allies.

It was a sunny day, lunch was at my house, Acheson sat at the head of the table, the sun streaming in behind. "Well," he began, "first they played the theme on the oboe, then they played it on the fife; then they let the strings pick it up and then they did it all in harmony." What theme? With great amusement, Acheson explained. The French had just accepted the Germans as co-equals in the army of the European Defense Community about to be formed: all of us had seen the treaty signed at the Salon de l'Horloge. But now, the treaty had to be ratified. And this morning the French cabinet had explained its problem to Acheson: the French Assembly would not accept the Germans as partners in Europe unless the American government accepted partnership with France in the Vietnam War. It was a classic case of French logic which adds up to befuddlement, and Acheson described the ministers of France, at their table, one by one, as they made their case. "It was as if they were telling a story to a child," he said, "each one adding a new line. The Prime Minister starts by saying, 'The pig came down the road to the stile,' and the next one adds, 'Then the goose came down the road to the stile,' and the third one adds, 'After the pig came down the road, then the goose came down the road, and after the goose came the farmer's son. . . .' " Whatever the specific tale Americans heard abroad in those days, it always ended with the same message: America must help. America must exercise its moral authority—and moral authority meant America must send arms, or send money, or both.

Acheson had given his hearing to the French cabinet that day, as if a proconsul were granting audience. Their logic had a certain merit which the future was to bear out—that if they lost Vietnam, they must almost certainly lose North Africa thereafter, and the effect within the Empire would be contagious. Acheson had pressed the French on why they could not reform their empire, which they called the "French Union." He told us he had

brought up the case of Tunisia, the most Francophile of
the French colonies in North Africa. Could they not make
reforms there in good time and soon? asked Acheson.
Otherwise they would someday face the same revolt as in
Vietnam. Then, said Acheson to us, "Do you know what
they said?" The French had answered they would if they
could, but their problem was they had already thrown the
friendliest Tunisians, the ones they *could* negotiate with,
in jail. And how could you negotiate with people in
jail?

Acheson shrugged his shoulders, in that eloquent
gesture of his. But no matter what the pressure from
France, he continued, we were not going to make common cause with the French in Indo-China. He had repeated to the French that we were already paying one
third the cost of their war. That we sympathized with
them. But American public opinion simply would not
stand for our joining the colonial war in Vietnam. Acheson did not argue either the strategy or the morality of
France's war in Vietnam. He was insistent only on the
central point: American public opinion would not tolerate
a spread of the Korean War to Indo-China. Suddenly, I
recognized that public opinion had become sovereign to
this man, who had outbraved it so often.

This response of Acheson to American public opinion was strange to me. Here was this elegant spokesman
of American power in Paris, visibly afraid of what the
senators from Nebraska or Wisconsin might say. Acheson
was vulnerable in a way that no European could understand. He had grown more bitter about Congress in each
of his visits, and ever more passionate on the subject of
Joe McCarthy, and how McCarthy might wreck his carefully thought-out policies. At the end, he would talk in
terms of "I" and "them." If he spoke of "I and them," we
knew he was talking of Acheson versus Congress. If he
used "we and them," we knew he was talking about
America versus the Communists. This contrast between
his certain power abroad and his uncertainty about his
Washington base intrigued me. His power base was Harry
Truman's confidence; Truman had won his power from

the American voters; so long as Acheson held Truman's confidence he was a great man; if Truman lost power, Acheson lost all leverage on affairs. Thus it was the American voter who was the true power source.

Dwight D. Eisenhower was even more important in leading my thoughts homeward.

Eisenhower had neither the elegance nor the sophistication of Acheson, but he, too, had learned, by 1952, where the source of power was. In America, the source of power ran to the people, and whatever persuaded them to believe and vote. Eisenhower had wielded power in its military form in the war, but had been bewildered and bothered by both Roosevelt and Churchill because they wielded a superior form of power. Eisenhower had found administration of the Pentagon after the war a bore; had found being president of Columbia University also a bore; had done a first-rate job as Commander in Chief of NATO, but was now, in early 1952, beginning to be bored there, too. At that point in his life, as a world hero, there was no place higher to which any man could appoint him; only the people could vote him up from where he was to the Presidency, which he now coveted. Watching Eisenhower stalk the Presidency taught me the first lesson in watching candidates, in trying to separate the public from the private man.

I had made the mistake so many observers did of considering Ike a simple man, a good straightforward soldier. Yet Ike's mind was not flaccid; and gradually, reporting him as he performed, I found that his mind was tough, his manner deceptive; that the rosy public smile could give way, in private, to furious outbursts of temper; that the tangled, rambling rhetoric of his off-the-cuff remarks could, when he wished, be disciplined by his own pencil into clean, hard prose.

Ike's simplicity was there, all right, but it was an imperative, a decisive simplicity. His job was to see that the ungirt and unarmed NATO powers of 1949 met specific military targets and commitments by 1952. He jotted down the targets in a little hip-pocket notebook:

so-and-so many divisions with component units due from the Dutch, the Belgians, the Italians, the French, the British, the Pentagon, on such-and-such a timetable of dates. On inspection in alliance countries he would pull out his little notebook, compare performance to promise, and treat prime ministers, foreign ministers and defense ministers of the lesser countries as if they were corps commanders in his wartime coalition. Foreign leaders who had read only of the benign victor were astounded; but they fell into line so smartly one could almost hear their heels click. They trusted Eisenhower as a general and some, personally, came to have affection for him. They were all politicians, and their collective fear, when he arrived in late 1950, had been that he would give the NATO job a whirl, organize the headquarters, leave the field force half-finished, then spin out of it for a Presidential fling. By 1952, they had changed their minds: the defenses were organized, or at least so well under way that the same prime ministers were individually urging him to drop the NATO command and run for President of his country, a job they felt his countrymen would surely, joyfully, yield him.

It was obvious to all of us reporters that Eisenhower's run for the Presidency was as much the story we had to cover as the defense of Europe. From the fall of 1951, we had begun to report the parade through Paris of movers and shakers trying to see Eisenhower. Such people are now in Presidential language called "campaign strategists." There was our old friend Paul Hoffman returning for a visit in 1952, telling us about the campaign he was putting together; there were Thomas E. Dewey and Herbert Brownell, purse-lipped; there was Harold Stassen, open to the press as always, hoping the headlines of his visit would amplify his importance. There was Henry Cabot Lodge, so sure of his own Massachusetts Senate seat (which he was to lose to John F. Kennedy that year) that he felt he could spend full time on the Eisenhower campaign. All were lavish with statements, predictions, prognoses. But none could come away with a flat-out quotable commitment from Dwight D. Eisenhower that his hat was in the ring.

Time wore on into the primary season, into his surprise New Hampshire victory, but Eisenhower's position was still obscure. Editors clamored for the story of our Paris candidate. He troubled us. Those of us who, as military correspondents, were accredited to his headquarters at Marly-le-Roi outside Paris were sternly instructed that anyone who brought up politics, or Eisenhower's candidacy, in the general's presence would be forthwith escorted out of the general's presence. Bang. Finally, under the joint persuasion of the most honored of the Paris press corps, Preston Grover of the AP and our friend General C. T. Lanham, Ike yielded. He could not, he said, discuss politics in a U.S. Army headquarters; but he would accept the invitation of our group for a private, off-the-record, all-secret lunch on politics at Grover's home.

He came to our lunch of eight people two days after the March 18 Minnesota primary of 1952; and he was an Eisenhower none of us had ever known in the field, in his office or on maneuvers. He was pink-cheeked as always, but bubbling, expansive, joyful. The Minnesota primary, just over, had been contested by both Senator Robert Taft of Ohio and Stassen, Minnesota's favorite son. And Eisenhower, not listed on the ballot, on a *write-in vote,* had come in second to Stassen with 37.2 percent of the total to Stassen's 44.4 percent on the regular ballot! (Ike's one-time chief, Douglas MacArthur, it should be noted, won only one half of one percent of the vote that day.) Following Eisenhower's New Hampshire victory a week earlier, it was a phenomenal showing, an earthquake. There could no longer be any dodging the reality that Ike was the leading Republican candidate for President of the United States.

His good mood that day was too irrepressible to quench. He had Politicians' Euphoria, a condition I later came to recognize on election-night victories—that moment of vulnerability when candidates are at their loosest and most expansive. Ike held a drink in his hand, and teetered back and forth on his heels, and I found myself in a corner encouraging his indiscretion. Von Krupp had just been freed from Allied imprisonment; and since that was the headline of the day, two of us launched him on that subject. This set him off in the raconteurial manner which was his best conversational mode. There was nothing we could do about Krupp now in 1952, said Ike; we had to let Krupp go free; but he didn't like it. If he had to do it over again, he would do it differently. Shoot all the war criminals you're going to shoot right away, then let the rest go free, said Ike. Like the Malmédy massacre of American GI's by Nazi storm troopers. He felt we should have caught, convicted and shot the S.S. killers immediately after victory; all shooting after a war should be done within six months. He did not like the Nuremberg trials, either. But the trials had been Roosevelt's idea. And thus he went from the conquest of Germany to Roosevelt, with anecdote after anecdote about Roosevelt. And as he talked about Roosevelt we edged him closer and closer to what he thought a President should be, while his own admiration for and exasperation with Roosevelt came through. He picked out Roosevelt's vast geographical knowledge as his most extraordinary quality, and then, with irritation, spoke of the difficulty of pinning Roosevelt down to specifics, the stubbornness of Roosevelt, his own inability to get clear instruction from him. When we had Eisenhower going on Roosevelt and the Presidency, with many a marvelous reminiscence, we sat down to lunch and Grover said flatly that since we were forbidden to talk politics at Ike's military headquarters, we were here to talk politics in his, Grover's, home. So—how about it?

At which Eisenhower took over, as if on cue.

Yes, he was glad to talk to us; as friends; off the record; he needed advice; he didn't know what to do; we must be his counsel.

What he wanted most, he said, was to keep the United States Army from being sucked into politics. It's bad for Americans to think of military figures in a political way; and now here he was, a general and a political figure. He made a rather impassioned speech about the vital separation of military from civilian in American life. But there it was. He'd made the mistake, on January 7, of stating he would never run for the Presidency unless there was a "clear-cut call to political duty" from the American people, and he shouldn't have used that phrase "clear-cut call." What was a clear call? he asked rhetorically. Was the New Hampshire primary a clear call? Was the Minnesota write-in a clear call? Minnesota, said Ike, was "fantastic."

He'd never sought the nomination, not once. Even in 1948, he went on, when the Democratic "bigwigs" told him he could have their nomination on a platter if he wanted it, he'd said no. And all he'd done since was listen. Then, when the Dewey-Duff people had come to him, he'd made no commitment to them, either. All he'd done was to promise them "not to pull the rug out from under them" if they did go to work for his nomination. He couldn't repudiate them now, could he? So now he *was* a candidate in uniform, looking for the honorable thing to do.

He grasped his Eisenhower jacket by the lapels and tugged it. "I can't, I won't drag this uniform through politics. It's been all my life," he said. We must help him; what should he do?

We all knew what he was going to do; but now we had been conscripted as advisers to tell him how to do it. This was turning out to be, as we all recognized, the first press conference of the Eisenhower campaign—yet it was not. He had made us a council of his friends, trusted military correspondents who were on his side. Few sophisticated political reporters today would let themselves be so trapped in confidence and thus barred from breaking a great story; but Eisenhower had more candidate skill than any amateur on a first run I have ever known.

It was a jovial lunch as we fell to at table. Grover, a bachelor, rarely gave his gifted cook an opportunity to prepare the kind of hearty Burgundian meals in which she specialized, so now for the great General Eisenhower she had outdone herself. The wine went round and round, the

pasties of ham curls stuffed with goose liver were piled
up. I tried to keep notes, not knowing these would be the
notes of my first exposure to a Presidential campaign,
then gave up, and tried to pin the afternoon in memory.

My notes reflect all the contradictions of impression
of anyone who met Eisenhower only occasionally: the
mixture of simplicity and astuteness, the beguilement he
could cast over any conversation he wanted; the boy-
scout sincerity; the shrewdness of manipulation; his understanding of the twisting corridors of government.

If he was going to run, he said—and by now it was
so obvious he would that we were all practically marching
into the White House with him—he must resign soon for
his conscience's sake. Thus, when should he cast off this
uniform? He couldn't lay down the NATO command
overnight. He had to give Bob Lovett (the Secretary of
Defense) at least six weeks to find another man for the
command. And he wanted to be home by May 15, if he
was going to run his own campaign. But resign to whom?
Truman had always been "decent and honest" with him.
He could not challenge President Truman except openly.
We found ourselves all agreeing with Ike's final thought:
to write the resignation letter to Truman in a sealed
envelope, but to send the envelope to Lovett for delivery,
with Lovett being told what was in the envelope. And
then leave it to both of them to decide how to announce
that General of the Army Dwight D. Eisenhower was
leaving the United States Army to campaign for the
Presidency.

There were other variations and subtleties of campaigning which we, all amateurs, discussed—matters
which today would be left to the professionals of politics.
Where should he make his first speech on homecoming:
at West Point? or back in Abilene, Kansas? or at Columbia University? And much more of tactics.

What I find most authentic today in the notes I
typed after that lunch was the spontaneous sound of the
Republican voice twenty-five years ago. Ike could have
had the 1952 nomination, I now know, on the ticket of

either party. But as he passed in conversation from the tactics of his resignation and nomination, I find my notes picking up his theme—a theme which then sounded fresh to me, but now, on the larynxes of Republican orators, sounds as old-fashioned as a lament from the Prophets. Ike was closing the lunch with his credo. After every lunch with a Presidential candidate, there comes the moment when the man clears his throat and very sincerely leans forward to tell you what it all really means. It is the moment of confessional. Usually, they *are* sincere, if not candid, and Ike was certainly sincere.

"The people have the right to know what I stand for," Ike began, and then went on thus: He didn't think any man should run for the Presidency without telling clearly where he stood. That didn't mean he wanted to talk about subsection C of the Taft-Hartley Act. He hadn't studied that. But his ideas were clear: this business of centralism in government. There was too much of the bureaucracy, too much looking to Washington. He wanted to get the federal government organized so it did not wipe out the states and the municipalities and the communities. He didn't want to have people looking to Washington for everything. He told us about the number of local governments that came to him (when he was President of Columbia) looking for federal aid to education. Ike told us that they attacked the problem wrongly. The problem was that the federal government was "taking so much money from everyone it left no resources for local government to run its educational apparatus. That was the problem. . . ."

This was the Eisenhower who, of course, years later decided, as he had to, that federal troops must be flown into Little Rock, Arkansas, to force that community to comply with the decision of the Supreme Court. This was the man who set up the Department of Health, Education and Welfare and *did* begin the modern chapter of federal aid to education. But the incantation against the central government went on, and on, and on, to be voiced later by every Republican candidate and President for the quarter century since.

Eisenhower closed the meal with an anecdote. Somebody brought up "luck," which caused him to explain why he had quit playing poker years ago: because he was getting too good at it, he said. It happened when he and "Georgie" Patton were both brigade commanders at an Army post back in the States. After one long session of poker-playing, he (Ike) and two other "poker sharks" discovered they had cleaned a young officer, named McElroy, out of all his savings. So they plotted to get together and in one night lose back to McElroy all they had won.

"It was the hardest damn thing," said Ike to us. But after they had successfully lost the money back to McElroy, Ike went to Patton, McElroy's brigade commander, and told him that McElroy didn't know the first thing about poker and had to be commanded never to play again. Which Patton did. At this point, Ike, who had held us laughing at the story as he told it in full detail, continued: "And do you know what McElroy said to me when we got him out of the game? 'Damn it, Patton ordered me to stop playing poker—just when my luck had started to change.' " Eisenhower waited a minute and then added, without any obvious connection: "He had two of the finest boys you ever saw. Made wonderful officers in the war. Still are wonderful officers."

Thereupon, as Ike rose, we all rose. We knew we had a candidate. Somehow, without meaning to, we had all become bound to confidence so we could not break the story from Paris of his resignation—and knew our Washington counterparts would break it instead. But we did not care.

I certainly cannot say that from the moment Ike rose and left us at Grover's home, I knew I was on the way back to America to pursue Presidents on the trail of power. But the lunch was a turning point. My stay in Europe was over, because the story was over; and Ike was leaving because he, too, knew the story was over. There would be any number of other divisions inserted in that fifty-odd divisional line of battle planned to ring Russia around; the accords of Lisbon, in February 1952, had blessed and made real all Eisenhower's plans for NATO. The decisions left to take were administrative, not policy, decisions. I would henceforth be covering an adventure that would never become a front-page story unless it was overtaken by the disaster of war. And so, sometime in early 1952, faced with this fading story, I began to face my own decisions.

I loved the life of Europe, and more particularly that of an American expatriate—but there was so little left to write about. Moreover, personal considerations were beginning to press. Money, for one thing, was running out; in four spendthrift years we had eaten up all the savings of *Thunder Out of China*. The two children were beginning to burble their baby words in French; they should be brought home to grow up as Americans. I also, like Acheson, sensed I was losing my base. Though I was as ferociously anti-Communist as our Secretary of State, I was being nipped at for my past reporting of China. Even my old friends at *Time* magazine referred to me in their columns as "pinko" Teddy White, which could be shrugged off; but the harassment of others was closing both my movements and my outlets. I was on the downhill side of the roller-coaster, not strapped in place, protected by no job. I had given myself these years in Europe not out of any idealistic purpose or passion but purely out of self-indulgence—because I liked following the big stories. Now the story clearly led back to the United States and Washington. It was time to plan homecoming. But that meant coming home on the punctuation of another book, on some impression of upbeat. For I did not like myself in my mirror. By 1952, I had become a professional free-lancer, and that was making me into the kind of reporter I did not want to be.

For the enlightenment of would-be writers and young reporters, I must strip the glamour from the term "free lance," as I came to know it in my last three years in Europe.

I had not chosen to become a "free lance." I was pushed into it in 1950 when the Overseas News Agency

began slowly, then ever faster, to sink. When they owed
me some $3,500 in back salary in 1950, and were falling
ever further behind, I pushed off as a "free lance" to
market my own writings; and discovered how very accurate the term is. A free lance in the waning Middle Ages
was a knight without an overlord; free lances were var-
iously horesmen, cavaliers, pikestaff men, who would rent
their lances and services to any master per battle or per
campaign; and then go their way without loyalty, without
home, seeking another fee. So it was in Europe when I
joined the still crowded company of free-lance journalists
—the star names left over from the war, the agile youngsters fresh from the States, all of them typing madly away
around the clock, peddling by mail or by agent their latest
effusion and waiting for the postman to bring back the
airmail letter which might, or might not, carry the check.

I fitted my time on any assignment, as they all did,
to the size of the check promised or estimated. I wrote of
Paris fashion openings, the underground market in gold, a
flying garage, the politics of the Isère, the best restaurants
of Paris, the plight of six million excess German women,
the falling Irish birth rate. In one year, while working on
my book, I managed to write in off hours some twenty-two
articles—and loathed all of them except those I wrote for
two men, Lester Markel and Max Ascoli. There I was
lucky. The imperious Markel, editor of the Sunday *New
York Times,* was exceeded in outrageous personal behavior only by Max Ascoli, editor of *The Reporter* magazine.
But both were men of impeccable courage. I had become
an outcast of American journalism early in the McCarthy
years. But neither Markel of the *Times* nor Ascoli of *The
Reporter* cared a pinch of powder for McCarthy's threats,
and continued to publish me on politics.

One does not grow rich, or even live comfortably,
writing politics as a free-lance reporter. It is a way of life
for writers of passion or narrow specialties, but not for a
man trying to connect political stories romantically to
history. For any major, complicated or delicate assignment a major magazine or newspaper relies on its own
staff men. The free lances they hire scavenge the leavings;

and Markel considered himself generous when he paid $250 for a month's work which made the first page of *The New York Times Magazine*. Of the work I did for Markel and Ascoli I was proud; of all the other work I felt like a rug merchant, proud not so much of the product as at having closed the sale.

So long as the stories of the Marshall Plan and the organization of NATO were being enacted, I could involve myself in my work. But as they faded my eye became more clinical, stripping an event or a phenomenon not for its meaning but for what was salable in free-lance commercial journalism, as television producers today strip any situation for its entertainment visuals.

One day my dear friend Theo Bennahum came upstairs to point out to me that I had become nothing more than a merchant of words. Theo was very fond of my children; he stood my three-year-old daughter Heyden in the middle of our round coffee table and made a speech which completely baffled the child. Waving his hands with great eloquence, Theo explained the difference between peddling stories, as I was doing, and peddling oil concessions, as he was. Oil concessions brought more money— much more money. Theo, though a Zionist, spoke fluent Arabic and was dealing with both Libyan and Algerian operators for American oil companies that later made much money in North Africa. Theo went on: I owed it to this child (here he hugged Heyden, a favorite of his) to drop this nonsense of journalism. I was now a family man. He would make me a partner in his growing enterprise, and we would get rich together. Theo loved writers, actors, sculptors, musicians, and collected them all. But journalism? Ach! He shrugged his shoulders. He had met so many brilliant men who claimed once to have been journalists themselves—but the more brilliant they were, the quicker they had left journalism. I must drop it.

But I could not leave journalism, even with Theo's kingly hand beckoning me to share the riches of African oil. I could not, I suppose, have left journalism at any time after I first followed a story in China, for what could money buy more exciting than a journalist can see?

Moreover, particularly at that time I could not leave, for ten years of my reporting and life were under attack. I could sense in my free-lancing that I was being silently extruded from print. The same thing was happening too often: editors back in New York would send me the encouraging instant response that a good editor usually gives a writer on first leafing through good raw copy. But then, a few weeks later, followed incomprehensible letters saying I had been "spaced out." And I recognized that, other than Markel and Ascoli, editors found me too "controversial" to print—except on gourmet food and Roman ruins.

The problems seemed always to be attached to my China past. Old China friends in the State Department were constantly in trouble; several required affidavits of their loyalty; new friends in the Army and the State Department in Europe warned that it was dangerous, or folly, to "stick your neck out"; but I persisted until, finally, I found myself involved in the case of Robert M. White, at long remove and by mail.

Robert White was my youngest brother, a scientist. I had loved him almost as a son when he was the young brother of our poverty, and later came to admire him with almost parental pride as the creator and director of the National Oceanic and Atmospheric Agency, which has framed America's policy in the waters and winds that wrap us round. At this time, however, he was a junior technical researcher, a specialist in the esoteric mathematical and computorial limits of long-range weather forecasting, working at the MIT labs on some project so sensitive that he has never yet told me of it. Then, in 1952, he wired me frantically that he was being removed, his clearance lifted, because he was the brother of the well-known subversive Theodore H. White! His message reached me in Germany; in Germany, I held NATO press card No. 6, which meant clearance, re-clearance, and over-again clearance by every security agency of the U.S. Army. My brother, however, worked on a U.S. Air Force project. His following letter revealed a rather stunned, Kafkaesque panic. Could the Air Force fire, for brotherhood, a man whose brother the Army had cleared? More than kinship binds my brother to me: respect and affection are the larger part of our friendship. He respected my work; did not want to involve me in his troubles; but I felt indignant that kinship with me should destroy a scientist so useful to the nation. I managed to pull the episode out of disaster only by a personal appeal to David Bruce, by then Under Secretary of State in Washington, who, with the help of Clayton Fritchie, another old friend in the Pentagon, managed to persuade authority that Dr. Robert M. White, scientist, was no subversive; and in no way tainted by kinship with his brother, Theodore H. White, co-author of *Thunder Out of China,* who happened also to be a trusted acquaintance of Bruce, Acheson, Eisenhower, et al.

If 1952 was disturbed by my alarm that my brother should be threatened by his blood tie to me, the next year, 1953, was further disturbed by two men named Cohn and Schine, fuglemen of Senator Joseph McCarthy. They had moved through Europe examining the books on the shelves of the USIA, and found in the Berlin library copies of *Thunder Out of China.* These had promptly been purged and burned, and the purge was duly reported in *The New York Times.* It was bad enough to be purged and burned, but to be publicly reported as subversive and burnable was even worse. I was on the public list for discard.

It was quite obvious, thus, that I would have difficulty going home again; that there would be no job waiting for me. I might, if I chose, join Theo in his business ventures; I might, if I wanted, become an expatriate, a permanent free lance; or join the growing colony of movie writers in Paris and London. But the only real option was to stake all on one more book, which would explain the American experience in Europe as *Thunder Out of China* had explained it in China. This was the option Nancy favored.

Of the faults of my first wife, Nancy, perhaps the greatest was her strange yet happy belief that with enough yellow paper, enough typewriter ribbons and enough cod-

dling, any man can write a successful book. My first two
books had been reviewed on front pages from coast to
coast; both had made substantial sums of money; it
seemed elementary to her that as soon as she could have
me seated once more before the typewriter to write another, all would be well. Moreover, since we were growing
poorer by the week, we must set aside enough money for
our passage home, yet leave enough to finish up our stay
in Europe in style. And so, carrying two servants with us
to cook and care for the children, we made our way to Le
Lavandou, on the Riviera, in 1952 and again in 1953.
Those were the last two years that the Côte d'Azur still
had any connection with the legend of the twenties, before
it was overwhelmed by the prosperity which, in the years
since, has made it as hideous as a sixty-mile-long Atlantic
City.

I dream again and again that I will come to Les
Mandariniers once more. Perhaps because we were so
happy there, the unraveling of our marriage began at Les
Mandariniers. It is not good to be too happy, and for
Nancy all the years thereafter until we separated were an
effort to reach back to the cloudless life of the Riviera,
when all we feared was the blacklist; and we laughed at
it; when our blood was young; and when Les Mandariniers was the hostelry where Americans as young as we, all
of them *doing* things, visited or overnighted—the then
unknown Julia Child, who liked to cook; and Jane Eakin,
who liked to paint; Irving London, who did research in
blood; Sasha Schneider, who organized music festivals;
Blair Clark, who was making his way with CBS; Mike
Bessie, who was to become my publisher.

Les Mandariniers was an old villa of whitewashed
walls, orange-tiled roof, parlors, dining rooms, seven bedrooms. Nine acres of vineyard and orchard ran down to
the edge of the Mediterranean, where the sun rose to our
left and set to our right. Below grew the lemon and
orange trees that were so fragrant and gave the villa its
name, and roses and mimosa, planted between the trees.
The villa belonged to a family of French diplomats in

Brazil, who had not seen it in years; we found it fusty and neglected since the war, but once the grand doors were opened and the rooms aired out, it was as if we lived on a balcony overlooking our private sea. This balcony, as well as the mansion itself, was overgrown with grapevines, which bore marvelous white and purple grapes, and was trimmed for beauty's sake with bougainvillea and oleander.

We could sit there with our guests, night after night as the sun set, and see the purple smudge of the Isle du Levant offshore. The Isle du Levant was inhabited by sun-worshippers, primitive postwar French nudists, who made the naked body seem startlingly pure as they pranced about. We, and our guests, were twenty years short of the liberation that came to American manners, so we were too shy to strip and prance with them. Nor did we recognize the threat that these innocent nudists would ultimately bring—which was to attract the perverts of all Europe to the area, particularly Germans, so that Le Lavandou became known for Riviera pornography and, with St. Tropez, twelve miles east, became a center of sexual experimentation.

In our day Le Lavandou was exactly as the old Baedeker volumes described it: a fishing village named for its famous lavender flowers. In those days it produced only fish and packets of dried lavender to be shipped all over the world. At night, in spring and summer, the odor of wild lavender came drifting down the escarpment above us, and we sat on the terrace and talked about what came to mind. The Saracens had held the islands on the rim of the horizon for generations after they had lost the mainland of the Riviera; the flora and fauna of the islands were distinctly North African, while where we sat was distinctly Roman-Europe. So we could talk a great deal about history; not only were there primitive ruins to look at, but authentic classical ruins, as well as the German blockhouses that had tried to stop the American Seventh Army from landing in 1944. After talking about history, we would wander off down to the port, where we would usually eat a bouillabaisse, before Lavandou's bouillabaisse became a tourist attraction. Bouillabaisse was then, in Lavandou, a fish stew made of trash fish, leftovers of the day's catch that the fishermen could not sell. And if we ate *bifteck,* we took for granted that it was horse meat.

Here, then, for all the long summer of 1952, after Eisenhower left, and for all the spring and summer of 1953, I worked on the book that would bring us home. Nancy was happy as a Riviera hostess; the children were happy because the caretaker of the grounds let them wander in and out of his chicken runs. I would rise at seven in the morning, and begin to write about Europe and its renascence. David, then two years old, would crawl upstairs from his bedroom and sit under the desk as I typed. He liked the sound of the typewriter, and I enjoyed his gurgling company. Then Heyden would romp in and together they would racket away until I called for help. The nurse would come to carry them off for breakfast and the beach, and I would go on writing until I went down to swim myself. It was a four-hour working day, from seven to eleven, and it is the way I wish all books could be written.

Politics were far away so that, in the book, I could look back on my experiences of the five years in Europe with some perspective. Only once did politics intrude, when in 1953, as I have said, Messrs. Cohn and Schine purged me from the USIA library in Berlin. This act was picked up by a local newspaper, which thereupon described me as another victim of resurgent American fascism. Madame LaTurque, the dark and handsome postmistress of Le Lavandou, came out from behind her *guichet* the day after that news and informed me that I was safe there in Le Lavandou; not only did she resent this fascist action of the American government, but all the villagers considered themselves friends of mine and the children. It was a touching moment; I thanked her, and explained that I felt in no danger of persecution but that, nonetheless, I would consider Le Lavandou my home and refuge forever. Which I did, as long as Le Lavandou remained Le Lavandou.

The episode of Europe in my life came to an end

with two events appropriately sequenced, the first historical, the second personal.

The historical ending came on June 17, 1953—when the workers rose in East Berlin, and Russian tanks mowed them down with machine gun fire. I had no sympathy with any Germans, but enough was left of my earliest political emotions to make me see as more than irony the killing of Karl Marx's German working class by Karl Marx's self-anointed Russian apostles. My book was then in galleys, and I listened to bad French radio trying to understand what was happening in Berlin. Momentarily, I thought of canceling book publication. In June 1953, it seemed that it might be there, at Berlin, that the final game might yet be played on the road to the Settlement. I had watched us build our strength in NATO for just this clash. Would Eisenhower use it? I waited, wondering for days whether my book of peaceful triumph and American vision was obsolete. But then I realized that Eisenhower preferred peace to victory; and that I would still have no coda, no last chapter of settlement or surrender, if I postponed publication—and so I let it go to print.

To print the book went. And the personal end of the European years came on July 20, 1953, a month after the Berlin uprising, when I had let the book out of my hands forever. We were sitting on our terrace in the early moonlight above the Mediterranean, and I was complaining to Nancy that beautiful as all this was, when we left we would leave as bankrupts. Then the telephone rang; the telephone had only recently been installed by the local Post and Telephone Administration as a grace to a writer who was being persecuted by American fascists. It rang with good news, for it was my then publisher, Thayer Hobson, calling from New York. The judges of the Book-of-the-Month Club meet there monthly for lunch, and when they rise with their decision, the president of that enterprise calls the lucky publisher to tell him. In those days, they generally broke at two-thirty in the afternoon, which meant at seven-thirty in the glowing twilight of the Riviera. Hobson had simple news: the judges had taken the new book, *Fire in the Ashes,* as their October choice.

I danced away from the telephone to tell Nancy the news, and she responded, "Well, at least it means we're living within our income again." So we were no longer bankrupt, and we could look on the Riviera, as the night stretched out from the hills to blacken the blue of the sea, and feel that life would always be generous or at least lucky.

There are pleasures in writing books which are difficult to describe. Among such pleasures is learning that a success pleases one's friends. At a victory at any election in America, at an award of any kind in Hollywood, the winners enjoy the delight shared by their friends even more than the imagined discomfiture of their enemies. I sent at least a dozen letters and telegrams to friends all around the world announcing the good news. We prepared for return to America with pride, as if we were the Scott Fitzgeralds coming home again.

But I was returning to the United States of the 1950s, a wondrous decade, when both what went right and what went wrong in our time began. And I was now, I hoped, upholstered with enough money to venture again into what could not be foreseen.

PART FOUR

AMERICA
1954-1963

THE HOMECOMER

He strode down the gangplank of the *Ile de France* to the old passenger pier on the Hudson River feeling, as always when he made a formal entry, like an impostor.

He was preceded by his wife and two stumbling children, followed by an authentic French nursemaid; at the end of the gangplank several friends were waving that bright morning's edition of *The New York Times*. The *Times* had chosen to review *Fire in the Ashes* a day before its publication, so that this morning, October 28, 1953, as he stepped ashore, there was a startlingly complimentary review by Orville Prescott. Another friend held up a copy of the *Saturday Review;* White's portrait was on that week's cover of the magazine. His diminutive agent, N. S. Bienstock, pulled clippings of advance reviews out of his briefcase and they were, without exception, more than satisfying in the manner the author later came to call "solid second-book reviews." Second-book praise is the very best kind, for at a writer's second book, reviewers decide that either the

473

first was a flash phenomenon, or the second book has "fulfilled" his "early promise." Thereafter the writer becomes an "author," and in due time, if he writes more, he becomes fair game for denunciation, indignation and exposure by the same critics. But all that lay far in the future—and the author stopped right there at the pier to read the reviews and share them with his wife, while his friends struggled baggage and furniture through customs.

Then, swollen with happiness, he drove off with wife, children and nursemaid to the hotel chosen for him. New York would be his home for twenty years and the bench marks scratched in memory began with the taxi trip from pier to hotel. He had wanted a hotel in a pleasant neighborhood, near enough to Central Park for the nursemaid to walk the children, and respectable enough to invite friends. Yet not too expensive. His agent, Bienstock, had guided him to the Van Dorn Hotel, one block from Central Park South, quiet, safe and pleasant. The homecoming suite consisted of two bedrooms, a large living room and a kitchenette; downstairs was a pleasant lobby where the children could romp. All this for fourteen dollars a day! The price lodged in his memory as fair, and bequeathed him a sense of outrage about hotel rates which rose as prices rose with American inflation for the next twenty-five years.

New York in the early fifties was a time and place to be pinned in memory and the first few weeks and months of his return were engraved there. He had seen New York first from a student's room at the YMCA at seventy-five cents a night; had seen it next as a vagabond foreign correspondent in 1941; had seen it as a man on the town in the early postwar years. But now he was seeing it at the beginning of a golden age, on the threshold of its great decade. Prices not only seemed reasonable to him; they became later almost legendary in recapture. That summer and fall of 1953, the peak rate of "inflation" was 2.1 percent—and in the next year prices would actually *drop* 1.4 percent, a phenomenon not to be repeated again in the next quarter century or, perhaps, ever. The city itself was also worth marking. That year, 1953, New York City was estimated to be at the midcentury plateau of its population: eight million people. It had taken three centuries to reach that size and thereafter, year by year, New York would shrink. That year, too, he would learn that one person was murdered almost every day in New York. In later years, the murder toll would rise to more than four persons killed a day, but he would accept the growing danger fatalistically. New York was then still predominantly a white city. Irish, Jews and Italians shared the political controls while leaving to traditional Protestants the financial, executive and cultural leadership of headquarters city; blacks and Hispanics together were only one sixth of the city's population. And the city was exuberant with vitality and good will.

Underneath the glow he could sense that many changes had taken place while he was in Europe. And three changes, outcroppings of history to come, soon intruded into personal life.

Television came first.

When he had left New York in 1948 he had never yet visited a private home with a television set.

Not only that; his early experience with television had so misled him as to disqualify him forever from any claim to prophecy. Once in 1946 he had agreed as a lark to go on a television show called *Town Hall of the Air;* and had to journey all the way to Schenectady, New York, where General Electric had an experimental TV studio. There, under the glare of lights hot enough to heat a furnace, he wilted so completely in a debate on China as to be incoherent. TV would not work, he was sure. In 1947, he had been a member of a study panel chosen by the Authors League to explore the enticing thought that writers might, someday, make money out of television. After a few months of this inquiry, he had decided that TV was one of the great mirages technology held out to innocents. Concluding that no writer, ever, anywhere, in our time, would make or earn a dollar by writing for the flickering tube, he had left that panel just before going to Europe—where nothing he heard from travelers from America could dissuade him from his conviction that television was a trick, an illuminated yo-yo that would fade away like a passing novelty.

Now he was back in New York, six years later. And like a Rip van Winkle, unaware of the television revolution, he went to visit his old friend Ed Murrow. Edward R. Murrow is a figure in American journalistic history as large as Horace Greeley, Walter Lippmann, Henry Luce or DeWitt Wallace, and we shall come to Murrow's significance later. But Murrow was then housed in a tiny award-cluttered office at 485 Madison Avenue. A single floor—the seventeenth—then held the entire News and Public Affairs Division of the Columbia Broadcasting System, an enterprise which now, with the swelling of television, sprawls over acres of space in half a dozen cities.

Murrow and White were both chain smokers, and puffing away furiously that afternoon, Murrow explained to White what television was doing to the network, to the country and to him. Then Murrow announced that he, Ed, had launched a new show called *Person-to-Person* only a month earlier. Would Teddy like to be exposed with his new book, *Fire in the Ashes,* on *Person-to-Person?* Tallulah Bankhead; the actress, was scheduled for the top half of the show; Teddy and his wife, Nancy, would be the bottom half; and Murrow would try to televise experimentally from the new apartment into which the Whites were moving. If White had had his druthers, he would have asked Murrow to expose him and the new book on the Murrow radio show; radio, he thought, was supreme, TV ephemeral. White wished to be gracious. If old Ed wanted help to kick this TV show off, White would agree—anything to please an old friend. Years later, when other books of his came and went, when he had learned what television was about, White would have begged for an Ed Murrow's attention. But then, not recognizing the dimension of

Murrow's kindness to him, he felt it was he doing the favor to Murrow, not vice versa.

White imagined that Murrow would come to his apartment with a sound man, a cameraman and, perhaps, a producer, as in radio days. The night of the telecast, however, two huge vans pulled up beneath his apartment windows; electricians strung cables up and down the exterior walls, while grapevines of wire trailed through the rooms of the still disarranged new apartment. Fifteen people and a producer rearranged White's packing cases and furniture to suit their script of a homecoming correspondent. Murrow did not come—he was downtown in some remote studio—but White could see on the monitor that it was as if White, Murrow and Nancy were all touch-close in the same room. The portrait of this person-to-person reunion of old friends, with all its illusion of intimacy, passed flawlessly.

Except there was no intimacy; this was a show that reached into eight million homes! White had come home in the fall of 1953, having left in 1948. When he left, some agency somewhere in Washington had just frozen television at the threshold of its expansion. By 1952, television could be frozen no longer; the ban had to be lifted; and hundreds of new stations were being installed, the lucky franchise-holders about to reap millions in profits from licenses that only rich gamblers could afford to seek. Television was bursting into the nation's imagination—commercially, artistically, technically. The print-and-word tradition of press and radio was being thrust aside for the visual immediacy that television could command. *See It Now* had been the title of the first Murrow experiment in television, but CBS owned the title to that show. *Person-to-Person* was the next Murrow experiment in television, as both artist and entrepreneur. It was one of the first efforts of a television performer to acquire a property right in what his own imagination has created.

Of all this White was unaware when television happened to him at the new apartment overlooking Central Park West. And then, within days, he recognized television's force. White received more mail from the fifteen minutes with Murrow than all the mail he had so far received on the book itself. People recognized him on the street, even years later. Old friends telephoned; cranks called in; so did salesmen; the mail was stuffed with brochures from world-savers. The power of this device, television, to move a novelty was so clearly continental that the writer felt the TV thrust behind his book as if a rocket had ignited under his saddle. He had barely made the bottom of *The New York Times* best-seller list the week before the Murrow show; the week after that show, the book began a swift, steady climb to the number four position. The week after that, the writer bought his own television set—one of the more than ten thousand Americans who *every single day during the mid fifties* were buying their first television sets, as the revolution surged through American manners and politics. And in a few years, his children were singing *"M-i-c-k-e-y M-o-u-s-e"* along with their entire generation, and he was buying them the mouse ears of the "Mouseketeers."

But television was not the only new, unsettling change to force itself on personal attention. Simultaneously, he became aware of Blacks, called "Negroes" then.

The blacks were at least as important—or more. He had known no "blacks" when he was a boy in Boston, but if he used the word "nigger," it brought an instant scolding from his mother. He had first encountered blacks in the U.S. Army in Asia, and was angry, as any decent person had to be, at the way they were segregated in labor battalions. There had been blacks in postwar New York, too, but they had lived safely tucked away up in Harlem, where, as a lark, young white people visited their nightclubs. But now, suddenly, in 1953, blacks were no longer invisible. It was not just that Earl Brown, an old friend of White's from the days when both were *Life* magazine writers, was on the City Council, the first black to be elected there. It was the visible phenomenon: blacks were everywhere. They had not yet made it behind the counter in central Manhattan, but they were shopping in Macy's, Gimbel's, even Bloomingdale's. Blacks were entering offices. Blacks were becoming reporters. Everywhere blacks were moving in.

It was as he himself "was moving in" that White first rubbed against the problem. White had returned from Europe proud of America's record there, and equally proud of what he had heard about the forward lurch of civil rights at home; he smiled, with a missionary's approving smile, at the neat white-collared blacks he was seeing for the first time in Manhattan— but he was at the same time pressed to find an apartment. The Whites were amateurs at apartment-hunting in Manhattan and immediately, on inquiry to their friends, ran into the snob divide: East Side, West Side. There were a dozen legitimate reasons, they were told, from prevailing winds to subway services, that made the East Side the better choice. But there was always, also, a hint, an unfinished reason: "Well, you know . . ." When pressed, liberals (and the Whites knew only liberals in those days) would say, "Well, you know . . . the neighborhood is changing," or "Well, you know . . . the West Side is O.K. if you live near Columbia," or ". . . if you know the block."

To "know the block," he soon learned, meant simply to know whether whites one by one were trickling away and blacks, one by one, trickling in. But the white and black countermigrations were not yet the overburdening problem of all American cities when he came to choose, as befitted a man of the world without prejudice, an apartment on Central Park West, overlooking the park. The apartment was large: three bedrooms, two maid's rooms, dining room, living room, study, modern kitchen, welcoming foyer—all for three hundred dollars a month. But his friends shook their heads: Wrong block. A recent survey had declared that the two cross streets Eighty-fourth and Eighty-fifth were the most dangerous that fed to the view on Central Park West

They were called "neighborhoods in transition." Obviously that meant that blacks and Puerto Ricans were moving in—and his apartment was at the corner of Eighty-fourth and Central Park West. The rumor did not seem important; the headshaking of friends seemed moved by prejudice rather than by judgment. The Whites believed in integration, would have felt like traitors to join "white flight," if the term had been coined then, and wanted to live on the West Side. So they moved in.

They lived there for a year, and before they left, had learned much about city street life. The new home was indeed in an area of transition. Neither the city nor any other authority knew then how to cope with the social rub and decay which can spread like an infection from two bad blocks to an entire neighborhood. White's rent was cheap because his block was infected. But because they were so early menaced, and opened on Central Park, and Central Park was too grand a city glory to be given up lightly, the city, in due time, mobilized with millions of dollars and special projects to save the Upper West Side from the blight that eventually ravaged Harlem and made desolate the South Bronx. By then, of course, the homecomers had moved away.

White watched with great interest what was happening on his two blocks, not knowing he was seeing the beginning of America's urban problem of the seventies and eighties. From his window, there was the vista of Central Park, the most splendid of all central-city parks anywhere in the world, and the most necessary green space to a city's survival. But down in the street, the microcosm of life he observed frightened him. One day he watched a black adolescent speeding on a bicycle on the sidewalk—not the street. The adolescent swerved away from a tottering old white woman, missed his swerve and tumbled her to the ground. The young black sped on. White helped the old lady up, knew he should not be race-blinded by one episode, tried to forget, could not. He watched, another afternoon, as three young black boys chased a white teen-ager down the block, throwing stones at him. White realized he was a coward when he moved to intervene, and found three black men on the stoop of a brownstone frowning at him for trying to rescue the white boy, who escaped. Other such incidents followed. It began to grow on him that the black-and-white problem in an area of transition always grated first with the rub of the youngsters, and unless a community had the help of both black and white parents, one had best get out of the way. He could not send his children to school here. The thought festered as he discovered that for the first time in all his life—in Irish Boston, in warlord China, in darkling Germany—he was afraid to walk the street outside his own house at night; that his wife felt unsafe going to the delicatessen on Columbus Avenue by daylight; that his children were not safe going to play in Central Park just below the window of his apartment house.

The problem was one of compression—two kinds of culture contesting in the pressure of closed city apartment blocks. It took White no more than six months from homecoming to pass through his particular adjustment to the confrontation. First, the blindness to the problem; then the bravado-disdain of the reality; then discomfort, and finally fear. Then, feeling like a deserter on a combat front, he decided to seek a house on the other side of the park, on the safe white East Side, the pleasant brownstone-and-apartment hive of the Establishment, where he had so many safe friends.

And it was here, from the safe East Side, that he began to see the dimensions of the third great change that had happened in his absence: Prosperity.

America in the 1950s was about to erupt in a well-being utterly without precedent in history. Figures often mislead, but one figure still staggers the imagination with the energy of the fifties. In those ten years, 1950–1960, the United States added one third as much more housing for common people as it had standing in 1950 from the exertions of all its previous three centuries.

Drunk on cheap gasoline, lured by new roads, urged by the butcher to upgrade from hamburger to steak, teased to new appetites by television, America was experiencing the Great Boom. And nowhere was the Great Boom more bountiful than in New York City.

It is not simply afterglow that makes New York in the fifties seem so exciting. The city was then truly rich: the wealthy were rich, the working people were rich, the municipality was rich. The city sprouted cubes of glass and stone as a meadow its flowers after rain. The wreckers' sheds surrounded a block one day, the dust and debris cascaded down next month, ironworkers shot steel cages into the sky the following month— and in one year in the 1950s 6.37 million square feet of office space (in twenty buildings) was being built in New York, probably more than in all the other big cities of the country combined. New York was, truly, headquarters city; the multinationals were reaching out and over the ocean to the continent the Marshall Plan had saved, and Manhattan was the place for them to be. Here, they and the great domestic corporations could find experts on Iranian oil and Arabian water resources, on German toilet and lavatory habits, French food and perfume specialists; financial wizards of high and low degree; and if Manhattan did not have the expertise, it could, almost overnight, import it.

Nor was New York's wealth and vitality visible only in the parlors, the offices and the changing skyline the homecomer observed. Beneath the skyscrapers and at midheight, all around the shores of the island and in the neighborhoods of its boroughs, the benign administration of New York's Mayor Wagner was building schools, hospitals and public housing as if the money had no end, and the tax rolls were ever-bearing bushes of money berries. There had long been a broader cultural underbase in New York City than in any other city of the Western world; London, in some years, might have better theater; Paris, better painting; Vienna, at one time, might have offered better music. But New York in the fifties reached an art level that it has never since, even in peril, let drop: whether in music, or in painting, or in architecture, or in dance, or in theater, New York was beginning to offer either the finest or the equivalent of the finest in the civilized world. And there remained, as there always would remain, the great museums—the Metropolitan, the Natural History, the Modern Art—as well as the opera, and the ballet, and that special flavor of sharp thought from the great universities. If New York was moving on the road to bankruptcy, it was doing so with reckless generosity, flogged on its course by fakirs, fantastics and philanthropists, public and private, of unrestrained and unbelievable good will.

In any given year of the 1950s, more creative imagination was probably on display in New York than anywhere else in the world. In the single year 1956, for example, when *My Fair Lady* premiered on March 15, one could also see the first performance of O'Neill's *Long Day's Journey into Night* and Chayevsky's *Middle of the Night;* or see the continuing performances of *Cat on a Hot Tin Roof, A View from the Bridge, Damn Yankees* or the Lunts performing in Lindsay and Crouse's *The Great Sebastians.* Money fertilized fantasy; fantasy nourished art. One could also see Cole Porter's *Silk Stockings;* or the 1956 Pulitzer winner *The Diary of Anne Frank;* or the Academy Award-winning *Around the World in 80 Days;* or hear Maria Callas's American debut at the Metropolitan Opera in Bellini's *Norma;* or watch the Met's new production of *The Magic Flute.* New York, at the dazzle of its splendor, was a simpler place than today. If, in 1956, the Yankees played the Dodgers for the World Series, Bronx against Brooklyn, all New York's papers took the spectacle for granted. No one guessed that it was the last New York City "subway series."

Nineteen fifty-six was still several years in the future when the Whites arrived back from Paris in 1953, but the excitement was building, and they could not stand apart from it. Both "Old New York" and "New New York" beckon to their homes people who "do

things," or people who "get things done." For such
celebrities New York has special graces; and though,
in New York, authors rank in celebrity well below the
reigning Broadway toast, to be a bestseller is an honorable ticket to the first row in the balcony. One is invited
out if one is a bestseller. And so the Whites were invited, and peered about them, wide-eyed; and once
they had moved from the West Side to the safe East
Side and established themselves in an East Sixties
brownstone, they were, momentarily, part of the excitement, and had their pick of it. On the East Side of Manhattan, in those days, in what White later came to call
the "perfumed stockade," lived the rain-makers and
the climate-makers. There was a banking world; and
New York's bankers, or at least the Federal Reserve
group in New York, were as influential in London as in
Washington; there were the advertising people, who
sold Jell-O, Fords and TV sets across the country; these
mingled with an independent Wall Street cluster; a
literary and publishing cluster; the world of the Bench
and the Bar; and a Hollywood-Broadway entertainment
cluster. In the early 1950s, for the first time since
Roosevelt, local politicians were beginning to meet such
social leaders. But leaders of the harsh underlying
worlds that provide outlet for New York's muscle were
still excluded: on the East Side, one met no one of New
York's great shipping industry; few leaders of its gar-
ment industry; or its construction industry; or its electronic industries. Nor, in fashionable New York gatherings, did one ever meet either a labor leader or a black
leader.

In the worlds of Manhattan outside the "perfumed
stockade," social life was masculine; wives invited the
people their husbands told them to invite. New York
politics, for example, were then entirely masculine, without a single great hostess, although women of brilliance
like Clare Boothe Luce or Anna Rosenberg could become power brokers in their own right. The more glamorous creative East Side life was, however, patrolled
by women, by great hostesses whose parlors made sta-

tions on the way up for young men who could leapfrog years of office drudgery by meeting the proper people at such parties in the evening. One either had to work very hard at the office, or be possessed of a talent that burst through restraint, or be lucky in meeting the right people.

In Upper East Side New York, no family pedigree was required for admission to the Round Table of Celebrities—money, or achievement, or passing notoriety would do. If one had such money, or solid achievement, or this year's publicity, the Court invited one in to its best parties, its best dinners, its best weekends. It was easy to be swirled up into this celebrity world. Except that it is very hard work to stay there and spin with the swirl. White found that a night out at a top-seeded New York party left him hung over and emotionally exhausted. Whereas a night out on the road following a story with other reporters had always left him fresh for the next day's work.

After a few months, White needed to be back at work, on some story or other. By January 1954, it was a craving: he needed to know what was happening from inside; not from the newspapers, but from his own reporting. He had closed his book *Fire in the Ashes* with the lines: "Which is why, now, for the first time in fifteen years the story of America's security lies chiefly at home. And why this correspondent, after fifteen years of following that story abroad, is coming home." He was looking for a way to track the story.

It was early in 1954, after months of New York's "celebrity" life, that White began to track the story once more. And 1954 was the very best year to pick up on the story of home, because later it was clear that 1954, not 1950, was the beginning of the decade.

Americans like to think of history in terms of decades—the "twenties," the "thirties," the "sixties." Europeans think of history in longer terms—the "Victorian Age" in England, "La Belle Epoque" in France, the "Weimar Republic" in Germany. American history is usually triggered by Presidential elections, calendar dates which remain important only if the new President uses his leadership to change the direction of events. But the strange, fluid decade of the fifties did not begin until halfway through Eisenhower's first administration —in 1954, to be precise. And ended only in November 1963, with the assassination of John F. Kennedy. That decade incubated not only the problems, but the abundance, the vitality, the passion that exploded in the tormented sixties. And into this decade, as one of its would-be chroniclers, White inserted himself in early 1954, looking, as always, for stories.

Consider that year as the opening of an era: the next twenty years of American history were to fall clearly away from several sharply defined peaks; but the two most spectacular peaks thrust up within seven weeks of each other in spring of 1954. On May 7, far away in Vietnam, the elite strike force of French general Christian de Castries, surrounded at Dienbienphu after eight weeks of siege, was forced to surrender by the Vietminh. On June 29, at a conference in Geneva, the French gave up, dumping the protection of a "South Vietnam" on a willing John Foster Dulles. John Foster Dulles's decision at Geneva would, even twenty years later, be causing the death of young Americans. But within that same month, on June 17, the Supreme Court of the United States outlawed segregation by race in all American public schools. By its decision in Brown versus the Board of Education of Topeka, it set a domestic revolution under way. The Supreme Court decision would change the color and character of American cities, alter the nature of American society, free millions of black people, but hammer into categories other millions of Americans previously unaware of their differences. Youngsters still sucking their thumbs in the summer of 1954, and dangling their knobby knees from the family couch as they watched Howdy Doody, would grow up to fight, to riot, to march, some to protest, some to die, because of these two watershed spring events.

But 1954, as the beginning year of a decade, had many immediate events which concealed the deeper drama that would later flow from Dienbienphu and *Brown* v. *Board of Education.* The sharpest political threat to the American system, as the year opened, seemed to come from within. Senator Joseph McCarthy of Wisconsin was unleashing the hounds of hate on the trail of his drunken whimsy. By midsummer, the Senate had passed and offered to the House a Communist Control Bill, outlawing membership in the Communist Party as an *ipso facto* crime. Yet by fall, McCarthy had passed his power point; the Senate was debating his censure; by December McCarthy *had* been censured. If there was drama in McCarthy—and, indeed, there was—it was as much historic as personal: he destroyed the respectability of hard-rock conservatives in the opinion of thinking Americans. Decent conservatives helped destroy McCarthy; then waited thirteen years for a new conservative leader, Richard Nixon, who, again, betrayed them. The political year 1954 closed finally on an event far beyond the measure of Joe McCarthy or Richard Nixon—the Congressional elections of 1954. That was the last year in our time that Republicans would enjoy control of both houses of the U.S. Congress. Deprived thus of control for the next twenty or more years, unable to propose and enact legislation, the Republican Party that year became a state of mind. For control of this state of mind, disorganized resistants warred with each other for the next twenty years to possess themselves of the heritage that had once made their party a vehicle of history and change.

Other events great and small were to make 1954 a lucky year of re-entry to America for a returning foreign correspondent. Dr. Jonas Salk had begun to inoculate schoolchildren in Pittsburgh with his antipolio serum; it worked. A runaway hydrogen bomb had been tested by Americans at Bikini island; it also worked, but no one yet knew its full reach. Hemingway won his Nobel Prize. Catton won a Pulitzer Prize for *Stillness at Appomattox.*

These events did not interest the returning reporter, who was political; he wanted to report how the United States was deciding on where and how it should go.

Who decides what is the central problem of history. To explore this central problem in America, White had enlisted on the staff of a magazine called, simply, *The Reporter.*

The Reporter reflected the personality of one man, and one man alone. That was Dr. Max Ascoli, political scientist.

White had met Ascoli before leaving for Europe, as long before as 1948; had written several articles for Ascoli as a free-lancer; then had been named Chief European Correspondent for *The Reporter* in 1951. Now Ascoli offered White the title of National Political Correspondent; it seemed the best way to explore the story in America, for Ascoli's view of America was both refreshing and inviting.

Ascoli was a strange man. It was not easy to like him, but impossible not to respect him. He had been a heroic anti-Fascist in Italy; a professor of law at the University of Genoa; had fled; arrived destitute in New York; taught at the New School; met his wife there as a student; enthralled her with both mind and personality, and married her. She happened to be Marion Rosenwald, an heiress to the Sears, Roebuck fortune; and so, when the war was over, she financed for him a magazine all his own.

The Reporter was a "liberal" magazine; but it was a "liberal" magazine with vigor, coldness and cut that stemmed directly from its editor-publisher-proprietor. For over a century most great "liberal" magazines have been subsidized by conscience-smitten heirs to great fortunes. *The Nation,* the oldest of them, was sustained for half a century by the Villard (railroad) fortune before passing on briefly to nurse from the Kirstein (department store) fortune, and then the Storrow (New England banking) fortune. The *New Republic* was endowed originally by the Straight (banking) fortune, then enjoyed a succession of benefactors, as have most other "liberal" journals, permanent or passing. Protected by great wealth, editors of such magazines are "free" to print the truth. They have educated two generations to dissent and, with their growing influence on campus, have educated the men and women who now edit the mainstream magazines. So much so, that it is almost a truism to say that what the "liberal" magazines publish now will be republished ten or fifteen years later as conventional doctrine by the mainstream magazines. But conscious of their own virtue, many such liberal publishers of such magazines are frequently abusive of their staff, pinchpenny in pay, intolerant of political deviation. The more firm and pronounced their liberal dogmas, the harsher and coarser can be their personal manners.

Even in this tradition of "liberal" publishers, Ascoli was excessive. In depth of learning and sheer brilliance of mind he was unmatched—as he was also in vileness of temper and exaggeration of ego. There was a histrionic brutality to Ascoli's manners; if he did not like a writer's work, he might scream with rage and throw the pages of copy into the air like a child kicking leaves into the wind. If he did like a writer's copy, his compliments were as niggardly as his envy and appreciation were apparent. *The Reporter* was his private principality; and in his court he behaved as the greater Medici behaved in Florence.

All Ascoli's shortcomings were more than balanced by his primitive virtues. He had courage, he had curiosity, he could be generous. The magazine reflected these qualities; Ascoli directed and edited an important magazine. His reporters first exposed the China Lobby of Chiang K'ai-shek, and their exposures wrecked it. He commissioned the first major investigative reporting of wiretapping; and he was among the first and most fearless antagonists of Senator Joseph McCarthy. Of all his qualities, however, the most attractive was Ascoli's mind: here was the academic political scientist, now a Maecenas and publisher, interested, as editor of a magazine, in the same questions that had interested him in his study. Ascoli's magazine eventually, in its nineteen years of life, from 1949 to 1968, became the favorite political reading of the nascent new governing class—those elites of scholarship, science and expertise who were becoming indispensable to American government. Ascoli's magazine reached a peak circulation of 178,000 subscribers, and for White, who later wrote for the *Reader's Digest* also (circulation: 18,000,000), the contrast in impact of the two magazines was most vivid in Washington. Call a man elected to Washington by the voters and tell him you write for the *Reader's Digest*—and he sits up, for the *Reader's Digest* means mass votes. No Washington politican responded to a call from *The Reporter* that way. But call a Washington bureaucrat at middle-level policy administration—and *The Reporter*'s call would be returned first. *The Reporter* spoke to men and women interested in making government work.

It was both the audience and the mind of Ascoli that drew White to *The Reporter* as its national political correspondent. The attraction recalled Luce's attraction; and the contrast of Ascoli and Luce in journalism was stimulating. Luce believed that men made history; thus had come about the institution of *Time*'s cover portrait. Luce's reporters were trained in pursuit of the anecdote, the quote, the personality. Ascoli, the scholar-tyrant of his magazine, held, however, that history was a study of changing institutions, and that institutions, rather than personalities, were the turntables of change. Whether the story was about New York City or the United Nations, Ascoli, the political scientist, insisted that the institution was the story. New York City, he felt, was obsolete, either too small or too large to govern five boroughs; a new metropolitan regional government was needed for the conurbation at the mouth of the Hudson. The United Nations, Ascoli held, was an institution that did not understand its own function: Was it a Great Power conclave? Or an aid-and-assistance dispensary for backward nations? Until it decided which it was, thought Ascoli, it held no future. Ascoli personally loved gossip as much as Luce, and would listen with dripping appetite at the backstairs rumors his reporters brought back. Behind his thick-lensed glasses, his eyes would gleam; his glottal stop and strange accent would bubble as he enjoyed the inner chronicles of the great. But as editor and in print, Ascoli was a man who sought meanings, large meanings, and always preferred the institutional to the personal in his pages.

Ascoli's academic curiosities coincided with White's weakness for political anthropology—how people in power behave, both before and after power. So they came together then, early in 1954, for a series of explorations of America in that changing year.

It was an exciting and rewarding year to start on what would become twenty-five years of reporting American politics. And the reporting started not with the politicians but with the institutions, each teaching a new lesson. A first handful of the new assignments gives, somehow, the range of the learning process.

• The very first, for example, was the U.S. Senate versus the U.S. Army—and the discovery of how frightened was the United States Army of the United States Senate, while the outside world White had just left was so frightened of that Army. Joseph McCarthy was bullying the civilian Secretary of the Army, and through him the khaki-clad institution led by its Chief of Staff, Ridgway. Matthew Ridgway was a first-class soldier, as adept at dropping a division by parachute from the air or lining up the corps artillery on the ridge as any field commander of his time. But Ridgway was a mute man, who knew no politics and despised what little he saw of them. Ridgway thus sat behind his desk at the Pentagon and glowered, not at White, the interrogator, but at Eisenhower, his hero, now President, who refused to defend the institution against the Senator. Ridgway called in a mutual friend, General "Tony" Biddle, a loquacious and intelligent diplomat-soldier, who, with Ridgway nodding, put out for White their opinion of Eisenhower. "What's he waiting for?" asked Biddle rhetorically. "There he [Ike] sits with his Commander in Chief's hat and it's raining outside. And he says, 'I won't wear my Commander in Chief's hat today; it'll get wet.' He's waiting for a sunny day so he can put the hat on and lead the parade. But you don't get that hat just to lead parades on sunny days." To which Ridgway added: "We're like men with our hands tied behind our back. McCarthy's only choice is whether to kick us in the groin or kick us in the face." Later the Army, institutionally, would try to buy up politicians; in those days it feared them.

• White's next exploration was in Texas. It was an exploration of how money gets into politics, and why Texas oilmen then seemed so much larger than life. It was the first reach White made at American politics as a process and he spiraled down into the way Texans combine, caucus and conspire to elect mayors, assemblymen, congressmen and senators. Texas politics were flavorsome with personalities the way Boston Irish politics always were, and were practiced, as in Boston, as an indoor sport. It was in Texas that White learned for the first time what he would learn again and again in California, Illinois, Wisconsin, New York, Michigan, Massachusetts: that each state of the Union has at least two parties, Democratic and Republican; but that each of these two parties has at least two and sometimes three or four rival factions; that to be an expert on grass-roots politics one must therefore try to understand the rivalries and personalities of two hundred or more factions in one hundred state parties of fifty sovereign states, which is impossible. White discovered that institutionally there simply was no national Democratic Party at that time; it did not then exist. All political parties were then built from the grass roots up by interlayers of favors and appointments, from the fixing of a traffic ticket, or a library fine, or zoning regulations, or the placement of school Stop signs, up to access to court decisions and the multimillion-dollar contracts. State parties, like the Texas Democratic Party, were bound to other state parties only in quadrennial grabs at the jugular—the Presidency, the greatest of all sources of favors and punishments.

Texas politics were unique only in the naked behavior of the state's Big Money: the two great oil companies, Humble and Magnolia, controlled the Texas state legislature as Southern Pacific had once controlled the California legislature. And the independent oil operators the truly Big Rich, much bolder than the big oil companies, were beginning an outreach into national politics so blatant, overt and ill-concealed that it backfired on them. In 1952, Texas oilmen had poured money into Congressional races in thirty states outside of Texas. Nothing in the leaky electoral laws of the day could stop them from trying to buy up congressmen by the dozen; one oilman, Hugh Roy Cullen, had bought his way into thirty-four campaigns! Though their money was unlimited, their understanding of out-of-state politics was not; and the outcry at what they did, or were trying to do, was the opening sound of a twenty-year battle to reform the electoral laws of the nation, which resulted, finally, for better or worse, in the emergence of a truly national Democratic Party.

• Certainly the most important, although the most baffling, of the long institutional explorations of that year was the exploration that White and Ascoli had agreed must be done on the American Scientific Establishment. J. Robert Oppenheimer was under closed-door trial before a loyalty and security committee. Both White and Ascoli, without ever having met Oppenheimer, admired him, and they agreed that White should investigate, then throw *The Reporter*'s considerable weight of influence behind the great physicist.

That story led on to uncharted frontiers and thickets. American science was the world's most creative; its creators and explorers had become favorites of the United States government and, above all, of the armed services. The hungry young doctoral candidates and youthful researchers White had known at college had vanished. A physicist now belonged to a new elite, pampered and funded by government. But they paid a price in freedom: investigators questioned their friends, brothers, sisters, rivals, about the loyalties, sobriety, sex habits, of the particular genius the government needed but could either spurn as untrustworthy or support and make rich and famous. The long investigation of the Oppenheimer case taught White some of the rudiments of the instrumentation of national defense, and even more about the politics of science. It taught another truth: each world of American endeavor, like each state, has within it a politics of its own. He encountered, in the purging of Oppenheimer, the politics of nuclear physics. He would eventually encounter the inner politics of coastal zone management; steel pricing; arts and humanities; health and hospitals; television networks; and at least another dozen constellations of purpose. Whenever such groups cannot settle their quarrels with their own leadership, they take them to a higher level; which brings most of them to the public judgment of government; and the place where all such quarrels and politics ultimately lock are on the desk of the President, where, White would finally discover, everything eventually locks.

In institutional terms, the Oppenheimer case had classic qualities. Scientists had forever left the days when, with a magnet, a bent wire, a particle emitter and a few dial counters, a single man could make a contribution of insight to physical science. The price of the ticket to explore inside the dancing emptiness of the atom had become so hideously expensive that only government could distribute such tickets. Each scientist wanted his share of government money to pursue the questions whose answers might shape mankind's history. Their differences of intellectual opinion had hitherto been critical only to scientists themselves. Now power and national security turned on their esoteric debates—as did huge wads of government money. An old Harvard classmate, Dr. Francis Friedman, a physicist who had worked on the first bomb, explained to White what had happened to the boy scientists with whom they had gone to school: "We [scientists] have briefly entered the riches of the medieval church, and are starting to resemble the fat friars grasping for temporal power through ecclesiastic politics."

Scientists White learned, fought each other and would at times destroy each other by the most personal attacks for reasons he could not fathom. But who could sit as judge in such quarrels? What does an institution like American science do when no outside jury of peers can be found which even vaguely comprehends the facts on which a quarrel hinges? White knew that he himself was absolutely incompetent to judge who was right, who was wrong, in the controversy over Oppenheimer's attitude to the H-bomb. He knew no one else, outside his scientist friends, who was competent to judge, either. And his scientist friends were split. White wished there was no such thing as an H-bomb, but he came down in his reporting unequivocally on Oppenheimer's side. He made up his mind not on the rights, the wrongs, the timing of America's development of a thermonuclear bomb—but on the politics of the matter, the politics that let policemen and FBI agents decide Oppenheimer's quarrel with another great scientist, Edward Teller.

The lesson was that the politics of institutions were passing out of control of the voters' understanding; and White would have to accept the fact that very much of what was about to happen would pass out of his understanding, too—not only missiles and bombs, computers and controls, but also inflation and deflation, black against white, pollution and environment. Henceforth, White would have to seek wise men he trusted, because he could no longer judge for himself. One of his acquaintances was Dr. Jerome Wiesner, a scientist-statesman permitted into every sanctuary of American military secrets who later became president of the Massachusetts Institute of Technology. Wiesner supported Oppenheimer, but would never reveal whether Oppenheimer or Teller was scientifically right or wrong in the controversy over "neutrons by the bucket." White took

Wiesner's word that the most elementary consideration of justice required Oppenheimer's clearance—but was even more impressed by Wiesner's description of his own role. "What do you do," asked Wiesner, "when you see something that can be disastrous to the country, when you find yourself one of the only dozen people in the country who understand it or have access to the secrets? This is a problem for every guy's conscience. I'm not prepared to sit on my butt and after this country has been demolished by an H-bomb say I could have prevented it, or it might have been otherwise. When we debate with the soldiers and the public has to be excluded, who represents the public?" Wiesner's question was unanswerable; but it meant accepting a world of politics by contending elites.

White had come to this point of perplexity about institutions when *The Reporter* published his articles on the Scientific Establishment in 1954. It was a fevered summer; White was enjoying the reporting of it; any number of interlocked matters were engaging public attention at the same time. There was the case of Joseph McCarthy versus the United States Army being tried on television before the entire nation. There was the case of the Atomic Energy Commission versus J. Robert Oppenheimer being tried behind closed doors, but smoke-signaled by a fringe of leakage reporting. And then there was a third case: of the United States versus John Paton Davies, a case being conducted in absolute secrecy.

It was this third and secret case that engaged White most closely. He might watch the McCarthy hearings on TV, and be caught up in the drama—but only as a citizen, not as a working reporter. The Oppenheimer hearings were, indeed, his professional assignment—and he was determined to forgo even-handed reporting and end with a clear defense of Oppenheimer. But the Davies case was another matter entirely. Davies was just too old a friend to forget or ignore.

Any man who becomes a friend of another before the age of twenty-five cannot cut himself loose; and when they were both young men, Davies was the very model of what White hoped an American diplomat would have been in China. Now, in 1954, the grapevine bore him the news that once more—for the ninth time— John Paton Davies was being investigated, this time by the State Department's Security Hearing Board. This redundant inquiry had been triggered by a TV attack on Davies by Senator Joseph McCarthy. White got in touch with Davies' lawyer and said that if any help or testimony was needed, he would be glad to journey down to Washington to testify. He remembers Davies' lawyer, Benjamin Shute, gulping on the phone and asking, in astonishment, "You mean you'll volunteer to do that?!" White was more than willing. He was in and out of Washington at all times on the Oppenheimer story; needed no expenses for travel or hotel; was indignant at what was being done to his friend; and felt that a principle was at stake.

He did not know what other hazards were at stake.

The secret hearings on Davies had been going on for weeks when White journeyed down to Washington to testify in the first week of July. White felt invulnerable. He was a well-known author. He represented a small but highly leveraged magazine. He knew President Eisenhower and was friendly with the White House staff. And his friend Davies was being assailed.

White testified sharply, intemperately. He tried to make one principle clear: A State Department officer, he insisted, must report the truth to his government no matter how unpleasant the truth. White reached back across the years to China days. If Davies had reported that the Communists were going to win in China, which turned out to be correct, he merited praise, not purging. The government must be informed correctly at all times; that's what we paid those men for.

White was thus feeling very noble, very effective, a detached but able master at this game of loyalty inquisition. He was proceeding on the assumption that the five men on the hearing board, listening to him, were actually a judicial panel, seeking justice. After an hour's closed testimony he hoped he might have turned their minds to a consideration of the merits of the case of John P. Davies, or, at least, given them some of the resonance of life in China at war, which was, after all, at the heart of Davies' behavior. White was so hoping, when a man with a blank face at the big table closed what was obviously the Davies folder, and opened another.

It must have been the White folder; and almost instantly, White realized that this was not a judicial hearing—it was a lynching party. Davies was to be lynched; and if White had to be gotten in the process, why, so be it.

"Mr. White," came the first question, "isn't it true that you made a speech to the Negro troops on the Burma Road urging them to a revolt during the war?"

With that question, White's composure cracked. He was facing the other America, where security had its own jurisprudence; and the politics of security required *them* to get *him*.

CHAPTER 9

The Fifties: Incubating the Storm

I still remember the room where the Davies security hearings were held, but no record in my diary, no note or recollection, brings back the address of the then secret hearings.

It was a nondescript building, two stories high, I think, somewhere on Twenty-second Street, Washington, Northwest. I had by then, in the summer of 1954, visited so many State Department outposts, at home and abroad, that it seemed as if I had grown up in State Department buildings. From the embassies in London, Paris, Warsaw, back through Rome, Cairo and Delhi, to Chungking and Peking; from the prewar State Department building, with its slatted doors and lazy fans, across from the White House, to the then new State Department building in Foggy Bottom—for fifteen years, from straw shack to marble palace, I had been at home in the offices of the State Department. But I had never seen an office like this: it might have been an abandoned book warehouse, or an old police station in New York. The yellow paint on its walls was peeling; the carpet in the anteroom was stained; it was the cloacal end of the State Department, through which it purged its human refuse. I walked upstairs to the designated hearing room, and as I waited to be admitted, two receptionists chatted, chewing gum, one inquiring of the other, "Hey, you got a Top Secret stamp, Doris? I've only got a Secret stamp." And then, fishing in her drawer, she said, "Oh, here it is now." Stenotypists relieved each other at twenty-minute intervals, as I watched the door. Then I was admitted.

It took several minutes before my eyes could adjust to the light in the room. It was sunny July in Washington outside, so the curtains and blinds had been drawn to keep out the heat, thus dimming the room to twilight. When my eyes did adjust from the glare of the antechamber to the half dark inside, I could see a long table at the end of the room, behind which sat five men, their backs to the window, so that one had to peer into their shadowed features to make out who they were. Their chairman, I learned later, was Lieutenant General Daniel Noce. I faced him for perhaps two hours that morning, but I have no recollection whether he was thin or fat, tall or short. To my right sat John Davies' counsel, Benjamin Shute, who had volunteered his services out of old friendship; and to Shute's right sat Davies himself—gaunt, almost sallow, his chin poked proudly into the air. In the years since we had known each other in China he had reached eminence. He had been First Secretary of the U.S. Embassy in Moscow, a member of the Policy Planning Staff of the State Department, Director of Political Affairs at the U.S. Embassy in Germany. But now he looked like a character in *Darkness at Noon*. I myself would have designed a far more dramatic stage set for the operation that was going on; but the room was too dingy and shabby to merit any description at all.

They were examining Davies' supposed "Communist connections." Later, in one of those breaches of secrecy of which the McCarthy primitives were so frequently guilty, I learned that Davies had devised an elaborate scheme to plant in Peking Americans considered "friendly" by the Chinese Communists and then milk them for the intelligence we needed. Because of this rather ingenious plan, Davies was now suspect of being a double agent. But the specific charge against him, for which I was called as witness, was that, during the war, by talking to the American press and explaining Stilwell's difficulties with Chiang K'ai-shek, Davies was deliberately undermining Chiang's government and preparing the way for a Communist takeover. The charges against Davies' behavior in Chungking during the war ten years earlier were preposterous. Of course Davies had talked to the press during the war. That was his job. He was Stilwell's briefing officer. We were war correspondents. He was supposed to tell us Stilwell's side of the dispute with Chiang. I may have been too contemptuous in tossing the charges back. But now, as they closed the questioning on Davies, and opened the unexpected dossier on White, the first charge hurled at me seemed preposterous—that I had tried to organize the Negro troops on the Burma Road for a revolt during the war.

It was so wild a charge that my memory, flicking wildly through recollection, could bring up nothing but humor and I was about to make a joke when it came to me: Why, yes, yes, of course, but they have it all wrong, all wrong.

What came back to me, as the charge was repeated, was a story swimming upstream through memory over a stretch of ten years. I tried to reel the story in through all that had happened between 1944 and 1954. Yes, I had indeed spoken to a gathering of black troops on the Burma Road during the war. Black Americans were then generally assigned under white officers to all-black, segregated labor battalions. At least one, perhaps several, such black battalions had hacked their way through the jungle to cut a road trace between the Ledo Road and the Burma Road which would end the blockade of China. The road had been essential to Stilwell's strategy; ultimately it was superior as an engineering feat to the Japanese bridge on the River Kwai. So, ten years earlier, in 1944, one night in Myitkyina, advance headquarters in the North Burma campaign, I had accidentally met a boyhood neighbor from Dorchester, now Lieutenant Gilbert of the Engineers. Under these jungle palms, we were very far from home in the Boston ghetto.

Gilbert, assigned like so many Jewish engineers to be officers in black battalions, said he was goddamn mad. His battalion was hacking away at the road trace; his black troops were eating their guts out; they had malaria, too, like the white troops; but they were not allowed in Myitkyina, our forward base. Their morale was shot; they didn't know what the hell they were doing over here; they might, for Christ's sake, just as well be in a Georgia chain gang—and they hadn't seen a white officer, except for a few officer engineers like him, since they had been dumped in the jungle. Would I do him a favor? I was a war correspondent, a big shot. Would I, for Christ's sake, come out and dine in the mess with his black troops, and then get up and make a speech, and tell them why it was so important to build this road through to China? He'd drive me out in his jeep, and drive me back the same night. Please!

For boyhood memories and because he was convincing, I agreed.

I had no distinct recollection now, ten years later in 1954, of precisely what I had said to those black Americans carving a road through jungle to help the Chinese defeat the Japanese, but I remembered what I had usually said on occasions like that. This "pep talk" must have gone quite simply: that the Japanese were the worst racists in the world after the Nazis; and we had to help the Chinese knock off the Japanese; this road would do the job; then after we knocked off the racist Nazis in Europe and the racist Japanese in Asia, we would all go home and knock off racism in the United States. So lift that ax, girdle that tree, bulldoze that road, got to get it through. Whenever I was called on to make a speech to troops, I was embarrassed, and I always tried roughly to balance snorting patriotism with facts, figures and profanity to prove that I was *not* an officer, but only a cynical newspaperman dressed up in the uniform of a war correspondent. That night as we drove back, Gilbert said I had done well, and the speech had disappeared into the pockets of memory until this question re-evoked it. I suppose today, pivoting to the new winds, I should be ashamed of the language I had then used. I called black troops "Negroes." But instead of calling on them to revolt, as charged, I had instead used the "Ol' Man River" theme: "Tote that barge, lift that bale."

I was flustering my way through that answer when, like a good prosecutor, the interrogator nipped it off with the next question.

"Is it true, Mr. White, that your wife is a member of the Communist Party?"

I can still remember my squeal. My voice tends to rise in anger or argument, and I squealed out in astonishment:

"My wife, Nancy?!"

"I don't know what your wife's name is."

From then on I was so angry I made little sense. While my speech on the Burma Road, ten years before, might have been connected, by lunatic imagination, to Davies at CBI headquarters, the accusation against Nancy had nothing to do with John Davies, or China, or anything at issue here. It was an attempt, simply, to intimidate the witness. I defended Nancy, spoke of her political indifference to all causes and stressed her background (her father was then president of his local Chamber of Commerce and considered Senator Taft a liberal). I was then queried about the political affiliation of Annalee Jacoby, my partner on *Thunder Out of China;* I defended her too against all charges (". . . she lost her husband, killed in the early days of the war . . . a loyal American"). I was asked to explain some poetry I had written. Since at the time I had never written any poetry, that defense was easily managed. They wanted to know whether I had quit or been fired at *Time* magazine, and for what reasons. And then I was asked to explain my presence at a list of meetings in 1946 and 1947, when China was being lost to the Reds.

Then I was dismissed. Davies and Shute sat through

several more days of such vivisection, while I flew back to New York immediately to push ahead with my series on the Oppenheimer hearings. On June 1, another security board had voted against reinstatement of J. Robert Oppenheimer's security clearance, thus denying him access to the secrets of American defense, which he had done more to revolutionize than any other man. So I was bitter and wrote and spoke intemperately about the sacrifice of Oppenheimer. And not until the morning of October 4 1954, did I realize that I had made it to the target list myself. I had, of course, been singed by the heat of the McCarthy passion well before; I had come to understand from friendly producers at CBS that I could not be cleared for appearance as guest or visitor on any show for that network; I had been branded nationwide as a candidate for all blacklists by a hit man's sheet known as "Counterattack," which had flourished by listing "known" subversives. But such public slander was common in McCarthy days, and I had never sensed the difference between the sting of slander and the fist of government when it squeezes until that morning in October.

I entered the passport office on Fifth Avenue in New York and stood in line to pick up my passport. I had left it there the previous week for routine renewal, and had been routinely told to pick up the renewed passport this Monday morning. I cannot remember the face of the man behind the desk, but after a few minutes' search, he blandly replied that my passport could not be renewed; I could not have it back; I fell under the "legislation."

It was like the click of unexpected handcuffs.

Giving up my passport has always made me feel naked, even if only for half an hour to a friendly concierge in a European hotel. And this time, I had not given it up; it had been taken from me; I had been gulled; I had been robbed; I was dazed. I could not yell, I could not fight. There was this man across the counter and I could not jump the counter and ransack the bureau for my purloined passport. The people behind me in the line were murmuring, the clerk was saying there was nothing he could do, and I stumbled out of line, knowing only that my need for the green booklet was both desperate and urgent. This was a Monday. Next Monday, a week hence, I was scheduled to fly to Germany. *The Reporter* had given me a two-month leave of absence, on loan to *Collier's* magazine, for whom I was to write a special survey on Germany Ten Years After Defeat. Unless I could free my passport immediately, I would have to tell both *The Reporter* and *Collier's* that the trip was off, that I was officially on the subversive list and thus disqualified now, and indefinitely, from any further reporting from overseas. A journalist without a valid passport is as crippled, professionally, as a chauffeur whose driving license has been lifted.

The problem posed that morning was one that was posed perhaps to hundreds of Americans in those years— and there were standard reactions. There was the reasoned reaction: Get a lawyer and fight it out. Or: Hit the press first, roar in protest and force them to martyrize you. Or: Crawl—seek them out, give the recantation in public, finger other names. Or: Quit—drop out of sight as fast as possible. In my case, I could do none of these. I could not quit: I would have to tell both *The Reporter* and *Collier's* I was on the subversive list and thus, passportless, have to break off my trip to Europe. I had no appetite for martyrdom; and even less appetite for crawling my way through the committees and boards, official and semiofficial, that in those mad days awarded badges of clearance or shame, honor, subversion or rehabilitation.

On quick reflection, it seemed to me that, first, the real malice was not against me but was snarling irritation on the part of some minor security officer, who must have been annoyed that I had volunteered to interfere in the crucifixion of John Davies. If I made a public fuss, it would frighten off any number of others from testifying for the accused officers of the China Division. That would play into their hands. Besides, there could be no real charges against me, for none were true. And lastly, if I did not know how to thread my cause through the State

Department, either I had wasted my years covering it—or in truth, someone positively wanted to get me, and then, of course, they would. I knew how to use State Department telephones from years of reporting; thus I won an appointment with a passport hearing officer for the next morning, Tuesday, in Washington; was off that evening for the capital; and then began an odd twilight stretch of life which went on for eleven weeks, until Christmas Eve.

When I flew down to Washington, I discovered my hearing officer was a thin, pale-faced man named Ashley J. Nicholas. He would not let me see the charges made against me. We sat in the same room, and he held them in his hands. But with old State Department courtesy, he let me take penciled notes of the charges as he read them forth. They were nonsense—the same charges that had been read to me at the Davies hearings, dropping the poetry charge, but adding that a Soviet organization called JILEK had taken me on a tour of either the Near or the Far East in 1948 or 1949. I said that my passports would show by their markings that I had not been in the Middle East since 1938 or in the Far East since 1945. Mr. Nicholas asked what I had been writing about since. This surprised me. *Fire in the Ashes* had then sold over a quarter of a million copies. I said that I had been writing about Europe. Had he heard of a book called *Fire in the Ashes*? I asked with feigned shyness. No, Mr. Nicholas had not. I felt that any officer in the State Department should be at least familiar with the records of others involved in foreign policy; but, gulping, I went into the degrading act of describing both my own book and my support of the American cause in Europe. I groveled.

Somewhere, in some passage of Hemingway, I had read his prescription for dealing with bureaucrats, which is never, never to argue with them, be they police officers, consuls, supplymasters, but always to meet them meekly and correctly within their own narrow rules. I now realized that Mr. Nicholas was such a bureaucrat, and I bowed, taking him quite seriously. His major doubt, as I spoke of my book, was my purpose in writing about

Europe. He averred that some people wrote about Europe only to take Americans' minds off the Far East: while the Reds were mopping up hundreds of millions out there, some people were trying to divert our attention to Europe! The concept was so bizarre and would have entrapped so many involved in the Marshall Plan, that I went into a name-dropping song-and-dance of my friends and acquaintances who also felt that Europe was important in itself: David Bruce and John McCloy; Lucius Clay and Alfred Gruenther; General—no, President—Dwight D. Eisenhower, and General Ridgway, Chief of Staff.

I can laugh now at the episode. I was there most of the morning persuading Mr. Nicholas that I did not fall under the legislation entitled "Limitations on Issuance of Passports to Persons Supporting Communist Movements." I procured a copy of *Thunder Out of China* for him to read. Then hurried to the Washington home of my artist friend William Walton, who had another copy of the book; and asked Walton for typewriter and paper to write my refutation of charges against me and the book. Walton, a man of great gaiety, would not let me take the matter seriously; he roared with laughter while he helped and edited and made all he could available to me. Together, in two hours, we put together a nine-page answer to charges; and Walton proved both wiser and less expensive than learned counsel. By early afternoon, Mr. Nicholas was wavering. By three, he had issued instructions that my passport would be marked "Valid for Travel to Germany, France and England," but only for two months' duration. After that, I answered more questions about China, and about *Thunder Out of China,* and found Mr. Nicholas growing somewhat apologetic. At the end of the afternoon, Mr. Nicholas said that he believed he could get the passport extended not just for two months but for a full year; and then, with a sensitivity that must have echoed back to his early days, when the State Department expected its officers to be gentlemen, he offered the thought that I really would not have to solicit letters of loyalty from important people I had known; "it might be embarrassing," he said. I nodded. And we agreed that when I returned from Germany, I would come to Washington, bringing my wife with me, to answer any relevant questions, and he would give us a formal hearing under oath.

So I was away two months in Europe, back in Germany, and wrote about it, and won an award, and later a new and more important job at *Collier's*. But it was a trip scored with schizophrenia. In Germany I was traveling the high road of old acquaintances who had achieved power (like Konrad Adenauer) or great wealth (like Willi Schlieker) or great eminence (like James Bryant Conant of Harvard, now Ambassador to Germany). But the passport in my inner pocket was a dirty passport, a subversive's passport, marked with the limitations and stigmata stamped there to indicate my suspect loyalty. And when I came home I would have to face more charges at Mr. Nicholas's hearing.

Nancy flew to meet me in Paris when I was done with Germany once more, and we had a lunch of asparagus and strawberries at the sidewalk terrace of La Crémaillère. It was a warm, sunny day, with Paris at its loveliest, and we wondered whether we should move back to Europe, where we had been so happy, or return to America and face the charges. It was unreal talk, of course, for both of us belonged to America, and there could be no other course but to go home—except that I was frightened and Nancy laughed because it was all nonsense.

I was home again very early in December and spent as much time working on my past for the hearing with Mr. Nicholas as I did over my survey of Germany for *Collier's*. I was charged with having attended five meetings with "subversives," and in researching my calendars of 1945–1946–1947, when supposedly I was losing China to the Reds, I found at least eleven more such meetings they had overlooked. The exercise in personal research was tedious, time-consuming, but ultimately very useful, for I prepared and sent ahead by registered mail a most meticulously detailed briefing paper for Mr. Nicholas, explaining precisely the nature of each meeting and why I had been there.

I was thus fully prepared for self-defense when I flew down to Washington, with my wife, to stand secretly before Mr. Nicholas on December 23, 1954. I was fearful of only one thing—the need to name names. But I had met that challenge on preliminary inquiries and had developed pat answers: "Yes, sir, I know many Communists, sir: Mao Tse-tung, Chou En-lai, Chu Teh, Ch'en Chia-k'ang, Ch'iao Kuan-hua, Huang Hua . . . No, I've never associated with American Communists, but I did know and report on French Communists, like Pierre Courtades, Jacques Duclos, Maurice Thorez. . . ." I anticipated a day, perhaps two days, of ugliness and unpleasantness. But nothing of the sort happened.

The final direct confrontation with State, as represented by Mr. Nicholas, turned out to be not only anticlimactic but painless, if not indeed pleasant. Mr. Nicholas had read my briefing paper; he seemed embarrassed. Far more importantly, however, Senator McCarthy's methods had been condemned by the full Senate of the United States only three weeks before, on December 2. Nancy was dressed as if she were chairwoman of the local League of Women Voters, and with somewhat the same hauteur of manner, stripped off her white glove to raise her right hand and swear that she was not then nor ever had been a member of the Communist Party. I, too, answered a number of perfunctory questions and swore my oaths. And then Mr. Nicholas became human. It was two days until Christmas, and, he volunteered, we'd probably like to fly back to New York with clean new passports, with all the dirty restrictions of the old wiped out. We certainly did want nice new clean passports. He suggested, then, that we go out, have lunch, come back, and he'd have the new passports ready; and we could still catch a plane back to New York. When we returned, the new passports were waiting, the new photographs still moist from being freshly pasted in place. Then we were off to the airport, and since the Virginia airport then sold no hard liquor, we celebrated on champagne until the plane was ready to take us back to New York as citizens free to travel anywhere.

I do not know how I would have behaved later had I not been able to clear myself then. John Davies was massacred judicially, purged finally by dictate of John Foster Dulles, deferring to the rock men. The hypocrisy of Dulles is Davies' story to tell. He spent fourteen years clearing his name. J. Robert Oppenheimer was removed from council on the most sensitive of all subjects in national defense. They were large men and their loss was national loss. I was small fry and men like me, suffering from similar charges, dropped out of journalism—to become press agents and real estate agents, to go into brokerage houses, to live in exile, to hide away if they could in TV. As for myself, no amount of self-reproach will reconcile me, even today, to the self-doubt that followed my clearance. From 1954 to 1972, I never wrote another article about the China I knew so well; and only four articles on Vietnam. It was not so much that I was afraid; I had stood up when I had to and the fear passed away in time. It was that I would never again be as sure of myself on anything as I had been on the need of our getting out of the path of the Chinese revolution. And unless I was that sure of myself, I would never again want to be a polemicist or an advocate in a national debate. I recognize now that I also consciously withdrew from a reportorial area of intense past interest to me—arms and defense, weaponry and combat. I had gone down that road far enough in reporting the Oppenheimer case to know I had made powerful enemies in the defense establishment, too; and so, deliberately, except for the years when I reported on Robert McNamara's pre-Vietnam leadership of the Pentagon, I wrote nothing about national defense, either. A self-censorship, imposed not by government but by prudence, circumscribed me—as it circumscribed countless others.

When, after almost twelve weeks of living within the cyclone, I recovered myself at the Virginia National Airport, my first thoughts were selfish: to protect my family, myself and my career. It would have been nobler and more heroic of me to have stood there and sworn to punish the faceless men who had put me through such anguish, and savaged such good men as Davies and Oppenheimer.

But I did not.

I meant to go on writing of politics in America, and clearance of charges meant that I could continue to do so. But I know that from then on and for years I deliberately ignored the dynamics of foreign policy and defense because too much danger lurked there; and for that shirking I am now ashamed.

It was years before the McCarthy experience faded from my sleep-tossing self-catechisms. More importantly, professionally I could not leave behind, nor could I ignore if I meant to go on writing of American politics, what McCarthy had done to those politics. The late Richard Hofstadter, the best of contemporary American historians, has described the "Paranoid Style of American Politics" as a constant in our long history. The McCarthy troopers modernized that style. There was, in their spurious scholarship, their score-paying nastiness, their flathead ambition above all in their intensity of cynicism, an absolutism that let them permit themselves any lie or any sin. The McCarthy episode thus not only affected my own life, but affected all American politics for several decades, and since I was choosing to report American politics as the control center of world decisions, I could not escape from observing the warping effect it had on the politics and elections that were my work.

So much of what I was to report about American politics for fifteen years was ridden by the ghost of that paranoid man that I wish I had stomached my disgust when he was riding high and made an effort to meet and interview him. Looking back, I can see that it was he who acidified American conservatism, making it wrathful and shrill. It was he who stripped it of its political tradition of intellectual respectability, deprived it of any voice that could be widely heard. He fouled the conservative terrain, turned simple patriotism into mindless flag-waving and, worst of all, so discredited the conservative point of view that conservative critics of the dominant liberal culture could not for years expect a reasonable hearing.

McCarthy was not, of course, unique. The thirty-year-long parade of men of his type had begun well before him, with J. Parnell Thomas, chairman of the House Un-American Activities Committee, who ended up in jail; and a phalanx of Southern racist demagogues whose ends are long since forgotten. But McCarthy was the first to win national attention as a leader; after him came Spiro T. Agnew; and then the climactic Richard M. Nixon. Few men of merit have wished to march publicly in this dreary procession. Perhaps only two conservative men of elective politics, Ronald Reagan and James Buckley, can now command the attention of thoughtful Americans, and another, Barry Goldwater, has in recent years won affection as well as respect. But for the most part, for the last twenty years, the decent grass-roots conservatives of the country have been leaderless, and thus unrepresented in the national political debate. For them the price has been bitterness; for American politics it may have been even greater.

Somewhere in McCarthy was buried the true tragedy of American conservatives: a total incomprehension of their own cause. Only the rarest American conservative, like a William F. Buckley, Jr., understands that America marks a pause in the normal flow of history, a departure from the usual pattern. In the past, successful societies have moved, it would seem inevitably, from simple success to the complex management of the success—with a Pharaoh, a Caesar, or a Chairman. And the Pharaonic or imperial state always required a mandarinate or a bureaucracy to manage its affairs. In modern Western history, the revolt against the closed state was led by Jean-Jacques Rousseau, John Stuart Mill—and Thomas Jefferson—all men known to history as classic liberals. For American conservatives to recognize these liberals as their true philosophical parents is very difficult; they must reach through the names to the idea, and the idea that the state may best be served by letting the individual express himself, in opinion as in business, seems alien to them. McCarthy did not even try to understand the idea he claimed to be defending. He rallied conservatives only because he could dramatize what seemed to be their enemy—Communism! McCarthy peaked in influence as Harry Truman and Dean Acheson fought Communism abroad, in blood and arms. But he ran around behind the lines like a crazed M.P.—loyal but paranoid, shooting wildly, randomly, cruelly, at friend or foe behind the lines, at anyone whom he could denounce, at the top of his lungs, as Red! Red! Red!

McCarthy was not only blindly cruel and historically ignorant, but politically reckless and myopic. He did not recognize that those who were gathering together in common defense against his attack were the forces of the near future in American politics, the nascent New Governing Class. His easy targets descended through a range of priorities—Communists, fellow-travelers, subversives, intellectuals, writers, professors, press and broadcasters. He lumped all of them together in one coast-to-coast web of conspiracy, pasted together with names, dates, meetings, letterheads, that had no connection with either the reality of the times or the linkages between them, or with Communism. But in the decade of the 1950s American universities were growing wildly; students and professors alike were first beginning to feel their way into politics. At the great foundations, new professionals of research and analysis were making the American government their central field of examination and inquiry. Within the press the first stirrings of professional change were showing as editors began to recruit political reporters from universities rather than the sports beat, and reporters and editors together began to talk back to their proprietors, who had, hitherto, treated them like hired hands. This growing class of people, what could be called the academic-media complex who would become so critically important in the next two decades, had to join ranks. And thrown together against McCarthy, by easy transfer of passion they turned against the entire Republican Party.

Fear, not hope, is the greatest glue of politics. Once

the impression sped in 1954 that no thinking or dissenting personality was entirely safe from McCarthy, McCarthy had to be eliminated from politics—and was. The credit for this elimination goes to decent Republicans and Democrats alike. But the cost was borne entirely by the Republicans: McCarthy had activated against that party the best brains and leadership of news room, media and campus. He had cut the Republican Party off from the intellectual dialogue of America; and the masters of that American dialogue were a far more formidable foe to encounter than the raddled Communist Party spokesmen, who fled in fear.

McCarthy's viral infection of American politics, particularly his penetration of the Republican Party by the temptation of the cheap win via the low blow, lasted for at least ten years and continues still, here and there, in domestic politics. But McCarthy's most lasting effect on American history may well have been on its foreign policy—for a direct line runs between McCarthy's terrorizing of the Foreign Service of the United States State Department and the ultimate tragedy of America's war in Vietnam.

It was Lord Acton who, in his inaugural lecture at Cambridge on the study of history a century ago, said: "I exhort you never . . . to lower the standard of rectitude . . . to suffer no man and no cause to escape the undying penalty which history has the power to inflict on wrong." The wrong done by the McCarthy lancers, under McCarthy leadership, was to poke out the eyes and ears of the State Department on Asian affairs, to blind American foreign policy. And thus flying blind into the murk of Asian politics, American diplomacy carried American honor, resources and lives into the triple-canopied jungles and green-carpeted hills of Vietnam, where all crashed.

One could see the beginning of McCarthy's impact of irrationality on diplomacy as early as the Korean War. In Korea, we fought armies commanded by P'eng Te-huai, launched by Mao Tse-tung. We had trained a generation of dedicated Foreign Service officers to speak and understand Chinese, to cultivate the leaders of Chinese

Communism, to understand what they planned. But all such China Service officers had come under the flagellation of McCarthy's rhetoric—they had not hated Communism enough. Some of these Oriental specialists could be saved by dispersion—shipped to such diplomatic posts as Kenya, Bonn, Iceland, where their expensive training was totally useless. Others were purged outright —as was John Stewart Service, purged in December of 1951. Thus, as truce negotiations at Panmunjon dragged on for two years, Service, the American diplomat who knew the Chinese Communist leadership best, was a purgee, working for a plumbing manufacturer in New York at nine thousand dollars a year. In the employ of this aging manufacturer, he invented a new and improved steam trap for radiators. But the United States Government would not seek his advice. Service had wined, befriended and spent countless hours of both purposeful and aimless conversation with the same Chinese Red leaders we now confronted across guns. They had respected and had liked him. But the terrorism of Joe McCarthy prevented the use of either Service, or Davies, or Vincent, or Ludden, or Sprouse, or anyone who knew anything about Asia, to help us address our problems in Asia.

The ultimate impact of McCarthy on American foreign policy, and thus on the world, came many years later, in Vietnam. The purging of the State Department had begun as an effort of John Foster Dulles to please his Republican right wing by sacrificing a few of the gallant China Service diplomats who had predicted too accurately and too eloquently the ultimate victory of the Communists. The purging ended with a State Department full of junior diplomats who knew their future career was pawn to political passion at home; who knew that prediction of a Communist victory would be equated with hope for a Communist victory; and who learned to temper their dispatches of observation in the field with what their political superiors in Washington or in Congress wished to hear. No field-grade American diplomat, in the long period between 1964 and 1975, had the courage flatly to predict the potential for disaster in Vietnam. Many rec-

ognized that potential; but none dared say it aloud or in
print until much too late. They reported what their political masters wanted to hear; McCarthy had ruined the
truth-tellers who had gone before.

Perhaps even today I harbor a sense of the deserter
for having gone on to other things once I was professionally cleared of loyalty-security charges. What if I, who
knew them as well as anyone, had made a vocation of
defending the China Service officers who were purged?
Could they have been saved? Would matters have been
different? Could I have helped them persuade the government, or the Congress, or the press, that it would be
best to stand apart from the quarrels of the Asians? The
Establishment had lined up to defend the U.S. Army and
Matthew Ridgway against the primitives of Joe McCarthy. But few rallied to the defense of the State Department officers, or even the Department itself, which was
accused of giving shelter to so many Communist spies. I
had made two tries—once for John Stewart Service, once
for John Paton Davies—and that was it. At the end of
1954, I ducked from the line of fire. And being freed of
the threat to my journalistic license, I abandoned forever
the old stories of America abroad to plunge into what
now fascinated me more: America at home.

In personal terms, my clearance of loyalty and security charges in 1954 meant that I was also freed of fealty
to Dr. Max Ascoli.

Had I not won my passport back, I would have had
slim choice: service to Ascoli, or expulsion from the
profession. Ascoli was so flamboyantly brave he would
have insisted on keeping me on his payroll, as a known
subversive, if only to taunt the primitives. But I would
then have been pawn to his will, his to move one step by
one step in any direction he chose, my writing his to
rearrange, paragraph by paragraph. His Florentine generosity was laced always with cruelty and mischief; after I
finally told him of my troubles with the State Department,
his manner to me became more warm and protective in

private, but more overbearing and demanding in public.

Our break was bound to come and it came over a matter of honorable intellectual difference—and coincided with the first cracking of my allegiance to the school of liberal journalism. If the various schools of journalism were divided as clerical orders are—Franciscans, Benedictines, Jesuits, et alii—the School of Liberal Journalism would be a leading order. The school believes that for every complicated problem there exists both an intellectual *and* a moral solution, and that they coincide. Ascoli's was the greatest liberal magazine of its time. His own intellectual frenzies and ego caused him to believe that there was *indeed* a solution for every problem and he, through his magazine, would deliver it. Since he was interested in institutions and we published in New York, it was obvious that something was wrong with the institution called New York City. Thus, once I was cleared of loyalty and security charges, he assigned me at the end of 1954 to a full-scale study of New York, and the perspectives to which its politics pointed.

All reporters owe gratitude to editors who turn them loose on a great assignment. The opportunity to spend months looking at New York, asking the proper questions, became for me a delirium of excitement, for even then, at its peak, the city was a perplexity. Few reporters are allowed to look at their city as a whole, and New York is a challenge to all reporters. Ascoli let me roam from the South Bronx to Far Rockaway, from the Board of Estimate to the Lexington Democratic Club. For three or four months, I spent my time learning New York as if it were a foreign country—and found that it fit into no known political theory. Ascoli was convinced, as always, that the problems of New York were institutional. I was convinced that they were political, ethnic and, above all, racial. This makes a difference in the thread of narrative reporting. Draft after draft rolled from my typewriter, grasping to catch the scene, from the night communications center of the police down at Centre Street to the sickbed of Gracie Mansion, from the clan chieftains of Italian, Jewish, Irish groups to the feverish little gatherings of earnest citizens who would someday become the reform movement. But as such essays rolled out, and I discarded each, it became obvious that with all my efforts, I would not be able to present Ascoli with the Solution, the Liberal Answer, to New York City's problems. Alas, in New York, even at that time, common sense was in conflict with morality; what had to be done by the dictate of common sense was uncommonly cruel. I was baffled and the reporting stalled.

I bore gratitude to Ascoli for turning over such an exploration to me. But I also bore him resentment for his manners and imperial insistence on rewriting what was mine to say. I prickled particularly when he dropped into conversation the odd fact that he had had a cost-account study done of his writers' work, and that I had turned out to be the most expensive. In a year, my average cost per word published had been fifty cents! I was sure that it would cost him more than that per word by the time I had found the ultimate solution to New York. It would be wise to leave, before the inevitable firing came upon me.

My leavetaking from Harry Luce had come over high principle and, however bitter, ended in a formal exchange of farewells of Oriental effusiveness. My leavetaking from the Overseas News Agency had been sad—a scratchy, miserable, transatlantic series of letters in which I pleaded that the New York office must pay me the six months' back salary they owed me; and then, finally, I quit in exasperation, mostly because I needed money. This leavetaking was different. I invited Ascoli to a fine French lunch, and, after telling him how forever grateful I would be for the opportunity of serving him, I realized that Ascoli was enjoying the farewell as much as I. He was spared both the pain and the cost of firing me; moreover, he waved aside my gallant offer to work as long as necessary to finish up the New York piece. He would have that sage and magisterial old New Dealer Adolph Berle rework my draft, for Berle knew what the facts really meant. Berle would sign the story and give the Solution. That sat well with me, for I knew a few more weeks or even months would give me no satisfactory answer to the problems of New York; and I was pleased, months later, to see that Berle had written a good piece, and been gentleman enough to refuse to sign half a dozen vignettes of New York street life which I had written. So they were run without a by-line months after I had taken my leave.

I was, I told Ascoli with some pride, joining *Collier's* magazine. *Collier's* was not as prestigious as *Life,* but easily equal to *Look* or the *Saturday Evening Post.* Apart from the little giant, *Reader's Digest,* these were the big four of the newsstands; each of them had a senior national political correspondent, and I was to fill that post for *Collier's.* The job was the journalistic equivalent of one of the great chairs of history at Harvard, Princeton, Columbia, or Yale. I felt, as I left Ascoli, that now after the years in the wilderness and my fright of Joe McCarthy, I was at last going back to the winning side.

And I could not have been more mistaken.

An enormous difference separated *Collier's* from *The Reporter.* It was not simply that *Collier's* sold 4,300,000 copies and *The Reporter* less than 200,000. Nor the difference in audience tone. Nor the presence in *Collier's* of those glossy advertisements that give commercial magazines so much of their flair. It was not that one came from the tradition of "mainstream" mass magazines and the other from the tradition of liberal "little" magazines. It was simply that their views of America were so different that I might almost have been reporting different countries to different peoples once I had crossed between their offices from one side of Fifth Avenue to the other. A friend hailed me in the street several months after I had made the change and asked, "What's happened to you? Since you left *The Reporter,* no one can find out where you're writing these days." Yet *Collier's* had more than twenty times the circulation of *The Reporter.*

At *The Reporter,* I had covered the wrinkled under-

side of American politics and leadership, examining the
cellular structure of our institutions as if preparing them
for Ascoli's surgical diagnosis. At *Collier's*, I was to
report what was actually happening to ordinary Americans. Both *Collier's* and *The Reporter* shared the same
Eisenhower years of prosperity and well-being. But their
views of America were entirely unlike, a *Rashomon* of
journalism. The high story in American science for *The
Reporter* was the inquisition and excommunication of J.
Robert Oppenheimer in the struggle over the hydrogen
bomb. For *Collier's* the high story of science in that
decade was Jonas Salk's triumph over polio—and *Collier's* effort to tell it first. For *Collier's*, the great women
of the world were led by Grace Kelly and Marilyn Mon-
roe, followed by Elizabeth Taylor and Kim Novak. For
The Reporter, Eleanor Roosevelt and Golda Meir were
leading ladies. At *Collier's,* the conquest of the do-it-
yourself workbench by the quarter-inch drill was a major
story; but the editorial director of *The Reporter* would
not have known which end of the quarter-inch drill to
hold in his hand. Both magazines reported America; and
reporting the same America first for one magazine, then
the other, was like reporting two different countries.

   In joining *Collier's* I had joined a magazine that had
no other purpose than to make money. But to make
money it needed an identifiable audience whose attention
it could sell to advertisers. Such an audience always
assembles around the personality of a great editor or
great publisher, and now *Collier's* was groping for such a
personality. It had been founded half a century earlier by
an Irish immigrant named Peter Fenelon Collier, who
made a fortune selling "library sets" on the installment
plan. Collier had a flair for capturing imaginations and
his magazine survived sixty-nine years of ups and downs.
When the winds blew to muckraking, *Collier's* muck-
raked. But whether for circulation's sake or not, *Collier's*
could, on occasion, stand against the wind; the magazine
supported women's suffrage and a national income tax
when they were unpopular, and, again against fashion,
cracked down on doctors, medical cheaters and chiselers.

Collier's, under later editors, peaked in the thirties and
forties as the only mass mainstream magazine supporting
Franklin Roosevelt. But then, after the war, it had erratically hawed this way and yawed that way, trying to find a
cause and a course to increase audience. A loud-mouthed,
colorful one-time Hearst executive came aboard as editor
—Lou Ruppel. His chef-d'oeuvre was a hysterical,
screaming, red-bordered issue in 1951 called "Preview of
The War We Do Not Want," describing America's war
with, and conquest of, Russia. Bombs whistled through
Collier's pages, raining death on Pinsk, Minsk, Vladivos-
tok, Rostov, Kiev. Flames spread across the center fold as
Moscow burned. The issue captured perfectly the spirit of
the anti-Red hysteria of the Korean War and was disastrous; even *Collier's* advertisers thought it coarse and
scary.

Ruppel was replaced by a shy and diffident opposite,
Roger Dakin. Dakin moved *Collier's* from anti-Commu-
nism to space-roving—prematurely, it turned out, for in
1952 and 1953, space exploration was still the domain of
fictioneers and Buck Rogers. Ruppel had told the world
what *he* thought they should think—at the top of his
lungs. Dakin's credo, as I discovered later in a basic
memo in our archives, differed: ". . . instead of editing
the magazine in terms of our own preferences, . . . standards . . . interests," he said, "we are making a studied
attempt to anticipate the preferences, standards and interests of our circulation . . . our primary assignment right
now is to build our circulation figures as a tool for our
advertising salesmen. All other considerations at the moment are secondary to newsstand sales."

This strategy also failed, and by the time I was
invited aboard *Collier's* as "talent," the board of directors, struggling to squeeze money and profit out of the
balance sheet, had given all authority to one man as new
president, editor in chief, chairman of the board, and
chief executive officer—Paul Smith.

Paul Smith was a good, if cocky, person. He had
been recommended to the motley group of financial interests that sat on the board by none other than Herbert

Hoover. Smith had once been a first-class reporter; then the San Francisco *Chronicle*'s financial editor; then, a boy genius, he became editor of the paper at the age of twenty-seven. He had given up that post on Pearl Harbor Day to join the Navy; quit the Navy to enlist as a combat marine; had hit the beaches, gun in hand, and was thrice decorated. He knew war, finance, publishing, great men, and how to use reporters. From Smith descended operational authority over the three magazines—*Collier's, Woman's Home Companion* and the *American*—which made up the magazine division (and biggest money-losers) of the Crowell-Collier Corporation.

Whether Smith meant to do so or not, his administration of the magazines defined for me the "cluster" theory of politics: that dominant groups tend to find each other by accident of kinship, schooling or nearness. When I first came aboard, I found the accents on the *Collier's* editorial floor oddly familiar: they were all Bostonian! Dakin came from Gloucester; his deputy, Gordon Manning, was from Boston University's School of Journalism; so was Manning's deputy, David Maness, who also came from Blue Hill Avenue. Jerry Korn, Homer Jenks and our queen bee, Diana Hirsh, were also Bostonians. This was the cluster Smith had inherited to edit and direct a magazine that sold best in the calico and chewing tobacco belt and outsold all others in Arkansas and Tennessee!

Over this Boston cluster Smith had now installed a new cluster of Californians: Kenneth McArdle, Ted Strauss, Dick Trezevant. The Californians and Bostonians together reached out to other names, and so there developed a group of younger writers who, over the years, became a recognizable *"Collier's"* cluster of talent of their own. A pensive and diffident Harvard boy came aboard on the strength of one superlative piece he had written on kite-flying in Thailand. His name was George Goodman; later, as "Adam Smith," he achieved fame as the author of *The Money Game* and other works that changed American financial reporting. Another contemporary youngster was Peter Maas; he felt a calling to go after the Mafia, and in his *The Valachi Papers,* opened up another genre of American investigative reporting. Then there was a Rhodes scholar out of Yale and Oxford named Robert Massie, who was interested at once in good writing and in Russia; he later wrote *Nicholas and Alexandra.* A fellow youngster from Yale never developed his by-line, which was Ray Price, because Price even then normally wrote as ghost for his superiors—the chief of whom was later Richard Nixon, whose best speeches, including both inaugurals, came of Ray Price's drafting. As important as or more so than any other youngster was Pierre Salinger, whose assignment was to investigate the Teamsters Union. Salinger insisted there were two men we must expose— Dave Beck of Seattle and Jimmy Hoffa of Detroit. We turned him loose. but his superb cross-country investigation was completed only the month the magazine died on the stone. Salinger was then urged to carry his data down to Washington. There he enlisted with Robert F. Kennedy, younger brother of the junior senator from Massachusetts, John F. Kennedy, who then aspired to a larger career; and Salinger followed that career upward. Salinger's best book was *With Kennedy;* Price's book, later, was called *With Nixon.*

The strangers from California, subordinate to the finance men of the board, directors of the new talent and the old staff, were open, decent, even-handed. While the youngsters—Salinger, Maas, Goodman, Massie, Price— were hassling over office space, page space, story assignments, the older-brother group of senior writers were given equal opportunity to show their talent. Vance Packard, then a minor writer, was encouraged to try what he wanted—and with *The Hidden Persuaders,* in 1957, rubbed open American consumer consciousness before Ralph Nader was even heard of. Editors such as Ted Strauss or Eugene Rachlis at *Woman's Home Companion* were encouraged to explore the New Woman. The unrecognized star of the older-brother group was the late Cornelius Ryan. Ryan had, for years, signed *Collier's* stories on outer space; as poet laureate of the space-cadet brigade, he had been mocked for his extravagant predictions that Americans were on their way to the moon. He was persuaded by the new leadership to try his hand at a different style of narrative, the episode-by-episode re-creation of large events. This style served *Collier's* well in its closing months as Ryan perfected it and brought to his reporting the quality that later produced his memorable books *The Longest Day* and *A Bridge Too Far*.

It was a pleasure working with men one respected, and though at *Life,* and later at CBS, I was to work with men who engaged my comradeship and respect as much as those at *Collier's,* none surpassed the *Collier's* team in talent. Alas, none were more misused. No one could tell us where we were going, or what we were to do, except to write well, which we did. No one harnessed us together, or gave us the beat, as was given at *Time* and *The Reporter*. We were a band of happy men, almost oblivi-ous of the advent of television except as a horn on a far hill. So must the singers of Zion have intoned their can-tillations in the temple after the legions of Rome had already arrived in Galilee.

And I was never happier than in this period. I was the political correspondent of *Collier's*. Whether *Collier's* knew what it wanted or not, whether the editors gave me the rhythm or not, I was where I wished to be—in the middle of the 1950s, in the age of Eisenhower, with a readership of fifteen to twenty millions, and a free pass into politics.

I cannot now deny my recognition that Eisenhower's years in Washington, from 1954 through 1960, were the most pleasant of our time. Once McCarthy had been eliminated, a placid quality probably never to be seen again slowly settled over Washington. Political fashion, of course, prevented me from saying that Eisenhower was an outstanding President during those years of his benign rule. Praise for any sitting figure of power had gone out of intellectual style years earlier, with the end of the war. Though Eisenhower was a holdover from that age of heroes, now that he was in politics as President, political writers had to write of him as political journalism re-quired; and convention required us to disdain him as an inert, good-willed but ineffective President. This presented me with a problem: how to write about the incumbent without seeming slavishly flattering or nastily picky.

There were two story streams, as there always are for a political writer: On the one hand were the challengers, the Democratic Party, that corrupt, civilizing and Americanizing force, the oldest continuing organized party in the entire world. Even at their worst, Democrats are not boring, and among the quarreling Democrats I was, of course, as happy as a dog loose in a meat market. But on the other hand, there was Eisenhower and his Republicans. Once Eisenhower had insisted on the condemnation of Joe McCarthy in 1954, he had stilled for a decade, until 1964, the permanent civil war in the Republican Party. Thereafter Eisenhower "presided." Like all Republicans since Theodore Roosevelt, Eisenhower was "managerial" rather than propellant, and of the seven "managerial" Republican Presidents who have sat in the White House since Theodore Roosevelt, only Eisenhower had any claim to greatness. Since I could not, then, see the great virtues in clean management, I missed the history lesson that Eisenhower was giving the nation.

Eisenhower's history lesson was quite simple: The Chief Executive, he felt, should do absolutely nothing new unless something new was absolutely inescapable. Then he did it quickly and very well.

The Republican story stream thus required a good deal of invention and imagination to make it interesting. Somehow, the personal excitement that once ran from the conqueror of the Nazis and the Commander in Chief of NATO had evaporated. Scribbled on memory is one visit I made to the Oval Office which seemed to sum up Eisenhower as President. Eisenhower was out when I arrived. The sun streamed in through the bulletproof glass panes behind his desk; the desk was immaculate except for one neat closed folder in its center; and on the closed folder lay his horn-rimmed glasses, askew, as if he had just stepped out to the men's room for a moment and would soon be back. Only he was out playing golf. The room drowsed. The entire administration seemed to drowse. My impression was of course a mistaken one; this room, as always, was the center of power. The man who was out playing golf was simply using its power in a way unacceptable to historians and reporters; he was letting slip the restraints of Presidential power on lesser power systems and letting them jostle each other down the road to their clashing or interlocking futures. He acted, as I have said, only when it was inescapable. And when he acted, it was usually as the master regulator.

It is the fashion these days to denounce bureaucrats, which is as silly as to denounce soldiers or professors. But it is not demeaning Eisenhower to say that he was not only a great commander and a great President, but a great bureaucrat. He knew the difference between bureaucratic nonsense and bureaucratic truths, and he could strain out of the alleged facts the dynamics that mattered. His ascent through the military bureaucracy had shaped him; and he liked to have complicated problems approach him properly, sorted and simplified, with supporting papers and options, through appropriate channels. He knew how to use government, and how government worked, and as a supreme bureaucrat, he let the lesser bureaucracies within the systems incubate in the 1950s those developments that seemed to him reasonable and manageable. These developments would, in the 1960s, change America unmanageably; but Eisenhower presided over their genesis with minimal drama. As, for example:

Item: The judical bureaucracy had already been swaying under the force of black protest for almost twenty years when, in 1954, Earl Warren, the Chief Justice whom Eisenhower had appointed, led the Supreme Court to its decision on color and race in American schools. Warren masqueraded as a judicial character, but he was, more realistically, a frustrated executive, a man of politics and also a moralist. When Warren and his Supreme Court forbade all states to segregate black and white children in separate school systems, Warren was setting history on the march—if only the President and the Executive branch would march, full-heartedly, with him. Eisenhower's own feeling about black and white has not come down to us; but for him, the Supreme Court *was* supreme, and when it came to exerting the absolute clutch of authority, it was Eisenhower who sent the 101st Airborne Division to Little Rock, Arkansas, in 1957. The Supreme Court had outlawed segregation, which was the appropriate way the matter should come before government. Though he had offered no leadership, Eisenhower as Executive enforced the judicial decision.

Item: As far back as the mid thirties, the engineers of the Bureau of Public Roads, as it was called then, had cranked up and sent to Franklin Roosevelt a plan for a national grid of highways. Highway bureaucrats exert one of the most irresistible forces in American government, second only to the revenue service bureaucrats. An elected Executive can say either yes or no to his highway bureaucracy—but their designs cannot be changed. For one reason or another, mostly the effort of the Great War, its dislocating aftermath, then the Korean War, Roosevelt and Truman both had stalled the highway bureaucrats' proposal for a national highway system. But now, in Eisenhower's time, the moment had arrived when a federal interstate highway system seemed inescapably necessary. Such projects come working their way to a President's personal attention in a cocoon of analyses and statistics, with a train of attendant advocates and denouncers. No President ever has time to unpeel all the layers of figures and interests in so monumental a problem as highways or energy, so he must go with the best advice that fits his own preconceptions. Eisenhower's instincts ran to good roads; as a country boy and military commander he loved roads; thus he leaned on Congress to give the nation its national highway system; and so America was on the march to the Suburban Society.

I make Eisenhower seem almost a tool of the bureaucracies; but as a managerial President, he was no one's tool and where he felt most certain, in military and foreign affairs, had not a moment's hesitation in overruling any bureaucracy. He demonstrated this virtue best against the chief diplomatic idealogue of the cold war, his own Secretary of State, John Foster Dulles. Dulles might

play at brinkmanship—but Eisenhower would have none
of it. Neither at the first Berlin uprising, in June of 1953,
nor at the conjunction of the Suez and Hungarian crises
of 1956, nor at any time, would Eisenhower risk war.
When Dulles, Radford and Nixon wanted the United
States to save the French at Dienbienphu in 1954, Eisenhower said no. Some urged an atomic strike. Eisenhower
said no. When it came to "unleashing" Chiang K'ai-shek
to hit the Communist mainland, Eisenhower said no.
Eisenhower understood military matters as no President
since George Washington, and no cheaper military-diplo-
matic stroke has been directed by any President of modern times than Eisenhower's personal stroke in Lebanon
in July of 1958. A Communist coup seemed possible
there. Resistance to the Communists required support.
Eisenhower responded with seventy warships of the Sixth
Fleet and nine thousand marines and paratroopers to
establish a beachhead just outside Beirut. Not a man was
killed. The Communist coup was averted, and within
weeks all Americans were out—safe. Chief Diplomat
Eisenhower was superb. Except for his one great blunder
in the Suez crisis of 1956, when he sacrificed American
interests for American pieties, he knew well the difference
between pieties and interests.

Where Eisenhower was weakest was as a politician.
Caustic biographers may make his political naïveté comic
—but it was part of his strength. He must be remembered
as a figure in a fading America, decent and tough, with
the virtues, the hypocrisies, the hero images, as guides.
He vibrated to an older American rhythm, as if he had
grown up reading McGuffey's Readers and his reading
tastes had never changed. As a boy he had undoubtedly
been thrilled by the relief of Cawnpore and the message
to Garcia, and as President he read Zane Grey Westerns.
He liked money; he apparently dallied with women but
above all he felt he must do what was right. His view of
the Presidency was simple: Congress passed the laws, the
Supreme Court judged the laws, the President did his best
to execute the laws. Apart from Eisenhower's belated
outrage at Joe McCarthy, he never gave any show of

understanding the manipulative political power and responsibility of the Presidency.

His blind spot for politics had struck me when I met him first in Europe, and twelve years later it was still there. In Europe I had once asked his opinion of Franklin Delano Roosevelt. Roosevelt was a great President, he said, Roosevelt loved maps and ships, but Roosevelt simply could not understand the way organizations should work. For example, Ike continued, take the Casablanca conference of 1943. On his arrival there, FDR had drawn Ike aside and told him to do something which, Ike knew, the British would vigorously object to. Ike explained to Roosevelt that even though he wore the American uniform, his was an Allied command; that he, Ike, represented all the Allies, so that all directives must be transmitted to him via the Combined Chiefs of Staff, in which the British had an equal voice with the Americans. Ike related that the President then nodded agreement. But the next day, after meeting with Churchill again, FDR once more asked Eisenhower to end-run the British; and again Eisenhower explained. The same thing happened yet again the next day. Then, finally, as the summit conference was breaking up, the President once more summoned Eisenhower, and once more Eisenhower explained why he could not follow his own President's orders. As Ike told it, it was a long story, full of repetitions, but it made his point: "No matter how much you explained to FDR, he never understood that in matters that big you just have to go through channels."

It was this insistence on "going through channels," bred into him as a soldier, that made Ike so poor a politician. At the Republican convention in San Francisco in 1964, the morning after Goldwater's nomination, the ex-President invited two reporters to breakfast—Felix Belair of *The New York Times* and myself.

All three of us had been up very late, and at least two of us—Belair and I—were slightly hung over. Ike, ever the Commander in Chief, had ordered toast, scrambled eggs and sausages for three. When we entered, the food was already on the table. And Ike greeted us by saying, "Do you guys feel as lousy as I do this morning?"

Then he said that the Goldwater nomination was a disaster for the Republican Party. But what could he, Eisenhower, have done to stop Goldwater? Should he have tried harder to intervene? Would it have been right for him, the ex-President, to try to dictate the nominee? Had he let Scranton down? Both of us, Belair and I, knowing how meticulously the Cow Palace coup had been put together by its craftmaster, Clifton White, assured the old chief that nothing could possibly have been done at the convention to stop it. Reassured, Eisenhower went on to a marvelous passage of introspection—as valid as it was naïve. "What's a conservative?" Eisenhower mused. "What's a liberal? I kept reading those papers, talking about inflation and deflation, and all I could make out was that if you let the budget float, prices went up, and if you pulled the budget tight, prices went up less, and if prices went up four or five percent a year, somehow you were a liberal, but if prices were kept under two percent, you were a conservative." Eisenhower did not think of himself as either conservative or liberal; nor was it Goldwater's conservatism that troubled him. Rather, he simply did not think Goldwater could win an election, and he was trying to explain to two acquaintances why he had taken no action to stop Goldwater—and at the same time was wondering why to himself.

Given a hard problem clearly defined, like the survey of a rough terrain or the conciliation of a major ally, Eisenhower could perform superbly—as, for example, landing more than 200,000 troops on one day under the guns of the Wehrmacht in Normandy; or landing nine thousand American troops on the beaches of Beirut; or landing one thousand paratroopers in Little Rock, Arkansas. Given a sense of what should be done, Eisenhower could usually figure out how to do it. And then he would *do* it expertly.

But from this charming personality followed a Presidential record that will puzzle historians who seek to thread arguments through facts. The Eisenhower legisla-

tive record offers, at first glance, one of the lowest
achievement scores made by any major President. But
when he was President, the American people were never
happier, or, at least, never more convinced of the opportunity to be happy.

The Eisenhower record, when squeezed down, tells
of a superb foreign policy—a matchless record of clean
decisions, starting with Korea, blemished chiefly by the
flinching from resolution in the Suez crisis.

At home, the record of Eisenhower as a propulsive
President is meager. He tried to reorganize the Post Office
and mail service, as every President in modern times has
done; he succeeded only in changing the olive-drab mail-
boxes and trucks to a decorative red, white and blue
which ornamented city blocks and village greens with gay
splotches of color. Benignly, he invited and presided over
the passage of the first Civil Rights Act of the century,
calling for a Civil Rights Commission and Civil Rights
Division in the Department of Justice which would protect the right of black people to vote. It was a moral and
high-minded act—but almost as completely ornamental in
effect as the new red-white-and-blue postal boxes.

The major structural change Eisenhower made in
government was in strengthening that push to centralization against which he had so vehemently protested as a
candidate in Paris. That change was embodied in the
creation of the Department of Health, Education and
Welfare, HEW. This monster agency has since come to
rival its sister gorgon, the Department of Defense, or
DOD, in every way—as the central target of the most
aggressive lobbies in Washington; as the richest spoils
system, over whose parts Congressional committees war
for jurisdiction; as the darling or villain of the most
animated, high-minded and do-good groups. In Eisenhower's time, in the 1959 "normal" budget, HEW spent
only one fourteenth ($3 billion) as much as the Depart-
ment of Defense ($42.2 billion). By the 1977 budget,
DOD expenditures had little more than doubled (to
$101.6 billion), while HEW "pure" social service costs
had jumped by more than ten times (to $42 billion). And

when one included in the HEW budget new and expanded
direct aid benefits, HEW's budget ran to $147.45 billion.
And its margin of spending was rising.

Eisenhower's purpose in setting up a Department of
Health-Education-Welfare was logical, simple and impressive. The President wanted to get a handle on what
was going on in the areas of social demand, the pressures
coming at the government from every angle, anticipated
and unanticipated. On paper, it seemed logical to channel
the demands of health, education, welfare in one stream
which would flow through one cabinet spokesman. But
the new department provoked the axiom that any department with a hyphen in its name simply does not know
what it is supposed to do; and HEW never has known,
then or now.

One may leave the history of the Eisenhower administration with the creation of HEW its crest. But one
cannot leave the history of the Eisenhower Presidency
there, for HEW was symbolic. HEW was an earnest
government effort to cope, to give reasonable response to
the new social problems the country was thrusting to attention as it throbbed with change. And Eisenhower, believing he could divorce politics from government, thought
that simple clean administration could answer the political questions simmering, and about to burst, under the
rubrics of "Health," "Education," "Welfare."

The 1960s were to prove Eisenhower's approach
politically naïve—but it did not seem so at the time. Most
of the stirrings about to pound their way into politics
were obscure. But whether it was television that incubated action in the streets or action in the streets that drew
television to it, none of these stirrings would be seen without drama. Drama brought their impact to politics, and
thus on the making of Presidents. But back then in the
1950s one had to leave Washington to get firsthand the
sense of movement "out there," the sense of what was
happening in the country.

Fortunately, at *Collier's*, the concept of politics was
broad enough, and the Eisenhower regime in Washington
so apparently unexciting, as to keep me out, almost con-

stantly, on the
Washington that
bined with what
assignment at *Collier*
ents that were going in
reached the manipulation a

An unworded but happy
reporting at *Collier's*. I could ch
assignments in agreement with Ken
But when necessary, McArdle could im
stories dictated to him by the magazine's
for advertising. My own choices were star
the northward migration of blacks from field
the contest for the Democratic Party's nominat
feuds and wars of the California Republican Party.
the stories forced on us by advertising needs, like
advent of the jet, or the building of the national highway
system, paradoxically enlarged my political understanding
most. Such advertising stories led me closest to the appetite systems and social pressures that worked on politics,
and whose rhythm in the fifties began to rock America.

The story of the jet airplane, for example, was
among a number of assignments I accepted with reluctance, and then came to find fascinating, as instructive in
politics as a political convention. McArdle had made no
attempt to coat the aviation assignment with honey. For
years, *Collier's* had granted a nationally famous *Collier's*
aviation trophy. But now it was losing travel and aviation
advertising and it needed an aviation story. McArdle did
not care how or when or at what point I began my
aviation story—so long as I wrote it well, with the history
accurate, and alerted the aviation industry to *Collier's*
welcome for the big jets. Unaware when I accepted the
assignment that new jets were even on the way, I was to
learn more about the rhythm of the fifties from the jet
than I could have had "The Rhythm of the Fifties" been
the title of the assignment.

The jet was an artifact—an airplane. So, too, in the
early fifties was television an artifact; so, too, was the new

The
fties
y by
hich

ition
ntici-
e on
vings
ound,
had
ng off
'Tex"
y, so
eing's
e end
ad no

Incubating the Storm

road looking for stories, for it was outside
politics in America were changing. Com-
had learned at *The Reporter,* my
exposed me to the critical ingredi-
American politics before they
d voting level.

(533)

compromise governed my
ose most of my own
McArdle, the editor.
ose on me those
desperate need
ly political:
o ghetto,
on, the
But
he

erican
ed of
traveling at the speed plateau of the old propellor pulled
planes. They wanted to travel faster, and more and more
they wanted to travel by plane. In the previous five years,
the number of Americans flying on scheduled airlines
had, actually, doubled—to 41,623,000. In the next twenty years that figure would grow to 220,000,000. Planes
had already crippled train service; by 1955, more than
three times as many passengers were traveling between
our cities by airplane as by train. Moreover, that year,
1955, had seen the old four-engine prop plane finally
overtake the even more cumbersome and obsolete ocean
liners; for the first time more travelers had *flown* out of
New York (432,692) then had *sailed* out (418,487).
Now this new Boeing 707 was going to put Los Angeles
within five hours of New York instead of eight, New
York within six and a half hours of London instead of
twelve, and rub its nose smack up against the barrier of
sound. There, said the 707 designers, at an average cruis-
ing speed of 545 miles per hour compared to the prop
planes' maximum speed of 340, air travel would rest for

some time—until the appetite for speed grew again, and designers found a way to build a Supersonic that could also make money.

The plane, like a chariot unearthed by archaeologists, led forward and backward. It led forward to a country that had not yet learned to design air terminals for the outgoing generation of planes but was now hurtling into the jet age. It led forward to the linking of continents and the crowding of hotels. It led forward to mazes of finance and huge profits.

But it was even more fascinating to trace the jet backward.

The jet had begun in private imagination; had been built by private enterprise; it was being placed in service by private companies. The airline pioneers thought of themselves as great individual adventurers, historic gamblers. Yet, however vehemently they protested their independence from government, they all wished to *use* the government, milk the government and be free of it at the same time.

The pioneers were still alive when I wrote their story. And as they talked to me, beneath their daring and the heroism and the adventure of flight, one heard the recurring theme of alternate dependence on and fear of government. As you reached backward, you discovered that at the very beginning of their good fortune lay a forgotten law called the Kelly Act of 1925. The Kelly Act had set out Contract Air Mail Routes—CAMs—to assist the flying freaks with post office subsidies. All modern major airlines have sprouted from such Contract Air Mail Routes. CAM 1 had been the Boston–New York run; its contractor was Colonial Air Transport, run by a recent Yale graduate named Juan Trippe, who abandoned that line to take up a contract to fly mail from Florida to Havana under a rubric called Pan American Airways. CAM 5 was a contract to fly mail over the Rockies, which a young San Francisco banker, William A. Patterson, linked to CAM 8 (Los Angeles–Seattle), then to CAM 18 (Chicago–San Francisco) and the New York–Chicago leg of National Air Transport, to make United

Airlines. CAM 9 (Chicago–Minneapolis) had grown into Northwest Airlines, which soon, with the jet, would reach from New York to Tokyo. The men I spoke with were proud of themselves. "This," said one, "is the industry of hashish-eaters. Nothing will ever seem as crazy a dream, nothing will seem as high or dark, as night-crossing the Alleghenies seemed in 1928."

It was C. R. Smith, then president of American Airlines, later the Secretary of Commerce, who could best make the story come together. Smith had the gift of making one see both private enterprise and government at work; aviation was the weaving together of private and public imaginations at once. For Smith, the marvel of aviation history was not the coming jet, but the old and obsolete DC-3. So many things had come together on time way back in 1935: A 900-horsepower engine, perfected by Curtiss-Wright in New Jersey just two years earlier! An automatic pilot, designed by the Sperry plant on Long Island, which meshed all panel instruments together so that the pilot could lock the plane on course and let it fly by itself! A rubber boot on the leading edge of each wing, just designed, which could flex back and forth, and break the grip of the ice demon! A Douglas designer's idea that, on takeoff, the undercarriage of the plane could be drawn up into its fuselage! Each innovation had a history of metallurgy, rubber, instrumentation, of its own. But what counted, what counted then *finally,* was the creation of a plane that could carry twenty-one passengers, or a payload of six thousand pounds, through the air at 185 miles an hour. "It was the first airplane," said Smith, "where, if you sold all the seats, you actually made a little money."

And with the DC-3 the airlines were off on that alternating sequence of triumph and corruption that locked them as partners to the government forevermore. The plane had freed airlines from direct out-of-pocket dependence on post office subsidies. But the government had still to support them. Flight had doubled, then tripled, then quadrupled before the war, so air traffic required traffic controls—and only government could pay for those invisible crisscross points and spiral electronic gateways in the sky. Government provided the radio beacons that replaced farmers' smudge pots. When the airlines learned to fly the Atlantic, and profit soared, profit depended on the safety of flight, and the presence below of ten "ocean station" beacon ships and air-rescue service provided by government. Government monitored instrumentation, safety, pilot licensing. What the government could give, the government could take away, and the dynamics of the industry thus pressed it into Washington politics, the airlines courting, bribing, stealing routes one from the other, leveraging out any favor, legal or illegal, they possible could.

I remember closing out my story for *Collier's* by standing on a ramp outside a Boeing test shed in Seattle. It was long before the days when environment had become a Sacred Cause, and pollution the Curse of Mankind. Boeing engineers were testing the raw jet engines that would power the 707 once in flight. The sound of the engine was barbarous; at full throttle it was as if someone were drilling away with a corkscrew in one ear, blowing a whistle up the tube of the other, while at the same time someone else was thumping my chest, *thud-thud-thud*, with a baseball bat. The Boeing engineers assured me they could solve the problem—and showed me a fitting, looking like a tube with rusty iron petals, which, they said, would cut the noise by half. They had to, they explained. If they didn't cut down the noise, they were sure that government would step in, and they hoped to slip this plane into American life without provoking government to intervene more than it already did.

There was, I agreed after six weeks on the story, nothing that could stop the jet. What it would do, what it would cost, how it would change life, no one could say. "We're buying planes," said C. R. Smith, "that haven't yet been fully designed, with millions of dollars we don't have, and we're going to operate them from airports that aren't ready, in a traffic-control system that can't handle them, and we have to fill them with more passengers than we know how to service."

But he was going ahead. That was the mood of the 1950s. Movement was of the essence, and the faster the better.

I had known Smith during the war when he was deputy commander of the Air Transport Command flying the Hump. He was a superb raconteur and so I knew some of his stories. He could recall how as a boy in Whitney, Texas, he would make the wagon trip to Hillsboro, the market town fourteen miles away, and it was a dawn-to-dusk trip. Now he was gambling $135 million as president of American Airlines on planes that would do the round trip New York–Los Angeles–New York in less than eleven hours, or the same time as the old round trip to market in Hillsboro.

Not all the stories I did for *Collier's* were as clear in perspective as the story of the jets. But all events that one could report, as they flowed together in families of development, flowed on the junction in Washington.

I was assigned, for example, again because we needed advertising, to do a major story on the proposed new national highway system. Highways had up until then been largely a statehouse, not a federal, story. But I was no more than days into this story when I realized that these proposed new highways meant not only life or death for scores of small cities and towns which would be zoned in or out of the mainstream by the planning, but that the plan as a whole was going to change America. At the center of all planning were the engineers in Washington and the Congress which would tax and pay for the roads; and there, in Washington, I learned about lobbies from the men who manufactured cement and the men who manufactured asphalt. Both groups supported the highway system, but each wanted roads built of its own paving materials. The asphalt and cement lobbies were feuding across Washington and the Capitol like the Hatfields and McCoys in the hills of Appalachia. Simultaneous with their war was the war of the truckmen versus the railroads; and the railroads, having lost one war—for passengers—to the airlines, were now losing another war—for freight—to the truckmen's lobby. Washington correspondents took such lobby wars for granted and were bored by them. I was only dimly aware of corruption in those days, but it was my sense that I could smell money burning like autumn leaves as the great National Highway Act passed in 1956.

The true significance of the act became crushing only many years later—when the nation realized that it had been placed on wheels, that Arab oil turned those wheels, that the entire civilization of the supermarket and the green lawn was subject to Arab blackmail. Even more importantly, the act promised a degree of painlessness that was politically narcotic, an anodyne provision that the new roads would be paid for by raising the tax on gasoline from two cents to three cents a gallon, the tax on tires from five cents to eight cents per pound, and the excise tax on buses, trailers and trucks from eight percent to ten percent; these taxes would accumulate automatically in a "trust fund" in Washington. Which "trust fund" continued thereafter for almost twenty years, untouchable either by the Executive or by Congress, to bend out of shape by its sheer swollen weight every reasonable plan for a national transport system to meet the needs of the seventies or eighties. But the lobbyists of the winners— the truckmen, the asphalt men, the cement men—all knew what they were doing: they were building into their fostering bureaucracy such powers, such resources, such legislative impregnability that only a national upheaval could wipe out the powers that later came to be lodged in such "iron triangles" of Washington. They were doing, I learned, what every lobby was doing—the schoolteachers with theirs, the bankers with theirs, the oil companies with theirs, the farmers of every variety with theirs.

Every single story I wrote for *Collier's,* political or not, led to Washington. I sought—and McArdle enthusiastically agreed—to do a story on the black vote in the big cities. Blacks in the big city had not even been a statehouse story before the Supreme Court's 1954 decision; if anything, they were barely emerging from the crime pages in the white newspapers. But, I found, black leadership had a clearer and sharper view of Washington than any other movement, large or small, across the country: Washington wrote the laws, the President then made the laws work. Blacks were still largely outlawed from the polling places in the South; but in the Northern cities, their votes were swelling to critical importance. Indeed, it was not too difficult to show that the vital margin of Truman's victory in 1948 had come from the black vote in three states—Ohio, Illinois, California. We would write and publish a story on the black vote.

In those days of the 1950s the black migration from the South was reaching its flood peak, the tide in some years exceeding a quarter of a million. Neither local, state nor federal government had made any preparation to receive the wandering blacks in the big cities; the cities were physically, politically, socially, ethnically and industrially totally unready to receive this flood. Only the black leaders, who still, in those innocent days, spoke of their people as Negroes, knew that the migration must end up in the streets, or else be channeled by Washington. My story lay in the slums, in the ghettos, in the clubhouses of men like Congressman William Dawson of Chicago, in the mechanics of getting black voters to the polls, in the grisly drama of a future nation where one race (black) dominated its big cities, and another, hostile race (white) surrounded them in suburbs and countryside. But the black leaders were ahead of me in perspective: they were then becoming, and have since become, the most powerful lobby in Washington. They had just proposed to Congress a bill to force the federal government to guarantee black registration and voting rights in the South; it was to be a decade before they got that bill passed by Congress, but they had a clear idea where the power lay. It lay in Washington, and they meant to increase that power of Washington again, and again, and again. Of all the forces urging power into Washington during the past twenty years, none has been stronger, more persistent, more long-lasting, than that of black protest.

All those who had a special claim to press on Washington were beginning to move in the 1950s—which meant schoolteachers, and peanut farmers, and sugar planters, and Zionists, and Croatian irredentists, and blacks, and university presidents, and research scientists, and fortune-hungry TV proprietors. Which left all the rest of the country with the conviction that Dwight D. Eisenhower was their proper President because he kept Washington from interfering in their lives as the Democrats had done—by conscripting boys for war, raising taxes or plaguing them with more forms to fill out. They, the vast majority, knew that Eisenhower not only knew nothing about the Sunday traffic jam on Highway 99 snaking over the hills into California's San Joaquin valley, but couldn't care less; knew nothing about arson in the South Bronx, which was just beginning, and couldn't care less. But that, vaguely, Eisenhower was for a good new highway program, as were they, and for giving the Negroes an even break, as were they. How the contending forces would work out from the happy "now" of the 1950s to the violence-torn 1960s neither he, nor they, nor the Democrats, could have foreseen.

The search for history implies, above all, a search for a center of control, for the pennant-ringed yurt of the nomad chief from which the order to ride goes out, for the contest of authority in and around the court which when resolved points the direction all must tramp. But the search for history, in the Eisenhower years, lay entirely outside these classic models. No one seemed to control. The search broadened out into a philosopher's puzzle of a society in full vigor—rushing where? The United States Government had inherited so much military power it need fear no one. It had so much confidence in American industrial supremacy that it felt it could tolerate any foreign economic penetration or commercial assault, fair or unfair. Government could posture as placid, and chuff up to its seat on the grandstand above the parade, and see the floats, the banners, the acrobats, the whirling dervishes, all pass by—while the beat and the throb of the band music grew faster and faster.

Figures and statistics trace the acceleration in black-

and-white terms. One could take the figures for the gross
national product, the GNP—which shot up from 286
billion to 506 billion dollars from 1950 to 1960! One
could take the stock market's Dow-Jones industrial index
—which shot up from 216 to 618 during the same decade. It took genius to lose money in the stock market in
those years, and individual share-owners who sought a
piece of the action rose in number from 6,490,000 in
1952 to 17,010,000 ten years later!

What was happening was the uncontrollable acceleration of American ingenuity, achievement and reward, as
Americans found the world open to them. Established
American industries, which before World War II had
made their foreign investments chiefly in England, or in
automobile plants in Europe, or oil wells in Arabia, were
joined by new American companies ambitious to become
multinationals. Americans now canned fruits and vegetables in France, made vacuum cleaners and undershirts in
Formosa, Korea and Hong Kong. My old friend Theo
was caught in this acceleration. Now he told me, with
liquid gestures, how he had worked out a deal for General Electric to buy up the entire French computer industry,
Machines Bull. Alas for both Theo and General Electric,
Machines Bull turned out to be a poor investment, because French technology was so far behind American
technology in computers and cybernetics that General
Electric had to get rid of it. But Theo's adventure in
buying up the French computer industry was only a detail
in the exuberance.

It would be entirely misleading to recapture the
American exuberance of the 1950s only in episodes of
high finance or international wheel-and-deal. The exuberance was there, for example, in the outburst of color—in
clothes, in shops, in architecture, in supermarkets, even in
the design of giant refineries. The Athenians, Romans and
Chinese, at their power peaks, had reveled in public
colors, too. Now the Americans outdid them. The exuberance was there on Broadway; in the new music; above
all in Hollywood, where, freed of block booking, independent producers were about to open the movie circuits

for anything their imaginations could conceive and their hustlers market. The fifties began with many odd departures. But how could one predict where a departure like the Diners Club would end? The Diners Club gave you a "credit card." By the end of the decade, everyone had a credit card, issued either from America's largest bank, the Bank of America, or its smallest shopping center. The credit card liberated America from the old doctrine of "cash and carry."

Technology moved equally fast. The transistor, a tiny device invented at Bell Laboratories in 1947, shriveled to fingernail size; then to microdot size; then was combined in circuitry wafers which defied the measures of weight and size. Those lucky enough to understand the exuberance in technology in the fifties grew rich by buying Xerox, IBM, Polaroid or a score of lesser companies sprouting along Silicon Gulch in California or Route 128 in Boston.

But the ultimate exuberance was just beginning—the exuberance later to be celebrated as freedom to choose one's "life-style." Physiologically effective oral contraceptives were unknown in 1950. By the end of the decade oral contraceptives and intrauterine devices were freely used by coeds and matrons alike. Alfred Kinsey's report on *Sexual Behavior in the Human Female* appeared in 1953, indicating that 26 percent of all middle-class women had committed adultery by age forty, while nearly 50 percent had experienced premarital intercourse. This simple report on such old realities probably undermined the resolution of more cautious women than any new code of seduction and acquiescence could have achieved. *Peyton Place* became a best-selling novel because it still had shock value; *Lolita,* only two years later, was a best seller because its artistic mastery obscured a sexual nastiness most critics ignored. Everybody was now supposed to be "with it"—but what being "with it" was, no one defined. "Beats" and "Beatniks" were coming in, as were rock-'n'-roll and Elvis Presley, all blended culturally in the huge new masticator of television. It was television, first sounding in the fifties, that would blare its way into the man-

ners of the sixties and then trumpet into the streets the
politics of a new America.

Television belongs in that family of mechanical devices that change civilization, of the order of magnitude
of the printed book. As soon as people learned to use it,
its use would change their lives. The men who took over
the television tubes sensed, almost at once, this potency.
The new masters were like Napoleon and his marshals
when they first learned how to mass artillery on the
battlefield and, defining their targets with an accuracy
and weight never before possible, went on to annihilate
their enemies.

The men who took over television came of every
political persuasion, and spanned the human range from
the utterly greedy to the doggedly noble. But what harnessed best and worst together was their common perception of the target. Audience was the target. And in shelling their rivals for American attention, the masters of
television, without any malice whatsoever, sent fleeing
bigots, babbits, fundamentalists, as well as old-fashioned
politicians, most thoughtful men and women, and most of
the poetry in public life. Television delivered instant excitement; television could excavate or carve such excitement out of public affairs. In the contest for mass audience, television routed all others. Among those others
sent fleeing in the rout were the mass magazines; and of
these the first and frailest was *Collier's,* my home when
the rout began, and to whose command staff I rose just
before the end.

There was no doubt that I was there, at the center,
at the opening of a chapter of American history, and
Collier's was a magnificent, if withering, perch from
which to watch the action unfold. The history of *Collier's*
magazine was woven into the history of the mass magazines; and for sixty years the history of such magazines
had been central to the history of American politics. The
collapse of *Collier's* was, thus, more than a commercial
bankruptcy. It was a political and social event, the first in
a train of such events which led to the domination of

American politics by television. And since I moved from junction to junction, I would like to linger at some length over the history that binds together American politics and American communications—and on how the crack-up came at *Collier's* as the 1950s speeded the American pulse.

Of the great mass magazines, *Collier's,* in its prime, might well have been classed in Category One of importance. Certainly not the most important magazine in that category, but nonetheless of major significance. It died when its time came to die as the time came for mastodons to die when the climate of America changed. Like a mastodon, *Collier's* knew it was dying but could not understand why.

All magazines have a life-and-death cycle; few last for half a century, and I can think of only six that have survived for a hundred years in America. The cycle usually depends on the vitality of one man or a succession of men who manage to capture and hold for a number of years the attention and mood of their time. To understand how very important the mood of the time is in the life cycle of magazines, one must distinguish between the different ancestors of the book and the magazine, for they are linked only by their use of printed words on paper pages. The ancestry of the book goes back to Greece and Rome and beyond; the book writer addresses himself to a reader, an audience of one. The magazine comes of entirely different ancestry—the ancient and medieval fairs, the Forum in Rome and the courtyard of the Temple in Jerusalem. A magazine is a fair, where merchants and peasants, townsmen and jugglers, bear-baiters and preachers, sex peddlers and elixir dispensers, offer their wares or entertainment. Long before there was a printed word, or even paper, in the Western world, there was a gathering on the fairgrounds, usually once, sometimes twice, a week, where men and women swapped news of weather, crops, kings, queens, assassinations, along with politics, gossip and ideas. The French Revolution was fermented by the talk at village fairs, the First Crusade was launched by the preachings of Peter the Hermit at the fairs of France, Caesar made his moves in politics coming up through the Forum and, according to legend, posting on its walls the world's first news organ, the *Acta Diurna*, an open account of the hitherto secret proceedings of the Senate.

Nowhere, however, did the magazine form reach so high a peak of national influence as in America—and hold it for more than a half a century, starting in the 1890s. Special circumstances gave it that opportunity here. America was, for one thing, huge. No local newspaper could reach from Maine to California; no New York or Washington newspaper could reach, as did Paris and London papers, half the country's reading population. But starting in the 1890s, any number of devices combined to give new mass magazines explosive impact on national life. The halftone photoengraving process permitted inexpensive photographic reproduction for a national population, which, though literate, was for the most part repelled by unbroken blocks of type on the printed page. The high-speed rotary press, another device, was perfected—presses which could spit out millions of copies a day. And most effectively, by the 1890s that giant device the national railway net was completed from coast to coast, border to border. A manufacturer could deliver stoves, pianos, beds, furniture and, soon, automobiles to one national market—if only a way could be found to reach the entire national market.

But to advertise to a national market meant to find a national audience—and with that imperative, there appeared not only the national magazine but the folklore figure known as a "national editor." The publisher knew he could buy the paper, build the presses, speed the run, physically deliver bound copies in millions, to satisfy the advertisers. But he needed an editor to assemble readers, and the impact of the national editor, or the national reporter for the national magazine, on American politics was prodigious.

This period of political breakthrough is remembered for the muckrakers who gave their name to an era. Yet the advent of the national magazine meant much more than the simple exposure of oil monopolies, sugar trusts, municipal corruption and packing-house filth. It meant that whoever was responsible for a *national* magazine had to think *nationally*. The Civil War had become inevitable as local newspaper editors inflamed sectional passions and pressed regional politicians sent to Washington to do their bidding. The new breed of national editor was different. Men like Edward Bok, Frank Munsey, Peter Collier, George Horace Lorimer and their peers were the only people outside the White House who, professionally, had to think of the concerns shared by people who lived in states as diverse as Minnesota, Oregon, Florida and Maine. Women's magazine editors, of course, could focus on cooking, child-rearing, feminine complaints, husbands and other problems that women shared. General mass magazine editors had it harder, but once they learned that every big city had a machine and the machine had a boss, a Lincoln Steffens could be turned loose; once they learned that everyone ate the meat of Chicago's packing houses, an Upton Sinclair could be turned loose; once they learned that every small town had a businessman or small manufactory or refinery in danger of being gobbled up by outsiders, you could turn the trust-busters loose. Collectively, national editors could command national attention; and once attention had been focused on a national problem by a vigorous editor and a vigorous writer, politics responded.

No political force in America can resist the cry for virtue—and the national mass magazines shrieked virtue. In its name they demanded a big navy (under the first Roosevelt), antitrust action, direct election of senators, the restriction of immigration in the twenties. They were *for* prohibition in the first quarter of the century and then, led by *Collier's, against* prohibition when the madness of that act of virtue became apparent.

These magazines were different from newspapers of their day, and more important. Newspapers, then, simply told what had happened yesterday. But magazine stories had to look fresh for a week or a month, the time it took for delivery to California or Seattle. They could not pause over what had happened yesterday; they had to write about what was going to continue to happen next week and next month. Their political power, nationally, thus was prodigious; and remained so for almost half a century. By 1940, if one has to fix a date, the magazines had become the dominant political medium of the nation. No greater demonstration of media authority has been exhibited in our time than when three East Coast magazine publishers forced the nomination of Wendell Willkie on the Republican Party in 1940—the publishers of *Life* and *Time, Look* and the *Saturday Evening Post*. (The fourth mass giant, *Collier's,* supported Franklin D. Roosevelt, in its idiosyncratic course of shrieking patriotism and erratic liberalism.)

The platform from which politicians preach is almost always the same as that from which merchants huckster their wares; by the end of the war, radio had begun to challenge the mass magazines; but radio could not deliver pictures, so its challenge was not deadly. But when, at the beginning of the 1950s, television came on the scene, then the magazines knew they were confronted by a force, a magnetic distortion, that would change the world in which they lived. And in 1955, when I joined *Collier's,* I was coming on board a vessel not only threatened by television but also riddled by years of corporate infighting, owned by widows and other heirs, by bank-managed estates and by Wall Street raiders, and now turned over to a group of delightful California amateurs who were expected to turn history around and make *Collier's* profitable.

The new team controlled three magazines (*Collier's, Woman's Home Companion* and the *American*) with a combined circulation of ten million copies and a readership audience of perhaps forty million—which even in the days of television is substantial. What none of us in the editorial leadership understood was the implacable logic of corporate life and the guillotine judgment of balance sheets. We were a division of a large corporation called "the magazines division," to distinguish our "profit" center from "the book division" and the "records, radio division." But our group, the magazines, was dragging the entire corporation down in red ink. All the corporation wanted was that the magazine group make money. And none of us on the editorial floor could explain to the corporation that paper processing in the magazine business is different from paper processing in the toilet-paper business, or the carton-folding, waxed-paper and disposable-diaper businesses. In the magazine business, to make money requires an ingredient of spirit and imagination which the readers, advertisers, *and* the writers can identify. And this spirit and imagination had already spoiled at *Collier's*. Earlier mismanagement had befuddled the staff and the heat of television had enfevered them. We were unsteady when I joined, and even shakier a year later, when I was called to the executive colors.

I was, at that moment in 1956, at play in the field of my choice—politics—reveling in the sights, sound and smells of the first national convention I ever attended, the Democratic convention at Chicago, when the call came. It was a message from McArdle telling me that our base was, apparently, crumbling; the *American* magazine was shutting down, the other two magazines were in danger, our chieftain and leader, Paul Smith, had to leave Chicago immediately for New York to face the financial crisis. But no one must know we were in trouble. Smith had reserved the corner table in the most fashionable Chicago restaurant, the Pump Room, for the duration of the convention; it must not remain unoccupied. Those who remained at the convention for Crowell-Collier must occupy that table and keep it filled with celebrities to refute all rumors of our financial troubles; let the wine flow, the steaks pass, the parties be jovial. I did my best, with some gusto, to make the *Collier's* table at the Pump Room seem the place to be; but then flew back to New York to hear McArdle deliver another, more personal message.

The message was simple: I must now stop reporting the campaign and American politics, for which purpose I had enlisted with *Collier's*. Since I had analyzed for *Collier's* the problems of Germany, of California, of the highway system, I was now to analyze *Collier's* for *Collier's*. What was happening to us? Why? Nor did I have a choice. McArdle was gently but stubbornly insistent. I must. And so, in mid campaign, wishing to follow the contest of Eisenhower and Stevenson to its November conclusion and write a story, for which I had chosen in my mind the title "The Making of the President—1956," I was called off. I was called away to examine the condition of *Collier's,* specifically, but more generally: How does one excite the American people? How does one reach them? How does one make a profit by entertaining, informing or educating them?

All the questions fitted together into what I called the "Audience Game." I had come across the Game while at the *New Republic* just after the war, when the Audience Game seemed exclusively a Manhattan sport. Trying to remake America with Henry Wallace and the *New Republic* I had become fascinated by "Audience": What makes people listen? What ping of editorial initiative draws what pong of reader response? What makes them pay to read?

By a variety of mechanical stratagems, we had tripled circulation at the *New Republic* to almost 100,000 in the one year 1947. When its publisher stopped flogging circulation on its upward course and a year later let the *New Republic* drop to its natural audience, its readership fell to almost exactly what it had been before Henry Wallace came. At *The Reporter,* which I had recently left, I had learned about paper costs, direct-mail costs, subscription-renewal figures—and begun to sense the connection of Audience to politics, but only vaguely. At *Collier's* on the editorial floor I had been amused by accumulated circulation folklore. Why was it, for example, that the picture of a dog, even the most appealing puppy, on the cover of our magazines sent sales down? While, whenever *Woman's Home Companion* needed a hypodermic, the picture of a pussycat sent sales shooting up at newsstands? Who stopped at newsstands to look at pussycats? Why did dog-lovers not buy magazines? Or:

why did a picture of a sports hero, either football or baseball, increase our sales so much in Boston and New England, while elsewhere a sports cover turned readers aside? And why did all the mass mainstream magazines experience the same phenomenon at the same unpredictable week each spring—when newsstand sales would drop by ten or twenty percent as spring fever swept the country like an overnight disease and the nation yawned? And why was Easter the worst time to send out a direct-mail reach for subscriptions and October the best?

Now, from August 1956 on, I sat in my Manhattan office, as a consultant to executives, invited to play *Collier's'* hand in the Audience Game, and discovered that neither folklore nor instinct was enough. The purpose of this game, in commerce as in politics, was to command attention. Attention could be sold. I was playing in a game crowded with experts who commanded more data and figures than I—yet the experts who had staffed or guided *Collier's* had been beaten by rival teams of experts and brought us to the edge of disaster.

I could look down from my windows and see the yellow taxis, the black limousines, and the buglike people scuttling across Fifth Avenue between them. But I could not guess what these people wanted to read when they got home. I could see out sometimes, from the other side of the building, to the soft gray hills of New Jersey. But how could we reach out beyond those hills and find the audience we needed in the great midvalley? At night, several times, I visited the home of our publisher, Paul Smith. From his high apartment I could see the automobile stream of golden lights on New York's East River Drive endlessly pouring onto the Triborough Bridge. What impulses, what purpose, carried them? How many would cross the Triborough Bridge, how many would stay in Manhattan? How many after crossing the bridge would fork south to Long Island or north to the mainland? And how many more would there be at six than at ten in the evening? And how many more leaving for a Fourth of July or a Labor Day weekend than on an ordinary winter weekend? Engineers who designed the bridge had had to make just those guesses. Then they built the answers in concrete. But the guesses we had to make were even more difficult, and would be countered by competitive experts, trying to outwit or destroy us.

It was a few weeks after taking up the new executive assignment that I realized that I, so confident in the world of politics, was in a world entirely new and strange. It was the world of the mass marketeer, the animal trainer. For the marketeer, all America was a collection of markets through which stalked, or slouched, or sauntered, the animal called "Them." The game was to prick or prod the animal, whistle, shriek or coo at it, but somehow tease the beast to pay attention. For the marketeer, all media— billboards and radio, junk mail and television, newspapers and magazines—were instruments to lure or club or tweak attention out of "Them." *Collier's* was only one dart in the marketeers' quiver called periodicals; if they chose to rent our pages to advertise, we might make money. If they did not, we would perish.

A parochial course in American history lay behind this science of markets, which set the rules of the game of Audience. Some historians say scientific marketing began with the orange growers of Southern California, who, at the beginning of the century, formed their Sunkist Orange cooperative and did the first real survey of the American market for oranges. Such historians believe that the orange growers of the Southland founded that school of opinion manipulation which came to its fullest expression in the promotions of Hollywood and the Nixon triumph of 1972. Others say that scientific marketing began in the middle twenties when the advertising genius William Benton, trying to snare a coffee account, canvassed, with his wife, Helen, door to door in New York, trying to establish what it was that people liked about coffee. But whether invented in Manhattan, Southern California or Vienna, the science of social measurements and ratings, the demographics of mass marketing, was a science well advanced by the time I came to my emergency post at *Collier's*. Amazingly, in retrospect, I had learned nothing of this science in covering politics, because politicians then were only at the very beginning of their experience in the mass manipulation of public opinion.

Gradually it dawned on me as an executive consultant that there was no longer any "Them" that we could reach. To make money, mass magazines like *Collier's* had to give up on "Them," leaving "Them" to television. Magazines would have to slim down and concentrate on the audiences defined as "upper-educated," "lower-educated," garden lovers, gourmets, housewives, mechanics, porno-lovers; or tribal, regional, professional or "cause" audiences. Except for such pocket giants as *TV Guide* and *Reader's Digest,* all other magazines had to choose which specific packs and tribes they wished to cut out of the shuffling horde called Audience, and then sell that specific slice of Audience to someone who sought that market. One of our intelligent advertising salesmen explained to me: "The idea is to tell your customer that you can do for him exactly what he wants you to do. All he can do for himself is lean out the window of his skyscraper and yell to the people down below. But how far will his voice carry? We tell him. We show him how to make his voice reach exactly the kind of people he wants to reach." Only we could not.

For this purpose, I massed columns of figures and statistics. But the competitive figures of other magazines gave me the outline of our problem best. One sheet placed on my desk said that in the first six months of 1954, the single most dramatic eruption in magazine publishing was the phenomenon of the new magazine called *TV Guide*. In one year *TV Guide* had gained 98 percent in circulation—from 815,000 copies to 1,647,000 sold each week at newsstands, as files of "Them" passed by the stands and each new purchaser of a television set purchased also the magazine that was its handmaiden. In that six-month period, *Life* magazine, the undisputed mass-culture giant of its time, had lost 21 percent of its circulation at newsstands! *Life*'s still pictures could no longer compete with the moving images on the tube. The leader of the general magazines at the newsstands was still the *Saturday Evening Post,* with its familiar illustrations. But the figures of its newsstand sales over the previous two years traced a gradual, graceful, persistent downtrend, as if it were a sailing vessel that had sprung a leak and was serenely but slowly settling into water. And *Collier's*—*Collier's* plunged and swooped, bobbed up and down erratically on graphs, charts and newsstands alike.

The reader must forgive me for lingering over such technical details as "newsstand" figures. But more than anything else that came over my desk, they caught my attention. Subscription sales can be engineered by any good circulation manager; newsstand sales, however, are impulse sales, the instant response of the passer-by to the editors' judgment of what will catch his attention. In the early postwar years, all the mass mainstream magazines had sold commonly between 1,500,000 and 2,000,000 copies a week at newsstands. In the dreary two years previous to my new troubleshooting assignment, I found *Collier's* had only twice sold more than 1,200,000 newsstand copies. One was an issue whose cover bannered the story of the Kinsey report on American women's sex habits. The other bore a scare cover, showing sinister doctors in surgical dress, with the bold statement: "Why Some Doctors Should Be in Jail." From there, our newsstand sales had gone steadily downhill until, at the end of April 1956, spring fever had caught the nation, with its invitation to May dalliance. People had stopped reading; and our newsstand sales had slipped to something under 500,000; 492,000 was the final bookkeeping tally!

So there was a crisis which we could conceal neither from ourselves, our rivals, our advertisers, nor—most important of all—from the corporate board of directors upstairs. The shrinkage in our newsstand sales had come so fast, the shrinkage in our advertising had followed it down so sharply, that the balance sheet was hemorrhaging red ink. I groped for solutions, exasperated that I could no longer report politics—but the figures on my desk rubbed my nose in what underlay politics.

The shrinking newsstand figures, which perplexed me so, told the clearest story. There were many reasons for the fall-off of newsstand sales, but the one we shared with most mass magazines was simple: the people, in all their packs and tribes, were on the move in the 1950s; they were leaving the cities; they were no longer stopping at the commuter station, the subway kiosk or the neighborhood variety store to buy either the evening newspaper or the weekly magazine. More and more they were driving home from work; they could not read and drive at the same time. Neighborhoods were slowly changing—and in the new suburbs, no newsboys yodeled the evening headlines. In suburbia, the headlines were smoothly delivered each evening by television, and television was learning to package the headlines with pictures in a developing American art form with which we could not vie.

Our problem at *Collier's*, both editorial and commercial as well as in advertising, was how to reach suburbia. And as I absorbed the conventional wisdom of our wise men in marketing, there rose on the imaginary horizon of the America whose politics I had just ceased reporting, the Symbolic Supermarket. If the 1920s had added the gas station and the movie marquee as entirely new features to the landscape of America, so the 1950s was adding to the same landscape two distinctive features of its decade—the supermarket and the television antenna. The two were symbiotically linked; between them they shaped and formed, as they continue to shape and form, the culture of the suburbs where, for almost thirty years, the growth of America has taken place while its cities decay.

For us, at *Collier's*, it was vital to show large advertisers that our magazines reached the people who shopped in suburbia, at supermarkets. The supermarkets in suburbia were the intersection not only of the highways and the television but also of the invisible computer. The computer was beginning to control inventories; it told the giant distributors what merchandise moved and what did not move off the shelves; it was beginning to measure the force of each advertising dollar spent—and all America was on a shopping spree.

If any decade could be called the decade of the

consumer, it was the fifties: the money rolled in, the living was easy, appetites expanded, and television nightly tickled greed. Twice in that decade the Bureau of Labor Statistics revised the consumer price index to make it reflect the changes in what the average American bought with his pay—an ever smaller percentage, it turned out, for food. Likewise for clothing. But more and more on housing, more and more for leisure, more and more for doctors and medicines. All essentials were easily met by the rising economy, but luxuries and indulgences, what the economists call "discretionary purchasing power," were themselves becoming an essential to the growing national economy, the growing national market. We at *Collier's* wanted our share of this growing market, but we were being shouldered away from the trough.

I would sometimes, after extended briefings, wonder what I was doing in this world, and at other times marvel at the insights it yielded into social politics. Our advertising salesmen proved most illuminating. I learned from them that thirty years earlier, toothpaste was something heavily advertised in upper-class magazines because poor people, nonreaders, generally used no toothpaste at all; and now, "every workingman son of a bitch and his wife brush their teeth in the morning." So toothpaste-makers now relied on television and the supermarket to move toothpaste because "both the doctor's wife and the plumber's wife get their Wheaties at the same place." Thus TV claimed the advertising dollar not only of the toothpaste-maker, but of the butcher, baker, and candle-stick-maker. I was told by *Woman's Home Companion* advertising salesmen that thirteen big national corporations controlled 70 percent of all grocery business in the United States. No family grocer any longer advised the housewife across the counter on her choice of flour or coffee; the TV set sold such goods. Television had changed merchandising forever. The big chains built and leased the supermarkets which would eventually in the seventies become the shopping malls. They structured them like warehouses, stacked the shelves with goods, arranged the filing lines so that the sheep trudged in proper sequence through the carefully planned maze. Then, if the advertising was done right, television simply blew the cans, packages and bottles off the shelves into the shopping carts, as an autumn wind blows leaves off the trees.

Since I had been so abruptly lifted out of political reporting to the status of troubleshooter, my new learning could not help but sharpen my political perceptions. Reaching the suburbs was not only the essence of *Collier's* problem; it was the essence of that decade in American politics; and the real supermarket candidate, I suddenly realized, was none other than Dwight D. Eisenhower. He was a nationally known, recognizable brand product: West Point-crafted, money back if it fails to please, tested in war, tested in peace, reliable, honest, safe, and look, it makes you smile. The election of 1956, which I had been covering with zest and delight until a few weeks before, was all over. I could recognize Adlai Stevenson for what he was: what our salesmen would call an upper-end-of-the-spectrum product. The Stevenson package, like *Collier's,* would not sell in the supermarkets or suburbs.

One of our advertising salesmen summed up our dilemma for me in a quick conference on what is now called the "demographics of the audience." Our problem, he explained, was that *Collier's* held the "tail end of the upper end of the socioeconomic stratum"; therefore, he went on, we were the most vulnerable of the big magazines to television. He did not use the metaphor of the shark, but *The Old Man and the Sea* had been favorite reading on Madison Avenue for several years, and the shark was television. It was gobbling up everything that moved, everything that glittered, everything that competed for attention. We, who were being nibbled off by television at the "tail end" of the spectrum of mass magazines, were victims of the shark, feeding higher and higher in the socioeconomic stratum once thought of as middle middle class. Television sets in the late 1940s and early 1950s had been bought largely from the bottom up—by the culturally illiterate, the lip-readers, people who could not sit down to read a book or magazine because their eyes formed the words too slowly to pass a message to the mind. These people, who enjoyed wrestling, baseball, Uncle Miltie, contests and the sight of characters they had previously only imagined from the sound of radio soap opera were television's original audience. From that base, in the early 1950s, television began reaching upward, engaging the literate and illiterate alike as it moved its cameras in on the real and imaginary dramas of American life.

There was no doubt that politics enlarged the television audience. Each convention and election year—1948, 1952, 1956, 1960—recorded a surge in sales. And so, too, did the spontaneous dramas of investigation as senators found they could play the role of gangbusters more effectively on television than in real life. With the Kefauver-Mafia hearings of 1951, a pattern was set. With the Army-McCarthy hearings of 1954, televised hearings were certified as a permanent ingredient of political drama. By the time of the Ervin-Watergate hearings in 1973, television was the place where it actually happened. When to such excitements were added the creative dramas of what is now called the "Golden Age of Television," television began to reach from the very bottom of American life to its top, from ghetto to gold coast, from slum to suburb. Only the national mass magazines had previously claimed such a national audience; television now delivered in reality what the magazines had once claimed as their inflated boast.

It was a hopeless contest. No mainstream magazine with any sense of decency could reach down to the cultural level of the slack-jawed audience that television assembled effortlessly every night. No newspaper could deliver the news more quickly, morning or evening, than the television news systems. No alarm could concentrate national attention more swiftly at one time and in one place more effectively than television. It would take over fifteen years to squeeze out all the mass mainstream magazines—Collier's, Look, Life, Post—but the great fair had passed away from the grounds where they pitched their tents, and *Collier's* was the first to close, the inevitable being the inevitable.

Henry Adams, in his *Education,* regards the death of the great quarterlies of the nineteenth century as a transition point in the cultural and political life of the republic —the end of the reflective, sober consideration of public life by an educated elite, the beginning of an intolerable speed-up of public affairs. The coming of television removed, almost unbearably, the filter of the time between the news event and its absorption. The nation and all its most urgent drive forces were in a hurry; and television could make one hear, see and feel the chant of "Freedom, Now!" better than anything anyone could write for *Collier's.*

We tried. We stressed again the one advantage words have over television: the ability to recapture the past, to structure a narrative, tell a story and reach the bottom of it. We began to draw back readers. By fall *Collier's* was well on the way back to its long-gone pre-eminence in straight narrative reporting—a tradition that had begun with Richard Harding Davis's coverage of the Russo-Japanese War and continued through Hemingway's reporting of World War II. That form of narrative reporting, the stringing together of episode upon episode of reality to make a driving drama, is a peculiarly American literary form, and *Collier's* had once pioneered the field. Triggered by a superlative story by Cornelius Ryan, on the sinking of the *Andrea Doria,* the magazine briefly, in September 1956, broke into a commanding newsstand lead over *Look.* From a low of 500,000 at newsstands in April it had reached over 900,000 in September, and the editorial command glowed.

The final weeks at *Collier's,* as our newsstand sales surged, were weeks of delusive self-congratulation, boyish gloating and a euphoria that grew more and more unrealistic as we approached disaster's edge and then tipped over the edge to oblivion.

Two very large lessons are legacies of the last few months at *Collier's.*

The first and most important lesson was freshman simple, and remains as true of politics as it does of communications: There are only two ways of gaining public attention in America. The attention-seeker must either buy attention with money or command it by a clear message. In the age of television, the former is easier— the most certain way of getting attention is by buying time on the tube; with enough money, a mass audience of any size can, briefly, be bought. The other way of getting public attention is to offer either identity or a message— which is more difficult. Magazine publishing can thrive only by offering a point of view. Only a sharp identity will cluster together random "people" who want to see what the magazine's editors see. Whether it be in woodworking, baby raising, fire fighting, personalities, foreign affairs or health foods, there is always a subtribe or a community among "Them" waiting for a voice to gather them. We, at *Collier's,* had no sharp identity, no point of view, and feared to carve out such an identity; we offered numbers to our advertisers and anthologies to our readers. Television could do both better. As we approached the cliff's edge, we also offered what I thought was the best collection of stories, mysteries, self-improvement pieces and narrative reporting of any mass magazine—but no particular vision of the world. And so we were doomed to perish.

The second lesson was one of the more memorable courses I have ever taken in life on the subject of money. I had first seen "money" as a tale of copper and paper, ending in the tragedy of inflation, critical to the larger story of China. I had seen money as the underlying story of the Marshall Plan, and described the billions of dollars mobilized in Congress as armies of the dawn sent to revive Europe. It had been easier for me to write of a billion dollars in politics then than to understand a million dollars while trying to save *Collier's.* At *Collier's,* a million dollars was a *true* million dollars—not a governmental "million," which is only an inflationary comma. At *Collier's,* a million dollars was real money meaning the same thing to poor boys hoping to get rich as to rich men fearful of growing poor.

The corporate money lesson, stripped of its larger dimensions, can be simplified thus: Money, not purpose, measures the metabolism of corporations. When money runs out and a corporation cannot pay its debts, its creditors take over, and its investors are wiped out, which terrifies all men who save. But no one cares what happens to its employees. *Collier's,* as a corporation, had been in debt. It hoped that its two magazines, *Collier's* and *Woman's Home Companion,* could win back an audience to attract advertisers who would fertilize the balance sheet with their advertising at $22,000 a page. We of the editorial departments were told to win back the lost audience; and we did. What we did not realize was that each new subscriber we won back, each new purchaser who bought either *Collier's* or the *Companion* at the newsstand, cost the corporation money.

This course in money thus ended with a grand demonstration of how pennies make dollars: To print *Collier's* required some twenty or twenty-five cents of paper, ink and production time for each copy. To express the physical product, the glossy, color-flecked, story-packed ten-to-twelve-ounce perishable magazine, from our printing plant, in Ohio, to our most distant delivery point, in Seattle, cost twenty cents more. Anyone buying the magazine at a newsstand in Seattle was thus buying for fifteen cents what cost the corporation forty or forty-five cents. Except that the corporation did not get back the full fifteen cents paid for the copy. After the wholesaler and newsstand distributor had taken their shavings, the company received only nine cents. Which meant each additional copy that our editorial efforts attracted to circulation increased the loss by twenty or thirty cents—or, as one multiplied pennies to dollars, a half-million circulation gain at newsstands brought a loss of some $100,000 an issue, or $2.5 million a year.

All this was predictable and inevitable but for the great *unless*—unless the large corporations who sought to reach the supermarkets chose to buy pages in the magazines. But they did not. The entire editorial reorganization, the consequent upward thrust of circulation, had been premised on the belief that the advertisers would return to make the company rich. *Collier's* had been consistently losing advertising to television for five years —down from 1,718 pages of advertising in 1951 to 1,008 pages in 1955. The downslide accelerated in 1956, even as circulation went up. The better we did on the editorial floor, unless advertising matched our growing audience, the more we added to corporate loss. By mid November, we in editorial were flush with confidence. I was proud of my share in this surge. Upstairs, where the board met, our success wrote our doom.

There is a rhythm to the financial year which I have since learned as a board member myself. The peak of the rhythm comes in late fall of the fiscal year, when accounts are reviewed and projections are made for the following year. Most publishing houses are run on a calendar year of accounting; and so, shortly before or after Thanksgiving, the board must decide what it will do for the coming year, starting January. Thus, at the beginning of the festive season, while the writers, peasants and editors are bringing in the sheaves and preparing Thanksgiving, the board sits to decide what to do the next year. In the case of a dying magazine, the board almost inevitably decides to harvest the Christmas advertising pages, which will show a profit—and close out the magazine as soon as the Christmas advertisers disappear, a week or ten days before the actual holiday itself. This is what colors the death of great magazines and publications with sentiment: they die usually just before Christmas, a time of rejoicing and wassail. And the employees of the dying magazine trudge home to tell their wives and children of short rations at a season when the survivors tell their wives and children of the size of the Christmas bonus.

So it was at *Collier's*. At their November meeting the board recognized that their investment in a better editorial "product" had not impressed the advertisers; that the better we, of the writing and editorial staff, did in assembling Audience, the more it cost them as a corporation. The magazines must die.

The news of impending death reached me only two weeks before it became public. I had hoped that once I had helped the recovery of the magazine's circulation, I could go back to do what I wanted—write of politics. So I was at the United Nations, beginning work on the story of the 1956 Arab-Israeli war, when I was called back across Manhattan to be told by McArdle that the magazines were probably going to die. We were losing too much money.

There is little I can remember of the last two weeks of *Collier's* and the *Companion*. I do recall trying to pull together a staff group that would seek new millions to buy the magazines, which we would then publish ourselves. I remember my rounds, which now seem so funny, among the New York rich, who regard money-seekers for arts-and-letters projects as a private parlor troupe of in-house entertainers; of coming to hate the hereditary rich, who usually fund such gambles in arts and letters, as much as the new and grasping rich, who were scuttling the magazines. And then, finally, in a spasm of indignation, a sudden change of role at the end. From my vision of myself as entrepreneur, buying the magazines, I was transformed into what I had imagined myself as a boy—a leader of the workers! Wtih a few companions, we organized the staff in protest to demand severance pay. Some, who were about to be dismissed penniless at Christmas season, had worked for thirty years for this organization that I had joined only eighteen months before. This seemed unjust, and the staff committee I had organized made the board see that their coldness was not only unjust but very dangerous. The staff committee of reporters and writers had political connections and knew the leverage of blackmail in a good cause. We won severance pay for all, but after the magazines were dead.

The most lasting of memories was a surprising recognition: the sense of affection that binds people to their working companions. Most people make believe they despise their jobs, their bosses, their corporate purpose, the people they meet every day. Only in Japan do workers openly demonstrate an affection for the corporate communities in which they work. At *Collier's* most of us discovered only in the last few days how much we genuinely liked each other. The prospect of not coming into the office the next day, not nodding to one's friends down the line, not poking one's head into the art-layout room, not waiting for the story conference, not flirting with the women at the water cooler, was devastating. This comradeship I had taken for granted at *Time* and *Life* magazines; had enjoyed again at the *New Republic,* at the Overseas News Agency and at *The Reporter.* But I had left those families of work always at my own desire or my own provocation. Perhaps my affection for *Collier's* remains longest because I did not want to go. I wanted to stay. Only after *Collier's* had vanished under me did I realize how much of an organization man I really was— either because of my rootless heritage, or the enjoyment I took in simple daily companionship. All through the next twenty years, many newsspeople would have to make that choice: to cling to organization at any cost or strike out alone, at great risk. Fewer and fewer in those twenty years would stand alone.

I did not know these were my choices at the time. It would have been easy to join the liquidation group at the corporate summit, who would make millions out of ending the magazines. But it was so much more exciting and pleasing to my conscience to become a leader of the workers.

From what few jottings remain in my journal, these scenes protrude through the haze:

• The crying of grown men and women who knew on Friday evening, December 14, 1956, that they would never work together again, recognizing for the first time how much they liked each other.

• The sign on the bulletin board that read: "We regret to inform you that there is no Santa Claus."

• My hatred of the cameras and crews of television, which had destroyed us. They came onto our floors trying to get pictures of the people who were crying, tears on their faces.

• All of us getting drunker and drunker as we boozed, and cartoons and designs of death heads appearing from the art department.

Then, finally, it was all over. I, as the spokesman of the dismissed workers, faced the television cameras in the lobby of the office building, and after that wandered out into the night. It was drizzling that Friday evening, and the *Collier's* offices were cater-corner from Saks Fifth Avenue, where the Christmas decorations had just been hung. The tinned music from the store's loudspeakers blared up and down the street, caroling "Peace on Earth, Good Will to Men." Through the rain I spied a taxicab with its lights welcoming, and ran across the street to hail it. I got in, and went home, and made up a little comforting story to tell Nancy, who was, as usual, unworried and undisturbed, regarding the whole adventure as a great lark; as she regarded all crises.

But I would never again be employed by anyone. I would never again have corporate shelter—neither the staff secretary and office; nor the simple medical insurance; nor the vitally important badge of accreditation that would pass me through police lines, or through war zones, or in and out of the White House and the Pentagon; nor the efficient travel office to make my reservations. I was, at this point, forty-one years old. At that age, in America, one should leave corporate shelter with great caution. One is, actuarially, a poor risk for employment. But I would, in the years to come, be both more alone and better rewarded than I had any reason to expect.

THE OUTSIDER

The roller-coaster of fortune had alternately swept him up and swung him down for almost twenty years. He should have grown used to the swoop-and-soar cycles by now. But it would take him months to realize how sharp this new dip was to be; how close to the end of his resources it would bring him, and how far away it would take him from any connection with the world of public affairs before finally, three years later, he would be able to return to politics.

There was, first, the *Collier's* matter to close. The leave-taking had been so unnatural, the friendships there so emotionally fused in the last few days of despair, that he clung to his old office for weeks after being sacked. As one of the co-chairmen of the staff committee, he found the struggle with management pretext enough to linger on the empty floor at his desk. By Wednesday after the Friday collapse he was meeting with the victorious liquidators of the magazines, demanding severance pay for all—and by ingenious

use of publicity, political leverage and discreet blackmail, his committee was in the next few months to wring
almost a million dollars for the casualties from the old
Crowell-Collier corporation, which then went on to
prosper mightily. For the first month he enjoyed the
fight; it distracted him from his own problems; and then
one man surprisingly revealed himself as a hero: Paul
Smith. Up to the end White had thought of Smith only
as a buccaneer. In defeat, however, Smith turned out
to be far better a man than at peak power as bombastic
editor and publisher. Smith made a private deal: If the
staff committee did not trigger creditors to press immediate bankruptcy on the corporation, he, Smith, with
or without the consent of the board, would sign as chief
executive officer a severance pay agreement for all
employees. Smith kept his commitment with impeccable
honor; so the board then fired Smith. And finally, after
trying his hand at several other New York jobs, his
spirit broken and his savings gone, Smith returned to
San Francisco. There, life carried him by a descending
spiral, down, down and down until several years later
he was carried off to a veterans hospital. Old friends
remembered him; one bequeathed enough money to
allow him to end his days in a decent convalescent
home.

   Not many suffered the same destruction of spirit
and evisceration of drive that Smith did. Most of the
younger men, between thirty and forty, prospered, as
if the unpotting from *Collier's* had caused their over-
crowded roots to thrive. Those pressing into their upper
forties were unfortunate—they had to scurry to seek
shelter in other institutions and accept whatever accident or contact brought them. One swashbuckling
executive could not abide the demotion forced on him
and founded a typing service which rented out typists
by the hour to advertising agencies with whom he had
once done business in the millions. Another, in Chicago,
committed suicide, in the delusion that his failure to sell
enough advertising had contributed significantly to
Collier's death. And the rest, particularly those over fifty,

simply withered away; when one met them later, reminiscence or recollection was embarrassing.

It was not until several months after the collapse that the pain of being separated from *Collier's* began to ache, as a cut begins to ache long slow minutes after the slash. It was when severance pay for the *Collier's* staff had been settled in principle, and the lawyers had begun to fuss over written detail, that White awoke one morning and realized that there was no office to go to, no meeting to attend, no interview scheduled. He was forty-one years old, without a job, and with no skill except as a reporter. He had nothing to do all that February day, the next day, or any day after that unless he himself made something happen, or found an organization that wanted him.

He had expected, almost daily, after the weekend of *Collier's* collapse, that he would be called with job offers. He was, after all, by then the winner of many awards, the author of two best sellers, a fringe roundsman of the East Side Establishment, and, in his exaggerated appreciation of his own importance, had felt certain that editors and publishers up and down New York would rush to acquire his talent.

But only two men called, and he had brushed them aside because their calls came so swiftly after the collapse that he did not foresee that such calls would be rare.

One call came, unsurprisingly, from Edward R. Murrow, then at the height of his power within CBS. Murrow offered him one of the reporters' places in CBS's Washington bureau. But television had not yet made its Washington correspondents important, and ninety-second snatches of radio or television reportage seemed impossibly concise to a man like White, who recognized himself as impossibly long-winded. TV news thrived on journalistic pemmican and White preferred fresh meat.

The other call came from Henry Luce, and that call was a surprise. The proprietor of *Time, Life* and *Fortune* had done as much to torpedo White ten years earlier as any single individual could have done. But now there came the familiar gruff, halting voice over the telephone, stammering an invitation to dinner at the University Club. Any invitation from Luce sounded like a command, but White was already lonesome. So he accepted. Dinner passed off excitingly, for they found themselves in agreement on almost everything but Eisenhower and China—particularly China, over which they argued violently, furiously and enjoyably. Then they went to White's house, and when White tried to resume the argument, Luce cut him off at once. It was time, said Luce, for Teddy to come home—to come home to the magazines where he had begun, whether it be *Time* or *Life* or *Fortune.* It was an act of generosity and peace-making, which laid the ground for a renewed friendship that would go on until Luce's death in 1967. But White could explain neither to himself nor to Luce why, sitting there together in warmth, under his own roof with his children sleeping upstairs, and knowing he must support a family—why he could not accept Luce's invitation to be safe. He said to Luce that he never again wanted to be caught on Christmas Eve without a job; he wanted to live outside an organization. Luce shook his head and said White could come back to the *Time-Life* magazines whenever he wanted. But what White wanted Luce could not give. He wanted both security and freedom. He wanted to go where and when he wished and to rest where and when he chose —and yet to command the weight and support of an organization, too. White could never recall afterward whether that was the night Luce first described him as an impossible combination of born organization man and born malcontent. But that in truth was what he was.

Had either Luce or Murrow made White such an offer three months later, White would probably have opted for safety in an organization. He had by spring explored the market for the kind of free-lance stories of public affairs or current history he had so much enjoyed writing at *The Reporter* and at *Collier's.* But such stories are jealously guarded privileges for the men who make their careers within publishing or broadcasting houses, and outsiders are unwelcome. He had, by spring, also explored the foundations and executive publishing structures, where he had some talent to offer. But he discovered that even his best friends, where he had entry, now regarded him warily. When he explained what he wanted to do, both they and he recognized that he would inevitably be a competitor for their jobs on his way up.

The next solution—what seemed to him the most desirable solution—was that he become a columnist. He thought that writing a good column was the highest form of journalism. It is a jeweler's showcase of the reporter's art, and American columnists at their best can rank with or surpass the greatest *feuilletonists* of European journalism, where the column has, for a century, been considered not only an art but a sparklet of history.

He was soberly warned off this adventure by none other than America's master columnist, Walter Lippmann. In public a high-minded, remote, Olympian figure, Lippmann was in private conversation as sharp, hard-headed and responsive as he was visionary and oracular in his published writings. Talking to White as older friend to younger, Lippmann was at his most pragmatic. It was useless, he said, to try to be a major, national columnist unless you had an assured outlet in either New York or Washington. Unless you appear in print in one, preferably both, of those two cities, the power centers did not know you existed. You were thus chopped off at the news source because you could neither help nor harm those you met on the power circuits in Washington. Moreover, said Lippmann, no one got rich from a column. Outside the big cities, the take from a column averaged three to five dollars per week per paper; the economics would not work for a beginning columnist unless he was underwritten by some major newspaper as he, Lippmann, was by the New York *Herald Tribune,* which both underwrote him and picked up most of his expenses. Lippmann went on to analyze the economics of being a columnist with the same cool logic he was then publicly applying to the national budget. Yet he had a further point: White could not be a columnist unless White had the knack for it. Lippmann had seen only White's books and articles; was White sure he could do the column?

And there Lippmann scored. White had been practicing columns as a form of finger exercise for two weeks since *Collier's* died. He believed that writing is like any other skill—if unused, it becomes rusty. Like an actor or singer without a role, he had thus been practicing at home, which had now become his office. White had discovered, doing such finger exercises, that a good column runs between eight hundred and twelve hundred words—and that he could scarcely clear his throat in eight hundred to twelve hundred words. White had grown up and lived too long in other schools of rhetoric. He could write books; he could write articles; he could write newspaper stories. He was like a runner who could do any distance from the one-thousand- to the ten-thousand-meter run, but was useless at the hundred-meter dash.

It was as he sat upstairs, hoping his wife would hear his typewriter clacking and be comforted by the belief that he was beginning a column, that the typewriter began to draw him to an idea, which he followed, thus stumbling, accidentally, onto the novel.

It is so difficult to say when an idea is born. Being unemployed, White was putting his papers in order—filing old notes, old stories, old clippings, in their proper places. Among them were wads of penciled notes on China; and not only notes, but private writings, efforts to recapture and put together what the jotted notes recalled. Unconsciously, his present fears ran together and merged with the memories reawakened by old notes of the war. He himself was now alone and on the outside, and had two children, a wife and responsibility. What caught him in the papers he turned was how completely he had been gripped by the great retreat from East China in 1944—first by the technology of explosive demolitions, then, next, by the refugee procession over a hundred miles of snow and desolation. These were all abandoned people, with no protection. How did a refugee decide when to abandon wife and children? If he himself could save only one of two children—which one?

While he bustled about and told friends of the column he was about to launch, he puttered privately at a story that he sensed must be there, somewhere, buried under the notes and the nightmares that kept him up, or awakened him, yelling, from sleep.

Since literature has become so elaborate an industry today, monitored and measured by professionals and distributors, White's barefoot view of literature then must seem impossibly old-fashioned. For White, literature divided into two parts: learning books and story books, books that taught lessons and books that entertained. He had never dreamed of being anything else but a reporter, and writing novels was so far from personal ambition as to be unthinkable. Yet he suffered from the exasperation of most reporters—the exasperation of being pinned to facts, when the facts cannot tell the story. Rare is the reporter who has not over and over again come home, having written the day's story, wishing he could have rearranged the facts so as to tell the true story. Then he tosses his notes in his drawer, or trash basket, or hopechest, and goes on to write the next day's story. Except that sometimes some happening—a battle, a riot, a convention, a crime, a breakdown in an interview—cannot be forgotten. Rereading his notes, the reporter finds his imagination and memory returning again and again to that episode, trying to rearrange the facts as they should have arranged themselves for the true story, though reality arranged them otherwise. Out of such rearrangements was born that respectable art form the American reportorial novel.

White's first novel came about because he was bored; he was unemployed; he detested job-seeking;

he was haunted by fears; and his nightmares were disturbing him. He had learned during the war that whenever he was particularly terrified, the best way of wiping out a bad time was to write it down in the morning. Then it was pinned like a butterfly on mounting paper, never to flap again. He had done this with a reporter's story of the East China retreat long ago. But now, as he sorted out the old notes, those memories had begun to flap again and he was trying to pin them down once more. This time, at the age of forty-one, he was trying to recapture what it was that had disturbed him in his twenties, in the explosions, the fires, the blastings, the shootings, with which his countrymen, the Americans, laid waste a belt of China from the rice paddies and orange groves of Kwangsi to the snow-covered plateau of Kweichou. So thus, finger-exercising, trying to put the notes of the China retreat together in a coherent sequence, he found himself gliding into a story at the typewriter. He would never have given up reporting to become a novelist; the fiction that each reporter carries in his knapsack a dream of being a novelist had seemed just that to him: a romantic fiction. Yet here he was spending the mornings typing away at notes that seemed to run together in quite different fashion than the facts they recorded; he was writing rather than going out to lunch, or going out to do the interviews required of the serious job-hunter or earnest free-lancer.

It was an indulgence, he told himself at first. But the memories kept insisting on rearranging themselves. And his wife urged him to go on with it; she had seen him put yellow paper in a typewriter several times before, type page one, and emerge a year later with a best seller. She was sure he could write a novel; all their friends did. He pointed out that they had only enough money saved to carry them for another year; their brownstone house on the East Side was preposterously expensive; the children were in private school; there was a maid, who had to be paid weekly. Just to make it through the year, he would have to cash in all his insurance. It was so chancy. But the story kept growing, and Nancy urged him to gamble.

By March, he found himself alone, chilled to the bone, in front of a fireplace in a cottage on New York's Fire Island, typing away at what was definitely a novel while the family finished the school year in Manhattan.

It was odd, camping as a bachelor on a sandbar in the Atlantic during a cold and rainy late spring, with no reading matter but jottings and war diaries of a lost China. He had no texts or documents with him except an army field manual on demolitions; and he was rewriting history from fragments which he, as a novelist, was now licensed to put together as he wished. The story he was writing began simply enough: with the Japanese ICHIGO offensive of 1944, when the front in East China had collapsed. White had followed that collapse and the retreat back to the highlands, and been especially impressed by the cool technical skill with which a rear-guard American demolition unit had achieved total destruction of highways, bridges, installations, ammunition dumps. Now, as he built the action again from the fragments in his notes, he could see it more clearly. When, finally, the novel built to its climax —the destruction of the highway and great ammunition dumps of Tushan—the characters seemed to be acting on their own. In his imagination Americans were doing what he had never seen them do in reality. Yet what they did in the novel was, somehow, more true than what they had done in fact years before—and, to his own numb astonishment, it would become true in deed, in Vietnam, years later, when the adventure of America in Asia miscarried. In his story, his imaginary Americans were burning and ravaging hundreds of miles of China at reckless personal risk and in total good will, to protect the Chinese from the Japanese. While the Chinese, beading the landscape in refugee knots and huddles, fled the Japanese and the Americans alike.

He called the story *The Mountain Road* and it raced up the road in one of those marvelous spurts

that make a writer feel his typewriter has taken off on
its own. He reached the climax of an almost finished
book, with only one chapter left to write, when the
typewriter stalled. The novel had climaxed with an
imagined berserk act of rage by the Americans, goaded
beyond restraint—a massacre that might have been a
foretaste of My Lai had Americans known that a My Lai
was in their future. It had taken only three months to
write all but the last chapter; it took almost three
months more to carpenter together an unsatisfactory
ending, for White had no solutions which would bridge
the truths that a novel required to the realities he then
perceived.

White insisted for years that it was a good novel,
except for the last chapter. The novel could not find
an authentic ending and White never understood why
until several years later, when he sneaked into a theater
to see for perhaps the tenth time the movie version of
his book. This time it was on a Saturday afternoon
in a run-down theater on New York's Forty-second
Street and a file of teen-agers occupied the row behind
him. They cheered whenever the crescendo of explosions reached a high point, as his movie-version demolition unit blew the screen apart more and more vividly.
Then came the technical climax White had written into
his novel: the blowing of the ammunition dumps at
Tushan, and the mad American destruction of the next
village. The explosions on screen were magnificent.
After that would come White's "message," the artificially carpentered last chapter now translated to film. But
with the sound of the last explosion still echoing from
the screen, the leader of the pack of teen-agers, who
had obviously seen the film before, rose and said to his
gang, "The hell with it. That's the best part of the
picture. The rest of it's crap." They rose and left, and,
as he watched the ending, the author had to acknowledge that the verdict was correct. The reportorial White
had written the ending, refusing to acknowledge guilt
in Asia. Fiction, however, required another ending—
the art form required an act or statement of conscience,

a recognition of guilt. The reality of the twenty-five-year-long American record in Asia was that of genuine good will exercised in mass killing, a grisly irony which White could master in neither film nor book. Asia was a bloody place; we had no business there; both novel and movie should have said just that at whatever risk.

White saw the film for the last time in 1960, when he was back in public affairs; he regretted he could not reissue the novel with a new last chapter of appropriate bitterness and irony. But of all his books, *The Mountain Road* remained his favorite. It had brought him a success at the lowest point of his life as a man on the outside; it was taken by a book club almost simultaneously with its sale to Hollywood. The two sales had released him from debt; had permitted him to pay his children's school tuition bills rather than beg for scholarships. It had let him plan a personal strategy with larger perspectives than immediate or twelve-month survival.

Having survived on the outside for a year, and with eating money now assured for at least another two years, White decided he would buy his re-entry into the story of American public affairs as a businessman —a publisher. No one, except a prosperous farmer, is more independent than a prosperous publisher.

In a frenzy of activity, White conceived and marshaled proposals and prospectuses.

• He floated a prospectus for a new publishing house to be called Contemporary Books. It would publish new books. One of the suggestions was that every four years such a publishing house would publish, quickly and first, a "Making of the President Series" which he would write. He found several interested investors in the East Side parlor cells of money. But the long trail he would have to crawl to raise enough money from the gambling rich to start such a publishing house appalled him. He let the scheme drop.

• He decided that he would start a Russian-American publishing house. This was before the days of

Solzhenitsyn. The only worthwhile Russian writing at the time was science fiction, which was of superlative quality. White wanted to establish a publishing house to translate Russian science fiction in New York. But dealing with the Russian government was far worse than dealing with the New York rich.

• White's most pedestrian idea turned out to be the only one that was at all profitable. He reasoned thus: What is the only book that everyone must buy every single year? Answer: a new desk diary. He thus organized, quickly, a small publishing enterprise to publish each year a new kind of diary, spacing each full week on two open-spread pages, to be called an "Executive Desk Diary," of the kind now common. The idea took root, became a company which still exists. But what appalled White was the exertion a business person had to put into the execution of even the simplest idea, like diary publishing. He had to find the right kind of paper at the right price; the paper had to be erasable, for people constantly erase and rescratch diary notes. Then the paper must be moved to the printer, from printer to bindery, from bindery to warehousing, from warehousing to sales people.

White came away from a year of exploring such publishing with an increased respect for the small entrepreneur who creates a business where none existed before. Businessmen brought things together: steel to construction sites, coal to ore, oil to port, books to bookstores. If they did it well, businessmen could make two and two add up not to four, but to five, six or even more. This quirk of the business system, he decided, is what irritates most intellectuals, who believe that always and invariably two and two must be four, as four and four must become eight, and if they do not, then someone is cheated.

• If diary publishing was White's simplest and only profitable business venture, by far the most instructive was his profitless introduction to the business of broadcasting—which taught him he was an amateur in a business that he should have known better than any other: news delivery.

He had been peddling news for many years, from the streets of Boston on. People needed news; they thirsted for news as they thirsted for water. And at this point, in 1958, the owners of broadcasting stations were beginning to realize, just as did the masters of the national networks, that it was the news, the instantaneous delivery of news, that bound the stations to the networks. The money-making programs of entertainment, comedy and drama could be produced by anyone and bought from the syndicates; but a station, if it was to get news from the world and its capitals instantly, while it was still news, had to tie into a network. It was inevitable that station owners would begin surreptitiously to explore whether they could throw off their servitude to the broadcast networks by creating their own cooperative news network. They wished to explore this possibility first with delivery of radio news, which was cheaper than television. And in spring of 1958 White was invited to become the consultant to an intermediate group of promoters, dealing with fourteen of the most important radio stations in the country, who wished to undo the national networks while there was still time.

The conspiratorial challenge to network news delivery was brought to White by a very intelligent businessman named Alfred Stanford, who published a boating magazine in Connecticut. Stanford was the "disintermediary." He could be repudiated. But the thought that Stanford carried from the principals to White was that if they—Stanford and White—could design a news-delivery system even partially as effective as the networks, then the station owners could unstaple themselves from dependence on the three national networks—first in radio news, then in television news.

White enlisted the help of a friend of Paris days, Blair Clark. Clark was a man of extraordinary vigor and imagination and would go on later to become a vice president of CBS, author of many of its news innovations, and campaign manager for Eugene McCarthy in 1968. As a lark, White and Clark put together a budget, a plan, a structure for creating a radio news-delivery system that would deliver two full hours of air-time news each day from all around the world, at a cost of only $1,500,000 a year. If the fourteen restless stations could find enough other stations to join them in revolt against the networks, it would cost each of fifty radio stations only thirty thousand a year. The arithmetical exercise in translating programming ideas, salaries and wire-lease costs into such a figure verged on the metaphysical.

White unveiled the proposed new network to the station manager at a secret meeting at the New York Yacht Club. It was the first time he had ever entered those raftered halls, the walls cased with the models of every winner of the America's Cup. He had never spoken to a more skeptical audience; he was overwhelmed by the importance of the call letters of the men gathered there—WGY (Schenectady) meant ownership by General Electric; WTIC (Hartford) meant ownership by Travelers Insurance Company; the initials of WJR (Detroit), KFI (Los Angeles), WHAS (Louisville) and the others meant equal clout. Such radio stations, each dominating its own region, needed news-delivery systems of their own to make money; their bondage to the networks came from the inability of money alone to summon up news. White explained about news—about the sounds of Sputnik beeping from outer space; about the then undeveloped gold mine of information in the Department of Justice; about how much cheaper it was to pump all Europe's news out of Paris rather than London; about what it would cost to have good reporters provide simple reporting, with or without frills, from anywhere in the world. Then he tossed in the ideas he and Clark had worked out about the commercial potential in providing garden news, bridge news, business news, movie news, book news, as well as news of law, medicine and taxes, all addressed to "you."

He was thoroughly surprised by the success of his promotion pitch. None of these men listening knew anything about news. Only that money could be made out of it, and the money the networks demanded of them for delivery of the news was exorbitant.

Weeks, then months, went by while a response was awaited. When, finally, the Columbia Broadcasting System became aware of the rustling and disturbance among its affiliate stations, it cracked down. When it cracked down, the restless stations decided that they would indeed finance a new news network—provided Stanford, White and Clark could give them a firm budget in two weeks, and firm commitment of news delivery in a few months.

A ridiculous scene followed. There were both Clark and White, proffered millions of dollars by sober businessmen for an idea they had conceived as a lark. One question remained: With whom were the conspirators dealing? With Clark or with White? White had assumed that once the idea was sold, Clark would be the executive, White would be the well-paid philosopher-guide. Clark had entertained a similar but opposite thought: White would be the executive, and Clark would tell White what to do. They bounced a ball back and forth across the room, catching and throwing. What had begun as a frivolity had been taken seriously. Did either one of them dare to challenge the established networks? Neither really wanted that burden and responsibility. Sheepishly, they telephoned Stanford and said neither one wanted to be the chief. They gave away their work, their prospectus and their programmed ideas to the promoter to do with as he wished. Stanford was furious, as he had good reason to be; he could promote but not produce. It was probably the silliest financial decision White ever made; the big networks were then still vulnerable as news gatherers. Fortunes might be made in organizing the news-delivery system against them.

It was probably also the closest White ever came to being rich. News was an ingredient of commerce; he knew both the raw stuff and how it was sold. He knew how money was made out of news. But he was more interested in how news originated. As a matter of fact, he was writing a book about that subject, a second novel.

He had usually come home each day from his business ventures to do more of the finger exercising at the typewriter which keeps the word skills from rusting. And again, as earlier with *The Mountain Road,* his typewriter had begun to take over from him. This time the story was about what he had learned in publishing, fictionalized from his experience at *Collier's,* in a novel to be called *The View from the Fortieth Floor.* It seemed more important to get said what he wanted to say about the news system in a novel, however melodramatic, than to shake the news system by organizing a radio news net.

White was another year writing this second novel and while he was so doing several recognitions came to him.

Recognitions are clearings in the jungle of life where space opens enough to let the mind turn.

In writing this second novel, he came across and passed through several such recognitions. He could never line them up in the precise sequence that led him back to public affairs. But later, when he attempted to cloak the accidents with an apparent logic of decisions, he thought the recognitions that came to him in writing the novels followed thus:

First was the recognition of how beautiful was the novel as a form and how satisfying it would be to do it well. Somewhere beyond the reach of his own typewriter, he recognized, was an art he could never master; a novel was even more demanding as a craft than writing a column. In France he had become an amateur painter and one of his paintings had won a local prize; what he learned most from being a bad painter, however, had been to appreciate good painting. Novels were like that, too. He learned from writing his own novels to appreciate the art of others. The great novelist sits as a creator, and people rise from his imagination, then wander across that stage of imagination, and in the world the novelist makes, they speak, or cry, or dance, or laugh, or avenge themselves on their enemies. There is no more masterful or lasting achievement of the human imagination than a great novel.

But White learned, from writing novels, that he could not dream of writing a great one. That lay beyond him. He had begun both novels as a form of therapy, as finger exercises. Both were successful in the sense that book clubs chose them, paperback publishers reprinted them, movie-makers purchased them, hundreds of thousands of copies were bought. Many people must have found them good reading—but White knew they were no more than entertainments, to be read quickly, then cast away and forgotten.

And with this recognition the reportorial half of his mind told the romantic half that the world of the novelist was not for him. The world of the novel in America was, he discovered, surveyed, staked out and parceled. Critics patrolled this storyteller's world like guards, penning novelists into designated corrals. There was the literary corral, patrolled from the universities, inhabited by writers who could not tell a story or make the reader turn a page, but who spun their shimmering sentences, as silkworms spin threads, in endless spirals into closed cocoons. A vast distance away was the world of schlock artists. A fist hit a mouth on the first page of their novels, a girl's nipple was rudely flicked on page two, and so on to the end. You could instantly tell these books by their covers—a high-bosomed heroine silhouetted against a moonlit castle, or plantation gates, or a shiny car, above a cutline which read: "Soon to be a Twentieth Century-Fox Production."

White's chosen corral of the novelists' world embraced the storyteller's patch, dominated at that time by men like Herman Wouk, James Michener, John Hersey. Hersey had, alas, just left the storyteller's patch to move over to the literary corral, writing novels appreciated more by academic critics than by his former readers. But Hersey had been followed in the novel, as in journalism, by a host of imitators and practitioners of what can be called the modern American novel of realities. From Herman Melville on down through Mark Twain and Stephen Crane to Hemingway and Hersey, a disproportionate number of America's best novelists have been essentially reportorial. Such novels were becoming more popular, reaching wider audiences in the 1950s; it was in that field White felt he was working; but even in this field he recognized he was very far from the best.

White might have continued with trying his hand at the novel, making money as he learned the sales tricks, but he could not quite bring himself to respect the world into which novels led him. It was a world that reeked of culture, was choked with pretensions. The more he met other novelists and spoke with them, the more appalled he grew at their self-importance; they took themselves seriously because critics took them seriously; the symbiosis between novelist and critic was more unhealthy than that between sports star and sportswriter. White was used to the companionship of reporters, the men of the press camp, the press bus, the late-night vigil, where the work was serious but the people involved refused to be solemn. In that world, every person was both writer and critic, and the greatest praise was the rare, curt comment from a rival: "Good lead yesterday, you son of a bitch." So to White it seemed a happier life to be a good reporter than a minor novelist, even though a minor novelist who sold to Hollywood and the paperbacks was two, five or ten times more prosperous than the best-paid reporter in China, Paris or Washington.

The writing of novels finally brought White to one final recognition that was absolutely critical for the next twenty years of his work: the nature of a story. He had never read a textbook on how to write a novel, but in the exhausting rewritings of his own two novels he had

learned to strain out of the blur of clichés that surrounds the art of the novel those particular clichés he
now recognized as truth. The first was: The novelist
must, above all, make the reader want to turn the page.
There followed in order: He must put his hero in trouble
immediately; next he must get the hero out of that trouble only to plunge him into worse. Then, if the novel is
working well, the characters move off by themselves
almost as if they have come alive—and all the writer
has to do is report how they behave when at night they
disturb his dreams.

This recognition of the nature of a story was critical because it explained to White what he had been
doing unconsciously for the previous twenty years in
reporting politics. From the first bombing of Chungking
to the closeout at *Collier's,* he had seen and written
about men in trouble. Now, if he ever got back to writing politics, he could encode what he wanted to do
in a simple formulation that was to last for a good ten
years of writing before he discarded it:

As follows:

History is Story. Politics, in the process of becoming History, is the story of a handful of men reaching
for the levers of power. Therefore one must seek out
the leaders as men. Leaders must act under pressure,
in circumstances they may or may not be able to
define. Their imperfect information describes forces,
thrusts, opportunities, menaces, real or imaginary, that
require decision. It was the intersection of the forces
in the personalities of the leaders that made both politics and history so exciting. After writing two novels
and making his heroes act under imaginary troubles,
he wanted to report public affairs—real men in real
trouble—as he had learned to do from writing novels.

Public affairs is an infection of the spirit that is
probably incurable. And White, after three years of
seclusion with novels, was aching to be back in the
arena, when he was invited to return in the happiest
possible way—with money.

He had been aware for several weeks that the Literary Guild was interested in his new manuscript. He was also aware that several Hollywood studios were interested. If either led to a happy result, he felt he must waste no more time or money trying to become a publisher. If once again he had enough money he would use that money simply to buy the time to do what he wanted most to do.

The desire was there. But the decision when it came was perhaps the swiftest major decision he ever made. It took him precisely four days, and was to govern the next twenty years of his life.

The episode opened pleasantly. It was New Members' Night at New York's Century Club, Thursday, October 15, 1959. He was paged to the telephone and over the phone came the staccato voice of his Hollywood agent, Irving Lazar. Lazar was a folklore character in the Hollywood menagerie—charming on social occasions, but snap-jawed and surgical at business. Lazar wanted a quick yes or no, right then. He, in Hollywood, had to make an instant call-back to Gary Cooper, a star who was one of White's favorites. Cooper had personally offered eighty thousand for the film rights to the new novel, plus escalator bonuses, if the Literary Guild (which did choose it) or another book club made it a selection. Cooper was tired of the "yup" and "nope" parts other producers offered him. The hero of White's new novel was loquacious, eloquent, almost incontinent of mouth; and Cooper wanted to buy and personally star in this image. Yes or no? Quick. For eighty thousand dollars plus escalators.

White, without consulting his wife, said yes.

The next day he drove out with Nancy and her closest friend, Muriel Grymes, to Fire Island. It was cold, blowy, rain-swept, and the fireplace blazed. Muriel Grymes was a beauty and a woman of courage; but she was a political innocent of the kind that would disrupt the coming decade. She was, for one thing, more involved in politics than White had ever been;

she had been one of the band of heroes and heroines who had launched the reform movement of politics in New York just after the war, when to oppose Tammany was to find your mouth full of your own teeth, or to pick. yourself up out of the gutter not knowing who had slugged you. Like all reformers, she confused her own pure conscience with the laws of nature. Adlai Stevenson was the captain of her conscience, and she quivered when Stevenson spoke. It always amused White to tease this good, beautiful and effective woman; she was so vigorously capable of organizing a single election district and so incapable of understanding how all 175,000 election districts in America must be fitted together by compromises that appear sordid to reformers. So, once again, he was retelling for her the story he had never written——the story of Stevenson against Eisenhower in 1956, and why Stevenson, for whom she had spent her energies to exhaustion, never had a chance from the start. He had been stopped from writing that story only because he had been summoned in midcampaign to help save *Collier's*. The articles he might have written had been, by some magic, stored up in his battery of memories and there they had fused.

He was relaxed, flush with the expected eighty thousand dollars of movie money, telling the story of 1956 and why Adlai should have waited for 1960 when he was promised serious support from Republicans who felt they could not abide Nixon. He was also teasing his high-minded friend with the sordid and mechanical details of a Presidential race which she chose to overlook; he did not realize that such moralists would tear the next decade of American politics apart. But, as he tried to explain to her the greeds and temptations of politics, he was talking as a novelist: with the conviction that the way to tell a story is to locate a hero in the middle of trouble; then to increase the trouble; complicate the trouble; bewilder the hero; and have him emerge with the stroke of decision or direction that resolved all. The weekend was all at once familial, celebratory and political. The idea thus formed: the best way to spend the Gary Cooper money was to use the time it bought to write public affairs again—but differently.

On Monday morning he was driving back from Fire Island to Manhattan with Nancy and Muriel, when he announced a decision. He would use the money to take the next two years tó write a book about how a President is made. The Presidency is the center of politics. The President's decisions make the weather, and if he is great enough, change the climate, too. But White had seen enough of politics to know that the decisions of state are always, inevitably, whether in China, France, England or America, prefigured by the politics that brought the leadership to power. He would write a book about the coming 1960 campaign— as a story. Muriel, who always thought of him as a cynic and possibly a closet reactionary, applauded immediately. She was all but sure he would be writing of her hero, Adlai Stevenson, in 1960. Nancy was far more dubious, having lived so long on the ups and downs of his book gambles. She said, "It's probably a good book if Kennedy wins. But if Nixon wins, it's a dog." And with that encouragement from his wife, the writer set off.

The idea was to follow a campaign from beginning to end. It would be written as a novel is written, with anticipated surprises as, one by one, early candidates vanish in the primaries until only two final jousters struggle for the prize in November. Moreover, it should be written as a story of a man in trouble, of the leader under the pressures of circumstances.

The leader—and the circumstances. That was where the story lay.

The writer knew he would never again be better positioned to do such a book. Reporting Presidential campaigns is very expensive, but he now had the money for two years of travel and writing. He had the

knowledge of circumstances, from ghetto to suburbs,
from missiles to inflation, from China to Germany. He
had covered the circumstances from which the pressures would converge, for *Collier's,* for *Life,* for *Time,*
for *The Reporter,* for *The New York Times Magazine.*
The Democratic contenders were John F. Kennedy,
whom he liked; Adlai Stevenson, whom he cherished;
Averell Harriman, whom he had known for so long;
Stuart Symington and Lyndon Johnson, whose counselors included some of his most ambitious friends;
and Hubert Humphrey, the evangelist of benevolence.
On the Republican side were Nelson Rockefeller, whom
he had come to know and admire; Dwight D. Eisenhower, the great presence; and Richard Nixon, whom
White disliked, but who was essential. They were all
colorful, virile, exciting men, but Nixon was critical
to the story—White had cast Nixon as the villain, as
in a novel.

All this White knew as a reporter.

What he did not know was even more important.
He did not foresee, for example, that the new book was
to come at the right time. It was to come after fifteen
postwar years when education had created an audience for such books—a literate reading class of men
and women who were developing an interest in stories
that explained what was happening to them. Politics
were about to pass from the control of specialists in
mobilizing illiterates to the control of specialists in
mobilizing the symbols that move the newly educated
to move their illiterate cousins.

Nor did he know that what would emerge from
the year-long adventure was an enchanting man who,
like White, believed that the hero is a man who masters the circumstances. If ever a man was made to
illustrate White's thesis of history as the intersection
of impersonal forces at personality points, it was John
F. Kennedy. Kennedy was the first postwar American
leader who could see how changed were the circumstances in the country which he had left for war twenty

years earlier. Moreover, and just as importantly in terms of a popular story, Kennedy was young, rich, heroic, witty, well read—and handsome.

White felt that 1960 was a good year in which to watch matters change. Eisenhower was leaving. Except for Harriman, there were none left of the high command of his war to challenge for the Presidency. If he meant to explore how men behaved under the stress of circumstances, here would be new leadership behaving under the stress of temptation. Most political stress rises from disaster. The new stresses in the United States were the torques of appetite and hope. Eight years of prosperity had supercharged the country with the energy about to erupt in the sixties. The United States still held total missile superiority over the Soviet Union; its navy was still unchallenged; it overmatched the Russians in ground troops on the line in Europe. Its security was close to absolute. Behind this security, forces were beginning to move. Millions of youngsters were graduating from college—and millions more were entering. More and more women were enjoying the same education and moving into the same jobs as men. Millions of blacks were moving into the big cities, and their leaders were beginning to teach the newcomers to flex muscle. All sorts of groups were about to burst from traditional enclaves; the old forms could not contain them.

White peddled the idea of a book on the Presidential campaign from publisher to publisher for several weeks. His original publishers, William Sloane Associates, were as decent as they could be. They had made so much money on his other books, they said, that they owed it to him to publish a book on this dreary subject of a Presidential campaign, too. It would not sell, but it was their obligation. Two other publishers were willing to lose money on a book about politics if White would vouchsafe that they could also publish his money-making commercial novels. And then White's old friend Mike Bessie, contemporary of John Kennedy, burst in enthusiasm for the idea. Bessie was founding his own new publishing house; wanted fresh manuscripts and ideas; thought there might, indeed, be an audience for books about politics, and was willing to publish this book about where the power comes from, how it is collected, how it is used.

Both author and publisher were lucky. They were walking unwittingly into the political awakening of the 1960s. Speaker Sam Rayburn had once told the writer, talking of one of his rich but lucky Texas oil friends, "He was playing the bass tuba the day it rained gold." So was White. He was entering a campaign which would not again be matched as a turning in American history until the campaign of 1976. Kennedy was the last of the candidates who played the game by the old rules; then, having won, he exercised the President's magisterial prerogative to change the rules. So that by the time he was killed, American politics were conducted as much in the streets as in Congress, as much in academia as in the cabinet, as much on television as at party caucuses. When John F. Kennedy was killed, America irrevocably left behind the America of Dwight D. Eisenhower. It was on the way to becoming the America of Lyndon Johnson, Richard Nixon and, ultimately, James Earl Carter.

But the exercise of 1960, for the writer, then rested entirely on personalities. And it began, after much preliminary research and reporting in Washington, with the writer waiting in snow-coated Wisconsin for a plane bearing John F. Kennedy.

And the senator, coming off, was saying, "Hi. Hi, Teddy, I heard you were writing a book about the campaign. Is Pierre treating you all right?"

CHAPTER 10

John F. Kennedy:
Opening the Gates

I still have difficulty seeing John F. Kennedy clear.

The image of him that comes back to me, as to most who knew him, is so clean and graceful—almost as if I can still see him skip up the steps of his airplane in that half lope, and then turn, flinging out his arm in farewell to the crowd, before disappearing inside. It was a ballet movement. The remembered pleasures of travel with him clutter the outline of history.

It is quite obvious now, of course, that he was the man who broke up the old pattern of American politics. All the sophisticated technology of election campaigning and analysis that has come since then has been just that—technology. He was the man who ruptured the silent understanding that had governed American politics for two centuries—that this was a country of white Protestant gentry and yeomen who offered newer Americans a choice for leadership only within their clashing rivalries. He made us look at ourselves afresh. Kennedy ended

593

sec 627

many other myths and fossil assumptions, and with him, an old world of politics and government came to a close.

But how the new world that he ushered in will take shape remains yet to be seen—and thus we cannot finally measure him.

Kennedy was, whether for good or bad, an enormously large figure. Historically, he was a gatekeeper. He unlatched the door, and through the door marched not only Catholics, but blacks, and Jews, and ethnics, women, youth, academics, newspersons and an entirely new breed of young politicians who did not think of themselves as politicians—all demanding their share of the action and the power in what is now called participatory democracy.

Kennedy was a substantially more conservative figure than either of the two Democratic Presidents who succeeded him, and he had a healthy suspicion of the Democratic liberals who now enshrine his memory. Even after he became President, he would growl about Adlai Stevenson and "the liberals," and he bet me once after he became President that in any contest between himself and Stevenson in Madison, Wisconsin, or Cambridge, Massachusetts, or Berkeley, California, Adlai would take him three out of three. Liberals, generally, could not see the weight and dignity in Kennedy until well on into the campaign year of 1960; with such outstanding exceptions as Arthur M. Schlesinger, Jr., they considered him a lightweight who had bought his Senate seat with his father's money. Practical politicians saw him more clearly. John Bailey, the "boss" of Connecticut, a veteran of the regular ranks of old politics, once described to me his movement in four years from Stevenson to Kennedy. He had supported Stevenson in both 1952 and 1956, said Bailey, because Stevenson had "heft," and that's what voters wanted in their Presidents. Bailey had probably never heard of the Roman civic phrase *gravitas,* the weightiness that is so becoming to a man of public affairs. But by 1958 Bailey could feel the "heft" he wanted in John F. Kennedy and was mobilizing for him. And by the time he was killed, John Kennedy was accepted fully for his *gravitas* by liberals, just as much as by politicians and common people who had elected him chiefly because he was elegant, gay, witty, young and attractive. It was this image that won him the election; that plus his superlative gamesman's skill at the game of politics; that plus the underswell of the times, with old prejudices breaking up and new forms of politics just beginning.

I had no feeling for Kennedy in the beginning except that he was one of the few men in the Senate who made literate copy and read books. His brother and I had been classmates at Harvard in 1938—classmates totally without contact, for Joseph P. Kennedy, Jr., and I were at opposite ends of the social spectrum; John F. Kennedy was two years behind, in the class of '40. I had first heard of him when John Hersey, whom I so admired, made Kennedy a national hero in a magnificent *New Yorker* story of the exploits of PT-109 during the war. But even though Hersey praised him, and Kennedy was a Harvard man, I could not accept the son of Ambassador Joe Kennedy as admirable; there must be some taint. Moreover, I had found his stand on Joe McCarthy weak.

What first intrigued me about Kennedy, however, was his gamesman's sense of politics. He seemed to see American politics cynically, yet hopefully, partly as amusement, more so as sport. Our first meeting was so casually conversational that I did not even make notes. It was early 1955; he was senator. As *Collier's* political correspondent, I had called him and he, astonishingly, said he had a date to lunch with his wife and would I come along.* Senators, and all other busy men, so rarely have time to date their wives at lunch that I accepted at once. We enjoyed ourselves, although I have no recollection of what the lunch was about. My lasting impression was of his grace: he was handsomer than his photos; still

---

*An axiom for young political writers should be to find out the relationship between a politician and his wife before accepting an invitation to lunch with both. A busy man who loves his wife is most responsive to interrogation in her presence. He sees her so rarely that when questioned about major matters of state, he seeks to impress her rather than the reporter. If a governor or senator

retained then, in 1955, an open, boyish countenance; and must have spent a good deal of time at the beach that summer, for with his bronzed face, his chestnut hair bleached almost to gold, he was picture-book handsome. It was the restlessness and grace of his movement, even at table, that I remember best—and the easy slurring of consonants that marks most upper-class Northeasterners.

Shortly thereafter, I find him in my notes talking of hard politics. I was writing a story for *Collier's* of the early jostling for the Democratic nomination of 1956. Kennedy made no bones: He liked Stevenson for '56, with open, unfeigned admiration. He was indifferent to Averell Harriman. He did not like Estes Kefauver: Kefauver was a loner, he said, had no friends either in the House or in the Senate; when he shook hands with you he was looking over your shoulder to see whether he should be with someone more important. The story that the bosses had "screwed" him in the 1952 convention was just untrue, said Kennedy; it was simply that Kefauver was a man without friends.

As for himself, he was quite aware that Stevenson was scouting for a Catholic running mate, and both he and Bob Wagner, then mayor of New York City, were being talked of. Kennedy appeared unenthusiastic; he didn't like to think of himself as a Vice President, going to banquets, not much power, rushing out to airports to greet people, a "hell of a job," he said. But he supposed if it came his way he wouldn't turn it down. He said I should talk with Albert Gore of Tennessee, implying that Gore really wanted the Vice Presidential slot.

He looked at himself quite impersonally. What was going against Stevenson? he asked, and answered: Take the Massachusetts delegation—they disliked Stevenson

---

does not like his wife, then the interview is worse than useless. She will interrupt constantly; explain what her husband really meant; contradict him; sometimes remind him to remember he is talking to a reporter. In the case of the Kennedys, his wife seemed to bask in his presence. She was as docile as Chiang Ch'ing seemed with Mao—an impression I later learned was deceptive in both cases.

because of his divorce, because of his eggheadry, because of Arthur Schlesinger. What Stevenson needed, he continued, was someone with a strong war record, a Catholic, someone who was married.

From that personal description of himself he went on to other personalities, then into Massachusetts politics, which he made fascinating in his description of chaos, anarchy and rival factions—McCormack's, Burke's, Kennedy's, Dever's, Hynes's, others, with the Republican *Herald Traveler* (then Boston's dominant newspaper) muddying the waters, usually supporting the least organization-loyal Democrat. (Kennedy was to bring the brawling Massachusetts party under his own personal and family control the following year, but with wry amusement he now described its customs as Margaret Mead might describe potlatch season among the Aleuts.)

Of Kennedy on the issues there is no reflection in my notes except for a fleeting reference as he talked of the game of party politics. The party had no objectives, he said. He, for example, sat on the Senate Labor Committee, and was surprised that no one was left on "the left" any longer. He was for taking a party position for a minimum $1.25-an-hour wage. At this high noon of Eisenhower's decade, he knew Congress would pass no higher minimum wage than one dollar. Even Paul Douglas wouldn't fight to get that wage up to a buck and a quarter. But the way Kennedy saw the game of politics, you have to lose a few now and then "before you can begin to hope to win a few in the end."

Aside from that remark, all our conversation was about personalities; as most of our conversations were to be until the campaign of 1960. Kennedy had an almost insatiable appetite for high- or low-level gossip, and he must have dealt with others as he dealt with me—with an amused, almost pickpocketlike skill of filching impressions or memories. Had I met Ray Jones? he asked. Ray Jones, the "Fox of Harlem," was one of the first respectable black leaders in New York politics, and I had written a piece about him. What was Jones like? Was he with LBJ? Was he available? Could he be trusted? (When I said yes, and Kennedy met with Jones privately, and Jones promptly leaked the meeting, Kennedy was furious with both me and Jones.) Had I met Chou En-lai? What was Chou really like? Did I really know Jean Monnet? What was Monnet really like? How did Monnet make the Plan work?

This, then, was my first impression of John Kennedy: that he was interested chiefly in personalities, that he saw politics as a game.

But personality led on to style, and this was where the image, radiating out through his circle of admiring staffmen and entranced newsmen, became the public persona—the dashing, impeccably tailored, handsome Boston Irishman with the Harvard gloss. He was by nature stylish, by twist of mind ironic, by taste a connoisseur of good prose. These qualities combined to convert the newsmen who followed him from reporters to a claque, of whom, I admit, I must be counted one. He read very carefully what newsmen wrote about him. If he liked what you wrote, he might tell you that it was a "classy" story and could even quote from it. He was also all those things newsmen wish to be but are not: he was always immaculate, changing suits and shirts as many times a day as the wrinkles of travel required. He was humorous at every level, in every idiom, with a twist of wry and a slight bite to his wit. His style was particularly attractive to women, to whom he applied the old British maxim "Treat a whore like a duchess, treat a duchess like a whore." One day early in the primaries, when he was still unprotected by guards, I saw him accosted in Wisconsin by a recognizable paranoid of the "patriot" school, a harridan, demanding why he did not support some local bill requiring loyalty oaths of students. After an interchange with his staff, who were trying to drag her away, Kennedy leaned over with immense courtliness and explained, as if he were explaining to his own mother, "But you see, when I enlisted in the Navy, they didn't ask me to take a loyalty oath, and when I entered Congress, they didn't ask me to take a loyalty oath. Everyone *should* take a loyalty oath, but we shouldn't ask only special groups to do it." The lady huffed and humphed down and disappeared, smiling and soothed.

He had a precise sense of his own style. One day, on his plane, the *Caroline,* he insisted I rewrite the dreary text for a Kennedy pamphlet to be put on the seat of every delegate at the Democratic convention. "You're the only professional writer on the plane," he said, "and you're getting free booze." I protested; I was a reporter, paid my own fare, was not part of his staff. I said I didn't know him well enough, but he insisted, so I did my best. And then he came back and said, "You're right. This would be good copy for Adlai. But it's not my style. It's too soft. My style is harder."

This sense of his own style made him a very self-confident human being. In Los Angeles, several months later, as he entered the final drive against Nixon, he made a speech containing a passage I considered superb political rhetoric. He said: "Mr. Nixon and I, and the Republican and Democratic parties, are not suddenly frozen in ice or collected in amber since the two conventions. We are like two rivers which flow back through history, and you can judge the force, the power and the direction of the rivers by studying where they rose and where they ran throughout their long course. . . ." I immediately tried to find out who had ghostwritten that lifting passage for him and I guessed that it was either his man Ted Sorensen or his man Dick Goodwin. I asked the question repeatedly and indiscreetly, and finally received from one of the Irish Mafia this message: "Tell Teddy White that no one wrote that for me; that bit about history collected in amber or frozen in ice is mine." It seemed, as the message was relayed back to me, that he must have spoken in stronger language, but the sense of pride in his own words and style was unmistakable.

Style, to Kennedy, was very relevant to politics. Indeed, style was the essence of personality; personality determined the quality of leadership; leadership was what the country needed and what he offered in the campaign of 1960. All these thoughts were put together in the opening speech of his 1960 campaign, an address at the

National Press Club, where he defined the issue of his candidacy. "That central issue," he said, ". . . is not the farm problem or defense. . . . It is the Presidency itself. . . . in the challenging revolutionary sixties, the American Presidency will . . . demand that the President place himself in the very thick of the fight, that he care passionately about the fate of the people he leads . . . reopen the channels of communication between the world of thought and the seat of power."

There could be no better man, thus, to follow in a campaign for the Presidency, a campaign for the conquest of power, than someone who believed as strongly as John F. Kennedy did in the ascendancy of man's will over man's fate—and the ascendancy of a leader over the circumstances of his time.

Moreover, the man was a joy to be with, one of the most attractive politicians of his era. Recall of Kennedy mixes laughter with pain, truth with nostalgia, the language of the street with the language of thinking people. He was realistic and romantic at once—and thus more difficult to see plainly in history than almost any other American President of our time. Those who knew him well loved him too much. Those who hated him did not know him at all. Between the conflicting memories was the man, and the man I followed wrapped me in such affection that I have never been able completely to escape.

It was the gamesman's attitude to politics that I found, at the beginning, Kennedy's most attractive quality, making him the most suitable candidate for the purposes of the book I was writing—the behavior of a man under political pressure.

One could pick up the gamesman almost anywhere, but he might like it best if I picked up the story at St. Patrick's Day, 1960, during the Wisconsin primary.

The game in Wisconsin was to knock Hubert Humphrey out cold. To do that, by Kennedy rules, meant to carry all Wisconsin's ten Congressional districts, of which the most Protestant and most hostile to him was the now abolished Tenth Congressional, a district of Lutheran dairy farmers, cut-over timberlands and iron mines where the ore was running out. If he could take all ten districts in this first primary, it would so impress other politicians that the convention itself might become no contest. It would be like running back the opening kickoff for a touchdown on the first play of the game.

Thus the stakes in Wisconsin as Kennedy saw them. But he had added a fillip: he would campaign through the cold Tenth Congressional District on St. Patrick's Day. It was the same Irish insouciance that later, when he was President, caused him to rename the Presidential yacht *Honey Fitz,* in honor of his grandfather, one of the more colorful rogues to be mayor of old Boston. Primaries were not then the media event they later became; the trailing press was thin to nonexistent by later standards; and *Life* magazine was, in those days, to a campaign what television coverage later became. *Life* had decided, coarsely but quite correctly, that the story of the Wisconsin test was Kennedy as a Catholic among the Protestants. Whether they wanted to or not, the photographers were going to have to get Kennedy visually in a Catholic setting to show him as the Catholic candidate. A picture of Kennedy conferring with the Pope would, of course, have suited *Life* best, but the editors would take what they could get. And there, down the road, as we drove along through the chilly day toward the town of Ladysmith, was a knot of black-robed nuns wearing green silk ribbons—about fifteen of the sisters from the Convent of Our Lady of Sorrows and the Servite High School of the Order of Sisters of Mary. It was a perfect picture, and several photographers were already there to see if the "Catholic" candidate would stop. Kennedy must have seen the trap instantly and known that the picture would run in every newspaper of the Protestant Tenth Congressional, as well as in all Wisconsin, and in *Life.* Then, as if reflecting his instant decision to take the challenge, the little caravan came screeching to a halt. As he got out, the photographers clicked away, the nuns pinned a bright-green ribbon on the candidate, and he entered the convent. The mother superior, a rotund, bespectacled lady, came out; she was so flustered that she thanked everyone, drivers, staffmen, newsmen, saying, "Now isn't that wonderful of him to come all this way to drop in to see us."

And off we drove. I liked the style and the way he played the game. I liked it a few stops later when it seemed that the grim, cold countryside had turned its back on him, and the rally at the town of Mellen consisted of five people. The rally's leader was obviously the town drunk; obviously Irish; obviously someone who had begun to celebrate St. Patrick's Day early. Since the toper did not see why we should stand in the cold, he invited Jack into the bar to have a drink. So Jack, and the toper, with Kenny O'Donnell and me following, all went into the bar. There Jack hoisted a quick Irish whiskey, expressed the hope this audience of one would vote for him in the primary, and made his way out. I have amused myself for years with the thought of the convivial drunk in some imaginary conversation saying, "Kennedy? Jack Kennedy and me? I knew him like this. Why, on St. Patrick's Day in 1960, he and I got drunk together in Mellen." And no one, of course, believing the old drunk, with the only eyewitness now left, White, too far away to testify.

It was a bad day, and at the end of it I joined Kennedy in his car. He was moody as he explained the larger dimensions of the game he was playing. This was cold country, he admitted. The Tenth Wisconsin Congressional was more than half the size of the state of Massachusetts, with fewer people in it than South Boston and Dorchester. But if he could carry this hard-rock Protestant place, he could carry anything; he could not see how the back-room bosses at the Democratic convention in Los Angeles could hold out against him, on what grounds, if he swept Wisconsin. He ran through some big names—all of them Catholics—and what their problems were. There was Albert Rosellini running for governor again in the state of Washington; practically every other name on his state Democratic ticket was Catholic, too, so Rosellini wanted a Protestant to head the *national* ticket. And David Lawrence, Catholic governor of Pennsylvania

—he needed to carry four state senatorial districts, all of them Protestant, for control of the state Senate; naturally, Dave Lawrence wanted a Protestant Presidential candidate to balance the ticket. Then there was the governor of Colorado, also a Catholic, and he, too, needed a Protestant. So he, Kennedy, needed to win this Tenth Congressional (which he later lost) to prove to other Catholics at the power joints that he was a viable candidate. If he did sweep Wisconsin, and carry the other primaries, then: "If they turn me down, the primary system is finished for good." After that we went on to talk about campaign money. He was angered by a story Sander Vanocur had written, which carried the phrase: "How much money Kennedy had spent no one will ever know." Kennedy went into a detailed description of his finances and the financing of his campaign and wound up by saying that it had cost him and "his friends" only $260,000 to get this far down the road. As it turned out in later years, Vanocur was right—no one will ever know what was spent on the Kennedy campaigns. John F. Kennedy probably did not then know himself. Later I learned that even Robert Kennedy did not know. Perhaps only Joseph Kennedy knew. But so far as the candidate himself was concerned that evening, he was playing it within the rules of the game. Kennedy's particular sportsmanship led him to accept the rules of any state, or any arena, whether national or international, high or low, clean or dirty—but he liked to win.

The gamelike quality he brought to politics occurs to me again and again, in images, flashes, recollections. It comes back pictorially, for example, from one afternoon on a bus in West Virginia—and John F. Kennedy is playing quarterback. He is going to make a speech at a factory. He gets off the bus and discovers the advance work is zero. I remember his eye sweeping the scene seeing the workers already coming off their shift. Then: Kennedy snapping his fingers at Kenny O'Donnell and Larry O'Brien, deploying them as if he were the football captain—Kenny to the back gate, Larry to the front gate, here's the literature, move them up to where I want to speak. And O'Donnell and O'Brien taking off at signal, like flanking guards, to cover the entrances and point the working men to the speaker. Gamesmanship in the West Virginia campaign ran all the way from the highest to the lowest level. One particularly happy afternoon, when everything seemed to be moving for Kennedy against Humphrey, we climbed aboard his plane at the end of day and I found him glowering. I asked what the trouble was. And he said it had been a perfect day, everything had gone well, but at the end of every perfect day something always went wrong. He'd just gotten word that Franklin D. Roosevelt, Jr. (who was stumping for him), had denounced Hubert Humphrey as a draft dodger. Kennedy was furious; West Virginia, like Tennessee, is a rifleman's, infantryman's state, where folk culture holds courage priceless, and so this was clearly a low blow. He'd told Roosevelt he did not want Hubert's war record brought into the campaign. It was dirty; he was browned off. It was not the way Kennedy played the game.

In West Virginia both Humphrey and Kennedy knew they were playing politics in one of the states where it was played at its worst. Kennedy's vote-buyers were evenly matched with Humphrey's; but others, too, were involved. Lyndon Johnson's friends were moving money into West Virginia to buy slates to support Humphrey against Kennedy; Adlai Stevenson's Ivy League friends were also moving money in, using Humphrey to stop Kennedy and deadlock the convention. At this degraded level, all were evenly matched, and thus, with his instinctive sense of the game, Kennedy decided that the wedge in his parameter of play must be the issue of Catholic against Protestant. Here he had Humphrey hobbled. No voter could prove his tolerance by voting for Hubert Humphrey, but any voter could prove to his own conscience in this state of ninety percent white Protestants that he voted without prejudice by voting for Kennedy. To this, finally, on the Sunday before the Tuesday primary, Kennedy addressed himself on local television, looking directly into the camera eye and the West Virginian audience.

"... so when any man stands on the steps of the

Capitol and takes the oath of office of President, he is swearing to support the separation of church and state; he puts one hand on the Bible and raises the other hand to God as he takes the oath. And if he breaks his oath, he is not only committing a crime against the Constitution, for which the Congress can impeach him—and should impeach him—but he is committing a sin against God."

Here, Kennedy raised his hand from an imaginary Bible, as if lifting it to God, and repeating softly, said, "A sin against God, for he has sworn on the Bible." It was nicely done—deft gamesmanship at a level where he had his opponent, Humphrey, checkmated; but also a stroke where history was the shaft, and the cutting edge was a truth that neither prejudice nor common sense could resist; John F. Kennedy was not the agent of the Pope, and one could not either see him or hear him and believe the old nonsense of prejudice.

Kennedy and Nixon both played their game on the new power field of modern communications; but whereas Nixon felt the publishers and station owners controlled the field, Kennedy concentrated on the players in the game—reporters, commentators, news personalities. He was certainly, as much as Nixon, among the first to understand the reach of television in politics, but he had also a sensitivity to the pride and prickliness of the vagabonds in the writing press which Nixon never even approached. Kennedy was interested in the politics of the media—its personalities, internal rivalries, best sellers, coming stars, fading giants, publishers' favorites, outcasts. He was interested in the newsmagazines like *Time* and *Newsweek*. Their internal politics of editor versus editor and putative replacements interested him as much as the politics, say, of Maryland and Delaware. On occasion, to a favorite of his, like Benjamin Bradlee, he would deliver an absolute scoop; or when William Lawrence later transferred from *The New York Times* to become Washington correspondent of ABC, he instructed Kenneth O'Donnell to give Lawrence, in his first few competitive weeks, any possible break in the news he could. Kennedy enjoyed the thought that he could, by a word or a story, make a man's reputation. To me, when I later won the Pulitzer Prize for my book on the campaign of 1960, he wrote a quick note of congratulation, saying: ". . . it pleases me that I could at least provide a little of the scenario." Like almost all the Kennedys, he had a particular irreverence for *The New York Times,* and enjoyed diddling it. I remember one comic occasion when he was toying with the *Times,* which began a passage of personal interchange that led to our friendship.

The occasion was the evening of June 27, the close of the Montana State Democratic Convention, the last stop on the preconvention route of 1960. Kennedy's private plane was just about to take off for the East from Helena, when someone told him of a story a news agency had just put out about him. He was incensed. It concerned a job offer he had purportedly made to Robert Meyner, then governor of New Jersey. Snapping the team to attention, clanging dimes into pay booths at the airport, he soon had Charles Roche on one phone, Kenny O'Donnell on another, himself on a third, all trying to reach New York with denials. He got the desk at *The New York Times,* switching as he spoke from his normal high Boston tenor to an imitation of the deep Burgundian voice of his press chief, Pierre Salinger. Salinger was off politicking elsewhere, and so, purporting to be Salinger, the candidate himself was dictating the denial to *The New York Times.* Now and then some stranger would pass by the open phone booth, recognize Kennedy, greet him, and Kennedy would stick out his hand, say, "How are yuh, good to see yuh," and go on with his imitation of Salinger to the *Times.*

It was a long way back from Montana to Cape Cod, whither Kennedy was flying home that night, and he talked until we crossed over the Missouri into Iowa. Blair Clark, who had been Kennedy's classmate at Harvard, was then reporting for CBS, and the three of us made convivial company as the plane winged home through the moonlight. Clark and I were drinking, but Kennedy wanted only tomato soup, into which he stirred great gobbets of sour cream. He was still annoyed by the story of his promise of a federal job to Meyner in return for support at the convention; it is a federal crime to make such an offer. Not only was the story untrue, he said, it was amateurish. "It's surprising," he went on, "how people in politics *don't* ask you for a job. No politician asks you directly for a job; they always do it through other people." What had happened was simple: one of Meyner's aides had asked Kennedy what, if he was elected, he had in mind for Meyner, and all Kennedy had said was that he couldn't conceive of any Democratic President of the United States not using Bob Meyner. As we unwound, the talk opened up into one of those rambling conversations which are the best nourishment of friendship, and that night, somehow, he won me.

I mentioned that Clark and I had been checking the lone bookstore in Helena for best sellers while he was politicking in the back rooms. How had his own book, *Profiles in Courage,* done there? he asked. We told him it was sold out. This annoyed him and he summoned the dozing O'Donnell from his seat and snapped that Harper's, his publishers, must be sure to stock a supply of his book wherever he traveled, particularly in Los Angeles during the convention.

Then we were into books. Clark asked when Kennedy would write another. Kennedy said he couldn't compete with professional writers. His problem was to get an idea *important* enough to sell a book, for it wouldn't sell on his writing. Then he asked Clark, why didn't Clark write a book about his great-great-grandfather Simon Cameron, Lincoln's first Secretary of War? Clark recalled that Lincoln had said of his Secretary of War that Cameron would steal anything except a red-hot stove—if the stove was nailed down. Astonishingly, Kennedy picked Clark up on the political detail and corrected him. The slur had come from Thaddeus Stevens, the radical Pennsylvania abolitionist, but Lincoln had enjoyed repeating it, always carefully attributing the slur to Stevens. Clark riposted neatly and said that the corruption was not the story of his great-great-grandfather. The real story in Simon Cameron was that he was the first man to mobilize the industry of a modern democracy for war.

Kennedy was interested in reputations and went on. He pointed out that Churchill had written the life of his great ancestor Marlborough, and observed that men of tarnished reputation could rely only on their descendants for rehabilitation. So might Clark do for Simon Cameron. After all, said Kennedy, quoting, it was Churchill himself who wrote of his ancestor that "In his youth he prized money more than passion, in his age money more than fame." From there we went on to what makes good historical writing. Kennedy cited a letter of Theodore Roosevelt's on the funeral of Edward VII as fine historical writing, better than Roosevelt's formal histories, which he thought "low-grade." At this point, he began to reel off a list of names of American historians which I found simply astonishing. I had thought of him simply as a games-player; he was not now trying to impress either Clark or me, but obviously his knowledge of history went far back beyond the roots of today's politics, and his reading had a range far beyond the needs of the gamesman. He said, winding up our talk about history, that if he ever wrote another book it would be about a politician dealing with events—exactly what I was trying to do!

We went on to current politics after a short while, as the plane rocked in the night stream, and began to discuss Kennedy's Vice Presidential options. He offered Stuart Symington's name first, then asked one of us to check the Constitution in the plane's little library to see whether Symington's birth in Massachusetts disqualified them from running on the same ticket. Then he brought up Lyndon Johnson. Six months ago he would have thought that LBJ was the best man outside of himself to be President; he still thought so, but now he also thought Johnson was an egomaniac. We were gossiping politics now. Take Adlai, he said—why is it you couldn't get the little old Irish ladies to vote for him? At another point he ran off the differences between Jews and Irishmen, then the differences between American Jews and Israeli Jews.

We then went on to "ethnics" in American politics. And I observed that "ethnicity" was a quality difficult to measure. For example: his father, the ambassador, who had graduated from both the Boston Latin School and Harvard, was still thought to be a Boston Irishman, while he himself, Jack, was thought to be a Harvard man. Why? said Kennedy. I said, The way you say "How are yuh?" —that sounds second-generation Harvard. Everyone else in Boston says, "How are you." Kennedy protested: "I do not. I say 'How are you,' not 'How are yuh,' " enunciating the syllables precisely as he spoke.

It was perhaps at this point that I think I moved or was drawn across the line of reporting to friendship. Somehow, being exhausted and slack-tongued with drink, I blurted out that no matter what he said, I just didn't like his father, old Joe Kennedy, and explained why. This saddened him. He leaned forward and said, "Teddy, you must meet my father someday; he's not like that at all." But he made no further attempt to persuade me to like his father, the old ambassador. Then I said that another thing I didn't like was what he had said about my teacher John Fairbank. In his first term as congressman, Kennedy had joined the pack and proclaimed that both John Fairbank and Owen Lattimore, another friend of mine, had been part of the Communist influence in the State Department which lost China to the Reds. Kennedy had no answer to that. But he put his head down in his hands, shook it, then said, as I recall, "Don't beat up on me. I was wrong. I know I was wrong. I didn't know anything then—you know what a kid congressman is like with no researchers, no staff, nothing. I made a mistake." His remorse was so real I could not press the matter; and then realized that inside myself I wanted to like this man, could find no reason for not liking him, and gave myself over to the loyalty of friendship.

We drifted on through the night, finally arriving in the early morning at Cape Cod, where I began to assemble some notes on Kennedy and history. It was on this trip that I learned the futility of trying to talk to a candidate about history. I had asked Kennedy if he could give me just a feel of where he wanted the American people to be after eight years of his Presidency—how far down the road he thought he could take them. At which he became annoyed, and considering me a friend but being nibbled to death by too many such questions, he said, "Jesus Christ, Teddy, you ought to have more sense than to ask me that kind of question now. There's the convention to get through first, then the election, then Congress. Ask me later."

So I was left to my own writer's measure of where the campaign of 1960 fit into history. I had read enough of previous campaigns and done enough reporting in the 1956 campaign to know that the "today" story, the morning and evening lead, is vital only to newspapers and television. The "today" story in any campaign runs an erratic course of slips of tongue, errors of scheduling, secret meetings, contrived statements, back-room deals, synthetic issues that flourish for a day or a week and then disappear. In 1960, there was the imaginary and nonexistent "missile gap"; Kennedy proclaimed (quite ignorantly) that the Russians were leading us in kill power at a moment when our superiority over the Russians was never greater; there was also the heated gas bubble of controversy that rose over Quemoy and Matsu, twin rock outcroppings off the coast of China, which Kennedy proclaimed (quite rightly) to be without significance. There were other such trivia and one-day flashes, but two episodes now seem to rise out of receding memory like great ridges leading directly to history. One was the Martin Luther King affair. The other was Kennedy's homecoming to Boston. Both were episodes in which concealed emotion erupted and hardened into visible landmarks of history.

The Martin Luther King affair, as I reported it then, was another Kennedy gamesman's move, a ploy to win black votes, while Richard Nixon, timid and cautious, could not bring himself to voice concern for a black leader whose life was in peril in a South Georgia jail. I wrote of it as a contest in gamesmanship on the part of two political gamesmen. But there was more to it, as I know now.

Kennedy had already tried to enlist Martin Luther King, Jr., the Lenin of the Black Revolt, in June of the campaign year. They had met at Kennedy's New York apartment, but had not quite vibrated to the same wavelength. King was more stubborn and messianic than was generally recognized at the time. The two had met once more, after Kennedy's nomination, in a hilarious French-farce misscheduling of black leaders in Kennedy's town house in Washington, in late August. By absolutely unpredictable mismanagement, Kennedy had been scheduled for two meetings at his home at once—one with Roy Wilkins and Robert Weaver of the NAACP, the other with their rival for black leadership, Martin Luther King, Jr. Lest it appear like "Negro Night at the Kennedys," said one of those present, they were separated into two parlors, unaware of each other. When Kennedy arrived, he ate dinner in one room with Wilkins and Weaver before sending them off directly to the airport with one of his aides.

He then sat down to confer with King. In the tight national race, black votes were vital, and King was the key man to sway them. But King had taken a nonpartisan stance and would not now be swayed to a commitment unless Kennedy came to the Deep South, to Atlanta, and there met publicly with King's Southern Christian Leadership Conference. Kennedy agreed in principle to a meeting, but wanted time to work out place, date, subject matter. King left disappointed. For the next few weeks negotiations hung fire. Nashville was discussed as a place to meet; so was Miami. But King wanted Atlanta. Talks continued, and then Kennedy's hand was forced by events.

It was impossible to conduct the campaign without taking serious note of Martin Luther King's public action. As the campaign wore on, among the many unorchestrated themes of concern making the usual blare, the "lunch-counter theme" rose loud and clear. It was a theme destined to swell later, but it first sounded in 1960 and it sounded because Martin Luther King made it ring nationwide. It is perhaps difficult to recall now that twenty years ago in large stretches of America it was legally forbidden for a black to eat a sandwich or sip a Coke at the same sit-down counter as a white. But on Wednesday, October 19, 1960, in the Magnolia Room of Rich's department store in Atlanta, a number of young black students had sat down in protest to order sandwiches at the same counter with whites. Martin Luther King had joined them and they were all arrested for violating Georgia's trespassing law. At which point, what had been considered normal background sound in an American campaign became a question pointed directly to two candidates—a symbolic question, which is the most important kind of question in politics.

The question ran thus: What does one say when a Martin Luther King is arrested for sitting down at a lunch counter, quietly insisting on his rights? Is this a civil right, a human right or a legal right? What does one say or do when all other protestors but Martin Luther King are released within five days yet he, on a technicality, is carted off in handcuffs to a jail in deep cracker country, where his life may be in danger? When his six-months-pregnant wife, who has always feared that white men will eventually kill King, believes he will be lynched now—how does one comfort her? Or more importantly, help her? This is one man's life, a black man, held in a state prison less than 150 miles from Plains, Georgia.

The moving spirit in all this now becomes the civil rights expert of the Kennedy campaign staff, Harris Wofford, Professor of Law at Notre Dame, an ardent humanitarian, a positive man. Wofford *insists* that Kennedy must act lest this black leader be murdered in jail by racists. On Wednesday, October 26, Wofford gets to Sargent Shriver, Kennedy's brother-in-law, who, in turn, reaches the candidate himself at O'Hare Airport in Chicago. Kennedy telephones from the airport directly to Mrs. King, expressing his concern and saying he is going to do all he can to make sure her husband is safe. He moves by impulse, not calculation, because no man of good will in his position can stand aside when a black leader is imprisoned on a technicality* and exposed to a possible prison knifing in a racist jail. But—and this is significant —Kennedy is upset, when he arrives in New York from Chicago, to find that his intervention has been made public. When questioned in New York, however, he says, yes, he has promised to do everything he can to see that Martin Luther King gets out of jail safely. Not knowing whether he would lose more Southern white votes than he would gain black Northern votes, unbriefed on the election balance, he must take a stand on instinct. It was a moment when gamesmanship ran concurrently with something stronger—with a sense of history, with a sense of the tide that was carrying America to far shores.

I had seen Kennedy play his stroke, during the campaign, from afar, for I was with Richard Nixon, his rival, that week. Through the crisis of King's transfer to the Reidsville state prison, I had sat on Nixon's campaign train in the Midwest, with Nixon unable to make up his mind how he wanted to play the game. Nixon was the Vice President; the machinery of the Department of Justice was his to use for intervention. But finally, unable to make up his mind in time, Nixon had passed, and thus lost. I like to think that Kennedy *wanted* King out of jail for humane reasons—and was on the way to that crest of his politics which later became the civil rights bill of 1963–1964.

The memory of Kennedy's action that week ranks with the memory of the last weekend of his campaign as occasions when campaign politics freeze a moment of history passing.

Kennedy need never have come back to New England in the last three days of the campaign; the game did not require it. His polls, as did Nixon's, told him how close were such crucial states as Illinois, Missouri and

*The technical charge was that the terms of a previous twelve-month suspended sentence—for driving with an expired license—had been violated by King's arrest at Rich's.

California. And New England was so safe for John F. Kennedy that time spent campaigning there was superfluous. Had he been an absolute gamesman he would have ended his campaign on the Pacific coast, fighting for the California vote, and then flown home to vote himself in Boston. But he wanted, out of style, to come home.

He had been changing during the campaign and my notes mark it in several ways: that he had become more sure of himself; that he was less shrill; that he spoke more slowly, not with the staccato of the primaries but letting the high pitch of the Kennedy voice take on a more tenor, singing quality. The rhythm of the campaign had been translating to the crowds as, in the cities, the surge came through the streets as candidates dream. I wrote: "One remembers being in a Kennedy crowd and suddenly sensing far off on the edge of it a ripple of pressure beginning, and the ripple, which always started at the back, would grow like a wave, surging forward as it gathered strength, until it would squeeze the front rank of the crowd against the wooden barricade, and the barricade would begin to splinter; then the police would rush to reinforce the barricade, shove back, start a counter-ripple, and thousands of bodies would, helplessly but ecstatically, be locked in the rhythmic back-and-forth rocking. One remembers the groans and the moans; and . . . the noise and the clamor." In the last two days he decided to bring all this back to southern New England, the most Catholic enclave of the nation, where all three states had, by then, in 1960, a Catholic majority and were thus safe. Yet he would close the campaign with them.

The final two days of the campaign began at half-past midnight in the dark morning of Sunday, November 6, as the Kennedy campaign caravan descended at the Bridgeport airport to give Boss John Bailey his promised day for Connecticut. Bailey's "day" for his state was to last only from midnight to midmorning Monday, but Kennedy meant to give this senior among his allies a full run for the effort Bailey had put in. Bailey, Irish Catholic, a Harvard Law School graduate, had grown up in ward politics, but his mind had a national reach that made him a transition character in New England political history. His Connecticut Democratic machine, whose control he shared with Governor Abraham Ribicoff, then purred with power from the smallest township in the Litchfield hills to the clotted wards of industrial Bridgeport, Waterbury, Hartford and the Naugatuck valley. Only Dick Daley of Chicago in his prime could call out such partisan troops as Bailey could put into the street, or pour into the polls, when he exerted himself. But at this point, Bailey was doing what he did that dark night as much out of artistry as out of loyalty and devotion, as a charioteer makes his horses prance when he wishes to impress.

It was for me, who had left New England twenty-two years earlier, a strange and throat-choking night. I had grown up contemptuous of the Irish-Catholic bosses of Boston's wards. But I had come to know and respect John Bailey on the national scene, and to embrace as friends the entire Kennedy entourage, once I had made my emotional peace with the candidate personally. And now John Bailey was showing Kennedy, and those of us on the press bus, what an old-fashioned machine could really do. There on the twenty-seven-mile route between Bridgeport, which made all kinds of steelware from ammunition to sewing machines, and Waterbury, which made all kinds of brassware from clocks to buttons, Bailey had turned out every Democratic mayor, first selectman, ordinary selectman, town committeeman, town treasurer, and their wives, husbands, children, along with citizen New Englanders who wanted Kennedy elected. Everywhere the machine had mustered the fire engines with their blinkers winking, the police cars with their red beacons revolving, the ambulances with sirens howling, to announce Kennedy's arrival. From bridges and overpasses and little buildings hung the signs, placards and banners hailing their homecoming Catholic prince.

The upheaval had begun here more than thirty years before, when politicians noticed in the Hoover sweep of 1928 that three Connecticut industrial towns—Bridge-

port, Hartford and New Haven, all of them Catholic—
had given Smith a majority. The three towns stood out
like Catholic islands in the tide that washed over solid
Yankee, Protestant, Republican Connecticut. If anyone
had pressed further into the census figures of 1930, they
would have discovered that more than two thirds of
Connecticut citizens were foreign born or the children of
foreign born—and these children would shortly be a voting majority. The foreign born, in those days, were largely
Catholic, with a bit of Jewish for flavoring. Bailey had
come to power by harnessing together a coalition of
groups in his native Hartford, which held three distinct
Democratic districts, one Irish, one Italian, one Jewish.
He had then built a statewide machine on his ability to
put together Irish, Italians, Poles, French Canadians,
Jews and a frosting of Yankee Democrats, for the tightest
control of his state of any politician in the East in November 1960. Now he had them all out, every single
group, on the industrial belt; but it was not only discipline
that had done it; it was yearning. In later years the
Catholics of Connecticut would split allegiances, as they
did everywhere, and share their votes with Republicans,
too. But that night, in 1960, they were coming into their
own, and as the cavalcade swept on with its Jewish
governor, Ribicoff, and its Irish boss, Bailey, and the
hero, all silhouetted at the head of the procession in the
night, the reception was more than political or ceremonial. It was tribal, roaring with atavisms and seething with
old repressions, until at three in the morning, on the green
of Waterbury, the mayor pleaded with Kennedy to send
the crowd home to bed. They had to work in the morning, he said, and Kennedy tried to send them home after
his speech, but they would not go, grown men joining
with women, yelling, "We love you, Jack, we love you,
Jack."

After which, in the last day of the campaign, the
tour flipped up to Maine, stopped back in Manchester,
New Hampshire (to denounce William Loeb, publisher of
the most biased paper in the nation, then and now),

touched down in Rhode Island, the most Catholic state of the union, and came back to Boston, late at night. But I remember best one vignette early that Monday morning, as our cavalcade took off from Waterbury through northern Connecticut. There, on a leaf-strewn autumn lawn, in a street choked with cheering Kennedy-lovers, stood a Yankee family, brave, isolated, unafraid. The placard on their lawn read "Henry Cabot Lodge for Vice President." Every member of the family—father, mother, children—had orange Lodge bumper strips pinned over their chests, like the sash of the French Legion of Honor, and they stood there, like a tableau of the Spirit of '76, all at attention, their thumbs on their noses, giving the full thumb salute to the Catholic candidate!

If Connecticut's reception had been tribal, Boston's was savage. I can remember the beating of the hands and the banging on the sides of the cavalcade's cars and buses. I can remember the inching of the press bus through the crowds, and clinically wondering whether we would have to run people down, because the candidate had a date with a nationally televised program from Faneuil Hall, the Cradle of Liberty. But as we came out of the grimy Sumner tunnel, up into central Boston, my scribbled notes as far as I can decipher them read: "Mounted police . . . white helmets . . . wild mobs . . . confetti . . . can't move . . . drum majorettes, shakos . . . men, navy pea jackets, army field jackets . . . more police, white helmets bobbing . . . choked . . . people screaming, mad . . . now two files of 20 cops, white helmets . . ." We managed to break through the screaming Celtic mob and get onto Washington Street, the narrowest main street in America, and the notes read: "People crowding into store windows . . . look like manikins . . . storms of confetti . . . total breakdown . . ."

From there we moved to the Statler Hotel, where the candidate changed clothes and with no other pause was off to two rendezvous: the first with his old Boston constituency at the Boston Garden, the second with his national constituency via a telecast from Faneuil Hall.

The Boston Garden rally was the kind of rally that political reporters, who see too many rallies, attend but ignore, which I did. But my notes now make it far more important than the Faneuil Hall speech. At Faneuil Hall, where Paul Revere had organized the Sons of Liberty, Kennedy spoke from a text drafted by his speechwriters; spoke to the nation. But at the Garden, in the sweaty hall of wrestlers, hockey players and sportsmen, next to the Old North Church of the revolutionary conspirators, he spoke to his own. He could look out over the audience and see it as it was: overwhelmingly political hacks, stalwarts, ward heelers, the pink-eyed predatory machine politicians down front; then the shawled Irish ladies of Boston, who used to go to any political rally if they were sure it wouldn't break up in a fight; and this time, a rather heavy sprinkling of Harvard and other students, who were the wave of the future.

What he had to do, he had to do fast, because he was due before television cameras and the nation in a very short time. But here, in this old tribal gathering in Boston, where the Celts and Gaels had finally, totally, overwhelmed the Anglos and the Saxons, he lingered. The chairman gave up on the introduction because the mob simply wanted to cheer. Outside, the police were clubbing latecomers (Boston police in those days used the club as an instrument of dialogue), and when they clanged down the corrugated iron gates on the Garden and the press tried to move through the mob, the police clubbed the press, too. But inside, Kennedy, oblivious to this, was doing a grace act, keenly conscious of the time and his rendezvous with television.

He ran through the list of Democratic candidates in Massachusetts, a necessary courtesy in American politics in any state, endorsing each and every one of them. The transcript records the list: ". . . my distinguished running mates of this state, Tom O'Connor . . . we need a Democratic senator from Massachusetts who will vote for progressive legislation . . . Joe Ward, who I am hopeful will be elected governor of Massachusetts . . . Edward MacLaughlin . . . the nephew of our beloved friend John Mc-

Cormack ... Tom Buckley ... John Driscoll ... Kevin White."

It was a totally Irish slate—what, in my boyhood, I had heard referred to as an "all-Green Ticket." John F. Kennedy gave them all his benison. Then he was moving out, trying to take the audience off home base: "I come here to Boston to this Garden which is located in the Eleventh Congressional District of the State of Massachusetts, which my grandfather represented sixty years ago, and which I had the honor of representing fourteen years ago when I was first elected to the House of Representatives ..."

He went on. But this time he was not playing the game of "remember," or what cynics used to call the game of "Irish Tag." "Irish Tag" was the contest among the Hibernians to pin one or another candidate as the candidate of "Beacon Hill," the man the Yankees had put into the race or backed. To tag someone with that label was once as effective as to tag someone today with the label of "racist." But John F. Kennedy was so far beyond that that he would have had to crumple his mind to recapture the rhetoric of his grandfather. The rhythms which had pitted the Fitzgeralds, the Walshes and Big Jim Curley against the Calvin Coolidges, Henry Cabot Lodges, Senior and Junior, and all the Saltonstalls, were burned away. He did not take this crowd in the Hall seriously; if he had come out for abortion, sodomy and divorce, this crowd would still have voted for him. But he loved them, as they loved him, and so, with his mind in free-gear association, he was piecing phrases together from the patches of all the speeches and rallies of the campaign of 1960, into what he wanted his father's, his mother's, his grandfather's people to see with him. Then, just as he had done in Los Angeles when he had reeled off his metaphor of the rivers of history, he now, in the presence of his own, pulled off the spool of inner rhetoric in his mind that I thought then, and think now, is perhaps the best explanation of why any man runs for the Presidency of the United States.

". . . I do not run for the office of the Presidency,"

he said, "after fourteen years in the Congress with any expectation that it is an empty or an easy job. I run for the Presidency of the United States because it is the center of action." He paused. Then, poking his forefinger at them from the platform, timing every word, gravely and slowly he went on: "and in a free society the chief responsibility of the President is to set before the American people the unfinished public business of our country. . . ."

The crowd rose and cheered, and he slipped away to Faneuil Hall to appear on national television, talking from a stiff text. The next morning he voted from a polling place at the old West End branch of the Boston Public Library, in what had once been the Jewish ghetto; and then he was off to Hyannisport. By the following morning he had been elected President.

For a man in search of history, the election of 1960 should have been a climax. And yet, for all the many words and pages I wrote of it, it was a passage that clarified itself only as time went by.

The two candidates, if they debated anything, debated foreign policy, and from their rhetoric it was difficult to decide which was the bolder or more dedicated cold warrior. Kennedy insisted "the country must move again," Nixon insisted he knew best how to "keep the peace without surrender." They ran off the same laundry list of partisan promises and denunciations that Democrats and Republicans had soiled by overuse since 1946. Both claimed they were speaking for tomorrow's decade, the 1960s, yet of the great civil rights battle that was to mark the decade, of the war in Vietnam, of the surge of female consciousness, of the eruption of youth, of the changes in life-styles, of abortion, of drugs, of the vast revolution in the tax system—not a single memorable speech or text comes down to me, either in recollection or in my notes.

The election of 1960 was apparently, and on the face of it, totally devoid of cause or issue. Yet it was devoid of cause only if one measured it against what came later—the election of 1964 with Goldwater's cause trenchant, the election of 1968 with bloodshed in the streets, the election of 1972 with McGovern's liberal pieties making him a stark target, the election of 1976 with Carter's managerial morality so crisp against the fresh memories of Watergate.

The election of 1960 was devoid of cause only if one failed to recognize that the man himself, John F. Kennedy, embodied the cause; and the cause was not borne by his tongue, his grace, his proposals. The cause lay in his birth: he was a Catholic, an ethnic from outside the mainstream of American leadership. To elect John F. Kennedy President was to make clear that this was a different kind of country from what history taught of it, that it was rapidly becoming, and would become in the next twenty years, so much more different in its racial and ethnic patterns as to make life in some of America's greatest cities completely unrecognizable.

Fundamentally, the politics of 1960 vented a demographic upheaval. Perhaps not since the time of the Gracchi had any eighty-year period seen so great a social and racial change in a political system as did America between 1880 and 1960. Between the time of the Gracchi (133 B.C.) and Caesar's thrust across the Rubicon (49 B.C.), the Roman Republic of farmers, yeomen, citizen soldiers and patrician leaders, which Polybius described as self-governing and eternal, vanished. Its own triumphs and laws had made its capital a gathering place at once of the powerful and the dispossessed, had enfranchised Sicilians, Alpine Italians, Spaniards, Jews, Gauls. Since Roman law made Rome the only legal place of voting, the new strangers exercised an entirely disproportionate influence as they filed through the *ovile* to cast their ballots and help choose Rome's leaders. Caesar put an end to the system because the Republic's old laws would not stretch over its new population, and rather than become a victim of those who manipulated the votes, he chose to drive the manipulators from Rome.

No such event is likely in the near future in America; but the demographic developments of the eighty years prior to Kennedy had changed America so profoundly that the significance of his election is incomprehensible if one does not try to measure the ethnic upheaval that transformed the America of John F. Kennedy's grandfather to the America of John F. Kennedy.

In 1894, the year that old John F. ("Honey Fitz") Fitzgerald first went to Congress from Boston, the United States Census had just made a first tentative but official guess at the religions of Americans. It estimated that a then startling thirteen percent of America's 64,361,000 population was Catholic—8,227,000. But these were people submerged in a Protestant culture, working-class folk, speaking bad English (some of the coastal Irish, fleeing hunger to reach Boston in the 1850s, still spoke only Gaelic); the few Catholic congressmen in Washington had less group influence than the Black Caucus today; and the Catholics were almost overwhelmingly Irish and German immigrants, with a sprinkle of French-speaking Catholics (in Louisiana), and Hispanic Catholics (on the Mexican border). Most of them were underclass—and most were suspect.

With the turn of the century, as the immigration figures record, another migration of Catholics to the United States began to flow from Italy, from Poland, from Bohemia, from French Canada. The United States was on its way to the modern torment between its principles and its prejudices, on the way to the yet unmade decision whether it is a place or a nation, an idea or a state. By the 1920s, Irish Catholics had gained leadership over most immigrant groups in the big cities—Boston, Buffalo, Hartford, New York, Chicago, all the way west to Omaha and St. Paul. Only hubris, however, could have explained Al Smith's adventure in 1928; with Catholics still estimated at only sixteen percent of the national population, and few yet accepted in leadership positions in education, journalism, industry or finance, Smith's campaign was hopeless. But cultures shape family life; and as the

Catholic birth rate rose, while the general birth rate dropped, estimates held that the count of Catholics in the United States was 21 million in 1940, by 1950 was over 27 million, by 1960 had reached 43 million, or more than a quarter of the population. A Catholic scholar, Dr. Donald Barrett of the University of Notre Dame, estimated that in the decade before Kennedy was elected, the Catholic population of the country increased by 35.8 percent, the general population by 16.6 percent, or in other words, as he put it, "forty-one percent of the total United States growth in 1950–1959 was derived from the Catholic sector of the population."

This, then, was the demographic surge that John F. Kennedy rode. But although statistics help define such surges for both politicians and scholars, it is not until the statistics are broken down into their segments that politicians can begin to plan strategies. In 1928, the statistics had broken *against* Alfred E. Smith, Catholic. In 1960, they now broke *for* John F. Kennedy. Four years earlier, Kennedy's in-house thinker, Ted Sorensen, and Kennedy's back-room friend, John Bailey, had prepared and circulated a broad-brush political/religious analysis of the fourteen states of the Union where Catholics were supposed to represent twenty percent or more of the voting population. They were trying to demonstrate that Catholic John F. Kennedy would, as Vice Presidential candidate, help rather than hurt the Democratic ticket in states that carried 261 of the 269 electoral votes needed to elect. By 1960, the demographics had raised Catholic voting proportions in every state in the Union, and in at least three states—Massachusetts, Rhode Island and Connecticut—Catholics were an absolute majority. In Massachusetts, the Democratic ticket that Kennedy hailed on election eve was Catholic from top to bottom; in Rhode Island the Catholics overbalanced Protestants until some reacted like Huguenots in Richelieu's France. In Rhode Island in 1960, governor, lieutenant governor, secretary of state, speaker of its House and president of its Senate, majority leaders of both houses, chief justice and three of the four associate justices of its supreme court—all were Catholic.* In the sixty-two counties of New York, then the largest state in the Union, the Democratic county committeemen in fifty-seven were Catholic; of the other five, two were Jewish and only three Protestant. In state after state, in a geographical pattern that no logic could comprehend, Catholics had become governors. From the far Northwest, stalked on the map by Washington, where Rosellini was governor, down the coast of California, where "Pat" Brown had recently been elected, across the Mississippi to Ohio, where Mike DiSalle was now governor—Catholic governors were becoming commonplace everywhere except in the Deep South.

An illuminating set of figures traced the breaking demographic waves as they rolled into Congress. In 1960, among the 434 members of the House of Representatives, Roman Catholics outnumbered congressmen of any other single denomination—98 Catholics as against 94 Methodists, 72 Presbyterians, 67 Episcopalians, 66 Baptists, and so forth down to 12 Jews. But in the Senate, matters were different—there, Catholics fell far short of their proportionate number in the electorate. Senators who listed themselves as Methodists came first (with 19); then came Episcopalians and Baptists, with 14 each; then came Catholics, with only 12. Such contrasting figures of House and Senate read as if, at the lower level of Congressional districts, Americans did trust Catholic congressmen to speak well and truly for them. But at the higher level of the Senate, where war and peace were made, where treaties and foreign policy were decided, where Supreme Court Justices were confirmed, Americans still preferred Protestants of the old tradition as custodians of national purpose. The House, which constitutionally has sole right to initiate taxation, responded to what the voters wanted; the Senate responded to what the nation needed.

*It should be noted how time has erased the sharp edge of confrontation. Rhode Island is now so thoroughly Catholic, and its Catholics so unafraid, that it is the only New England state that now boasts two old-stock Protestant senators, Claiborne Pell and John Chafee.

The flavor of history in 1960, and the old Protestant-Catholic perceptions of their roles in American politics up to then, comes back to me best by a reflection on the intertwined careers of John Bailey and Chester Bowles, both of Connecticut's Democratic Party. The party boss, Bailey, Catholic, was promised and received, once Kennedy was elected, the chairmanship of the National Democratic Party, symbolic patronage and favor dispenser. But Bowles, Unitarian, former governor of the state, was charged by Kennedy to direct the task force which would seek out the names of those who would conduct foreign policy and national defense. Evidently the Bowles appointment did not sit well with Bailey, for some time later, in a reminiscent mood, he told me the following story, echoing of the past: It was he, Bailey, as boss of the state Democratic machine, who had delivered to Bowles the nomination for governor of Connecticut in 1948. In a tight race, Bowles had won. The next year, Connecticut's Senator Raymond Baldwin had resigned, leaving a seat in the United States Senate to be filled by new Governor Bowles. Bailey wanted for himself the seat which was Bowles's to give; but Bowles turned him down. Bowles had decided to appoint his old friend William Benton as senator instead, because, so remembered Bailey, Bowles said that Benton was better qualified to deal with foreign affairs, war and peace, the United Nations and nuclear weapons, than a local Hartford politician. So it was that Benton became a United States Senator, and Bailey was left behind as the cigar-smoking boss of Connecticut. Thereafter the wheel of fortune turned: Bowles lost his run for reelection in 1950; served as Ambassador to India until 1953; and in 1954 Bailey was still boss, but Bowles was again applicant for the Democratic nomination for governor. Bailey, according to the story as he told it—and he told it with savor, punctuating it with his cigar smoke—received Bowles in the family house on Main Street, where he made his office in what was once the bedroom in which he had been born. Bailey listened to Bowles make his plea for support for the nomination. And then, again according to Bailey, he had replied, "Chet, five years ago when you were governor and I sat across the desk from you, you decided I wasn't fit to be a senator of the United States, it needed someone like Benton. Well, I've decided you aren't fit to be governor, and I'm going to support a Jew for governor, Chet, I'm going to support Abe Ribicoff for governor, a Jew, because I think he understands this state better than you do . . . and maybe I don't understand foreign affairs."

Thus, then, a very large degree of social prejudice, both of Protestant against Catholic and Catholic against Protestant, still hung over the election of 1960. But there was an issue involved in the religious face-off which never did surface in the campaign, an issue of two world views, of two contending philosophies, both of them changing, both letting slip from control cultures they once dominated.

American politics had derived from the Protestant ethic—the credo that man is responsible directly before God for his conscience and his acts, without the intervention or intercession of priests. That ethic had been translated into both government and daily life; men and women were responsible for their lives, and must strive to make them rewarding. No space of geography had ever been more inviting to such an ethic than America, with its endless, open, free and fertile land. There, if a man worked hard, plowed deep, neither slacked nor slothed, and took care of his wife and children, then either fortune or God would reward his efforts.

This American Protestant culture dominated politics until 1932—when all of it broke down in the marketplace, where hunger and unemployment mocked the Emersonian philosophy of self-reliance and independence. And it was Roosevelt, moving through this ravaged political culture, who saved it. He gave the Democratic Party its lasting political truth: in a modern industrial system, all individual effort must be braced by a government that guarantees opportunity for those who want to work, food for those who would otherwise starve, and pensions for the old.

Few analysts could perceive in Roosevelt, a High

Church Episcopalian, any great intellectual appreciation of either Protestant or Catholic theology as applied to politics. Nor could those who voted. But the Roosevelt philosophy of government echoed far more of the Catholic than the Protestant tradition in government. The Church had always, historically, allied itself to the State —to maintain the discipline of morality, to give mercy, feed the poor, teach the young, to instruct family life. Catholic cultures, historically, shared with governments authority over life-styles, manners, rituals, ceremonies— as far, in some cases, as the reach of the rack or customs of the bed. For centuries in Europe, the Church and State had between them embraced all life—while the American Protestant tradition had tried since the beginning of this Republic to separate the two in their responsibilities. For millions of American Catholics the Roosevelt way of government supplemented, in a way they could not explain even to themselves, the family tradition where Church and State were jointly the givers of alms, the keepers of hospitals, the comforters of the aged and the orphan. This requirement of mercy seemed imperative to millions of Protestants, too. Thus, while politically cementing the Catholics to the Democratic Party, Roosevelt split the Protestants into workingmen and entrepreneurs, into rich and poor, into liberals and conservatives. The religious forms remained; the bigotries remained; but catch phrases like "welfare," "death penalty," "birth control," teased different reactions out of different communities.

It was in Roosevelt's time that the cultures of the country, both Protestant and Catholic, began to change; the war speeded the change. By 1960, John Kennedy and Richard Nixon dueled on this shifting ground—the one, Kennedy, vaguely for enlarging the embrace and solicitude of government, the other, Nixon, extolling the Emersonian virtues of independence and self-reliance.

I reported the campaign of 1960 as it unrolled in no such philosophical manner. Had I done so, no one would have printed or read a paragraph of it. Nor did I have to—I was reporting for a book. For that book about 1960, the imperative was to concentrate first on the men, next on the game, then, lastly, on the religious issue. The reach of ideas in American politics I found totally unmanageable.

I had to report the religious issue with the few facts that surfaced: the Arkansas Baptist State Convention came out against a Catholic for President. So did "Protestants and Other Americans United for Separation of Church and State." So did a handful of others, including the Reverend Norman Vincent Peale. I had to supplement hard fact with vignettes, like the unforgettable memory of the two elderly ladies I had met in the rain in the West Virginia primary. Under a dripping umbrella I had huddled with Mary McGrory, another Bostonian, of the Girls Latin School, and heard the two mountain ladies explain why they were voting for Humphrey against Kennedy: "If our fathers had wanted a Catholic to be President," one said, "they would have said so in the Constitution." Millions of simple bigots thought that way. So did the Ku Klux Klan. So did slow-minded people.

What I left out of my reporting of the campaign of 1960 was the "nonevent." The most difficult problem for any reporter is to report what Conan Doyle caused Sherlock Holmes to describe as the importance of the "curious incident" of the dog that did not bark. What does not happen is, sometimes, more significant than what does. The largest thing that did not happen in 1960 was an orgy of prejudice. The organized Protestant churches refused to take a stand against John F. Kennedy. Every national conference of religion in the United States—Baptist, Episcopalian, Methodist, Jewish, Presbyterian, Congregational—declared its neutrality, and withdrew itself from political commitment.

I could, of course, writing irregularly, pay attention to whatever I wanted, when I wanted. And so generally I continued to consider the religious issue as part of the game, played largely on the court of communications, on schedules set by editorial "futures" calendars. The "futures" calendar of any editor lists the various rendezvous with events he may plan in advance to report. In 1960, Reformation Sunday would fall on October 30. On that day, traditionally, Protestant divines of the old school tell of the martyrs in the struggle for conscience against the dogmas of the priests. It is an occasion worth remembering. And with so many editors and reporters marking the date on calendars as a dramatic climax to the campaign, second only to the scheduled Great Debates on television, the Kennedy people knew they must move quickly to lance the religious issue before press and television heated it to a boil. They moved with great speed; they recognized that they required an event; they knew the best way to handle any tricky issue is to get it out in the open fast, where it can be cauterized by attention. Their problem was to separate Protestants into those whose ears were stopped and those whose ears absorbed new phrases. Roosevelt had divided the Protestant base by concern for livelihood; Kennedy had to cleave at a higher level.

The event that Kennedy strategy chose very early on was, of course, the well-remembered confrontation of Kennedy with the Greater Houston Ministerial Association in Texas on Monday, September 12, 1960.

His remarks were certainly the best of Kennedy's campaign statements:

> . . . because I am a Catholic, and no Catholic has ever been elected President, the real issues in this campaign must have been obscured. . . . So it is apparently necessary for me to state once again—not what kind of church I believe in . . . but what kind of America I believe in.

> I believe in an America where the separation of church and state is absolute—where no Catholic prelate would tell the President (should he be a Catholic) how to act and no Protestant minister would tell his parishioners for whom to vote. . . .

I believe in a President whose views on religion are his own private affair, neither imposed by him upon the nation or imposed by the nation upon him as a condition to holding that office. . . .

This is the kind of America I believe in— and this is the kind of America I fought for in the South Pacific and the kind my brother died for in Europe. No one suggested then that we might have a "divided loyalty." . . . and when they fought at the shrine I visited today, the Alamo . . . side by side with Bowie and Crockett died Fuentes and McCafferty and Bailey and Bedillio and Carey—but no one knows whether they were Catholics or not. For there was no religious test there. . . .

I am not the Catholic candidate for President. I am the Democratic Party's candidate for President, who happens also to be a Catholic. I do not speak for my church on public matters —and the church does not speak for me. . . .

But if the time should ever come . . . when my office would require me to either violate my conscience, or violate the national interest, then I would resign the office, and I hope any other conscientious public servant would do likewise. . . .

. . . if this election is decided on the basis that 40,000,000 Americans lost their chance of being President on the day they were baptized, then it is the whole nation that will be the loser in the eyes of Catholics and non-Catholics around the world, in the eyes of history, and in the eyes of our own people.

. . . without reservation, I can, and I quote, "solemnly swear that I will faithfully execute the office of President of the United States and will to the best of my ability preserve, protect, and defend the Constitution, so help me God."

The Houston statement ranks with Lincoln's "House Divided" speech and Bryan's "Cross of Gold" as one of the great speeches of American political campaigns—a moment when politics reach up and touch history. What it did was to invite intelligent Protestants to forsake a tradition that had become cramping. And with the victory it forecast, it also released millions of Catholics from the cohesion that had bound them together against Protestants. Catholics were about to dissolve into their constituent groups—city people against suburban people, businessmen against union men, rich against poor, Irish, Germans, Italians, Poles, French and Spanish-speaking into what in the next twenty years would become known as "ethnics," contesting in politics for spoils and honors.

Politics are built on myths, and an old American myth was about to break up. The United States had no official religion. Yet a formidable if unofficial agreement underlay all politics: that America was not only a Christian country but a Protestant country. Inherited myth and political consensus both held that only men of the Protestant tradition and ethic could be entrusted with the sacred office of the Presidency. With Kennedy, the old myth was to be shattered—but a new ethic and a new consensus would have to take the place of the old.

The next twenty years of American politics and life would be spun around that search for a new consensus and a new ethic.

We will come to that story later down the road.

For the moment, the dissolution of the old consensus is the central story of the election of 1960.

Technically, as well as politically, the election of 1960 was a close-run thing, its story told by many people.

But as it fades now, one can see that second in importance only to the outcome was the total size of the vote. In the election of John F. Kennedy, 63.8 percent of all Americans eligible to vote actually cast their ballots! That percentage of turnout of eligibles had not been

reached since Taft defeated Bryan in 1908; and, after
Kennedy, has not happened again since.

No crisis, no disaster, no depression, no war, stirred
Americans in 1960—nothing but the personalities of the
candidates and the religion of one of them. Yet the
national vote bulged upward over the 1956 total by more
than six million votes, or eleven percent. Only once in the
half century had there been so remarkable an increase in
national turnout—when, in 1928, the national total
jumped by an unbelievable 25 percent over the turnout in
1924. That election of 1928 also pitted a Catholic (Al
Smith) against a Protestant (Hoover), and the Catholic
had lost. This time the huge total and the even more
remarkable percentage of eligibles who did vote buried
the oldest religious rift in the oldest nonreligious republic
in history.

Political scientists and historians often read into
election returns the lessons and portents that become
visible only years later. My own bewildered attempt to sift
immediate meaning from the figures that rolled in on
election night in 1960 convinced me that election figures
speak only of the past—of what has already happened in
the minds and divisions of Americans. They tell nothing
of the future.

To me reading the election returns of 1960 thus,
with an eye to the past, the close returns and the staggering totals concealed interesting crosscurrents. The most
heavily Catholic states took the election in stride. New
York, with its polyglot population and large Catholic
minority, increased its total vote by only three percent as
against the national jump of eleven percent. The predominantly Catholic states—Massachusetts, Rhode Island and
Connecticut—also jumped their vote by less than the
national average—by five percent, four percent, nine percent, respectively. In Texas, however, which Johnson and
Kennedy carried, the vote went up by eighteen percent. In
California by nineteen percent. Brushing with a broad
stroke across the continent, it was apparent that Catholics, who in the 1950s had more and more split their vote
to favor Eisenhower and the Republicans, had now come

back with a bang to the Democrats; while Protestants, pouring out in huge numbers, seemed to split their vote between the two candidates.

Only when one broke the macropolitical national figures down to their micropolitical districts, wards and precincts did it become clear how much prejudice influenced voting. In Nelson County, Kentucky, for instance, four predominantly Baptist precincts gave Kennedy thirty-five percent of their vote against sixty-five percent for Nixon. But five predominantly Catholic precincts gave Kennedy eighty-eight percent and Nixon only twelve percent! There were three key precincts to be followed in 1960 in Philadelphia—precincts with a registration fifty-three percent Republican, but overwhelmingly Catholic. They switched to Kennedy in 1960 by seventy percent! And then there was the incredible performance of Aroostook County in Maine, where the best potatoes in the United States were once grown by some of the hardest-rock Protestants in New England. Aroostook County's vote went up by fifty-one percent and went anti-Kennedy, anti-Catholic by 55.8 percent, while Maine was carried by Richard Nixon by only 59,449 votes.

But on the other hand, when one lifted to the macropolitical level of national politics, one could not escape the overwhelming fact that the Protestants had, in this faith-founded Republic, cast the votes that made Kennedy President. The gross figures, insofar as the analysts could separate them, read that blacks had given Kennedy seventy percent of their votes (although he was the least favorite Democrat among blacks in the primaries) and that his own Catholics had given him between seventy-eight percent of their votes (according to Gallup) and sixty-one percent (according to CBS-IBM figures). What was most significant, however, in the macropolitical picture of the country was the Protestant vote. Kennedy received a minority of the Protestant vote—by estimates running from 46 percent to 38 percent. But that number was so large as to make it the major constituency of the new Presidency. Whether one took the low estimate or the high estimate, of his 34 million votes, something between 22.5 million and 18.6 million were Protestant votes. He had campaigned in the suburbs, campaigned in the South, campaigned in the supermarkets, campaigned in the schools; his themes and his voice, added to his tactical skills, had penetrated the Protestant conscience of the nation; and so he was President.

None of this was at all clear on election night 1960 at Hyannisport, Massachusetts. The Kennedy command post was in Bobby Kennedy's house in the family compound; the press headquarters was at the nearby Hyannis Armory, festooned with bunting and wired up for television. All through that night, as the booze ran out in the armory, and the returns stuttered to the deadlock that was apparent first in the command center, then across the nation, the election result became more and more obscure, and the only apparent certainty was that whoever won would have won by the accident of counting and not by a national mandate of purpose.

At about ten o'clock in the morning after Election Day, with the result still unknown, I joined a small group of friends, the Massachusetts core cluster of the Kennedy drive, in the back room of the armory, where the news tickers were chattering away with the cascade of figures that commentators and reporters were desperately trying to compress in paragraphic wisdoms. By now, every newscast on the air voiced a different reading of the incomplete returns; but in this group of professionals it was accepted that the election hung on the results in California and Illinois. Missouri, Texas, Hawaii, were all still too close to call, but California (thirty-two electoral votes) and Illinois (twenty-seven electoral votes) were the prizes.

All of us in the room were hypnotized by the news tickers, as if they were talking to us, with the clackety-clack of the old-fashioned machines that makes melody in memory for men who grew up with them. There were in the room, as I recall, Larry O'Brien, Kenny O'Donnell and Dick Donahue; I was pleased to be in this professional company, watching them read the figures not for

history, as I was, but for real. There were countless
precincts "out" in Illinois, as the professional politicians
in the "Land of Lincoln," Republicans and Democrats
alike, played games with the vote totals of the missing
precincts they held in closed hands.

Even in the most corrupt states of the Union one
cannot steal more than one or two percent of the vote; an
authentic election landslide is irrefutable. But in an election like that of 1960 (or 1968 or 1976), minuscule
percentages of theft, vote fraud and corruption may carry
with them the Presidency of the United States. So it had
been all through the previous night; and in Illinois, as the
Associated Press news ticker now choked out late results,
the power of the Presidency turned. The AP was pressing
its reporters for returns, and the reporters were trying to
gouge out of the Republican and Democratic machines
their vote-stealing, precinct-by-precinct totals. The tickers
read, in a sequence I cannot possibly reconstruct from my
notes, something like this:

". . . With so-and-so many precincts still unreported,
Nixon leads in Illinois by 11,000 votes." Then: "Four
hundred precincts in Cook County have just reported and
with 712 precincts still out, Kennedy now leads by 7,000
votes." Then: "New returns from downstate give Nixon a
lead of 5,000 votes, with Cook County precincts still
unreported."

The vote kept seesawing; it was the first time I had
read precincts with professional politicians; and these
professional politicians understood the game. It was
downstate (Republican) versus Cook County (Democratic), and the bosses, holding back totals from key precincts, were playing out their concealed cards under pressure of publicity as in a giant game of blackjack. There
was nothing anyone could do in Hyannisport except hope
that Boss Daley of Chicago could do it for them. Daley
was a master at this kind of election-night blackjack
game. So were the men I was with in the back room—all
of them tense until the AP ticker chattered its keys once
more and reported: "With all downstate precincts now
reported in, and only Cook County precincts unreported,

Richard Nixon has surged into the lead by 3,000 votes." I
was dismayed, for if Nixon really carried Illinois, the
game was all but over. And at this point I was jabbed
from dismay by the outburst of jubilation from young
Dick Donahue, who yelped, "He's got them! Daley made
them go first! He's still holding back—watch him play his
hand now." I was baffled, they were elated. But they
knew the counting game better than I, and as if in
response to Donahue's yelp, the ticker, having stuttered
along for several minutes with other results, announced:
"With the last precincts of Cook County now in, Senator
Kennedy has won a lead of 8,000 votes to carry Illinois's
27 electoral votes." Kennedy, I learned afterward, had
been assured of the result of the game in Illinois several
hours before. Later that evening, Kennedy told his friend
Ben Bradlee of an early call from Daley, when all seemed
in doubt. "With a little bit of luck and the help of a few
close friends," Daley had assured Kennedy before the
AP had pushed out the count, "you're going to carry
Illinois."

The Senator and President-designate appeared shortly thereafter in the Hyannis Armory in Republican Barnstable County, Cape Cod. Barnstable Township had voted its Protestant prejudice the previous day, preferring
Nixon over John F. Kennedy by 4,515 to 2,783.

He strode up on the platform, with all the cameras
ranging for focus. He was puffy-eyed, but still handsome.
He had insisted that his father now appear with him in
public, and also his pregnant wife. It was noticed that the
elegant and controlled John F. Kennedy had tears in his
eyes. (I have observed that most men, when elected
President and first sensing that they have it all in their
hands, break down and wipe tears from their eyes.)

He spoke briefly, gracefully, composed as the camera held on his face; but his hands below camera level
quivered and shook as he tried to hold his papers. He
stepped down from the platform and, suddenly, we all
noticed that there was an elastic membrane of Secret
Service men separating us from him. Through such a

guard all of us would now have to pass, but they had been well briefed in recognition of key personnel. He spoke first as he descended to the old Massachusetts guard—O'Donnell, O'Brien, Donahue. He had special words of greeting for all within touch distance; for myself a taunting "O.K., Teddy, now you can go ahead and write that book of yours." And somewhere in that ten minutes he uttered a phrase which has scored itself on my memory, although I can find it neither in my notes nor in any transcript.

It remains in my memory thus: "The margin is thin, but the responsibility is clear." The echo has returned to me on every election night in America, however thin or large the margin. Politics, in the United States, beget power; and when the votes are counted, however thin the margin, the man who has that margin cannot escape the responsibility of power.

John F. Kennedy had no slightest intent of cringing from the power his politics had brought him. His politics had been based on proving that his Catholic descent was no breach with the continuity of the American past, that he would defend the purposes of America at home and abroad. No candidate I have followed in twenty years tried more eloquently (and successfully) to pin his campaign to the American past. He ran the thread back to the beginning of the Republic, and the Connecticut legislature of 1789, where a Colonel Davenport, its speaker, refused to suspend session for an eclipse of the sun. "The day of judgment is either approaching or it is not," said Davenport. "If it is not, there is no cause for adjournment. But if it is, I choose to be found doing my duty. I wish, therefore, that candles may be brought." He told that story from coast to coast, to great applause. In Montana he quoted Thoreau: "Eastward I go only by force. Westward I go free." In Kentucky he told his audience of Henry Clay. Everywhere he could make people laugh over the Jefferson-Madison butterfly-and-delegate-hunting expedition up the Hudson valley; or call them to reflection with his stories of Lincoln. His campaign, it sometimes seemed, was a transcontinental lecture in American history; the stories not only entertained but gave a lift to his audiences, making them see their connection with America's past.

Even down to the first night after his election, he was trying to prove that he was in the continuity of history as taught in Civics courses. Clark Clifford, one of the *genro* of Washington, had earlier urged him to reappoint several key Washington officials as public servants above politics. So, also, had urged political scientist Richard Neustadt of Columbia. Two such public servants were J. Edgar Hoover and Allen Dulles, masters respectively of American internal and external intelligence services. No one, at that time, had any idea how far out of political control these two services had run, but that first night after his election, Kennedy dined with friends, the Benjamin Bradlees and William Walton, with whom he could relax, and who, presumably, knew little or nothing of intelligence practices. Walton and Bradlee, iconoclasts both, argued that night that the first thing Kennedy ought to do as President was to get rid of J. Edgar Hoover; the second, to get rid of Allen Dulles. None were more surprised than these closest of social friends when the first two appointments announced by Kennedy were, nonetheless, Hoover and Dulles. The fact that amateurs Walton and Bradlee were right and President Kennedy wrong would not be apparent until at least fifteen years later. But Kennedy was seeking, I think, to prove that he would not violate the older American tradition of *pro patria*—that, indeed, he would use the power instruments as responsibly and as unpolitically as any of his predecessors. And for the next five months Kennedy remained with this conviction—until the Bay of Pigs, when he learned that power has its own politics, which have nothing to do with electoral politics.

I doubt whether Kennedy himself sensed the hinge he turned in American history. For he turned it not as a Catholic but as the spokesman of his generation in American leadership. His religion sat as comfortably and unconstrictingly on him as their religions had rested on Roosevelt and Churchill. I doubt whether Kennedy ever read St. Thomas Aquinas or St. Augustine. The demands on him of his faith and his God were, unlike Jimmy Carter's, easy to live with. The hinge Kennedy turned was, above all, the hinge of time, which moves by quanta, not by tick-tock. In his inaugural address he would say it as he felt it. At the age of forty-three, he was of a new generation of Americans, who saw the world differently from their fathers.

". . . Let the word go forth," he said in the snow of his inaugural, "from this time and place, to friend and foe alike, that the torch has been passed to a new generation of Americans, born in this century, tempered by war, disciplined by a hard and bitter peace, proud of our ancient heritage, and unwilling to witness or permit the slow undoing of those human rights to which this nation has always been committed. . . ."

It was, indeed, a new generation of Americans. Across the board, and up and down through the Kennedy cabinet and ranks, were the colonels, the majors, the captains and enlisted men who had staffed, manned, bombed, stormed and conquered in the outburst of power that was America's entry into world leadership in World War II. They were men brought up to believe, either at home or abroad, that whatever Americans wished to make happen would happen. They were men not only of unprecedented vigor and combat experience. They were also men who wanted to explore new ideas. Kennedy was as much the symbol of their leadership as the actual director. Many were men of new stock, and a whole generation of new Americans was about to follow them to political command and influence—men whose fathers had never felled a tree, guided a plow or broken the sod of the plains.

But for all that these men thought of themselves as a new generation, they, too, would have to grapple with enduring American problems: Black and White, War and Peace, Bread and Butter. The election of 1960 had settled only one matter: religion. Kennedy had defined that matter well enough to remove it from politics. Religion might become, and did, a personal motivation in many politicians over the next twenty years. But it was no longer a political cleavage at the electoral base. Other cleavages, just as emotional, would soon be opening—and the Kennedy administration would drive some of the entering wedges.

CHAPTER 11

Camelot

No American prejudice faded, I think, more quickly than the religious prejudice that vexed and underlay the election of 1960. It began to fade within weeks after Kennedy's election, even before his inauguration, as it became clear that what he wanted to do with power was connected neither to Papal nor to Protestant purpose.

Exactly what he did want to do with power was not clear immediately—either to the public or to him. But his relish of the power was so apparent that one is tempted to think he used the spectacle to amuse and entertain the suspicious and the adoring alike. Quite simply: Kennedy made millions of Americans realize, as only highborn Establishmentarians and professional politicians had realized before, how much fun and frolic attend life in politics and government. For the first time since Roosevelt, the White House had the quality of a court. At this court a young queen danced at dazzling balls, handsome children held birthday parties, people laughed, and the great seemed human. One could not possibly imagine Papal legates in black garb lurking in dark corners. That old issue religion, which had cost so many thousands of lives in the history of the Anglo-American tradition, vanished in the light.

For me, watching a transition in administration for the first time, this relish of power, this light-heartedness, remains best captured in a memory of my first visit to Washington after the election, in early December 1960. Hurrying to write my book about the campaign, I needed essential documents and facts and so I went to see two friends in their temporary adjacent offices—Robert Kennedy and his Harvard football teammate Kenneth O'Donnell.

I had expected some new sense of gravity and austerity would have come to rest on them since the election, for it was obvious that Bobby was closest to the new power and Kenny was of the inner circle.

But not so. I walked into this new center of power, where, supposedly, they were scrutinizing the names of those who would make up the new Kennedy cabinet and government, and there they were, both in shirtsleeves. But Bobby was wearing a new black homburg hat atilt on his head, strutting in a cakewalk, while O'Donnell applauded. I laughed at the Mr. Gallagher and Mr. Shean scene. Bobby was a fine mimic, better than his brother, the President, though not as good as his younger brother, Teddy, who would become senator. Bobby explained: Alex Rose, chief of the hatters' union, had sent the homburg. Rose was also boss of New York's Liberal Party, which had supported Kennedy to the full reach of Rose's critical exertion in the campaign just over; Kennedy had carried New York State by the margin of Rose's Liberal votes. Now Rose had sent the hat with a plea that both Bobby and the President, for God's sake, wear hats in the inauguration ceremonies. Appearing hatless so often during the campaign, they had imperiled the jobs of thousands of hatworkers. The black homburg, which Rose thought fitting for Bobby, made him look like a minor thug and so both Bobby and Kenny were laughing at the favors politics demanded. But Rose was a friend, the hatters union needed work, the President and his entourage must set an example.*

When they got through playing, I spent an hour asking questions for my book, and then, when O'Donnell had left, Bobby wanted to ask *me* for advice.

Bobby's problem was serious: Jack wanted to name *him*, Bobby, Attorney General. What should he do? Was it proper for the President to name his brother Attorney General? I have no clear recollection of my own advice to Bobby. I have notes only of Bobby's reaction to his brother's suggestion: Bobby ran through the power structure as he saw it. He would have liked to be in the Pentagon. If someone like Gates had been held over as Defense Secretary, he might have been useful there as part of the action. But Jack had chosen McNamara, and McNamara would want to run his own show. No point, either, in his running for the Senate—they'd call him his brother's mouthpiece. Then there was the governorship of Massachusetts. Ethel, his wife, was in favor of that. The state was so corrupt, there was so much to be done—but what could you do to keep yourself busy between now and 1962, when the governorship came up again? Now Jack had asked him to be Attorney General. He had already consulted with Clark Clifford on this, and Clifford had said: Take it. Then Bobby repeated that he didn't think the President should appoint his own brother to the post. He added, "I told him, 'If you announce me as Attorney General, they'll kick our balls off.' " "Well, what did Jack say to that?" I asked, and Bobby replied, "You know what he said? He said, 'You hold on to your balls and I'll make the announcement.' " Which, of

*Neither Bobby nor the President, it should be noted, liked the image of the homburg. When informed that the two Kennedys preferred to wear silk toppers at the inaugural, Rose stretched his union to the utmost once more. The Kennedy brothers had extremely large heads and required size 7¾ hats, of which none were in stock. Rose finally found an aging hatmaker who could still customize silk hats to rush order, and shipped off three to Washington, the extra being for Larry O'Brien.

course, two days later, the new president-elect did.

John F. Kennedy enjoyed such use of power. To acquire power was the purpose of politics, the goal of the game. He had appointed Robert McNamara as Secretary of Defense, and McNamara had gone to visit outgoing Secretary of Defense Thomas Gates the same day that Kennedy had gone to visit outgoing President Eisenhower. McNamara telephoned Kennedy and said, "Say, I've just spent the afternoon with Gates, and I think I can do his job." To which Kennedy replied, "I've just spent the afternoon with Eisenhower, and I think I can do his job, too." Much later, I talked with James Tobin, who had been invited to join the Council of Economic Advisers. Tobin told me that he had not wanted to be on the council and thought of himself (then Sterling Professor of Economics at Yale) as a scholar. According to Tobin, he had responded to Kennedy's invitation to join the council by saying, "I think you've got the wrong man—I'm an ivory tower economist." To which Kennedy had said, "That's the best kind. I'm going to be an ivory tower President."

It was all gay in the first few weeks, all aglitter, all bravado.

Yet it comes to me now that underneath the bravado, he, like all new Presidents, was groping. They all do as they try to reach for control of the levers and pedals in their first few months—as a buyer gingerly tests the brakes and gas pedals of the new car he has driven off from the dealer's. Kennedy, however, was groping not only for control of unfamiliar instruments; he was pushing out into an unknown stream, guiding the power around the bend into a new country, new times, and the unexplored landscape of the 1960s.

Foreign policy was then, surprisingly, the most clearly defined of the problems he must encounter on that landscape. After the instant disaster of the Bay of Pigs and the taut confrontation with the Russians on access to Berlin, by his first autumn in office he had brought his instruments well in hand and, then, gradually, moved to the mastery of the missile crisis and the test-ban treaty.

Domestic policy was far more difficult. But that, too,

he learned to master after some groping. It had been easy to speak in the campaign of what must be done, or *should* be done, to make America a better place to live in. And Kennedy had understood, as Eisenhower had not, what particularities of scholarship, learning, expertise and science must be gathered in to define what was happening to the changing American people, let alone prescribe remedies. As senator from Massachusetts, he had also been the senator from Harvard and the Massachusetts Institute of Technology, whose relationship to American learning at that time was that of the Ruhr to German heavy industry. He had, naturally, used his Harvard and MIT scholars to recruit other scholars and learned men from across the country to help in his campaign—and more importantly, to staff his new government. Of the many departures that began in the brief Kennedy Presidency, none, probably, outranks in importance his elevation of the traditional American scholar from brilliant eccentric (like a Joseph Henry or a Robert Oppenheimer) to the status of a Chinese mandarin—a wise man who does more than advise, a wise man who jostles in the court for control of the action. Under Kennedy, the kind of men whom Roosevelt had gathered to guide the New Deal's economics and devise arms for the war were subtly but irrevocably brought together in a phantom corps of mandarins who would later achieve dominant power as the New Governing Class under Jimmy Carter. Kennedy knew how to use such people; they were valuable; they could tell him what was happening at home even better than abroad. He was the first to recognize that no modern President can govern without such mandarins—and also to recognize that such men, in turn, must be governed by the President with an iron hand.

There remained then, his major problem: the Congress of the United States. He had spent fourteen years in that Congress, but as President his groping would be most conspicuous in his relations with it. Congress reflects all the splits and divisions in the American people, by color, status, ethnic origins, regions, constituencies; as it should. But the President reflects the unity of Americans, what is best for all. Thus, from the beginning of American political history, the war between Congress and President has been a constant war over direction. Unless both President and Congress choose to do nothing—which is sometimes, as in the 1950s, a wise policy.

I did not understand this struggle over directions, except from books, when six weeks after Kennedy had been elected, I first went to see him in the White House. I found him strangely uncertain of himself, quite unlike the self-confident man of the campaign; I realize now that he was giving me a privilege in letting me see him grope. But I wanted a page of his thinking for my book; and on his mind that day was his problem with Congress. Had I listened more closely rather than pushing my own questions on him, I might have recorded a better bench mark from which to measure the pace and the controls by which, more than two years later, he learned to master the Presidency.

This first talk was peculiar. As I entered the Oval Office, the President rose from behind his desk, shook hands, then promptly unbuckled his belt, zipped open his pants and stripped to his underwear. He must have seen the shock on my face, for he laughed and explained that his tailors had come down from New York to measure him for a new suit and had been waiting all afternoon to get in. Since I was the only one on his appointment list that day whom he knew well enough to undress before, he assumed I wouldn't mind if they fitted and measured him while I was there. The door opened on the other side of the Oval Office and three tailors entered, who pinned, chalked, measured for five or six minutes as we talked.

It was casual talk while the tailors were present. We talked about his election and he called the victory a "miracle," insisting that the historic comparison had to be with Al Smith. Had I noticed the change in Philadelphia? Smith losing by 150,000 in 1928, and himself carrying the city by 300,000? He asked if I had read the newly published official transcripts of the outdoor campaign rallies—his and Nixon's. "Did you ever read such shit?" asked Kennedy, commenting on Nixon's off-the-cuff stumping. Queer man, Nixon, said Kennedy. In direct conversation Nixon was smart, very smart. But his mistake in the campaign had been talking "down" to the American people; in a Presidential campaign you have to talk "up," over their heads.

Finally, the tailors left and he began to talk almost as he used to. The Congress of the United States, it appeared from his mood, had replaced Stevenson, Humphrey and Nixon as contenders in his competitive gamesmanship. He had just carried off the first successful move by a President against the House Rules Committee in years. He had forced Congressman Howard Smith, the committee's Virginia chairman, to accept a congressman of Kennedy loyalty on the committee. The dictatorial Virginian had until then decided alone on the blocking and unbottling of national legislation. Kennedy wanted the right to get the President's proposals considered; and had won. But Congress, he said, was still "one hell of a problem." Look at the narrowness of the vote on the feed-grain bill that very day—a margin of only seven. I was aware that Kennedy knew as little as I did about feedgrains, corn, wheat, pigs, beef, or from which side of a cow you take the milk. But I was surprised by the intensity of his emotion and of his commitment to this feed-grain bill. I have no idea to this day whether that bill was good, bad, practical or chimerical. The best agricultural mandarins had devised it; therefore as President he must move the bill by skill, stealth, seduction or pressure through to a Congressional majority. In an exception to the rules of American Presidential elections, he had won the Presidency while his party was simultaneously *losing* twenty-one House seats and two in the Senate. This left him in trouble, vote by vote,* which he would, I am sure,

---

*I spent several hours the next day with Kennedy's vote-counters and gamesmen in the Congressional contest. Larry O'Brien was captain for persuading Congress, and each bill was a fight. Religion, said O'Brien, had cost them their normal Presidential ma-

have detailed to me as neatly as he had detailed conven-
tioneering a year earlier.

But he must have seen the distress on my face as he
talked of his game rival, Congress. I wanted to close my
book with an interview of great loftiness, and he, with a
sense of the reporter's craft, interrupted himself and
asked, "Am I saying what you want? Was there any
particular kind of question you wanted to ask?"

I said yes, about foreign policy. And he began to
pull foreign-policy issues out of his head. He was saying
what he felt I needed for a toga-clad portrait of the
President, and we went through Laos, the Congo, Russia,
South America, in great haste. Then, when we came to
personalities, with Lumumba in the Congo, and Wang
Ping-nan in Warsaw, he came alive, as he always did when
talking personalities. Suddenly he asked me whether he
should write a letter directly to Mao Tse-tung and Chou
En-lai and settle the Laos matter with them directly. I
ducked and said I needed more than thirty seconds to
think that one over; later, I did agree, wrongly, with his
State Department advisers that the time was unpropitious
for him to make the direct approach to Mao which his
instinct told him was necessary.

Kennedy had, by this time, relaxed, his legs hooked

---

jority; they were short ten or twenty votes on every critical issue.
The Chicago and Philadelphia congressmen said the hell with the
feed-grain bill, that's for farmers; what's for us? And trying to keep
the New York delegation in line! And after that, I had the picture
from O'Brien's deputy, Dick Donahue, who marveled at the political blindness of Kennedy's nonpolitical appointees. The President,
for example, had appointed Bob McNamara simply for quality.
Thus McNamara had insisted on quality, not political, appointees
as his deputies. So that up and down the line, said Donahue, who
was in charge of patronage, every other appointee also insisted on
quality deputies. Arthur Goldberg, for example, wanted to get his
minimum-wage bill through Congress—but at the same time, he
wanted quality appointees in his department. Donahue ran on
about the afflatus that comes to all appointees to national office:
"Even the hacks we appointed refuse to accept other political hacks
in their departments. But how do you get high-grade bills through
without paying off in low-grade appointments?"

over the wastebasket; but I sensed O'Donnell outside
trying to hurry me out of the room, because Lyndon
Johnson, the Vice President, was waiting. Kennedy urged
me to stay, but I, like almost anyone else who visits a
President and wants to be able to come back, knew I
must break off; I had run through my time and he was
simply dodging a session with Johnson. He walked me to
the door, and there ended with what was on his mind at
the beginning: Congress. He said, "The trouble with the
Eisenhower years was that nothing moved. Inertia. How
can you get things going? Congress is unused to thinking
in national terms because it hasn't been summoned to
think in national terms . . . every man worries about keeping his seat safe. All of them got used to the deflationary
psychology of Ike's regime. Now they *have* to learn to
think in national terms. . . ."

I ducked away, quickly making mental notes on the
change of scenery in the office, scarcely hearing him as I
left, for I knew his staff had trusted me to be in and out
in my allotted time. But I should have stayed and let him
ramble on about what really bothered him—which was
his relationship with Congress.

A President and his wise men can only propose; but
Congress disposes. It is when President and Congress
agree that American history marches forward, but I did
not grasp the simplicity of that theorem then. I made the
mistake of letting myself be bored by the game of Congress versus Kennedy for the next two years, well on into
the spring of 1963, when I could finally sense that Kennedy, the gatekeeper, had learned the President's trade, and
begun to shake matters out of their mold.

Until that spring of 1963 the Kennedy legislation is
of little excitement and, in retrospect, is most interesting
only when matched against the legislation of the Eisenhower administration. Then what becomes fascinating is
how little turning showed in the passage from eight years
of Republican government to a new Democratic regime.
It is as if, until the beginning of 1963, the tides of the
postwar world had been carrying Truman, Eisenhower
and Kennedy in the same direction, to the same ends,

sometimes a bit faster, sometimes a bit slower. Initiatives seemed born far outside politics, and only partisans could argue precisely where credit or blame lay, in which administration, for which chapter of events. New Dealers could argue that the national highway system was first traced out under Roosevelt, but Republicans could argue that Eisenhower transformed the plan from paper to concrete. Democrats could argue that Kennedy first launched the nation into space; but Republicans could argue that the ballistic missile program began under Eisenhower and Americans walked on the moon under Nixon. Until the spring of 1963, then, the Kennedy legislation flowed in this stream, nuanced only here and there by his instincts or his mandarinate.

There was, for example:

• Housing. Neither Eisenhower nor anyone else probably ever thought of his Highway Act as being the single most important act to influence housing in the postwar generation. The fact that it was so became apparent only much later. Yet on housing per se, Eisenhower among Republicans was a "liberal." He began by authorizing loans for 35,000 public housing units in 1954, jumped that to 45,000 public housing units in 1955, dribbled a sizable $200 million into college housing (on a federal loan program), took Harry Truman's urban renewal program of 1949 and pumped another $500 million into that. No system of legislation is, however, as complicated as legislation on public housing, and Kennedy, apparently, was bored by it. He contented himself simply by adding budgetary zeros to the dominant housing thinking that had begun with Truman and continued through Eisenhower and which he fertilized: with over one billion dollars more for college housing, with an added two billion dollars for urban renewal and planning, and thus, down the line. One can detect a Kennedy deflection, a gatekeeper's signal, only in a single Executive Order, No. 11063, not cleared with Congress, which banned discrimination by race in housing built, bought or financed with federal assistance of any kind. A President's

Committee on Equal Opportunity in Housing was set up to establish and oversee enforcement, a forerunner of the institution of the New Orthodoxy.

• Or, for example, the Kennedy legislation on health.

Some of the first nodules of American thinking on public medicine had been visible in the bud by 1947 under Harry Truman—federal funding for fellowships, training, medical research, hospital construction. Eisenhower's speed-up in the development of medical services for Americans followed hard on the Truman initiatives. He raised health concern to an executive policy level in his establishment of the Health, Education and Welfare Department. But Ike explored further ground. In 1958 he authorized a national conference on the problems of the aging, and by 1960, sent his men before the House Ways and Means Committee to use for the first time the word "Medicare," which, ultimately, would become a program that would cost the government half as much as the entire U.S. Air Force. Ike's "Medicare" proposal was rejected by Congress; so, too, was Kennedy's when he offered it in different form. There was nothing revolutionary about Kennedy health programs. Eisenhower in his eight years raised federal health appropriations from $221 million to $840 million in 1960; in his three years, Kennedy raised the federal health budget from $1 billion to $1.6 billion in 1963. But one can detect almost no turning in purpose—nothing except the old Republican/Democratic difference in which the Republicans promise to increase spending more slowly and the Democrats promise to increase spending more quickly. If one scrutinizes the record closely, one can detect a tiny blip of concern that must be personally Kennedy's—a first six-million-dollar appropriation in 1963, to be stretched over three years, for research into the education of handicapped children, an area of grief in his family's life, as it is in the lives of hundreds of thousands of other American families.

For all the rest of domestic policy—whether in education, space, environment, roads, urban affairs—the course of American life as decided by agreement of President and Congress was a continuum from Truman through Eisenhower through Kennedy until the beginning of 1963.

And then John F. Kennedy presented to Congress two bills, the first on tax reform, the second on civil rights, which became, respectively, the Tax Reform Act of 1964 and the Civil Rights Act of 1964 under Lyndon Johnson. They were really Kennedy's acts, however, and in the adventure of watching Kennedy become President in history as well as in name and in law, they were as important as his campaign for election. The first, the revenue reforms, reflected his full absorption of the thinking of the new mandarin scholars. The second, the civil rights bill, reflected the shouting in the streets. In submitting both to the consent of Congress in 1963, he best showed what he had now learned of the purposeful use of power.

The revenue proposals of 1963 came first, in January. Even had it stood alone, the revenue bill would have signaled a revolution in thinking. Basically, all governments—monarchies, tyrannies, democracies and republics—rest on taxes, which is the charge demanded of people by their rulers for safety and "civilization." But whether in Rome or Peking, in America or Switzerland, the inner arguments all revolve on who should pay how much of the cost for this "civilization." In the American Republic both historic parties believe that taxes should encourage "growth," as well as support "services," and all promise more for everybody at every election. They split over an historic distinction—Republicans believe the best way to encourage growth is by tax policies that encourage investment; Democrats believe that the best way to encourage growth is by tax policies that encourage consumption. Until the time of Kennedy, both these divergent philosophies bowed to the "theology of the budget," which held out for generations the mirage that someday, sometime, the revenues of government would equal the costs it must bear. The tax legislation proposed by John F. Kennedy finally, and forever, threw away the "theology of the budget," and accepted a budget which was more like a compass indicating government directions than a bookkeeping balance sheet of income and outgo. Moreover, so said the scholar mandarins, who now, for the first time, replaced the businessmen accountants as the chief influence on budgeteering, the conjunction of the times invited a policy that was irresistible for this political, games-playing President. After being deciphered from the hieroglyphics of specific proposals, their advice held simply that now was a good time to cut taxes for everybody.

The original Kennedy revenue formula was a marvelous and still fragrant compost of conservative and liberal thinking on taxes. Rich and poor alike would benefit. The only reasonable modern proposal on capital gains taxes was included, a proposal recognizing both the ravages of inflation and the greed of speculation. The maximum tax on true capital gains would be 19.5 percent! But simultaneously, short-term speculators and options holders would be deprived of capital gains shelter. Kennedy's was still a good bill as it was ground up, chewed, examined and amended in the constitutional way. As finally passed by Congress, it cut taxes for the very poor to encourage consumption (no couple who made less than four thousand dollars a year would have to pay any taxes). It cut taxes for the very rich from 91 percent to 77 percent, with further cuts down to 70 percent in following years. The bill cut taxes for both corporations and their workingmen: withholding taxes from workingmen's pay checks were cut from 18 percent to 14 percent; corporation taxes were cut by giving a tax credit (i.e., real cash) to companies that put new investments into industry.

Kennedy's revenue proposals slipped the leash on budgetary dogmas and a hundred years of Puritan ethics applied to money: budgets need not balance! Miraculously, the proposals, once passed a year later, worked better than could possibly have been anticipated. Whether it was in their encouragement to investment or their encouragement to consumption, or both, the mandarins had come up with the most successful formula since scholars had translated Einstein's $E=mc^2$ into Hiroshima. It was a spectacular success; its very success enticed the quantifiers and scholar economists to think that they might, at any time, apply their other formulas to reality with equal success. This added up to later tragedy. But at the time, the thinking of the tax bill was the most successful demonstration of cool thinking applied to hot issues yet, and thus revolutionary. Had it not been overshadowed by the second of the great Kennedy bills, the civil rights bill of 1963, it would have marked Kennedy's peak in domestic affairs.

But the civil rights bill was so large it overshadowed all else. Moving the bill to national consideration, Kennedy passed from his personal pose as gamesman and his political role as gatekeeper to the grand posture invited by the American Presidency—that of the man who presides, in fact as well as in theory, over the management and meshing of the great affairs of state. Only in his management of the missile crisis did Kennedy so fully play the President as in the civil rights bill—and the civil rights bill would affect American life longer and more deeply.

The authors of the civil rights bill of 1963 are anonymous—black people, street people, young people, moral people. But whoever the authors, its publisher was John F. Kennedy. He could take the story from the streets and publish it as vital national policy.

This ability to contrast what the streets say with what history tells us is not particularly difficult in the story of black and white in America. What is difficult is to face openly the depths of indignation or to respond reasonably to the excesses of hate and fear, white and black, that intertwine in American life. One may start with indignation either at the black chieftains of Africa who sold their own people away as animals, or at the white slave traders who bought black captives for transshipment as beasts. The politics of black and white can begin with the story of Nat Turner's rebellion in 1831, or with the Plessy-Ferguson decision of 1896, which gave up half the victory of the Civil War to the South by accepting the "separate but equal" doctrine. For John Kennedy, rising black indignation had paralleled his own rise in national politics. The year-long bus strike that began on December 5, 1955, in Montgomery, Alabama, had nicked one of the edges of racism when Kennedy, then a junior senator, was ill and in bed. Autherine Lucy had made her protest in 1956. There is no record of a Kennedy position. His campaign of 1960 had been accompanied by obbligatos from the student lunch-counter sit-ins in the South. He had given his support to Martin Luther King in October of that year. Yet he was still uncommitted and perplexed about blacks. He had said to me during the campaign—and I agreed—that there is no group more difficult to understand in America than the blacks, because no group shows a larger difference of culture between leaders and led.

Kennedy's election had not stilled black indignation, which was deeper than any single personality, either black or white, could control. So, as President, he had faced successively the crises of the Freedom Buses of 1961; of Ole Miss and the confrontation with Governor Ross Barnett of Mississippi in 1962; and then finally, climactically, the battles of Birmingham, Alabama, out of which came the Civil Rights Act of 1963–1964.

Birmingham, Alabama, then a city of some 360,000 people, of whom 140,000 were black, was generally recognized as one of the two meanest cities in the South—the other being Jackson, Mississippi. It was a violent, race-hating city in which blacks lived then almost as fearfully as whites now live in Newark, New Jersey. In the six years prior to the climax of 1963, Birmingham had seen fifty old-fashioned cross-burnings and eighteen racial bomb blasts. And it was this city that Martin Luther King had chosen in the fall of 1962 to break wide open. "I contended," King later told me, "that Birmingham was pivotal. That we had to go there. . . . If we could break through the barriers in Birmingham—if Birmingham went—all the South would go the same way."

The Birmingham drama had begun in best Shavian, not Shakespearian, fashion—with trivia as subject of protest. Blacks were not allowed to sit down at the same lunch counters as whites, even in the department stores which thrived by their patronage. Nor could blacks use the same water fountains or toilets in those stores, if they could use any at all. Black picketing of these Birmingham stores, in this meanest city, began in April of 1963, with the simple insistence of a few black volunteers that they be served their coffee and rolls at the same counter as whites in the stores where they traded. Arrests followed, forty protesters a day, for three days; then 125 arrests; then 100 more. On Good Friday, April 12, 1963, Martin Luther King, Jr., himself led a parade of black protest that moved no more than eight blocks before he was arrested and jailed. He was once again released on Kennedy's personal intervention; but now he proposed to mobilize students for the protest. Robert Kennedy telephoned King to plead against the use of children in politics; but King was firm, and said that no matter what happened to them, it was no worse than segregation. And so, at the beginning of May, students and young children began to fill Birmingham's jails, until the jails would hold no more, and the primitive police chief of Birmingham, Eugene ("Bull") Connor, decided that he had to take more violent action. Martin Luther King described it as "the day the jails were full with no place to put any more." Then television took over and drama became national politics.

The Birmingham riots were made for television, and the sight television brought the nation was unprecedented: official violence, naked in the streets. Bull Connor's police brought their dogs, and television showed the dogs reaching up to snap at the flesh of women's thighs. Since the police could hold no more black protesters in jail, they tried to disperse protesters in the streets with fire hoses whose high-pressure streams could peel bark from trees; and the hoses thrashed and flailed at women and children, whipping up ladies' skirts in flaring visible obscenity.

was there to broadcast the jump. George Wallace, then governor of Alabama, had decided personally to bar black students from the University of Alabama's summer session at Tuscaloosa. Kennedy, privately informed that Wallace wanted not a showdown but a show of pictorial significance, promptly federalized the Alabama National Guard and sent them, guns ready, to force the governor to admit black students to his state's university because federal law demanded it. In 1957, Ike had used the 101st Airborne Division of the U.S. Army in Little Rock; in 1962, Kennedy himself had used some sixteen thousand troops of the 82nd and 11th Airborne Divisions and the Second Infantry of the U.S. Army at Old Miss; now he used only Alabama's own men, its own National Guard, called to the colors for the occasion. There was no resistance. Wallace gave up.

But a President can (or should) use force only within the rule of law. And the most demeaning of the humiliations which at that time were bringing blacks to surge in the streets were beyond the reach of any law.

What to do?

That evening, having vanquished George Wallace by their prearranged show of force, the President took to the air to make ready the way for the new civil rights bill he would introduce the next week in Congress. It was one of the half-dozen best speeches of an eloquent career in politics.

Like all good speeches, it bore a single message—the need of new laws for a new time. The message concerned the American people, and how the laws must stretch over our diverse origins. The old code read that for every wrong perpetrated against the law, the law itself provides a remedy. But no law covered the humiliations in dignity that blacks suffered not only in Tuscaloosa, Alabama, but all across the South; and thus, since no laws governed, there was no remedy. What Kennedy was about to propose was an entirely new jump in the jurisprudence of civil rights. Such a bill had been under preparation by a handful of men in Robert Kennedy's Justice Department for several weeks. They had come to realize that no government could any longer safeguard tranquillity if no law gave government authority to remedy the human as well as the legal grievances of black against white. To abolish discrimination, which was real and vicious, law— and marshals of the law—would have to go where no laws ever went before.

There was, to be earthy, the "pee-pee question," sanitized in Congressional debate as the problem of "public accommodations." The "pee-pee question" was, however, tragic, not comic. As one black witness before Congress quietly explained it: what if you are black and driving down a road in the South and your little girl must go pee-pee. How can you tell a little girl she can't use the toilet at the next gas station because she is black and that most gas stations reserve their restroom facilities for whites only. This is an intolerable private agony; but no law, at that time, could remedy it. Just so, no law touched segregation at lunch counters, in hotels, in boarding-houses, at movie theaters or supermarkets. Equal but separate rights for the blacks had been sanctioned by the Plessy-Ferguson decision in 1896; segregation had been officially hammered into federal practice and federal facilities by no less a liberal than Woodrow Wilson. Law had begun to reach out to shelter blacks once more only with Eisenhower's Civil Rights Act of 1957. But that act had reached only to public, not into private, life; it had emphasized the strengthening of the Supreme Court's school decision of 1954 and the general validity of voting rights for black and white alike. Eisenhower's act had succeeded moderately: schools were being draggingly integrated; Southern blacks were being slowly admitted to voting (400,000 black registrants in the ten years between 1952 and 1962). Kennedy's legislation proposed to go much farther, and since it was a point where history turned, we must examine it briefly now, so that later we may trace from it the Jurisprudence of Equal Opportunity that would color all the politics of the 1970s.

The civil rights bill put before Congress by John F. Kennedy on June 19, 1963, eight days after Alabama's young men were mobilized to put down Alabama's governor, floated on the indignation of the nation at what television had shown it. But the bill was immensely more complicated than the emotions that floated it. Up until that time, almost all postwar black progress had come either from the Supreme Court or by Executive Order of a President. (A prototype of Executive Order was Truman's abolishing segregation in the armed forces in 1948, issued to amplify the Selective Service Act of that year.) The first postwar bill voted into an act of Congress to protect black rights under law was Eisenhower's in 1957—but that bill restrained itself to public, governmental, official activities only. The U.S. Government, said that bill, must not discriminate by race.

The Kennedy civil rights bill of 1963 carried the concept of "discrimination" light-years forward. Not only must government not discriminate, it said; neither must private groups, offering public accommodations or services, discriminate.

The civil rights bill of 1963, enacted as the Civil Rights Law of 1964, was thus revolutionary, by John F. Kennedy's own decision. It not only strengthened the ability of the federal government to oversee voting rights everywhere in the country, but it went on. It made the federal government's Department of Justice the sword and paladin of black rights everywhere—with the right to prosecute local governments that discriminated, the duty to institute suits against local government where schools were not properly balanced for race. It subordinated the distribution of federal money to federal interpretations of racial justice—i.e., no federal funds would be given to any state, town, jurisdiction or county that was found to discriminate against blacks. Since the South was, then, the most favored regional beneficiary of federal funds, it meant no locality in the South could use federal funds, taxed from the North, to build schools, hospitals, museums or swimming pools that blacks could not use.

And then, critically, most importantly, finally, the law guaranteed all blacks access to all accommodations newly defined as "public." Blacks must not be excluded from schools, colleges, hotels, motels, restaurants, sports arenas, theaters, whether managed by governments, or conglomerates, or the hypothetical "Mrs. Murphy," owner of a hypothetical boardinghouse. If Mrs. Murphy had six or more rooms to rent in her boardinghouse, she could not exclude anyone who knocked to enter, whether he was an itinerant black carpenter, a black preacher, black tourist or black mystery.

The Civil Rights Act of 1963–1964 moved the United States into an area of life that neither it nor any other government of modern times had tried to penetrate before. "Equal Justice Under Law" was a dogma of American life as much accepted in the observance as any dogma can hope to be. But now, by this new act, equal justice under a passive law would scarcely be enough. By this new law, the federal government propelled its Department of Justice out into the states, cities, communities, to discover injustice and bring it into court. No longer need the federal government wait for the NAACP to come before the bar to plead for justice; it must outdo the black leadership with its own new definitions of racial malefactions. The Attorney General would be entitled and enjoined to scourge the South wherever, from statistical inference, it would be reasonably believed that blacks were being denied their right to vote. Abruptly, the cry of twenty years of liberals for a "fair employment practices" act became old-fashioned. The new law demanded "equal employment opportunity," and for enforcement set up an Equal Employment Opportunity Commission. Whoever, even remotely, did any business with the federal government would, eventually, fall under the police power of this office. The government had already opened what it could of governmental function—army, bureaucracy, welfare, schools, universities. Now it would open private places—private centers of study, hitherto closed; every restaurant, toilet or motel along any highway construed as falling under the Interstate Commerce authority of the federal government. If a university accepted a federal research grant, or if a magazine accepted an Army advertisement for recruits, it would become a federal contractor, subject to scrutiny that would grow and grow in the next fifteen years to a tangle of inexplicable complexities, thicketed with no less than eighteen overlapping bureaucratic agencies.

Of all the great events in domestic history since the war, the Law of Unintended Consequences might later claim this Kennedy legislation as one of its finest demonstration pieces. A new jurisprudence was opening up, not intending to but nonetheless destined to establish new special privileges. Not only blacks, but also, successively, Asian Americans, Indian Americans, Hispanic Americans, Aleut Americans, would all soon, under the new Jurisprudence of Civil Rights, be able to claim special, compensatory rights. And then, as the new Jurisprudence of Civil Rights developed over the years, it could, and would, increasingly be invoked by women, youth, prisoners, gay people of both sexes. A law intended to unify would divide Americans by categories. And government would be summoned to intrude as authority into areas previously left to community law or custom to decide.

No departure of the Kennedy administration, neither the tax bill, nor the confrontation with Khrushchev in the missile crisis, surpasses in importance the reach of the Civil Rights Act of 1963–1964. Even in 1963 I thought the Civil Rights Act, as proposed by Kennedy, a beautiful piece of historic law-making. But all would depend on its execution. What might derive from it, I was only just beginning dimly to discern. I wish there had been time to talk with him about it.

What might have happened had John F. Kennedy lived to preside as the Jurisprudence of Civil Rights took hold and developed into the Jurisprudence of Life-Styles can only be a guess.

But I think he would have moved more slowly—and explored the terrain just conquered more cautiously before rushing on to occupy more. I had rejoined the Time-Life family in 1962 and spent the fall months of 1963 working for *Life* magazine on a nationwide survey of the big cities. What did the civil rights bill mean to the cities if it passed? Could this bill, proposed to meet conditions in the small-town South, offer remedy to Northern cities where blacks were so conspicuously swelling in number? The tone of my story was completely jarring in the happy, hopeful fall of 1963. RACIAL COLLISION IN THE BIG CITIES, the story was headed, as the correspondent, Theodore H. White, warned that matters might go to bloodshed and riot unless the laws were wisely, cautiously and fairly implemented. The flip-page headlines read: RUSHING TO A SHOWDOWN THAT NO LAW CAN CHART . . . NEITHER WHITES NOR NEGROES WILL LOOK THE GRIM FACTS SQUARELY IN THE FACE . . . WITHIN TWO DECADES, NEGROES MAY BE IN THE MAJORITY IN MOST OF THE LARGEST U.S. CITIES . . . TO THE FRUSTRAT-ED NEGRO LEADER, THE WHITES BECOME A CONSPIRACY, and then, announcing the next part of the series, *Life* promised that White would hold forth soon on NEGRO DEMANDS—ARE THEY REALISTIC?

Life gave the story enormous space, but space at the back of the magazine so as not to detract from the effervescence that was so much more characteristic of the Kennedy time. The issue caught a moment. It opened with a marvelous story on Broadway, which was all a-tinsel that fall with glitter and success. A young new playwright, Neil Simon, had opened a hit called *Barefoot in the Park*. He would become the most successful play-wright since George Bernard Shaw, but *Life* shared the story of his triumph with Simon's new young male lead, Robert Redford; with a new and beautiful actress, Eliza-beth Ashley; and the new young director, Mike Nichols. It was a sprightly issue for sprightly times: new toys for the children at Christmas, new make-up protector masks for fasionable ladies. The advertising offered food spe-cialties that ran literally from soup to nuts, as well as whiskey, the new stereos, electric ranges, shampoos—and automobiles. The automobiles fairly screeched off the page, "Zavoooom!," boasting their acceleration and pow-er under the hood; energy shortages were inconceivable with gasoline at thirty cents a gallon.

The date on the cover of the issue read November 22, 1963, and it fairly reflected the end of one decade and the beginning of the next. Most of the magazine was happiness-packed, but mine was not the only somber note in the issue. On the page opposite the advertisement for Pontiac's new LeMans hardtop was an editorial of ominous portent. It was entitled PRESS THE WAR IN VIETNAM. *Life* (and Harry Luce) could scarcely restrain their enthusiasm for the recent overthrow of Diem and Nhu ("the stain on the coup," they called Diem's assassination) and urged, "Now is the time to pour on more coal." But aside from this exhortation at the front of the magazine to lay it on in Vietnam, and my doom-saying on future black riots at the end of the issue, the magazine reflected the carefree happiness of a Thanksgiving time when all was going well. *Life* magazine's great editor, Edward K. Thompson, gave it a touch of history for echo by beginning one of those series in which he, a country boy, could indulge his yearning for color, pageantry and self-improvement all at once. George Hunt, the managing editor, had decided to precede my frightening piece on the blacks in the cities with the first part of this series of nostalgic fluff—Europe at peace in 1913, half a century before, as La Belle Epoque and the Golden Yesterday both vanished. *Life* had inserted a fold-out centerpiece, with a painting it had commissioned, of the 1910 funeral of Edward VII, showing all the panoply of a century gone to legend. Kings and Kaiser followed on foot behind a riderless black horse. And in the custom honored since the death of Genghis Khan, the leader's horse paced behind the coffin, saddle empty, riding boots reversed in the stirrups. It was all so long ago. But by its next issue, *Life* would have the riderless horse prancing through Washington in real life.

The moments of history that crease the memory are rare, but come more frequently in our time than a hundred years ago because communications are instant. A triad of memories marks my generation: the strike at Pearl Harbor; the death of Franklin Roosevelt; the killing of John F. Kennedy. Each of us could write his own history of our time if we could but recall not *where* we were, which all remember, but what we *thought* when those accidents changed our world.

I was beginning the campaign of 1964. I was lunching with an old war-correspondent acquaintance, James Shepley, at that time assistant publisher of *Life,* since risen to president of Time Incorporated. Since he had been so close to Richard Nixon in 1960, and had so contemptuously broken with him later, I was trying to find out from Shepley what he knew, or did not know, about 'Eisenhower's scheduled weekend in New York. Eisenhower was rumored to be joining a secret cabal to find a candidate other than Rockefeller to stop Barry Goldwater's public pursuit of the 1964 Republican nomination. Whether Shepley knew of the conclave or not, I do not recall. I remember only a waiter leaning over us and saying, "Mr. Shepley, the radio says Kennedy has been shot." We both rose, paying no bill; by journalistic instinct we homed on the news ticker in *Time*'s office; read the clatter and chatter as researchers, reporters, editors, all likewise interrupted at lunch, began to crowd the room; and the ticker then spat out its final bulletin. It was Friday afternoon, *Life*'s closing day, and the presses were about to roll—all seven million copies of the magazine. Shepley and I dashed to the office of George Hunt, the managing director of *Life,* just as he swung back from lunch, peeling off his coat with the same flourish as a matador twirling a cape. Before giving Hunt a chance to speak, I yelled, "This is my story." And Hunt, a former marine commander, said, "O.K. Get going now—to Dallas." There was no time for reflection, and I passed the hat, for covering a story needs cash; everyone in the room peeled off bills until I had almost three hundred dollars, and I rushed out, en route to Dallas. On the way to the airport I told the cab to pause, ran into my house to drag out clothes, typewriter and shaving kit, and, pointing the driver to Idlewild Airport, begged him to speed. But the cab's blaring radio was now announcing that Kennedy's body was being taken to the Dallas airport, thence to be flown to Washington, and I ordered the cab to get to the La Guardia-Washington shuttle. I would intercept the

President at homecoming. In Washington, I pressed dollars into the hands of a bewildered cabdriver, hired him for the night, and made my way out to Andrews Air Force Base, which is the private landing pad for all Presidents.

I did not know what I might see there, or whether a conspiracy was afoot, or whether the Virginia Military District was cordoned off—but I felt that since I had attended so many trips of this graceful man for so long, I should be there for his last arrival in Washington. So all the rest of the evening, and the next day and the day after, was spectacle, as the surrender of the Japanese aboard the *Missouri* had been spectacle. All through those days the scenes tumbled before the eye, and I was filing them to New York, desperately, as a newsman does when history breaks raw in pieces before him and he does not know which fragment to pursue. Except that this time, unlike the time of the surrender, I was crying as I wrote, and only now does any sequence unfold, or any meaning come from what I saw and reported.

There were the fragments I jotted in my notebook, little fragments first: the cabdriver saying, "I sure hated to see that man go," then dodging through airport traffic; then suddenly, on the parkway out to Andrews, I saw the embankments flecked with youngsters: teen-agers sitting in their white shirts and pretty dresses on the brown fall grass, called out to watch the cortege pass by radio's incessant tapping of the news, and all of them silent, knees bent under their chins, waiting, waiting. Then Andrews Base itself: guards on the perimeter, guards on the interior, guards about the airstrip, grim Air Force Police with white caps and black-holstered pistols; helicopters dropping down, roaring, red lights winking from rotor staff, white belly lights making a cone of light below, the sound of hand-held radios turned down low, muttering. Then, above the tin sound of radio, the live patter of broadcasters talking into their microphones as the television cameras assembled, and the technicians, with then unnoticed virtuosity, made visual-relay hookups from the field to the pickup points of the national net; and in the spreading light of television, slowly, I watched them arrive.

I had been long enough in politics now to know most of these people at sight, some only by name, some by call of friendship, but it is strange, now in recollection, how they grouped. The old ones huddled with the old, the young ones with the young, as at any family funeral. Among the old ones towered tallest Averell Harriman, now a bit stooped—but he had, after all, been part of government since Franklin Roosevelt's time. Around him clustered Everett Dirksen, his hair wispy and windblown, and Mike Mansfield, Arthur Goldberg and Hubert Humphrey, who, finally, joined the older men. The younger men stood in their own group apart—Sorensen, Schlesinger, Bundy, Franklin Roosevelt, Jr., Ralph Dungan, Angier Biddle Duke, others. All were quiet; no one spoke except for the newswomen assigned to this particular stakeout. In the eyes of the networks then, women were of no great importance, and thus, by perversity, were assigned to interview these men in their grief. A half-moon had now burnished its way through the evening mists, the lights of the television producers were spreading, they had just made their microwave relay connections to Washington—when, in all this, the blue-and-white airplane of the President, *Air Force One,* came gliding in soundlessly. The pilot had landed downwind, cut the plane's engines and let it roll silently into its proper place of arrival, almost precisely in proper camera focus for the entire nation.

I can remember no one breaking ranks from the edge of the little group that represented what there was of the United States Government at the field. There was no one to give them orders, except within the plane. Only the Air Force ground personnel moved to the opening plane. The others stood and swayed, for in the United States no one calls: "The King is dead—Long live the King."

First the rear door of the plane opened and through the darkness appeared the red-bronze coffin, carried by the bearers, O'Donnell, O'Brien, Powers, to the crane lift, which lowered it to the ground. Then Jacqueline Kennedy, her raspberry-colored suit still smeared and stiff with blood, appeared, helped by Robert Kennedy into the gray Navy ambulance that carried the coffin. And then that was away, with its red beacon light unwinking; and still no one moved to follow it, for the leader was now about to appear, a new President, for the first time, before them and the entire nation.

Lyndon Johnson emerged from the front door of *Air Force One*. And after a few words into the cameras, Johnson was up and away by helicopter. McGeorge Bundy, a man with a command presence, had arranged for the transfer. It was he who, by telephone, had been urging the new President back from Texas from the moment of Kennedy's death, and it was Bundy who had coordinated with McNamara the scene at Andrews Air Force Base. Johnson had instructed Bundy that he wanted only cabinet officers to meet him at the airport to confer. But half the cabinet of the United States was, at that moment, winging back from the mid-Pacific to join him. Johnson needed to know whether any problem rose overseas that he must meet that night. Bundy and McNamara jointly urged in the confusion that a third man, George Ball, Under Secretary of State, be asked to join them in the helicopter. So when they lifted off the field, the helicopter lights winking red from its rotor staff and sweeping white from its underbelly, these four were the government of the United States facing the world if conspiracy had made confrontation necessary. According to Bundy, Johnson asked the little trio in the President's helicopter, the men who should know, whether there was anything they felt he must decide that night. McNamara said no. Then Ball said no. Then Bundy said no. Kennedy had left the nation in a rather impressive defense posture; no one would tempt America's retaliation in a moment of weakness.

I watched the helicopter take off, scuttling through the air, as helicopters do, to the White House, and do not remember how I moved from there. I followed out to the hospital where they had taken Kennedy; saw Mrs. Kennedy for a moment, still bloodstained, and so numb of expression I could not bring myself to speak to her, and then made my way through the streets toward the White House. There at the gates, as the autumn leaves blew down Pennsylvania Avenue, people strolled silently, mostly young couples, in a *paseo* of mourning; the fountains played; and the upstairs chambers were lit. It must have been well on to midnight when I remember approaching the gate, preceded by a young man who declared he was the Assistant Attorney General and "I have a proclamation and memorandum for Mr. Johnson to sign." The guard checked him by phone, then corrected him: "The President is expecting you." The gate clicked open, the young man passed; I passed, too, showing my credentials; and there, inside the White House, were none but weeping people. I retreated from the grieving and wandered late at night to knock on the door of Averell Harriman's home, feeling I knew him now, after so many years, well enough to ask shelter. He took me in, then and for the next three days, and through his house, from morning until dark, revolved one of the many wakes of John F. Kennedy's friends.

I would slip out of the house to pick for fragments of the story, and then dart back in to sit and watch on television to find out what was really happening. Television had finally come of age politically that fall with the half-hour television news shows that were to change the dynamics of American politics. But the full, final acceptance of television as the nation's supreme forum was earned only by its performance over the assassination weekend. And for those of us of the older reporting crafts, to be in Washington then, that weekend, was to live through not only bereavement but bewilderment. Sitting with friends in Harriman's parlor and watching the tube was to be in touch with reality, to be part of the national grief. But to slip out, to do one's reportorial duty, to ask the questions that must be asked, was a chore, for television tugged one back, irresistibly, to emotional participation. Television observed the nation with countless cameras, forty-four camera eyes in Washington alone. The splendid reportorial staffs of all three networks surpassed themselves.

Thus, now, as I review my notes, it is difficult to know which of them I took from the tube in Averell Harriman's house, and which I took from observation or conversation at the White House and elsewhere. I know I bowed before the coffin and paid respects as I filed by, with family friends, in the black-draped East Room, where the candles burned; I know I listened to the chanting, and I remember the smell of incense in the cathedral at the funeral services. I know I rode in the funeral cortege and helped persuade Averell Harriman to wear his high silk hat, for this was ceremony and the throng watching the cortege craved ceremony. I know I watched in the dusk at the burial in Arlington Cemetery as Cardinal Cushing prayed in his dry and rusting Irish-lilted Boston voice, and blessed the taper with which the widow lit the flame that would burn over his resting place. But almost everything else I wrote, and that others wrote, came from the spectacle of television; and the spectacle of television, so splendid, unifying and steadying a force that weekend, made John F. Kennedy's burial a tribal ceremony and made the man into a myth. With that myth politics would grapple for years to come.

More than any other President since Lincoln, John F. Kennedy has become myth. The greatest President in the stretch between them was, of course, Franklin D. Roosevelt; but it was difficult to make myth of Franklin Roosevelt, the country squire, the friendly judge, the approachable politician, the father figure. Roosevelt was a great man because he understood his times, and because almost always, at the historic intersections, he took the fork in the road that proved to be correct. He was so right and so strong, it was sport to challenge him. But Kennedy was cut off at the promise, not after the performance, and so it was left to television and his widow, Jacqueline, to frame the man as legend. For four days, as never before in history, an entire nation was invited into the sorrow and private mourning of the family of its chief.

The nation, almost as much as his family, must have craved for some end to the ceremonies, some stop to the open ache. What it needed was a last word, and this Jacqueline Kennedy provided.

Quite inadvertently, I was her instrument in labeling the myth, because she was concerned about history and wanted me to help him be remembered—and so, after a long night's talk, she urged my using the word "Camelot" to describe it all. And her message was his message—that one man, by trying, may change it all. Whether this is myth or truth I still debate.

It happened this way:

On the weekend of the assassination I had held *Life* magazine open long hours beyond its closing time at enormous expense in order to write the story as it should be written. I stayed in Washington until the funeral on Monday, then came back to New York, sleepless and sad, to await my mother, who was to join us for Thanksgiving.

I left the house the morning after Thanksgiving to visit my dentist, and was taken from the dentist's chair by a telephone call from my mother saying that Jackie Kennedy was calling and needed me. It seemed like an outer ripple of the instabilities that rock a time of crisis, but I came home immediately to find my mother, then quite old, alone in the house and absolutely unable to describe the tangle of calls that had come in—from the Secret Service, from Hyannisport, from Washington. Making a call back to Hyannisport, I found myself talking to Jacqueline Kennedy, who said there was something that she wanted *Life* magazine to say to the country, and I must do it. She would send a Secret Service car to bring me to Hyannisport. I called Thompson of *Life* and asked him to hold its run. I called the Secret Service, and was curtly informed that Mrs. Kennedy was no longer the President's wife, and she could give them no orders for cars. They were crisp. I called and learned I could rent no plane because a storm hovered over Cape Cod. I telephoned my brother, then chief of the weather service of the United

States, who said that no planes would land or take off in New England that night because it was either an old-fashioned northeaster or a full-scale hurricane blowing up on the cape we both knew from boyhood. I hung up on him and went to give his report to our mother—at which point it became quite apparent that she, unused to this kind of excitement, was having a heart attack. This complicated the problem, for if the widow of my friend needed me and my mother needed me, what should I do? Nancy made that decision; she called our family doctor, Harold Rifkin, and he said he would come now, immediately, holiday weekend or not, and preside at my mother's bedside; but that I must go to comfort the President's widow.

In a rented limousine, with a strange chauffeur, in a driving rainstorm, I made my way back to New England. The driver stopped now and then at gasoline stations, so I could telephone to New York, find how my mother was doing, learn she was stable. Then finally I told the chauffeur to gun the car into Hyannisport.

It was now quite late on Friday, November 29, a week after the assassination. Once more I had asked *Life* magazine to hold its presses open as it had the week before. Without hesitation, the editors had agreed to my suggestion. They would hold until I found out what Jacqueline Kennedy wanted to say to the nation. But since it cost thirty thousand dollars an hour overtime on Saturdays at the printing plants for me to hold up *Life,* they hoped I could let them know soon whether there was a story there. At that sum per hour; desperately worried about my mother; still unstabilized by the emotions of the assassination, I entered the Kennedy home in Hyannisport very briskly.

It was obvious, instantly, that my brisk mood was wrong. She had been trying to escape for days. No single human being has ever endured more public attention, more of the camera-watching, the camera-angling, the microphones intruding, the tears caught glistening, the children's hands curling in her own, than she had in the telecasts of the assassination and the ceremonies. She had performed as people rarely do, flawlessly, superbly. I know now she wanted to cry, and she could not. She had fled from Washington and the squeeze of observation to Hyannisport, to be away from it all. But still with her, in the room when I entered, were the good-willed comforters: Dave Powers, the family friend; "Chuck" Spalding, Jack's classmate at school; Pat Lawford, the President's sister; and Franklin Roosevelt, Jr.—who, curiously, was the only one who noticed my need to call New York to find out how my mother was faring.

She did not want anyone there when she talked to me. So they left. They, too, had been sleepless for too long, and knew I was a "friendly." I sat down on a small sofa, looked at her, the journalistic imperative forcing reportage almost automatically into my notes: ". . . composure . . . beautiful . . . dressed in black trim slacks, beige pullover sweater . . . eyes wider than pools . . . calm voice . . ." And then she began to talk.

A talk with Mary Todd Lincoln a week after Lincoln's assassination would not have been nearly as compelling, for Jacqueline Kennedy was a superior wife, a superior person, and wise. But as she began to talk, I realized that I was going to hear more than I wanted to—that she regarded me, and had summoned me, as a friend who also happened to be a journalist, rather than a journalist who could make precise in print what was unclear in her mind. I had brought a tape recorder, but I left it unopened, and sat and listened, for she was faced with a problem, and she wanted to share it with me as both friend and reporter. She was without tears; drained, white of face.

Then, in the most lucid possible manner, she was making a plea that was both unreal and unnecessary. She had asked me to Hyannisport, she said, because she wanted me to make certain that Jack was not forgotten in history. The thought that it was up to me to make American history remember John F. Kennedy was so unanticipated that my pencil stuttered over the notes. Then I realized that there was so much that this woman—who regarded me as one of Kennedy's "scholar"

friends rather than an "Irish" or "swinging" friend—
wanted to say that if indeed I was a friend (as I still feel
myself to be), my first duty was to let this sad, wan lady
talk out her grief. And let *Life*'s presses wait for whenever I could get back to them.

What bothered her was history.

Over the telephone, before I had undertaken to
come to Hyannisport, she had angrily commented on
several of the journalists who by now were writing the
follow-up stories, assessing the President, just dead, by
his achievements. She wanted me to rescue Jack from all
these "bitter people" who were going to write about him
in history. She did not want Jack left to the historians.

Well, then, I said, concerned for her sorrow, tell me
about it.

At this, then, there poured out several streams of
thought which mingled for hours. There was the broken
narrative, the personal unwinding from the horror, the
tale of the killing. Then there was the history part of it.
And parts too personal for mention in any book but one
of her own.

My notes run in patches and ups-and-downs, for
Jacqueline Kennedy, that night, talked first of her personal anguish, then of what she thought history might have
to say of her husband, and then wandered from his
childhood to Dallas, trying always to make clear to me
that I should make clear to the people how much magic
there had been in John F. Kennedy's time. She thought
her husband was truly a man of magic, which is a lovely
thought in any wife. But since magic is so difficult to
capture in any conversation, I must rearrange the sequence of my notes, which, as so often happens, reflect
the jagged jumping of phrase to thought to another
thought rather than the story she sought to tell and the
message she wanted to give.

We talked for a few moments aimlessly and then the
scene took over, as if controlling her.

". . . there'd been the biggest motorcade from the
airport. Hot. Wild. Like Mexico and Vienna. The sun was
so strong in our faces. I couldn't put on sunglasses. . . .

Then we saw this tunnel ahead, I thought it would be cool in the tunnel, I thought if you were on the left the sun wouldn't get into your eyes. . . .

"They were gunning the motorcycles. There were these little backfires. There was one noise like that. I thought it was a backfire. Then next I saw Connally grabbing his arms and saying no, no, no, no, no, with his fist beating. Then Jack turned and I turned. All I remember was a blue-gray building up ahead. Then Jack turned back so neatly, his last expression was so neat . . . you know that wonderful expression he had when they'd ask him a question about one of the ten million pieces they have in a rocket, just before he'd answer. He looked puzzled, then he slumped forward. He was holding out his hands. . . . I could see a piece of his skull coming off. It was flesh-colored, not white—he was holding out his hand. . . . I can see this perfectly clean piece detaching itself from his head. Then he slumped in my lap, his blood and his brains were in my lap. . . . Then Clint Hill [the Secret Service man], he loved us, he made my life so easy, he was the first man in the car. . . . We all lay down in the car. . . . And I kept saying, Jack, Jack, Jack, and someone was yelling he's dead, he's dead. All the ride to the hospital I kept bending over him, saying Jack, Jack, can you hear me, I love you, Jack. I kept holding the top of his head down, trying to keep the brains in."

She remembered, as I sat paralyzed, the pink-rose ridges on the inside of the skull, and how from here on down (she made a gesture just above her forehead) "his head was so beautiful. I tried to hold the top of his head down, maybe I could keep it in . . . but I knew he was dead." It was all told tearlessly, her wide eyes not even seeing me, a recitative to herself.

Then, as I now pick my way through the notes, she described how, when they came to the hospital, they tried to keep her from him, "these big Texas interns kept saying, Mrs. Kennedy, you come with us, they wanted to take me away from him. . . . They kept trying to get me, they kept trying to grab me. . . . But I said I'm not leaving. . . ." The narrative continued, as she lived the horror of the hour. "Dave Powers came running to me at the hospital crying when he saw me, my legs, my hands were covered with his brains. . . . When Dave saw this he burst out weeping. . . . I remember this narrow corridor, I said I'm not going to leave him, I'm not going to leave him. . . . I was standing outside in the corridor . . . ten minutes later this big policeman brought me a chair."

Dr. Burkley (Rear Admiral George G. Burkley, U.S. Navy, personal physician to the President) came out and saw her and insisted she needed a sedative. She countered that she had to be in that room when he died. Burkley took up her cause, brought her into the operating room, insisting "it's her prerogative, it's her prerogative." Dr. Malcolm Perry (the operating surgeon) wanted her out. She remembered him as a very tall, bald man. But she said, "It's my husband, his blood, his brains, are all over me."

Then it was over. The hunt for the priest. The priest entered to give extreme unction. Then they pulled the sheet up: ". . . There was a sheet over Jack, his foot was sticking out of the sheet, whiter than the sheet. I took his foot and kissed it. Then I pulled back the sheet. His mouth was so *beautiful* . . . his eyes were open. They found his hand under the sheet, and I held his hand all the time the priest was saying extreme unction." By this time, or slightly earlier, her gloves had stiffened with his blood and she gave one of her hands to "this policeman," and he pulled the glove off. Then: ". . . the ring was all bloodstained . . . so I put the ring on Jack's finger . . . and then I kissed his hand . . . and then I asked Kenny, do you think it was right . . . and Kenny said you leave it where it is . . . and he brought me the ring back [later] from the Bethesda Hospital. . . ."

Interspersed with the memories, spoken so softly, in the particular whispering intimacy of Jacqueline Kennedy's voice, was constantly this effort to make the statement—the statement she had asked me to come and hear. It would stutter out over and over again with an introductory: "History! . . . History . . . it's what those bitter old men write," or just: "History . . ." But that was what she wanted to talk about; so, thus, I pull together here fragments of disjointed notes; and as I run the notes through my retrieval of memory for meaning, her message was quite simple:

She believed, and John F. Kennedy shared the belief, that history belongs to heroes; and heroes must not be forgotten. We talked from eight-thirty until almost midnight, and it was only after she had rid herself of the blood scene that she tracked clearly what she wanted to say:

". . . But there's this one thing I wanted to say. . . . I'm so ashamed of myself. . . . When Jack quoted something, it was usually classical . . . no, don't protect me now. . . . I kept saying to Bobby, I've got to talk to somebody, I've got to see somebody, I want to say this one thing, it's been almost an obsession with me, all I keep thinking of is this line from a musical comedy, it's been an obsession with me.

". . . At night before we'd go to sleep . . . we had an old Victrola. Jack liked to play some records. His back hurt, the floor was so cold. I'd get out of bed at night and play it for him, when it was so cold getting out of bed . . . on a Victrola ten years old—and the song he loved most came at the very end of this record, the last side of *Camelot*, sad *Camelot*: . . . 'Don't let it be forgot, that once there was a spot, for one brief shining moment that was known as Camelot.'

". . . There'll never be another Camelot again. . . .

"Do you know what I think of history? . . . When something is written down, does that make it history? The things they say! . . . For a while I thought history was something that bitter old men wrote. But Jack loved history so. . . . No one'll ever know everything about Jack. But . . . history made Jack what he was . . . this lonely, little sick boy . . . scarlet fever . . . this little boy sick so much of the time, reading in bed, reading history . . . reading the Knights of the Round Table . . . and he just liked that last song.

"Then I thought, for Jack history was full of heroes. And if it made him this way, if it made him see the heroes, maybe other little boys will see. Men are such a combination of good and bad. . . . He was such a simple man. But he was so complex, too. Jack had this hero idea of history, the idealistic view, but then he had that other side, the pragmatic side. His friends were his old friends; he loved his Irish Mafia.

"History!" And now she reverted to the assassination scene again, as she did all through the conversation, which had swung between history and death. ". . . Everybody kept saying to me to put a cold towel around my head and wipe the blood off [she was now recollecting the scene and picture of the swearing in of Lyndon Johnson on *Air Force One* at Love Field, as the dead President lay aft]. . . . I saw myself in the mirror, my whole face spattered with blood and hair. I wiped it off with Kleenex. History! I thought, no one really wants me there. Then one second later I thought, why did I wash the blood off? I should have left it there, let them see what they've done. If I'd just had the blood and caked hair when they took the picture. . . . Then later I said to Bobby, What's the line between history and drama?"

At some point in the conversation she had said to me, "Caroline asked me what kind of prayer should I say? And I told her, 'Either Please, God, take care of Daddy, or Please, God, be nice to Daddy.'"

What she was saying to me now was: Please, History, be kind to John F. Kennedy. Or, as she said over and over again, don't leave him to the bitter old men to write about.

Out of all this, then, being both a reporter and a friend, I tried to write the story for which *Life*'s editors were waiting in New York. I typed in haste and inner turmoil in a servant's room and a Secret Service man, who had been sleepless for days, burst in on me and snarled, "For Christ's sake, we need some sleep here." But I went on; and in forty-five minutes brought out the story she was waiting for, her message that Americans must not forget this man, or this moment we styled "Camelot."

Life was waiting, and at 2 A.M. I tried to dictate the

story from the wall-hung telephone in the Kennedy kitchen. She came in while I was dictating the story to two of my favorite editors, Ralph Graves and David Maness, who, as good editors, despite a ballooning overtime printing bill, were nonetheless trying to edit and change phrases as I dictated. Maness observed that maybe I had too much of "Camelot" in the dispatch. Mrs. Kennedy had come in at that moment, having penciled over her copy of the story with her changes; she overheard the editor trying to edit me, who had already so heavily edited her. She shook her head. She *wanted* Camelot to top the story. Camelot, heroes, fairy tales, legends, were what history was all about. Maness caught the tone in my reply as I insisted this had to be done as Camelot. Catching my stress, he said, "Hey, is she listening to this now with you?" I muffled the phone from her, went on dictating, and Maness let the story run.

So the epitaph on the Kennedy administration became Camelot—a magic moment in American history, when gallant men danced with beautiful women, when great deeds were done, when artists, writers and poets met at the White House, and the barbarians beyond the walls held back.

Which, of course, is a misreading of history. The magic Camelot of John F. Kennedy never existed. Instead, there began in Kennedy's time an effort of government to bring reason to bear on facts which were becoming almost too complicated for human minds to grasp. No Merlins advised John F. Kennedy, no Galahads won high place in his service. The knights of his round table were able, tough, ambitious men, capable of kindness, also capable of error, but as a group more often right than wrong and astonishingly incorruptible. What made them a group and established their companionship was their leader. Of them all, Kennedy was the toughest, the most intelligent, the most attractive—and inside, the least romantic. He was a realistic dealer in men, a master of games who understood the importance of ideas. He assumed his responsibilities fully. He advanced the cause of America at home and abroad. But he also posed for the first time the great question of the sixties and seventies: What kind of people are we Americans? What do we want to become?

For twenty-five years, from the day of my graduation and departure for China, I had been fascinated by the relationship of Leader to Power, of the State to Force, of the Concept to Politics—and most recently of the Hero to his Circumstances. I had given unquestioning loyalties to all too many men, as one does when one is young, and I would give guarded affection to several more in years to come. But I would never again, after Kennedy, see any man as a hero. A passage of my own life had closed with a passage in American politics.

EPILOGUE

Outward Bound

The storyteller was unaware of passing a divide as he left the Kennedy compound that night. It was still raining as he reached the main highway to New York, and there he was on familiar ground. Except for the sadness and the personal ache, all seemed as it had been before. He did not know then that he and everyone else in America had, that week, passed through an invisible membrane of time which divided one era from another; and that Jacqueline Kennedy's farewell to Camelot was farewell to an America never to be recaptured.

Even less did he know that he himself was outward bound once more—as definitely set away from his most recent past as he had been set away from his traditional past when he left Boston after the great hurricane of 1938, twenty-five years earlier. Now in the drizzle of this waning blizzard he tried to sleep, and dozed fitfully until the gray dawn showed him he was coming into New York. His mother had survived the night; she would be up and around again in a few weeks. So he must be up and off immediately to Washington and then on the campaign trail of 1964, with neither pause nor reflection.

This next leg of his journey would last fifteen years and carry him away from all his certainties to questions he could then, in 1963, neither define nor expect to have to ask.

That week of the Divide, however, he had been quite certain of both questions and answers. If he had been awakened from his doze that night on the road, he would have ribboned off an almost perfect specimen of American liberal thinking from the standard spool. All the proper words and ideas would have come out in the right order, without hesitation. And had he been asked to summarize what he had learned of the American experience at home and abroad, he would have answered, doubtless, with the mothering cliché of the time: that America was that unique country whose political faith could be summed up as Opportunity.

Opportunity was just as much the north point on his political compass as he was a personal examplar of how Opportunity was supposed to work in America. He had, for example, first traveled this route between Massachusetts and Manhattan as an adolescent hitchhiker. Later, he had learned how to hustle a ticket: In Depression days, a round-trip fare between Boston and New York cost only two dollars for the forty-eight-hour weekend; and if you were smart enough to buy an unused stub from a one-way traveler, at either Boston's South Station or New York's Grand Central, you could make the trip for fifty cents each way. Now the Opportunity that had lured his father to America seventy-two years before had rented him a limousine and chauffeur, given him status, recognition, access to the great, and a comfortable brownstone house in New York to return to. That same Opportunity had taken his youngest brother from the same house on Erie Street, through the same Boston Latin School, the same Harvard, over these same roads down to Washington, where he was now director of the U.S. Weather Service, monitoring this blizzard, and about to become the chief environmental scientist of the United States, responsible for surveillance of air, oceans, inland waters, coastal zones, hurricanes, whales, porpoises, and God knows what else. His other brother, still in Boston, edited textbooks in American history. It was appropriate that this road was numbered U.S. 1. This same coastal road had carried John Adams down from Boston to New York to Philadelphia to attend the First Continental Congress in 1774 as a young man of thirty-nine; it later carried the same Adams down to a new capital named Washington, D.C., as President of the United States at age sixty-one. And from Washington, D.C., somewhere down the road, stretched all those promises and opportunities White and his brothers and countless others, including all the Adamses, had enjoyed.

In White's thinking, Opportunity was what set American history off from the history of all other lands. The frontier had been Opportunity. The American school system was Opportunity. The enterprise system was Opportunity. He could not conceive then that this American faith, Opportunity, was about to tangle itself in the same contradictions as caused the French Revolution to make Liberty a synonym for Terror, the Chinese Revolution to make Liberation a synonym for Conquest.

To that first tenet of his then political faith he would at this time have added as the second tenet a belief in heroes, and the conviction that great men could move affairs for the good.

Heroes were not necessarily part of the faith of all American liberals; the Marxist wing of American liberalism, to which he had leaned when he was young, held that the dialectic of history made personalities unimportant. Such "liberals" believed that Marx's "locomotive of history" moved on preset rails to a predestined end. The engineer might slow or speed the pace but could not deviate from the track. Exposure to events had forced White to abandon the myths of Marxism completely. In twenty-five years of reporting, he had met so many definitely *good* men in places of high or critical power, he simply could not ignore the importance of heroes in history. Whatever the entries on the balance of violence, his net judgment was that Chou En-lai was a man who had done more good than harm. And there was no doubt that, against all odds, Jean Monnet, Pierre Bertaux, Konrad Adenauer and others he had known in postwar Europe had well served the cause of liberty and humankind. And then there were the Americans. Starting with Joseph Stilwell, following on with Paul Hoffman, David Bruce, Averell Harriman, countless others, his memory was crowded with the recollection of men who had used power, used it well, made a difference in the lives of other people. You could not understand history if you did not include such men as a critical ingredient.

All nations, of course, had their heroes, but there seemed to be something distinctive about American heroes, just as there was something distinctive about American history. Perhaps that was because an American hero was to be remembered not as other heroes, for his conquests, but for the degree by which he enlarged Opportunity.

The distinctive line of American hero had begun well before Abraham Lincoln, with Jefferson, but Lincoln was the greatest of the saints in the American faith of Opportunity. Lincoln had not only freed the slaves; he had opened land to moneyless homesteaders; he had passed laws to endow colleges with land grants and open them to all youngsters who sought learning as Opportunity; he had called into being a National Academy of Sciences, which opened government by a wee crack to the learning of wise men; he had given millions of acres to railroad men to open the West. He was hallowed as the victorious War President, but his monuments in the faith of Opportunity were prodigious. So, too, were those of the first Roosevelt, the second Roosevelt and Harry Truman.

So, too, John F. Kennedy.

Much would be written or whispered later about John Kennedy which would either amuse or sadden those who thought Camelot had been for real. What was later written about Kennedy and women bothered White but little. He knew that Kennedy loved his wife—but that Kennedy, the politician, exuded that musk odor of power which acts as an aphrodisiac to many women. White was reasonably sure that only three Presidential candidates he had ever met had denied themselves the pleasures invited by that aphrodisiac—Harry Truman, George Romney and Jimmy Carter. He was reasonably sure that all the others he had met had, at one time or another, on the campaign trail, accepted casual partners. The noise, the shrieking, the excitement of crowds, and then the power, the silent pickup and delivery in limousines, set the glands alive in women as in men. What was far more important in assessing Kennedy was the demerit history would have to mark against him for failing to tighten control over those instruments of Presidential power which had already passed beyond the law and would go further. What would later be revealed of the American intelligence services should have engaged Kennedy's intervention; and did not receive it. Such revelations, however, would come only far down the road and White would have to grapple with them only much later.

But the balance was already struck in his mind as he rode home to New York that night, and would not change. Kennedy had done so much good, had so enlarged opportunity that he qualified in the line of American greatness. Kennedy had let slip so many old restraints, invited so many new kinds of people into the arena of American power, that the power system would have to adjust to accommodate them—party system, information system, industrial system, administrative system. America would begin to be a different kind of nation shortly after John F. Kennedy's death, and because of him.

In the imaginary conversation about history he might have had with a questioner that night on that road from Massachusetts down to Manhattan, he would have added many other dogmas of the liberal catechism. But he would have left out a critical ingredient: Accident.

Not until many years later would the storyteller appreciate the importance of accident. Yet if you believed in heroes, then this belief led you to a contemplation of accident—because accident, raising the hero to attention or striking him down, could deflect history itself. That week the accident of assassination had led to just such a deflection. It would not be apparent for some time, but the locomotive had slipped its brakes. It seemed to be going in the same direction, but it careened ahead with a runaway good will and power to a point where the tracks disappeared over the horizon.

That entire November week had been a blur for White, but one scene would grow sharper over the years, and would acquire the stark outlines he would later describe as the Scene of the Accident.

Five days before this drive down the road, on the Sunday after the killing, he had been in Washington. The television cameras had been trained on the catafalque of Kennedy in the rotunda of the Capitol, but Lyndon Johnson had slipped away from the camera eye to speed by back street to the White House. There he would preside over a conference that had been called by Kennedy to discuss America's future course in Vietnam; 16,732 Americans were already engaged "unofficially" in war there. The brother dictators, Diem and Nhu, had been murdered three weeks before. Now Johnson, having moved up the scheduled date of the meeting, presided over the council Kennedy had invited: the Secretaries of Defense and State, McNamara and Rusk; National Security Adviser Bundy and CIA Director McCone; Ambassador to Vietnam Henry Cabot Lodge; Chairman of the Joint Chiefs of Staff Maxwell

Taylor, and several others. Should they go on in Vietnam or not?

White remembered waiting in the lobby of the White House for the answer; and remembered Pierre Salinger, the spokesman, climbing on a table, his eyes red-rimmed from weeping, to give a briefing. Most questions were about the ceremonies of Kennedy's funeral. The room was crowded; it smelled of the trench coats of reporters, still moist from the previous day's drenching rain; all were tired, drained emotionally. Someone thought, as if mechanically, to ask Salinger: What did they just decide to do about Vietnam in there? Salinger, too, was tired, and put his hand behind his ear as if to hear the question better. He had just said that Lyndon Johnson's policy was to continue John Kennedy's policy. Then he answered, as if in disbelief at the question, that of course we would go on. There would be no change in Kennedy's policies, at home as abroad—in Vietnam as in everything else. Johnson would carry on.

The answer, however I may misremember the words, was authentic to the spirit of the day. And reflected a classic accident. White later tried for a long time to find out what, indeed, lay in Kennedy's mind in that critical week, his last—whether Kennedy indeed would have gone on to full-scale war in Vietnam or not. Much later, he was assured by Kenny O'Donnell, who knew Kennedy's inner thinking as substantially as anyone but Robert Kennedy and Ted Sorensen, that Kennedy meant *not* to go on. According to O'Donnell, Kennedy had just pledged to Senate Majority Leader Mike Mansfield not only the immediate withdrawal of one thousand of the sixteen thousand American troops then in Vietnam, but the withdrawal of *all* of them after the 1964 election. When O'Donnell asked Kennedy how he meant to do that, Kennedy had quipped, "Easy. Put a government in there that will ask us to leave."

If that had been Kennedy's intention—and White had no reason to doubt O'Donnell's word—then the ac-

cident of assassination had led on to the death of fifty
thousand American men and more than a million Vietnamese! Kennedy, as President, had been free to
maintain or reverse course. Lyndon Johnson, just installed by the accident of assassination to preside over
this council, could not, politically, repudiate the apparent course of the dead President, who lay still unburied in the rotunda.

But there was more than that to the effect of accident. Accident could affect more than a single deed
or a series of deeds. It was, for example, more than
the accidental linking of a hemophiliac prince, a neu-
rotic mother, a mad monk, a weakling emperor, that
brought down Czarist Russia. It was the consequent
breakdown in Russia of the central switchboard of governing ideas, the discontinuity of thinking. In American
history, for certain, the tragedy of Abraham Lincoln's
assassination lay in the disconnection of his governing
ideas from the political process which was then churn-
ing with new movement. The erratic course that power
took when the radical Republicans of Congress and
the greedy Republicans of business made an alliance
to give America the excesses both of reconstruction
and of industrialization was not *entirely* accidental. The
forces were there, forces of greed and forces of ideals.
But the accident of Lincoln's death freed them both to
rush on to excess. The yoking ideas had been cut
apart.

So, too, with the assassination of John F. Kennedy.
So much vitality, so much prosperity, so much education, so much sheer military power, had built up in the
America of the 1950s and 1960s that the country invited outreach, exploration, experimentation. A surplus
of energy, learning, appetite, made all things seem
possible. But ideas and programs still had to be sequenced, meshed together and pushed through Congress to law and action. In the American system, control of that agenda of proposal, legislation and action
lies with the President. Whether he recognizes it or
not, a candidate's campaign has been an exercise in

fitting ideas to the times. As President, he is supposed to pull them together. And if the elected President is removed by accident, then something can snap—coherent control of ideas over events and the agenda of events. Kennedy was to be replaced as President by a man of boundless power appetite and reckless historical ambition, who simply did not understand ideas. With unwitting good will, he would plunge America into a new war in Asia, and hasten the decay of the nation's great cities. That President would in turn be succeeded by a man of equal historical ambition who did not understand the central idea of America itself, a President who would elevate the petty malice of all men in power to policy—and thus to crime. It would be eleven more years before accident would bring back a President whose character the storyteller could trust, and several more years before another President would offer America a set of ideas that had some internal coherence, however violently debatable.

If the larger ingredients of the storyteller's thinking about history seemed certainties on that drive home in 1963, the most certain of them would have been unspoken, almost unrecognized—his assumption of American Goodness and Virtue.

All his reporting up to that time had, finally, convinced him that America, however much she might err, worked Good around the world.

Yet the years to come would shake the storyteller's conviction—not because America ceased to seek to do Good but because the Good that Americans increasingly sought would encase itself in an absolutism of spirit that led from self-righteousness on to brutality. He was about to see virtuous scholars and planners threaten or wipe out the communities of America's great cities; and observe selfless men plunge America into the most gainless of wars, wasting the youth of two nations. The questioning of America's purpose, of America's virtues, of America's faith in Opportunity would boil out into the streets and politics of the nation in what, in his later reporting, he would call the Storm Decade. But the storyteller himself would first come to recognize his own fear of American Virtue and Good Will only in 1976 when, as if stumbling over his own mistakes, he returned to visit his hometown, Boston.

No city in America has been more sharply transformed in its outer face and political dialogue than Boston. From the russet-red city of patricians and bigots of his youth to the glowing and vibrant central city of today, with its dazzling architecture of plazas and skyscrapers, the old Hub has been transformed. But the elderly poor fear Boston. White families leave Boston. The rich, the young, the learned and the oppressed congregate there. Boston is a city where, finally, Virtue is proclaimed triumphant on the hills and even the thieves have learned to talk publicly like saints.

It was in Boston, thus, quite appropriately, at the beginning of the campaign for the Presidency in 1976, that the storyteller found himself in February of that year rubbed, personally, against what thirty years of triumphant and ascendant Good Will had done to the neighborhood of his youth.

It happened this way:

George Wallace, a racist candidate, was particularly strong in South Boston, and so White had decided to spend an afternoon there to measure the Wallace strength in the coming Massachusetts primary. It took very little reporting to find out how much fear and hatred ran all through these neat old wooden homes of working-class Irish; so on impulse, White asked his cabdriver to take him from South Boston to Erie Street in Dorchester, to see the house in which he himself had been born. The driver, a student, turned, asked if White knew the neighborhood, then said he'd have to ask for ten dollars more to go there because it was so dangerous.

It irritated White to pay ten dollars over the meter to go back to his birthplace. But as they penetrated the neighborhood, he began to understand. He had seen this kind of desolation in other American cities—the blank places, the burned-out hulks, the boarded windows, the caries of the inner urban community. But this had been home. Frightened at being fearful of the streets where he had once courted girls and played hit-the-ball, he nonetheless went on. The Christopher Gibson School, where Miss Fuller had taught him American history, had been burned out only a few years earlier. No one could account for the fire; or how the school was vandalized. The city had razed it; and at the top of Morse Street, where the school had once been, stretched a blank, empty parking lot. The little Hebrew school on Bradshaw Street, where he had first learned and then taught the language of the Bible, had also been vandalized. It, too, had been razed to the ground, the site covered with blacktop paving.

He guided the driver around the corner to Erie Street. The old trees had vanished. He knew the chestnut trees of New England had gone in the blight, but all the others, the oaks and elms and maples, had been slashed away here, too. Those few shops still standing in the small marketplace were boarded up and shuttered. Empty lots and tumble-down near-ruins flanked the silent street where gardens once grew and mothers strolled with babies. The driver had speeded up on this desolate street and had overshot the mark, when White realized he had passed his own house. He asked the driver to back up. And there it was—a derelict of a house, with a tin number plate saying "74" on the doorpost. It *was* 74 Erie Street, standing by itself, the neighboring houses on either side and behind long since torn down. But it took minutes for the leaning shanty to restructure itself in mind's eye and conform with the memory of the little crimson house of childhood with its beautiful New England garden. The old steps to the porch were rotting and twisted; the house itself was askew; on the upstairs floor where his grandmother had reigned as tyrant, the windows were either smashed, open to the wind or boarded up. Four bells with names attached indicated that four families now

lived on the bottom floor, which had once housed
David White and his family. He could see that his mother's bedroom, in which he had been born, was still
intact and inhabited. But its windows looked out not
on a flower garden but on a junkyard, with three
wrecked cars and two trees which might be either alive
or dead. No shrubs showed, no flower tubs were left.

White was peering over the wire-mesh fence of
what had been the garden of his birthplace when several black children materialized, yelling, "Hey, man,
what y'doing?" Then followed a dignified but scowling
black man, who challenged, "What you doing here,
man?" When White said he had been born in this house
sixty years before, the man in coveralls responded bel-
ligerently, "You putting me on, man?" White told him
about the cherry tree, the day lilies, the garden, the
tulips, as they all had been. Gradually the man's suspicion faded; they exchanged names and telephone
numbers. The owner of the shanty was this man's
brother; if White wanted, he should telephone and
they'd let him visit inside. The black man offered the
information that there was still a pear tree in back and
the old grapevine had still been there when they'd
moved in several years before. Beyond that, there was
no connection of this place with time past, or home with
recollection.

Then White left the street which once, on summer
nights, had been fragrant with the odor of baking
bagels and on summer days loud with the sound of
boys playing knuckle games with the shiny golden
chestnuts that came from Wolcott Street. It was gone,
all gone. The Opportunity America had given him to
leave this street had somehow left it a plague street,
full of fearful black people in an America that did not
understand itself. He knew it was the last time he would
see the house itself. Next time he returned, if he ever
did, it would certainly be gone—gone the way of the
Christopher Gibson School and the Beth-El School. It
would be demolished, burned down for the insurance
money or paved over in some urban renewal project.

The next morning White was up and out of reverie and coursing through the campaign of 1976 with Candidate Morris Udall. Congressman Udall was the last emissary of the yearning and hopeful sixties to the politics of the seventies, and that day he was going to campaign in White's old neighborhood. Udall stopped first at Eliot Square. As a boy, White had delivered groceries from his uncle's store in the square to the lace-curtain Irish and modest Protestant families of that sedate neighborhood. But the square now was reminiscent of Essen or Berlin—wiped out, as the South Bronx of New York City was wiped out. Some federal program had built a concrete-and-brick blockhouse pharmacy on old Eliot Square. The local poverty specialists explained to the candidate how only the federal government could provide pharmacies on this ancient and historic square. But when White had been a delivery boy, forty-five years earlier, there had been several prosperous and thriving little pharmacies on this same square, serving the Irish and Yankee families of the neighborhood. Now only government could erect and fortify a pharmacy which would not be raided by the under-Goths for drugs or sacked by vandals as the buildings roundabout were sacked. The "poverticians" so proud of this federal pharmacy they had erected knew no history; they had no historic memory of Eliot Square as it was when it was safe, and corner pharmacies could send little boys safely to deliver prescriptions to neighbors' homes at night. The program people proudly displayed to the candidate their pharmacy and explained its interconnections with Medicaid and Medicare. The candidate listened as all watched a file of very old and tottering white ladies, led by a beautiful and understanding young black social worker, entering the drugstore. She told them they must each keep one hand on the shoulder of the lady ahead as they lined up for their medicines. The government provided the medicine, and their guide; and the guide took them back to their old folks' home. But there was no community any longer.

The rest of that morning had prodded White to further speculation. From Eliot Square, Mr. Udall drove with his following entourage to Egleston Square, then to Blue Hill Avenue, down which the candidate sped, never seeing the side streets, where the decay gnawed its way through block after block. The candidate stopped, after three miles of high-speed cavalcade, at a typical urban border-line barrier of high tension, a spot in Boston called Mattapan Square. There the fleeing whites and the advancing blacks still mingled— the most genteel of the blacks, the most forlorn of the whites. It was a "photo opportunity." The good and conscientious candidate from Arizona, aspiring to be President over an urban America, spoke briefly. Someone of his local staff had misled Udall to believe that he was seeing a pastoral of urban harmony, although, indeed, he was seeing a way station on the route of flight from disaster. He praised this tranquil "community" which proved that integration could work, invoked brotherhood, peace and the need of the federal government to do more, and then his campaign sped off to the pure white suburbs in the liberal belt that now surrounds inner Boston. The liberal belt gave Udall his only victories in the Massachusetts primary. The fearful whites of South Boston voted for George Wallace; the fearful blacks of White's native Dorchester voted for Jimmy Carter; everyone else voted for Henry Jackson. Jackson carried Massachusetts. But White knew that no federal program, nor any federal promise, could restore the tranquillity and quiet of the streets of his boyhood. And that this campaign would not seriously affect how Americans lived.

Now, in the second year of the Presidency of James Earl Carter, the storyteller could look back and study his own surprise. He was coming to the end of a book entirely different from the one he had meant to write and had promised his friends and readers.

His grand scheme, way back then in the days before Kennedy, had been to write one book every four years about how a President is made. And thus, if he exercised that scheme every election year from 1960 to 1980, he would place on the shelves six books covering a quarter of a century of American politics.

Now he could not; and it was probably that week spent on the Massachusetts primary in 1976 more than anything else that had derailed the grand scheme. No one had planned the desolation of his birthplace. Indeed, every bit of goodness in national, state and Boston politics had been mobilized against this kind of desolation, as well as countless millions of dollars— and had failed. The storyteller had been trying to fit the story to vote totals. Yet there had to be some other connection between purpose and power in America than the mechanics of elections, some more reasonable way of passing judgment on good intentions than simply by counting votes.

As the campaign of 1976 wore on, the storyteller had applied himself to both the roadwork and the homework of the contest; chased the candidates, attended the debates, trudged in the primaries, pushed at the rallies, pontificated on television on election night. But when it was over and the time came to write it down, he found that what had been happening in America could no longer be carved up into arbitrary four-year chunks, packaged in Presidential elections. This time, in 1976, the Americans had chosen a President whose good will and morality could not be questioned—but whether he could control the forces of good will, or check their absolutism, or guide them through their clashes and controversies to compromises of common sense, was entirely unclear.

It would take much time to see the meaning and perspective of the 1976 campaign for the American Presidency; and he would be able to tell that and the story of 1980 only after he had established for himself, as well as for his readers, his credentials of experience. He had begun that way as soon as the election was over, but what he had achieved, he realized, was a story of the sights, sounds, persons and episodes he had witnessed as he had been whipped around in the slipstream of American power. Accident had drawn him into that slipstream as one of its chroniclers; he had seen American power peak at the moment of victory in Asia; seen it used with majesty to save liberties and people in postwar Europe; then followed it home to find out where the power came from, and found the trail led to politics.

Thus it was quite obvious to the storyteller long before it could have become apparent to the reader that he would need two books to tell this story. The first book, which is this, would have to tell how he had seen American power used. The second would necessarily have to go back in time and overlap, because it would be about how men reach for power, which means politics. In politics it is not the way things really are that counts, but the way they appear to be. Control of appearance and communications varies from country to country, as do their politics. In America this kind of control had been changing before Kennedy, would change even more quickly after the assassination. Thus, what was about to happen in American politics would be so dramatic that it made an entirely different story.

The moment of break between the two stories had to be the killing of John F. Kennedy, the moment he marked for himself as the "Divide," or the "Discontinuity." Until that moment he had believed that it was only Opportunity, as a faith, that pre-eminently distinguished American politics from the politics of other countries. With Kennedy's passage, it was retrospectively clear that the old English political culture had lost control over the other peoples who had filled America's vast spaces and clotted cities. The polyglot peoples of America had no common heritage but only ideas to bind them together. Power at Kennedy's death still lay in the established order. But politics would reshuffle those who controlled the power; and a changing culture would change those who controlled politics. The happy, tranquil decade that had run from 1954 to 1963 was about to give way to the Storm Decade of the sixties, which ran from 1963 to 1974. And all the contending groups under the surface of the old political culture would emerge, claiming special privilege under the banner of Opportunity.

What would be really at issue was whether America would be transformed, in the name of Opportunity, simply into a Place, a gathering of discretely defined and entitled groups, interests and heritages; or whether it could continue to be a nation, where all heritages joined under the same roof-ideas of communities within government. The revolution of the Storm Decade and its aftermath would be a testing of whether the old ideas that had made America a nation could stretch far enough to keep it one; and whether a new culture could nourish a political system as strong and successful as the one that was passing away.

ACKNOWLEDGMENTS

I have been blessed with so many friends over the years that this book of memories would have to stretch for another chapter if I were to list all those who helped the story on the way from Dorchester, Massachusetts, to Bridgewater, Connecticut.

Gratitude insists, however, that I specifically acknowledge those who helped me to nail these recollections into readable form.

My wife, Beatrice Kevitt Hofstadter, sustained this book not only with her affection and devotion but with her wisdom as a professional historian and her skills at contemporary research. My editor, Simon Michael Bessie, has for almost twenty years encouraged me with his enthusiasm and craftsmanship—but this time he contributed to my work beyond any call of affection or duty. Richard Clurman prodded me into the action at chapter one—and closed his support two years later by scrutiny and comment on the entire manuscript. Hedva Hadas Glickenhaus has done so much for me in so many ways— as editor, researcher, critic, conscience and manager— that I can find no way of specifically thanking her except to style her, as she is, indispensable.

INDEX

ABC (American Broadcasting Company), 605

Academic world: involvement in government, 456, 644, 645, 653

Accident, role of, in history, 261, 687–90

Acheson, Dean, 375, 401, 415, 418, 427, 439, 449–53, 461, 465, 513

Acta Diurna, 546

Acton, John Emerich Edward, Lord, 514

Adams, Henry, 28, 559

Adams, John, 53, 685

Adenauer, Konrad, 415–16, 423, 425–427, 508, 686

A. F. of L. (American Federation of Labor), 52

Africa: Allied World War II landings in, 180–81; French presence in, 451–52; postwar economic dependency on Britain, 383–84, 389–90

Agnew, Spiro T., 512

Airlines, origins of, 535

Airplanes: B-25s, 286; B-29s, 222, 229, 289–91, 300, 303; B-47s, 447; Boeing 707, 534, 537; C-46s and C-47s, in Hump airlift, 189, 292; C-87s, 292; DC-3s, 291–92, 536; Japanese Zero, 104; jets, 533–38; P-40s, 104, 186

Air power and air war: vs. ground war, 186–89, 191, 221, 228; against Japan, in World War II, 188–91, 221, 222–23, 286–94, 296, 300; Sino-Japanese war, 104, 111–15; U. S. commitment to, 191, 316; in Vietnam, 191

Alabama, civil rights confrontations in, 655–56, 658–61

Aldridge, James, 174

American Airlines, 536, 538

American Black Chamber, The (Yardley), 105 n.

American Broadcasting Company (ABC), 605

American Commonwealth, The (Bryce), 142

American Federation of Labor (A. F. of L.), 52

American magazine, 522, 548, 549

American Revolution, 252, 260, 269

American Weekly, 109

Andrea Doria, S.S., 559

Anhui province, China, 152, 153

Arabs, in Palestine of 1938, 85–86

Arkansas Baptist State Convention of 1960, 628

Army-McCarthy hearings, 558

Arnold, General H. H. ("Hap"), 191, 289

Aroostook County, Me., in 1960 election, 633

Ascoli, Marion Rosenwald, 488

Ascoli, Max, 462, 488–91, 493, 516–519

Asia: American policy in, 221, 252, 562–63, 689–90; Japanese comeback in, 401, 435; Japanese prewar expansionary thrust in, 143, 148; MacArthur's legacy in, 146, 148–149

Associated Press (AP), 108, 433, 635–36

Athens, Tenn., 1946 local election in, 330–31

Atkinson, Brooks, 233, 235

Atlanta, Ga., civil rights demonstrations in, 612

Atom bomb, 291, 295–96, 300, 301, 444–47

Atomic Energy Commission, 496

Atsugi airfield, Japan, 296–98

Atlee, Clement, 382, 390

"Audience Game," the, 550–57, 560

Auschwitz concentration camp, 406, 408

Australian Broadcasting Commission, 117

Authors League, 475

Aviation, 533–38

Avukah (Torch) Society, 76, 85

Bailey, John, 594, 614–16, 623, 625–626

Baldwin, Raymond, 625

Ball, George, 669

Bankhead, Tallulah, 476

Bardot, Brigitte, 352, 354

Barnett, Ross, 655

Barrett, Colonel David D., 246, 248, 251, 264 and n., 267 n., 270, 271

Barrett, Donald, 623

Baton Rouge, La., racial violence in, 658

Baxter, James Phinney, III, 68

Bay of Pigs disaster, 638, 644

BBC (British Broadcasting Corporation), 357

Bean, Nancy. *See* White, Nancy Bean

Beaverbrook, William Maxwell Aiken, Lord, 382

Beck, Dave, 523

Belair, Felix, 530

Belden, Jack, 342–43

Belgium, 401; and European unity movement, 439; and Marshall Plan aid, 396

Bennahum, Midge, 353

Bennahum, Theo. 353, 463, 542

Benton, William, 552, 625, 626

Berle, Adolph, 518

Berlin, 409, 412, 418–19, 444; airlift, 292, 408, 412, 446; blockade, 409, 412, 418, 442, 446, 449; crisis of 1960, 644, 1953 uprising in East Berlin, 469, 528; USIA library in, book purge, 465, 468

Bertaux, Pierre, 686

Bessie, Simon Michael ("Mike"), 466, 490–91

"Bestsellerdom," 334, 478

Bevin, Ernest, 381, 449

Bible, the, 38–40

Bidault, Georges, 431
Biddle, General Anthony J. D., Jr. ("Tony"), 491
Bienstock, N. S., 473–74
Birch, John, 314
Birmingham, Ala., civil rights demonstrations in, 655–56
Birth control, 543
Birth rate, 622–23
Bismarck, Fürst Otto von, 425
Bissell, General (Stilwell staff), 184–185
Bissell, Richard, 374–75
Blacklisting, 340, 342–43, 463–65, 504
Blacks, 29–30, 46, 331, 333, 360, 486, 527, 590, 654–61; in armed forces, 478, 501–03, 660–61; in Boston of 1976, 694–96; in Congress, 333–34, 622; discrimination against, 478–79, 612, 650, 654–61; in New York City, 475, 479–80, 597; northward migration of, 533, 540, 663; race demonstrations, 611–12, 655–59; vote of, 531, 540–541, 660–61, 662; vote in 1960, 611, 613, 633
Bojessen, Chris, 88–89
Bok, Edward, 547
Bond, William Langhorne, 104
Bonn, Germany, 407, 408, 410–17, 424
Book-of-the-Month Club, 328, 334, 469
Book reviews, 334–36, 473–74, 584
Borodin, Mikhail, 210
Boston, Mass., 173, 692; ethnic groups of, 28–30, 46–48; Irish of, 28–30, 46–48, 492, 618–19; Jewry, 27–30, 42–49; Kennedy's 1960 campaign visit to, 617–20; in 1976, 692–96; political machines, 331, 492–93; public schools, 49–55; shoe industry, 56; South Boston, 692, 696; Yankees, 48
Boston *American*, 21
Boston *Globe*, 79, 86, 87, 89, 116
Boston *Herald Traveler*, 597
Boston Public Latin School, 53–55, 57, 68
Bowles, Chester, 625–26
Boylston Hall, Harvard, 68–69
Bradford, William, 50, 52, 295
Bradlee, Benjamin, 605, 636, 638
Bradley, General Omar, 180, 186, 189
"Brain remolding," as term for "consciousness raising," 256
Brewster, Kingman, 374
Bridge Too Far, A (Ryan), 524
Brinkley, David, 657 *n.*
Brinkmanship, in U.S. foreign policy, 528
Brinton Crane, 71, 85
British Army of the Rhine, 487
British Broadcasting Corporation (BBC), 357
British Commonwealth, 380, 389
British Empire, 85–86, 357, 380; and world trade, 377–79
British journalism, 356–57

British Labour Party, 390–91, 414, 442
British Navy, 149, 377
Broadcasting, 578–80; news delivery, network vs. independent station, 378–80. *See also* Radio; Television
Brown, Earl, 478
Brown, Edmund ("Pat"), 624
Brownell, Herbert, 454
Brown v. Board of Education of Topeka (1954), 486, 487
Bruce, David, 372–73, 375, 439, 445, 448, 465, 507, 686
Bryan, William Jennings, 631
Bryce, James, Lord, 142
Buchan, John, Baron Tweedsmuir, 77
Buchwald, Art, 352
Buck, Paul, 71
Buck, Pearl, 335
Buckley, Thomas, 619
Buckley, William F., Jr., 512
Buddhism, 40
Buffalo, N.Y., 622
Bundy, McGeorge, 668, 669, 688
Bureaucracy, 526–28
Burgess, Thornton, 30
Burke, James A., 597
Burkley, Rear Admiral George C., 677
Burma: campaign of World War II, 186, 223, 224; independence, 380; Japanese occupation, 177–78, 181, 189–90
Burma Road, 498, 501; reopening of, 294
Burroughs Newsboys Foundation, 61, 84
Bus boycott, Montgomery, Ala., 655
Bush, Vannevar, 374

Caesar, Julius, 55, 423, 438, 546, 621
California: in 1948 election, 540; in 1960 election, 614, 632–33, 634; state politics, 492–93, 624
Callender, Harold, 433
Cambridge, Md., race riots in, 658
Cameron, Simon, 607–08
Cannibalism in Honan famine of 1943, 198–99, 206
Canton, China, 98, 250; 1927 insurrection, 162
Capitalism, 52, 57; demise in Britain, 378–79
Carter, Jimmy, 331, 621, 639, 645, 687, 691, 696, 697; mentioned, 337, 590–91
Casablanca Conference of 1943, 529
Castries, General Christian de, 486
Catholic Church, traditional social role of, 626–27
Catholics, 614–15, 622–27, 628–29; candidates and officeholders, 601–602, 604–05, 621–25; census figures on, 622–23; in Congress, 622, 623–624; vote of, 615–16, 622–24, 632–633
Catroux, Diomede, 358
Catton, Bruce, 487–88

CBS (Columbia Broadcasting System), 169, 433, 476, 477, 504, 524, 569, 580, 581, 606, 633, 657 n.

Century Club, New York, 586

Chafee, John, 624 n.

Chambers, Whittaker, 276, 278, 280

Chang Fa-kuei, General, 212, 223

Chang Hsueh-liang, Marshal, 212

Chang Tso-lin (Manchurian warlord), 136, 136 n.

Chang Tsung-chang (Chinese warlord), 136 n.

Charlottesville, Va., racial violence in, 658

Ch'en Chia-k'ang (ambassador), 163, 245, 270, 509

Chengchow, China, 196, 197 n., 199, 204

Chengtu, China, 218; U.S. air base at, 289–90

Ch'en I, General, 242

Chennault, General Claire, 15, 104, 184, 185–92, 210, 221, 222, 223, 229, 286–87, 289; feud with Stilwell, 184–92, 221, 223; proponent of air power, 186; 187–89, 228–29

Ch'en Yun, 249

Chiang Chien-tsai, Dr., 280

Chiang Ch'ing (wife of Mao Tsetung), 260–61, 596 n.

Chiang K'ai-shek, 129, 208–14, 220–237, 248, 250, 251, 260, 336, 342, 528; American advisors of, 102–05; assessment of, 208, 213–14; background of, 102, 152, 209; characterization of, 208–09, 212–13, 259; China Lobby of, 489; and Chou En-lai, 158, 164, 212; and Communist Chinese, 150–52, 166; and Communist insurrection, 307–309; Communists perceived as his real enemies, 184–85, 223, 232, 234, 236–37, 258; his demands for U.S. war aid, 180–81, 183–85, 190, 222, 228–29, 399; detained at Sian in 1936, 134–35, 164, 212; "fascism" of, 336; and foreigners, 209–210, 211; and Honan famine, 204–208, 213; and Hurley's Nationalist-Communist truce mission, 267, 270–71, 279, 312–15; incompetence of, 137–38, 166, 180, 185, 192–93, 208, 213, 215–16, 221–22, 228; and Japanese surrender, 307–09; Luce's and *Time*'s support of, 271–73, 274–76, and n., 275–76, 278–79, 317; in New Fourth Army Incident, 154, 155–58, 252 "off with his head" ("ch-iang pi") attitude toward enemies, 211–13, 229; "one China" maxim of, 314; personal budget of, 218; political convictions and goals of, 209–10; pro-airwar, with Chennault, 188–89, 190, 210, 229; quoted, on the Communists, 156–57; quoted, on the Japanese, 157; recognition by Stalin's Russia, 314; reduction to figurehead threatened, 223–27, 232, 262; relationship with Stilwell, 183, 184–85, 190, 222, 223–27, 228–37, 240, 241, 501; Roosevelt's repudiation of, in Stilwell affair, 223–26, 227, 229, 240–41, 242; Roosevelt's reversal on, in Stilwell affair, 235–236; Stilwell quoted on, 180, 208, 210–11, 225–27, 233–35, 236–37; U.S. support of, in 1945, 315–18; mentioned, 89–90, 136, 162, 169–170, 289

Chiang K'ai shek, Mme. (Mei-ling Soong), 102, 109, 184, 205, 210, 212, 216

Ch'iao Kuan-hua (foreign minister), 163, 509

Chicago, Ill., 47, 333, 377, 549, 648 n.; black vote, 540; ethnic groups, 27, 29–30, 622; in 1960 election, 636; political machines, 331; racial strife, 658

Child, Julia, 466

China, 32; breakup of Nationalist-Communist alliance against Japan, 158–59. 185, 221, 252, 258–59; civil war anticipated, 234, 240. 241–42, 266, 276, 277–78; civil war between Communists and Nationalists, 162, 306–18, 323–24, 403; concepts of one vs. two Chinas, 313–14; defense of her freedom as a factor contributing to World War II in Pacific, 221–22, 315; foreigners in, 85–86, 209; foreigners seen as "barbarians," 209; historiography of, 255–56; "loss of, to the Reds," 266, 335–36, 500–01, 503, 508, 610; Mandate of Heaven, 214; myth of Dr. Fu Manchu, 75, 336; a nation of villages and peasantry, 119–23, 132–33; 1939 population of, 133; *pao-chia* system of government, 104; paper currencies, 214–15, 252; Quemoy and Matsu controversy, 610; racial consciousness and pride in, 208–09; roads of, 121–22; time-keeping in, 121, 131; warlords, 98, 136 and n., 151–53, 156, 214, 313. *See also* China, Nationalist Republic of; China, People's Republic of; Communists, Chinese; Nationalists, Chinese.

China, Nationalist Republic of: American advisory system, 103–06, 181, 209–10; American influences in, 101–04; American pressure for rapprochement with Communists, 231–33, 258, 262, 266–71, 278–79, 312; American relations with, 169–170, 181, 183–85, 190, 214, 217, 220–26, 242, 252, 258, 312–16; budgets of, 216–17; collapse of economy of, 190–91, 215–21; conscription system of, 166, 213; corruption in, 185, 203, 218–19, 221–222; government of, 89–90, 98–99, 101–04, 114–15, 137, 185, 192–93, 200–01, 203, 233; government deterioration, 214–23; Honan famine of 1943, 193–208; inflation, 215–20; Japanese attack on, 76, 87, 89–90, 98–99, 106–07, 111–15, 120, 122–138, 151–53, 155, 158, 184–85, 193–194, 204, 214, 250–51, 258, 294–95,

575; Japanese ICHIGO offensive (1944) and collapse of East China front, 211, 221–23, 228–29, 234, 248, 295, 574–75. Japanese surrender in, 306–10; "liberated areas" of Communists in, 248, 250–51, 258, 267, 306–08, 316; monetary policy, 104–05, 213–18; National Military Council, 267–68, 279; New Fourth Army Incident, 150–58; paper currency, 104, 190, 200, 214–15, 216–19; railroad seizures by Red Army, 307–08, 316, 403–404; Stilwell's role in, 179–85, 221–26; taxation, 200–02; tax revolts, 219; treaty with Soviet Union, of 1945, 313–14; U.S. air bases in, 187–88, 191, 220–23, 287, 289–91; war reporting from, 107–111. *See also* Chiang K'ai-shek; Nationalists, Chinese

China, People's Republic of, 118–19, 162, 240, 501, Cultural Revolution, 256, 261; invasion of Korea, 394, 514; leadership of, 245; Nixon's visit to, 168–69; relations with U.S., 164, 514–15, 647–48; relations with U.S.S.R., 164. *See also* Chou En-lai; Communists, Chinese; Mao Tse-tung

China Information Committee, 91, 106–11, 117

China Lobby, of Chiang K'ai-shek, 489

Chinese language, 118–19, 126 *n.*

Chinese Nationalist Army, 129–30, 135, 153, 155, 209, 228–29, 232, 242, 248, 251, 258; airlifted into Communist-controlled regions by U.S., 315–16, 318–19; corruption in, 185, 203; reopening of Burma Road by, 294–95; Stilwell's mission, 181–84, 185, 188, 222–23, 224–27, 293; tax collection in grain, 200–01; used against Communists rather than against Japanese, by Chiang, 154, 156, 184–85, 222–23, 258

Chinese press, 107, 360

Chinese Red Army, 241, 244, 245, 248, 250–51, 267; orders to, after Japanese surrender, 306–07; 312; vs. Soviet Army, in Manchuria and near Mongolia, 313. *See also* New Fourth Army.

Chinese studies, at Harvard, 69–70, 72, 75–76

Chin Tso-jen (chief of conscription), 231

Chou Chih-jou, General, 183

Chou En-lai, 17, 159–69, 180, 220, 241, 245–47, 249, 509, 686; background and career of, 162–65; character and personality of, 159–162, 164–66; and Chiang K'ai-shek, 158, 164, 212; host to Nixon, 168–169; and Mao Tse-tung, 164–65; 256–57; Monnet compared with, 435–36; in negotiations with Hurley and Chiang, 264, 269–71, 278, 312; and New Fourth Army Incident, 154, 157–58; quoted, on

Chiang K'ai-shek, 158; and U.S., 164, 649

Christianity, 40, 43, 252

Chungking, China, 90–106, 150, 156–57, 205, 223, 230–31, 296, 304–05, 317, 501; Communist HQ at, 153–155, 160–63, 221, 306; Communist-Nationalist truce negotiations of 1944 at, 270–71, 278–79; Communist-Nationalist truce negotiations of 1945 at, 312, 314–15; description of, 95–99; 100–01; government of, 98–103, 115, 138; Japanese air raids on, 106, 111–15; after Japanese surrender, 307–08; population of, 99; talks on New Fourth Army withdrawal in, 153–155, 158–59

Chungtiao Mountains, Shansi, China, 126

Church and State, 626–31

Churchill, Sir Winston, 182, 224, 381, 382, 390, 397, 435, 453, 529, 608, 638

Chu Teh, General, 242, 244–45, 246, 249, 264, 306, 313, 509; General Orders No. 1 to 7, August 1945, 307, 312

Cities, U.S.: black migration to, 539–40, 663; black vote in, 539–540; ethnic "ballet" in, 29, 479–80, 622; racial confrontations in, 479–481, 486, 540–41, 658, 663–64; urban problems, 479–81, 691–96

Civil rights, 478–79, 610–13, 620; movement, 655–61

Civil Rights Act of 1957, 631, 660

Civil Rights Act of 1964 (Civil Rights Bill of 1963), 541, 613, 651, 654, 655–56, 659–63

Civil Rights Commission, 531

Civil War, American, 547, 654

Civil War, Chinese, between Nationalists and Communists, 162, 306–317, 323–24, 403; anticipated, 234–235, 240–42, 266, 277–78

Clark, Blair, 466, 579–81, 606–08

Clark-Kerr, Sir Archibald (later Lord Inverchapel), 141–42

Clay, Henry, 52, 637

Clay, General Lucius D., 186, 400–401, 409–10, 411–13, 418, 424, 448, 507

Clemenceau, Georges, 437

Clifford, Clark, 638, 643

Code-cracking, 105 and *n.*

Cohn, Roy, 465, 468

Cold War, 348, 352–53, 394–95, 443–444

Collected Works of Mao Tse-tung, 246

Collier, Peter Fenelon, 520–21, 547

Collier's magazine, 505, 508, 519–24, 532–33, 537–38, 539, 544–45, 547, 548–65, 567–69, 570–72, 582, 589, 595–96

Collingwood, Charles, 343

Colorado, in 1960 election, 603

Columbia Broadcasting System (CBS), 169, 433, 476, 477, 504, 524, 569, 580–81, 606, 633, 657 *n.*

Columnists, 571–73

Index

Common Market (European Economic Community), 68, 367, 439

Communism, 441–45; damage of McCarthyism to U.S. ability to handle, 513–16; as global threat, 424–426, 440–45, 513; and Lebanon crisis of 1958, 528; parties of the West, 347–49, 443–44 (*see also* Communists, in America; Communists, of Europe); threat to Western Europe, 361, 364–65, 392–395, 422, 426, 445, 446

Communists, Chinese, 123, 150–69, 231, 240–61, 278, 443–44, 509; alliance with Nationalists ended, 158–60, 185, 220–21, 252, 258; American pressure for rapprochement with Nationalists, 231–33, 258, 262, 266–71, 277–79, 312–13; American relations with, in 1944–45, 231–32, 233, 240–42, 248, 251–52, 258, 312–16, 448; America seen as potential ally by, 232–33, 241–42; call for insurrection in August 1945, 307, 312; Chungking HQ of, 154–55, 160–63, 220, 306; control of "liberated areas" behind Japanese lines by, 232–33, 248, 250–51, 258, 267, 279, 306–308, 316; founders' meeting of 1921, 162; guerrilla warfare of, 132, 151–52, 251, 316; hatred of walls, 133; Hundred Regiments Offensive of 1940, 251; intellectuals attracted to, 219–20, 250; and Japanese surrender, 306–07, 308–310; leadership of, 159–60, 162–63, 241–42, 244–46, 248–49, 253–61; New Fourth Army, 152–55, 250, 312; New Fourth Army massacre, 150, 155–58, 252; 1927 uprising, 162–63; partisan warfare of, 250–251, 259–60; Politburo, 248–49, 253–54; popular support for, 204, 248; relations with Soviet Union, 164, 209, 257, 277, 314, 316; and religion, 160; revolution of, 240, 242, 260–61, 271, 272, 278, 307, 323, 342, 403, 685; revolutionary order of insurrection of August 1945, 307–08, 311; seen as real enemy by Chiang K'ai-shek, 184–185, 232, 232, 234, 236–37, 258; Seventh Party Congress (1944), 242, 248; in Shansi province, 122, 127, 129–35, 138, 151, 231, 306; Stilwell's contacts with, 223, 230–232, 237; Yenan HQ of, 156, 158, 168, 220, 231, 232, 237, 243, 248, 252–53, 307. *See also* China, People's Republic of; Chinese Red Army; Chou En-lai; Mao Tse-tung

Communists, in America, 443–44; Communist party outlawed, 487, 515; at Harvard, 65–66; and Henry Wallace, 337–38

Communists, of Europe, 348, 443; Eastern Europe, 314, 443; French, 347–49, 431, 432, 438–39, 441–45, 509; German, 413–14, 418–19, 422–423; Italian, 443; Russian, 160, 257 (*see also* Soviet Union); as thugs, 443–44

Comptoir des Produits Sidérurgiques, 398

Compton, Karl, 296

Conant, James Bryant, 62–53, 65, 69, 79, 374, 508

Confucius, 260, 275 *n.*

Congressional elections: of 1946, 333; of 1952, oil money in, 492–494; of 1954, 487; of 1960, 647

Connally, John, 676

Connecticut: Bailey-Bowles political rivalry, 625–26; Catholic stronghold, 616, 623–24, 632–33; Democratic voting coalition of 1960, 615–16; in 1960 election, 616, 625–626, 633; 1960 Kennedy visit to, 615–17

Connor, Eugene ("Bull"), 657 and *n.*, 658

"Conquistador" (MacLeish), 14

"Consciousness raising," origin of term, 256

Conservatives, American, 68–69; damage of McCarthyism to, 487, 512–13

Contract Air Mail Routes (CAMs), 535

Cook County, Ill., in 1960 election, 635–36

Cooper, Gary, 586–88

Council of Economic Advisers (U.S.), 644

"Counterattack," 517

Courtades, Pierre, 509

Crimson (of Harvard University), 64, 66, 102

Cripps, Sir Stafford, 382, 389–90

Crowell-Collier Corporation, 522, 549, 568
   See also Collier's magazine

Crump, Boss of McGinn County, Tenn., 330–31

Cullen, Hugh Roy, 493

Cultural Revolution, China, 256, 261

Curley, James ("Big Jim"), 47–48, 57, 619

Cushing, Richard Cardinal, 671

Czechoslovakia, Communist takeover of, 442

Dakin, Roger, 521

Daley, Richard J., 615, 635–36

Danielli, Dr., 196

Davenport, Colonel (Speaker of Connecticut legislature in 1780), 637

Davies, John Paton, Jr., 241–242, 244, 245, 247–48, 251, 263–64 and *n.*, 271; charges of subversion against, 496–98, 499–503, 506–11, 515–16

Davis, Richard Harding, 559

Dawson, William, 333, 590

De Gaulle, Charles, 17, 182, 428, 435

"Delegate broker," term, 436

Democratic Party (U.S.), 492, 525, 541, 620; basic social philosophy, 626; claims of achievements, 650–52; of Connecticut, 615–16, 625–26; fiscal philosophy, 652–53; National, 492–94, 625; 1952 National Convention of, 596; 1956 National Convention of, 549, 596; in 1960 election, 615, 620, 633, 647–48; 1960 Presidential hopefuls, 589; 1964 National Convention of, 657 *n*

Demographic changes of 1880–1960, effect on politics, 621–624

De Murville, Couve, 410

Depression of 1930's, 20–22, 33, 55

Detroit, Mich., 27; racial strife in, 658

Dever, Paul A., 597

Dewey, Thomas E., 454, 457

Diem, Ngo Dinh, assassination of, 665, 688

Dienbienphu, French surrender at, 486, 487, 528

Dirksen, Everett, 668

DiSalle, Michael J., 624

Dixie Mission, in Yenan, China, 231, 241, 244, 264, 268

Dixie Mission (Barrett), 264 *n.*, 267 *n.*

Dollar, U.S. vs. Chinese dollar, rates of exchange, 216–217; devaluation of, 369; dominance of, 367–69; vs. pound sterling, 383–85

Domei (Japanese news agency), 271, 277

Donahue, Richard, 634, 636, 637, 648*n.*

Donald, W. H., 210

Donzerre-Mondragon power project, France, 392

Dorn, Brigadier General Frank, 299

Douglas, Paul, 597

Doyle, Sir Arthur Conan, 628

Dragon by the Tail (Davies), 241, 264*n.*

Driscoll, John, 618

Duclos, Jacques, 509

Dudley, Hall, Harvard, 66, 79

Duff, (Senator James Henderson), 457

Duhig, Charles, 65–66, 79

Duke, Angier Biddle, 668

Dulles, Allen, 638

Dulles, John Foster, 164, 434, 449, 510, 516, 528

Dumbastapur, India, U.S. air base, 292

Dungan, Ralph, 668

Duranty, Walter, 174

Durdin, F. Tillman, 109

Eakin, Jane, 466

East Indies, Dutch, 355; Japanese thrust into, 146, 178; U.S. air strikes on, in World War II, 290

Economic Cooperation Administration (ECA), 369

Economic Planning, 396, 437–38, 653–54

Eden, Sir Anthony, 382, 427, 450

Education, 589, 590, 651–52. See also Hebrew education

Education (Adams), 559

Education of a Poker Player, The (Yardley), 105 *n.*

Edward VII, King of England, 608, 665

Egypt, 163, 380, 383

Eisenhower, Dwight D., 186, 449, 453–61, 524–33, 589–90, 632–33, 644; characterization of, 453, 457–458; domestic and legislative record of, 460, 530–32, 541, 645, 649, 650–52, 660–61; federalist philosophy of, 459–60; federal troops sent to Little Rock, 460, 527, 659; foreign policy record of, 528, 530; and Goldwater's 1964 candidacy), 529–31, 537; NATO Commander, 446, 453, 458, 461; 1952 Presidential candidate, 454–60; 1956 Presidential candidate, 550, 557, 587–88; political naïveté of, 528–29; as President, 469, 491, 524–33, 541, 649–50, 660–61; quoted, on Roosevelt 528–29; mentioned, 180, 437, 465, 467–68, 486, 497, 507, 590–91, 597.

Elections, 587–88, 593–94, 595; corruptive practices, 330, 492–94, 634–635; effect of McCarthyism on, 511–12; ethnic vote, 47–48, 630; issue of religion in, 601–02, 605, 611, 616, 623–34, 638–41, 646–47; voter turnout, 631–32. See also Congressional elections; Presidential elections

Eliot, Charles William, 62

Eliot, T. S., 214

Elisaeff, Professor, 74

El Paso Company, 353

Emerson, Ralph Waldo, 30, 626

Engels, Friedrich, 255

England. See Great Britain.

Equal Employment Opportunity Commission, 662

Equal opportunity, jurisprudence of, 660, 661–663

Equal Opportunity in Housing, President's Commitee on, 650

Equal protection under the law doctrine, 662

Erhard, Ludwig, 425

Ervin-Watergate hearings (1973), 558

Establishment, the, shifts in, 369, 372–78, 375

Ethnic groups, 608–09, 621–23; in American cities, 28–30, 46, 479–80, 622–23; voting, 47, 630

Europe, 344–45, 366, 388–89, 401, 403–06, 447–48, 467–69; Americanization of, 360, 394; Communist threat to, 361, 363–64, 365, 392, 393–95, 422, 426, 445, 446; defense of, against U.S.S.R., 445–48, 454, 590; Eastern Communist parties of, 314, 443; economic history of, 71–73; formal peace displaced by unity movement, 426, 439, 441; Jewry of, 41–42; Marshall Plan for, 343, 344, 347, 349, 360, 361–362, 365–77, 391–401, 445; Marshall Plan benefits, 392–94, 399; postwar bankruptcy of, 362–65; postwar industrial revival, 393–94; steel production, 398, 421–22, 439; unity movement, 67–68, 373–74, 404–05, 421, 427–29, 435, 438–41;

Europe (*cont.*)
  U.S.-Soviet confrontation in, 445–447, 469, 590; Western Communist parties of, 348, 441–45; World War II in, 143, 184, 222, 229, 234, 284–85, 315
European Coal and Steel Community, 439, 440, 445
European Defense Community, 426, 433, 440–41, 451
European Economic Community. *See* Common Market
European Recovery Program (ERP), 363, 369. *See also* Marshall Plan
Ezekiel, Mordecai, 18

Fairbank, John King, 72–76, 78–80, 609
Fairbank, Wilma, 72
Falkenhausen, General Ludwig von, 210
Fascism, 76, 89, 170; of Chiang, 336
FBI (Federal Bureau of Investigation), 336, 369
Federal aid: non-discrimination requirement, 662; Eisenhower and, 459–60
Feng Yu-hsiang, General, 136 and *n.*
Figaro, Le, 359
Fire in the Ashes (White), 72, 469, 473, 476, 485, 506
Fischer, Heta, 419
Fitzgerald, F. Scott, 284, 372
Fitzgerald, John F. ("Honey Fitz"), 601, 619, 622
Flickinger, Lieutenant Colonel Donald D., 292–93
Flying Tigers (U.S. China Air Task Force), 185, 186–90
Foreign aid, U.S., 399, economic, to postwar Europe, 361, 363–65, 392–394, 398 (*see also* Marshall Plan); military, to Vietnam, 399, 486, 688; war, Chiang K'ai-shek's demands for, 180–81, 182–83, 190, 221–22, 228–29, 399
Foreign policy, U.S.: brinkmanship, 528; China policy, 221–22, 242, 315–16, 336, 341, 510–11, 514–16, 528; China's defense by U.S. as invitataion to Pearl Harbor, 221–222, 315; China's "loss to the Reds," 266, 335, 501, 503, 508, 610; Chinese Communists, U.S. relations with, in 1944-45, 231–33, 240–41, 242, 248, 251–52, 258, 312–316, 442; Chinese Nationalists, U.S. relations with, 169–70, 181, 182–85, 190, 214, 217, 220–37, 242, 252, 258, 312–16; Chinese Nationalists and Communists pressed for rapprochement by U.S. (Hurley negotiations), 230–33, 258, 261–62, 265–71, 278–79, 312; Chinese events of 1944-1945 misread by U.S., 272; Communist People's Republic of China and U.S., 164, 515, 647–49; dilemma of Japanese surrender to Chiang's vs. Mao's troops, 309–10, 312–13; effect of McCarthyism on, 514–16; under

Eisenhower, 528, 530–31; European defense against Soviet Union, 424–427, 444–48, 454; and European unity movement, 406, 440; under Kennedy, 644–45; lack of occupation policy for Germany, 399–400, 409–10; relations with Britain, 423–24, 442; relations with Britain in world trade arena, 376–86, 389–90, 391; relations with France, 348–50, 359–60, 392–93, 424, 427–429, 432–35, 450–52; relations with postwar Germany, 398–402, 407–419, 423–28; in Vietnam, 191, 399, 434, 451–52, 514, 515, 688–90 (*see also* Vietnam, South; Vietnam War)
Foreign Relations of the United States, China (State Department papers), 267 *n.*
Forman, Harrison, 193
Formosa, 212; U.S. air raids on, in World War II, 287–88
Forrestal, James V., 262
Fortune magazine, 115, 169, 172, 569–70
France, 401, 427–32; colonies of, 451–52; Communists in, 347–49, 431, 432, 438–39, 441–45, 509; and European unity movement, 404–05, 427, 435, 438; Fourth Republic of, 348, 431–32, 434; government crises and changes, 429–32. Monnet Plan for postwar reconstruction, 436 437–39; in 1948-1949, 347–51, 358–360; 1950 Marshall Plan benefits, 392–94, 397–99; and postwar Germany, 408–11, 414–15, 425, 426, 433–34, 439, 451; steel production and cartels, 397–99; U.S. relations with, 349–50, 360, 423–24, 427–29, 432–35, 451–52; war in Vietnam, 428, 434, 445, 451, 452, 486, 528 (*see also* French Indo-China); World War II Resistance, 359, 360
Fraternelli, Father, 196
Freedom Buses, 655
Free-lance reporting, 461–62
French Indo-China, 143–46, 427, 435, 452. *See also* France, war in Vietnam
French National Assembly, 429–30, 433, 451
French press, 355, 358–60, 430
French Revolution, 215, 252, 260, 545; Terror, 357, 685
French Union, 451
Friedman, Francis, 494
Fritchie, Clayton, 465
Fukien province, China, bubonic plague in, 231
Fuller, Miss (teacher), 49–52, 55, 295
Fu Manchu, Dr., myth, 75, 336

Gallup polls, 1960, 633
Gates, Thomas, 643, 644
Gavin, General James M., 186
General Electric Company, 353, 475, 542, 580
General Union of Red Workers (China), 312

Geneva Conference of 1954, 164, 434 486

Georgia, civil rights struggle in, 610–12

German-Americans, 30, 622

German Federal Republic, 416–19, 424; Allied High Commissioners of, 418, 424, 426; Allied occupation statute, 426; Basis Law of, 410, 414–18; "Contractual Arrangements" with Western Allies, 426–27; economic "miracle" of, 401, 424, 425; and European unity movement, 404–05, 421, 438–39; genesis of, 410–19; postwar economic beneficiary of U.S. aid, 386, 401; rearmament of, 425–26; relations with France, 426, 433–34, 438–39, 451; role of political parties in, 416; as U.S. ally, 424–27; vote of no confidence device in lower house, 416–17. *See also* Germany

Germany, 405–08, 508; Allied occupation policy, 363–64, 390, 399–402, 411–14; Communists of, 414, 419, 422; demilitarization of, 425; dismantling of Ruhr industries, 421–23; East-West split, 410; Nazi, 378, 406, 414, 417, 422–23; 1945 surrender of, 301; people of, 418–424; postwar conditions in, 363–66, 400–01, 426; Soviet threat to, 444–447; U.S.-Soviet cold war confrontation in, 469 (*see also* Berlin blockade); Weimar Republic of, 215, 416; Western, economic reconstruction of, 386, 400–01, 424; Western, occupation statute, 426; Western, political reconstruction of, 408–18 (*see also* German Federal Republic); World War II Allied advance against, 222, 234–235

Gilbert, Lieutenant, 502–03

Goddard, Robert Hutchings, 18

Goldberg, Arthur, 648 *n.*, 668

Gold standard, 377–78

Goldwater, Barry, 37, 291, 512, 530, 621, 666

Good Earth, The (Buck), 335

Goodman, George, 522, 523

Goodwin, Richard, 599

Gore, Albert, 596

Gouverner, C'est Choisir (Mendès-France), 434

Government: bureaucracy, 526–28; federalism vs. centralism, 459–60; financing of, 215–16, 651–54; managerial, 524–27; "no confidence" vote provisions in Europe, 416–17, 430; Pharaonic/static, vs. dynamics of free trading world, 395; Protestant vs. Catholic ethic and tradition in, 626–27; protective role as basic justification for, 121, 133–34, 137, 196

Government regulation, 537

Governors, U.S., Catholics as, 602–603, 624

Graves, Ralph, 680

Great Britain, 405, 423–24; capitalist-socialist schizophrenia of, 379–83; and European unity movement, 438–39; fails to fit into Marshall Plan, 376–86, 391; Labour government and policy, 376, 379–83, 385, 387–89, 390–91, 438–39, 442; postwar course of, compared to that of West Germany, 399–401, 423–24; and postwar Germany, 390, 408–09, 410–11, 414–16, 424–25, 426; postwar problems of, 364, 376, 380–86 (*see also* Pound sterling); views of Soviet Union, in 1949; 390–91; views of the U.S., in 1949, 382–85, 389–91; World War II, 184, 222, 315

Greater Houston Ministerial Association, 629

Greeley, Horace, 476

Gross national product (GNP), U.S., 542

Grover, Preston, 433, 455, 456, 457

Gruenther, Alfred, 507

Grymes, Muriel, 586–88

Guerrilla warfare, of Chinese Communists, 132, 151–52, 251, 316

Gunther, John, 174

Hachette, 359

Haiphong, Vietnam, World War II bombing of, 285

Haldeman, H. R. ("Bob"), 17

Hall-Patch, Sir Edmund, 382–84, 433

Halsey, Admiral William F., 298

Han Fu-chu, General, 157

Hanoi, Vietnam, 90, 144–46; World War II bombing of, 285–86

Harlem, N.Y., 30, 478, 480

Harper's Magazine, 331

Harriman, E. H., 375

Harriman, Marie Whitney, 370–71, 397

Harriman, W. Averell, 370–72, 375, 397, 445, 448, 668, 670–71, 686; Marshall Plan administrator, 369–73, 397–99, 401, 445; as Presidential candidate, 589–90, 596

Harvard Club of China, 102

Harvard University, 22, 28, 53, 54, 58, 61–79, 368, 609, 645; Chinese studies at, 68–69, 70, 72–73, 74–76; History Department, 66–68, 70–71; Oriental Department, 74; ROTC at, 76–77; student body division into white men, gray men, and meatballs, 63–65; tutorial system, 73

Harvard Graduate School of Business Administration, 62

Harvard-Yenching Institute, 68–69, 75, 78

Hawaii, in 1960 election, 634

Health services, U.S. policy, 651

Hebrew College of Boston, 38

Hebrew education, 37–41, 42–43, 49

Hemingway, Ernest, 487, 506, 559, 584

Herald Tribune (Paris), 352

Heroes, role of, in history, 590, 678, 686, 687–88

Hersey, John, 116, 139, 326, 583, 595

Herzl, Theodor, 41

Heusinger, Adolf, 424
Hidden Persuaders, The (Packard), 523
Highway lobby, 538–39
Hill, Clinton, 676
Hill, Colonel David ("Tex"), 288
Hiroshima, Japan, 305, 421
Hiroshima (Hersey), 326
Hirsh, Diana, 522
Historiography, 71, 228; Chinese, 255–56; vs. journalism, 14–15, 22, 110, 116, 228, 317–19, 323–24, 404–05
History, 514–15, 678–79; American, nature of, 70–72, 683–84; definitions of, 405, 490, 585, 590; at Harvard University, 66–68, 70–71; Jewish, 40–43; role of accident in, 261, 687–90; role of heroes in, 590, 678, 686, 687–89
Hitler, Adolf, 41, 48, 76, 408, 412, 415, 420–23, 425, 438
Hobart, Alice Tisdale, 335
Hobson, Thayer, 469
Hodges, General Courtney Hicks, 301
Hoffa, James, 523
Hoffman, Paul Gray, 369–70, 371–74, 401, 435, 448, 454, 686
Hofstadter, Richard, 511
Hollywood, Calif., 27, 543, 552, 577, 584, 586
Holocaust, the, 40, 406, 408
Home relief, Great Depression, 57–58
Honan famine of 1943, 193–204, 271, 274; causes of, 200; Chiang K'ai-shek and, 204–08, 213; death toll of, 201–03
Honan province, China, 192; Japanese occupation of, 204, 220–21
Hong Kong, 90–91, 150, 172; World War II bombing of, 285–86
Hoover, Herbert, 148, 262, 521–22, 615–16, 632
Hoover, J. Edgar, 638
House Judiciary Committee, 64, 65
House Rules Committee, 647
House Un-American Activities Committee, 512
Housing, U.S. programs, 650
Houston, Texas, Kennedy campaign statement on religion in, 629–30
Ho Ying-chin (minister of war), 166, 236
Hsueh Yueh, General, 229, 231
Huang Hua (foreign minister), 266, 509
Huilungshan, Mount, battle at, 294
Humble Oil & Refining Company, 493
Hump, the, airlift over, 189–90, 222, 291–93, 538
Humphrey, Hubert H., 247, 369, 647, 668; 1960 Presidential candidate, 589, 600–01, 603–05, 628
Hundred Regiments Offensive of 1940, China, 251
Hungarian uprising of 1956, 528
Hunt, George, 665–66
Huntley, Chet, 657 *n.*

Hurley, Major-General Patrick J., 223, 225, 231, 261–62; career of, 262; China negotiations of, 261–271, 279, 312
Hydrogen bomb, 487, 495–96
Hynes, John Bernard, 597

ICHIGO offensive, 1944, 221, 575
Ideas, 17–20, 41–43; brokerage of, 435–37; carried by the young, 127, 137; clad in slogans, 254; use by Chinese Communists, 252, 255, 259
ILA (International Longshoremen's Association), 444
Illinois: in 1948 election, 540; in 1960 election, 613–14, 634, 635–36; politics, 492, 636
Immigrants, 47–48, 51–52, 622
Immigration Act of 1924, 51, 389
Imperialism, Western, 86–87; British Labourites and, 380–81, 391
India: August 1942 uprising in, 178–79; economic dependence on Britain, 380, 383, 390; independence, 380; Japanese World War II threat to, 178
Indian Congress Party, 178
Indo-China: French in, 143–46; Japanese expansionary thrust in, 143, 144–45
Indonesia, Japanese expansionary thrust in, 143–46
Inflation, 215, 653; in China, 214–15, 216–21
Inner Mongolia, Japanese surrender in, 310
Intelligence services, U.S., 105, 638, 687
International Longshoremen's Association (ILA), 444
Investment incentives, 653–54
Iowa, U.S.S., 301
Irish-Americans, 30, 59, 608, 622; of Boston, 28–29, 46–49, 492, 619, 622–23; of New York City, 47, 474–75
Islam, 40
Israel, 85, 163
Italian-Americans, 30, 622; of Boston, 28, 46; of New York City, 475
Italy: Communists of, 443; and European unity movement, 438–39; exchange of pounds for dollars, 1949, 385; Marshall Plan aid to, 385, 392

Ives, Burl, 354
Jackson, Henry, 696
Jacksonville, Fla., race demonstrations in, 658
Jacoby, Annalee, 230, 279–80, 318, 324, 334, 340, 503
Jacoby, Melville, 230
Japan, 274, 294–95; air war against, in World War II, 187–91, 220–21, 222–23, 286–94, 296, 300, 304; Americanization of, 305; attack on Pearl Harbor, 174–75, 315; Burma occupied by, 178, 181, 189; China war, 76, 87, 89–90, 98–99, 106–07, 111–15, 120, 122–38, 150–53, 155–

56, 158–59, 185, 194, 204, 214, 250–51, 258, 293–95, 575; ICHIGO offensive of, and collapse of East China front (1944), 211–12, 220–223, 228–29, 234–35, 248, 295, 574, 575; industrial revival of, 401, 435; MacArthur's legacy in, 146–49; occupation of, 296–300, 399–400; postwar economic beneficiary of U.S., 386, 401; postwar reconstruction of, 386, 400–01; prewar expansionary thrust of, 143, 148; surrender of, 296–97, 301–04, 404; surrender of troops in China, 306–310; threat to India, 177–79; tonnage losses from Chennault's Flying Tigers, 191–92; U.S. World War II strategies against, 183–85, 187–89, 190, 252

Japanese air force, 287, 288–89, 291

Japanese army, 124–26; MacArthur on, 147

Japanese navy, 252; MacArthur on, 147, 149–50

Javits, Jacob, 333

Jefferson, Thomas, 512, 637, 686

Jenks, Homer, 522

Jet airplanes, 533–39

Jewish history, 40–42

Jewry, 608–09; in American cities, 27–30; Americanization of, 36, 42–43; of Boston, 27–30, 42–47, 49; members of Congress, 624; of New York City, 28, 42, 475; Orthodox, 36, 42–43; Orthodox education, 37–43, 49; in Palestine of 1938, 84–86; sects, 42–43; as voting bloc, 47. *See also* Zionism

JILEK (Soviet Organization), 506

John Birch Society, 314

Johnson, Howard, 45

Johnson, Lyndon B., 36, 262, 591, 597, 647; 1960 Presidential candidate, 588–89, 604–05; 1960 Vice Presidential candidate, 608–09; 632–33; as President, 652, 669–70, 679, 688–90; and Vietnam, 688–90, 691

Jones, Ray, 597

Journalism, 174, 265–66, 310, 461–464, 571–74, 583–84; and blacklisting, 339–40, 342–44, 462–65, 504–05; British, 356–57; columnists, 571–73; European *feuilleton*, 571; foreign correspondents, 432–433; freelance reporting, 461–63; vs. historiography, 14–15, 22, 110, 116, 228, 317–19, 323–24, 404–05; "inner few" device of, 432–34, 435, 455–58; liberal, 336–37, 344, 488–89, 517; magazine, 338–39, 488–89, 531, 547, 559–60; magazine vs. daily, 116, 547–48; military and defense correspondents, 445–446; misuse of editorial power, 271–72; muckraking, 547; narrative reporting, 559–60; political, 524–525, 533, 585; war propaganda from Chungking, 107–11; war reporting, 192–93, 228, 284–85, 444–446

Judaism, 40. *See also* Jewry

K'ang-Ta University, Yenan, China, 255

Kansu province, China, tax revolt of 1943 in, 219

Kao Tzu-li, 252

Kapital, Das (Marx), 255

Katz, Milton, 372–75, 397–98, 401, 445

Kefauver, Estes, 331, 596

Kefauver-Mafia hearings (1951), 558

Kelly Act (1925), 535

Kennedy, Caroline, 679

Kennedy, Edward M., 642

Kennedy, Ethel S., 643

Kennedy, Jacqueline Bouvier, 596 *n.*, 668, 670, 671–80, 683–84

Kennedy, John F., 159, 163, 523, 589–590, 593, 594, 641–63, 687, 688–90, 698–99; assassination of, 486, 665–671, 675–77, 680–81, 687; assessment of, 611–14, 655–57, 659–661; "Camelot" epitaph, 672, 678–81; domestic and legislative record of, 645–63; foreign policy record of, 644–45, 648–49, 688–90; gamesman's view of politics, 595–96, 597–605, 610–11; impact on politics, 590–91, 593–95, 638–39; inaugural of, 639, 642–43 and *n.*; knowledge and love of history, 607–09, 636–38, 678; 1946 entry into politics, 333; 1952 Senatorial race, 455; 1960 Presidential candidate, 588–91, 599–624, 627–37, 639, 646–47; and 1960 religious issue, 601–03, 604–05, 611, 615–16, 621–624, 626–27, 628–34, 638–39; 1960 runningmate's choice, 608–09; personality and style of, 593–94, 596, 598–600, 613–14; political philosophy of, 593–99, 627–28; as President, 590–91, 638–42, 644–63, 690; relationship with Congress, 645–648, 649, 651–52; and Vietnam, 688–90; and women, 687; mentioned, 15, 17, 36, 102

Kennedy, Joseph P., Jr., 593, 595

Kennedy, Joseph P., Sr., 595, 603, 609

Kennedy, Robert F., 523, 603, 634, 642–43 and *n.*, 669, 678, 679, 689; Attorney General, 643, 656–57, 659–60

Kenny, General George Churchill, 301

KFI Radio (Los Angeles), 580

Khrushchev, Nikita, 663

King, Coretta, 612

King, John 64

King, Martin Luther, Jr., 450, 610–613, 655–58

King, Martin Luther, Sr., 611

Kinsey, Alfred, 543, 554

Kissinger, Henry, 168

Kleiman, Robert, 433

Knox, Frank, 262

Koo, Wellington (ambassador), 102

Korea, 148–49; invasion of 1950, 391, 393–94, 442, 445

Korean War, 240, 245, 398, 403, 435, 441–42, 452, 514, 521, 531; effect

Korean War (*cont.*)
on European events, 424–26, 435, 440, 444
Korn, Jerry, 522
Krueger, General Walter, 301
Krupp, Friedrich Alfred, 456
Krupp steel works, 421–22
Ku Klux Klan, 628
Kung, H. H. (finance minister), 102, 166, 170, 216–17
Kung, Mme. (Ai-ling Soong), 216
Kung P'eng, Mme. (asst. foreign minister), 163, 165
Kunming, China, U.S. air base at, 187, 286, 287
Kuomintang, 258, 268, 271, 274. *See also* Nationalists, Chinese
Kweilin, China, U.S. air base at, 223, 229, 287

Labes, Emmanuel, 85
Lampoon (of Harvard University), 64
Langer, Rudolph Ernest, 374
Lanham, General C. T., 447, 455
Laos, 648
Laski, Harold, 389–91
Lattimore, Owen, 609
Lawford, Patricia Kennedy, 674
Law of Unintended Consequences, 399–402, 408
Lawrence, David, 602
Lawrence, William, 605
Lazar, Irving, 586
Lebanon crisis of 1958, 528
Left-Wing Communism, an Infantile Disorder (Lenin), 255
LeMay, General Curtis E., 191
Lenin, Vladimir Ilyich, 209, 255, 257
Levy, Raoul, 352, 354
Leyte Gulf, battle of, 251
Liberalism, 68, 337, 395, 480, 512, 594–95, 683–86
Liberal journalism, 335–37, 343–44, 488, 517
Liberal Party, of New York, 642
Li Chi-sen, General, 212
Life magazine, 115, 169, 271, 280, 304, 326, 478, 519, 524, 548, 553, 558, 564, 569–70, 589, 601, 663–66; "Camelot" story on Kennedy, 672–675, 678–80; "*Life* Looks at China" article, 275; "Press the War in Vietnam" article, 665; "Racial Collision in the Big Cities" article, 663–64
Li Fu-ying, General, 157
Lincoln, Abraham, 52, 302–03, 607, 631, 637–38, 657, 671, 686, 690
Lingling, China, U.S. air base at, 287
Lin Piao, General, 162, 164, 220, 242, 245, 256, 313, 403
Lippmann, Walter, 476, 571–72
Li Shou-wei, General, 153, 154, 157
Litchfield, Edward H., 412, 413
Literary Guild, 586
Little Rock, Ark., 459, 527, 530
Liu Shao-ch'i (Chinese Communist Party leader), 242, 249, 254
Lloyd George, David, 437

Lodge, Henry Cabot, Jr., 454, 617, 619, 688
Loeb, William, 616
Lomasney, Martin, 47
London, Irving, 466
London, 85, 386–87, 393, 482; world trade and banking center, 377–78
London *Times*, 193
Longest Day, The (Ryan), 524
Longfellow, Henry Wadsworth, 30, 49
Long March, of Mao Tse-tung, 74–75, 132, 163, 245
Look magazine, 519, 548, 558, 559
Lorimer, George Horace, 547
Los Angeles, 377; Boyle Heights, 30; Kennedy's 1960 campaign appearances in, 599, 607, 619
Lovett, Robert A., 262, 446, 458
Lowell, Abbott Lawrence, 62
Lowell, Amy, 30
Lowell, James Russell, 49
Loyalty-security charges, 497–98, 499–506, 508, 514–16
Luce, Clare Boothe, 170, 174, 278, 484
Luce, Henry R., 115, 149, 169–74, 205, 280, 325–28, 337, 338, 359, 476, 490, 518, 569–70; as a Christian, 171, 273–74, 275–77, and *n.*; in Chungking, 169–72; as an editor, 173–74, 273–74; misuse of editorial power by, 271–77; as a patriot, 170–72; support for Chiang K'ai-shek, 271–79, 317, 319; and Vietnam, 665
Luce, Henry Winters, 171, 174
Lucy, Autherine, 655
Ludden, Raymond, 515
Ludendorff, Field Marshal Erich, 223
Lumumba, Patrice, 648
Lunch-counter sit-ins, 611–12, 655

Maas, Peter, 523
McArdle, Kenneth, 522, 533, 539, 549, 563
MacArthur, General Arthur, 149
MacArthur, General Douglas, 143, 146–49, 171, 178, 184, 245, 287, 295, 305, 317, 401; and Japanese surrender, 296–98, 300–03, 404; General Order No. 1 on Japanese surrender, 308–10; lack of understanding of American politics, 146–150; as Presidential candidate, 455; return to Philippines, 222, 251–52; mentioned, 180
McCarthy, Eugene, 580
McCarthy, Joseph, 274, 333, 452, 462, 465, 487, 489, 491–92, 496–97, 512–16, 524–25, 528, 595; Senate censure of, 487, 509; Senate Committee hearings, 558
McCarthyism, 335, 339, 462, 500, 504, 512–13, 514–16
McCloy, John, 507
McCone, John A., 688
McCormack, John, 597, 618–19
McDaniel, Joseph, 374
McGovern, George, 337, 621
McGrory, Mary, 628
McKinley, William, 147–48, 302

McLaughlin, Edward, 618
McMinn County, Tenn., 1946 local election in, 330–31
McNally, James B., 340
McNamara, Robert, 17, 510, 643, 644, 648 n., 669, 688
Madison, James, 269, 637
Magazine journalism, 116, 338, 488–89, 519–24, 547, 559–60
Magazines: circulation and the "Audience Game," 550–55, 557, 560; edged out by TV, 553–62; "liberal," 488, 519–21; life cycle of, 545; mass, national, 490, 519–21, 544–55, 556–64; vs. newspapers, 116, 545–48; newsstand vs. subscription sales, 553–55; quarterlies of nineteenth century, 558
Maine, in 1960 election, 616, 633
Making of the President 1960, The (White), 606
"Making of the President" Series, 577, 588–89, 696–98
Malaya, 146; Japanese expansionary thrust into, 143; postwar trade, 383, 389
Manchester Guardian, 116
Manchuria, 135, 151; Chiang K'ai-shek's concessions to Stalin in, 314; Chinese Red Army in, under Lin Piao, 245–46, 307, 314–15, 403; Japanese surrender in, 310; Soviet Army in, 308, 313–14; U.S. airlift of Chiang's troops into, 316; U.S. air strikes in, 290
Maness, David, 522, 680
Mann, Horace, 49
Manning, Gordon, 522
Mansfield, Mike, 262–63, 668, 689
Mao Pang-chu, General, 183
Mao Tse-tung, 74, 131, 162, 220, 232, 237, 241–42, 249, 254, 256–61, 403, 648; character and personality of, 256–59; choice forced on, of Russian over American connection, 313–16; and Chou En-lai, 164–65, 257; doctrine of revolution of, 260–61, 270–71; "enemies of the people" term, 259; family losses of, 257; godhood of, 256, and Japanese surrender, 306, 307, 309; his knowledge and reading disorganized, 257, 259–60; knowledge and understanding of his people, 260–61; and Korean War, 514; in negotiations with Hurley and Chiang K'ai-shek, 260, 264–67, 269–71, 312–15; 1944 interview with, 258–61, 266; and Nixon's visit, 164–65; order of insurrection of August 1945 by, 307–08, 312; "the people are the sea" phrase of, 132; Stalin and, 314; statement after New Fourth Army massacre, 155–56, 252; as a teacher, 209, 247, 256–57, 259; wife of, 260, 595 and 596 n.; mentioned, 17, 103, 336, 509
Marie, André, 428
Markel, Lester, 462
Marketing, scientific, 552–56

Marshall, General George Catlett, 180, 190, 222, 233, 375, 401; and Chiang K'ai-shek vs. Stilwell episode, 222–24; genesis of his foreign aid plan, 365, 368–69, 394–95; and MacArthur, 149; ranking of World War II priorities by, 184–85. *See also* Marshall Plan
Marshall Plan, 15, 68, 72, 343, 344, 347, 349, 360, 361–62, 365–77, 391–402, 404, 405, 422, 445; administrators, 369–75, 396; assessment of, 393–402; benefits, 392–94, 399; Britain's failure to fit into, 376–86, 391–92; counterpart funds, 367–68, 396; goal and doctrine of, 378, 381; mechanics and management of, 366–68, 396; motives for, 362–65, 394–95; Paris headquarters of, 356, 366, 370, 373–75; press policy of, 396–98; production stressed over social benefits, 380, 391, 393–94, 396, 399
Martin, "Pepper," 304
Martin, Robert, 108, 113
Marx, Karl, 43, 255, 469, 685–86
Marxism, 43, 685–86
Mason, George, 269
Mason, Colonel Gerry, 292
Massachusetts, 48, 643; Catholic stronghold, 618, 623–24, 633; in 1960 election, 619, 635; 1976 primary, 692, 696–97; politics, 492, 597
Massachusetts Institute of Technology (MIT), 28, 645
Massie, Robert, 523
Mass media. *See* Media, Mass
Mayer, René, 431
Ma, Yin-ch'u, Professor, 212
Mayne, Wiley, 64–65
Mazanowski, Ray, 288
Media, mass, 513–14, 544–64; political coverage, 544–45, 548, 558, 604–06. *See also* Magazines; Newspapers; Press; Radio; Television
Medicare program, 651
Megan, Bishop Thomas, 195–96, 207
Memphis, Tenn., racial violence in, 658
Mendès-France, Pierre, 434
Merriman, Roger Bigelow ("Frisky"), 66–68
Meyer, Eugene, 368
Meyner, Robert, 606–07
Michigan, state politics, 492
Middle East, 163, 380, 386; oil resources, 385–86
Military, the, relationship with civilian sector, in democracy, 447, 456. *See also* War, role of politics in
Mill, John Stuart, 512
Minnesota, 1952 primary, 455, 457
Minorities, U.S. proctection of, 663
Missile crisis of 1962, 645, 663
"Missile gap," 1960 campaign issue, 610
Missile program, U.S., 590, 610, 650
Mississippi, civil rights struggle in, 655, 657–58
Missouri, U.S.S., 301–04, 403

Missouri, in 1960 election, 613–14, 634

Mitchell, General William ("Billy"), 18, 186

Moch, Jules, 431

Money Game, The (Smith), 522

Mongol Dynasty, 215

Mongolia: Inner, Japanese surrender in, 310; Soviet-Red Chinese hostilities near, 314

Mongolian Communist army, 307

Monnet, Jean, 17, 68, 369, 373, 425, 435–41, 445, 448, 449, 686; Plans of, 435–39

Monnet, Sylvia, 437

Monnet Plans, 436–39

Montgomery, Field Marshall Bernard, 189, 222

Montgomery, Ala., bus boycott, 655

Morrill, Justin, 68

Morton, Thruston, 333

Moscow Conference of Foreign Ministers, 1947, 365, 394

Mountain Road, The (White), 575–77, 582

Muckraking, 546–47

Mueller, Kurt, 419

Multinational companies, 353–54, 482, 542

Munich Crisis of 1938, 84–85

Munsey, Frank, 547

Murrow, Edward R., 343, 476–78, 569–70

Mydans, Carl, 328

NAACP (National Association for the Advancement of Colored People), 611

Nader, Ralph, 523

Nan Han-ch'en, 252

Napoleon Bonaparte, 428, 438–39, 544

Nation, The, 488

National Academy of Sciences, 686

National Association for the Advancement of Colored People (NAACP), 611

National Association of Manufacturers, 52

National Broadcasting Company (NBC), 169, 433, 657 *n.*

National Highway Act of 1956, 539, 650

National Intelligence Agency, 105

Nationalists, Chinese (Kuomintang), 123, 150–60, 258, 268–69, 271, 274–275, 277–78; breakup of alliance with Communists, 158–59, 184–85, 220–21, 252, 258; Communists seen as real enemies of, by Chiang K'ai shek, 184–85, 223, 232, 234, 237, 258; defeat by Communists, 403; and Japanese surrender, 308–09, 310; New Fourth Army withdrawal agreement, 153–54, 158; New Fourth Army massacre by, 150, 155–59; in Shansi province, 122–23, 127, 129, 133–35, 231. *See also* Chiang K'ai shek; China, Nationalist Republic of; Chinese Nationalist Army

National Oceanic and Atmospheric Agency, 464

National Relief Commission, China, 109

NATO (North Atlantic Treaty Organization), 444–47, 453–54, 458, 461, 469

Nazism, 378, 406, 414, 418, 422; guarding against revival of, 408, 409–10, 412, 418–19

NBC (National Broadcasting Company), 169, 433, 657 *n.*

Nehru, Jawaharlal, 170, 178

Nelson, Donald, 223

Netherlands, the; and European unity movement, 439; Marshall Plan aid to, 392

Networks, national boardcasting, 579–581

Neustadt, Richard, 638

New Deal, 77, 645, 650

New Fourth Army, Red Chinese, 150, 152–59, 250, 312; massacre of, 150, 155–59, 252–53

New Hampshire: 1952 primary, 455, 457; in 1960 election, 616

New Republic, 336–38, 339, 488–89, 550, 564

Newspapers: vs. magazines, 116, 545–546, 547–48; vs. TV, 558

Newsweek magazine, 304, 433, 605

New York City, 173, 318, 323–24, 333–34, 473–75, 490–91, 517–19; banking and big business, 482, 484; blacks in, 478–80, 601; book reviewing in, 334–36, 473–74; crime, 480–81; cultural life, 482–83; Harlem, 30, 478, 480; Irish role in government, 47, 622; Jewry of, 27–28, 42; Manhattan East Side vs. West Side, 479–81, 484–85; of 1950s, 474–76, 481–85; "perfumed stockade," 484; political machines, 331, 476; population, 475; prosperity of 1950s, 482–85; Puerto Ricans in, 475, 480; racial strife, 481, 658; reform movement vs. Tammany Hall, 587; South Bronx, 480, 541, 695; Upper East Side, 484–85; Upper West Side, 479–80; "white flight," 480

New Yorker, The, 326, 595

New York *Herald Tribune,* 571

New York State: Catholic vote, 624, 632–33; in 1960 election, 631–33, 642–43; politics, 492–93

New York Times, The, 108, 233, 236, 354, 433, 462, 465, 473, 478, 529, 605–06

New York Times Magazine, The, 463, 589

Nhu, Ngo Dinh, assassination of, 665, 688

Nicholas, Ashley J., 506–08, 509

Nicholas and Alexandra (Massie), 523

Nieh Jung-chen, 242

Ningsia Province, China, tax revolt, 219

Nixon, Patricia, 168–69

Nixon, Richard M., 64, 65, 88, 487,

512, 523, 666; in China, 168–69, 246; 1946 entry into politics, 333; 1960 Presidential candidate, 587–589, 599, 605, 610, 613, 620, 627, 633, 635–36, 647; 1972 election, 552; as President, 650, 691; rapprochement with China, 164; as Vice President, 528; mentioned, 17, 491

Noce, Lieutenant General Daniel, 500

Normandy, D-day beaches of, 349

North Atlantic Treaty Organization (NATO), 444–47, 453–54, 458, 461, 469

North Korea: invasion of South Korea by, 394 (*see also* Korean War); Japanese surrender in, 310

Northwest Airlines, 536

Nuremberg trials, 456

O'Brien, Lawrence, 603, 634, 637, 643 *n.*, 647–48 *n.*, 669

O'Connor, Thomas, 618

OCTAGON Conference, Quebec, of 1944, 224

O'Donnell, Kenneth, 602–04, 607, 634, 637, 642–43, 649, 669, 677; on Kennedy's intentions in Vietnam, 689

OEEC (Organization for European Economic Cooperation), 366–67, 382

Ohio: in 1948 election, 540; in 1960 election, 624

Oil companies, 539; and national politics, 492; in Texas politics, 493

Oil for the Lamps of China (Hobart), 335

Okinawa, 296, 297

Old, Don, 291

Ole Miss (University of Mississippi), integration of, 655, 659

Olmsted, Brigadier General George, 315

Omaha Beach, 350

Operation Gymnast, 180

Opium, 97, 99, 146

Oppenheimer, J. Robert, 374, 493–96, 497, 504, 510–11, 520, 645

Organization for European Economic Cooperation (OEEC), 366–67, 382

Overseas News Agency, 343, 350, 461–62, 518, 565

Pabsch, Anton F., 413, 414

Pacific, World War II in, 184, 191, 222, 252, 281, 284–304, 315

Packard, Vance, 523

Palestine, in 1938, 85

Pan American Airways, 535

Panmunjon, truce negotiations at, 515

Pao-chia system, China, 103

Paper currencies, 214–15, 252

Paris, 85, 343, 347–53, 354–59, 393–394, 418, 427, 482; European Defense Community contract signed (1952), 426–27; museums, 355–56; 1944 liberation of, 374–75; U.S. press corps, 432–33, 455

Paris Herald Tribune, 352

Paris-Soir, 359

Partisan warfare, doctrine of, 250, 260

Partisans of Peace, 442

Passman, Otto, 333

Passport limitations legislation, 504–508

Patterson, William A., 525

Patton, General George, 180, 186, 189, 222, 460

Peace movement, 442

Peace treaties, 404, 426, 438, 441; European unity movement as substitute for, 426, 438–39, 441; strong defense as substitute for, 444–48

Peale, Norman Vincent, 628

Pearl Harbor, Japanese attack on, 174–75, 315, 665

Peking, China, 87, 98, 152, 403; destruction of walls of, 133; Nixon's visit to, 168–69, 246

Pell, Claiborne, 624 *n.*

P'eng Chen (Chinese Communist leader, later Mayor of Peking), 255–56

P'eng Te-huai, General, 242, 245, 249, 514

Pennsylvania, in 1960 election, 602–603

Perry, Dr. Malcolm, 677

Perry, Commodore Matthew C., 301

Pershing, General John J., 375

Person-to-Person (TV show), 476–77

Philadelphia, 47, 331, 648 *n.*; in 1928 election, 646; in 1960 election, 633, 647; racial strife in, 658

Philippines, 146, 222, 251–52, 295; army of, 147; Japanese thrust into, 143–44

Picasso, Pablo, 442

Pinay, Antoine, 431

Planning, 396, 437–38. *See also* Economic planning

Plessy v. *Ferguson* (1896), 655, 660

Pleven, René, 431, 433

Plimmer, Dennis, 387

Po Ku, 249

Poland, 222, 315, 405–06

Political journalism, 524–25, 533, 585

Politics, 17, 125–26, 137–38, 585, 589, 641–42, 698–99; "cluster" theory of, 522; demographic-ethnic transformation of 1880-1960, 621–24; effect of McCarthyism on, 511–15; electoral, 493, 638 (*see also* Elections); ethnic groups in, 47–48, 631; of institutions, 494–98; issue of religion in, 601–02, 605, 611, 616, 622–34, 638–41, 646–47; Kennedy's impact on, 590–91, 593–95, 638–39; Kennedy's gamesman's view of, 594–96, 597–99, 600–05, 611; local machines, 330–31; and mass media, 544, 548, 538, 605–06; money and, 490; North vs. South, 331; role in war, 148, 154, 181–182, 183–85, 235–36; source of power in, 411, 452, 698–99

Polo, Marco, 94, 215

Polybius, 621

Potsdam Proclamation, 307

Pound sterling, 378, 380, 383–86; crisis of 1931, 384; devaluation crisis of 1949, 381, 385, 386; vs. dollar, 383–85
Powell, Adam Clayton, 333
"Power broker," origin of term, 436
Powers, David, 669, 674, 677
Prescott, Orville, 473
Presidency, 587–88, 599–600, 619–20, 691; abuses of power of, 687, 691; vs. Congress, 645–47, 649, 691
Presidential campaigns, 532, 691; financing of, 603; primaries, 601–02
Presidential elections: of 1908, 632; of 1924, 632; of 1928, 615–16, 622, 632; of 1932, 47; of 1936, 47; of 1940, 548; of 1948, 540; of 1952, 453–55, 456–60; of 1956, 549, 557, 587, 596, 632; of 1960, 587–91, 598–607, 610–21, 623–24, 626, 627–636, 639, 647; of 1964, 529–30, 621, 666; of 1968, 621, 635; of 1972, 552, 621; of 1976, 14, 19, 331, 390, 621, 635, 692, 697
Press: British, 356–57; Chinese, 107, 360; conferences, 432; French, 355, 358–60, 430; Kennedy and, 604–06; power of, 272. *See also* Journalism; Newspapers
Price, Ray, 523
Profiles in Courage (Kennedy), 607
Progressive Party, U.S., of 1948, 338
Prohibition, 30–31
Protestant ethic, 626, 627–28, 631
Protestants: in Congress, 624–25; and Kennedy, 627–29, 633–34, 636–37; split on role of government caused by Roosevelt's approach, 626–27, 629, 633
"Protestants and Other Americans United for Separation of Church and State," 628
Protestant vs. Catholic issue, in politics, 601–02, 604–05, 611, 622–634, 638–39
Public housing, in U.S., 650
Public opinion, mass manipulation of, 552–53
Publishing, blacklisting in, 340, 342–343, 463–65, 504–05
Puerto Ricans, in New York City, 475, 480

Quebec Conference of 1944, 224
Quemoy and Matsu, islands of, 610
Queuille, Henri, 431
Quezon, Manuel, 147

Rachlis, Eugene, 523
Racial discrimination, 478–79, 612, 650, 654–61
Racial strife, 479–81, 486, 540–41, 611–12, 655–60, 663–64
Radford, Admiral Arthur William, 528
Radio, 548, 558; news delivery, network vs. independent stations, 579–582
Railroads, U.S., 534, 538
Ramadier, Paul, 428
Rayburn, Sam, 591
Reader's Digest, 274, 490, 519, 553

Reagan, Ronald, 512
Reconstruction Finance Corporation, 368–69
Reed, John, 243
Religion, 39–40; Chinese vs. Soviet Communist stance toward, 159–60; role in elections and office-holding, 601–02, 605, 611, 616, 622–34, 638–639, 642, 647
Reporter, The, 462, 488–90, 493, 496, 505, 519–20, 524, 533, 564, 570, 589
Reporting. *See* Journalism
Reportorial novel, 573–74, 581, 584
Republican Party (U.S.), 487, 492, 525, 620; claims of achievements, 650–51; damage of McCarthyism to, 514; fiscal philosophy of, 652–653; loss of control of Congress, 487; 1940 Presidential nominee, 548; in 1946 elections, 333; in 1960 elections, 620, 633; 1960 Presidential hopefuls, 589; 1964 Presidential choice, 529–30, 666; opposition to Nixon in, 587; philosophy of federalism, 459–60
Reserve Officers' Training Corps (ROTC), at Harvard, 76–77
Reuss, Henry, 374
Reuter Agency, 108–09
Revolutions: genesis of, 126–38, 219–220; Mao's doctrine of, 259–61, 271; role of intellectuals in, 249–250
Reynaud, Paul, 433
"Rhapsody on a Windy Night" (Eliot), 214
Rhode Island: Catholic stronghold, 617, 623, and *n.*, 632; in 1960 election, 633
Ribicoff, Abraham, 615, 616, 626
Ridgway, General Matthew, 444, 491–92, 507, 516
Rifkin, Dr. Harold, 673
Roche, Charles, 606
Rockefeller, Nelson A., 397; 1960 Presidential candidate, 589; 1964 Presidential candidate, 666
Rodino, Peter, 333
Roman Catholic Church, traditional social role of, 626–27
Rome, Republic of, 621
Rommel, Field Marshal Erwin, 178
Romney, George, 337, 687
Roosevelt, Franklin D., 21–22, 47, 48, 57, 262–63, 269, 285, 289, 375, 456, 521, 548, 686; assessment as President, 671–72; basic social philosophy of, 626–28; and China, 182, 184, 223, 240, 264; and Chiang-Stilwell deadlock, 223–26, 227, 229, 231–33, 235–36; comparisons with Kennedy, 639, 641, 645, 665–66, 671–72; Eisenhower on, 528–30; and Henry Wallace, 337–38; and highway system, 527, 650; MacArthur's opinion of, 149; in Stilwell-Chennault feud, 190; mentioned, 37, 76–77
Roosevelt, Franklin D., Jr., 63, 604, 668, 674

Roosevelt, Theodore, 525, 547, 608, 687
Rose, Alex, 642–43 and *n.*
Rosellini, Albert, 602, 624
Rosenberg, Anna, 483
Rosenzweig, Sammy, 45
ROTC (Reserve Officers' Training Corps), at Harvard, 76–77
Rousseau, Jean-Jacques, 512
Ruhr district, Germany, 420, 421–23, 439, 645
Ruppel, Lou, 521
Rusk, Dean, 688
Russia. *See* Soviet Union
Russian-Jewish immigrants, 33, 34
Ryan, Cornelius, 343, 523, 559

Sacco, Nicola, 32
Sacramento, Calif., racial strife in, 658
Saigon, South Vietnam, U.S. advisers, 435
Salinger, Pierre, 523, 591, 606, 689
San Francisco *Chronicle*, 522
Saturday Evening Post, 336, 519, 548, 553–54
Saturday Review, 473
Saunders, Brigadier General Laverne G. ("Blondie"), 290
Scherman, Harry, 334
Schine, David, 465, 468
Schlesinger, Arthur M., Jr., 64–65, 374, 594, 597, 668
Schlesinger, Arthur M., Sr., 71
Schlieker, Willi, 420 and *n.*, 508
Schmid, Carlo, 415
Schneider, Sasha, 354, 466
Schoenbrun, David, 433
School integration, 486, 487, 527, 655–56, 658–61
Schumacher, Kurt, 414, 427
Schuman, Robert, 428, 431, 439, 449
Schuman Plan, 439
Science and the Modern World (Whitehead), 74
Scientific Establishment, 494–95
Scranton, William, 530
Secret Service, 636, 672, 676
Security, national. *See* Loyalty-security charges
Seeckt, General Hans von, 210
See It Now (TV show), 477
Selective Service Act of 1948, 661
"Separate but equal" doctrine, 654, 660–61
Service, John Stewart, 515
Sevareid, Eric, 87, 343
Sexual Behavior in the Human Female (Kinsey Report), 543, 554
Shanghai, China, 152, 159, 377, 403; Chinese Communist founders' meeting at, 162; international settlement in, 87, 311; Japanese air raids on, 113–14; Japanese occupation of, 98, 311; Japanese surrender at, 305–06, 309–12; 1927 uprising, 163; in 1939, 87–90; in 1972, 88
Shansi province, China, 246; campaign in, 117, 122–37, 138, 151–52, 193, 231, 307
Shaw, Irwin, 352

Shaw, Marian, 352
Sheldon (Frederick) Traveling Fellowship, 78, 84
Sheng Shih-tsai (Chinese warlord), 165
Shepley, James, 666
Shigemitsu, Mamoru, 302, 303
Shih Yu-san, General, 157
Shinchiku, Formosa, Japanese air base, 287–88
Shriver, Sargent, 612
Shute, Benjamin, 497, 500, 503
Sian Incident of 1936, 135, 164
Simons, Hans, 412, 413
Sinclair, Upton, 547
Singapore, 86, 177–78
Sino-Soviet Treaty of 1945, 314
Six-Day War of 1967, 41
Sloane, William, 334, 590
Smathers, George, 333
Smith, Adam (*pseudonym* of George Goodman), 522
Smith, Alfred E., 616, 623, 632, 646
Smith, C. R., 536–38
Smith, Howard, 647
Smith, Paul, 521–22, 549, 551, 568
Snow, Edgar, 79, 87, 316
Socialism, in Britain, 378–81, 387–88, 390–91, 438, 442
Socialism, Utopian and Scientific (Engels), 255
Sokolovsky, General Vassily D., 409, 412
Solzhenitsyn, Alexander, 578
Soong, T. V. (prime minister), 102, 184, 235, 437
Soong sisters, 210, 216. *See also* Chiang K'ai-shek, Mme.; Kung, Mme.; Sun Yatsen, Mme.
Sorensen, Theodore, 599, 623, 668, 689
South Dakota, U.S.S., 301
Southeast Asia, 142–48; Japanese thrust into, 142–43, 148
Southern Christian Leadership Conference, 611
Southern Pacific Railroad, 493
Soviet Red Army: clash with Chinese Red Army near Mongolia, 314; in Europe, 400, 443–44, 445–48, 469; move into Manchuria, 307–08, 313–314
Soviet Union, 160, 378, 404–05, 408–409, 441–42, 590; British views of, in 1949, 390–91; Communist Chinese relations with, 164, 209, 257, 277, 312, 316; invasion of Korea, 394, 426, 441–42; in possession of atom bomb, 444–45; and postwar Germany, 409–10, 412, 414–15, 417–419, 426, 446, 469; Treaty with Chiang's China, 1945, 314; Western Europe threatened by, 365, 395, 446
Spaatz, General Carl, 301
Space program, U.S., 650, 651–52
Spanish-American War, 62
Spanish Civil War, 76, 80, 90
Spalding, Charles ("Chuck"), 673
Speer, Albert, 430
Speidel, Hans, 424
Sprouse, Philip Dodson, 515

Stalin, Joseph, 182, 257, 276 n., 348, 378, 426; and Mao, 314; recognition of Chiang K'ai-shek by, 314; Western Europe coveted by, 365, 395

Stanford, Alfred, 579, 581

Stassen, Harold, 454

Steffens, Lincoln, 547

Stern, Isaac, 354

Stevens, Thaddeus, 607

Stevenson, Adlai E., 594, 608, 647; 1956 Presidential candidate, 550, 557, 587–88, 596; 1960 Presidential candidate, 587–88, 597, 604

Stillness at Appomattox (Catton), 487

Stilwell, General Joseph Warren, 15, 149, 159, 177, 179–85, 205, 221–37, 239, 240–42, 289, 293–94, 301, 501, 686; assessment of, 234–37; background and career of, 180–81, 233, 235–36; character and personality of, 185, 186, 187, 234; Commander-in-Chief to-be of Chinese ground forces, 223–26, 232–35, 262; contacts with Chinese Communists, 223, 231–32, 236–37; death of, 339; dismissal of, 233–36; dismissal episode distorted in *Time* magazine, 271–72, 274, 276–77; and Dixie Mission in Yenan, 231–32; feud with Chennault, 185–92, 220–21, 223 229; proponent of ground support in China, 186, 189, 190–92, 221, 229; quoted, on Chiang K'ai-shek, 180, 208, 210–11, 225–27, 233–34, 237; relationship with Chiang K'ai-shek, 182, 184–85, 221–22, 223–27, 228–37, 501; violation of oath of secrecy, 233

Stilwell, Mrs. Joseph W., 226, 339

Stilwell Papers, The (White, ed.), 339

Stimson, Henry L., 105 n., 262, 375

Stock market, in 1950s, 542–43

Storm Decade, the, 692, 699

Strauss, Edward, 522, 523

Suburbia, 527, 539, 554–57

Subversion charges, 497–98, 499–506, 508, 514–15

Suez Crisis of 1956, 381, 528, 531

Sullivan, Ed, 332

Sun Fo, Dr., 102

Sung dynasty, 215

Sun Yat-sen, 210

Sun Yat-sen, Mme., (Ching-ling Soong), 206

Supermarket culture, 555–57

Symington, Stuart, 589, 608

Szechwan province, China, 94–95, 98, 137–38

Taft, Robert A., 455, 503

Taft, William Howard, 632

Ta Kung Pao (newspaper), 218

Talleyrand-Périgord, Charles Maurice de, 356

Tang En-po, General, 197–98, 203

Tax Reform Act of 1964, 652–54

Taylor, General Maxwell, 688–89

Teamsters Union (U.S.), 444, 524

Technology of 1950s, 543

Television, 475–78, 543–44, 548–49, 553, 555, 556–60; advertising, 556–557, 562; campaign coverage, 601, 605; coverage of civil rights strife, 656–58, 661; coverage of Kennedy assassination and funeral, 671; news, 558, 569–70, 578–80, 657 n.

Teller, Edward, 495

Teng, Fa, 249, 254

Test-ban Treaty of 1963, 645

Texas: in 1960 election, 633, 634; state politics, 493

Third World, alliance against Israel, 163

Thomas, J. Parnell, 512

Thompson, Edward K., 665, 672

Thoreau, Henry David, 637

Thorez, Maurice, 500

Thunder Out of China (White and Jacoby), 334–36, 339, 343, 461, 465, 503, 507

Time Incorporated, 364, 433, 663, 666

Time magazine, 109, 115–17, 139, 140, 143, 150, 160, 166, 170, 173–174, 186, 205, 230, 236, 271, 278, 279, 281, 304, 306, 310, 317, 319, 324, 325–28, 337, 338, 461, 503, 524, 548, 564, 569–70, 589, 605–06; Chiang K'ai-shek legitimized by, 272, 276, 278, 317; cover portrait, 172, 490; Stilwell episode distorted in, 270–72, 276–78

Tito (Josip Broz), 182, 363

Tobin, James, 644

Todros, Reb, 33

Tokyo, Japan, 298, 304, 422

Tokyo Bay, 296, 297–98, 301

Town Hall of the Air (TV show), 475

Trade. *See* World trade

Trahison des clercs, le, 219

Translations, inadequacy of, 268

Travelers Insurance Company, 580

Trezevant, Richard, 522

Trippe, Juan, 535

Truckers' lobby, 538, 539

Truman, Harry S., 148, 337, 338, 390, 452–53, 458, 513, 686–87; domestic programs under, 527, 649, 650–51, 661; election victory of 1948, 540

Tsai, Huang-Hua ("Golden Flowers"), 109

Tung Pi-wu (Chinese Communist founding father), 162

Tunisia, 452

Turner, Nat, 655

Tushan, China, munitions depot at, 228, 575, 576

TV Guide, 553

Two Tactics (Lenin), 255

Udall, Morris, 695–96

Ulbricht, Walter, 415

Umezu, Yoshijiro, 302–03

Unintended Consequences, Law of, 399–402, 663

Union of Soviet Socialist Republics (U.S.S.R.). *See* Soviet Union

United Airlines, 536

United Nations, 490; Chinese delegation of 1945, 164; 1948 meeting in Paris, 355

U.N. Relief and Rehabilitation Administration (UNRRA), 363

United Press, 108

United States: British views of, in 1949, 383–85, 389–91; civil rights legislation in, 531, 541, 614, 652, 654, 655–56, 660–63; fiscal policies, 652–54; foreign affairs (*see* Foreign aid, U.S.; Foreign policy, U.S.); health legislation, 650–51; housing programs, 650; interstate highway system, 527, 533, 538–39, 651; prosperity of 1950s, 481–85, 542, 556, 590; source of political power in, 449, 452; space program, 650; Storm Decade of 1963–1974, 590, 656–59, 691, 698–99; tax reform, 652–54; World War II, military priorities ranked, 184

United World Federalists, 428

Universities, 513; integration of, 655–656, 658–60

University of Alabama, 659

Urban renewal program, U.S., 650

U.S. Air Corps, in China, 186–90, 223, 228–29; Air Transport Command, 189 (*see also* Hump, the, airlift over); Eleventh Bombardment Squadron, 285–88, 329–30, 332; Twentieth Bomber Command, 289–91

U.S. Air Force, 651

U.S. Army, 186, 446; blacks in, 478, 501–03, 660; in China, 574–76 (*see also* U.S. Air Corps, in China); in Europe, 363, 400–01, 407; 445, 446–48, 590; McCarthy and, 491–92, 496–97, 515–16, 558; in the Philippines, 147; in Vietnam, 575, 576, 688

U.S. Census statistics on Catholic population; of 1890, 622–23; of 1930, 616; of 1940, 1950, and 1960, 622–23

U.S. China Air Task Force (Flying Tigers), 185, 186–90

U.S. Congress: and aid to Europe, 363–64, 365, 367–68, 369–70, 392, 396, 398; blacks in, 333, 622; Catholics in, 622, 623–25; and civil rights legislation, 540–41, 652, 659–660; Communist Control Bill, 487; and interstate highway system, 527, 539; Kennedy's relationship with, 645–47, 649, 651–52; lobbies in, 538–39; Republican control lost, 487. *See also* Congressional elections; U.S. House of Representatives; U.S. Senate

U.S. Department of Defense, 531

U.S. Department of Health, Education, and Welfare, 459, 531, 651

U.S. Department of Justice, 580, 658–659, 661–62; Civil Rights Division created in, 531

U.S. Foreign Service, 514–15

Usher, Abbott Payson, 71–72

U.S. House of Representatives: composition analyzed by religion (1960), 624–25; Judiciary Committee, 64, 65; Rules Committee, 647; 1960 Democratic losses in, 647; Un-American Activities Committee, 512

USIA (U.S. Information Agency), 465, 468

U.S. Navy, 222, 590; MacArthur on, 149–50; Pacific Third Fleet, 299, 301

U.S. News & World Report, 433

U.S. Senate, 491, 624–25; composition analyzed by religion (1960), 623–625; McCarthy, 487, 509; McCarthy hearings, 558; 1960 Democratic losses in, 648; Watergate hearings, 558

U.S.S.R. *See* Soviet Union

U.S. State Department, 267 *n*., 505–507, 509, 514, 515; China Division, 506, 515–16, 609–10, 649; Security Hearing Board, 497, 499–503

U.S. Supreme Court, 526, 661; *Brown v. Board of Education* (1954), 486, 487, 527, 661; *Plessy v. Ferguson* (1896), 654, 661

U.S. Weather Service, 672, 685

Valachi Papers, The (Maas), 522–523

Vanocur, Sander, 603

Vanzetti, Bartolomeo, 32

Versailles, Treaty of, 404

Veterans of World War II, 324–25, 330, 332–33

Vietminh, 486

Vietnam: French role in, 143–46, 428, 434–35, 451, 452, 486, 528; Geneva Conference of 1954, 164, 434, 486; impact of McCarthyism on events, 514–15, 516; people of, 144–45

Vietnam, South: overthrow of Diem and Nhu, 665, 688; U.S. aid to, 399, 486, 688

Vietnam War, 114, 117, 146, 164, 182, 240, 283–84, 289, 428, 432, 445, 451–52, 486, 514, 575, 576, 620; Eisenhower and, 528; Johnson and, 688–90; Kennedy and, 688–90; U.S. air power in, 191–92

View from the Fortieth Floor, The (White), 582

Vincent, Colonel Clinton ("Casey"), 288, 515

Vishinsky, Andrei Y., 411, 449

Vote: black, 531, 539–40, 660–61, 662; black, in 1960, 611, 613, 633; ethnic blocs, 47, 631; fraud, 634–635; religious blocs, 615–16, 622–624, 626–29, 632–33; turnout, 631–632

Wagner, Robert F., Jr., 482, 596

Wallace, DeWitt, 274, 476

Wallace, George, 659, 692, 696

Wallace, Henry A., 231, 336–38, 550

Wallace, Mike, 657

Walton, William, 507, 638

Wang Ping-nan, 648

Wang Shih-chieh (minister of information), 232, 279
War, role of politics in, 148, 154, 181–82, 184–85, 235
War crimes: German, World War II, 456; Japanese, in China, 124–25
Ward, Joseph, 618
Warlords, Chinese, 98, 135–36 n., 151, 152–53, 155–57, 214–15, 314
Warren, Chief Justice Earl, 526
War reporting, 193, 228, 285, 445–46; on Sino-Japanese War, 107–11
Warsaw, Jewish ghetto of, 406
Washington, George, 62, 260, 528
Washington, D.C., 324, 490, 591, 642; McCarthyism in, 496–97, 499–508, 524–25; Eisenhower years, 524–33; lobbies, 538–41; regulatory politics, 537, 538
Washington *Post*, 433
Watergate scandal, 621; Senate Committee hearings, 558
Wavell, Field Marshal Sir Archibald Percival, 178
Weaver, Robert, 611
Wedemeyer, General Albert C., 304, 315
Weimar Republic, 215, 416
Weinberger, Caspar, 64
Westphalia, Treaty of, 404
West Virginia, 1960 primary, 604, 627–28
WGY Radio (Schenectady), 580
Whampoa Military Academy, 164
WHAS Radio (Louisville), 580
White, Alvin (brother), 59, 684
White, Clifton, 530
White, David (father), 20, 29, 32–35, 37, 55, 57–58
White, Frank, 433
White, Gladys (sister), 58, 334, 341
White, Kevin, 619
White, Mary Winkeller (mother), 19, 29, 34–37, 57, 334, 341, 673
White, Nancy Bean (wife), 340–42, 343, 345, 350–51, 354, 403, 465–68, 469–70, 476–77, 503, 508, 565, 575, 586, 588, 589, 673
White, Robert M. (brother), 59, 341, 464–65, 673, 684
Whitehead, Alfred North, 74, 276 n.
Whittier, John Greenleaf, 30, 49
Widener Library, Harvard University, 61
Wiesner, Jerome, 495–96
Wilkins, Roy, 611
William Sloane Associates, 334, 590
Willkie, Wendell, 548
Wilson, Edmund, 372
Wilson, Woodrow, 660
Winkeller, Samuel, 28–31, 34, 35–36, 37
Winkeller, Mrs. Samuel, 34–37, 41–42
Winship, Laurence, 79, 86
Winship, Thomas, 79
Wisconsin: 1960 primary, 591, 600–602; politics, 492

With Kennedy (Salinger), 523
With Nixon (Price), 523
WJR Radio (Detroit), 580
Wofford, Harris, 612
Woman's Home Companion, 522–23, 548, 550, 556, 561, 563
World Peace Movement, 442
World trade, 367–69, 376, 377–81, 391–95, 403–04, 542; "automatic" mechanisms of, 378–79; dollar v. pound sterling in, 382–86; U.S. problems of 1970s, 369, 401
World War I, 284; American code cracking, 104–05 and n.
World War II, 169–70, 174–75, 177–178, 221–22, 284–85; defense of free Poland and free China as factors in, 221–22, 315; in Europe, 143, 183–84, 221–22, 229–30, 234–235, 284–85, 315; Japanese code broken, 105; in Pacific, 184, 191, 222, 252, 281, 284–305, 315; ranking of American priorities, 183–85; strategies of Marshall, 183–85, 190; strategies of Stilwell vs. Chennault, 187–89, 190–92, 222–23
WTIC Radio (Hartford), 580
Wu, K. C., 115
Wu, P'ei-fu (Chinese warlord), 136 n.

Yangcheng county, Shansi province, China, 127–28, 137
Yang Hu-cheng (Chinese warlord), 137
Yangtze valley, China, 98, 170, 214, 222, 279, 314, 403; New Fourth Army movements in, 150–55
Yardley, Herbert O. ("Osborne"), 104 and 105 n., 106
YCL (Young Communist League), 57
Yeh Chien-ying, General, 162, 242, 246, 264
Yeh T'ing, General, 155
Yellow River, China, 123, 151, 194, 200, 221, 222, 313
Yenan, China, 151, 240–61, 411; Communist HQ in, 155, 158, 168, 220, 237, 243, 248, 252–53, 306–07, 312; Dixie Mission in, 231, 241, 243–44, 264, 268
Yenching University, Peking, 171
Yen Hsi-shan (Chinese warlord), 151, 231
Yokohama, Japan, 296, 298–301, 304
Young Communist League (YCL), 57
Young People's Socialist League (YPSL), 57
Young Worker Zionists, 57
Yu Fei-p'eng, General, 181
Yunnan province, China, tax revolt in, 219

Zionism, 38, 40–41, 75–76